Y0-BQZ-661

MECHANICS
OF MATERIALS

Top left: Courtesy U.S. Steel Corp. *Top right:* Courtesy Bethlehem Steel Co. *Center:* Courtesy U.S. Steel Corp. *Bottom left:* Courtesy Bethlehem Steel Co. *Bottom right:* Courtesy U.S. Steel Corp.

MECHANICS OF MATERIALS

by Alvin Sloane

Late Associate Professor of Mechanical Engineering in the Massachusetts Institute of Technology

DOVER PUBLICATIONS, INC.
NEW YORK

Published in Canada by General Publishing Company, Ltd., 30 Lesmill Road, Don Mills, Toronto, Ontario.
Published in the United Kingdom by Constable and Company, Ltd., 10 Orange Street, London WC 2.

This Dover edition, first published in 1967, is an unabridged and unaltered republication of the work originally published by The Macmillan Company, New York, in 1952. A separate *Solution Manual for Mechanics of Materials,* prepared by the author and containing answers to all of the problems in this text, is available from Dover Publications, Inc., for 75¢.

Library of Congress Catalog Card Number: 66-29185

Manufactured in the United States of America
Dover Publications, Inc.
180 Varick Street
New York, N. Y. 10014

This book is dedicated
to the memory of

ALVIN SLOANE / May 1, 1901 — May 25, 1959

Preface

This is a textbook written for the engineering student.

In preparing it, the writer has attempted to express the fundamental theorems of Mechanics of Materials in prose which is clear, direct, and satisfying to that student. It is designed to challenge his imagination by not talking over his head—and to deliver a message of engineering philosophy which shall offer a true perspective of the profession. It will not dictate, but invite; and it will try to anticipate the questions which will arise in the student's mind. At the same time, the subject will be presented fully, with no attempt at false simplification, or evasion of fundamental proof.

The engineering student contributes individuality, ambition, and perseverance to an educational project—he ought, therefore, to be welcomed as a partner by his teacher and his textbook. Courses in Applied Mechanics furnish one of the most fertile territories in the curriculum for the nurturing of this philosophy of common effort. It is our hope that the teacher will find here an ally which will enhance his contribution to the venture.

In this branch of mechanics—the Mechanics of Materials—engineering students first encounter the opportunity of witnessing the liaison between axiom and application. The necessity for departing from the comfortable security of rigid law and positive rule and of introducing expedient assumption can effectively demonstrate the compromise between theory and practice which is engineering. And it can inspire devotion to the further research and study which will enhance our understanding of the materials with which the engineer must work. When so enriched, an educational career becomes significant and stimulating.

The first courses in Statics and Dynamics, which precede this subject in the training of an engineer, focus attention upon *method* in engineering thought. The vigor of the "free body" philosophy of those subjects is the tangible evidence of teaching sincerely devoted to the growth of mental power in the progress of the student, as distinguished from training in the gathering of information alone. This process should be continued as the student advances into this second level of his study of mechanics, and the teaching effort of this stage must embrace a similar devotion to the forging and refinement of planned reasoning as the basic weapon of attack.

The writer believes that integrated organization of the course content in the Mechanics of Materials can encourage logical thinking. To insure coordination, the predominant feature of the subject—the basic beam or flexure theory—is treated as a fundamental core. The theories of longitudinal shear and of deflection are corollary to this theory, and next appear as natural and correlated branches. Additional, organic growth supplies such factors as the theories of torsion, of combined stress, and of failure.

In this book, this pattern of coordination is constantly followed, and the study of detached and disjointed elements—a form of "parcel-collection" education—is vigorously eschewed. Two examples of this devotion to coordinated growth in the integration of the course may be cited. Mohr's circle, as applied to plane stress, moments of inertia, and plane strain, has become a vital and valued ally in the current solution of problems in mechanics. In this text it has, therefore, been discussed in the earliest treatment of simple stress and made available for constant use as the field of discussion expands.

The necessity, as well as the advisability of introducing limitations and assumptions in the exploration of the basic theories, has received more attention than is customary, for it is our belief that only when the bases upon which these theories rest are truly appreciated does the student become more than an unworthy "formula-substituter" destined for mediocrity in an engineering profession which demands sincere understanding.

The position of the chapter devoted to the mechanical properties of materials is somewhat unusual. This subject matter is now being given by many schools in courses devoted to engineering materials and is not germane to the development of the course in Mechanics of Materials, except where it is needed to supply vocabulary and a background of definitions. Since we are concerned with the coordinated growth of ideas concerning stress and strain, this material has been placed beyond the articles devoted to the primary development of the subject. Where such material is given as a part of the Mechanics of Materials course, the chapter may be considered earlier with no inconvenience.

The wide range of difficulty of courses in Mechanics of Materials is recognized by the device of printing in prominent type the articles of major importance. Articles of secondary importance, which may be omitted from less extensive courses, are printed in smaller type.

The problem material has also been planned to afford flexibility in presenting courses of differing extent. They vary between the limits of the orthodox problem which illustrates in simple and direct fashion the application of each theory, and those which challenge the imagination as well as objective planning of a comprehensive method of attack. The book may be used for either the abridged course which is customarily offered to the student whose future field of action in mechanics may be limited, or in the more extensive course intended for the student whose training must be more rigorous.

The author acknowledges, with gratitude, the counsel and cooperation so generously afforded him by his colleagues of the faculty of the Massachusetts Institute of Technology.

ALVIN SLOANE

Cambridge, Mass.

Table of Contents

CHAPTER I

Introduction to Mechanics of Materials

CHAPTER II

Bending. The Basic Flexure Theory

CONTENTS

CHAPTER X
Mechanical Properties of Materials

CHAPTER XI
Additional Uses of Mohr's Circle

Appendix

MECHANICS
OF MATERIALS

CHAPTER I

Introduction to Mechanics of Materials

1. The Free Body of Mechanics. In all of the branches of mechanics, effective solution of problems rests upon the development of a *directed* attack. The engineering method of thinking—*conscious planning of the direction of thought*—is opposed to haphazard assembling of facts.

The dreams of early philosophers crystallized, after having been fortified by observation, into axioms upon which engineering progress has been built. Engineers—the appliers of pure science to the practical problems of man—have accepted or rejected earlier theory, observed the possibilities of new concepts and, again, after carefully testing them, accepted or rejected. The body of engineering knowledge grows as new dreams or schemes, arising from philosophical speculation, prove their worth or expose their fallacies.

In all of this process, the engineer dispassionately appraises and coolly tests possibilities of practical application, free of prejudice and serving as an efficient and effective agent as he brings to bear the power of planned reasoning. In his explorations of the field of mechanics, as in all other branches of engineering action, the engineer may not wander as whim suggests, but must travel by careful definition of the objective and painstaking plotting of the most effective channel toward that objective.

In mechanics, the bases of concern are tangible—this is the science which concerns itself with the influence of forces upon bodies. These bodies may be minute or colossal, they may range in size from a humble particle to a great planet. The body may be a part of a machine or structure, or a group of such parts, or the entire structure. In every case, the engineer insists upon exact definition of the body which, when isolated from its neighbors and allowed to stand alone, becomes the *free body* of mechanics.

When such a free body has been isolated for study, the influence of the surrounding bodies is noted. These may be bodies in contact with the free body under investigation, which exert force by the direct contact, and thus control or restrain the motion of the free body. In addition, the pull of gravity or of magnetic fields may produce force.

The appraisal of all of the sources of force acting upon the free body sets the problem, and conclusions may now be drawn, making use of the Newtonian axioms of motion, to predict the state of motion of the body, to solve the problem of evaluating previously unknown forces, or to determine the nature of the deformation of the free body.

Such a building of firm foundation is characteristic of all successful essays in engineering analysis—the setting of the problem, the careful organization of all of the factors pertinent to its solution must precede the application of laws, formulas, or techniques of investigation of the unknowns which are to be evaluated.

The investigations which we shall pursue in the subject of the Mechanics of Materials, also called Strength of Materials, or Resistance of Materials, concern themselves primarily with the distortion or change of shape of the free body.

In the fundamental courses in Statics and Dynamics which have, in the education of an engineer, preceded this subject, the free bodies have generally been assumed to be *rigid*. No matter what forces may have been applied, we have idealized, or simplified, the preliminary stages of the problems of mechanics by an assumption which has enabled us to draw conclusions which were approximate—they applied only as the extent of the fallacy introduced by such approximation was of negligible concern.

In our present studies, we advance beyond such a stage of approximation and admit that when forces are applied to free bodies, they are capable of deforming those bodies.

2. Mechanics of Materials. The branch of mechanics which investigates the development of stress in loaded bodies, and the accompanying deformation of those bodies is called the Mechanics of Materials, or the Strength of Materials.

The body of fundamentals of axiom or law forms the science of this subject—the applications to engineering design comprise the art.

The undergraduate course in Mechanics of Materials presents a very challenging opportunity to the engineering student. In this subject, he must depart from the comfortable security of rigid body and axiomatic law, and venture to realize that, in the dynamic progress of science, all is not known—the behavior of materials but imperfectly understood and the necessity for making assumptions introduced. Such assumptions may have validity—their introduction is forced by the impossibility of reducing all of man's endeavors as he schemes, dreams, and builds, to a mathematical equation. The validation of assumptions is the challenge which stimulates scientific research and the development of engineering application of fundamental research.

The study of the mechanics of behavior of materials, as they are utilized in machine or structure has had a long and interesting historical development. This growth has culminated in the form of two basic theories which, together with their corollaries, form the core of the course in Mechanics of Materials.

The primary or basic theory is the *flexure*, or beam, theory—its corollaries are the theories of *longitudinal shear* and of *deflection*.

In addition, the basic theory of *torsion* furnishes essential background.

Other theories and practices, notably those devoted to combination of the patterns of stress and of deformation, continue the development of the knowledge which the engineer must bring to the design of machine or structure. When the engineering student has at his command a sympathetic understanding of the limitations as well as the potentialities of these basic theories, he is equipped with one of the most effective factors in his engineering training.

As we enter such a study, it is desirable that we first establish a vocabulary of the subject, and the succeeding articles will be devoted to definition of those terms which will arise in our fundamental concepts. When we have built a vocabulary, we shall examine the basic theories and strengthen our ability to employ them in applications taken from engineering practice.

STRESS

3. Stress. *Stress* is internal force. It is defined as the force transmitted through a plane section of a free body. For example, the rod shown in Fig. 1-a is suspended from a ceiling, and subjected to a load, P, at its lower end. The rod is in equilibrium and we shall, at the moment, neglect the weight of the rod itself. We wish to determine the stress or force transmitted through any plane section, like a-a.

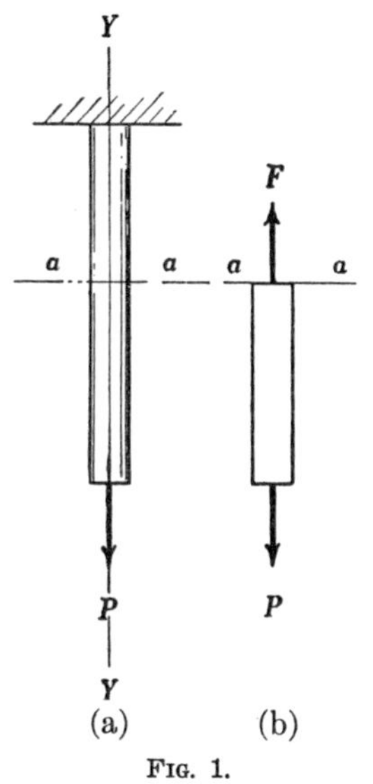

Fig. 1.

The tools with which we investigate are the conditions of equilibrium. These conditions, in an orderly analysis, must be applied to the system of *external* forces acting upon an isolated free body. Figure 1-b presents the isolation of the portion of the rod which lies below section *a-a*. The external force system acting upon this free body consists of the load P and the force exerted by the neighboring upper portion of the rod. This force is distributed over section *a-a*, which is the top surface of the isolated body. The resultant of this distributed force is shown as F.

Applying the condition of equilibrium, $\Sigma Y = 0$, we find that $F = P$. The stress in the rod—the force transmitted through a typical section *a-a*—is therefore equal in magnitude to P. We note that force F of Fig. 1-b is pulling upon the isolated free body, tending to elongate it. Such stress is called *tension*. Had the load P, applied to the bottom of the rod, been applied vertically upward, force F would have been revealed as pushing upon the isolated portion, tending to contract it, and the stress would then be called *compression*.

The term stress has thus far been employed to describe resultant or total internal force. The force F of Fig. 1 is distributed over the cross-sectional area at section *a-a*. It is the resultant of distribution which may be either uniform or variable over that area. In either event, $F = \int s\, dA$, where s is the intensity of stress. If the distribution is uniform, s is a constant, and $F = sA$. The assumption of uniform distribution is generally proper when the resultant force passes through the centroid of an area, except when cases of stress concentration arise, such as those noted in Art. 13.

The term s is intensity of stress, or force per unit area, which we shall call *unit stress*. The term stress, in current usage in engineering literature, is synonymous with unit stress. We shall differentiate, in our discussions, between the intensity of stress and the resultant stress by referring to the former as stress or unit stress and to the latter as total stress.

The rod which we have employed as an illustration has called our attention to two forms of force transmitted through the plane sections of a loaded body—we have viewed examples of tensile and compressive stress. Each of these stresses is perpendicular to the cross-sectional area upon which it acts, and is therefore referred to as a *normal stress*. The definition of stress, however, has not confined our consideration to normal stresses. Figure 2-a illustrates the presence of another kind of stress. When a horizontal force P is applied to the member at its central section, as shown, and the member is restrained by forces F_1 and F_2, equidistant from P, force is transmitted through horizontal sections *a-a* and *b-b*. To discover the magnitude and direction of such internal force, the free body lying between sections *a-a* and *b-b* has been isolated and, together with the accompanying system of external forces, is shown in Fig. 2-b. The forces acting upon the top and bottom faces are distributed over those surfaces. The sum of these forces is

$$F_1 + F_2 - P = 0 \qquad (\Sigma X = 0)$$

If a moment axis be set on the line of action of P,

$$+F_1 \times \frac{l}{2} - F_2 \times \frac{l}{2} = 0 \qquad (\Sigma M = 0)$$

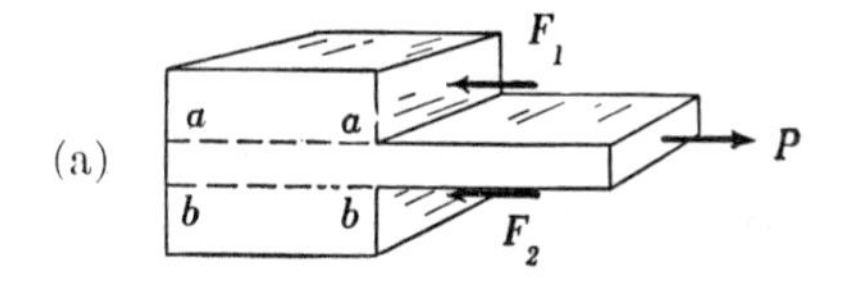

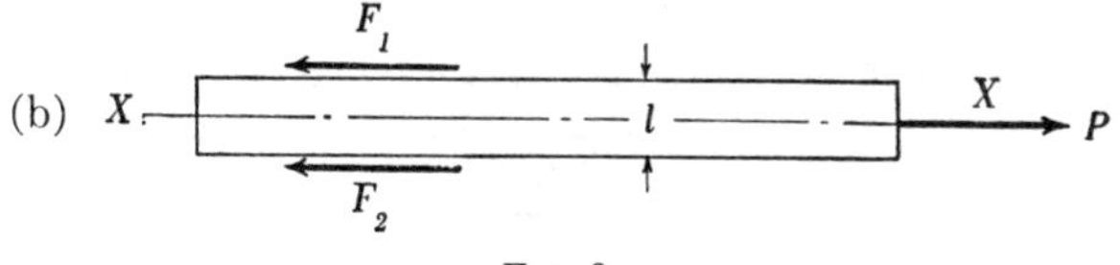

FIG. 2.

Then each force is $F = P/2$. Internal force is therefore transmitted through sections *a-a* and *b-b*, and stress is developed along those surfaces. Such stress is exerted parallel to the surface and is called *shearing stress.*

Stress may, therefore, be acting normal to the surface, or parallel to it, or it may be oblique to the surface, in which event it will have normal and shearing components. Such a possibility is illustrated in Fig. 3.

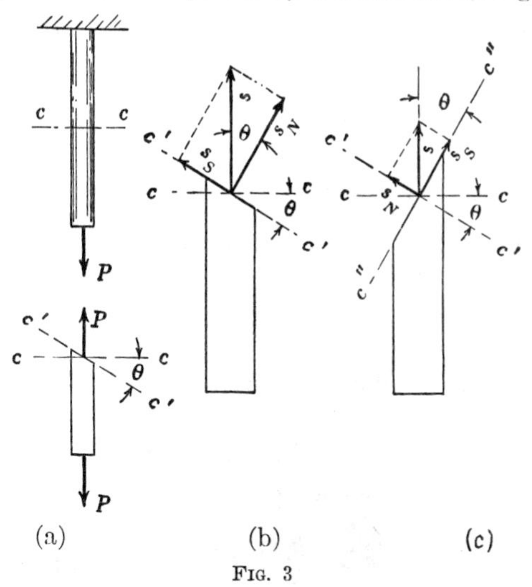

FIG. 3

The isolation of Fig. 3-a establishes the magnitude and direction of the total stress transmitted through an oblique section c'-c' of a loaded body, as P. This total stress is oblique to the section on which it acts.

Assuming that the distribution of stress over the area is uniform, (usually a proper assumption when the resultant force passes through the centroid of the section) the unit stress on the section in the direction of P (Fig. 3-b) is

$$s = \frac{P}{A'}$$

where A' is the cross-sectional area of the body at section c'-c'.

$$A' = \frac{A}{\cos\theta}$$

in which A is the area of the right cross-section at section c-c.

Then $$s = \frac{P\cos\theta}{A}$$

Such a resultant unit stress may be resolved into rectangular components, s_N and s_S perpendicular to and parallel to section c'-c', respectively (Fig. 3-b).

The normal component of the unit stress s is

$$s_N = s\cos\theta = \frac{P}{A}\cos^2\theta \tag{1}$$

and the shear component is

$$s_S = s\sin\theta = \frac{P}{A}\sin\theta\cos\theta \tag{2}$$

When $\theta = 0°$, $$s_N = \frac{P}{A} \times 1 = \frac{P}{A}$$

and $$s_S = \frac{P}{A} \times 0 \times 1 = 0$$

When $\theta = 90°$, $$s_N = \frac{P}{A} \times 0 = 0$$

and $$s_S = \frac{P}{A} \times 1 \times 0 = 0$$

The maximum normal unit stress in the body therefore occurs upon the right section c-c.

The maximum shearing stress will occur when $\theta = 45°$, for, at that inclination, we find the maximum product of $\sin\theta\cos\theta$,

and $$s_{S(\text{max.})} = \frac{P}{A} \times 0.7071 \times 0.7071 = \frac{P}{2A}$$

One observation, which will be of significance as we proceed, may be noted in the case of shear stress.

Figure 3-c shows another section c''-c'' through the loaded body. c''-c'' is perpendicular to c'-c'.

The cross-sectional area of the body at section c''-c'' is

$$A'' = \frac{A}{\cos(90 - \theta)} = \frac{A}{\sin\theta}$$

and

$$s = \frac{P}{A/\sin\theta}$$

The shear stress on c''-c'' is

$$s_S = \frac{P\cos\theta}{A/\sin\theta} = \frac{P}{A}\sin\theta\cos\theta$$

Then the shear stresses on planes which are mutually perpendicular are equal in magnitude.

The body which we have been considering has been subjected to the simplest type of loading—a single force applied axially. The analysis of the resulting stress conditions has yielded the simple expressions noted in equations (1) and (2). As we advance, we shall find that stress analyses may yield more complex expressions, but that in *all* cases the method of attack which we have employed here—the cautious isolation of a free body and the appraisal and evaluation of the force system exerted by the contacting bodies—furnishes an equally effective method of attack which we may pursue with confidence.

The relationship between the direct stress on the right section produced by the axial loading, and the normal and shear stresses induced on the oblique sections furnishes us with an opportunity of observing the influence of the role which graphical or pseudo-graphical solutions may play in the solution of problems in mechanics. The following article considers such solutions.

PROBLEMS

Note: In each of the problems of the following group it is assumed that all stresses are distributed uniformly over the areas upon which they act.

1. Determine the maximum allowable load P which may be placed on the cylinder. The allowable unit stress in compression is $s_C = 16{,}000$ psi; the allowable unit stress in shear is $s_S = 8800$ psi. The cross-sectional area of the cylinder is $A = 10$ sq. in. *Ans.* 160,000 lb.

2. Determine the maximum allowable load P which may be placed on the block if the allowable unit compressive stress is $s_C = 12{,}000$ psi and the allowable unit shear stress is $s_S = 4500$ psi.

3. A hollow square column supports a uniformly distributed load whose resultant is a force $R = 153{,}900$ lb. If the unit compressive stress in the column must not exceed 2500 psi, determine the length of sides a of the square hole. *Ans.* 6.2 in.

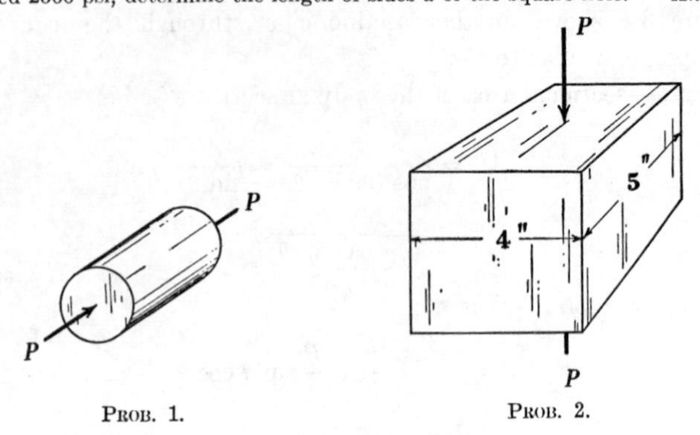

PROB. 1. PROB. 2.

4. The frame consists of a boom CB, of 3 in. diameter, and a supporting cable CA, of 1 in. diameter. Determine the unit stress in CA and CB.

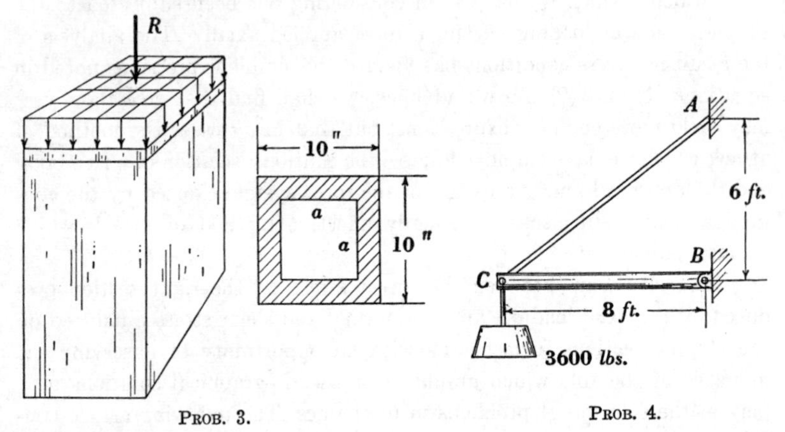

PROB. 3. PROB. 4.

5. The total stress in member AB is 30,000 lb. (tension). The cross-sectional area of the member is 6 sq. in. Determine:

a) The maximum unit normal stress.

b) The maximum unit shear stress.

c) The normal and shear stresses on the plane indicated as b–b.

6. The shear stress on an oblique plane of an axially loaded body is 6000 psi. The oblique plane is inclined at an angle of 60°, with the axis along which the load acts. Determine the normal stress on the oblique plane. *Ans.* 10,400 psi.

7. The normal stress on an oblique plane of an axially loaded body has a magnitude which is twice that of the shear stress on the same plane. Determine the angle between the oblique plane and the axis of the body along which the load acts. *Ans.* 63.4°.

8. The shaded cylindrical test bar (½ in. diameter) is mounted between two supports and force F is applied midway between the supports. If the ultimate strength of the material in shear is 48,000 psi, determine the load F which will cause failure by shearing. *Ans.* 18,800 lb.

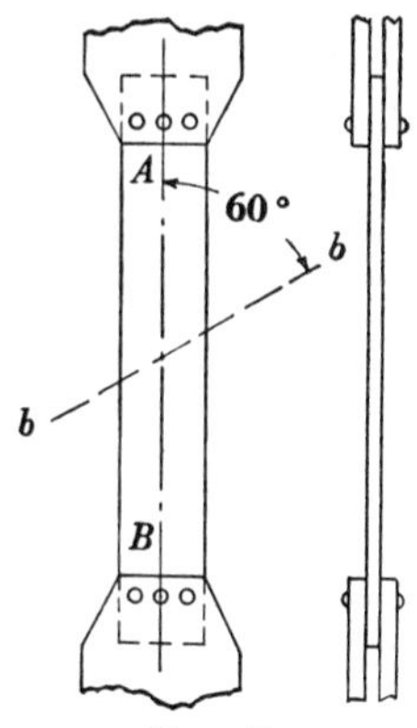

PROB. 5.

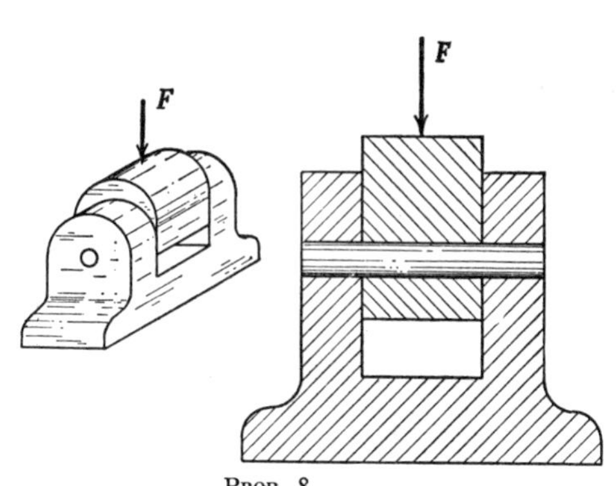

PROB. 8.

9. Determine the required cross-sectional areas of members AB, AC, and DE of the truss shown if the allowable unit normal stress in all members is 20,000 psi. All members are pin-connected.

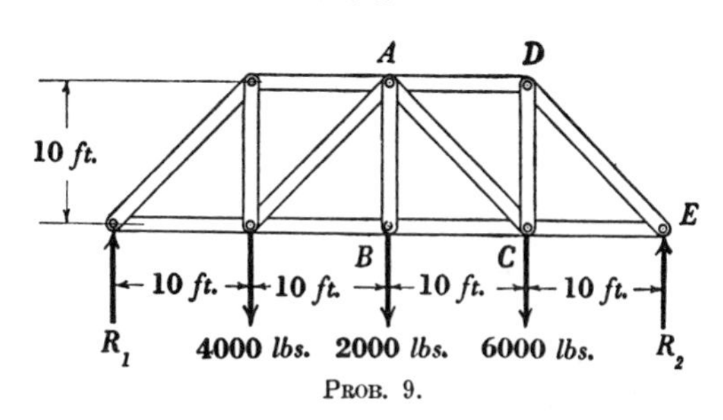

PROB. 9.

10. The cylinder head is held on the cylinder by 12 bolts. The diameter of the bolts is ½ in.; the inner diameter of the cylinder is 12 in.; the internal pressure in the cylinder is 140 psi. If the pressure which the washers exert on the surface of the cylinder head must not exceed 1600 psi, determine the minimum diameter of the washers. *Ans.* 1.14 in.

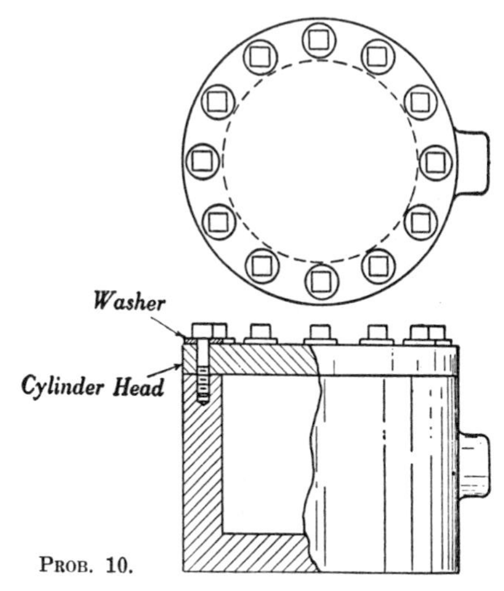

PROB. 10.

4. Graphical Solutions. Such solutions are translations of analytical equations into the language of the drawing. In graphical form, the relationships of the equations are frequently presented more clearly than when they appear as the symbols and terms of analytical equations, so that many of their trends and relationships may be noted by inspection of the drawing. The solution of the graphical equations is accomplished by introducing

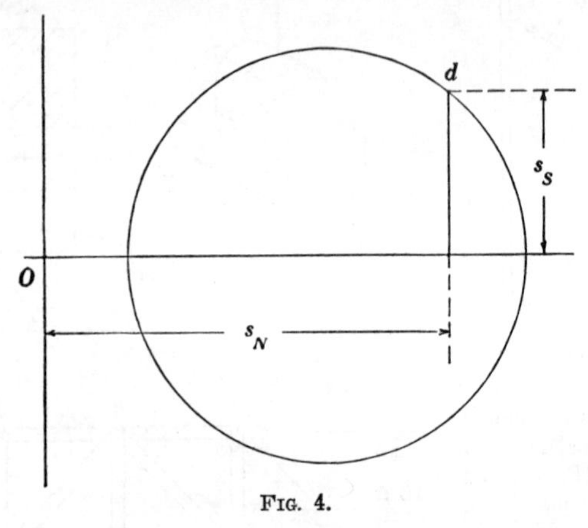

FIG. 4.

a scale into the drawings, and by measuring the scalar distances—often a much simpler technique of solution than substitution of literal or numerical values in analytical equations. In the *pseudo*-graphical solution, the relationships are also set in the form of a drawing which need not be to scale but which clearly indicates the geometrical pattern of the factors involved. The drawing is then used to guide the calculations, which become simple geometrical or arithmetical operations.

The graphical solution of equations (1) and (2) of the preceding article was the product of the fertile mind of Otto Mohr (1835–1918), a German mathematical philosopher who contributed a series of graphical techniques to the science of mechanics.

This graphical solution is one of the most useful tools in the field of mechanics, and we shall discuss its details so that we may have an effective weapon at our command.* *Mohr's circle* is a graph, like that of Fig. 4, which is plotted on rectangular coordinates. The circumference of the

*Mohr's circle is a graphical solution of an equation of a particular form, and not just a technique of solution of stress problems. It may, therefore, be used whenever an equation of the particular form is encountered. Such applications arise, most notably, in the equations expressing the relationships of moments and products of inertia about inclined axes, and in the relationships of plane strains at a point of a loaded body. These opportunities of effective solution by Mohr's circle are discussed in Arts. 92 and 93.

circle is the locus of a series of points which represent the state of stress on all of the planes which may be passed through a given point of a loaded body. Abscissae of the circumferential points represent normal stresses, and ordinates of the same points represent shear stresses.

The conventions used in plotting follow: Tensile stresses are plotted as abscissae to the right of the origin, compressive stresses to the left. Positive shear stresses are plotted as ordinates above the origin, negative shear stresses below. The assignment of the quality "positive" or "negative" to shear stress is illustrated in Fig. 5. This figure shows an elementary prism at a point of a loaded body. The shear stresses acting upon opposite faces of such a prism are always equal in magnitude and opposed in direction, as we shall prove in later discussions. The pairs of opposed shear stresses form couples. When such a couple tends to rotate the prism clockwise, the shear stress is called positive. Conversely, when the opposed shear stresses on opposite faces of the prism tend to cause counter-clockwise rotation, the shear stress is negative. In Fig. 5 positive shear stresses are shown.

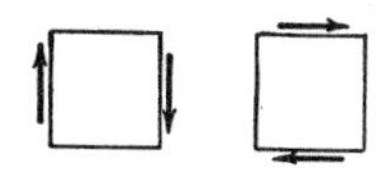

Positive Shear Stress

FIG. 5.

In Fig. 4, the point d represents the state of stress on one of the oblique planes which may be passed through a point of a loaded body. The abscissa of point d lies to the right of origin O, and the normal stress on the oblique plane is tensile. The ordinate of point d, which represents shear stress, lies above the origin O and the shear stress on this oblique plane is, therefore, positive.

Let us now discover which plane a point like d of Fig. 4 represents. In addition, let us confirm the validity of Mohr's circle by comparing the evaluation of normal and shear stress which it yields with the values we have already derived and expressed in equations (1) and (2). We shall employ, as an example of a loaded body, a rod suspended from a ceiling, as in Fig. 6, carrying at its lower end a load P, which is applied along its axis. The weight of the rod itself will be assumed to be negligible.

Point B is one point of the rod, and any number of planes may be passed through it. One of these planes is the right section c-c, whose area we shall call A. This section c-c has, acting upon it, a normal unit stress

$$s = \frac{P}{A} \text{ (tension)}$$

In Fig. 7, a Mohr's circle has been drawn to portray the condition of stress at point B of Fig. 6. This circle is constructed as follows:

$$Ob = s = \frac{P}{A} \text{ (tension)}$$

We draw a circle with Ob as diameter. We may determine, using this Mohr's circle, the stress on any other plane than the right section c-c. For example, c'-c' (Fig. 6) is *any* other plane section passed through the

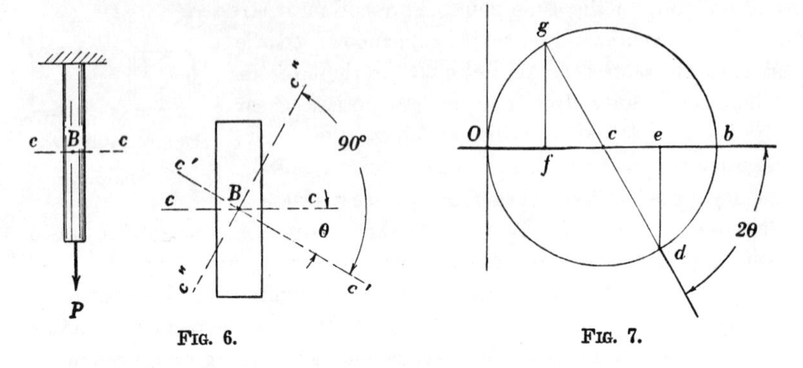

FIG. 6. FIG. 7.

body at point B. This plane is located at an angle θ from plane c-c, clockwise. We now proceed from point b of Fig. 7, which is representing plane c-c to point d, located at angle 2θ, clockwise, from b. (Mohr discovered that his circle would always be correct if angular distances of the circle are made *twice* those of the angular distances between plane sections of the loaded body.) This move establishes d as the point describing the state of stress on plane c'-c'. The abscissa of point d is Oe, and the ordinate is de. Since abscissae represent normal stresses, Oe is the normal stress on plane c'-c'. Let us see if Oe agrees with the value of normal stress given by the analytical equation (1).

From the geometry of Fig. 7, we note that

$$Oc = \frac{Ob}{2} = \frac{P}{2A}$$

and

$$ce = \text{Radius } cd \times \cos 2\theta$$
$$= \frac{P}{2A} \times \cos 2\theta$$

Then

$$Oe = Oc + ce$$
$$= \frac{P}{2A} + \frac{P}{2A} \cos 2\theta$$
$$= \frac{P}{2A}(1 + \cos^2 \theta - \sin^2 \theta)$$
$$= \frac{P}{A} \cos^2 \theta$$

Then Mohr's circle does yield a value of normal stress which agrees with that given in equation (1).

The ordinate *de* should, similarly, yield the proper value of shear stress, if we are to have confidence that the circle presents a proper method of solution.

$$
\begin{aligned}
de &= \text{Radius } cd \times \sin 2\theta \\
&= \frac{P}{2A} \times 2 \sin \theta \cos \theta \\
&= \frac{P}{A} \sin \theta \cos \theta
\end{aligned}
$$

which is in agreement with equation (2).

We have already noted (page 7) that unit shear stresses on planes which are mutually perpendicular are equal in magnitude. Point *g* of the Mohr's circle of Fig. 7 represents the stress on a plane of the loaded body. This plane is c''-c'' located, as shown in Fig. 6, at an angular displacement of 90°, from plane c'-c', since points *d* and *g* are 180° apart on the circumference of the Mohr's circle, which operates with twice the angular displacements of the planes of the loaded body.

The shear stress on plane c''-c'' is represented by ordinate *fg*, which is equal in magnitude to *de*. (*fg* and *de* are corresponding sides of the congruent triangles.) This equivalence of the shear stresses acting on mutually perpendicular planes further confirms the equivalence of the results yielded by Mohr's circle to their counterparts in the analytical equations.

(a)
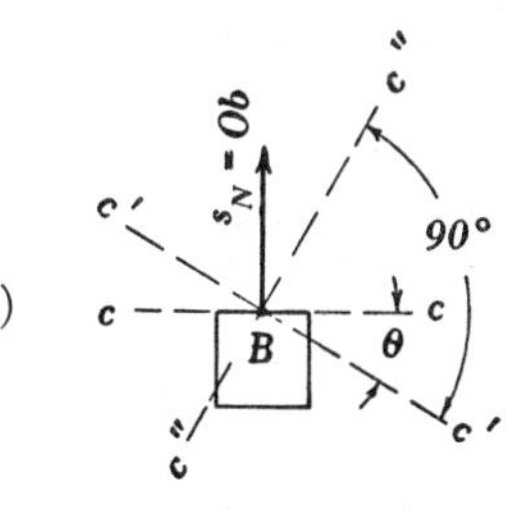

(b)
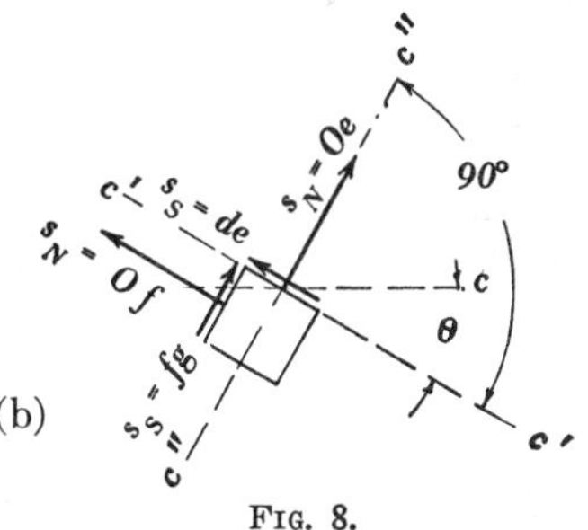

FIG. 8.

The Mohr's circle, in addition to indicating the magnitudes of the normal and shear stresses, reveals their direction. For example, Fig. 8-a shows an elementary prism isolated, as shown, at point *B* of Fig. 6. The normal stress on the face of the prism at section *c-c* is $s_N = Ob$ (Fig. 7).

In Fig. 8-b, the results obtained from the Mohr's circle have been plotted to indicate their direction as well as their magnitude. For example, plane c'-c' is located at an angle θ, clockwise from plane *c-c*. Then, proceeding clockwise from point *b* of Mohr's circle (Fig. 7) through an angle 2θ, we arrive at point *d*, representing the stress on plane c'-c'. The abscissa of point *d* is *Oe*, which indicates tensile stress, for it lies to the right of origin O. This stress has been plotted on an elementary prism in Fig. 8-b. The prism is oriented to show plane c'-c' as an upper face, and the tensile stress Oe is plotted—the vector directed away from the prism face to indicate tension.

The shear stress on plane c'-c' is de (Fig. 7), which indicates negative shear since it lies below the origin of the Mohr's circle. This stress has, therefore, been plotted in Fig. 8-b as a vector directed upward to the left, in accordance with the conventions which we have previously adopted for shear (see Fig. 5).

Plane c''-c'' of the loaded body occurs (Fig. 8-a) at an angular displacement of 90° from plane c'-c'. Then the stress on plane c''-c'' of the body is represented by point g, 180° away from point d of Fig. 7. The normal stress on this plane is Of, which is tensile, and the shear stress is fg, which is positive. These results are plotted on the prism of Fig. 8-b.

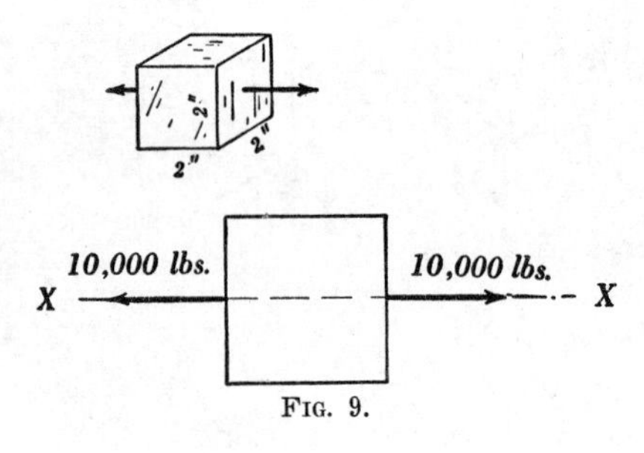

FIG. 9.

Illustrative Example. The 2 in. cube of Fig. 9 is subjected to an axial load of 10,000 lb., applied as shown. We are to determine the normal and shear stresses on a plane through the center of the cube whose normal, or axis, makes an angle of 30°, counter-clockwise with the indicated X-axis. It will be assumed that all stresses are uniformly distributed over the plane areas of the body.

The solution, by Mohr's circle, is indicated in Fig. 10-a. The normal stress on the plane perpendicular to the X-axis is

$$s_N = \frac{P}{A} = \frac{10{,}000}{4} = 2500 \text{ psi (tension)}$$

The solution may be purely graphical and all values translated, by assigning a scale, into linear distances, or a pseudo-graphical routine may be adopted, as follows, with a sketched circle serving as a guide to our computations.

To the right of origin O s_N is laid out as the distance Ob. A circle is next drawn with Ob as its diameter. Now we establish point d, lying at an angular distance twice $30 = 60°$, from b as indicated. The desired normal stress is Oe, and the desired shear stress is de.

$$\text{Radius } cd = Oc = 2500/2 = 1250 \text{ psi}$$
$$ce = cd \cos 60° = 1250 \times 0.5000 = 625 \text{ psi}$$
$$s_N = Oe = Oc + ce = 1250 + 625 = 1875 \text{ psi (tension)}$$
$$s_S = de = cd \sin 60° = 1250 \times 0.8660 = 1083 \text{ psi (positive)}$$

These results of our analysis are plotted as Fig. 10-b.

Analytical equations (1) and (2) are simple in form, and Mohr's circle presents no marked superiority as a means of their solution over direct substitution in the equations. It does enable us, however, to note the

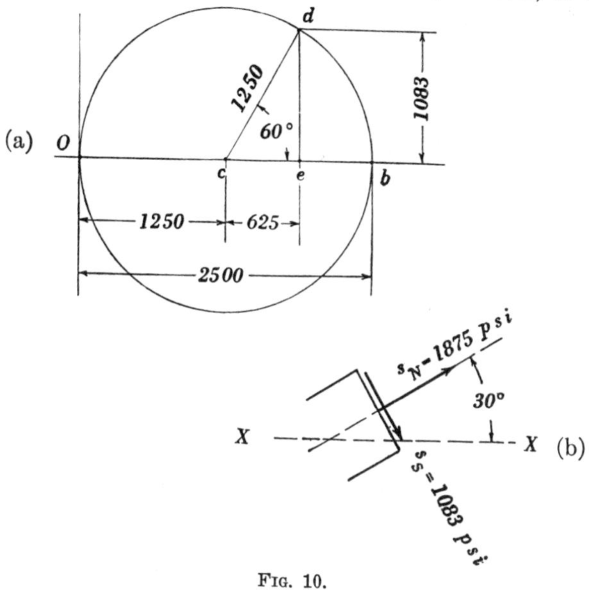

FIG. 10.

relationships of the unit stresses on the several planes through a point much more readily than by inspection of the analytical equations.

For example, we note in Fig. 11 that a Mohr's circle has been drawn, representing the state of stress on all of the planes through point B. Any

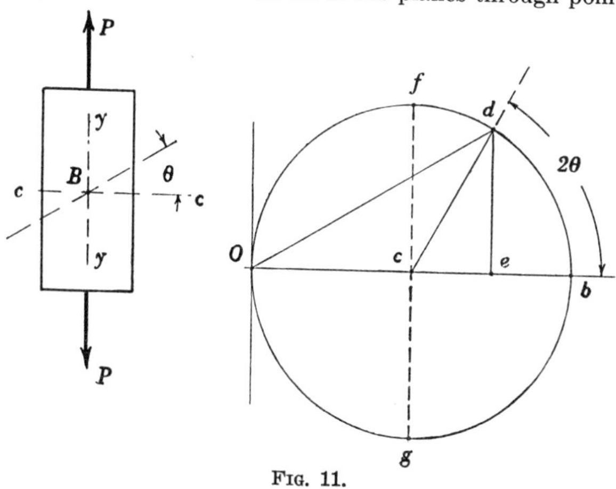

FIG. 11.

chord, like Od, drawn from the origin to a point on the circumference, is the vector sum of the normal and shear stresses Oe and de, and therefore represents the resultant unit stress on the section.

Then the maximum resultant unit stress on any plane through point B of the loaded body is Ob, the normal stress on the right section c-c. The minimum resultant unit stress is represented by point O itself, and is equal to zero. This stress occurs on a plane of the body which is inclined at 90° with plane c-c and is therefore the longitudinal plane indicated as y-y.

These maximum and minimum normal stresses are called the *principal stresses* at point B of the body, and the planes upon which they act are called the *principal planes of stress* for the point.

We also note by inspection of the Mohr's circle of Fig. 11 that the points O and b have ordinate distances equal to zero. Then *there is no shear stress upon the principal planes.*

We further note that there are two planes upon which the greatest shear stress occurs, which are represented by points f and g of the circumference, because the ordinates cf and cg are the largest ordinates and represent therefore maximum shear stress. Points f and g, on the Mohr's circle, are located at $2\theta = 90°$ from the principal planes represented by points O and b. It follows that the planes of the body on which maximum shear stresses occur must be inclined at $\theta = 45°$ with reference to the principal planes.

We have thus far employed Mohr's circle to indicate its value as an exploratory device to analyze the relationship of the stresses on the planes which pass through a typical point of an axially loaded body. As we advance into our subject, we shall encounter more complex forms of loading; we shall then find that Mohr's circle affords very definite advantage over the analytical method.

5. General Case of Plane Stress. We shall now consider the state of stress upon the many planes which may be passed through any point of a loaded body. We shall limit our discussion to the case of *plane stress,* which arises when all of the loads that are applied to the body are confined to a single plane.

Point O of Fig. 12 is any point of a body subjected to plane stress. A very small triangular prism at point O is indicated, bounded by faces Oa, Ob, and ab. The body is assumed to be of unit depth. The resultant external forces acting upon the body lie in a single plane at the central section of the body parallel to its front and rear faces.

Such a force system is capable of inducing stress on the three longitudinal surfaces of the triangular prism. Such stresses may be perpendicular, parallel, or oblique to the surfaces upon which they act. In any case, however, all possibilities are included when we indicate upon each face a normal and shear component of stress, as shown in Fig. 12.

The lengths of faces *Oa*, *Ob*, and *ab* have been established as very short, and it will therefore be assumed that all stresses are uniformly distributed over the faces upon which they act.

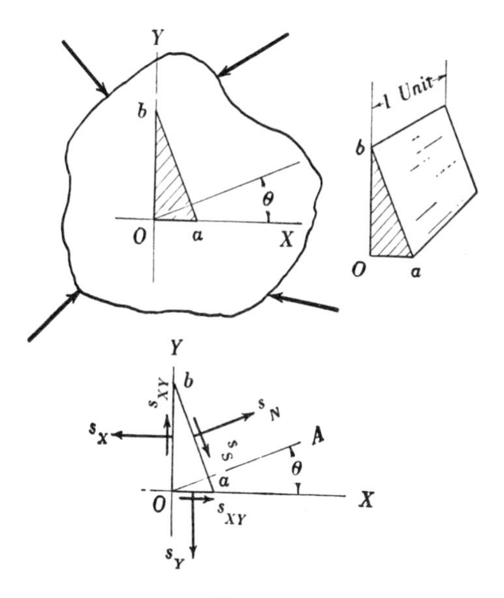

Fig. 12.

We shall adopt a system of nomenclature to avoid, as far as may be possible, the use of many modifying subscripts and exponents as symbols.

Any plane will be identified by the name of the axis to which it is perpendicular. For example, the plane indicated as *Ob* is perpendicular to the *X*-axis and is called an *X*-plane; *Oa* represents a *Y*-plane, and *ab* an *A*-plane. The *A*-axis is inclined at any angle θ from the *X*-axis, and plane *ab* therefore represents any oblique plane at point *O* of the body.

Normal stresses on the *X* and *Y* planes will be associated with the plane upon which they act, by using as subscript the letter identifying the plane. For example, the normal stress on the *X*-plane *Ob* is s_X.

We have noted, in a previous discussion, the equality of the shear stresses acting upon mutually perpendicular planes of axially loaded bodies. Now that we are investigating the development of stress in bodies whose loading is not confined to one axis, we should note the similar development of such equality of the shear stresses.

Figure 13 shows an elementary prism subjected to shear stress in a single plane. If the prism is in equilibrium, the shear stresses on opposite faces must be equal and opposite to satisfy the conditions of equilibrium $\Sigma X = 0$ and $\Sigma Y = 0$.

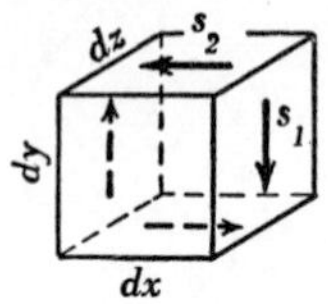

Fig. 13.

For equilibrium the condition of equilibrium $\Sigma M = 0$ must also be satisfied.

The shear forces acting upon the right and left faces are $s_1\, dy\, dz$, which are opposed in direction and which together form a couple of magnitude $s_1\, dy\, dz\, dx$, which is directed clockwise.

Similarly the shear forces acting upon the top and bottom faces form a couple of magnitude $s_2\, dx\, dy\, dz$.

This latter couple must be equal and opposite the couple exerted upon the right and left faces.

Then

$$s_1\, dy\, dz\, dx = s_2\, dx\, dy\, dz$$

or

$$s_1 = s_2$$

and *shear stresses on mutually perpendicular planes of loaded bodies are equal in magnitude and oppositely directed.* It is well to note here that whenever shear stress is set up on any plane of a body in equilibrium, shear stress of equal magnitude is always induced upon the perpendicular plane.

Since the shear stresses on the X- and Y-planes of Fig. 12 are equal, they are indicated by the same subscript, and are called s_{XY}.

The shear stress on plane ab is typical of shear stress on any oblique plane of the body, and for the present will be identified as s_S. The normal stress on plane ab is, similarly, typical and will be designated as s_N.

Our goal is the evaluation of s_N and s_S, the normal and shear stresses, respectively, on any oblique plane of a loaded body. These will be evaluated in terms of the stresses on the X- and Y-planes and the locating angle θ.

In accordance with the philosophy of the free body and its force system, we therefore proceed to apply the conditions of equilibrium to the isolated triangular prism. The Newtonian conditions of equilibrium apply to external *forces*, rather than unit stresses. We must, therefore, summarize the influence of the forces acting upon the faces of the triangular prism.

Figure 14 shows a resolution of the stresses indicated in Fig. 12, into components which are either parallel or perpendicular to the A-axis.

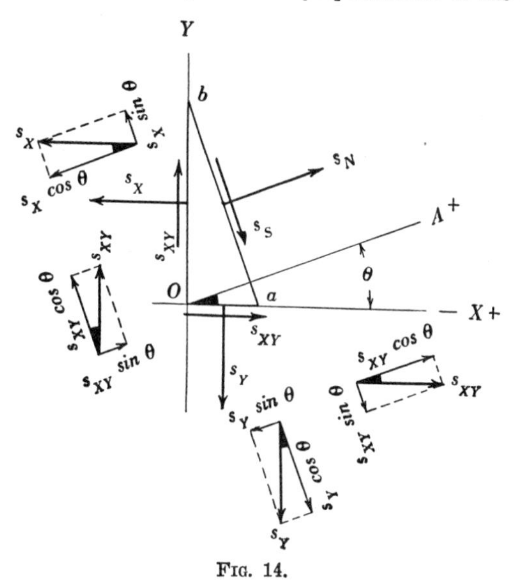

FIG. 14.

Applying first the condition of equilibrium $\Sigma A = 0$ to all forces parallel to the A-axis,

$$s_N(ab \times 1) + s_{XY} \sin \theta(Ob \times 1) - s_X \cos \theta(Ob \times 1) + s_{XY} \cos \theta(Oa \times 1) - s_Y \sin \theta(Oa \times 1) = 0$$

Substituting $$Ob = ab \cos \theta$$

and $$Oa = ab \sin \theta$$

$$s_N(ab) + s_{XY} \sin \theta(ab \cos \theta) - s_X \cos \theta(ab \cos \theta) + s_{XY} \cos \theta(ab \sin \theta) - s_Y \sin \theta(ab \sin \theta) = 0$$

and $$\mathbf{s}_N = \mathbf{s}_X \cos^2 \theta + \mathbf{s}_Y \sin^2 \theta - 2\mathbf{s}_{XY} \sin \theta \cos \theta \quad \textbf{(3)}$$

If now we summarize the forces which act in a direction perpendicular to the A-axis, we have

$$-s_S(ab \times 1) + s_{XY} \cos \theta(Ob \times 1) + s_X \sin \theta(Ob \times 1) - s_{XY} \sin \theta(Oa \times 1) - s_Y \cos \theta(Oa \times 1) = 0$$

and $$\mathbf{s}_S = (\mathbf{s}_X - \mathbf{s}_Y) \sin \theta \cos \theta + \mathbf{s}_{XY}(\cos^2 \theta - \sin^2 \theta) \quad \textbf{(4)}$$

Equations (3) and (4) present analytical expressions which evaluate the normal and shear stresses on all of the oblique planes through a point of a loaded body.

The form of such expressions indicates that these stresses vary sinusoidally as a function of the locating angle θ, and that they must rise to a maximum, then descend to a minimum.

We shall, therefore, differentiate the equation for normal stress (3) and set the first derivative equal to zero, to discover the angle θ locating the planes of maximum and minimum stress which have already been defined as the principal stresses.

$$\frac{ds_N}{d\theta} = -2s_X \cos\theta \sin\theta + 2s_Y \sin\theta \cos\theta - 2s_{XY}(\cos^2\theta - \sin^2\theta) = 0$$

Then

$$(s_Y - s_X) \sin\theta \cos\theta = s_{XY}(\cos^2\theta - \sin^2\theta)$$

or

$$\frac{(s_Y - s_X)\, 2 \sin\theta \cos\theta}{2} = s_{XY}(\cos^2\theta - \sin^2\theta)$$

$$\frac{2 \sin\theta \cos\theta}{\cos^2\theta - \sin^2\theta} = \frac{2s_{XY}}{s_Y - s_X}$$

and

$$\mathbf{\tan 2\theta = \frac{2s_{XY}}{s_Y - s_X}} \qquad \mathbf{(5)}$$

There are two values of 2θ, differing by 180° which have the same tangent. Then there will be two values of θ, differing by 90°, which will result from substitution in equation (5). Each of these values will locate a principal axis and its accompanying principal plane. Upon one of these planes, the normal stress will be maximum, while upon the other it is minimum.

We have found, in the simpler case of the axially loaded body, that the value of shear stress is zero on principal planes. This may be confirmed in the present case as well.

If, in equation (4), expressing shear stress on all oblique planes, the value of shear equal to zero is introduced,

$$s_S = (s_X - s_Y) \sin\theta \cos\theta + s_{XY}(\cos^2\theta - \sin^2\theta) = 0$$

then

$$-\frac{(s_X - s_Y)\, 2 \sin\theta \cos\theta}{2} = s_{XY}(\cos^2\theta - \sin^2\theta)$$

and

$$\tan 2\theta = \frac{2s_{XY}}{s_Y - s_X}$$

which agrees with equation (5) and proves that the shear stress is zero on the principal planes.

Equation (5) locates the principal axes, and determines the principal planes. When these have been located, equations (3) and (4) may be used to determine the principal stresses.

Illustrative Example. At a point in a loaded body, the following stress values are known (Fig. 15-a):

$$s_X = 5000 \text{ psi (tension)}$$
$$s_Y = 2000 \text{ psi (compression)}$$
$$s_{XY} = 2000 \text{ psi (positive on the } X\text{-plane)}$$

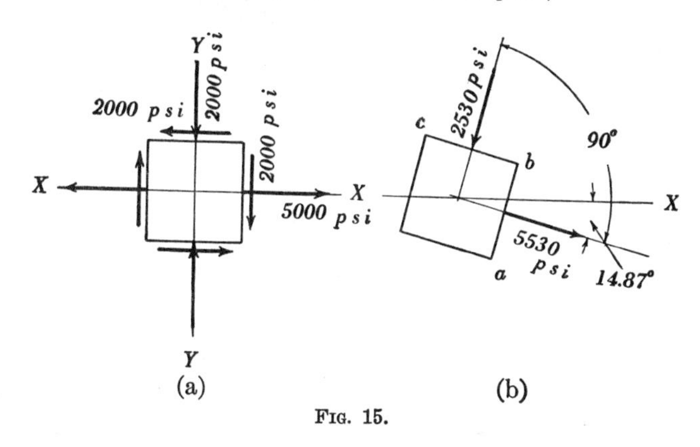

FIG. 15.

The principal planes are to be located, and the principal stresses determined.

Since we are making use of analytical equations, a proper system of signs must be employed. In the derivation of the equations we have employed tensile stresses in the case of both s_X and s_Y. These tensile stresses were introduced into the equation as positive quantities. We shall in this illustrative example, therefore, denote tension as positive and compression as negative. In the derivation, a positive shear stress was encountered on the X-plane, and written into the equations as positive. If a negative shear stress occurs on the X-plane, it must therefore be entered in the equations as a negative term.

We first proceed to locate the principal axes. Substituting in equation (5),

$$\tan 2\theta = \frac{2 \times 2000}{-2000 - (+5000)} = -0.5714$$
$$2\theta = -29.74°; \qquad \theta = -14.87°$$

The solution orients one of the principal axes at an angle of 14.87° clockwise from the X-axis, as noted in Fig. 15-b. One principal plane is normal to this axis, the other being perpendicular to the first. These principal planes are denoted as *ab* and *bc*.

The principal stresses may now be evaluated by substitution in equation (3).

$$\sin(-14.87°) = -0.2566$$
$$\cos(-14.87°) = +0.9665$$

$$s_N = (+5000)(0.9665)^2 + (-2000)(-0.2566)^2 - 2(+2000)(-0.2566)(+0.9665)$$
$$= 4670 - 132 + 992 = +5530 \text{ psi}$$

The second principal stress may be determined by introducing the value $(90 + \theta) = +75.13°$ in equation (3).

$$s_N = (+5000)(0.2566)^2 + (-2000)(0.9665)^2 - 2(+2000)(0.2566)(0.9665)$$
$$= +330 - 1868 - 992 = -2530 \text{ psi}$$

The location of the principal planes and the plotting of the principal stresses are illustrated in Fig. 15-b.

One readily available method of checking the evaluation of the principal stresses just determined may be applied if we note the relationship of the normal stresses on any two mutually perpendicular planes.

If the normal stress on any plane whose axis makes an angle θ with the X-axis is called s_N, and the normal stress on a perpendicular plane called s_N', we find by substitution in equation (3) that

$$\begin{aligned} s_N + s_N' &= s_X \cos^2 \theta + s_Y \sin^2 \theta - 2s_{XY} \sin \theta \cos \theta + s_X \cos^2 (90 + \theta) \\ &\quad + s_Y \sin (90 + \theta) - 2s_{XY} \sin (90 + \theta) \cos (90 + \theta) \\ &= s_X \cos^2 \theta + s_Y \sin^2 \theta - 2s_{XY} \sin \theta \cos \theta + s_X \sin^2 \theta + s_Y \cos^2 \theta \\ &\quad + 2s_{XY} \sin \theta \cos \theta \\ &= s_X(\cos^2 \theta + \sin^2 \theta) + s_Y(\cos^2 \theta + \sin^2 \theta) = s_X + s_Y \end{aligned}$$

which proves that *the sum of the normal stresses on a pair of mutually perpendicular planes is a constant,* the sum being always equal to the sum of the normal stresses on the basic X- and Y-planes.

In the present example, the sum of the two principal stresses is

$$+5530 + (-2530) = +3000$$

which agrees with the sum of the normal stresses, s_X and s_Y which is

$$+5000 + (-2000) = +3000$$

6. General Case of Plane Stress by Mohr's Circle. The pseudo-graphical solution by Mohr's circle which we employed in our treatment of the simple, axially-loaded body may be used as an efficient technique in the general case. We proceed to plot the circle as follows (Fig. 16):

It is assumed that s_X, s_Y, and s_{XY} are known, and that s_X and s_Y are both tensile, with s_X greater than s_Y. It is also assumed that s_{XY}, the shear stress on the X-plane is positive (Fig. 16-a).

Then $Ob = s_X$ and $bd = s_{XY}$ are laid out to establish point d of Fig. 16-b. Similarly, $Oe = s_Y$ and $ef = -s_{XY}$ are laid out to establish point f.

The diameter of the Mohr's circle, which is now drawn, is df. As before, we shall have confidence that this circle correctly evaluates the state of stress at a point of a loaded body if we are able to determine that it yields results which are consistent with equations (3), (4), and (5).

According to the circle of Fig. 16-b, Og and Oh are the principal stresses for the given point, and the angle between points d and g is $dcb = 2\theta$.

$$\tan 2\theta = \frac{bd}{bc} = \frac{s_{XY}}{(s_X - s_Y)/2} = \frac{2s_{XY}}{s_X - s_Y}$$

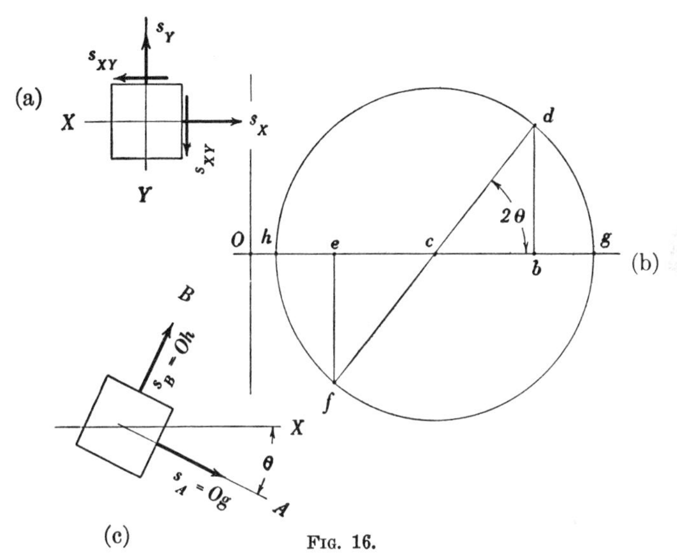

FIG. 16.

The angle is clockwise from point d, representing the stress on the X-plane, to point g, and the equation may therefore be written

$$\tan 2\theta = -\frac{2s_{XY}}{s_X - s_Y} = \frac{2s_{XY}}{s_Y - s_X}$$

which is in agreement with equation (5).

We shall now investigate the relationship between the values of stress yielded by the Mohr's circle and those given in equations (3) and (4).

Figure 16-c shows the principal axes located by points g and h. These have been called axes A and B. The $A-$ and $B-$ planes perpendicular to these axes are principal planes.

Equation (3) may be written as follows to evaluate the normal stress on the X-plane ($s_X = Ob$) in terms of the stresses on the $A-$ and $B-$ planes:

$$s_X = s_A \cos^2 \theta + s_B \sin^2 \theta - 2s_{AB} \sin \theta \cos \theta$$

Since the $A-$ and $B-$ planes are principal planes the shear stress, $s_{AB} = 0$, and

$$s_X = s_A \cos^2 \theta + s_B \sin^2 \theta$$

If now we turn to Fig. 16-b we note that

$$s_X = Ob = Oc + cb$$
$$= \frac{Og + Oh}{2} + cd \cos 2\theta$$
$$= \frac{s_A + s_B}{2} + \frac{s_A - s_B}{2} \cos 2\theta$$

But $\cos 2\theta = \cos^2 \theta - \sin^2 \theta$

and $1 = \cos^2 \theta + \sin^2 \theta$

Substituting these values,

$$s_X = s_A \cos^2 \theta + s_B \sin^2 \theta$$

and the Mohr's circle correctly evaluates the relationship of the principal stresses to the stresses on the other planes.

Similarly, the evaluation of the shear stress $s_{XY} = bd$ may be checked against that given by equation (4).

Substituting, $s_{XY} = (s_A - s_B) \sin \theta \cos \theta$

By Mohr's circle,

$$s_{XY} = bd = cd \sin 2\theta$$
$$= \frac{s_A - s_B}{2} \sin 2\theta$$

But $\sin 2\theta = 2 \sin \theta \cos \theta$

and $s_{XY} = (s_A - s_B) \sin \theta \cos \theta$

Illustrative Example I. In the illustrative example of the preceding article the following data were given:

$$s_X = 5000 \text{ psi (tension)}$$
$$s_Y = 2000 \text{ psi (compression)}$$
$$s_{XY} = 2000 \text{ psi (positive on the } X\text{-plane)}$$

We shall again solve this problem, in this case making use of a Mohr's circle as our technique of solution. We shall also observe the location of the planes of maximum shear, and evaluate the maximum shear stress.

The given values are shown in Fig. 17-a. The Mohr's circle is plotted as Fig. 17-b.

$Ob = 5000$ (to the right of the origin, for tension)
$bd = 2000$ (above the origin, for positive shear)

Point d is now determined. Point f is similarly established with

$Oe = -2000$ psi (to the left of the origin, for compression)
$ef = -2000$ psi (below the origin, for negative shear)

The circle is now drawn with df as diameter.

Point c, the center of the circle, will lie at a distance of 1500 from the origin O.

The first principal axis, which we will call the A-axis, represented by point g, will lie at an angular distance 2θ from point d.

From the circle,

$$\tan 2\theta = \frac{bd}{bc} = \frac{2000}{3500} = 0.5714$$

$$2\theta = 29.74°; \qquad \theta = 14.87°$$

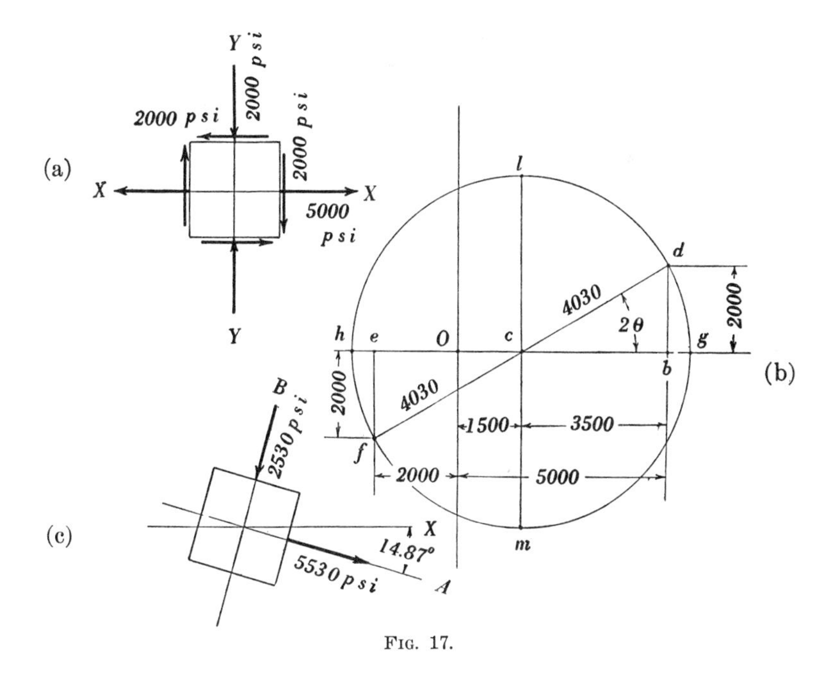

FIG. 17.

The A-axis has been drawn, in Fig. 17-c, at an angle of 14.87° with the X-axis. It will be noted that the angular displacement from d to g on the Mohr's circle is clockwise; on the plot of Fig. 17-c the A-axis is therefore oriented clockwise from the X-axis.

The other principal axis, called the B-axis, represented by point h of Fig. 17-b is located at 90° from the A-axis in Fig. 17-c.

We can now determine the values of the principal stresses. The radius cd is first evaluated:

$$cd = \sqrt{(3500) + (2000)^2} = 4030 \text{ psi}$$

Then $$Og = Oc + cd = 1500 + 4030 = 5530 \text{ psi}$$

Since this abscissa lies to the right of the origin, the stress is tensile.

$$Oh = Oc - cd = 1500 - 4030 = -2530 \text{ psi}$$

Since Oh lies to the left of the origin, the stress is compressive.

These principal stresses have been shown acting on the principal planes in Fig. 17-c.

The planes of maximum shear are represented by points l and m of Fig. 17-b. Point l lies at an angular distance $2\theta = 90°$ from point g, measured counter-clockwise. A C-plane is shown in Fig. 18, located at 45° from the A-plane. On this C-plane the shear stress has magnitude cl = radius cd = 4030 psi, and is positive, for point l of Fig. 17-b lies above origin O.

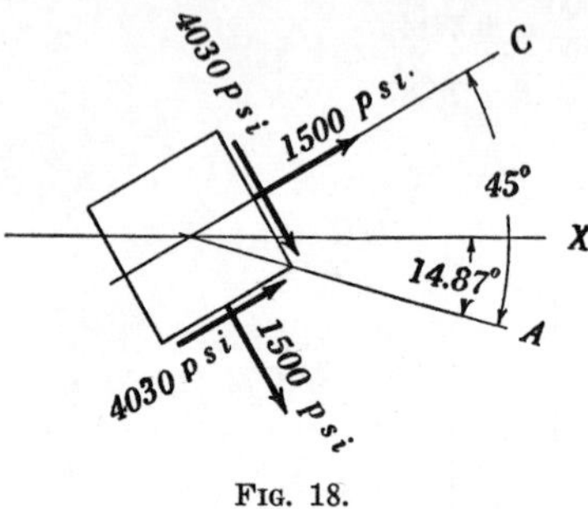

FIG. 18.

It should be noted that while the principal planes, or planes of maximum and minimum normal stress have no shear components, there is a normal stress acting on the planes of maximum shear; in this case, for example, the maximum shear planes have acting upon them a normal stress of 1500 psi tension.

Illustrative Example II. It is quite possible that there may be a shear stress at a given point of a loaded body which is of greater magnitude than the values revealed by the usual Mohr's circle, as in the preceding problem. This possibility may be present even in the cases of plane stress, which we are considering. To reveal whether or not such a greater shear stress is present, it is necessary that we investigate *all* of the planes which may be passed through the given point.

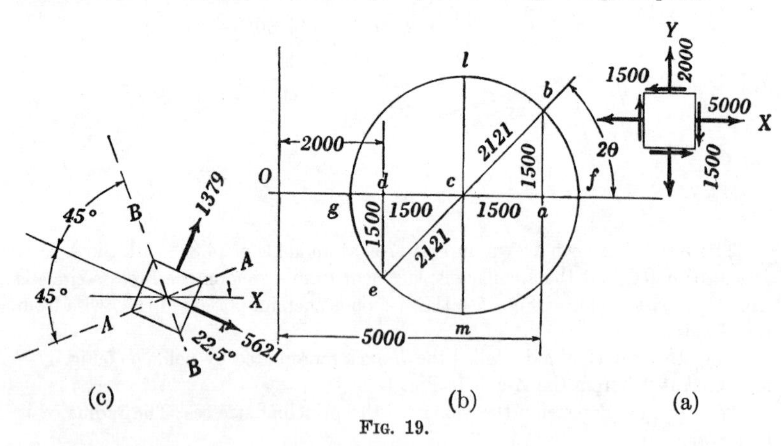

FIG. 19.

Figures 19 and 20 are intended to assist us in such a consideration of all planes. If we carefully investigate the series of small prisms which are shown in these figures we shall establish a method of attack upon the problem of maximum shear stress in cases of plane stress.

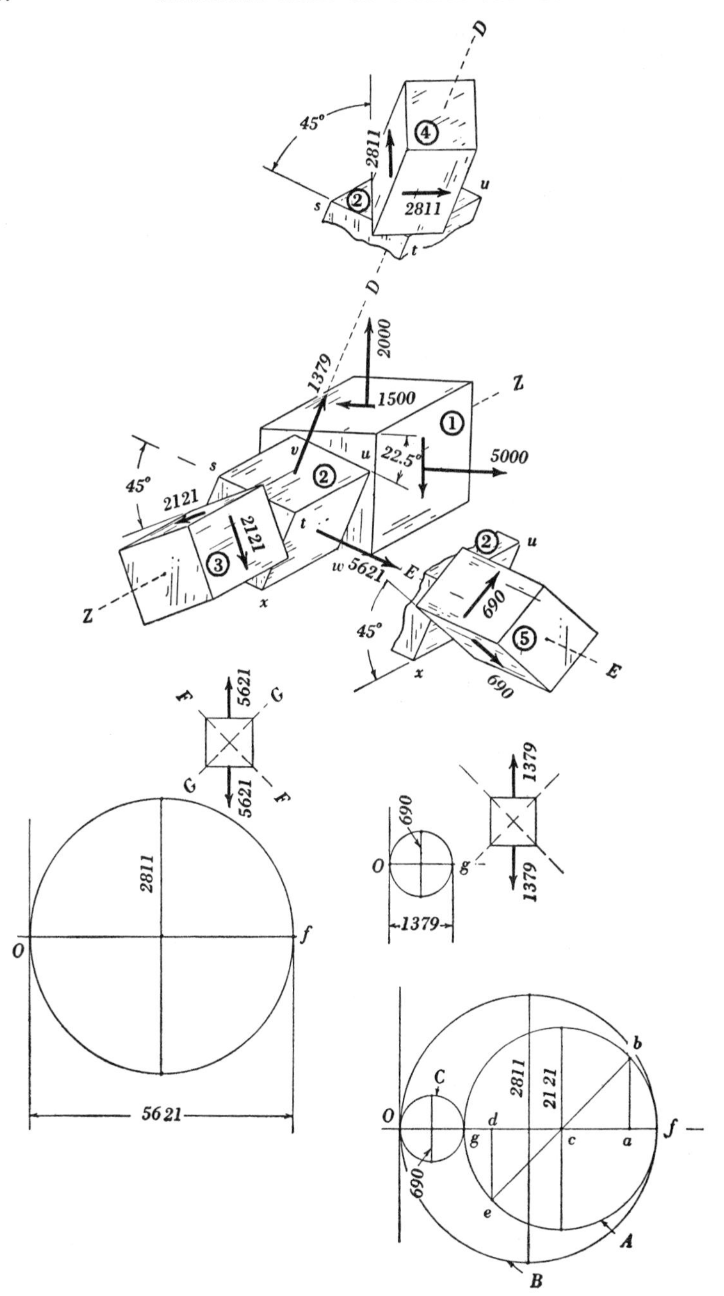

D
45°
4
2811
2
2811
s
u
t
D
2000
1379
1500
Z
1
5000
22.5°
u
v
s
2
45°
2121
2121
3
t
2
u
w 5621
E
Z
x
690
45°
5
x
690
E
5621
F
G
G
5621
F
1379
690
O
g
1379
1379
2811
O
f
5621
C
2811
2121
b
O
d
g
c
a
f
690
e
A
B

Fig. 20.

The given data of the problem follow:

$$s_X = 5000 \text{ psi (tension)}$$
$$s_Y = 2000 \text{ psi (tension)}$$
$$s_{XY} = 1500 \text{ psi (positive on the } X\text{-plane)}$$

These data have been plotted on the small prism of Fig. 19-a.

Our first step in the analysis is to locate the principal planes and then to determine the principal stresses as we have done in preceding problems. The Mohr's circle which represents this first step in our attack is shown in Fig. 19-b., where

$$Oa = s_X = 5000$$
$$ab = s_{XY} = 1500$$
$$Od = s_Y = 2000$$
$$de = -s_{XY} = -1500$$

The radius of the circle is

$$cb = \sqrt{(1500)^2 + (1500)^2} = 2121$$

and the maximum principal stress is

$$Of = 2000 + 1500 + 2121 = 5621 \text{ (tension)}$$

The minimum principal stress is

$$Og = 2000 + 1500 - 2121 = 1379 \text{ (tension)}$$

The principal planes are located as follows

$$2\theta = \tan^{-1}\frac{ba}{ca} = \tan^{-1}\frac{1500}{1500} = 45°$$

and $\theta = 22.5°$

The principal stresses, properly displayed on the principal planes, are shown in Fig 19-c.

There are two planes, each making an angle of 45° with the principal planes, which will be planes of maximum shear stress. These planes are indicated as the lines *A-A* and *B-B* in Fig. 19-c.

We now turn our attention to the series of prisms which is illustrated in Fig. 20-a. Prism ① shows the stresses of the original data. Prism ② has been inclined at 22.5° with the top face of prism ① to show the principal stresses in position on the principal planes. Finally, prism ③ is shown, inclined at 45° with the top face of prism ②, so that it will serve to show the maximum shear stresses in position on the planes of maximum shear. (There are, of course, normal stresses on these planes of maximum shear. These normal stresses are of no interest to us in the present study, and they have been omitted from the drawing, which is of sufficient complexity to occupy us without burdening it with unnecessary detail).

Our survey has thus far revealed two planes of maximum shear, each inclined at 45° with the principal planes. These are the planes which we see as we look along axis *Z-Z* of Fig. 20-a.

This series of planes is not, however, the only group of planes which may be passed through the center of the original prism ①.

Let us now consider the axis *D-D* of Fig. 20-a. This is the axis along which the principal stress of 1379 psi acts. Looking along this axis from the top of the drawing we see face *stuv* of prism ②. The maximum principal stress of 5621 psi appears, perpendicular to face *tuwx*. Our observation is recorded as the small prism of Fig. 20-b, accompanied by a Mohr's circle to represent the series of planes which has *D-D* as a common axis. This Mohr's circle reveals, by its radius, a maximum shear stress of magnitude

$$\frac{Of}{2} = \frac{5621}{2} = 2811 \text{ psi}$$

on planes *F-F* and *G-G* which are inclined at 45° with principal plane *tuwx*. The presence of this large shear stress is shown on prism ④ (Fig. 20-a), which is inclined at 45° with line *tu*. This shear stress is greater than the one of 2121 psi previously noted, but we must patiently introduce one more observation before we shall have considered every possibility of a maximum shear plane.

We now turn to axis *E-E* of Fig. 20-a. Looking along this axis from the right side of the drawing, we note principal plane *tuwx*, and the minimum principal stress of 1379 psi. This observation is recorded in Fig. 20-c, together with the Mohr's circle for all of the planes which have axis *E-E* as a common axis. This Mohr's circle reveals a maximum shear stress of magnitude

$$\frac{Og}{2} = \frac{1379}{2} = 690 \text{ psi}$$

This shear stress is indicated, in position on the proper 45° plane on prism ⑤.

We have already noted, in our previous discussions, that planes of maximum shear are always inclined at 45° with the principal planes. We have now surveyed *every* plane which is inclined at an angle of 45° with a principal plane and have therefore weighed every possibility of the presence of a maximum shear plane, and have determined all possible maximum shear stresses.

The maximum shear stress for the point which we have considered is, therefore, 2811 psi.

The relationship of the three Mohr's circles which we have employed in effecting the complete solution of our problem is indicated by plotting them on common co-ordinates in Fig. 20-d.

Circle *A* is the original circle of Fig. 19-b, which served to orient the principal planes and to determine the principal stresses. Circle *B* is that of Fig. 20-b, and circle *C* is that of Fig. 20-c. These are the Mohr's circles which appeared when the views of the principal planes were taken. These circles are tangent at the origin *O* and at points *f* and *g*, representing the principal stresses. It will be noted that whenever, as in this case, *both* of the principal stresses are tensile, the maximum shear stress will be the radius of the circle which, like *B*, has for its diameter the maximum principal stress. This condition will also prevail when both of the principal stresses are compressive. When, however, the two principal stresses are of opposite nature, the radius of the original circle *A* will be the maximum shear stress.

PROBLEMS

11. The value of s_X is 5000 psi (tension). Determine the normal and shear stresses on a plane whose axis makes an angle of 45°, clockwise, with the X-axis.

Ans. s_N = 2500 psi (tension); s_S = −2500 psi.

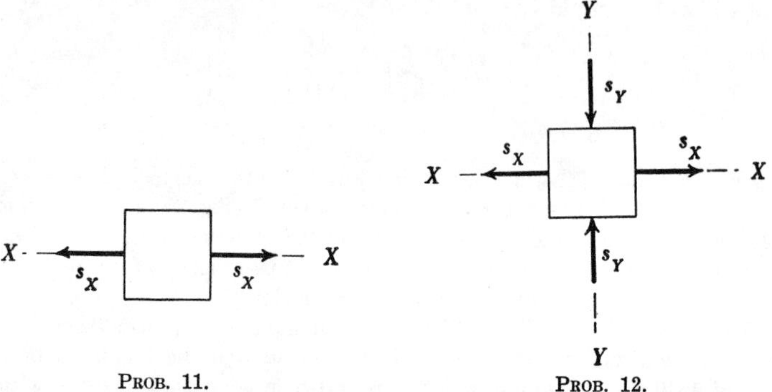

PROB. 11. PROB. 12.

12. s_X = 5000 psi (tension); s_Y = 2000 psi (compression); s_{XY} = 0. Locate the planes of maximum shear stress, and determine the value of maximum shear stress.

13. s_X = 5000 psi (tension); s_Y = 1000 psi (tension); s_{XY} = 2000 psi (positive on the X-plane). Determine the following:

a) The location of the principal planes.
b) The principal stresses.
c) The maximum shear stress.

Ans. a) −22.5° and +67.5°;
b) 5828 psi (tension) 172 psi (tension);
c) 2914 psi.

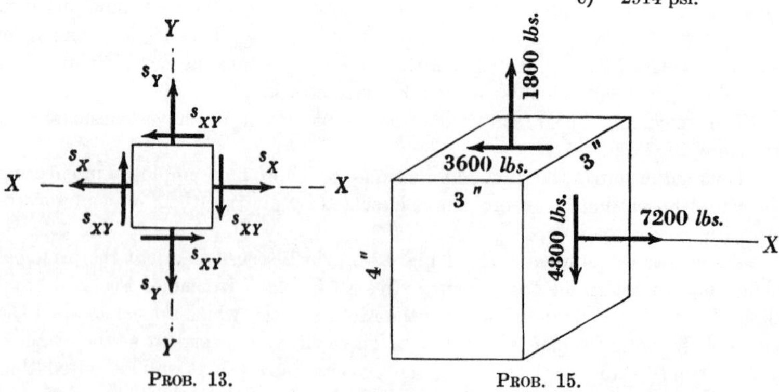

PROB. 13. PROB. 15.

14. s_X = 6000 psi (compression); s_Y = 0; s_{XY} = 2000 psi (positive on the X-plane). Locate the principal planes, determine the principal stresses and the maximum shear stress.

Ans. 6610 psi (compression) at +16.9°;
610 psi (tension) at −73.1°;
3610 psi.

15. The forces acting upon two faces of a prism are shown. Equal and opposite forces are acting upon the opposite faces to preserve the equilibrium of the prism. Assuming that all stresses are uniformly distributed through the prism, determine the following:

a) The location of the principal planes at the center of the prism.
b) The principal stresses.
c) The maximum shear stress.

Ans. a) $-31.7°$ and $+58.3°$.
b) 847 psi (tension) and 47 psi (compression).
c) 447 psi.

16. The external forces acting upon two faces of a small test block are shown. Equal and opposite forces act upon the opposite faces. Assuming that all stresses are uniformly distributed through the block, determine the normal and shear stresses on the diagonal plane *abcd*.

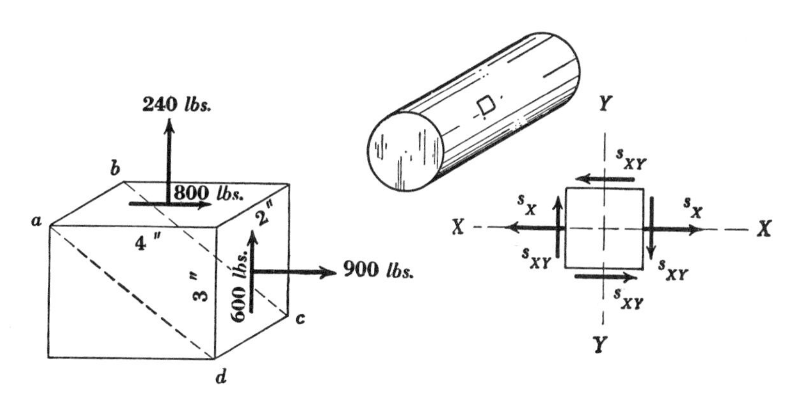

PROB. 16. PROB. 22.

17. $s_X = 1200$ psi (tension); $s_Y = 200$ psi (tension); $s_{XY} = 600$ psi (negative on the X-plane). Locate the principal planes and determine the principal stresses.

Ans. 1480 psi (tension) at $+25.1°$;
80 psi (compression) at $+115.1°$.

18. $s_X = 30{,}000$ psi (tension); $s_Y = 10{,}000$ psi (tension); $s_{XY} = 5000$ psi (positive on the X-plane). Locate the principal planes and determine the principal stresses.

19. $s_X = 30{,}000$ psi (tension); $s_Y = 10{,}000$ psi (compression); $s_{XY} = 5000$ psi (positive on the X-plane). Locate the principal planes and determine the principal stresses.

20. $s_X = 5000$ psi (tension); $s_Y = 1000$ psi (compression); $s_{XY} = 1000$ psi (positive on the X-plane). Locate the principal planes and determine the principal stresses.

Ans. 5160 psi (tension) at $-9.2°$;
1160 psi (compression) at $+80.8°$.

21. Determine the maximum shear stress for the stress conditions described in Prob. 20

Ans. 3160 psi.

22. A small prism at the surface of a shaft is shown. The stresses acting upon the prism are $s_X = 6000\,r^3$ psi; $s_Y = 0$; $s_{XY} = 4000\,r^3$ psi, where r is the radius of the shaft, in inches. If the maximum principal stress is 27,000 psi, determine the radius of the shaft.

Ans. 1.50 in.

23. At a point A of a loaded beam, $s_X = 2400$ psi (tension); $s_Y = 0$; $s_{XY} = 1600$ psi (negative on the X-plane). Locate the principal planes for point A, and determine the principal stresses. Ans. 3200 psi (tension) at $+26.6°$; 800 psi (compression) at $+116.6°$.

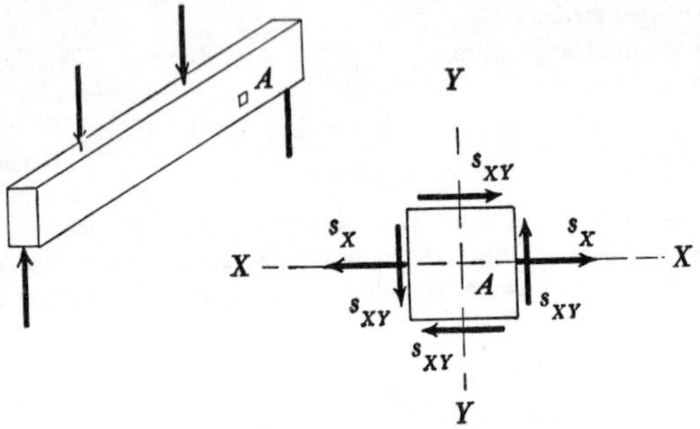

PROB. 23.

7. True Stress. Much of the information concerning the metals which engineers use is gleaned from a tension test. In this test, a bar of the metal is placed between two jaws which then move away from each other, stretching the specimen. We shall discuss in Chapter X, in detail, the mechanical properties of materials which are observed through such testing.

One feature of this test is of present interest. It is customary to employ the original or unreduced area, A, of the specimen in computing the unit stress at any load, P, by the formula

$$s = \frac{P}{A}$$

This practice is honored by long usage, and tolerated because of its ease of application; it has impeded, however, the harvesting from the simple tensile test of data which might be used in correlation with those gleaned from torsional, combined-stress, and impact tests, to greatly enhance our knowledge of materials. To attain its maximum usefulness the tensile test should also provide more data concerning the plastic range of materials than it does at present, information which could be most helpful in the metal-working processes of rolling, drawing, and extrusion.

As the tensile specimen stretches, its cross-sectional area will, of course, be reduced. A more accurate computation of unit stress must insist that the *true* unit stress at any load P will be the quotient obtained by dividing the load by the *actual* area of the specimen under that load, assuming that the stress is uniformly distributed.

Extensive research* has indicated the merit of obtaining the true stress-strain pattern of materials, and this more accurate information is gaining acceptance in industrial engineering practice.

It is our present intent to prepare the student for the practices which he will encounter in current design procedures. He will find that we are still using the apparent stresses taken from the tensile test as our design criteria. He should, however, be made aware of the fictitious nature of the constants derived from the usual tensile test so that he may realize that there are avenues of investigation leading toward greater knowledge, which are ever engaging the attention of researchers and that, as he progresses along the roads leading to professional practice he, too, may seek opportunity to make contributions.

The case of true stress versus the apparent stress of current practice is one example of approximation which is typical. The engineer, in the practice of his art, frequently departs from the theories of the underlying science. The original cross-sectional area of the tensile-test specimen is readily available from simple measurement at the start of the test. The instantaneous values of the decreasing area necessary to the evaluation of true stress are more difficult to ascertain. Engineers have, therefore, been content to accept the apparent stress. However, improvements of testing techniques are being developed and it is most probable that true stress data will become increasingly available.

We shall, as we proceed with our subject, note other examples of engineering approximation. In all cases, the approximation must be a justifiable one. The approximation may justify itself by virtue of the current state of our limited knowledge of a material or of a process which demands that some basis of operations be employed until more accurate information becomes available. However, in the use of approximation we must never invite the possibility of failure of the machine or structure by tolerating, in design, approximations whose order of magnitude is unknown and unconfirmed by empirical observation.

In addition to the introduction of approximation, we shall find that we are obliged to make assumptions in developing some of the theories which serve as basis for design procedure. Such assumptions must be checked before we may have confidence that the results are valid. In some cases, mathematical logic may be the basis of checking assumptions. Such rational approaches are ever the goal of the engineering profession, and enormous strides have been made in recent years toward that objective. Another channel of approach to the checking of assumptions consists of the

*See Article and Bibliography of C. W. MacGregor in Hetenyi: *Handbook of Experimental Stress Analysis*, Wiley (1950).

improvement of the instruments and techniques of testing, in laboratory or field, so that the actual behavior of materials or of loaded bodies may be observed with a high degree of precision. This necessity furnishes the motivation for much of the research which the engineer, in partnership with other scientific workers, performs.

8. Working Stress. Factor of Safety. The formal school career of an engineering student would be most comfortable, and probably least inspiring, if all of the material which must be placed at the command of the engineer were known and its boundaries rigidly fixed. Fortunately, such a static sinecure is not available; this is a dynamic profession which is constantly in flux. Our horizons constantly expand, and the challenge of exploration of new territory is ever presented. Our present study of the fundamentals of the behavior of materials cannot be reduced to exact formulas in which we may substitute values or rigidly rationalized theories which we must accept with docile submission.

In the fixing of the allowable or working stresses in materials we must respond to a situation which is, for the engineering student, a new and disturbing one. In the elementary courses in mechanics which have preceded this subject in the engineering curriculum, our preparation has assumed that we were not yet sufficiently mature to be entrusted with the facts of the engineering life. Such material has been postulated upon premises of palatable axioms, or dictated as arbitrary law which must be accepted without question. Now we must adopt a more demanding philosophy which insists upon facing reality.

The mechanical properties of materials (which are discussed in Chapter X) are measured in materials-testing laboratories. The results of such tests vary in their accuracy, and hence in their validity, with such factors as the reliability and the precision of the instruments which are employed. Other factors may also play a part in the value of such tests; for example, the rapidity with which a tensile specimen is deformed may very materially affect the test results. In some cases, as in the tensile test, the specimen must be a small coupon or test bar which, while chemically a fair specimen of the material, may not represent a fair sampling of the mechanical properties of the whole structural member or machine part. Any assumption that the material, even within the confines of a small test specimen is absolutely homogeneous and isotropic* may be far from true. The crystalline structure may vary, or the specimen may contain imperfections that will lead to local concentrations of stress.

In the face of such obstacles some order must be brought into the practice of dependence upon test results or the designer would have no

*The word isotropic means "having the same physical properties in all directions"

framework of reference in which to operate. Convenience, or expediency has dictated many of our present practices. This has been the natural result of a search to effect a working liaison between the testing laboratory and the designer's desk.

The absolute evaluation of the properties of materials must ever wait for the perfection of those materials or of the rational or empirical tools of measurement, but progress in the use of the materials can never await such idealistic perfection. We are, therefore, obliged to compromise by accepting, in general, relative measurements of properties. In the selection of available materials to be assigned to service in a machine part—if comparison of several materials can be made—the relative merits will dictate the choice of the best material.

For example, the preceding article has discussed the apparent stress which is determined in the usual tensile test versus the true stress actually present in the test specimen. If several kinds of steel are subjected to the same test, comparison may be made of their properties and desirability, whether or not the true stress is determined. Such establishment of relative values must rest upon a common background of testing technique, which will insure that fair comparisons have been made. Each tensile specimen must be of the same size and shape as the competing specimens—the manner in which the axial load is applied, the rate at which the specimen is deformed, the temperature of the medium in which the test is performed must be identical for all specimens.

To insure the fairness of these comparative tests, the engineering profession has evolved a series of rules. These rules appear as the codes or standards of groups of engineers or of societies like the American Society for Testing Materials. Such devices are destined to effect uniformity in testing equipment and techniques and to assure universality of understanding of the test data. Constant effort is devoted to improvement of testing as well as to dissemination of information and the encouragement of the adoption of standard procedures.

The engineer must, however, be aware of the current limitations of our knowledge. He must never assume that the properties of materials announced in handbooks are absolute and irrevocable, but must be alert so that he may establish a proper perspective in the use of commonly accepted values.

In addition to the approximations made in announcements of the properties of materials, a proper philosophy of engineering must embrace caution in predicting the future of machine or structural members. Such members may find themselves confronted by service conditions different from those which their designer had anticipated. They may be subjected to occasional or regular overloading, greater speeds, or higher temperatures. The materials of which the parts are made may not be as uniform in their composition as the test specimen. When materials are fabricated, the method of fabrication may itself introduce stress, as in the placing of rivets or bolts, or in the welding of joints.

Time effects are an additional source of concern—materials may deteriorate in use so that the ability of the part to resist load or deformation may be appreciably lowered. For example, corrosion in the case of steel, or decay in the case of timber, will influence their strength properties. If the part is used at elevated temperatures, creep, or gradual change in dimension, may occur at constant load, even though the material is not stressed beyond the proportional limit.

These factors are all of serious concern to the designer, who must make the decision as to which materials are to be used, and who must prescribe the dimensions of the units or parts which will be made of those materials. And yet another source of doubt rises to plague his decision. The action of the parts is predicted by means of theories of the mechanics, or behavior, of bodies under load. We shall be engaged, in the major portion of this text, with an examination of those basic theories. We must, from the start, appreciate the fact that despite the efforts of mathematical philosophers, scientists, and engineers to reduce to a rational pattern the mechanics of materials under stress, many of those theories still rest upon assumptions. These assumptions may be true—they could not have prevailed through some generations of engineering experience, had not pragmatic trial indicated that they are at least approximately true. The latitude of approximation which is now tolerated by the assumption may, in some cases, be narrowed as refinement of the basic theory advances through additional research. In other cases, the assumption is so very nearly true that the empirical evidence already gathered confirms the validity of the assumption, and further expenditure of effort and money in refining the basic theory is unwarranted.

To effect a convenient design basis in the face of the obstacles which have been outlined above, it is customary in engineering practice to follow one of two established paths.

The maximum stress which will be permitted in a loaded body is called the *working stress*. Synonyms which are widely used are the *allowable stress* and the *design stress*. The working stress may be fixed, for cases of static loading, through the test data obtained from the simple tension test. Theories of failure are discussed in Art. 69 and concern themselves with the criteria which offer a medium for determining the working stress. For the present, we shall be content with a description of the simplest of the approaches to a design basis.

In the case of ductile materials, of which steel is typical, the yield point is determined in the tension test. Yield point is the stress at which, in the test, the stretched specimen suddenly exhibits a marked yielding, or elongation. This property is defined and discussed in detail on page 404. The yield point is the most critical property of such materials for they fail, characteristically, by yielding or deforming plastically. For brittle materials, which characteristically fail by fracturing, the ultimate strength is established as the critical property by testing. The ultimate strength of a material is the unit stress in the tensile test specimen when the specimen offers its greatest resistance to failure by tension. For a more detailed description, see page 405.

In both cases, the stresses determined in the test are arbitrarily reduced by dividing them by a factor of reduction which is intended to insure that the greatest resisting stress which the designer will demand of the material will lie well within the limits of its elastic range, so that neither permanent deformation nor fracture need be feared. This factor of reduction is called the *factor of safety*, which is a dangerous misnomer for it conveys the impression that it guarantees safety. In view of the uncertainties which preclude exact knowledge of the materials themselves, and the difficulty of determining the precise nature of the distribution of stresses in loaded bodies, the factor of safety is more properly a factor of ignorance through which an effort is made to compress the range of uncertainty to limits based upon the current knowledge of the engineering art.

If the stress at yield point is called $s_{\text{Y.P.}}$, the ultimate stress s_U, and the working or allowable stress s_W, the factor of safety will be

$$\text{F.S.} = \frac{s_U}{s_W} \quad \text{for brittle materials} \tag{6}$$

$$\text{F.S.} = \frac{s_{\text{Y.P.}}}{s_W} \quad \text{for ductile materials} \tag{7}$$

Prof. C. Richard Soderberg* of the Massachusetts Institute of Technology has proposed a more logical factor for allowable stresses. This is the *factor of utilization*, which is the reciprocal of the factor of safety defined above. If the load at failure is called P_0 and the actual load placed upon the body is called P, then the factor of utilization is

$$u = \frac{P}{P_0} \tag{8}$$

*For a more detailed discussion of working stresses, see "Working Stresses," by C. R. Soderberg in Hetenyi: *Handbook of Experimental Stress Analysis*, Wiley (1950).

Such a factor indicates the actual use which is being made of the material in relationship to its potentialities. A factor of utilization of 1 thus indicates that the material is being utilized to its limiting value, and represents the condition of failure.

Either of the above forms of factor is dependent for its value in design upon the criteria or standards which are employed as basic theories of failure, and must be used in conjunction with them. The maximum stress, maximum strain, maximum shear, and the von Mises-Hencky theories of failure are discussed in Art. 69.

The second avenue of approach to working stresses is the arbitrary announcement by organized groups of engineers or by codes like the building codes of various cities. For example, in structural engineering, it is common practice to accept the following values as allowable stresses in structural steel members: tension, 20,000 psi; compression, 20,000 psi; shear, 13,000 psi. The Boiler Construction Code of the American Society of Mechanical Engineers gives the following allowable stresses for steel plates and rivets: tension, 11,000 psi; compression, 19,000 psi; shear, 8800 psi. Such announcements as these have already considered the nature of the material as well as a factor of safety, which will be an average compromise for the conditions that will normally be faced by the type of member for which they are intended.

In the discussions of this article only static or gradually appplied loading at normal temperature has been considered. Later articles of the text consider impact loading and repeated loading which may result in fatigue failure.

The following Articles (9 to 12) are devoted to some common examples of bodies under load to illustrate the techniques which are employed in the analysis of stress for simple cases.

These discussions are intended to establish background for more complex situations and to offer some examples of the compromise between theory and practice, which is the constant concern of the engineer.

In each case we shall pursue the investigation to enhance our understanding of the fundamentals of the mechanics of materials; we should appreciate the fact that no one of these discussions is intended to be exhaustive. The intimate detail of design, for example, is the concern of the specialist in each particular field, and is beyond the scope of our present intent.

9. The Thin Hollow Cylinder and Sphere. Hollow cylinders, like those which are used as tanks and other pressure vessels, are classified as "thin" hollow cylinders when there is a very great difference between the thickness of the wall and the diameter of the cylinder. They are placed in a category because the theory applying to stress in thin hollow cylinders makes use of approximations which are only permissible for such cylinders and which would lead to untenable conclusions if the thickness of the wall is a very appreciable portion of the entire diameter of the cylinder. As we discuss this theory we shall note the introduction of approximation.

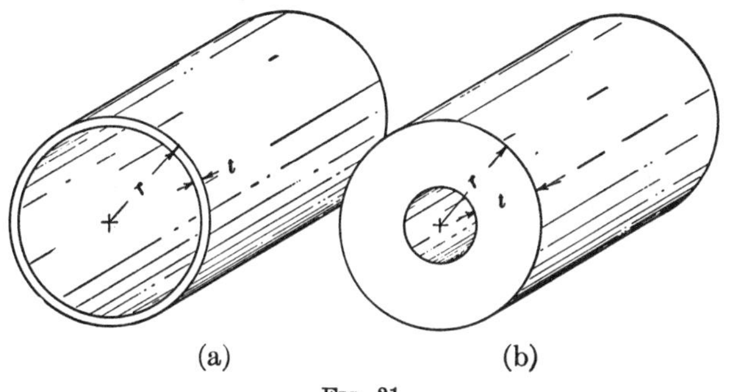

Fig. 21.

This type of classification into broad categories occurs very frequently in the subject of mechanics of materials. While there is great comfort in exact classification which would make it possible to decide quickly upon the assignment of a specific theory to each problem as it arises in stress analysis, such precision is impossible. There are no rigidly defined lines of demarcation between the region where one theory applies, and that in which another theory takes over. There is much overlap in adjacent areas—for example, loaded bodies of certain dimensional nature behave very much like bodies of somewhat different dimensions until the dimensional contrasts become extremely marked.

The development of engineering judgment is a process of learning through experience the extent of the broad areas in which a basic theory may be applied, and the limits of those areas which suggest that the theory must be rejected as inapplicable.

Certain areas of agreement in basic behavior, while not rigidly bounded by exact dimension begin to be apparent as our engineering judgment matures.

We do form some mental picture of men as we classify them in groups labelled "short," "of medium height," or "tall." Similarly, we accept a cylinder like that of Fig. 21-a as a "thin" hollow cylinder, and reject placing the cylinder of Fig. 21-b in such a category. The cross-sectional area of the wall of a tank which is of the nature of the cylinder of Fig. 21-a can be approximately determined as $2\pi rt$, but the cross-sectional area of a given gun barrel in which the relative sizes of wall and radius are those indicated in Fig. 21-b could not be determined, even approximately, by such an expression.

When internal pressure is built up in such cylinders, it is reasonable to assume that the stress in the thin wall of the first case is distributed fairly uniformly, but the stress in the thick wall of the second case varies very appreciably.

Testing confirms the truth of the foregoing statements. The thin hollow cylinder, designed and built as a tank under the above assumptions, will yield, when tested, the results anticipated by the theory. The thick hollow cylinder will yield results which are so very different that the theory has no validity.

To the embryonic engineer such a development is, at first, dismaying—he would prefer to have each basic theory assigned to a specific case which he can at once recognize as belonging in a rigidly bounded dimensional category, rather than a range whose end regions overlap. He must therefore learn to assign the use of basic theories to cases which lie, obviously, well within the questionable end ranges. For example, in the thin hollow cylinder now being considered, wall thickness greater than $\frac{1}{20}$ to $\frac{1}{10}$ of the total diameter become suspect. When the ratio of diameter to wall thickness is greater than 10, the cylinder will be amenable to treatment by a theory which rests, as does this one, upon such assumptions as the approximate cross-sectional area and uniform distribution of stress. The factor of 10 which has been suggested is intended to indicate a possible range of value, rather than an absolute boundary.

When the difference between the thickness of wall and the diameter is not so marked as to suggest immediately that the cylinder is a thin hollow one, the engineer questions the validity of such a theory and seeks, through research and further investigation, methods of analysis which will narrow the assumed range of approximation.

We have dwelt upon the philosophical approaches to the assignment of applicable theory in this case because similar decisions must be made as our subject progresses. In all cases, the engineer's attitude is one of caution. Theories may be developed as a basis of attack, but their underlying assumptions must constantly be challenged, and accepted or rejected as observation and experience confirm or invalidate such assumptions.

Figure 22-a shows a thin hollow cylinder or tank. It is assumed that the ends of this tank are sealed, and that a fluid pressure whose intensity is p exists within the tank. The radius of the tank is r, and the thickness of the wall is t.

The fluid pressure tends to expand the circumference, and a tensile stress is built up along such a longitudinal surface as *ab*.

Here, as in all essays in the field of mechanics, effective attack upon problems is based upon the selection of a free body, and appraisal of the force system which acts upon that isolated free body.

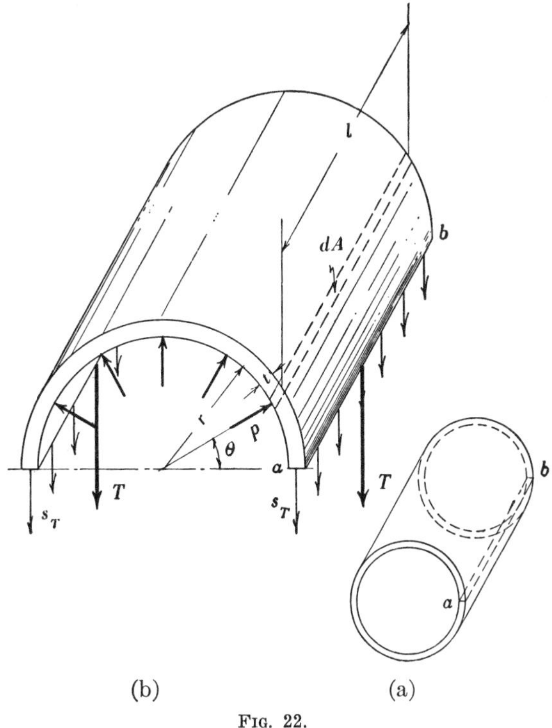

Fig. 22.

To evaluate the tensile stress in the wall of the cylinder, we isolate as free body a thin half-ring, as shown in Fig. 22-b.

The force system consists of the pressure of the fluid—(the weight of the free body is assumed to be of negligible magnitude)—which acts normal to the inner surface of the tank. The resultant of this distributed pressure is resisted by the resultant tensile forces developed on the two lower surfaces of the wall; these forces are indicated as T.

dA is an elementary area running along the inner surface for the entire length l.

The resultant force acting on dA caused by the internal pressure is

$$dF = p\,dA = p\,rd\theta\,l$$

The vertical component of dF is

$$p\,rd\theta\,l \sin \theta$$

and the sum of all such vertical components is

$$P = \int_{\theta=0}^{\theta=\pi} p\,rd\theta\,l \sin \theta = 2p\,r\,l$$

It will be observed that $2rl$ is the projected area on the horizontal plane of the semicircular ring, and the resultant pressure is, therefore, equal to the intensity of pressure, p, times the projected area.

We have already assumed that since this is a thin hollow cylinder, the tensile stress in the wall is uniformly distributed.

Then
$$T = s_T\,t\,l$$

where s_T is the unit tensile stress on the longitudinal bottom surface.

Applying the condition of equilibrium,

$$\Sigma Y = 0$$
$$+P - 2T = 0$$

or
$$2p\,r\,l = 2s_T\,t\,l$$

and
$$s_T = \frac{pr}{t} \tag{9}$$

This stress is called the *hoop tension.* This name arises from the fact that if two of the half-rings which we have isolated as the free body were bound by a hoop of cross-sectional area $t \times l$, s_T would be the tensile stress in the hoop.

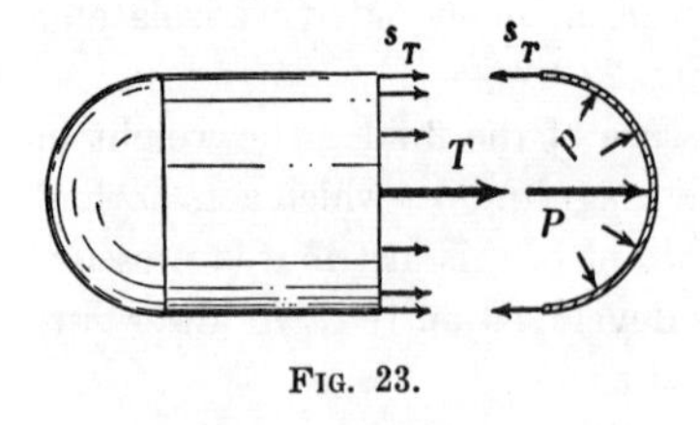

FIG. 23.

The stress in an end seam, or the stress on a transverse section of the tank, may be found by noting (Fig. 23) that the resultant pressure on the hemispherical end is

$$P = p\pi r^2$$

in which p is the intensity of pressure, and πr^2 the projected area of the hemisphere.

The force P must be equal to the force T, which is the resultant tensile force developed over the surface of the thin ring, forming a cross-sectional area of the wall.

Since
$$P = T$$
$$p\,\pi r^2 = s_T\,2\pi\,r\,t$$

and
$$s_T = \frac{pr}{2t} \tag{10}$$

This stress is called the *end* or *longitudinal tension.*

We should note that the end tension is one-half as great as the hoop tension. It follows that if a tank is built in the form of a thin hollow sphere, rather than a hollow cylinder, only one-half as great a tensile stress will be developed in the walls.

Illustrative Problem. The tank shown in Fig. 24 is subjected to an internal pressure of 400 psi. The diameter of the tank is 30 in., and the thickness of the wall

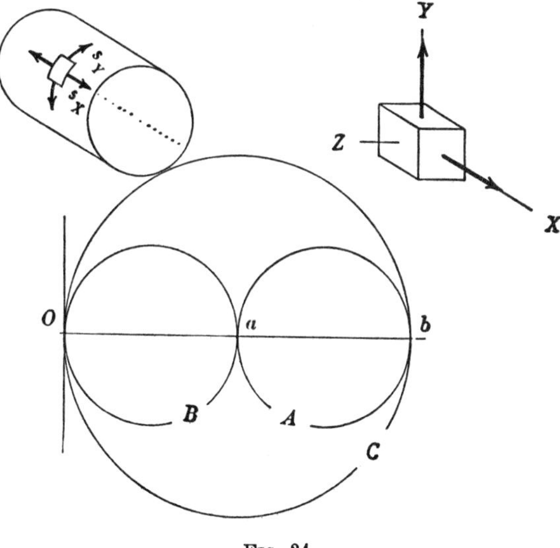

FIG. 24.

is ½ in. We are to determine the maximum shearing stress in the wall of the tank.

The hoop tension in the wall is found by using equation (9).

$$s_Y = \frac{pr}{t} = \frac{400 \times 15}{\frac{1}{2}} = 12{,}000 \text{ psi}$$

and the end tension is, by equation (10),

$$s_X = \frac{pr}{2t} = 6000 \text{ psi}$$

The intensity of pressure in the radial direction (Z is perpendicular to X and Y) of 400 psi, may be assumed to be negligible.

Since both of these principal stresses s_X and s_Y are of the same nature, the series of three Mohr's circles, discussed on page 29, is necessary to appraise all possibilities of maximum shear.

The first Mohr's circle (A) is drawn as in Fig. 24 with

$$s_X = Oa = 6000$$

and

$$s_Y = Ob = 12{,}000$$

This circle represents the group of planes of which the Z-axis is a common line or axis.

If now we consider the series of planes having the Y-axis as a common axis, circle B will be the Mohr's circle which represents these planes.

Finally, the series of planes having the X-axis as a common axis will be represented by Mohr's circle C.

The maximum shear stress will be the radius of the largest circle (C) which is

$$s_{S\,(\text{max.})} = \frac{Ob}{2} = \frac{12{,}000}{2} = 6000 \text{ psi}$$

PROBLEMS

24. The pressure in a cylindrical tank is to be 250 psi. The diameter of the tank is 3 ft., and the allowable tensile stress in the wall is 12,000 psi. Determine the minimum thickness of the wall. *Ans.* 0.375 in.

25. Determine the required thickness of the wall plate for a boiler, whose diameter is 6 ft., if the internal pressure is 150 psi; the allowable tensile stress of the material is 12,000 psi; the efficiency of the longitudinal joint is 85 per cent, and the efficiency of the end joints is 75 per cent.

26. What is the safe internal pressure in a hollow sphere if the thickness of the wall is $\frac{1}{4}$ in., the diameter is 20 in., and the allowable tensile stress in the material is 7000 psi. *Ans.* 350 psi.

27. A cylindrical tank has a diameter of 4 ft. The thickness of the wall is $\frac{3}{8}$ in., and the internal pressure is 200 psi. Determine the maximum shear stress in the wall. *Ans.* 6400 psi.

28. When the piston is at the forward end of its stroke, the pressure in the cylinder is 200 psi. The inner diameter of the cylinder is 10 in., and the allowable tensile stress in the wall is 10,000 psi. The efficiency of the welded end joint is 90 per cent. Determine the minimum wall thickness.

29. Determine the maximum permissible pressure of the fluid contained in a spherical tank, having a 10 ft. diameter, wall thickness of $\frac{3}{8}$ in., allowable tensile stress of 16,000 psi, if the efficiency of all joints is 85 per cent.

30. Determine the maximum hoop and end tensions in the tank shown. The wall thickness is $\frac{1}{4}$ in., and the internal pressure is 250 psi. *Ans.* Hoop tension: 24,000 psi.
End tension 8340 psi.

31. A cylindrical standpipe is 8 ft. in diameter and 25 ft. tall. When the standpipe is filled with water, determine the maximum hoop tension in the $\frac{3}{8}$-in. wall. Weight of water: 62.5 lb./cu. ft.

32. The tank shown is fabricated by welding hemispherical ends to a piece of welded pipe. The allowable tensile stress of the material is 12,000 psi. The efficiency of the longitudinal joint is 80 per cent, and the efficiency of the end joints is 60 per cent. The wall thickness is 0.1 in., and the diameter of the pipe is 8 in. Determine the safe pressure in the tank.

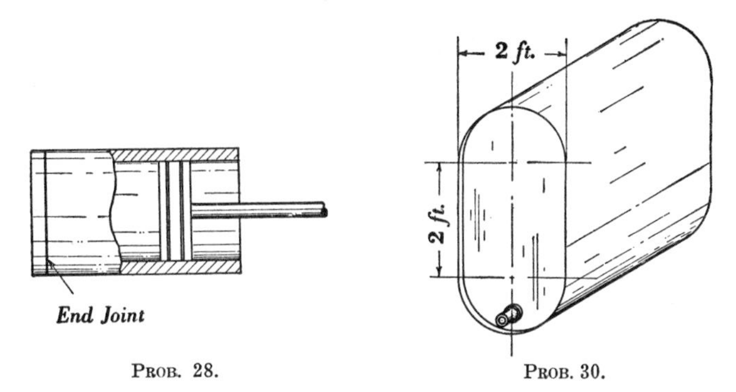

PROB. 28. PROB. 30.

33. Determine the diameter of the largest spherical tank which may be fabricated of ⅜-in. steel plate, having an allowable tensile stress of 16,000 psi, if the tank is to be subjected to an internal pressure of 300 psi. *Ans.* 6.67 ft.

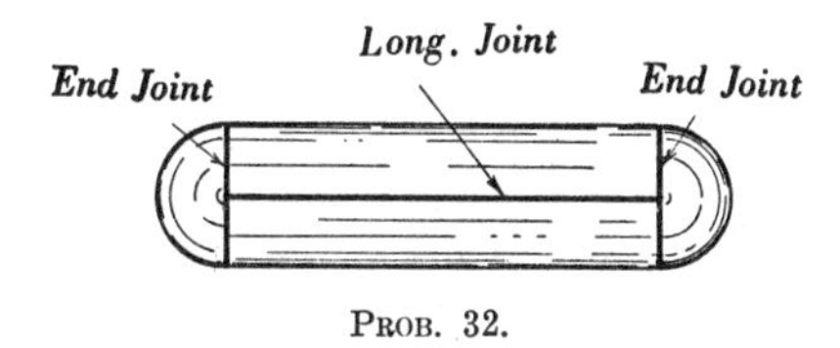

PROB. 32.

34. A tank is to be fabricated of ¼-in. plate. The maximum allowable shear stress in the metal is 9000 psi, and the maximum tensile stress is 20,000 psi. The tank is cylindrical. Determine the maximum radius of the tank if the internal pressure is 200 psi.

10. Riveted Joints. Riveted joints furnish another opportunity for us to appraise the distribution of stress in loaded bodies, when assumptions and approximations are employed to minimize the difficulty of designing in the face of complexities of stress distribution.

The simplest form of riveted joint—the lap joint—will be discussed to furnish a background of terminology and of stress considerations. Figure 25-a shows the details of a lap joint. Two plates which overlap are shown fastened together with a single row of rivets. This type of joint is called a *single-riveted lap joint*.

To isolate a free body for appraisal of the force system, we select the "repeating section," shown as Fig. 25-b. This specimen portion of the entire joint includes the region for which one rivet is responsible, and is exactly duplicated throughout the joint. It therefore furnishes a proper sampling of the conditions faced by each of the remaining sections.

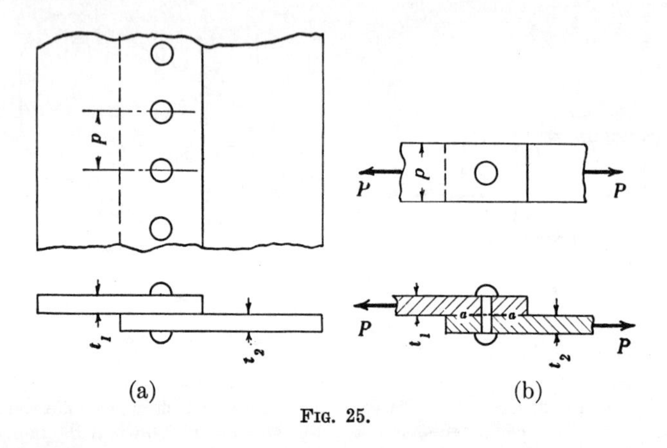

FIG. 25.

If the pitch, or distance between the centers of the rivets, is p, the width of the repeating section is also p.

We now examine all of the possible methods of failure of the repeating section. There is more than one manner in which the joint may fail, and each of the possibilities must be investigated. Just as a chain will fail at its weakest link, the riveted joint will be no stronger than its source of minimum strength.

1. Failure by Shearing of the Rivets. If loads P are applied as shown in Fig. 25-b, the rivet will tend to shear on section a-a. The measure of its ability to resist is a force

$$R_1 = s_S\, A \tag{11}$$

in which s_S is the allowable shear stress in the rivet and A the cross-sectional area of the rivet.

Certain assumptions are being made in fixing the total resistance R_1. First, it is assumed that the shear stress in the rivets is uniformly distributed. Second, the influence of friction between the plates has not been credited, even though it may be appreciable. Since rivets are usually heated, placed in the plate holes, and allowed to cool, there will be appreciable pressure between the plates. In engineering practice, the assistance of friction in preventing relative motion of the plates is not recognized. Third, the assumption is made that there is no bending of the rivets, which is not true, for it will be noted that the balanced forces P do not have the same line of action, and that their resultant is therefore a couple which does tend to bend the plates and rivet. These assumptions are made justifiable by assigning lower values to the allowable stresses than pure theory would suggest and, in the case of the possibility of bending, providing rivet heads of sufficient strength to resist the destructive action of the tendency to rotate.

2. Failure by Crushing. Under the influence of the loads P (Fig. 26) it is possible for the plate material behind the rivet—the shaded region—to crush, for this region of the plate is subjected to a compressive action called *bearing pressure* or *crushing.* The same action may tend to crush the rivets themselves. If, for example, the rivets were made of steel and the plates of soft wood, it is evident that the pull exerted by the forces P would cause the rivets to crush the wood. The ability of our repeating section to withstand such failure is the resistance to crushing.

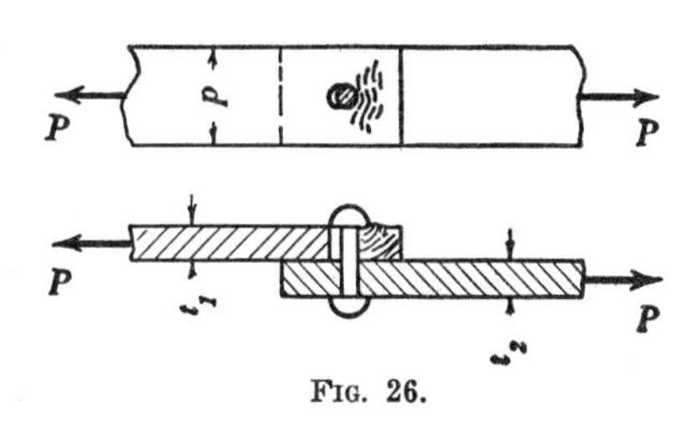

FIG. 26.

$$R_2 = s_C\, d\, t_1 \qquad \text{or} \qquad s_C\, d\, t_2 \tag{12}$$

in which s_C is the allowable compressive stress in the plate, d the diameter of the rivet, and t the thickness of the plate. (If t_1 and t_2 are equal, the plates will resist crushing equally well; if the thicknesses are different, the thinner plate will fail first.)

This resistance to crushing is analogous to the case discussed in Art. 9 for the thin hollow cylinder, where we found that the resultant pressure is the product of the intensity of pressure and the projected area of the surface subjected to pressure.

3. Failure by Tearing of the Plate. When plates, like those of Fig. 27 are subjected to the loads P, tensile stress is set up in the plates. The resultant resistance of the plates to failure by tension, or tearing, will be least in value at the section of the rivets, for it is there that the available area is smallest, as indicated in the figure.

The resistance to failure by tearing of the plate is

$$R_3 = s_T(p - d)t \tag{13}$$

in which s_T is the allowable tensile stress of the plate material, p is the pitch, d the diameter of the rivet, and t the thickness of the thinner plate.

The area subjected to tension is $(p - d)t$, and it is assumed that the tensile-stress distribution is uniform.

4. Margin or Lap Failure. It is conceivable that if the rivet is placed near the edge of the plate, as indicated in Fig. 28, the metal between the rivet hole and the edge of the plate will be forced out, a failure which is a

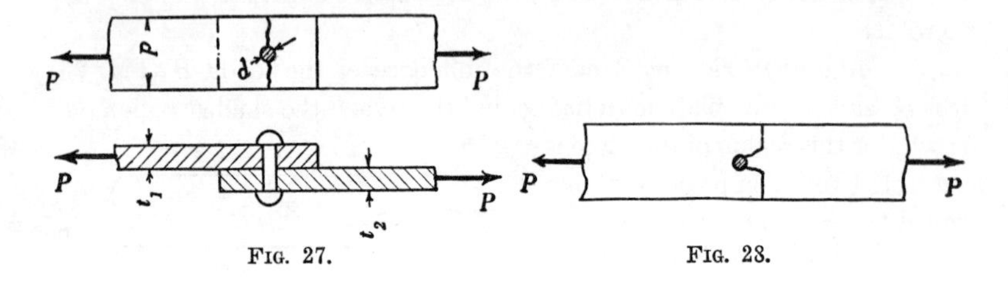

FIG. 27. FIG. 28.

combination of shearing and tearing. To protect a joint against such failure, the distance between the center of the rivet and the edge of the plate, called *lap*, is made 1¾ to 2 times the diameter of the rivet. This arbitrary value is the result of practical experiments.

The foregoing possibilities of failure have appraised the problem of the riveted joint from the viewpoint of total resistances based upon allowable stresses.

In practice, the problems usually faced by the designer are the determination of the pitch and the prediction of the resulting efficiency of the joint.

The following quantities are usually encountered as fixed:

The diameter of the rivets is fixed by shop practice, which considers the nature of the structure. The plate thicknesses are fixed in the problem-specific plates are to be joined. The physical properties of allowable stress are fixed by codes. Then, in the quantities to be used, only the pitch need be determined. The procedure is to evaluate resistances R_1 and R_2. The weaker of these fixed resistances is then substituted for resistance R_3 and the pitch determined.

The *efficiency* of the joint is defined as the ratio of the strength of the riveted joint to the strength of undisturbed plate.

The strength of the joint is R_3, which has already been made equal to the weaker of resistances R_1 and R_2.

Then

$$\text{Eff.} = \frac{s_T(p - d)t}{s_T pt} = \frac{p - d}{p} \qquad \textbf{(14)}$$

Riveted joints are built in many forms, which are grouped into two basic classes: the lap joint, already discussed, and the *butt joint*, illustrated in Fig. 29. In this form of joint, the two plates which are to be joined are placed in line, or butted, and cover plates used as indicated, to furnish support for the rivets.

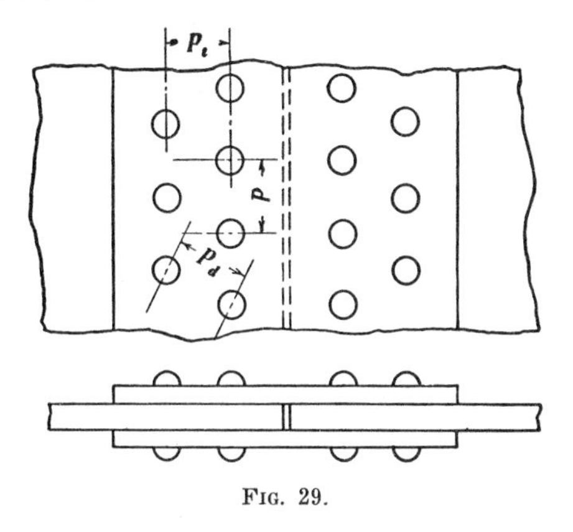

FIG. 29.

If a single row of rivets is used, the joint is a *single-riveted* joint, and if two rows of rivets are used, the joint becomes a *double-riveted* joint. Other patterns have been employed, making use of three or more rows.

When two or more rows are used, as in Fig. 29, the distance between rows of rivets, p_t, called the *transverse*, or back, pitch, is usually fixed by the minimum clearance requirements of the rivet-heading tool as $p_t \geqq 2.5d$, where d is the diameter of the rivets. When the rivets are staggered, the diagonal pitch, p_d, must be great enough so that tearing of the plates on the diagonal line between rivet centers will not occur. This condition will be fulfilled if

$$2(p_d - d) \geqq p - d \tag{15}$$

Illustrative Example I. The single-riveted lap joint shown in Fig. 25 is to be analyzed to determine the allowable load per rivet, the pitch, and the efficiency of the joint.

The following data are given:

$$d = \text{diameter of rivets} = 13/16 \text{ in.}$$
$$t = \text{thickness of plates} = 3/8 \text{ in.}$$

The allowable stresses will be those recommended by the A.S.M.E. Boiler Code.

$$s_T = 11{,}000 \text{ psi}$$
$$s_C = 19{,}000 \text{ psi}$$
$$s_S = 8800 \text{ psi}$$

One repeating section of the joint is indicated in Fig. 25-b.

The cross-sectional area of one rivet is 0.5185 sq. in., and the resistance to failure by shearing is, by equation (11),

$$R_1 = s_S A = 8800 \times 0.5185 = 4560 \text{ lb.}$$

The resistance to failure by crushing is, by equation (12),

$$R_2 = s_C\, dt = 19{,}000 \times \frac{13}{16} \times \frac{3}{8} = 5790 \text{ lb.}$$

The allowable load per rivet is the least of these values, or $R_3 = 4560$ lb.

Then, by equation (13) $\quad R_3 = s_T(p - d)t = 11{,}000\left(p - \frac{13}{16}\right)\frac{3}{8} = 4560 \text{ lb.}$

and $\quad p = 1.92$ in.

The efficiency of the joint is, by equation (14),

$$\frac{p-d}{p} = \frac{1.920 - 0.813}{1.920} = 0.577 \text{ or } 57.7 \text{ per cent}$$

Illustrative Example II. Compare the efficiency of a double-riveted lap joint with the single-riveted lap joint of Example I. Use values given in Example I.

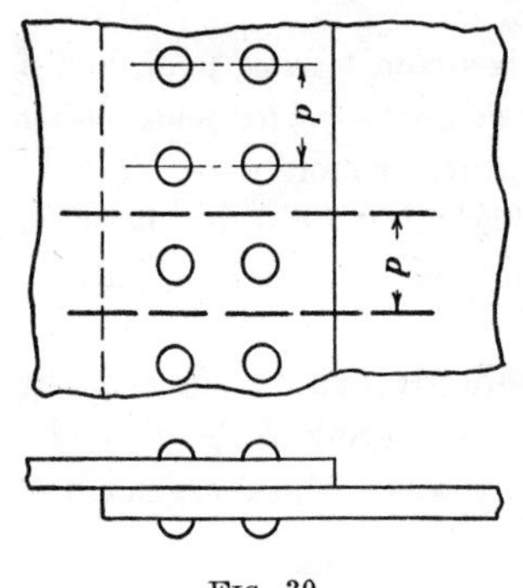

FIG. 30.

We find here (Fig. 30) that the load is carried by two rivets in each repeating section. In order to produce failure, two cross-sectional rivet areas must be sheared, and the resistance to failure by shearing of the rivets is, by equation (11),

$$R_1 = 2s_S A = 9120 \text{ lb.}$$

Unless two projected bearing areas are crushed, the joint will not fail, and the resistance to failure by crushing is, by equation (12),

$$R_2 = 2s_C dt = 11{,}580 \text{ lb.}$$

The possibility of failure by tearing of the plate is investigated by fixing the pitch, employing equation (13),

$$R_3 = s_T(p - d)t$$

$$9120 = 11{,}000\left(p - \frac{13}{16}\right)\frac{3}{8}$$

$$p = 3.02 \text{ in.}$$

The efficiency of the joint is, by equation (14),

$$\text{Eff.} = \frac{p-d}{p} = \frac{3.02 - 0.813}{3.02} = 0.731 \text{ or } 73.1 \text{ per cent}$$

Illustrative Example III. A double-riveted butt joint is shown in Fig. 31. The main plates carry a load of 5000 lb/in. The pitch of the rivets is 3 in., the diameter of the rivets is $\frac{13}{16}$ in., the thickness of the main plates is $\frac{1}{2}$ in., and the thickness of the cover plates is 3/8 in. The ultimate stresses of the A.S.M.E. Code are: tension, 55,000 psi; compression, 95,000 psi; shear, 44,000 psi. The factor of safety of the joint, based upon these ultimate stresses is to be determined.

A repeating section is shown in dashed outline. The total load on the repeating section will be 5000 × 3 = 15,000 lb.

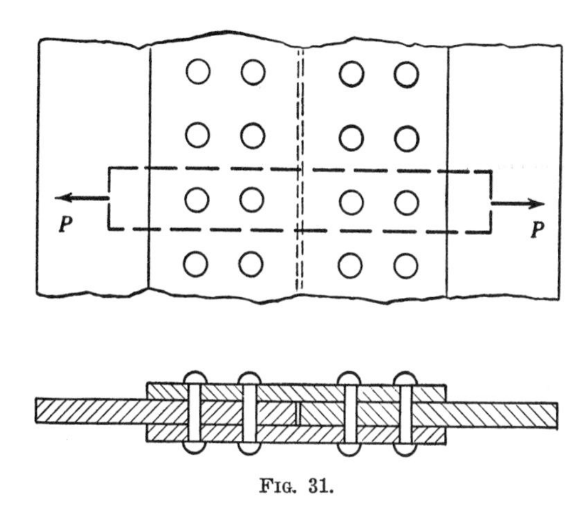

Fig. 31.

We first explore the possibility of failure by shearing of the rivets. These rivets are subjected to *double shear*—two cross-sectional areas of each rivet must be sheared to produce failure. The cross-sectional area of one rivet is 0.5185 sq. in. Each rivet is subjected to a total load of 15,000/2 = 7500 lb.

Then the shearing stress developed in the rivets will be, using equation (11),

$$s_S = \frac{7500}{2 \times 0.5185} = 7240 \text{ psi}$$

The main plate has a thickness of 1/2 in., while the cover plates have a combined thickness of 2 × 3/8 = 3/4 in. The main plate will, therefore, tend to crush first and, applying equation (12),

$$7500 = s_C dt = s_C \times \frac{13}{16} \times \frac{1}{2}$$

$$s_C = 18{,}460 \text{ psi}$$

The main plate, with its lesser thickness, will tend to tear in advance of the cover plates. Applying equation (13),

$$15{,}000 = s_T(p - d)t = s_T\left(3 - \frac{13}{16}\right)\frac{1}{2}$$
$$s_T = 13{,}710 \text{ psi}$$

The factor of safety will be

a) based upon shear, $\text{F.S.} = \dfrac{44{,}000}{7240} = 6.08$

b) " " crushing, $\text{F.S.} = \dfrac{95{,}000}{18{,}460} = 5.15$

c) " " tearing, $\text{F.S.} = \dfrac{55{,}000}{13{,}710} = 4.01$

The joint is therefore credited with a factor of safety of 4.01 based on the ultimate stresses.

Illustrative Example IV. Whenever possible, the resultant load applied to a riveted joint should have a line of action which passes through the centroid of the group of rivets. This condition, however, cannot always be fulfilled, and eccentric loading, like that illustrated in Fig. 32, may be encountered.

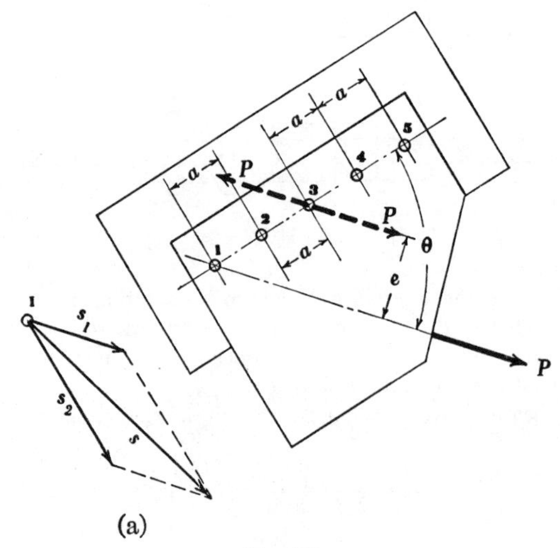

FIG. 32.

In such cases, the load P may be resolved into an equivalent system consisting of a force P applied at the centroid, and a couple Pe, where e is the distance from the centroid to the line of action of the original load P.

It is assumed that force P, acting at the centroid, is divided into equal parts, and that there is a direct unit shearing stress in each rivet

$$s_1 = \frac{P}{nA} \tag{1}$$

where n is the number of rivets and A is the cross-sectional area of each rivet.

Couple Pe will tend to rotate the plate and this twisting will induce a secondary shearing stress in each rivet. The shearing force in each rivet—F_1, F_2, etc.—is assumed to vary directly with the distance of the respective rivets from the centroid, and to have a line of action which is normal to the line joining the center of the rivet with the centroid of the group.

Then $$Pe = F_1 \times 2a + F_2 \times a + F_4 \times a + F_5 \times 2a \qquad (2)$$

To illustrate the application of these principles to the eccentrically loaded joint of Fig. 32, let us assign the following data, and determine the shearing stress in each rivet: $P = 5000$ lb.; diameter of rivets = ¾ in.; $a = 3$ in; $\theta = 50°$.

The direct shear stress in each rivet will be, by equation (1) above,

$$s_1 = \frac{5000}{5 \times 0.442} = 2260 \text{ psi}$$

To establish the secondary shear stress caused by twisting moment, we must first solve equation (2).

$$Pe = 5000 \times 6 \times \sin 50° = 22{,}980 \text{ in-lb.}$$

Then $$22{,}980 = F_1 \times 6 + F_2 \times 3 + F_4 \times 3 + F_5 \times 6$$

From the assumption that these total forces vary with their distance from the centroid,

$$F_1 = F_5; \qquad F_2 = F_4; \qquad F_1/F_2 = 6/3$$

Substituting these values in terms of F_1,

$$22{,}980 = 6F_1 + \frac{1}{2}F_1 \times 3 + \frac{1}{2}F_1 \times 3 + 6F_1 = 15F_1$$

$$F_1 = \frac{22{,}980}{15} = 1532 = F_5$$

$$F_2 = \frac{1}{2}F_1 = 766 = F_4$$

The secondary unit stress in rivet 1 will be

$$s_2 = \frac{1532}{0.442} = 3466 \text{ psi}$$

The resultant unit shearing stress in rivet 1 will be s, the vector sum of s_1 and s_2 (Fig. 32-a).

$$s = \sqrt{(2260)^2 + (3466)^2 - 2 \times 2260 \times 3466 \times \cos 140°} = 5400 \text{ psi}$$

The unit shearing stress in the remaining rivets will be

Rivet 2: 3760 psi
Rivet 3: 2260
Rivet 4: 1450
Rivet 5: 2263

PROBLEMS

Note: Table XVI, page 462, which gives the areas of circles, will be found useful in riveted-joint problems.

35. Determine the maximum allowable value of load P. Diameter of rivets = ⅞ in. Allowable stresses in shear, compression, and tension are

$$s_S = 10{,}000 \text{ psi.}$$
$$s_C = 20{,}000 \text{ psi.}$$
$$s_T = 12{,}000 \text{ psi.}$$

Ans. 15,470 lb.

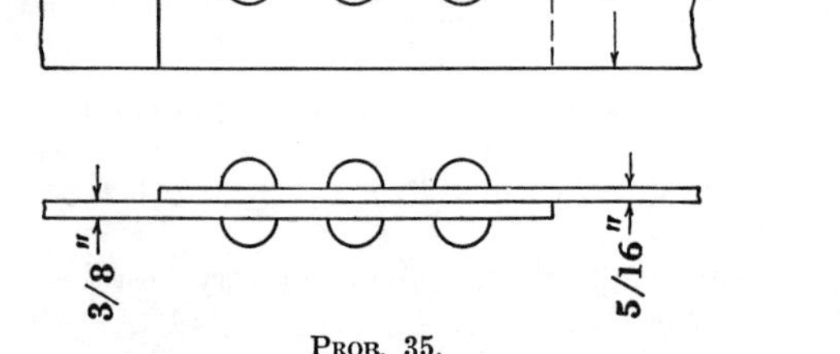

PROB. 35.

36. The joint shown is a double-riveted lap joint. The maximum allowable stresses are

$$s_T = 15{,}000 \text{ psi.}$$
$$s_C = 20{,}000 \text{ psi.}$$
$$s_S = 10{,}200 \text{ psi.}$$

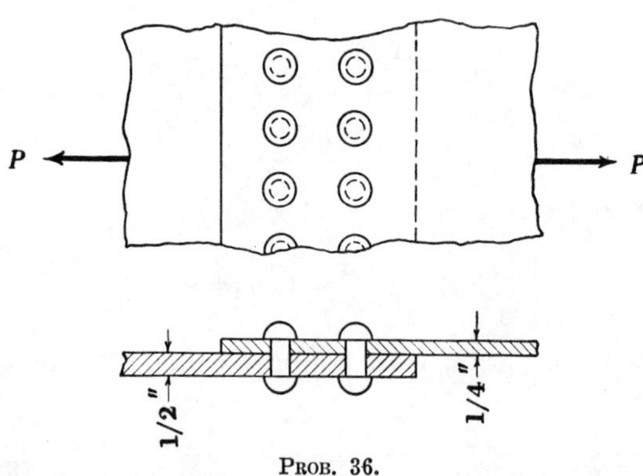

PROB. 36.

Determine:

a) The size of rivet to yield equal resistance to failure by shearing and crushing.
b) The pitch of the rivets.
c) The efficiency of the joint.

37. Determine the pitch of the rivets and the efficiency of a single-riveted lap joint. Diameter of rivets = ⅞ in. Thickness of each plate = ½ in. s_S = 11,000 psi; s_C = 22,000 psi; s_T = 15,000 psi. *Ans.* 1.76 in.; 50.2 per cent.

38. Determine the pitch of the rivets and the efficiency of a double-riveted lap joint, using the same data as in Prob. 37.

39. An 8 in. × 8 in. × ½ in. angle is used to fasten two ½-in. plates. The total stress in the angle is 30,000 lb. The diameter of the rivets is ¾ in. s_S = 7500 psi, s_C = 15,000 psi. Determine the number of rivets required at each end of the angle.

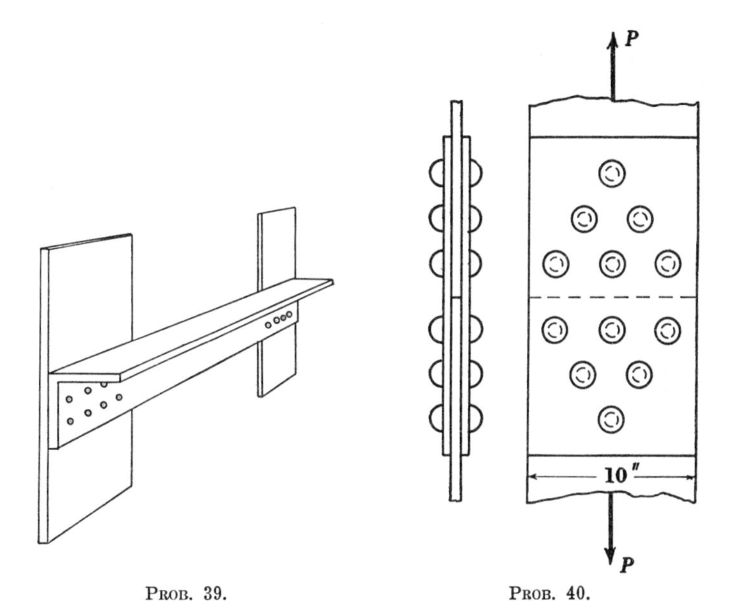

PROB. 39. PROB. 40.

40. The butt joint shown carries an axial load, P. The maximum permissible value of P is to be determined under the following conditions:

Diameter of undriven rivet = ¾ in. (In calculating resistances to failure by *shearing* and *crushing*, use the undriven diameter; in calculating resistance to failure by *tearing* of the plates, use ⅞ in.)

The allowable stresses will be those of the American Institute of Steel Construction (A.I.S.C.):

Tensile stress in plate, s_T = 20,000 psi.
Shearing stress in rivets, s_S = 15,000 psi.
Crushing or bearing stress, s_C = 32,000 psi (single shear).
s_C = 40,000 psi (double shear).

Thickness of main plate = ½ in.; thickness of cover plate = ¼ in. *Ans.* 73,800 lb.

41. Determine the maximum load which can be supported by a structural joint, per repeating section, if the pattern of the rivets is the same as that of Prob. 40.

Diameter of undriven rivet = ⅞ in. (add ⅛ in. in tearing)
Thickness of main plate = ½ in.
Thickness of cover plates = ⅜ in.
Allowable stresses: A.I.S.C. (see Prob. 40)

42. The load P is 4000 lb., and the diameter of the rivets is $\frac{3}{4}$ in. Determine the shearing stress in each rivet of the eccentrically loaded joint shown.

Ans. Rivets 1 and 4, 7580 psi; Rivets 2 and 3, 3310 psi.

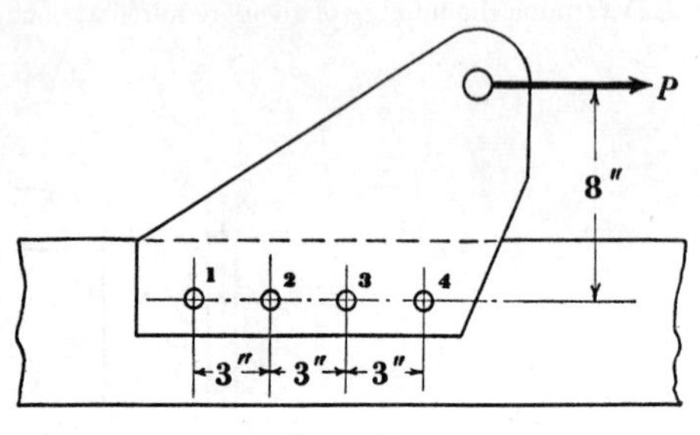

PROB. 42.

43. The load P is 2500 lb., and the diameter of the rivets is $\frac{5}{8}$ in. Determine the shearing stress in rivets 1, 2, and 3 of the eccentrically loaded joint shown.

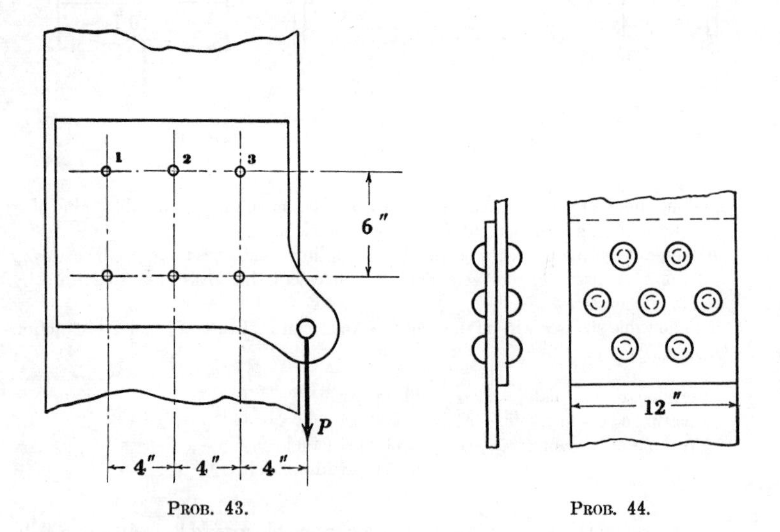

PROB. 43. PROB. 44.

44. Two plates, 12 in. wide and $\frac{1}{2}$ in. thick, are joined by a lap joint, as shown, using $\frac{3}{4}$ in. rivets. There are two rivets in the inner row, three rivets in the second row, and two rivets in the outer row. Determine the maximum allowable tensile load which may be applied axially to the plates, using the A.S.M.E. Boiler Code allowable stresses (see page 38).

Ans. 27,200 lb.

Courtesy James F. Lincoln Arc Welding Foundation

Courtesy Bethlehem Steel Co.

Courtesy Republic Aviation Corp. Aluminum Co. of America

11. Welded Joints. The welded joint offers an additional example of the compromise which must be made between rational analysis and empirical observation, when complexities of behavior, or lack of complete knowledge of the fundamental nature of stress distribution is encountered.

Three types of welded joint are shown in Fig. 33. (a) illustrates the butt joint, (b) a lap joint using fillet welds, and (c) the spot-welded joint. In

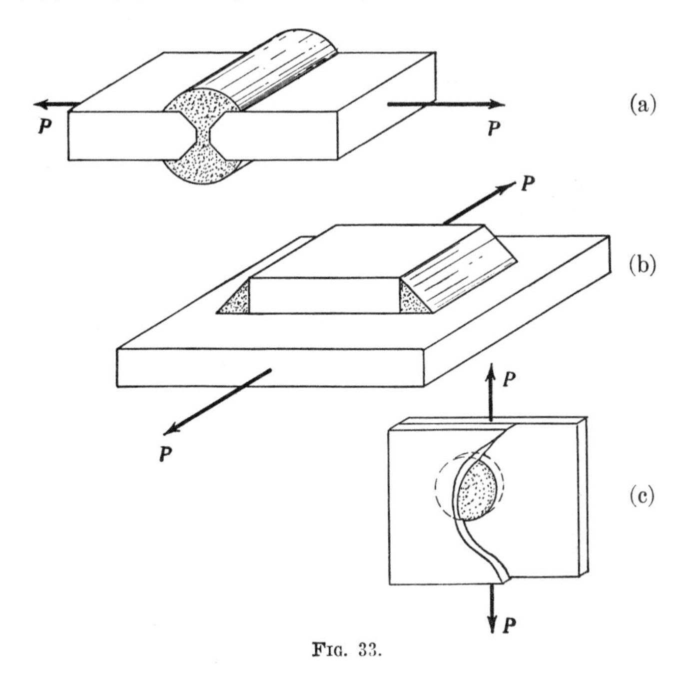

FIG. 33.

all of these forms, the joining of the metals is accomplished by heating them to the fusion temperature of the material. At the same time, additional metal is applied in the butt or fillet joints by melting a filler rod, and by depositing the rod material as indicated by the shaded portion of the joint. The heat may be supplied by a burning gas, by an electric arc, or by igniting a chemical mixture of iron oxide and powdered aluminum, known as thermit.

The strengths which are available to the designer are based upon the process used, and additional factors must be considered such as the skill of the welder, which varies with individuals. When weld metal from filler rods is deposited, oxygen and nitrogen are absorbed from the atmosphere, an objectionable feature in that the strength of the joint and its ability to resist corrosion are lowered. To overcome this difficulty, the arc and the molten weld metal may be shielded from the atmosphere, or a deoxidizing agent in the form of a hydrogen jet may be employed. When such shielding is used, higher allowable stresses become available to the designer.

Codes of the American Welding Society and similar sources are available in engineering literature, and may be consulted for allowable stresses.

We shall use, in our examples, the following values, which are those generally accepted for shielded arc welds.

$$s_S = 13{,}600 \text{ psi}$$
$$s_C = s_T = 16{,}000 \text{ psi}$$

The butt weld of Fig. 33-a is designed on the assumption that the normal stress is distributed uniformly through the weld.

If force P produces tension, the allowable force is

$$P = s_T \times t \times l \tag{16}$$

in which s_T = allowable stress in tension,

t = thickness of the thinner plate, and
l = length of the weld.

Similarly, for compressive loading,

$$P = s_C t l \tag{17}$$

The lap joint of Fig. 33-b may have fillet welds along the sides, as indicated, or along the end, or in both places. The fillet weld is assumed to fail in shear along the *throat* of the weld which, as shown in Fig. 34, is defined as the plane surface inclined at an angle of 45° with the *leg* of the weld. The leg is, as indicated, the side of the largest isosceles triangle which may be inscribed in the weld.

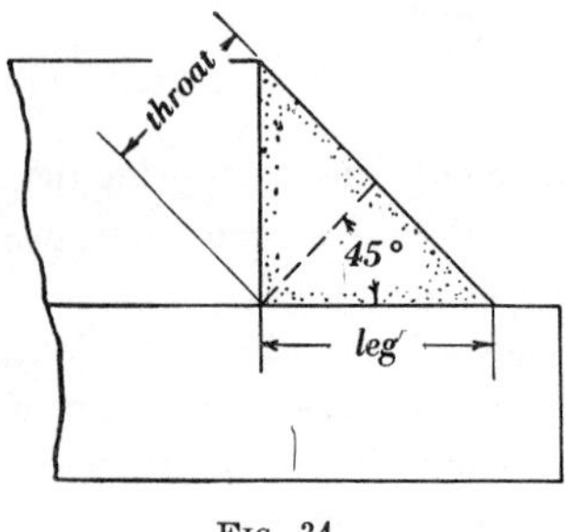

FIG. 34.

The area of the throat surface is then 0.707 times the area of the leg surface.

Then the allowable load is

$$P = s_S \times 0.707t \times l \tag{18}$$

in which s_S = allowable stress in shear,

t = width of leg, and
l = length of weld.

The end fillet is designed upon the same basis as the side fillet.

The spot-welded joint (Fig. 33-c) is used in fastening thin plates only and, most commonly, for aluminum sheets. The empirical design procedure assumes that the weld will fail in shear in the plane of contact between the plates, and

$$P = s_S A \tag{19}$$

in which s_S = allowable shear stress of the material and
A = area of the "spot" or circle of weld.

Illustrative Example I. Plate A (Fig. 35) is to be welded to plate B, using side fillets of equal length. If a load $P = 75{,}000$ lb. is applied, acting at the centroid of plate A, determine the lengths of the side fillets. The leg of the welds is ⅜ in.

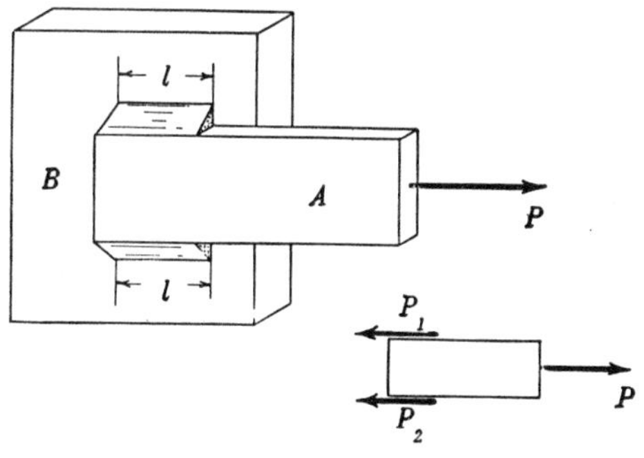

FIG. 35.

If plate A is isolated as a free body, the system of external forces in equilibrium consists of P, the resultant applied load; P_1, the force of resistance exerted by the top fillet weld; and P_2, the force of resistance of the bottom fillet. Substituting in equation (18),

$$P_1 = s_S \times 0.707t \times l$$
$$= 13{,}600 \times 0.707 \times \frac{3}{8} \times l = 3606l$$
$$P_2 = 3606l$$
$$P_1 + P_2 = P = 75\,000$$
$$2 \times 3606 \times l = 75{,}000$$
$$l = 10.4 \text{ in}$$

Illustrative Example II. In Example I the only problem facing the designer has been that of providing of a sufficient length of weld to resist the applied load.

The case presented in Fig. 36, however, poses an additional problem. In this case, it is necessary, in addition to determining the required total length of weld, to provide that this length be divided into proper segments at top and bottom so that no tendency to rotate will be developed in the joint.

The angle section is to be welded to a flat plate. Side and end fillets are to be used. These are indicated as fillets a, b, and c. The angle is a standard $8 \times 8 \times \frac{1}{2}$

in. structural angle, having a cross-sectional area of 7.75 sq. in.; an allowable tensile stress $s_T = 20{,}000$ psi, and with its centroid located as shown in Fig. 37. All fillets are to have leg = ½ in.

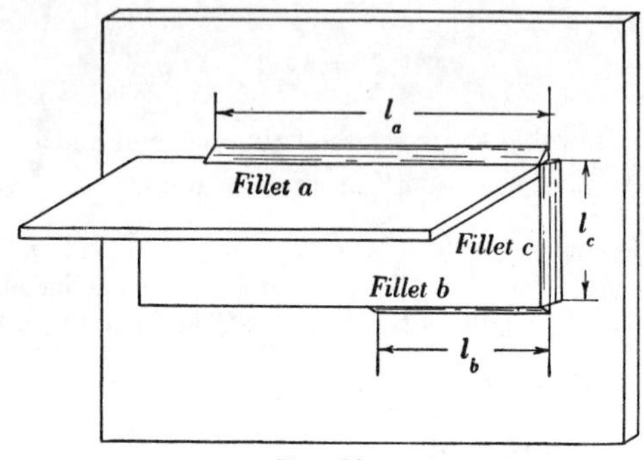

FIG. 36.

The angle section carries the maximum allowable load, and the lengths of the welds are to be determined. It is assumed that the resultant load, P, on the angle acts through its centroid.

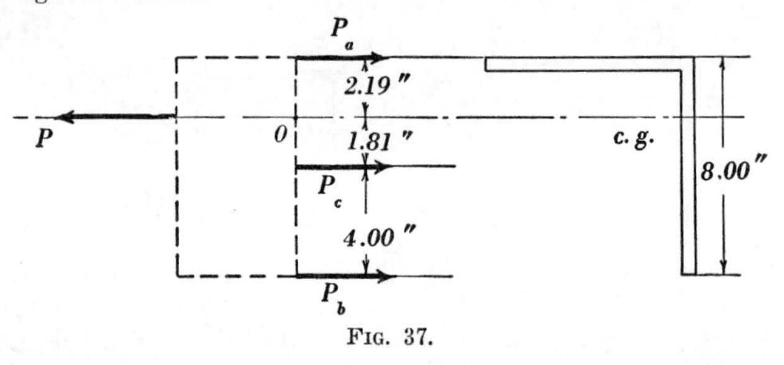

FIG. 37.

The isolation of the angle as a free body is shown in Fig. 37. The system of external forces acting upon the free body consists of P, the resultant load; P_a, P_b, and P_c, the resisting forces exerted by the three fillet welds.

For equilibrium, the sum of the parallel forces must be equal to zero ($\Sigma F = 0$) and the sum of their moments about any axis perpendicular to their plane must be equal to zero ($\Sigma M = 0$).

$$-P + P_a + P_b + P_c = 0 \qquad (\Sigma F = 0)$$

The force P is the maximum allowable load on the angle section.

$$P = 7.75 \times 20{,}000 = 155{,}000 \text{ lb.}$$

The resisting force exerted by each fillet weld is, by equation (18),

$$P = s_S \times 0.707t \times l$$

For fillet a,

$$P_a = 13{,}600 \times 0.707 \times \frac{1}{2} \times l_a$$
$$= 4808 l_a$$

For fillet b,

$$P_b = 4808 l_b$$

End fillet welds, like fillet c, are run across the entire run of the end of the angle, and

$$P_c = 13{,}600 \times 0.707 \times \frac{1}{2} \times 8$$
$$= 38{,}460 \text{ lbs}$$

P_c is assumed to act at the center of the weld.

Then, $$4808 l_a + 4808 l_b + 38{,}460 = 155{,}000 \quad (1)$$

To prevent rotation, the sum of the moments of all of the forces about any axis must be equal to zero. Selecting an axis of moments on the line of action of force P_b,

$$\Sigma M: \quad +P_a \times 8 + 38{,}460 \times 4 - 155{,}000 \times 5.81 = 0$$
$$P_a = 93{,}340 \text{ lb.}$$

and $$l_a = \frac{93{,}340}{4808} = 19.41 \text{ in.}$$

We now select an axis of moments on the line of action of P_a, and

$$\Sigma M: \quad -P_b \times 8 - 38{,}460 \times 4 + 155{,}000 \times 2.19 = 0$$
$$P_b = 23{,}200 \text{ lb.}$$

and $$l_b = \frac{23{,}200}{4808} = 4.83 \text{ in.}$$

These results may be checked by substituting in equation (1) above,

$$4808 \times 19.41 + 4808 \times 4.83 + 38{,}460 = 155{,}000$$

PROBLEMS

Note: In the following problems, use shielded arc value for welds: $s_S = 13{,}600 \times 0.707 \times \text{leg}$, unless otherwise noted.

45. If load $P = 50{,}000$ lb., determine the required length of fillet welds **1** and **2**. Both welds have ⅜ in. legs. *Ans.* 6.93 in.

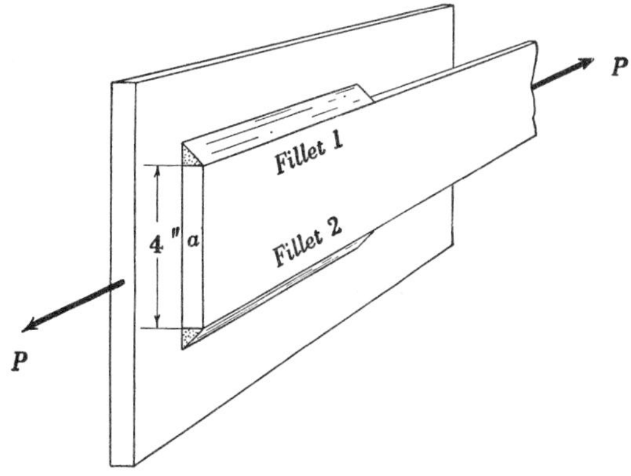

PROB. 45.

46. Determine the lengths of fillets **1** and **2** of Problem 45 if the leg of weld **1** is held at ⅜ in. while the leg of weld **2** is increased to ½ in.

47. Determine the lengths of fillets **1** and **2** of Problem 45 if a fillet weld with ½ in. leg is run along the entire length of end *a*, fillet **1** has a ⅜ in. leg, and fillet **2** has a ½ in. leg.

48. A 3 in. × 3 in. × ½ in. angle is to be welded to a plate as shown, using side fillet welds. Load P is 50,000 lb. $\bar{X}$-$\bar{X}$ is the centroidal axis of the angle section. Determine the lengths of the fillet welds if the allowable stress of the weld is 10,000t lb. per in., where t is the leg. *Ans.* $l_1 = 9.2$ in.; $l_2 = 3.1$ in.

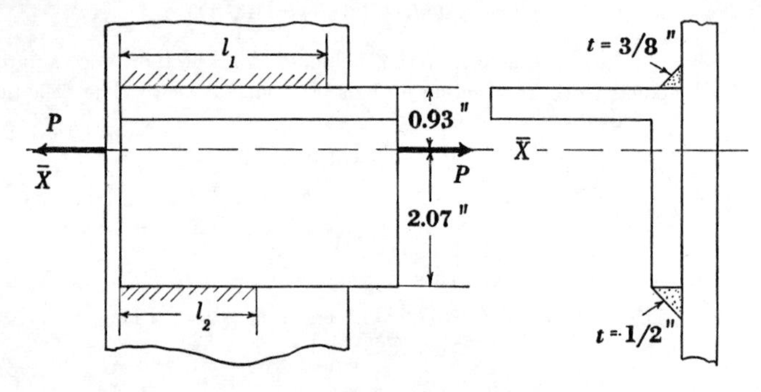

PROB. 48.

49. A 4 in. × 4 in. × ⅜ in. angle is welded to a plate as shown. The allowable stress in the welds is 8000t lb./in., where t is the leg of the fillet. Determine the maximum allowable load P and the length of fillet l_1. $\bar{X}$-$\bar{X}$ is the centroidal axis of the angle section.

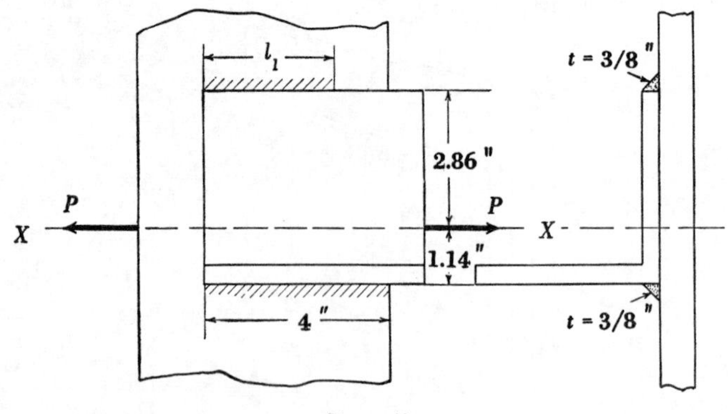

PROB. 49.

50. Determine the length of weld required at the top and bottom of the angle sections shown. The allowable tensile stress in the angle sections is 18,000 psi. The angles are 5 in. × 3½ in. × ½ in., each having a cross-sectional area of 4 sq. in., and a centroidal axis at $\bar{X}$-$\bar{X}$. The allowable load per linear inch of weld is 4000 lb.

Ans. Top, 12 in; bottom, 6 in.

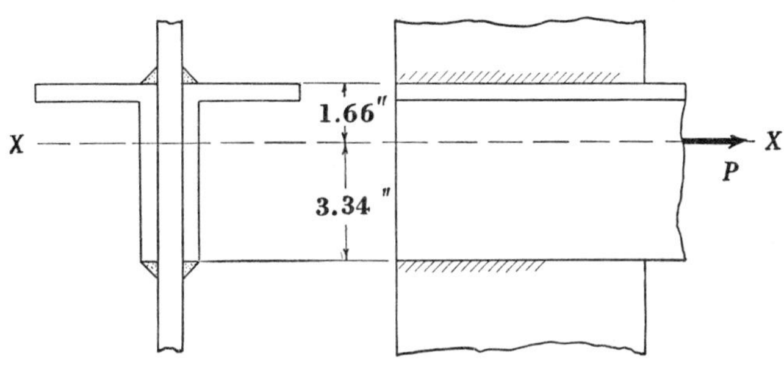

PROB. 50.

51. The bracket shown is welded to a flat plate. The maximum load is 60,000 lb., parallel to the long axis of the bracket, and acting through the centroid. All fillets have ¼ in. legs. Determine the length of fillets **2** and **3** if the end fillet **1** is run across the entire length of the end of the bracket.

Ans. l_2 = 8.01 in.; l_3 = 12.45 in.

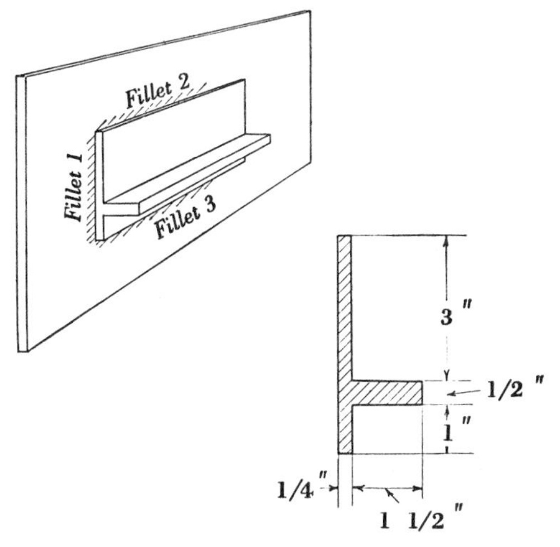

PROB. 51.

52. A load of 40,000 lb. is applied at the centroid of the track bracket. Side fillet welds are used at top and bottom, with ⅜ in. legs. Determine the lengths of the welds.

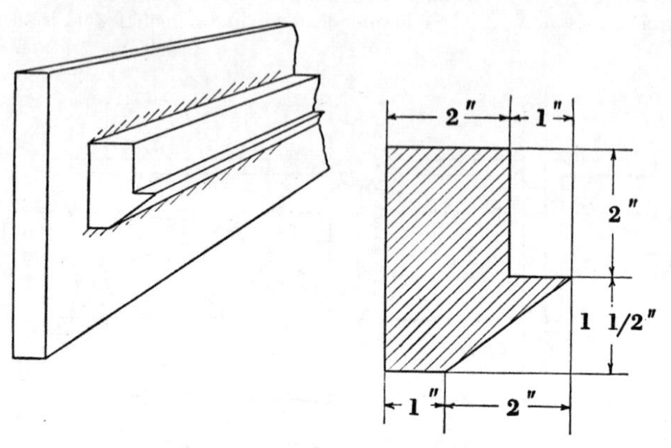

PROB. 52.

12. Simple Dynamic Stresses. Our chief concern in the basic study of the mechanics of materials lies in the field of statics, and deals with bodies in equilibrium.

We are, however, aware of the fact that moving parts of machines are affected by forces which have their origin in acceleration. The influence of acceleration in some elementary cases is noted in this article to suggest the method of attack. More elaborate cases deserve very extensive study, and, as the engineering curriculum progresses, become the concern of courses in dynamics which deal more exhaustively with dynamic stresses and the accompanying deformations.

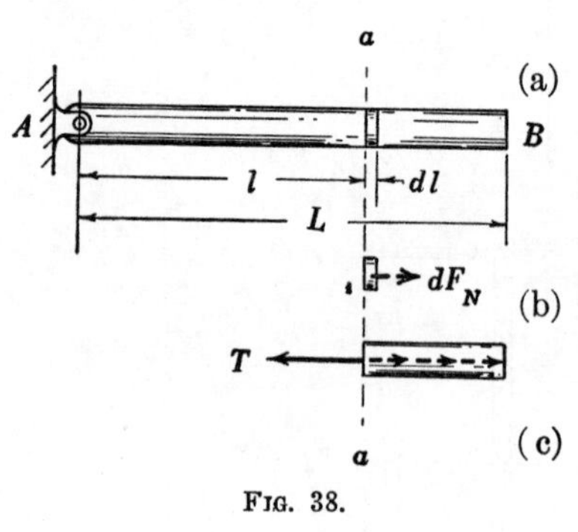

FIG. 38.

The rotating rod shown in Fig. 38 offers one example of stress distribution when acceleration is present. Rod AB rotates, in a horizontal plane, about a fixed axis at A.

The weight of the rod per unit of length is δ, its angular speed in radians per unit of time is ω, which is constant, and the total length is L.

Figure 38-b shows an isolation of an elementary portion of the rod of length dl, at section a-a, located at distance l from the fixed axis at A.

The rotation of this elementary mass in its circular path about A produces a normal, or radial, acceleration, $a_N = \omega^2 l$, and a centrifugal force

$$dF_N = \omega^2 l\, dm = \omega^2 l \frac{\delta\, dl}{g}$$

If we now consider the portion of the rod lying between the section *a-a* and end *B*, which is shown as an isolated free body in Fig. 38-c, we find that the tension exerted on this body is T, and the total centrifugal force opposed to T is

$$\int dF_N = \int_l^L \omega^2 l \frac{\delta\, dl}{g} = \frac{\omega^2 \delta}{2g}(L^2 - l^2)$$

Then the unit tensile stress in the rod at any section will be

$$s_T = \frac{T}{A} = \frac{\omega^2 \delta}{2gA}(L^2 - l^2) \tag{20}$$

The maximum tensile stress will be developed at the axis when $l = 0$, and

$$s_{T\,(\text{max.})} = \frac{\omega^2 \delta L^2}{2gA} \tag{21}$$

Another example of the influence of rotation upon the development of stress may be observed in the rotating thin ring of Fig. 39.

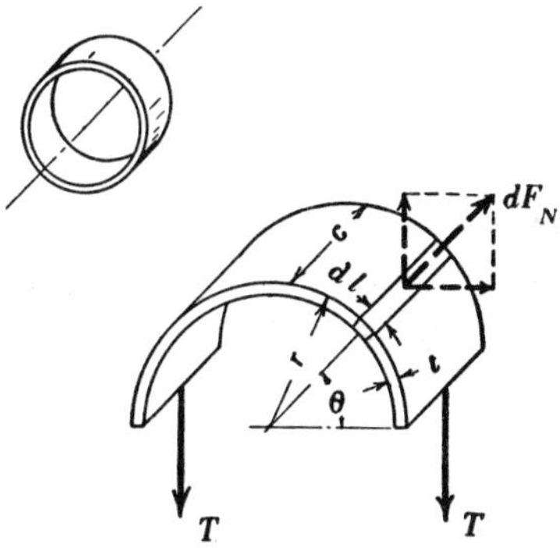

An elementary segment of the ring will have an acceleration, if the ring is rotating at constant angular velocity, of $a_N = \omega^2 r$ and the centrifugal force will be

$$dF_N = \omega^2 r \frac{dw}{g}$$

where ω = angular velocity of ring, in radian units,

r = radius of ring

$\frac{dw}{g}$ = mass of the elementary segment

Fig. 39.

If the weight density of the ring is called δ,

$$dF_N = \frac{\omega^2 r \delta (tc\, dl)}{g} = \frac{\omega^2 r \delta (rtc\, d\theta)}{g}$$

and the vertical component of this centrifugal force will be

$$dF_N \sin\theta = \frac{\omega^2 r^2 \delta tc \sin\theta\, d\theta}{g}$$

The total centrifugal force acting on the indicated half-ring will be

$$P = \int_{\theta=0}^{\theta=\pi} \frac{\omega^2 r^2 \delta tc \sin\theta\, d\theta}{g} = \frac{2\omega^2 r^2 \delta tc}{g}$$

This force is balanced by the total stresses, T, acting on the bottom surfaces of the half-ring,

$$T = s_T\, t\, c$$

Then

$$2T = P$$

and

$$2s_T\, t\, c = \frac{2\omega^2 r^2 \delta tc}{g}$$

$$s_T = \frac{\omega^2 r^2 \delta}{g} \tag{22}$$

which is the hoop tensile unit stress in the ring.

Since the velocity at the circumference of the ring is $v = \omega r$, the equation, in terms of surface velocity, may be expressed as

$$s_T = \frac{v^2 \delta}{g} \tag{23}$$

PROBLEMS

53. Determine the maximum surface velocity of a rotating ring if the material weighs 450 lb. cu. ft., and the tensile stress must not exceed 4000 psi. *Ans.* 203 ft./sec.

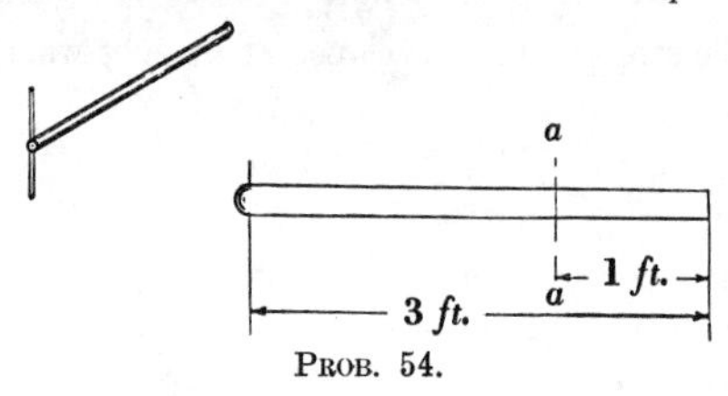

PROB. 54.

54. A rod, weighing 480 lb/cu. ft., rotates in a horizontal plane at constant angular speed of 600 r.p.m. about a vertical axis at its end. The diameter of the rod is 2 in. Determine the tensile stress at section *a-a*, and the maximum tensile stress in the rod.

55. The rim of a flywheel is made of cast iron, weighing 0.26 lb./cu. in., and the allowable stress is 6000 psi. If the wheel has a diameter of 4 ft., determine the limiting speed, in r.p.m., assuming that the influence of the hub and arms may be neglected. *Ans.* 1190 r.p.m.

56. If the maximum tensile stress in the rod of Prob. 54 must not exceed 6000 psi, determine the limiting angular speed.

13. Stress Concentration.

In our previous discussions of stress the loaded bodies have been of uniform cross-section throughout their entire length; in addition, the cross-sectional areas have been solid. We have,

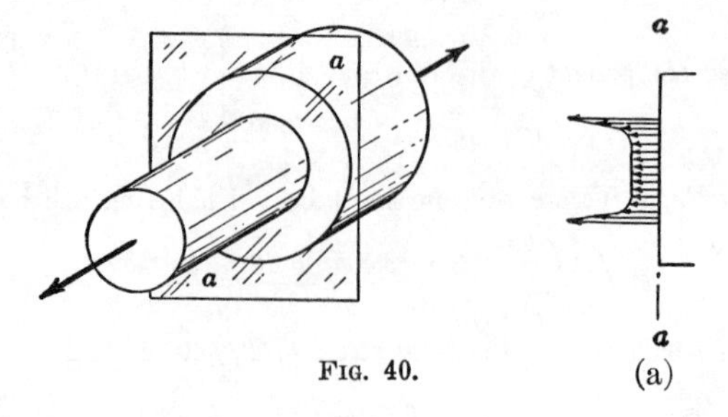

FIG. 40. (a)

in such cases, assumed that the stress across each section is uniformly distributed.

When, as in the shaft of Fig. 40 (whose diameter changes) or in the plate of Fig. 41 (which contains a hole), the constant nature of the cross-section is disturbed, the assumption of uniform stress distribution can no longer be tolerated. Laboratory investigation of such bodies has revealed that the stress may vary greatly across such sections as *a-a* of Fig. 40 or *b-b* of Fig. 41. The qualitative pattern of stress distribution is indicated in Figs. 40-a and 41-a. Quantitatively, the magnitudes of the stresses will be dependent upon the nature of the material and upon the size of the disturbing factor, or discontinuity, which is the hole, square corner or fillet, notches, and the like.

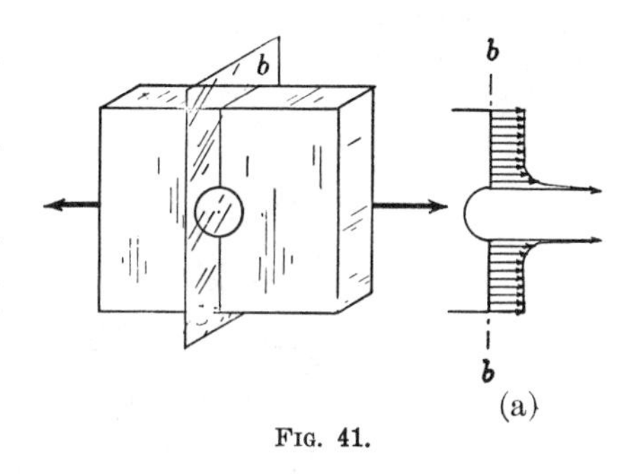

FIG. 41.

Some discontinuities are intentionally introduced, in the form of different diameters of shafts, screw threads, or holes; others are accidental "stress raisers" like scratches or other tool marks which disturb machined surfaces.

Stress concentration in ductile materials is rarely of concern when they are subjected to static loading, for local plastic yielding in the region of the stress raiser will tend to relieve the concentration. In brittle materials, even under static loading, stress raisers may invite failure. In repeated loading (see Fatigue, Art. 79) stress concentration is always a source of danger.

The subject of stress concentration is treated in books on machine and structural design. This brief discussion is intended to alert the engineering student to the menace presented by stress raisers.

The relationship between maximum unit stress, $s_{max.}$, and the average unit stress across the section, s_0, is usually expressed as

$$s_{max.} = ks_0$$

where k is the *factor of stress concentration.*

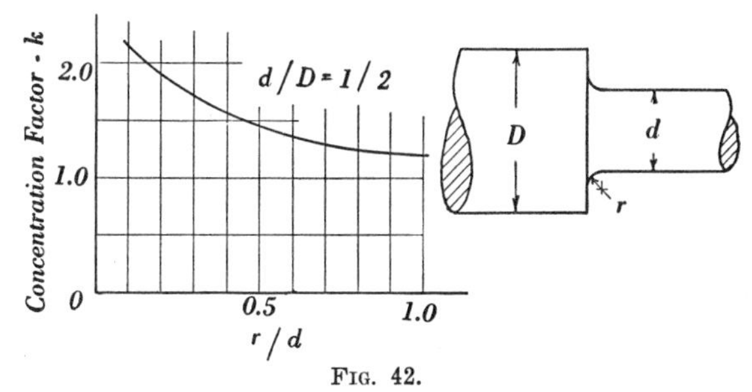

FIG. 42.

A suggestion of some of the magnitudes involved is noted in the case illustrated in Fig. 42. In this case, the member is loaded axially by a static load. The two diameters, D and d, are joined by a fillet curve of radius r. When $D = 2d$, and $r = d/4$, the value of k is about 1.8. For a theoretical plate of infinite width with a central circular hole the value of k is 3. For finite widths there is no marked reduction in the value of k for ratios of hole diameter to plate width of less than $\frac{1}{4}$. Values of k are available in the literature for many types of members when subjected to axial, bending, torsional, or repeated loading.*

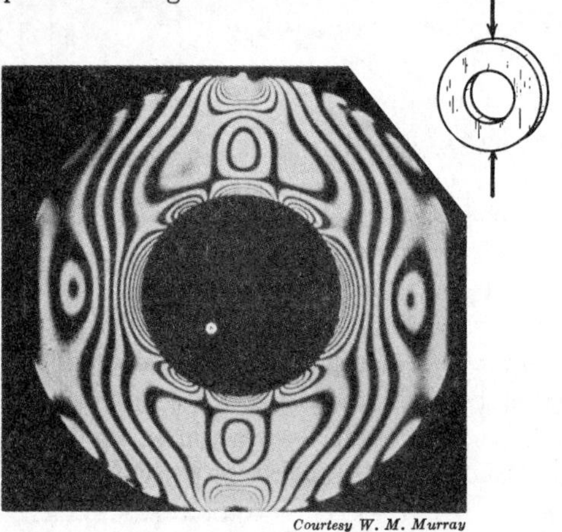

Courtesy W. M. Murray

FIG. 43.

Some approaches to the evaluation of stress concentration are available mathematically through the theory of elasticity, but most of our knowledge of the magnitudes involved has come through experimental determination and, most notably, through the use of *photoelasticity*. In photoelastic analysis, polarized light is passed through a loaded scale model of the member which is being studied. The scale model is made of a plastic possessing favorable optical properties. The polarized light beam will produce color bands which will indicate the state of stress in the model and therefore represent the state of stress in the actual member.

When photographed in black and white, the colored stress bands appear as alternating black and white stripes, as shown in Fig. 43. Each dark band in the picture represents the locus of points at which there is the same difference between the principal stresses, or constant shear stress (see discussion of principal stresses in Art. 5). To evaluate, quantitatively, the magnitude of stress, a small tensile specimen of the model material is used as a calibration device, and comparison of the loaded model is made with the calibrating specimen.

*See Roark: *Formulas for Stress and Strain*, McGraw-Hill Book Company, Inc., 1943.

The photographs reveal regions of stress concentration where the white space between black stripes is small, and many black bands are grouped. In these regions, therefore, the designer must guard against possible failure by providing relief from high factors of stress concentration.

Figure 44 shows a photoelastic study of a beam which is freely supported

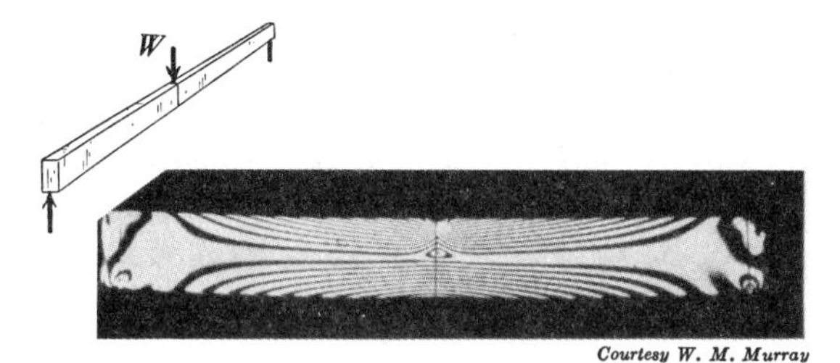

Courtesy W. M. Murray

FIG. 44.

at its ends, and loaded with a concentrated load W at mid-span. The most severely stressed section of the beam is indicated by the vertical line at the section where the load is applied.

Figure 45 indicates the advantage of increasing the radius of a fillet curve in a corner where stress concentration takes place. The model has

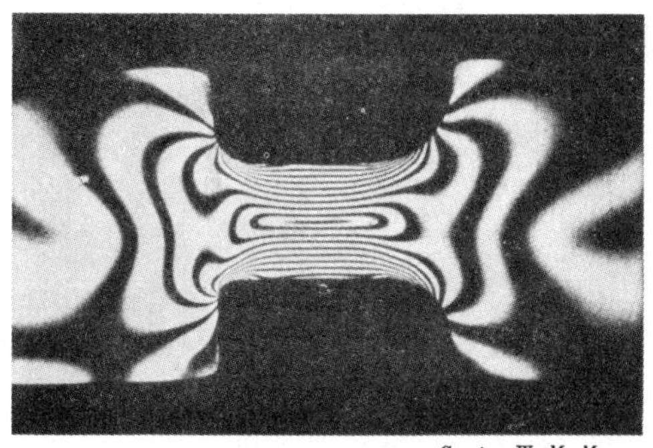

Courtesy W. M Murray

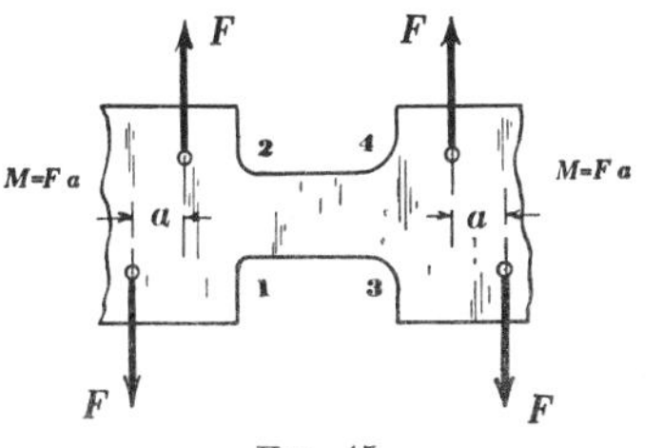

FIG. 45.

been loaded by couples $M = Fa$ so that the central section has been subjected to pure bending. Fillet 1 is the fillet of smallest radius, and fillet 4 has the greatest radius. The increase of radius will, as shown by the grouping of the respective stress bands of lines, diminish the factor of stress concentration.

STRAIN

14. Strain. When members, like the tensile and compressive specimens shown in Fig. 46, are subjected to loads, like P, they are deformed. If the total deformation, indicated in the illustration, is called δ, the deformation per unit of original length, l, is

$$e = \frac{\delta}{l}$$

This "unit deformation" is called *strain*. It is assumed, in defining strain by such an equation that the unit deformations are uniform over the entire length of the body.

The application of the load P, in either of the cases shown in Fig. 46, causes, in addition to the longitudinal strain, a lateral strain. The lateral dimension of the specimen under the tensile loading will decrease, and that of the specimen under the compressive loading will increase. The relationship between the lateral and longitudinal strains is a property of the material, and is formally expressed as a ratio, called *Poisson's ratio*. If this ratio is symbolized as μ,

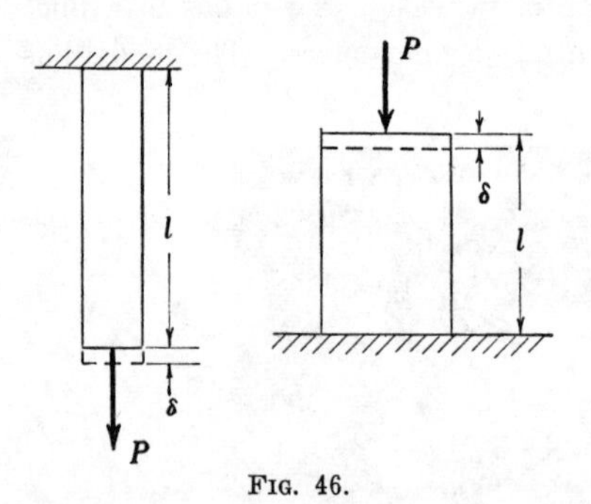

FIG. 46.

$$\mu = \frac{e_{\text{lateral}}}{e_{\text{longitudinal}}}$$

The values of μ for some of the common engineering materials, which are assumed to be isotropic, that is, to exhibit the same elastic properties in all directions, follow:

TABLE 1

Material	*Poisson's ratio*
Cast iron	0.27
Steel	0.30
Aluminum	0.33
Copper	0.36
Lead	0.43
Rubber	0.40
Concrete	0.14

When Poisson's ratio for a material is known, the change in volume of a loaded body made of that material may be determined.

We shall consider here the case of a bar subjected to axial tension only. Later, under the sections devoted to combined loading and stress, similar analysis of strain relationships will be made.

Figure 47 shows a bar subjected to an axial tensile load P. The solid lines indicate the shape of the body before loading; the dotted outline indicates its shape after the load is applied. The original length is l, and the original cross-sectional area is A. The final length will be

$$l_1 = (1 + e)l$$

The final cross-sectional area will be

$$A_1 = (1 - \mu e)^2 A$$

Then the final volume will be

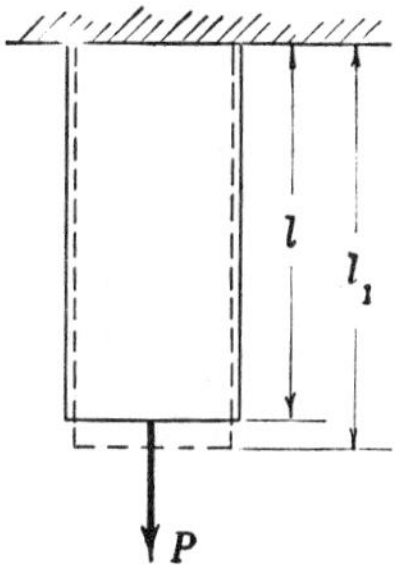

Fig. 47.

$$l_1 A_1 = (1 + e)(1 - \mu e)^2 lA$$

or the ratio of final volume, V_1, to original volume, V, is

$$\frac{V_1}{V} = (1 + e)(1 - \mu e)^2 = 1 - 2\mu e + \mu^2 e^2 + e - 2\mu e^2 + \mu^2 e^3$$

Since e is a quantity much smaller than 1, its powers other than the first are negligible in comparison with the first power, and,

$$V_1 = V(1 - 2\mu e + e) \quad \textbf{(24)}$$

When a bar, like that of Fig. 48, is subjected to tensile loads acting in mutually perpendicular directions, the elongation in each direction will depend not only

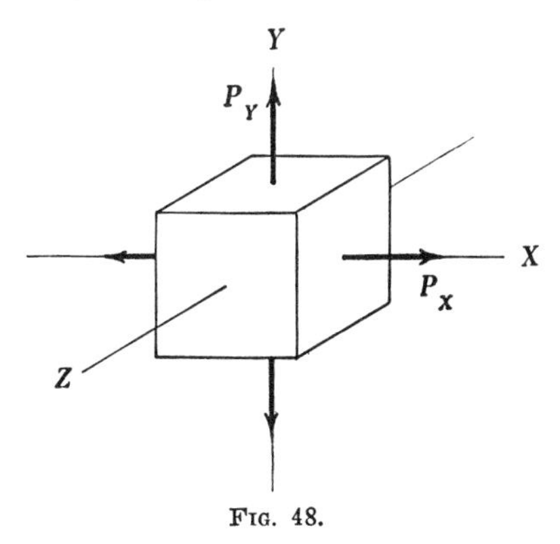

Fig. 48.

upon the individual stress in each direction but will be affected by the stress in the other direction.

The strain, for example, in the direction of the X-axis caused by s_X will be

s_X/E. In this direction there will also be a contraction which will be $\mu s_Y/E$. The total strain in the direction of the X-axis will be

$$e_X = \frac{s_X}{E} - \mu\frac{s_Y}{E} \tag{25}$$

In the direction of the Y-axis there will be a strain

$$e_Y = \frac{s_Y}{E} - \mu\frac{s_X}{E} \tag{26}$$

The X- and Y-planes of Fig. 48 are principal planes of stress, for the resultant stresses are normal to the planes and have no components of shear. Then e_X and e_Y are *principal strains*, that is, strains in the direction of the principal axes.* In the general case of three-dimensional stress, with all three of the principal stresses tensile, the value of each principal strain will be determined by the influence of the direct stress in its own direction plus the contributions of Poisson's ratio in the remaining two directions. For example,

$$e_X = \frac{s_X}{E} - \mu\frac{s_Y}{E} - \mu\frac{s_Z}{E} \tag{27}$$

and

$$e_Y = \frac{s_Y}{E} - \mu\frac{s_X}{E} - \mu\frac{s_Z}{E} \tag{28}$$

$$e_Z = \frac{s_Z}{E} - \mu\frac{s_Y}{E} - \mu\frac{s_X}{E} \tag{29}$$

Shear Strain. The definition which has been established for strain in the cases of tension and compression finds analogous expression in the case of shear.

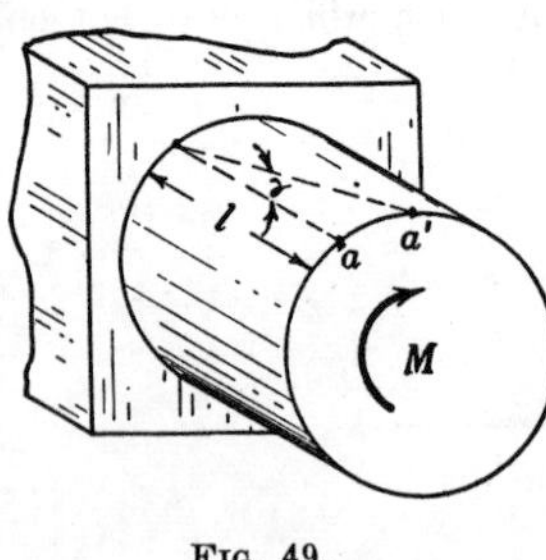

FIG. 49.

If a twisting moment is applied to a specimen, as indicated in Fig. 49, while the left end of the specimen is held rigidly, a point, like a of the right face, will move to location a'. This is a deformation which occurs in a specimen of length l. Shear strain, a deformation per unit of length, is defined as aa'/l. It will be noted that aa'/l is the tangent of the angle γ, which changes its value with the displacement of the point a. The angle γ is the measure of the shear strain and in practical cases is very small. For small angles, tangent and angle expressed in radians may be interchanged, and

$$\gamma = \frac{aa'}{l}$$

The angle γ is the form usually employed in expressing shear strain.

*See Arts. 94 and 95 for further discussion of principal strains.

PROBLEMS

57. The tensile stress in a rod is 15,000 psi when the rod is loaded axially. $E = 30 \times 10^6$ psi. Determine the axial strain. *Ans.* 0.0005 in./in.

58. If Poisson's ration for the material of Prob. 57 is $\mu = 0.30$, determine the lateral strain.

59. If the longitudinal strain in an axially loaded steel bar is 0.0012 in./in. when the lateral strain is 0.0004 in/in., determine the value of Poisson's ratio for the material.

60. A cylinder of aluminum, having a diameter of 4 in. and a length of 6 in., is subjected to a tensile load whose resultant lies in the axis of the cylinder. If the total longitudinal elongation is 0.006 in., determine the volume of the cylinder when loaded ($\mu = 0.33$). *Ans.* 75.42 cu. in.

61. Determine the loaded volume of the cylinder of Prob. 60 when the axial load is reversed to cause compression. *Ans.* 75.37 cu. in.

62. A block of metal, 3 in. high, is subjected to a shearing force which distorts the top surface through a distance of 0.0036 in. Determine the shearing strain. *Ans.* 0.0012 radians.

STRESS VS. STRAIN

15. Stress vs. Strain Relationships. Many of the materials used in engineering applications show definite relationships between the properties of stress and strain, which have been discussed in the preceding articles.

When stress varies directly with strain, the behavior of the material is said to conform with *Hooke's law.* Hooke was a seventeenth-century mathematical philosopher who first observed direct relationship between applied force and deformation experimentally.

Expressed as an equation, Hooke's law becomes

$$s = Ee$$

where E is the constant of proportionality between stress, s, and strain, e. This constant is called *Young's* modulus, or the *modulus of elasticity* (the word *modulus* means "measure of").

If we replace s by its equivalent, P/A, and e by δ/l,

$$\frac{P}{A} = E\frac{\delta}{l}$$

or the total deformation

$$\delta = \frac{Pl}{AE} \tag{30}$$

This equation supplies a very useful tool. Many of the problems of statics in which the number of unknowns exceeds the number of available conditions of equilibrium, and hence are statically indeterminate, can yield to attack when this equation becomes an additional ally. In the illustrative examples which follow, we shall observe the effectiveness of this analytical tool.

Illustrative Example I. In Fig. 50 rods A, B, and C are mounted, as indicated, between the jaws of a testing machine so that when a load, P, is applied, bar *de* is lowered but remains horizontal. Assuming that *de* is rigid so that it does not bend, we wish to determine the unit stress which will be developed in each rod.

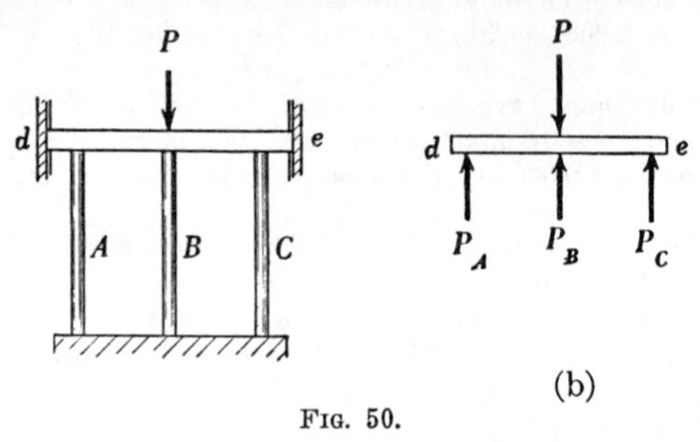

FIG. 50.

The length of each rod is 20 in. The cross-sectional area of rods A and C is 1 sq. in., and that of B is 0.75 sq. in. The modulus of elasticity for rods A and C is $E_A = E_C = 30 \times 10^6$ psi; the modulus of elasticity for rod B is $E_B = 20 \times 10^6$ psi. $P = 40{,}000$ lb. This resultant is acting at the midpoint of *de*. Rod B is equidistant from A and C.

Isolating *de* as a free body, as in Fig. 50-b, we find that there are three unknown external forces, P_A, P_B, and P_C, and we must seek three simultaneous equations to accomplish a successful solution.

From Statics, we have available the two conditions of equilibrium, for a parallel, coplanar force system, $\Sigma F = 0$, and $\Sigma M = 0$.

If a moment axis is selected on the line of action of P_B, we prove that $P_A = P_C$.

If now we apply
$$\Sigma F = 0$$
$$2P_A + P_B - 40{,}000 = 0$$

To assist these conditions of equilibrium, we introduce the equation of deformation [equation (30)].

For rod A,
$$\delta_A = \frac{P_A \times 20}{1 \times 30 \times 10^6}$$

For rod B,
$$\delta_B = \frac{P_B \times 20}{0.75 \times 20 \times 10^6}$$

But the conditions of the problem announced that *de* will remain horizontal and rigid, and
$$\delta_A = \delta_B$$
$$\frac{P_A \times 20}{1 \times 30 \times 10^6} = \frac{P_B \times 20}{0.75 \times 20 \times 10^6}$$
$$P_A = 2P_B$$

Then
$$2P_A + P_B = 5P_B = 40{,}000$$
$$P_B = 8000 \text{ lb.}$$
$$P_A = 2P_B = 16{,}000 \text{ lb.}$$
$$P_C = P_A = 16{,}000 \text{ lb.}$$

The unit stresses in the rods will be

$$s_A = \frac{16{,}000}{1} = 16{,}000 \text{ psi}$$

and

$$s_B = \frac{8000}{0.75} = 10{,}670 \text{ psi}$$

Illustrative Example II. The shaft of Fig. 51-a is composed of three sections, securely fastened to each other. All of the indicated loads are assumed to act along

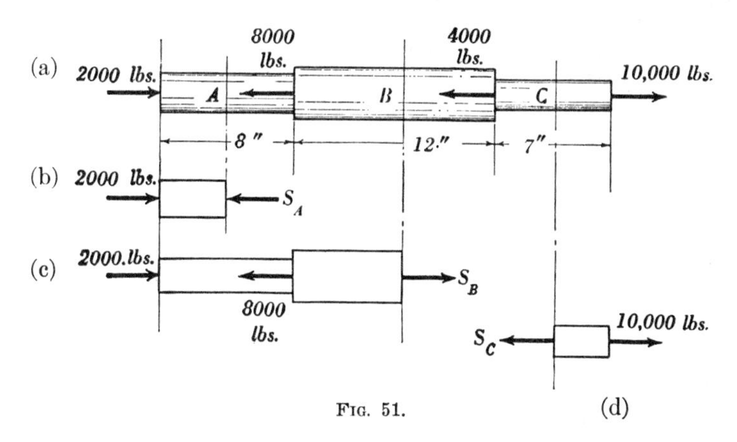

FIG. 51.

the geometric axis of the shaft. The total elongation of the shaft is to be determined.

Section A has a cross-sectional area of 0.5 sq. in., and $E_A = 16 \times 10^6$ psi; B has a cross-sectional area of 1.0 sq. in. and $E_B = 30 \times 10^6$ psi; C has a cross-sectional area of 0.40 sq. in., and $E_C = 14 \times 10^6$ psi.

To use the deformation relationship, $\delta = PL/AE$ [equation (30)], the total stress in each section must be known.

If a free body is isolated, as indicated in Fig. 51-b, we find that the total stress in section A may be obtained from the condition of equilibrium.

$$\Sigma X = 0; +2000 - S_A = 0 \qquad \therefore S_A = 2000 \text{ lb. (compression)}$$

Similarly, the total stresses in sections B and C are found by making use of the isolated free bodies of Fig. 51-c and 51-d.

$$S_B = 6000 \text{ (tension)}$$
$$S_C = 10{,}000 \text{ lb. (tension)}$$

The total elongation is

$$\delta = -\frac{2000 \times 8}{0.5 \times 16 \times 10^6} + \frac{6000 \times 12}{1 \times 30 \times 10^6} + \frac{10{,}000 \times 7}{0.4 \times 14 \times 10^6}$$
$$= -0.0020 + 0.0024 + 0.0125 = 0.0129 \text{ in.}$$

Illustrative Example III. A steel bolt is inserted in a sleeve as in Fig. 52. A nut is placed on the bolt so that it rests against the sleeve. If the nut is now tightened through one-quarter turn, determine the unit stresses in the body of the bolt and in the sleeve.

The length of the sleeve is 15 in.; its cross-sectional area is 1.0 sq. in., and E for the material is 14×10^6 psi.

The bolt has a cross-sectional area of 0.3 sq. in., and E for steel is 30×10^6 psi. The pitch of the bolt thread is $\frac{1}{16}$ in.

This problem furnishes an excellent opportunity to apply the method of *superposition.*

Very frequently we shall encounter problems in which the combined efforts of a group of bodies which exert force upon each other presents an involved pattern of actions. If we consider the sources which exert force in individual steps or stages, we can then add their effects to determine the combined action established by all of the factors when acting simultaneously.

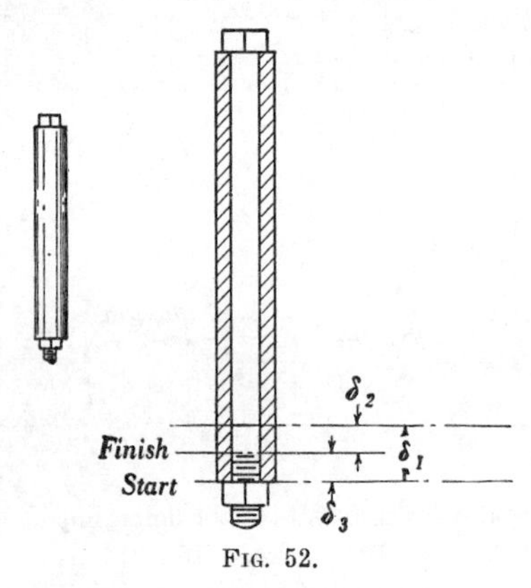

FIG. 52.

For example, let us first consider, in our present problem, the influence of the turning of the nut on the bolt. To establish a starting stage in our series of effects to be superimposed, we may imagine that the sleeve has been removed and the nut is in the starting position indicated in Fig. 52. If now the nut is rotated, it will move freely along the axis of the bolt and, in $\frac{1}{4}$ turn, will be raised through an axial distance

$$\delta_1 = \frac{1}{4} \times \frac{1}{16} = \frac{1}{64} \text{ in.}$$

If the sleeve is now assumed to be forced into the remaining space, the bolt will be elongated some distance, which is indicated as δ_2. The sleeve itself must have been contracted from its original length. This contraction is shown as δ_3.

During elongation δ_2 a tensile stress is set up in the bolt; during contraction δ_3 a compressive stress is set up in the sleeve.

The final length of the sleeve is equal to the final length of the enclosing distance between nut and bolthead, and the finish line of both bodies is indicated.

Then

$$\delta_1 = \delta_2 + \delta_3$$

or

$$\frac{1}{64} = \frac{P_{\text{bolt}} \times 15}{0.3 \times 30 \times 10^6} + \frac{P_{\text{sleeve}} \times 15}{1.0 \times 14 \times 10^6}$$

However, the total compressive force which the nut exerts on the sleeve is balanced by the total force which the sleeve exerts on the nut and, in turn, is the total tensile force acting on the bolt.

Solving the equation for

$$P = P_{\text{bolt}} = P_{\text{sleeve}}$$

$$\frac{1}{64} = 1.667 \times 10^{-6}P + 1.071 \times 10^{-6}P = 2.738 \times 10^{-6}P$$

$$P = 5710 \text{ lb.}$$

The unit stress in the bolt will be

$$s_T = \frac{5710}{0.3} = 19{,}030 \text{ psi}$$

and in the sleeve will be

$$s_C = \frac{5710}{1.0} = 5710 \text{ psi}$$

Illustrative Example IV. A load of 10,000 lb. is supported by members AD, BD, and CD (Fig. 53-a). The total stress in each of the members is to be determined. The members are identical in material and cross-sectional area.

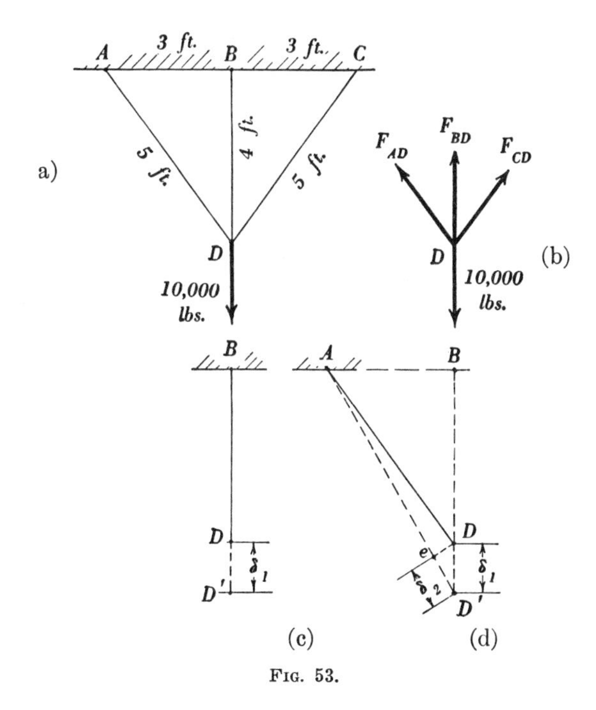

FIG. 53.

This problem presents an additional opportunity for us to note the manner in which the deformation equation $\delta = PL/AE$ [equation (30)] may be added to the conditions of equilibrium in facing a statically indeterminate case.

Figure 53-b illustrates the isolation of the pin at D as a free body. The system of external forces acting on the free body is shown, and we note the presence of three unknowns.

From Statics we have available but two conditions of equilibrium, $\Sigma X = 0$ and $\Sigma Y = 0$—the conditions for a concurrent, coplanar, force system. These two conditions are insufficient for the complete solution. With them, however, we can organize a first stage in the attack.

Applying $\Sigma X = 0$,

$$+F_{CD} \times \frac{3}{5} - F_{AD} \times \frac{3}{5} = 0$$

Therefore $$F_{CD} = F_{AD}$$

Applying $\Sigma Y = 0$,

$$+F_{AD} \times \frac{4}{5} + F_{BD} + F_{CD} \times \frac{4}{5} - 10{,}000 = 0$$

or $$2F_{AD} \times \frac{4}{5} + F_{BD} = 10{,}000 \qquad (1)$$

If now we consider the relationship of the deformations of the members we shall have available another and simultaneous equation containing the same unknowns as equation (1).

Here we shall employ, as in Illustrative Example III, the technique of superposition to appraise individual effects, which will then be combined to summarize the total action.

We shall first assume that the member BD is removed from the structure (Fig. 53-c). The deformation of this member will be found by substitution in equation (30),

$$DD' = \delta_1 = \frac{F_{BD} \times 4}{A \times E}$$

We now consider the remaining members. Member AD is shown in Fig. 53-d. Under the loading the point D will move to D' and the final length of this member will be AD'. If Ae is made equal to AD, the total elongation of AD is eD'. Since the deformations of such a structure are very small, it may be assumed that angle $AD'B$ = angle ABD, and that

$$eD' = \delta_2 = \frac{F_{AD} \times 5}{A \times E}$$

Tne final location of point D' is the same for the entire structure, whether we have been considering one member or another, and

and $$\delta_2 = \delta_1 \times \frac{4}{5}$$

Then $$\frac{F_{AD} \times 5}{AE} = \frac{F_{BD} \times 4}{AE} \times \frac{4}{5}$$

and $$F_{AD} = \frac{16}{25} F_{BD} \qquad (2)$$

Equations (1) and (2) may now be solved simultaneously, and

$$F_{BD} = 4940 \text{ lb.}$$

$$F_{AD} = F_{CD} = 3160 \text{ lb.}$$

PROBLEMS

Note: The value of the modulus of elasticity of the metals used in the problems is given in the following table. These are *average* values—the mechanical properties are affected by the composition of the material, and by such processing as heat treatment.

TABLE II. MODULUS OF ELASTICITY

Material	E
Steel	30×10^6 psi
Cast iron, gray	15×10^6
Cast iron, malleable	25×10^6
Wrought iron	28×10^6
Brass	15×10^6
Bronze	12×10^6
Copper	16×10^6
Aluminum	10.3×10^6
Magnesium	6.5×10^6

63. The steel rod has a cross-sectional area of 4 sq. in. and a length of 6 ft. Determine the load P which will cause a total deformation of 0.036 in. *Ans.* 60,000 lb.

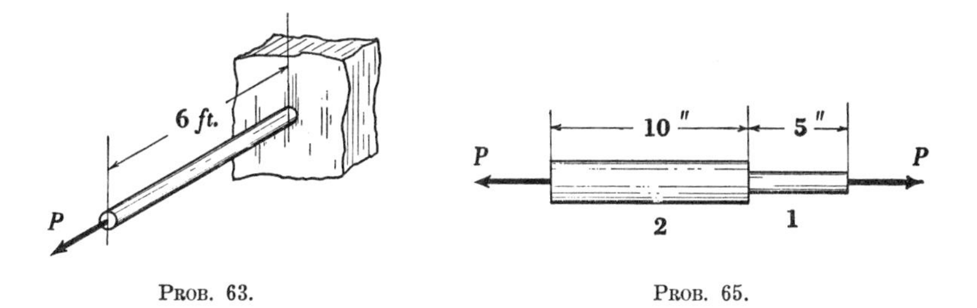

Prob. 63. Prob. 65.

64. A weight of 500 lb. is suspended from a steel cable, which has a diameter of 0.2 in. Determine the unit stress in the cable, and its elongation if the length of the cable is 40 ft., assuming that the weight of the cable itself may be neglected.

65. The cylindrical machine part is made of malleable cast iron. The diameter of section **1** is 1 in., and the diameter of section **2** is 2 in. Determine the unit stress in each section if $P = 10{,}000$ lb.

66. Determine the total deformation of the machine part of Prob. 65, when the axial load of 10,000 lb. is applied. *Ans.* 0.00382 in.

67. Blocks of two different materials are compressed between the jaws of a testing machine, which applies an axial load P. The total axial deformation of the two blocks is 0.002 in. Determine the unit stress in each block. Block **1** is made of copper, and $l_1 = 3.00$ in.; block **2** is made of aluminum, and $l_2 = 2.50$ in. The blocks have the same cross-section. *Ans.* 4650 psi.

68. The allowable stress in the hollow cast iron column shown is 6000 psi. Determine (a) the safe axial load P; (b) the amount the column will contract under this load. Length = 7.5 ft.

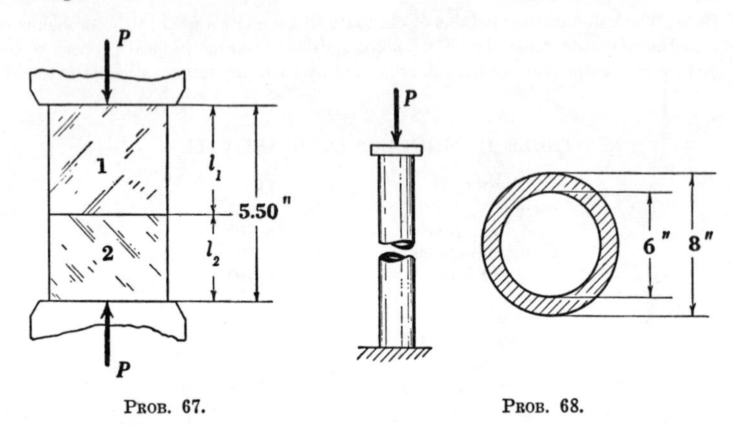

PROB. 67. PROB. 68.

69. The bar is held rigidly in unyielding walls, and load P applied along its axis at section a-a. Determine the forces which the wall exerts on the bar at its ends.

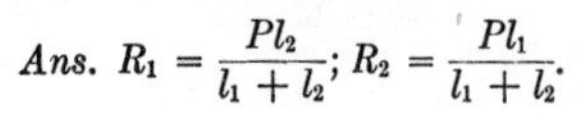

Ans. $R_1 = \dfrac{Pl_2}{l_1 + l_2}$; $R_2 = \dfrac{Pl_1}{l_1 + l_2}$.

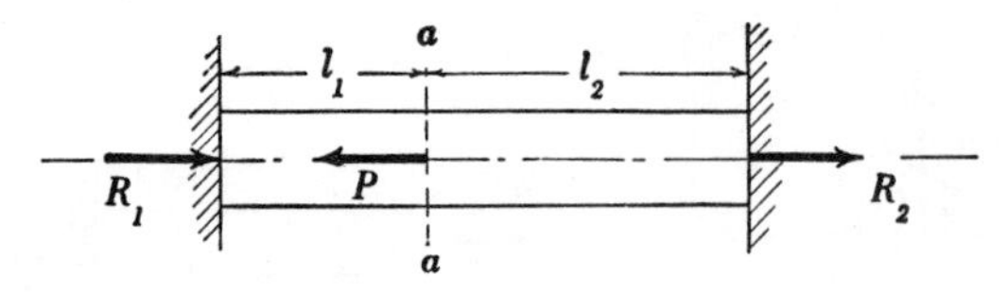

PROB. 69.

70. The loads P_1 and P_2 are applied along the axis of the rod. Areas: section **1**, 2 sq. in.; section **2**, 1.6 sq. in.; section **3**, 1.2 sq. in. Determine the unit stress in each section. Assume that the walls do not yield, and that all sections are made of the same material.

Ans. Section **1**: 8860 psi (compression); section **2**: 1430 psi (tension); section **3**: 10,230 psi (tension).

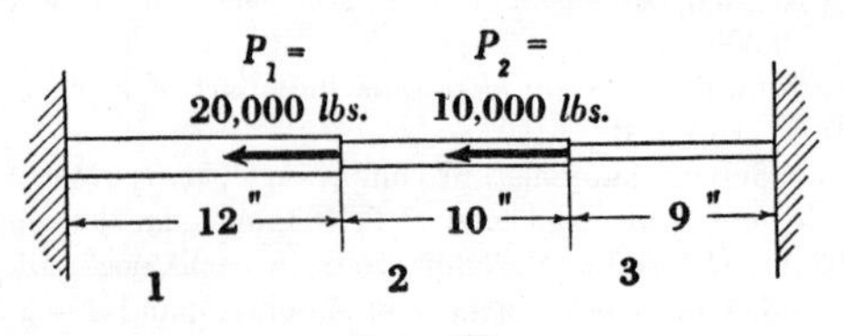

PROB. 70.

71. Determine the total elongation of a rod, of length L and density w when suspended in a vertical position from a ceiling. The rod has a uniform cross-section throughout its entire length. *Ans.* $\delta = wL^2/2E$.

72. The top of the tapered column is 6 in. square, and the bottom is 12 in. square. $E = 1.3 \times 10^6$ psi. What will be the axial load P if the column contracts 0.1 in.?

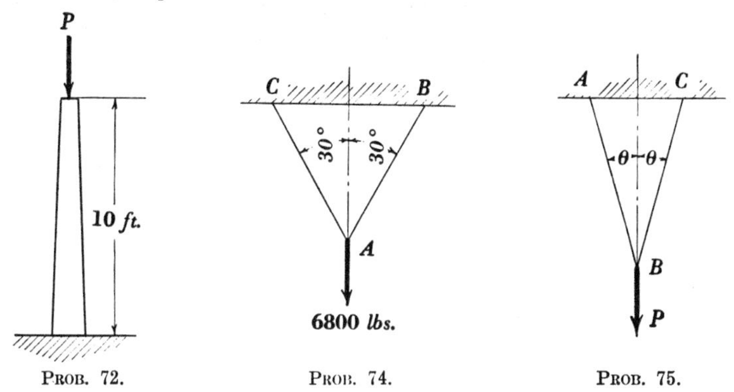

PROB. 72. PROB. 74. PROB. 75.

73. Determine the elongation of cable CA of Prob. 4. The cable is made of steel.

74. Determine the diameters of rods AC and AB if the allowable stress in each is 20,000 psi. A, B, and C are pin joints.

75. Rods AB and CB are of equal length L and are made of the same material. They have the same cross-sectional area A. Determine the amount point B will be lowered when load P is applied. *Ans.* $PL/2AE \cos^2 \theta$.

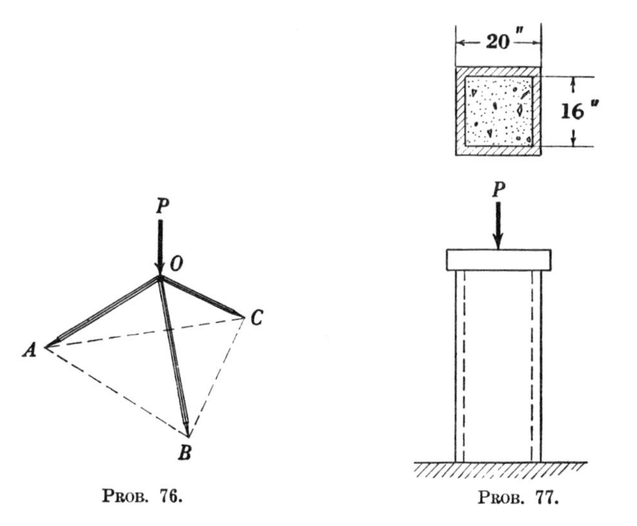

PROB. 76. PROB. 77.

76. Three steel legs, each 3 ft. long, are used as a tripod to support the load $P = 3000$ lb. O is a ball-and-socket joint. Points A, B, and C form an equilateral triangle with 3 ft. sides, lying in a horizontal plane. The load P is vertical and its line of action passes through the centroid of triangle ABC. The allowable unit stress in the steel legs is 12,000 psi. Determine the required cross-sectional area of the legs, and the amount point O is lowered.

77. The square cast iron column shell is filled with concrete. Load P = 167,000 lb. Determine the unit stress in each material, using $E = 2 \times 10^6$ psi for concrete. The column cap through which load P is applied is rigid.

78. A gray cast iron core A, of 5 in. diameter is placed in a steel tube B, 0.1 in. thick. The resultant of a uniformly distributed axial load is P = 200,000 lb. Assuming that the strains are the same in both materials, determine the unit stress in each material. *Ans.* A: 8760 psi; B: 17,500 pi.

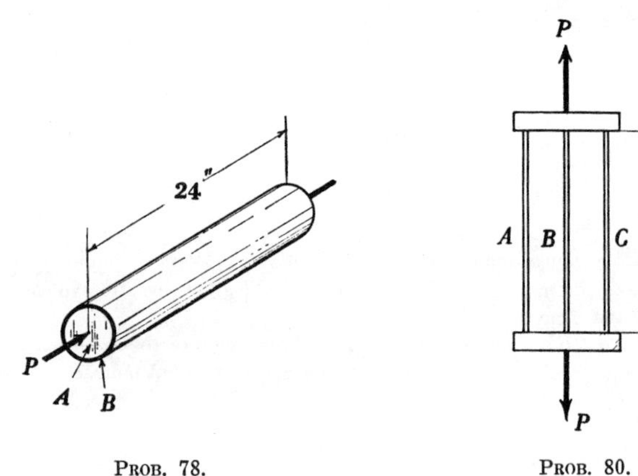

PROB. 78. PROB. 80.

79. Determine the total deformation of the assembly of Prob. 78. *Ans.* 0.014 in.

80. Three rods of the same length and same cross-sectional area are held between holders which apply an axial load P. Rods A and C have the same modulus of elasticity E_A and rod B has a modulus of elasticity E_B. A and C are equidistant from B. Assuming that the holders do not bend, determine the total elongation of the rods.

Ans. $\dfrac{PL}{A(2E_A + E_B)}$

81. Rods A and C are steel rods, having a diameter of ¾ in.; B is a copper rod, having a diameter of 1 in. (see figure for Prob. 80). The length of all rods is 30 in. Determine the unit stress in each rod when P = 15,000 lb.

82. Determine the total elongation of each rod of Prob. 81 when the load of 15,000 lb. is applied.

83. Rods A and C are made of steel, and the allowable stress in these rods is 10,000 psi. Rod B is made of aluminum and the allowable stress is 6000 psi. All rods have a cross-sectional area of 6 sq. in. The length of A and C is 6 ft.; the length of B is 4 ft. Determine (a) the safe load P, assuming that the beam ab is rigid. (b) If the length of rod B is increased to 6 ft., determine the safe load P. *Ans.* a) 150,900 lb.; b) 140,600 lb.

84. Rods A and B are made of steel, and rod C is made of brass. The area of A and B is 0.6 sq. in., and the area of C is 0.4 sq. in. Determine the unit stress in each rod, assuming that beam D is rigid and remains horizontal. *Ans.* A and B: 7140 psi; C: 3570 psi.

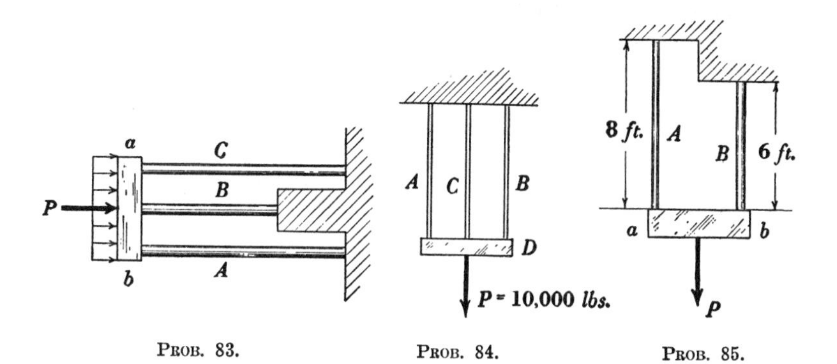

PROB. 83. PROB. 84. PROB. 85.

85. Steel rod A has a cross-sectional area of 1 sq. in., and an allowable tensile stress of 16,000 psi. Brass rod B has a cross-sectional area of 2 sq. in., and an allowable tensile stress of 9000 psi. Determine maximum allowable load P, assuming that beam ab is rigid, and remains horizontal.

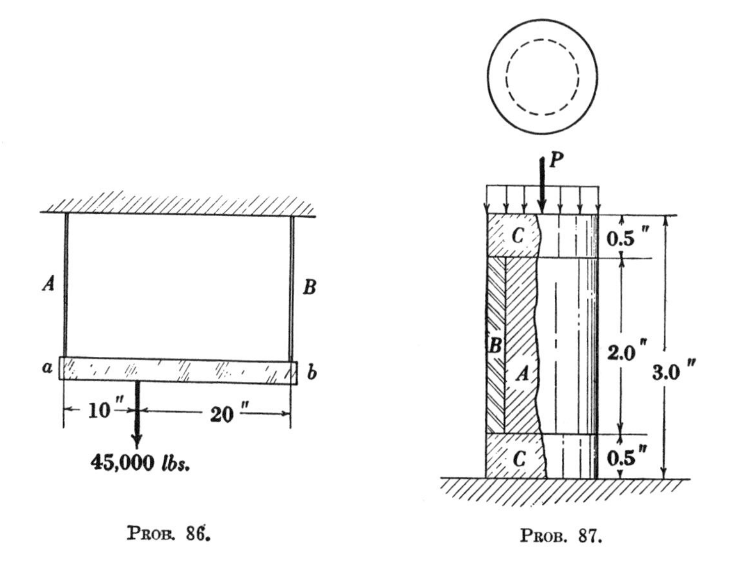

PROB. 86. PROB. 87.

86. A rigid bar, ab, supports a load of 45,000 lb. ab is supported by rods A and B. Rod A is made of steel. Rod B is made of aluminum, and has a cross-sectional area of 3 sq. in. Assuming that ab is rigid and remains horizontal, determine the cross-sectional area of rod A.

87. Two views of a circular test piece are shown. The piece consists of

A: Cast iron (gray) core; Area = 0.45 sq. in.
B: Steel shell; Area = 0.55 sq. in.
C: Copper caps; Area = 1.00 sq. in.

When a uniformly distributed load whose resultant is force P is applied, the total length decreases from 3.00 to 2.9946 in. Determine the load P and the unit stress in each material. Assume that the caps do not bend. *Ans.* $P = 36{,}400$ lb.
$s_A = 23{,}500$ psi.
$s_B = 47{,}000$ psi.
$s_C = 36{,}400$ psi.

88. The beam OA is supported on a pin joint at O, and by rods AB and CD. The rods are made of bronze, and each has a cross-sectional area of 0.75 sq. in. Angle $AOB = 30°$. AB and CD are perpendicular to OA. When load W is applied, a strain gage placed on AB shows that the longitudinal strain in that member is $\frac{1}{6000}$ in./in. Determine the magnitude of load W, assuming that beam OA does not bend.
Ans. 10,000 lb.

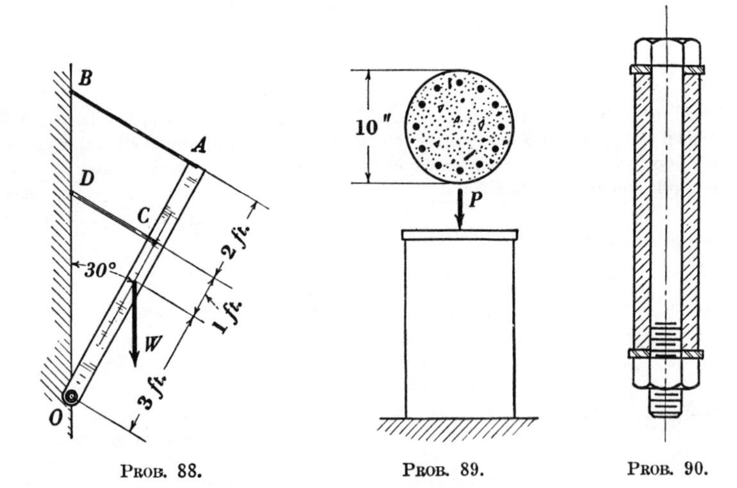

PROB. 88. PROB. 89. PROB. 90.

89. The concrete column is reinforced by 12 steel rods, each having a cross-sectional area of 0.1963 sq. in. The modulus of elasticity of the concrete is 7.5×10^5 psi. The allowable stress in the concrete is 800 psi, and the allowable stress in the steel is 20,000 psi. Determine the maximum load P which may be placed on the column.
Ans. 85,100 lb.

90. A steel bolt is placed in a brass sleeve. The diameter of the bolt is $\frac{3}{4}$ in. and the outer diameter of the sleeve is $1\frac{1}{2}$ in. The length of the sleeve is 24 in. The pitch of the bolt thread is $\frac{1}{8}$ in. If the nut is turned through $\frac{1}{4}$ turn, determine the unit stress in each material. *Ans.* Steel: 23,400 psi; Brass: 7810 psi.

91. A cylindrical bronze casting C, having a diameter of 6 in. and a length of 12 in., is compressed by tightening the four nuts a through one-eighth turn. The bolts c are made of steel, with a diameter of $\frac{1}{2}$ in. and pitch of thread = $\frac{1}{16}$ in. Determine the total deformation of the casting, and the unit stress in the casting. The bar A is rigid.

92. The beam AC is supported on a pin joint at O, and by steel rods AB and CD. Rod AB has a cross-sectional area of 1.5 sq. in., and a length of 2 ft. Rod CD has a cross-sectional area of 1 sq. in., and a length of 5 ft. Determine the unit stress and total deformation for each rod. Assume that there is no bending of the beam AC.

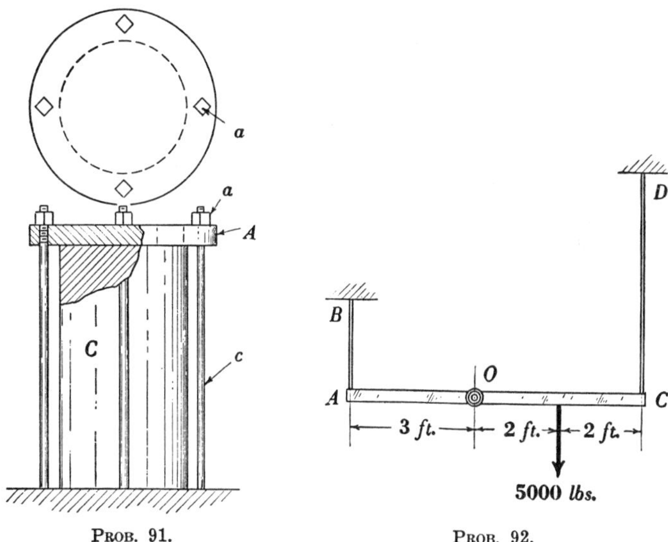

PROB. 91. PROB. 92.

93. The beam OB is supported on a pin joint at O, and held in position by rods AC and BD. The length of each rod is 5 ft. Rod AC has a cross-sectional area of 0.4 sq. in., and rod BD has a cross-sectional area of 0.2 sq. in. Both rods are made of steel. W = 13,200 lb. Assuming that there is no bending of the beam, determine the unit stress and the elongation of each rod. *Ans.* AC: 12,000 psi, 0.024 in.; BD: 30,000 psi, 0.060 in.

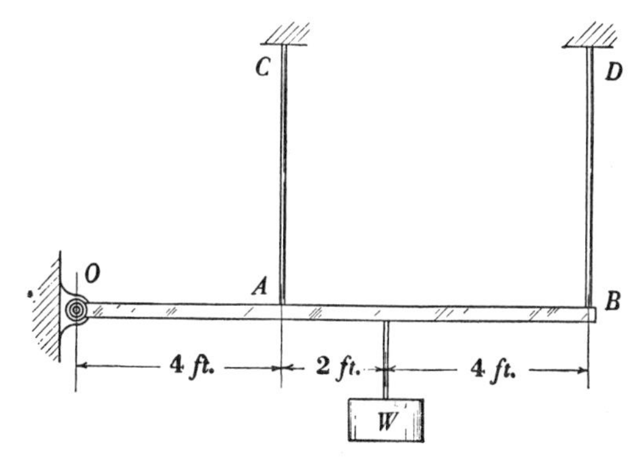

PROB. 93.

16. Modulus of Rigidity. The modulus of elasticity is the constant of proportionality in the stress-strain relationship $s = Ee$, whether the loading produces tension, compression, or shear.

When, however, the relationship between the shearing stress and shearing strain is considered, we express the relationship as

$$s_S = G\gamma$$

where s_S = the shearing stress,
γ = the shearing strain (see Art. 14), and
G = the modulus of elasticity in shear, usually called the *modulus of rigidity*.

The modulus of rigidity for a given material, while identical in concept with the modulus of elasticity, is quantitatively different. For example,

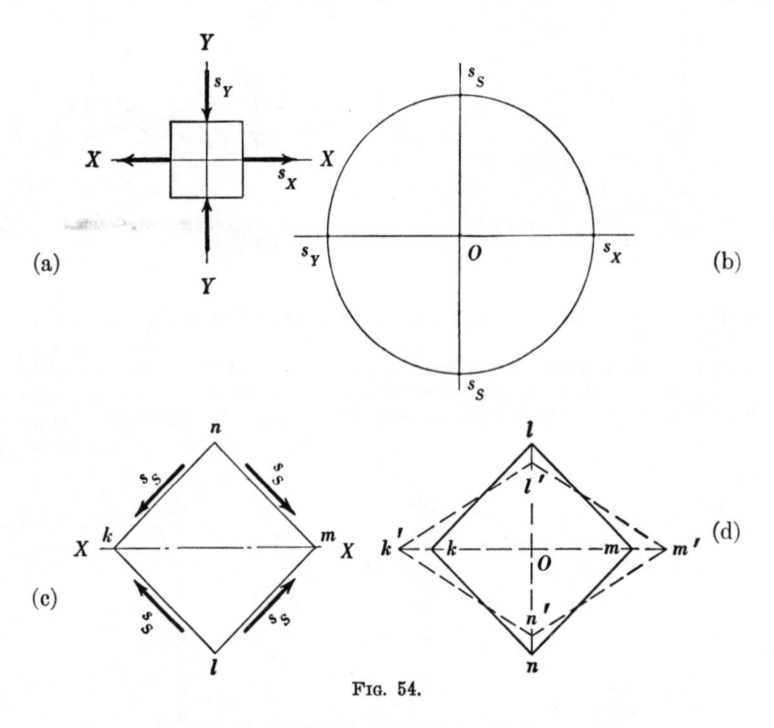

FIG. 54.

the modulus of elasticity of steel in tension or compression is $E = 30 \times 10^6$ psi, while its modulus of rigidity is $G = 12 \times 10^6$ psi, the modulus of elasticity of aluminum is $E = 10.3 \times 10^6$ psi, and its modulus of rigidity is $G = 3.85 \times 10^6$ psi.

17. Relationship of E, G, and μ. The determination of Poisson's ratio by direct measurement is difficult because of the extremely small magnitude of the lateral strains. It is possible, however, to determine the ratio from the relationship of the moduli of elasticity and rigidity as determined from tensile and torsional tests.

If we observe the free body of Fig. 54-a, we note that it has, acting upon its faces, the tensile stress s_X and the compressive stress s_Y, which are assumed to be equal in magnitude.

The unit elongation of the prism in the X-direction will be

$$e = \frac{s_X}{E} + \mu\frac{s_Y}{E} \tag{1}$$

Mohr's circle for this state of stress appears in Fig. 54-b. We note that there will be two planes of maximum shear which are inclined at an angle of 45° with the X- and Y-planes. These planes are shown in Fig. 54-c. On these planes of maximum shear, the normal stresses are zero.

The shear stresses will deform the prism $klmn$ into the form of a rhombus $k'l'm'n'$ as shown in Fig. 54-d. The deformations have been greatly exaggerated so that we may note the relationships of the angular and linear displacements.

The total length of diagonal km after application of the loading will be $k'm'$.

The unit deformation in the X-direction will be

$$e = \frac{k'k + mm'}{km} = \frac{mm'}{Om}$$

The shearing strain γ is the total change of angle at the corners of the prism. For example,

$$\begin{aligned} \gamma &= knm - k'n'm' \\ &= 2(Onm - On'm') \end{aligned}$$

and

$$\frac{\gamma}{2} = Onm - On'm'$$

as indicated in the figure.

By the definition of shearing strain given in Art. 14 and illustrated in Fig. 49,

$$\frac{\gamma}{2} = \frac{mm'}{Om} = e$$

But

$$\gamma = \frac{s_S}{G} \quad \text{and} \quad \frac{\gamma}{2} = \frac{s_S}{2G}$$

Then

$$e = \frac{s_S}{2G} \tag{2}$$

We may now equate the values of e given by equations (1) and (2), and

$$\frac{s_S}{2G} = \frac{s_X}{E} + \frac{\mu s_Y}{E}$$

If we return to the Mohr's circle of Fig. 54-b, we note that s_S, s_X, and s_Y are numerically equal.

Then

$$\frac{s_S}{2G} = \frac{s_S}{E} + \frac{\mu s_S}{E}$$

$$\frac{1}{2G} = \frac{1}{E}(1 + \mu)$$

and

$$G = \frac{E}{2(1 + \mu)} \tag{31}$$

Illustrative Example. A bronze specimen has a modulus of elasticity $E = 17 \times 10^6$ psi., and a modulus of rigidity $G = 6.5 \times 10^6$ psi. Determine Poisson's ratio for the material.

By equation (31)

$$G = \frac{E}{2(1 + \mu)}$$

$$6.5 \times 10^6 = \frac{17 \times 10^6}{2(1 + \mu)}$$

$$\mu = 0.308$$

18. Stress Effect of Temperature Change. Thermal Stress. When a body is subjected to change of temperature, its dimensions will increase or diminish as the temperature rises or falls. If the body is constrained in its dimensional change by neighboring bodies, stress will be produced.

The influence of temperature change is noted through the medium of the coefficient of thermal expansion, ϵ, which is defined as the unit strain produced by a temperature change of one degree. This physical constant is a property of each material, and values of ϵ for several materials are given on page 89.

If the temperature of a bar of length l is changed $\Delta t°$, the deformation of the unrestrained bar will be

$$\delta_T = \epsilon \, l \, \Delta t$$

We can best observe the nature of the development of stress resulting from a change of temperature, or thermal stress, by investigating an actual case.

The rod of Fig. 55 is fastened at its ends to two rigid plates. We are to determine the stress in the rod after a temperature drop of $\Delta t°$. It is assumed that the end plates do not yield.

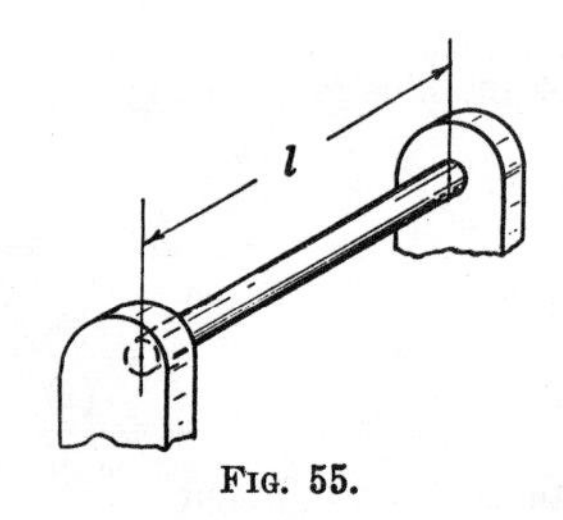

FIG. 55.

Here, again, the method of superposition is effective, and we shall attack the problem in stages.

First, we assume that the end plates are removed, and the temperature drops. The total contraction of the rod will be

$$\delta_T = \epsilon \, l \, \Delta t$$

Second, we assume that the end plates are now placed on the contracted rod and that they stretch it back to its original length. During such stretching stress is developed in the rod.

Then

$$\delta_T = \frac{Pl}{AE} = \epsilon \, l \, \Delta t$$

and

$$\frac{P}{A} = s = \epsilon E \, \Delta t \tag{32}$$

If, as in most practical cases, the end plates do yield an amount δ_1, the deformation during which stress is developed is

$$\delta_T - \delta_1 = \frac{Pl}{AE}$$

Illustrative Example. Sections **1** and **2** of a machine part (Fig. 56) are securely fastened to each other and mounted in a retaining framework as shown.

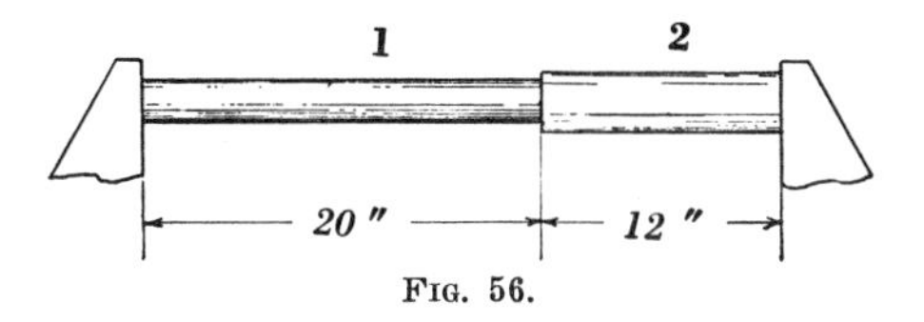

Fig. 56.

The coefficient of linear expansion (°F.) for section 1 is $\epsilon = 6 \times 10^{-6}$; its cross-sectional area is $A = 1.0$ sq. in.; its modulus of elasticity is $E = 30 \times 10^6$ psi. The corresponding values for section **2** are $\epsilon = 14 \times 10^{-6}$; $A = 2.0$ sq. in.; $E = 18 \times 10^6$ psi.

The unit stress in each section is to be determined if the temperature drops 80°F. There is no initial stress in the part before the temperature change takes place, and the end walls do not yield.

If the part is isolated as a free body, the total contraction due to the change of temperature will be

$$\begin{aligned}\delta_T &= 6 \times 10^{-6} \times 20 \times 80 + 14 \times 10^{-6} \times 12 \times 80 \\ &= 2.304 \times 10^{-2} \text{ in.}\end{aligned}$$

Then $$\delta = 2.304 \times 10^{-2} = \frac{P \times 20}{1 \times 30 \times 10^6} + \frac{P \times 12}{2 \times 18 \times 10^6} = \frac{P}{10^6}$$

and $$P = 23{,}040 \text{ lb.}$$

Unit stress in section **1** $$s_1 = \frac{23{,}040}{1} = 23{,}040 \text{ psi}$$

Unit stress in section **2**, $$s_2 = \frac{23{,}040}{2} = 11{,}520 \text{ psi}$$

PROBLEMS

Note: The values of the coefficient of linear expansion (°F.) for engineering metals of average composition are given in the following table.

TABLE III. COEFFICIENT OF LINEAR EXPANSION

Material	*Coefficient*
Steel	6.5×10^{-6} in./in./°F
Cast iron, gray	6.0×10^{-6}
Cast iron, malleable	6.6×10^{-6}
Wrought iron	6.7×10^{-6}
Brass	10.4×10^{-6}
Bronze	10.0×10^{-6}
Copper	9.3×10^{-6}
Aluminum	12.5×10^{-6}
Magnesium	14.5×10^{-6}

94. The steel rod *AB* is securely restrained by holders at its ends. The length of the rod is 6 ft. and its cross-sectional area is 2 sq. in. If the temperature falls 100°F., determine the unit stress in the rod. Assume that the holders do not yield, and that there is no initial stress in the rod. *Ans.* 19,500 psi (tension).

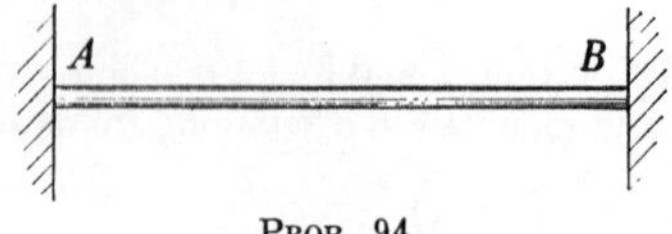

Prob. 94.

95. If the rod *AB* of Prob. 94 is made of aluminum, and all other conditions are the same, determine the unit stress in the rod. *Ans.* 12,875 psi (tension).

96. If there is an initial stress of 4000 psi, compression, in the rod *AB* of Prob. 94, determine the unit stress in the rod after the temperature drop.

97. If the supporting holders of Prob. 94 yield 0.01 in. determine the total pull of the rod on the holders after the temperature drop.

98. A steel shaft, 25 ft. long and having a cross-sectional area of 3 sq. in., is held rigidly at one end and by a partially yielding holder at the other end. If the temperature drops 40°F., and the holder yields 0.024 in., determine the unit stress in the shaft. *Ans.* 5400 psi

99. A gray cast iron bar, 100 in. long, having a cross-sectional area of 2 sq. in. and initial stress zero, is mounted in end holders. Determine the amount the holders must yield when the temperature drops 100°F. if the unit stress in the rod must not exceed 6000 psi.

100. Section **1** is made of aluminum and has a cross-sectional area of 1 sq. in. Section **2** is made of steel and has a cross-sectional area of 1.2 sq. in. Determine the unit stress in each material if the temperature is raised 100°F. The supports do not yield. *Ans.* Section **1**, 14,700 psi; Section **2**, 12,300 psi

Prob. 100.

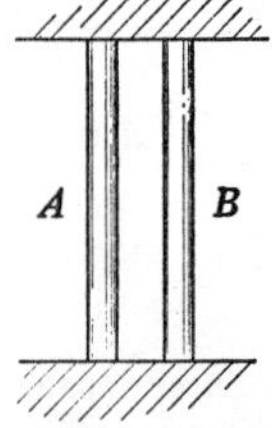

Prob. 101.

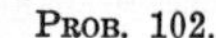

Prob. 102.

101. The two bars of different materials are mounted between rigid holders. The lengths and cross-sectional areas are the same in both bars. Determine the ratio of the unit stresses in the two bars when both are subjected to the same change of temperature if *A* is made of steel, and *B* of aluminum.

102. The 20,000-lb. rigid block rests on three supporting struts *A*, *B*, and *C*. *A* and *C* are made of brass, and *B* is made of steel. All struts have the same length, and each has a cross-sectional area of 5 sq. in. Determine (a) the total stress in each rod and (b) the amount the temperature must be raised to force the brass rods to carry the entire load. *Ans.* (b) 34.2°

103. The assembled series of rods are securely fastened to each other, and held in unyielding walls at the ends. Sections **1** and **4** are made of steel, and each has a cross-sectional area of 2 sq. in. Section **2** is made of aluminum and has a cross-sectional area of 1 sq. in. Section **3** is made of brass and has a cross-sectional area of 1.6 sq. in.

If the maximum allowable stress in the brass is 9000 psi, determine the maximum rise in temperature to which the assembly may be subjected. *Ans.* 63°F.

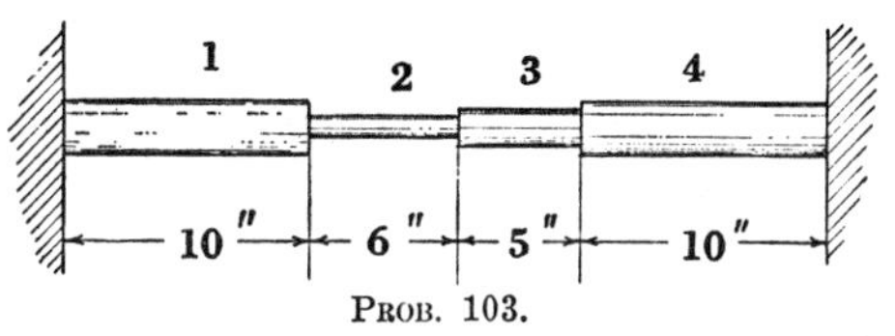

PROB. 103.

104. The steel rod AB has a cross-sectional area of 0.01 sq. in. The constant of the spring is 500 lb./in. Determine the unit stress in AB after a temperature drop of 100°F., assuming that the walls are unyielding. Neglect the effect of temperature on the spring. *Ans.* 1440 psi.

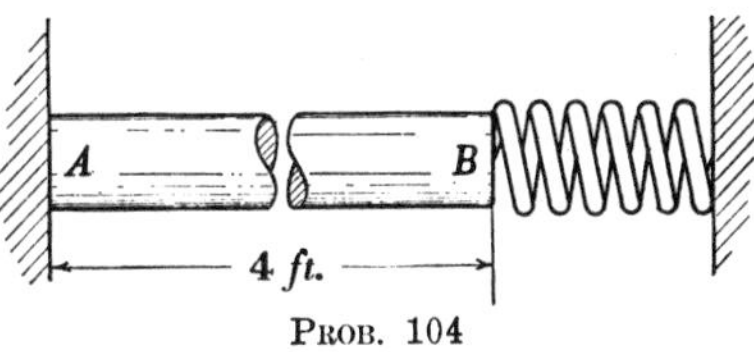

PROB. 104

105. An aluminum band is placed on a 12 in. diameter core, and the nut is tightened until the unit stress in the band is 12,000 psi. Determine the amount the temperature must be raised to relieve the stress in the band completely. Assume that the effect of the temperature change on the core is negligible. *Ans.* 93.2°F.

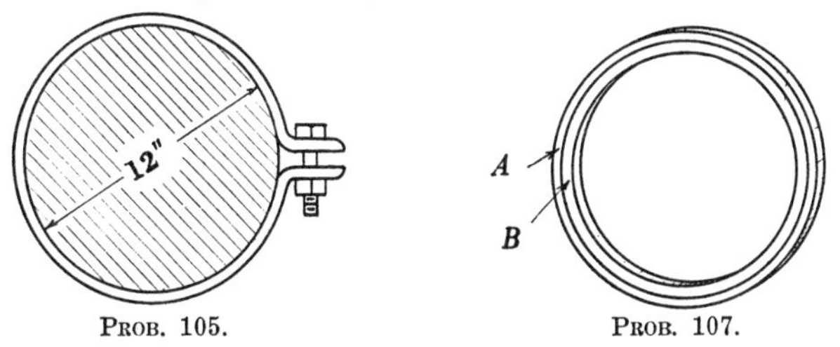

PROB. 105. PROB. 107.

106. A copper hoop is placed on a steel hoop so that it just fits snugly. The diameter of the hoops is 18 in. Determine the amount the temperature must be raised to produce a clearance of 0.001 in. between the hoops.

107. The copper hoop A is 1 in. wide by 1 in. thick, and the steel hoop B is 1 in. wide by 1.5 in. thick. Diameter = 20 in. The hoops fit together with zero clearance at room temperature. Determine the pressure between the hoops and the unit stress in each material when the temperature is lowered from room temperature at 70°F. to 0°F. *Ans.* Pressure, 231 psi;
s_A, 2310 psi;
s_B, 1540 psi.

108. The rods of Prob. 84 are subjected to a temperature drop of 100°F. while supporting the load of 10,000 lb. Determine the unit stress in each rod, assuming that D remains rigid. *Ans.* A and B, 5470 psi; C, 8580 psi.

109. How much must the temperature of the rods of Prob. 84 be elevated in order to force rods A and B to carry the entire load of 10,000 lb.?

110. Assuming that there is no bending of the beam AC of Prob. 92 and that the temperature drops 50°F., determine the unit stress in rods AB and CD.

111. Assuming that there is no bending of the beam OB of Prob. 93 and that the temperature rises 60°F., determine the unit stresses in rods AC and BD. *Ans.* AC: 6680 psi; BD: 34,300 psi.

112. A strip of copper, ½ in. × 1 in. × 18 in., is brazed between two strips of steel, ¼ in. × 1 in. × 18 in., as shown. If the temperature rises 200°F., determine the unit stress in each material. *Ans.* 5840 psi.

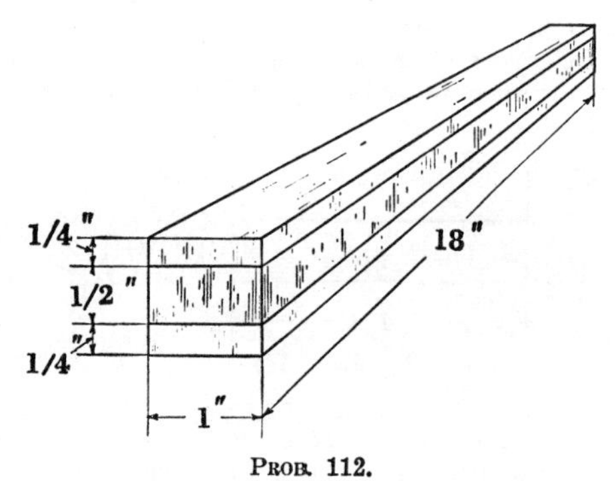

PROB. 112.

CHAPTER II

Bending: The Basic Flexure Theory

19. Beams. The core of the subject of Mechanics of Materials consists of the application of the theories of behavior of beams in bending.

The term *beam* has broader significance here than in ordinary architectural or structural practice. Any prismatic, straight bar which is subjected to transverse forces—that is, forces perpendicular to the long axis of the bar—is a beam. We shall have need, in developing the discussion of theories underlying the analysis of stress behavior, for further limitation of such loaded members, and for more rigid boundaries in classifying those loaded bodies which are embraced by the term beam. For our present purposes the simple definition given above is quite adequate.

Beams are, then, loaded transversely. Qualifying adjectives are used to distinguish the various manners in which such loaded members are supported. The *simple* or freely supported beam (Fig. 57) is supported by forces which, like the loads, are perpendicular to the longitudinal axis of the beam. Such supports offer no restraint parallel to the longitudinal axis. Two types of simple beams are shown in Figs. 57 and 58—the former is supported at its ends; the latter is an *overhanging* beam, with the end sections projecting beyond the supports.

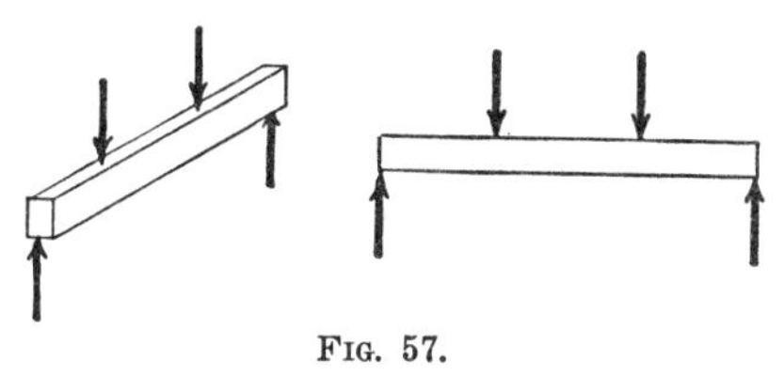

FIG. 57.

When a beam is supported by being built into walls or fastened to columns, as shown in Fig. 59, it is called a *built-in* beam. The beam of

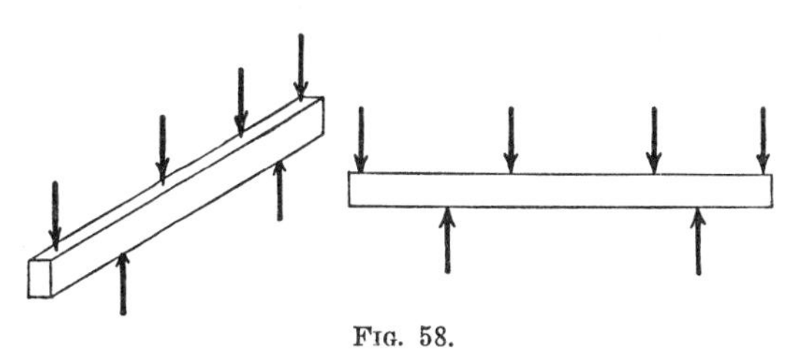

FIG. 58.

Fig. 60, rigidly supported by a wall at one end, with the other end free, is known as a *cantilever* beam.

20. Shearing Force. The beam of Fig. 61-a is loaded by forces W_1, W_2, and W_3, and freely supported at its ends by the supporting forces R_1 and R_2. The weight of the beam is assumed to be negligible.

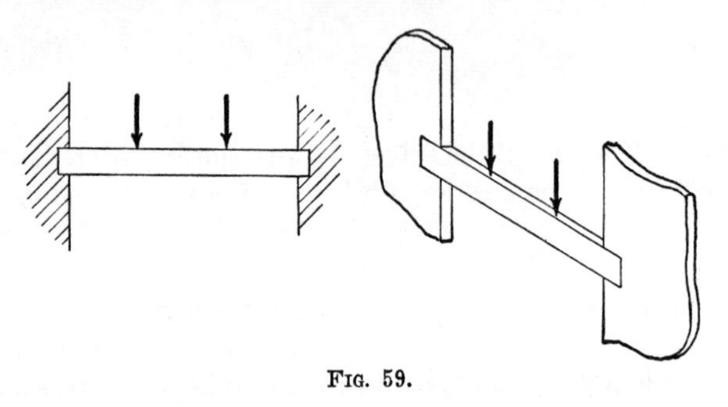

FIG. 59.

Any right section of the beam—for example, section A-A—is acted upon by some distributed force system. These internal forces are stresses, and our concern is with their evaluation.

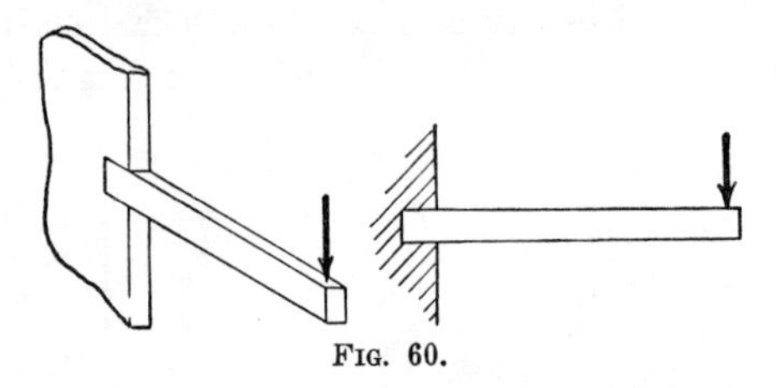

FIG. 60.

If we isolate as a free body the portion of the beam which lies to the left of the plane A-A, as shown in Fig. 61-b, we find that in addition to force R_1 some force is acting which represents the influence of the neighboring body—the portion of the beam lying to the right of A-A. This force must have a vertical component, for the isolated free body is in equilibrium. This vertical component is shown as V in Fig. 61-b. It is the resultant of a system of unit stresses which are parallel to section A-A and are, therefore, shear stresses. V is called the *shearing force* at section A-A of the beam.

To evaluate V, we apply the condition of equilibrium, $\Sigma Y = 0$.

$$+R_1 - V = 0$$

and

$$V = R_1$$

V will always be equal in magnitude to the sum of all the vertical forces acting on the isolated portion of a beam taken either to the left or right of the isolating section upon which V acts.

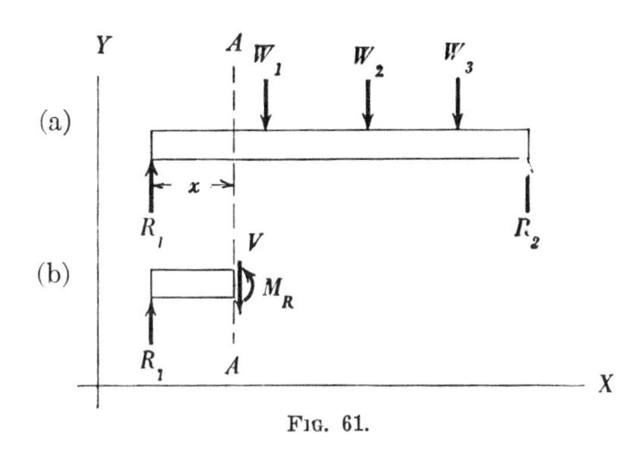

FIG. 61.

The sign of shearing force is established, arbitrarily, by the convention illustrated in Fig. 62. If as shown in Fig. 62-a, a force acts so as to tend to make the portion of the beam to the left of the shearing section, A-A, move upward relative to the portion on the right, the shearing force on section A-A is positive. Figure 62-b illustrates the convention for negative shearing force. The force R_1 of Fig. 61, produces positive shearing force on section A-A.

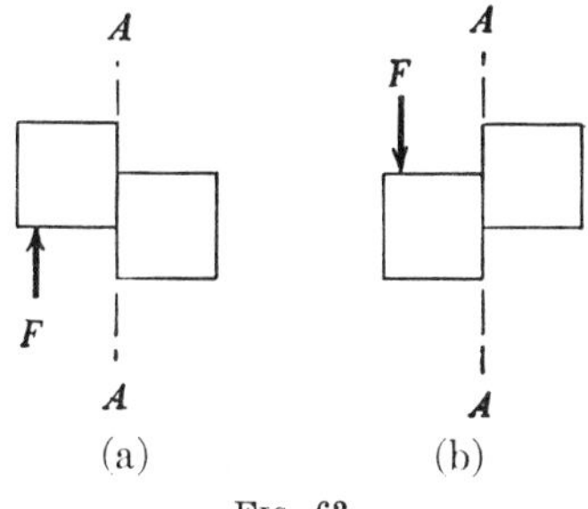

FIG. 62.

21. Bending Moment. The isolated free body, lying on the left of section A-A of Fig. 61-b, could not remain in equilibrium if only forces R_1 and V were acting upon it, for they form a couple of magnitude R_1x, which would, if left unbalanced, cause rotation of the free body. It follows that the portion of the beam lying to the right of A-A must be exerting a torque or moment equal and opposite to that of couple R_1x, in addition to shearing force V. This moment, indicated as M_R is the resultant of a system of normal unit stresses acting upon section A-A.

When a beam is loaded—for example, as shown in Fig. 63-a—it will sag. The lower fibers will stretch while the upper fibers contract. (The term fiber, as used here, means the geometric lines which comprise the prismatic beam.) Then the lower portion of the beam is in tension while the upper portion is in compression. The exact nature of the distribution of these tensile and compressive stresses will be discussed in later articles. Let us note, for the present, that there will be a resultant tensile and a resultant compressive force acting normal to section *A-A* as in Fig. 63-b, where these normal forces are represented by R_T and R_C.

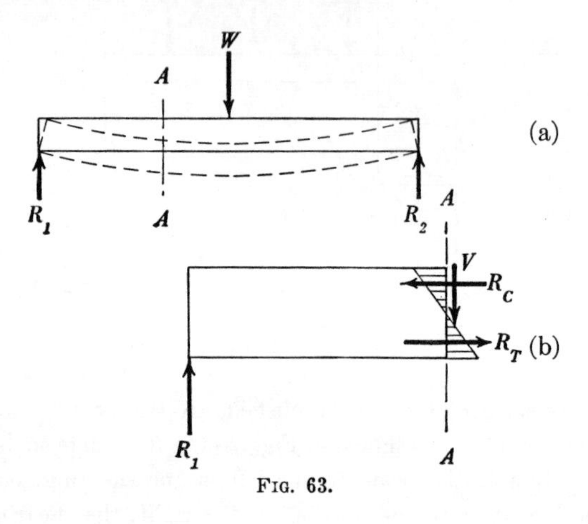

FIG. 63.

Since the isolated body is in equilibrium, $R_T = R_C$. Then the resultant of the normal stresses is a couple. It is this couple which must balance the couple R_1x of Fig. 61-b. This moment is called the *moment of resistance*

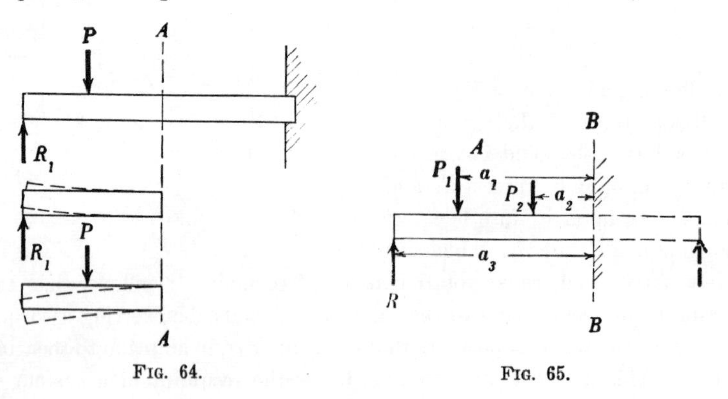

FIG. 64. FIG. 65.

at section *A-A*. The couple which it balances (R_1x) is known as the *bending moment* at section *A-A*.

We have illustrated principle by a simple example in which only one external force (R_1) is acting on the free body to the left of section *A-A*.

If more than one external force acts upon such a free body, the bending moment will be the sum of the moments of all the external forces acting on either side of the section.

The convention which is employed in establishing a sign system for bending moment is illustrated in Fig. 64. If a force like R_1 tends to bend the portion of the beam to the left of section A-A so that the bottom fibers are stretched, the bending moment at A-A caused by that force is *positive.* A force, like P of the figure, tends to compress the bottom fibers, and causes *negative* bending moment at A-A.

To determine the sign of the total, or resultant, bending moment at any section of a beam (for example, section B-B of Fig. 65) it is convenient to assume that the portion of the beam lying to the right of section B-B is held rigidly, and then to note the influence of each of the external forces to the left of the section.

R will cause a bending moment of magnitude Ra_3 at section B-B. This bending moment is positive, for it tends to produce tension in the bottom fibers of the beam. P_1 produces a negative bending moment of magnitude P_1a_1 at section B-B, and P_2 produces a negative bending moment of magnitude P_2a_2.

The net bending moment at section B-B will be the algebraic sum of these three moments, which is

$$M = +Ra_3 - P_1a_1 - P_2a_2$$

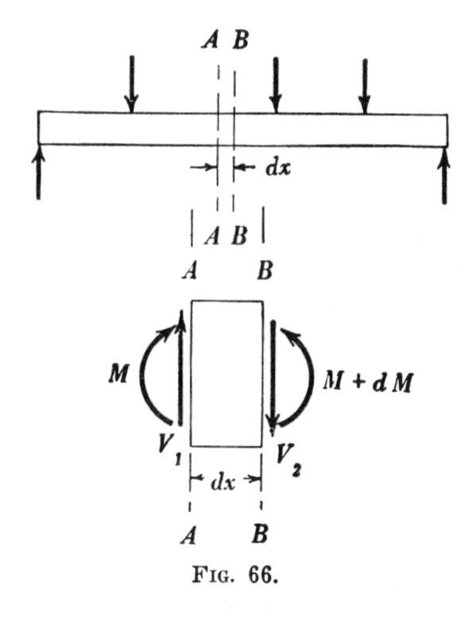

FIG. 66.

22. Relationship between Shearing Force and Bending Moment. If we examine the free body of Fig. 66, we shall have an opportunity of noting the relationship which exists between the shearing force, discussed in Art. 20, and the bending moment, discussed in Art. 21.

The free body is the portion of a beam lying between right sections A-A and B-B, at a distance dx apart. If the entire beam is in equilibrium, this isolated portion must be a free body in equilibrium.

The system of external forces acting on the body comprises V_1 and V_2, the shearing forces on faces A-A and B-B, the bending moment M on the left face, and $M + dM$ on the right face.

It is assumed that the weight of the free body itself is negligible, and that there are no other vertical forces acting upon this portion of the beam.

Applying the condition of equilibrium,

$$\Sigma Y = 0$$

$$+V_1 - V_2 = 0$$

and

$$V_1 = V_2$$

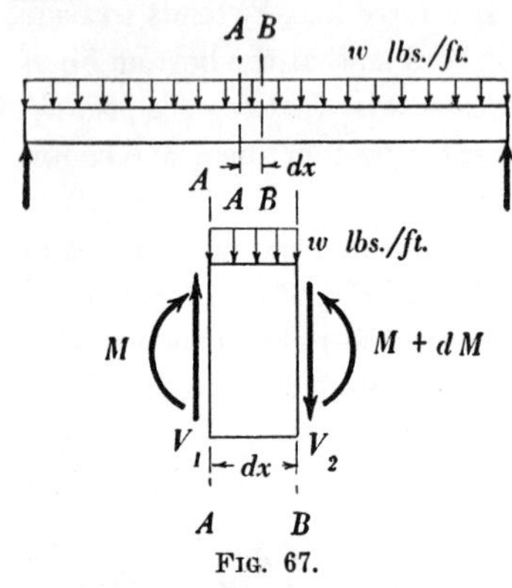

FIG. 67.

The two shearing forces have as their resultant, therefore, a couple of magnitude $V\,dx$.

Applying the condition of equilibrium,

$$\Sigma M = 0$$

$$+V\,dx + M - (M + dM) = 0$$

$$V\,dx = dM$$

and

$$V = \frac{dM}{dx} \tag{33}$$

Shearing force is therefore the *first derivative of bending moment with respect to x.*

If, as in Fig. 67, the free body has, in addition to the forces previously noted, a distributed force of intensity w lb./ft. acting upon it—which might be the weight of the body, or an applied load—we may again apply the conditions of equilibrium to note the shearing force–bending moment relationship.

Applying $\Sigma M = 0$, taking moments about an axis at section B-B,

$$+M - w\,dx\left(\frac{dx}{2}\right) - (M + dM) + V_1\,dx = 0$$

The second term is the product of two differentials and is so small that it may be neglected.

Once again,

$$V = \frac{dM}{dx}$$

Then, in all cases, shearing force is the first derivative bending moment with respect to x.

This is a most useful relationship, for our usual concern with bending moment consists of determining its maximum value. To establish this value we may determine the location of the section of the beam at which the shearing force, as first derivative, is equal to zero. Maximum (or minimum) bending moments will occur at such sections. We shall observe these relationships in the following article.

23. Analysis of Shearing Force and Bending Moment. To enhance our understanding of shearing force and bending moment we shall survey the development of both of these factors in actual beams. The survey is to determine the shearing force and bending moment for every section of each beam. The results of a complete survey may be most clearly observed when they are reported graphically. The description of shearing forces will therefore be plotted as a graph, called the *shearing force diagram.* In such a graph, ordinates represent shearing force, with abscissae representing distances along the span of the beam. Similarly, the description of bending moment will be plotted as a graph, called the *bending moment didgram,* in which ordinates represent bending moment, and abscissae are again distances along the span of the beam.

Illustrative Example I. The overhanging beam of Fig. 68 carries concentrated loads of 2400 lb., 3000 lb., and 540 lb., located as shown. The beam is supported by forces R_1 and R_2. The shearing force and bending moment diagrams are to be drawn.

The entire beam is taken as a free body to evaluate the supporting forces. The most effective routine consists of applying $\Sigma M = 0$, taking a moment axis at the line of action of each supporting force in turn. $\Sigma Y = 0$ may then be applied as a check upon the results.

$$\Sigma M_{R_1} = 0$$
$$-8R_2 + 2400 \times 3 + 3000 \times 7 + 540 \times 10 = 0$$
$$R_2 = 4200 \text{ lb.}$$

$$\Sigma M_{R_2} = 0$$
$$+8R_1 + 540 \times 2 - 3000 \times 1 - 2400 \times 5 = 0$$
$$R_1 = 1740 \text{ lb.}$$

Checking,
$$\Sigma Y = 0$$
$$-2400 - 3000 - 540 + 1740 + 4200 = 0$$

We have now evaluated all of the external forces acting on the beam.

To establish the shearing force, each range of loading must be investigated. A range of loading is defined as a portion of the beam in which no new load is applied. For example, the first range of loading is the 3-ft. distance between R_1 and the 2400-lb. load.

In this range of loading, a typical section, like A-A, may be taken at any distance x from an origin at R_1.

An equation may now be written, expressing the value and sign of the shearing force at section A-A.

$$x : 0\text{–}3 \text{ ft.}$$
$$V_x = +1740 \text{ lb.}$$

We note that the shearing force in the first range of loading is constant, and the resulting portion of the shearing force diagram is a straight, horizontal line, as plotted in Fig. 68-b. We should at this time note the influence of a concentrated force upon the shearing force diagram. In practice, the concentrated force cannot be produced physically, for all forces, whether exerted by neighboring bodies or by the influence of gravity, require finite extent of contact with free bodies. The concentrated forces of engineering practice are in reality the resultants of distributed forces. In many cases, however, the region of distribution is so limited in its extent that the forces are assumed to be localized at a point.

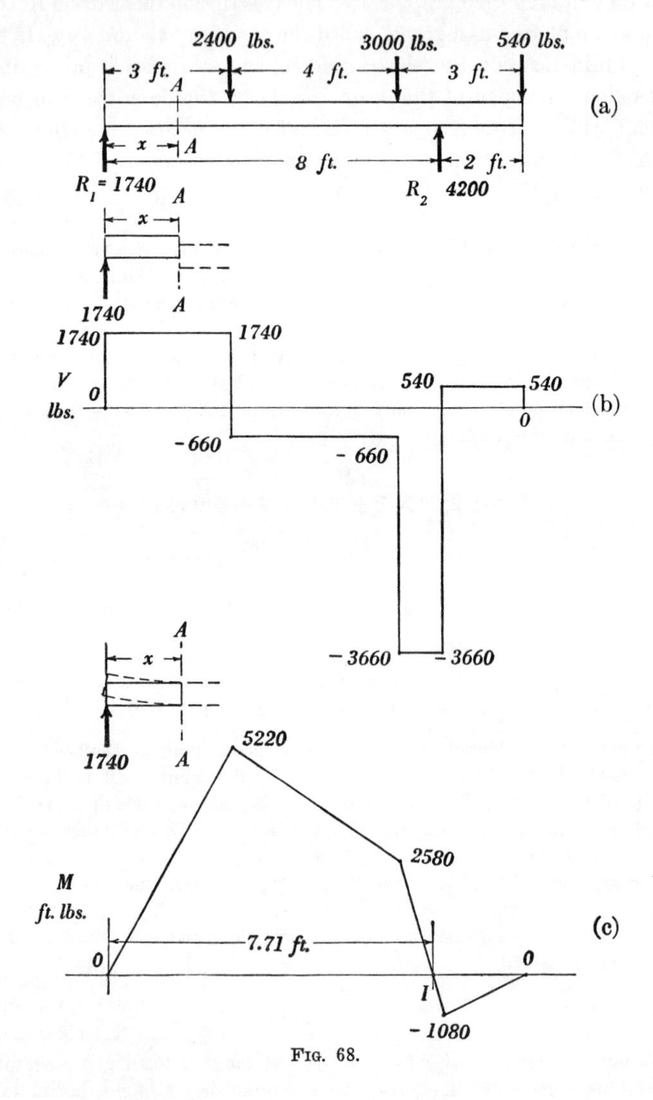

FIG. 68.

In the present instance, the value of shearing force in the first range, ($V_x =$ 1740 lb.) actually applies to values of x which are greater than zero, and less than 3 ft. Since the supporting force R_1 is taken as a concentrated force, its entire influence is assumed to be felt at a point. Just to the left of this force, the shearing force in the beam is zero; immediately to the right of it, the shearing force has become 1740 lb. This change is revealed in the diagram by the vertical line at the left end, whose lower end is labeled 0 lb., and whose upper end is labeled 1740 lb. The zero value of shearing force applies to a section of the beam at an infinitesimal distance to the left of the supporting force, while the magnitude of 1740 lb. applies to a section an infinitesimal distance to the right.

Another instance which illustrates the influence of a concentrated force occurs at the end of the first range of loading, when $x = 3$ ft. We find, as we approach the 2400-lb. load from its left, that the shearing force continues at its constant value of 1740 lb. As we pass the 2400-lb. load and enter the second range of loading ($x = 3$–7 ft.), the entire influence of this concentrated load is immediately introduced. The shearing-force diagram again follows a vertical line. The equation of shearing force in the second range of loading is

$$x : 3\text{–}7 \text{ ft.}$$
$$V_x = +1740 - 2400 = -660 \text{ lb.}$$

In these equations, the origin of x has remained at the left end of the beam. We must be cautious to assign such equations only to the finite values of x to which they apply—such equations are not continuous through new ranges of loading, but are limited to the regions bounded by the introduction of new forces.

The technique which we have employed in establishing values of shearing force is applied in the two remaining ranges of loading, and the complete shearing force diagram appears as Fig. 68-b.

The bending moment diagram (Fig. 68-c) is developed and plotted by making a similar exploration of each range of loading.

In the first range of loading, the equation of bending moment is

$$x : 0\text{–}3 \text{ ft.}$$
$$M_x = +1740x \text{ ft-lb.}$$

This is an equation of the first degree and its graphical counterpart is a straight line, as shown in the diagram. Since only two points are required to determine the straight line, values $x = 0$ and $x = 3$ may be introduced in the equation.

At $x = 0$, $\quad M_x = +1740 \times 0 = 0$
$\quad x = 3$, $\quad M_x = +1740 \times 3 = +5220$ ft.-lb.

The equation of bending moment in the second range of loading is:

$$x : 3\text{–}7 \text{ ft.}$$
$$M_x = +1740x - 2400(x - 3)$$

We note here that no such distinction between the sections bounding a concentrated force, as was made for shearing force, is necessary. Changes in bending moment require finite change of moment arm, and the bending moments acting on sections an infinitesimal distance apart are equivalent.

The completed bending-moment diagram is shown as Fig. 68-c.

We have already noted, in Art. 22, equation (33), the relationship between shearing force and bending moment, $V = dm/dx$.

Then
$$\int dM = \int V\,dx$$

$\int V\,dx$ is the area under the curve representing shearing force, and the change of bending moment between two sections of a beam is represented by the area of the shearing-force diagram between those sections.

For example, the area under the shearing force curve of Fig. 68-b, between sections at $x = 0$ and $x = 3$ ft. is $1740 \times 3 = 5220$ ft.-lb. This value, obtained by graphical integration through evaluation of area agrees with the value obtained by determining the bending moment as the product of force and moment arm.

Another approach to the determination of bending moment may be made through analytical integration.

The equation of shearing force in the first range of loading is

$$V_x = 1740$$

Then
$$M = \int V\,dx = +1740x + C_1$$

When $x = 0$ $M = 0$,
$$\therefore C_1 = 0$$

Then
$$M = +\,1740x$$

is the equation of bending moment for the first range.

The equation of bending moment in each of the other ranges may likewise be determined, by analytical integration, if we are careful to evaluate the constants of integration by noting the boundary conditions for each range as we integrate. For example, in the second range

$$x\ :\ 3\text{–}7 \text{ ft.}$$
$$V_x = -660$$
$$M = \int V\,dx = -660x + C_2$$

When $x = 3$, $M = +5220$, and $C_2 = +5220 + 660 \times 3 = +7200$

then, at $x = 7$, $M = -660 \times 7 + 7200 = +2580$ ft.-lb.

In addition, we can always determine *maximum* bending moment by using the shearing force diagram as an exploring device.

Since $V = dM/dx$, the section of maximum bending moment may be located by setting this first derivative equal to zero, and solving for x. This step is equivalent, graphically, to noting where the shearing-force curve crosses the zero axis, changing in value from positive to negative. When the location of the section of maximum bending moment is determined, the value of that moment may be established by taking moments about an axis at that section.

It will be noted that the shearing force diagram of Fig. 68-b crosses the zero axis $x = 3$ ft., and at $x = 8$ ft. These are sections at which bending moment will have a maximum value.

The value of bending moment at $x = 3$ ft. is $+5220$ ft.-lb. (see Fig. 68-c) which is the maximum *positive* bending moment in the beam. At $x = 8$ ft., the bending moment is -1080 ft.-lb., which is the maximum *negative* bending moment in the beam.

One other section of the beam is of interest, particularly to the structural designer. At point I of Fig. 68-c, the bending-moment diagram crosses the zero axis, changing from positive to negative values. The curvature of the beam itself will reverse, for positive values of bending moment represent sections of the beam at which the bottom fibers are in tension, while negative values indicate sections where the bottom fibers are in compression. Such a point as I is therefore called a *point of inflection* of the beam. The bending moment at point I is zero. The equation of bending moment in this range of loading (with x measured from an origin at the left end of the beam) is

$$M_x = +1740x - 2400(x - 3) - 3000(x - 7) = -3660x + 28{,}200$$

To locate the point of inflection, we set the value of bending moment equal to zero.

Then $$M_x = -3660x + 28{,}200 = 0$$

and $$x = \frac{28{,}200}{3660} = 7.71 \text{ ft.}$$

Illustrative Example II. When a beam is subjected to distributed loads, the techniques which we have employed in the preceding example are still valid and effective. The natures of the curves representing shearing force and bending moment are, however, altered. To illustrate this difference, we shall analyze the beam of Fig. 69-a, which is loaded with a uniformly distributed force of 100 lb./ft. and supported upon uniformly distributed supporting forces whose intensities are indicated.

The shearing force equation in the first range of loading is

$$x : 0 - 4 \text{ ft.}$$
$$V_x = +160x - 100x = +60x$$

This is an equation of the first degree, and the straight line representing shearing force may be plotted when two values are determined.

At $x = 0$ $$V_x = +60 \times 0 = 0$$
$x = 4$ $$V_x = +60 \times 4 = +240$$

The equations of shearing force in the remaining ranges (values of x have been taken in each equation from a common origin at the left end of the beam) follow:

x : 4–11 ft. $$V_x = +640 - 100x$$
x : 11–13 $$V_x = +640 - 100x + 480(x - 11)$$
x : 13–16 $$V_x = +640 - 100x + 960$$

The shearing force diagram (Fig. 69-b) indicates two sections of maximum bending moment, lying in the second and third ranges of loading, respectively. These sections are located by setting the values of shearing force in those ranges equal to zero.

When $$V_x = +640 - 100x = 0$$
$$x = 6.4 \text{ ft.}$$

When $$V_x = +640 - 100x + 480(x - 11) = 0$$
$$x = 12.21 \text{ ft.}$$

All of the equations of shearing force are of the first degree, and the shearing force curve is composed entirely of straight lines. It will be noted that no concentrated forces are present on the beam, and there is, therefore, no vertical-line portion of the curve.

We now prepare to plot the bending moment diagram by writing the equations of bending moment in each range of loading. The bending-moment equation for the first range is:

$$x: 0\text{–}4 \text{ ft.} \qquad M_x = +160x\frac{x}{2} - 100x\frac{x}{2} = +30x^2$$

This is an equation of the second degree, and the bending moment curve is parabolic (Fig. 69-c).

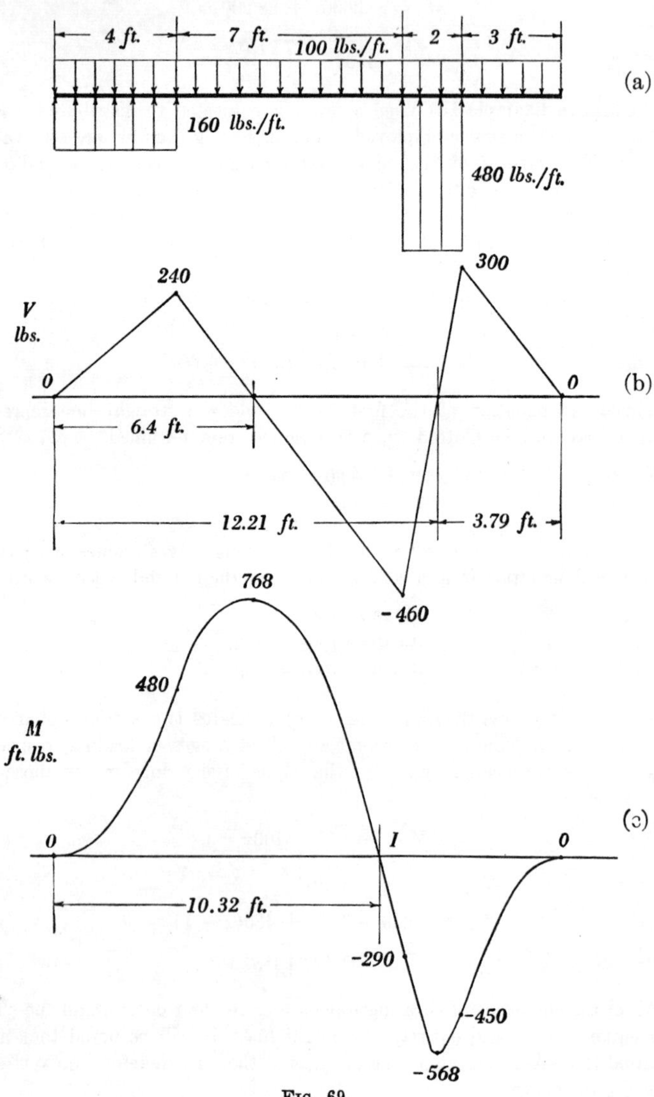

FIG. 69.

The remaining bending moment equations will be

$$x: \text{ 4–11 ft.} \qquad M_x = +640(x-2) - \frac{100x^2}{2}$$

$$x: \text{11–13} \qquad M_x = +640(x-2) - \frac{100x^2}{2} + \frac{480(x-11)^2}{2}$$

$$x: \text{13–16} \qquad M_x = +640(x-2) - \frac{100x^2}{2} + 960(x-12)$$

All portions of the bending moment diagram are parabolic. They are now plotted by inserting values of x in the equations, and the completed diagram is shown as Fig. 69-c. The maximum positive and negative bending moments are computed by inserting the values of x which locate the sections where the shearing force diagram crosses the axis which were found above.

$$\text{When } x = 6.4 \text{ ft.,} \qquad M = 640(6.4-2) - \frac{100(6.4)^2}{2}$$

$$= +768 \text{ ft.-lb.}$$

$$x = 12.21 \text{ ft.,} \quad M = 640(12.21-2) - \frac{100(12.21)^2}{2} + \frac{480(12.21-11)^2}{2}$$

$$= -568 \text{ ft.-lb.}$$

The preceding shearing force and bending moment equations have been developed in each case, from an origin at the left end of the beam. The resulting equations may become cumbersome if we persist in always continuing to explore throughout the beam span from one end. For example, with origin taken at the right end of the beam, a first range of loading ($x =$ 0–3 ft. from right) would yield the simple expression, $M_x = -100x^2/2$. This method of approach may be used in the interest of simplification and is always effective if used to check results previously obtained by proceeding from the left.

The maximum bending moment may also be determined by computing the area under the shearing force curve. For example, the area of the shearing force diagram of Fig. 69-b between $x = 0$ and $x = 6.4$ ft. is

$$A = \tfrac{1}{2} \times 4 \times 240 + \tfrac{1}{2} \times 2.4 \times 240 = 768 \text{ ft.-lb.}$$

It will be noted that the bending moment curve of Fig. 69-c crosses its zero axis in the second range of loading (origin at left end). Then

$$M_x = 640(x-2) - 50x^2 = 0$$

and

$$x = 10.32 \text{ ft.}$$

This value locates the point of inflection of the beam.

Illustrative Example III. A cantilever beam is shown in Fig. 70. It carries a single concentrated load W, at its free end, and is rigidly supported by the wall at the right end. The beam is shown as an isolated free body in Fig. 70-b so that we may make a proper analysis of the force system supplied by the wall.

We note first that the wall must exert an upward force of W lb., in order that $\Sigma Y = 0$ The two forces, W, form a couple of magnitude WL. In order that $\Sigma M = 0$, the wall must supply, in addition to the upward thrust W, a moment equal and opposite to WL. The wall exerts a downward force, F, on the upper surface of the beam. The total upward force must therefore be $W + F$. The two forces F form a couple of magnitude $F \times a = W \times L$.

The forces F and $W + F$ are actually distributed forces, acting over the top and bottom surfaces of the beam which are located within the wall. The distance a will be dependent upon the nature of this distribution. The shearing force diagram will cross the axis of the beam at or near the surface of the wall, and the maximum bending moment is therefore WL. The shearing force and bending moment diagrams are shown in Figs. 70-c and 70-d, respectively.

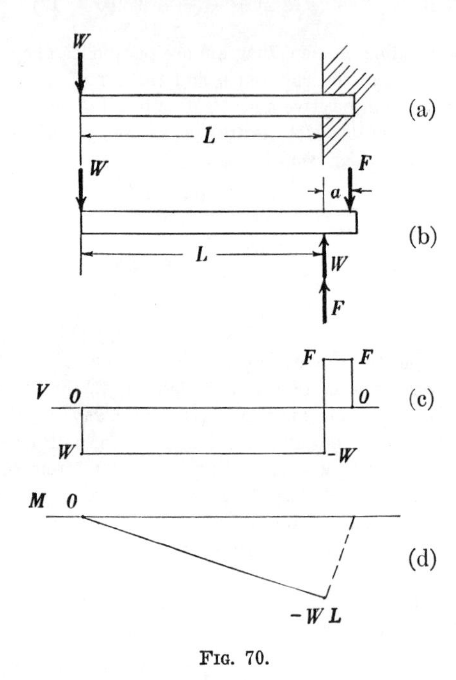

FIG. 70.

Illustrative Example IV. In each of the preceding illustrative examples, the loads have been applied at fixed locations.

The engineer also encounters loads whose positions along the span of the beam do not remain fixed—for example, the *moving* loads applied by the wheels of a moving vehicle as it crosses a bridge. Such a case is illustrated in Fig. 71. W_1, W_2, and W_3 are the loads exerted by some moving wheels, which remain at constant distance a from each other. We are to determine the maximum bending moment in the beam.

A shearing force diagram for a beam loaded with concentrated forces, and freely supported at its ends only, will cross the zero axis but once, yielding maximum bending moment under one of the concentrated loads.

Let us assume that this section of maximum bending moment occurs under load W_1, which is located at distance x from the left end of the beam.

The loads W_1, W_2, and W_3 may be replaced by their resultant W_R located at distance b from W_1 (Fig. 71-b).

Applying the condition of equilibrium $\Sigma M = 0$, and taking the right end of the beam as an axis of moments,

$$+R_1 l - W_R(l - x - b) = 0$$

and
$$R_1 = \frac{W_R(l - x - b)}{l}$$

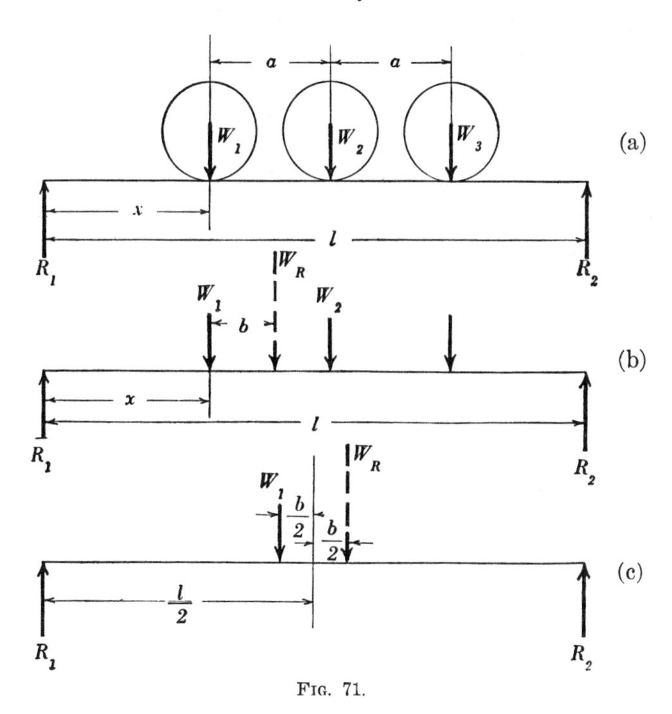

Fig. 71.

The bending moment at load W_1 will be

$$M_x = \frac{W_R(l - x - b)x}{l}$$

To establish the value of x at which M_x will be maximum, we set the first derivative of M_x with respect to x equal to zero.

Then
$$\frac{dM}{dx} = \frac{W_R}{l}(l - 2x - b) = 0$$

and
$$x = \frac{l}{2} - \frac{b}{2}$$

This evaluation has determined the location of W_1, which will give maximum bending moment in the beam as W_1 moves along its span.

Examination of this situation as shown in Fig. 71-c shows that W_1 produces maximum bending moment in the beam when it is as far away from the center of the beam as is W_R, the resultant of all the loads.

The solution of the problem has, thus far, rested upon the assumption that load W_1 is responsible for the maximum bending moment in the beam. It is quite possible that loads W_2 or W_3 are the ones responsible, and the shear diagram may cross its zero axis beneath either.

Each of those loads must, therefore, be subjected to the same procedure we have employed with regard to W_1. Each must be placed, in turn, at the position which will enable it to exert maximum bending moment. This will occur, in each case, when the load under investigation is placed as far away from the center of the beam as is the resultant, W_R. In each case, we compute the maximum bending moment in the beam. The greatest of these three bending moments will be the maximum bending moment developed in the beam by the moving vehicle.

PROBLEMS

Note: The following group of problems is intended to offer adequate preparation in determining shearing force and bending moment—elements which must later be used in the investigation of stresses in beams. In each case, the complete shearing force and the complete bending moment diagrams are to be plotted. The maximum shearing force, and the maximum positive and maximum negative bending moment should be reported. In beams which have a point of inflection, the location of that point should also be determined and indicated.

The practice of neatness in plotting encourages training in orderly calculation—a most essential trait of the engineer. Care in arithmetical computations is the tangible expression of a calm, orderly procedure in problem attack. Many of the difficulties which the engineering student encounters in calculations are due to impatience—the arithmetical operations seem to present the least inviting aspect of his chosen profession, and he is tempted to rush through them. The development of caution can never be more fruitfully encouraged than in the assigned problems of his daily educational experience, and he should, at that period of his professional career, resolve to foster that patience.

In plotting shearing force and bending moment diagrams, the relative magnitudes of these properties should be indicated so that their relationship may be readily observed.

Problem paper, available at engineering-college bookstores, which has a grid of lines forming ⅕- or ¼-in. squares, is most convenient. The diagrams may be plotted on such paper, free-hand, by using the grid to establish ordinate and abscissa lengths. A more accurate scaling is, in general, superfluous, for the results which are to be obtained from the graph will be computed and preclude the necessity of using such accuracy as drawing instruments would provide.

Since such a sketch is of comparatively small scale, and since only the plotted magnitudes are used in further computations of stress, every plotted point should be labeled to indicate its value. The procedure of plotting the diagrams on such paper is illustrated in specimen Prob. 113.

Probs. 113-132, incl. Plot the shearing force and bending moment diagrams. Report the maximum shearing force, maximum bending moment (positive and/or negative) and the location of any points of inflection.

Probs. 133-138, incl. Determine the maximum shearing force and the maximum bending moment. Where both positive and negative bending moments are present report the maximum positive and the maximum negative bending moments.

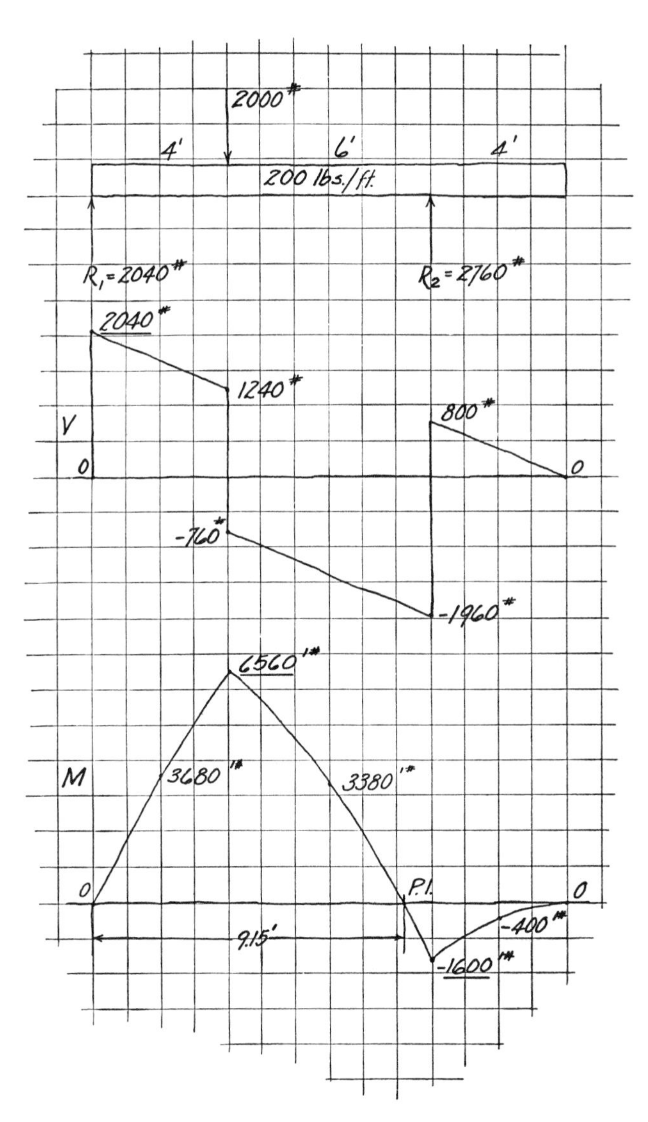
2000#
4'
6'
4'
200 lbs./ft.
R1=2040#
R2=2760#
2040#
1240#
800#
V
0
0
-760#
-1960#
6560'#
M
3680'#
3380'#
0
P.I.
0
-400'#
9.15'
-1600'#

PROB. 113.

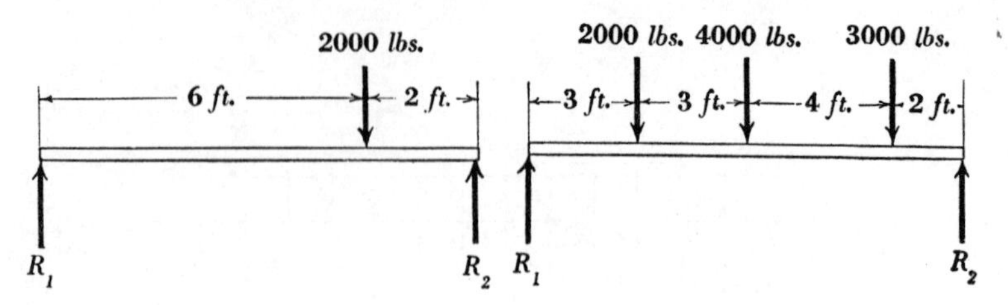

PROB. 114.

PROB. 115.

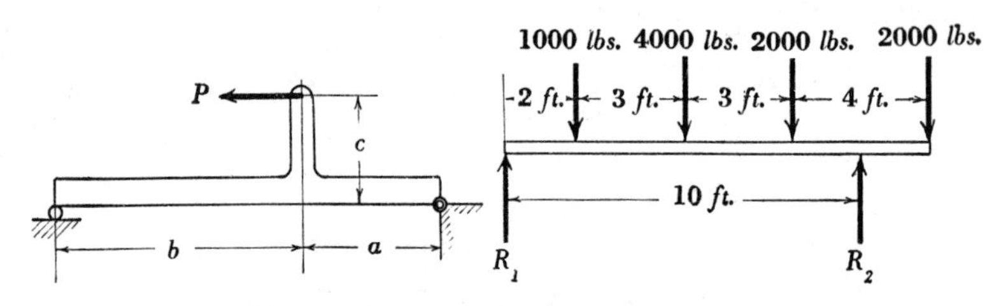

PROB. 116.

PROB. 117.

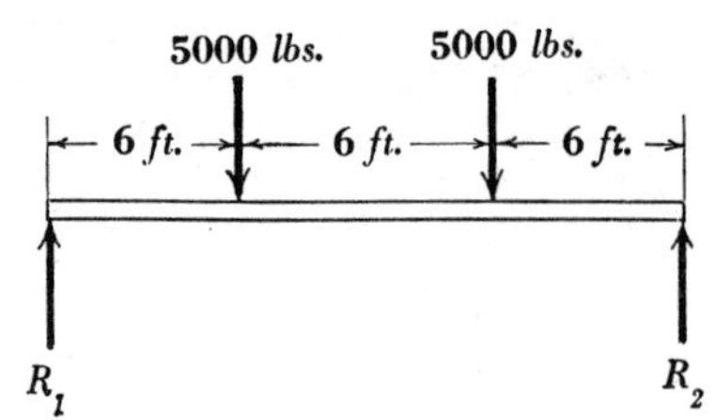

PROB. 118.

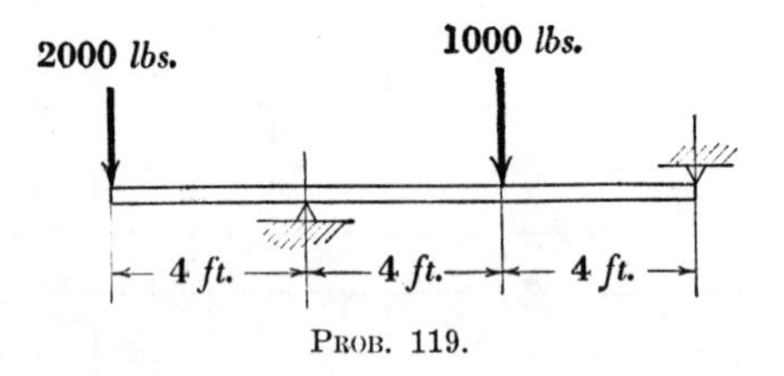

PROB. 119.

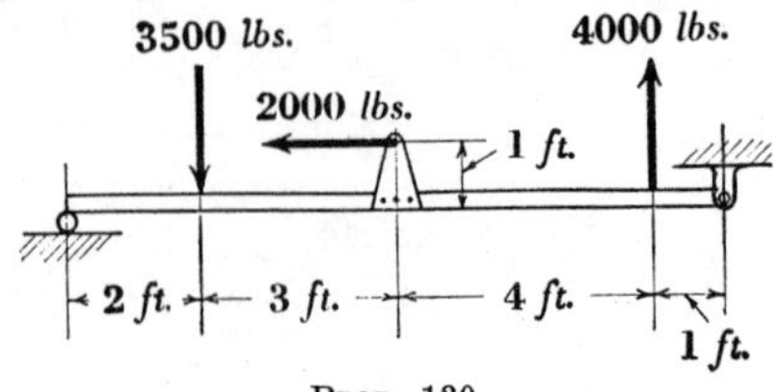

PROB. 120.

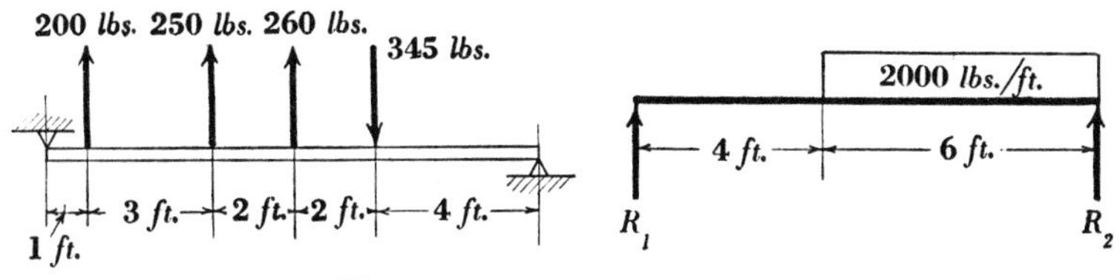

PROB. 121.

PROB. 122.

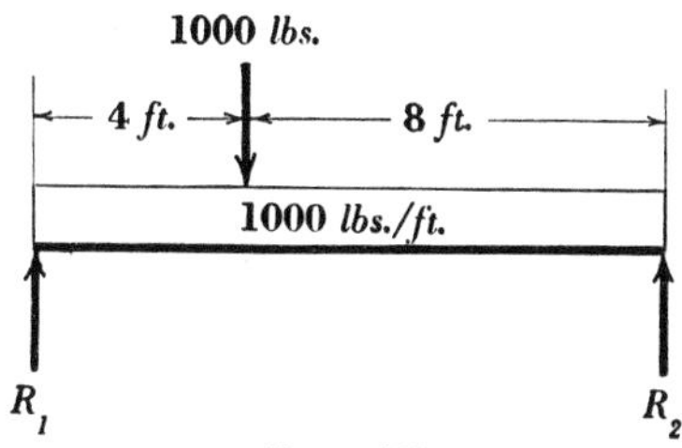

PROB. 123.

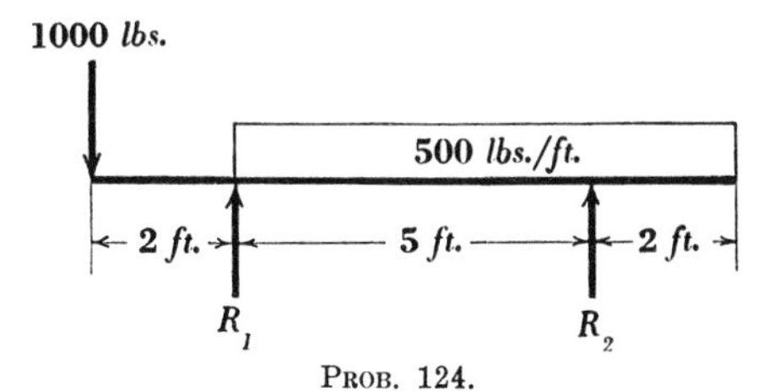

PROB. 124.

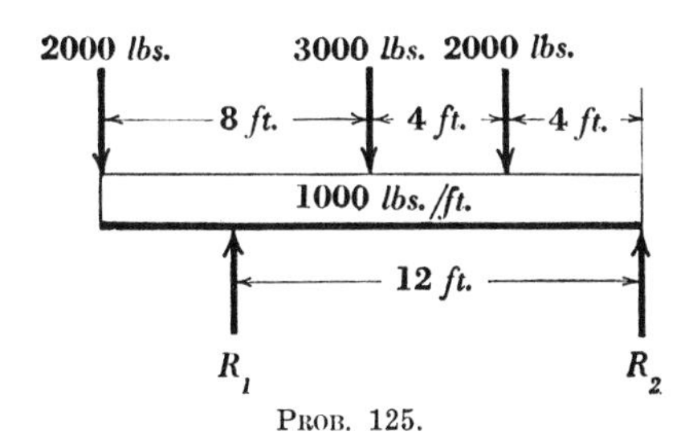

PROB. 125.

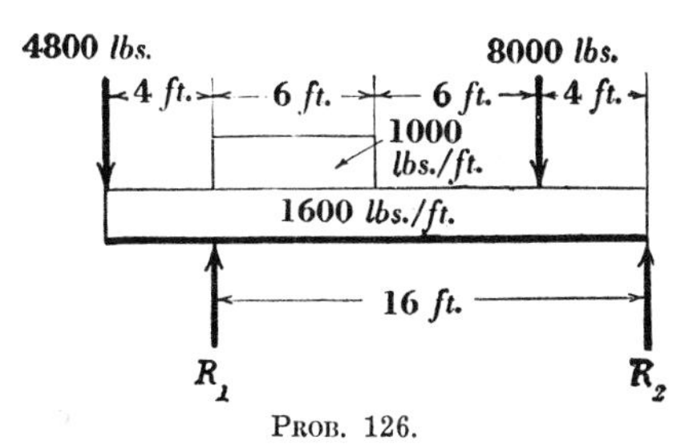

PROB. 126.

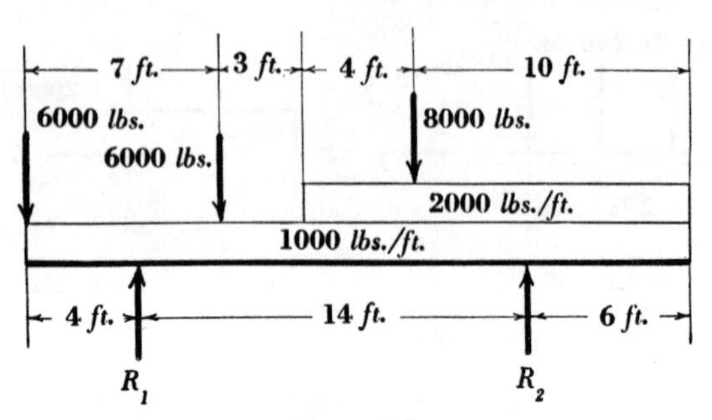

PROB. 127.

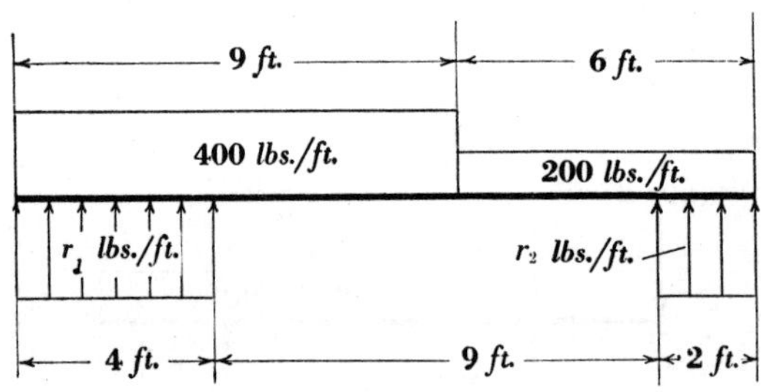

PROB. 128.

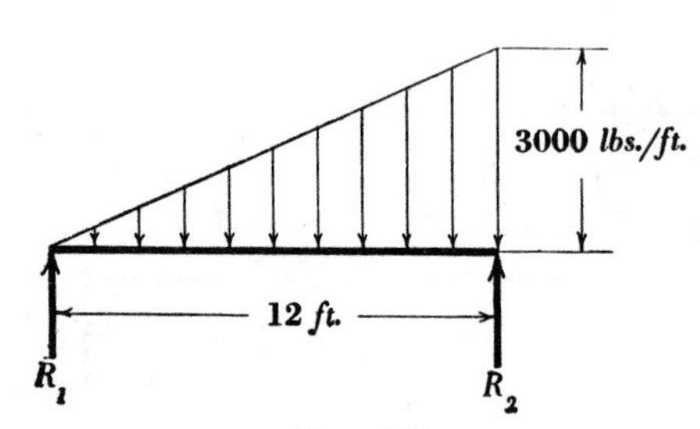

PROB. 129.

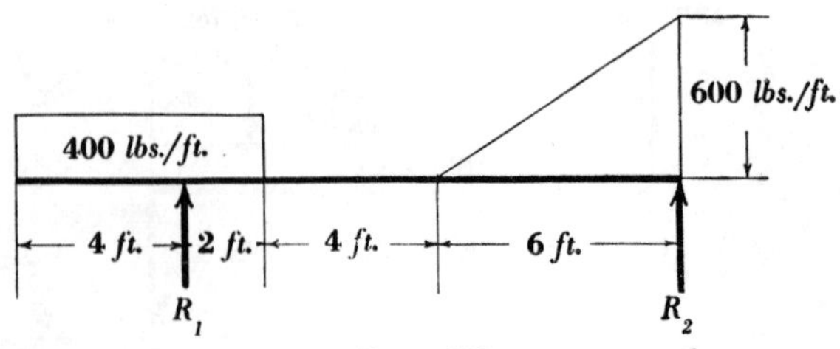

PROB. 130.

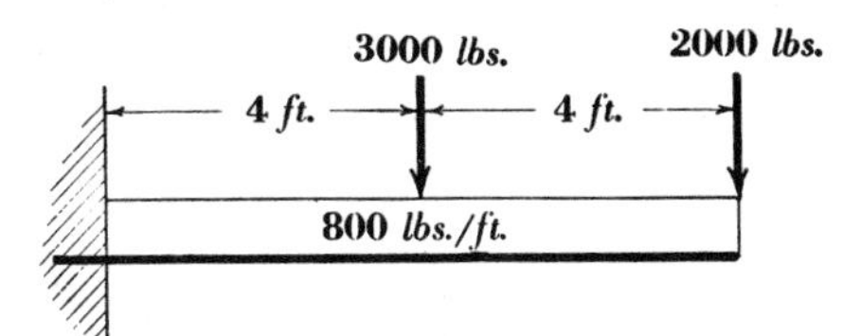

PROB. 131.

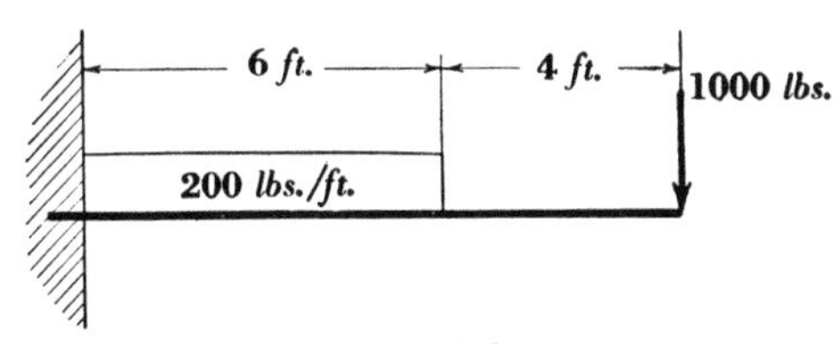

PROB. 132.

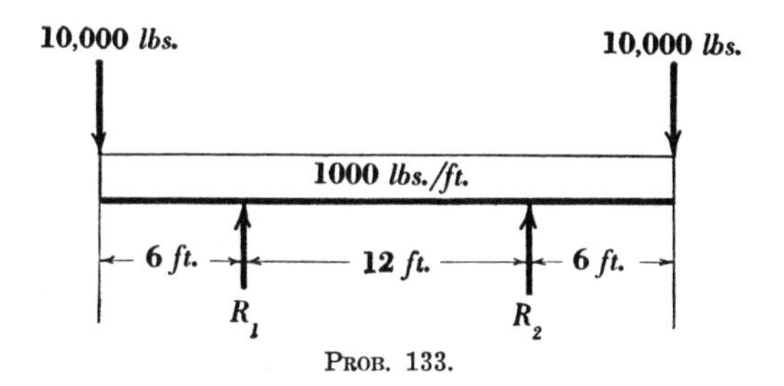

PROB. 133.

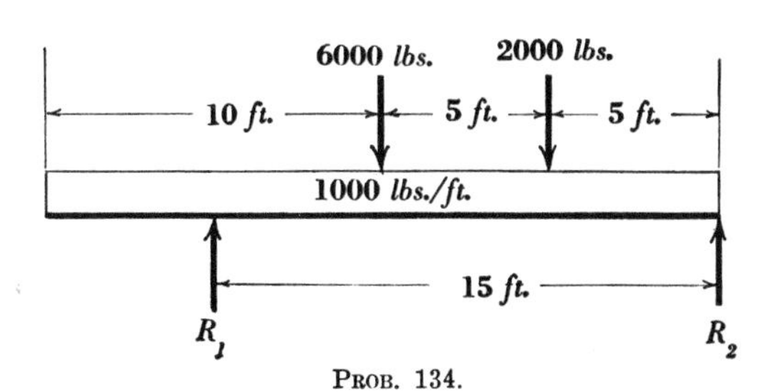

PROB. 134.

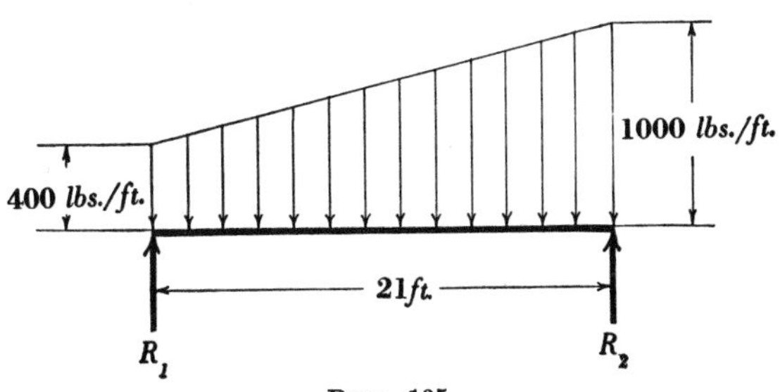

PROB. 135.

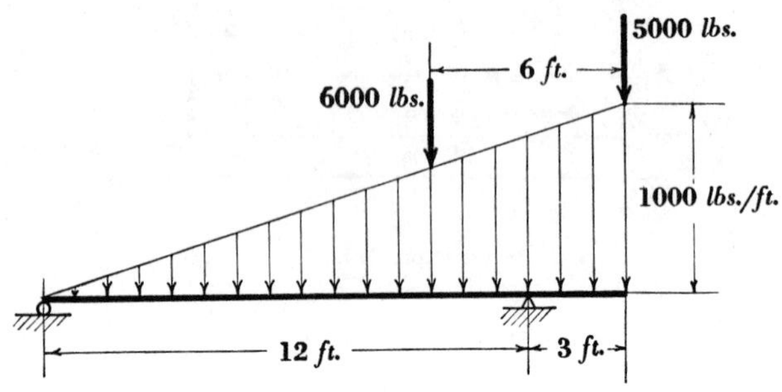

PROB. 136.

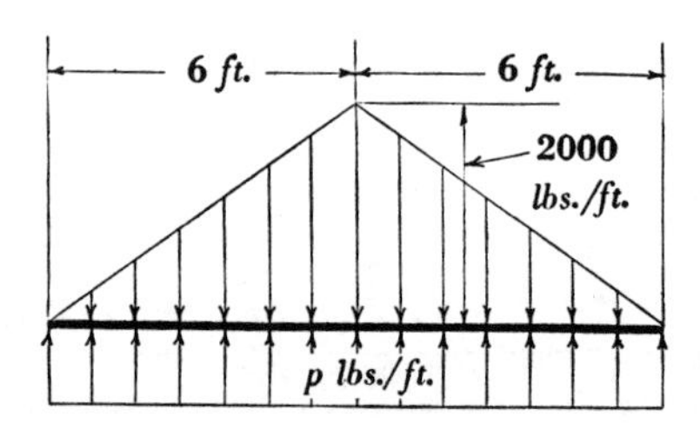

PROB. 137.

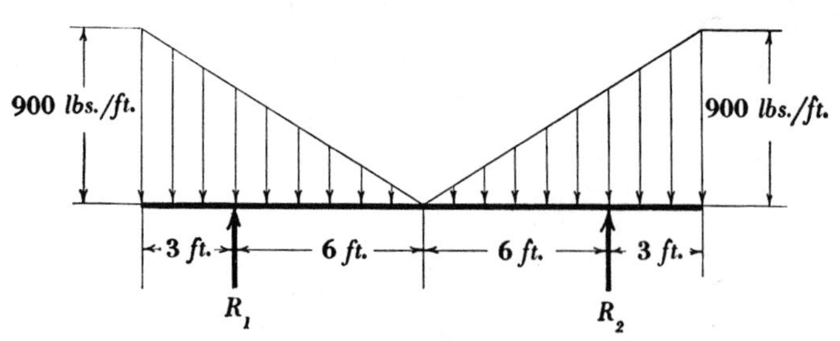

PROB. 138.

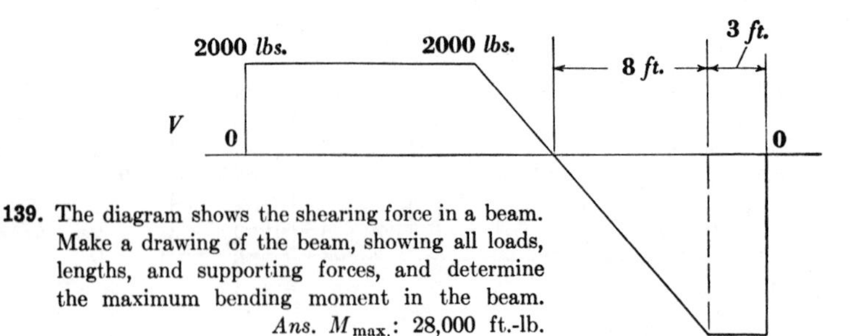

139. The diagram shows the shearing force in a beam. Make a drawing of the beam, showing all loads, lengths, and supporting forces, and determine the maximum bending moment in the beam.
Ans. $M_{\text{max.}}$: 28,000 ft.-lb.

PROB. 139.

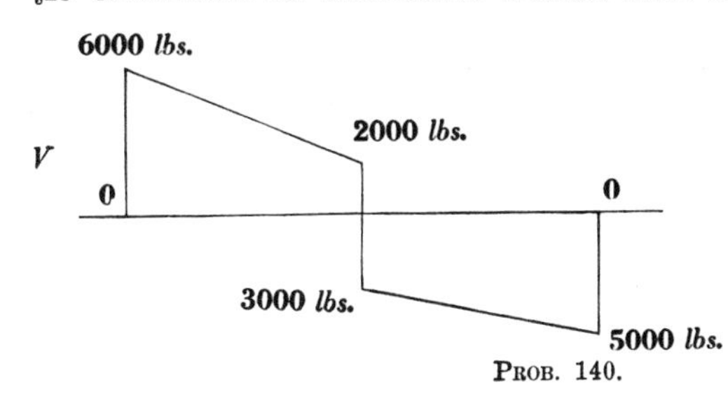

PROB. 140.

140. The diagram shows the shearing force in a beam. The maximum bending moment in the beam is $M = 20{,}000$ ft.-lb. Make a drawing of the beam, showing all loads, supporting forces, and lengths along the beam.

141. The beam shown is built into walls at its ends. The shearing force and bending moment at end AA are 6000 lb., and $-12{,}000$ ft.-lb., respectively. Determine (a) the bending moment at 4 ft. from AA; (b) the bending moment at mid-span, and (c) the location of the points of inflection *Ans.* (a) 4000 ft.-lb.; (b) 6000 ft.-lb.; (c) 2.54 and 9.46 ft.

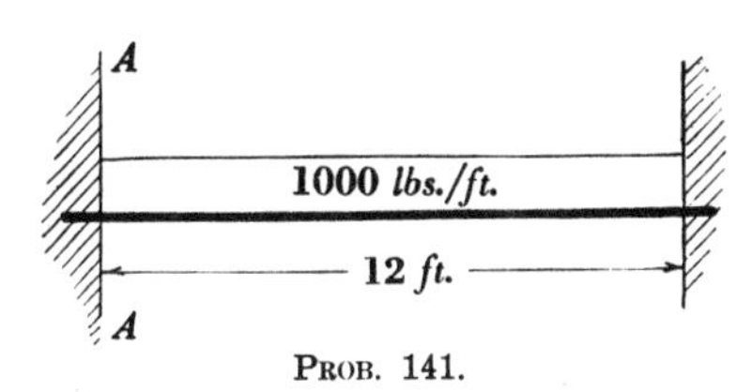

PROB. 141.

142. The beam shown is made of three sections, fastened together by pin joints at A and B. The beam carries a uniformly distributed load of 900 lb./ft., and is supported by concentrated forces R_1, R_2, R_3, and R_4. Determine the maximum shearing force, maximum positive, and maximum negative bending moments in the beam. *Ans.* $V_{\text{max.}} = 4500$ lb.; $M_{\text{max.}}$ (positive) = 4050 ft.-lb.; (negative) = -7200 ft.-lb.

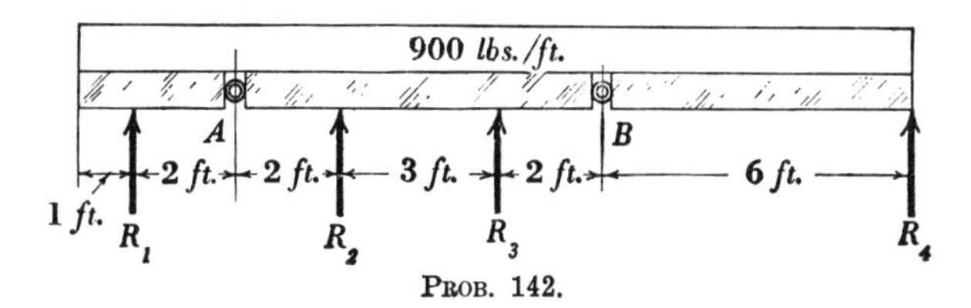

PROB. 142.

143. The beam is built into a wall which exerts a negative bending moment $M_1 = -12{,}000$ ft.-lb. as well as a shearing force. The beam rests on support R. Determine the maximum bending moment in the beam.

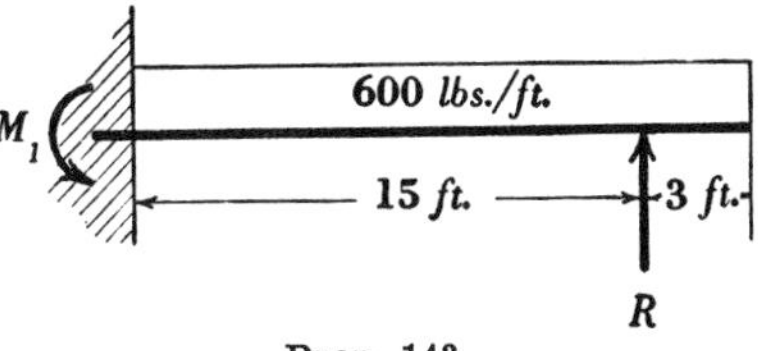

PROB. 143.

144. The moving crane is supported on beams as shown. Determine the maximum bending moment in the end beams. $W_1 = 1500$ lb.; $W_2 = 3500$ lb.; $W_3 = 2800$ lb. The beams are freely supported at their ends. *Ans.* 52,070 ft.-lb.

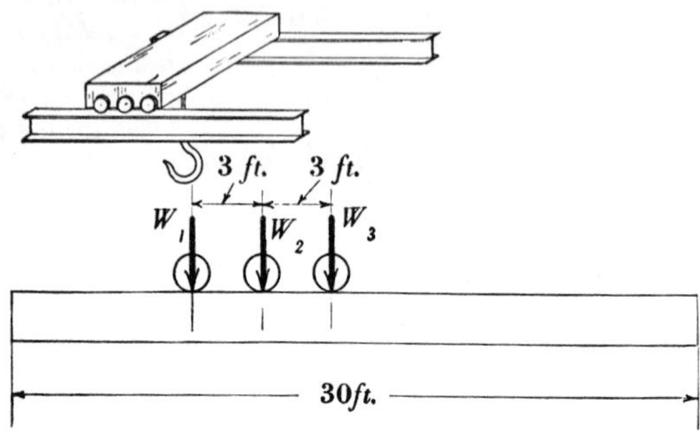

PROB. 144.

24. Graphical Determination of Bending Moment. When a beam is subjected to several concentrated loads, graphical methods of determining bending moment present advantage in that the number of operations necessary to a solution are minimized. This is of particular value when the bending moment at many sections, rather than the maximum bending value, are to be determined.

As in all other engineering graphical solutions, the validity of the results is dependent upon the precision of the drawing, which is largely a function of the scale employed as well as the care used in drafting. Large-scale drawings should, therefore, be used.

The graphical solution of bending moment is based upon the force polygon, and the string, or funicular, polygon. These are discussed in the textbooks of the elementary courses in Applied Mechanics, and this discussion will, therefore, concern itself only with the application of such polygons to bending moment problems.

The beam shown in Fig. 72 carries the indicated loads and is freely supported at its ends.

The supporting forces R_1 and R_2 may be determined graphically or analytically. The former method presents no advantage over the simplicity of the analytical solution.

A force polygon is now drawn, as in Fig. 72-b. Bow's notation has been inserted in the space diagram of Fig. 72-a as indicated by the circled letters and the corresponding letters are used on the force polygon. The lines *ab*, *bc*, and so on, have been drawn to scale to represent forces AB, BC, etc., of Fig. 72-a.

We now draw a horizontal line through point *a* of the force polygon, and establish a pole, P, anywhere on this horizontal line. Rays from P to points *a*, *b*, *c*, etc., are now drawn and the string polygon constructed on the space diagram of Fig. 72-a with each string parallel to its respective ray.

The resulting string polygon represents, to scale, the bending moment diagram for the beam. Ordinate *lm* is the bending moment at section LM of the beam; ordinate *no* is the bending moment at section NO, and so on.

The proof follows. The bending moment at section LM is the algebraic sum of the moments, taken at section LM, of forces R_1 and W_1. It is therefore the moment of the resultant of R_1 and W_1 about an axis at LM. This resultant appears on the force polygon as distance ac, and has a line of action which is determined by the

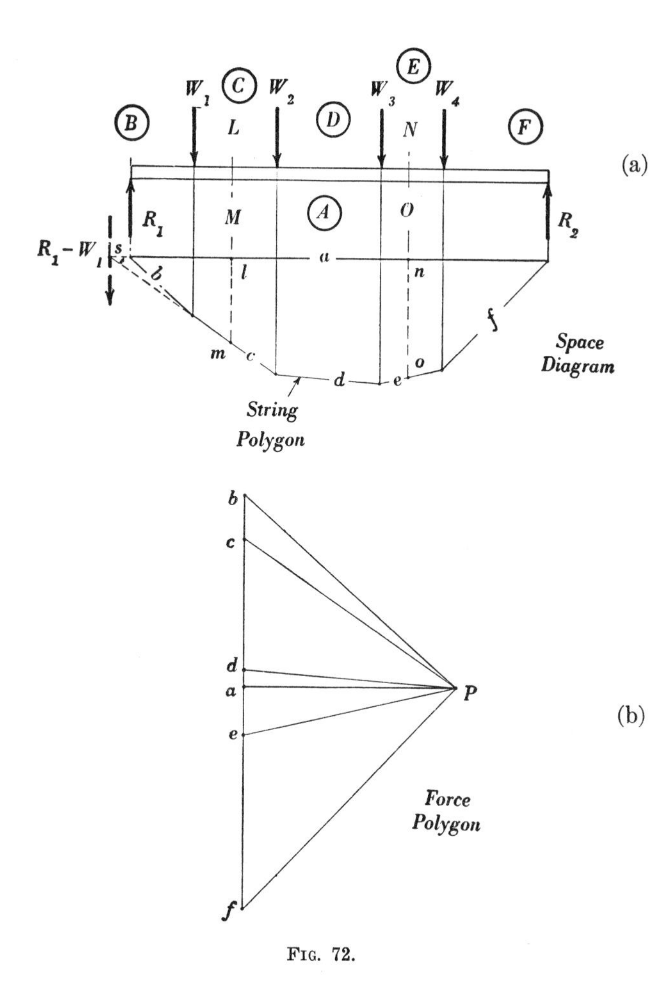

FIG. 72.

string polygon. One point on this line of action is point s, the intersection of the c and a strings.

The bending moment at section LM is therefore

$$M = (R_1 - W_1) \times \text{distance } sl.$$

The triangle *slm* of the string polygon is similar to triangle *acP* of the force polygon. Then

$$\frac{lm}{sl} = \frac{ac}{aP}$$

and $$lm = \frac{ac}{aP} \times sl$$

But $$ac = R_1 - W_1$$

Then $$lm = (R_1 - W_1)sl \times \frac{1}{aP}$$

and the bending moment at section *LM* is

$$M = lm \times aP$$

aP is the constant horizontal distance of the force polygon from pole to force line, and may be evaluated as force in pounds by applying the scale of the force polygon.

lm is a distance of the space diagram and may be evaluated as distance in feet by applying the scale of the space diagram.

The bending moment at section *NO* is, similarly,

$$M = no \times aP$$

25. Bending Stress. The Basic Flexure Theory. The discussion of the moment of resistance in Art. 21 called our attention to the presence of unit stresses normal to the right sections of beams. Such stresses are known as *bending stresses*. Other synonymous adjectives are used to describe such stresses in engineering literature—*fiber stress* and *flexural stress* are two of the most common.

To evaluate such stresses, we have need of a fundamental theory which shall be direct and simple in its application. Thus far beams have been described only as "members which are transversely loaded." To accept such a broad definition, without careful regard for the geometry of the beam, the nature of the material of which it is composed, and the manner in which it may be loaded, would be to introduce many variables, and to preclude the possibility of evolving a simple basic theory.

We shall, therefore, adopt certain limitations in all of these factors. The theory which results after such qualifying limitation may, of course, only be applied to beams which fulfill the limiting conditions.

We can later build corollaries of the basic theory as tools with which we may attack the problems of beams which lie outside of these limitations.

The theory, applicable to beams which do conform to the limitations, is called the *common theory of beams*, or the *flexure theory*.

Limitations of the Flexure Theory. The first limiting conditions which we shall impose will be geometrical.

1. The beam must be straight. A beam may be considered to be a solid composed of geometrical rods or lines, called fibers, parallel to the long axis of the beam. These lines must be straight before the loading is applied; after loading, the lines will become curved, for loading causes bending. The radii of curvature after loading, however, are very long and beams, in general, remain sensibly straight after loading. The limitation is imposed in order that the unit strains discussed under the assumptions which follow may be proportional, and beams which are composed of curved lines before loading are excluded.

2. The beam must be of *uniform cross-section* throughout its entire span.

3. The dimensional nature of the beam must be restricted in order that failure produced by other causes than the development of bending stresses will not be involved. A very thin plate used as a beam may fail by twisting, lateral buckling, or wrinkling. A beam which has a very short span relative to its cross-sectional dimensions will, likewise, manifest other types of failure.

While, as in other cases of loaded bodies which we have discussed, exact, rigidly defined categories of dimension cannot be established, some concept of proper dimensional relationships may be suggested. In Fig. 73,

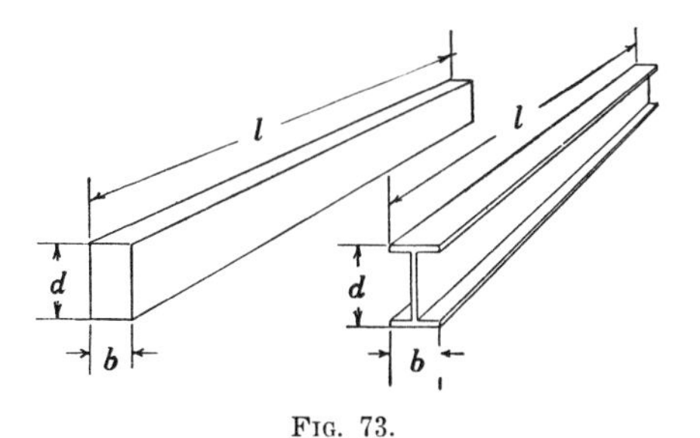

FIG. 73.

the span of the beam is called l; b and d are its breadth and depth, respectively. The following values suggest the range of dimensional values to which the flexure theory may properly be applied.

The length, l, should be at least ten, and not over twenty, times the depth.

The depth, d, should not be more than four times the breadth, b.

It does not follow that beams whose dimensions lie outside of these limits will immediately violate the predictions of the flexure theory—they are intended to suggest that there is a necessity for caution which the engineer must be alert to employ when obvious deviation from such dimensional limitation arises. In most of the common cases of beams employed in machine or structural practice, the dimensions will be found to lie within such limits, and behavior according to the flexure theory may be predicted safely.

4. When beams are composed of non-homogeneous and non-isotropic material, their behavior as concerns bending stress may present a complex pattern. In the use of this theory, therefore, such materials are precluded.

Most of the materials which are used in structural or machine members do satisfy this limitation when the beam is composed of a single material. In the case of reinforced concrete, containing steel, and similar combinations where a partnership is effected between materials each of which presents desired properties to the total structure, the flexure theory is unsatisfactory. Many of these beams may be designed, however, by such

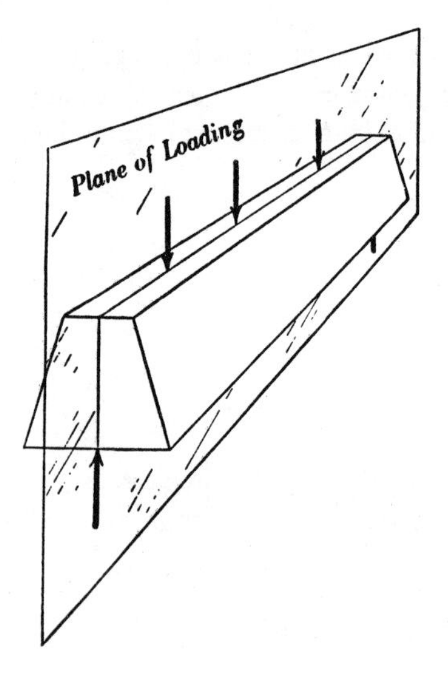

FIG. 74.

methods as the transformed section discussed in Art. 50, in which a technique of analysis based upon the flexure theory is applied.

The remaining limitations are concerned with the manner in which the loads are applied to the beam.

5. All external forces must be applied in a single plane, called the

plane of loading. If the loads include distributed forces, their resultants must be located in the plane of loading.

6. The plane of loading must have as its trace or intersection with each right section of the beam, an axis of symmetry of the cross-section, as in Fig. 74. This condition bars the use of cross-sectional areas which do not have axes of symmetry as suitable beam sections for consideration under the flexure theory.*

7. All loads (and supporting forces) must be perpendicular to the longitudinal axis of the beam.

8. The beam must be in equilibrium.

Now that the necessary limitations have been imposed, we shall make certain assumptions to take advantage of the conclusions which these assumptions will permit. No assumption, however, is left unconfirmed by

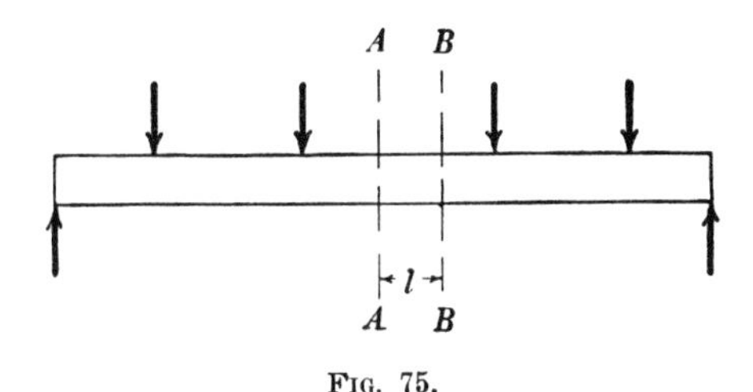

Fig. 75.

the engineer. The validity of the following assumptions has been proven by laboratory trial and by long experience, which has shown that the assumptions are reasonable, and that when beams are designed according to the flexure theory, they will behave as the theory has anticipated. The assumptions may, therefore, be accepted with confidence that they are true within the limits of accuracy demanded by the use to which each assumption is applied.

Assumption I. The right sections of a beam, which are plane before the beam is loaded, remain plane surfaces when the beam bends.

In Fig. 75, two right sections, A-A and B-B, are shown. The distance between A-A and B-B is l and all of the fibers of the beam between those sections are of length l before loading.

*This limitation is also satisfied if the plane of loading has, as its intersection with each right section of the beam, a principal centroidal axis of inertia, as noted in Art. 54, whether or not the intersection is an axis of symmetry. Most beam sections do have an axis of symmetry which serves as the plane of loading, and the present limitation causes no difficulty. When the principal axis is not also an axis of symmetry, the more general form of the flexure theory, as presented in Art. 54, will supply a proper method of attack.

When load is applied, the beam will bend, as shown in Fig. 76. Since sections A-A and B-B are assumed to remain plane surfaces, they will converge at some point, like O. The bottom fibers of the beam will be stretched, and the upper fibers will contract. At some intermediate layer of the beam, the fibers are still of length l. These fibers comprise the *neutral layer* of the beam.

If we examine a fiber at distance y from the neutral layer (Fig. 76) we find that its length is $l + el$, in which l is the original length and e the unit strain. The distance from the neutral layer to the line of convergence of sections A-A and B-B is the radius of curvature, r. Then, from the geometry of the figure, we note that

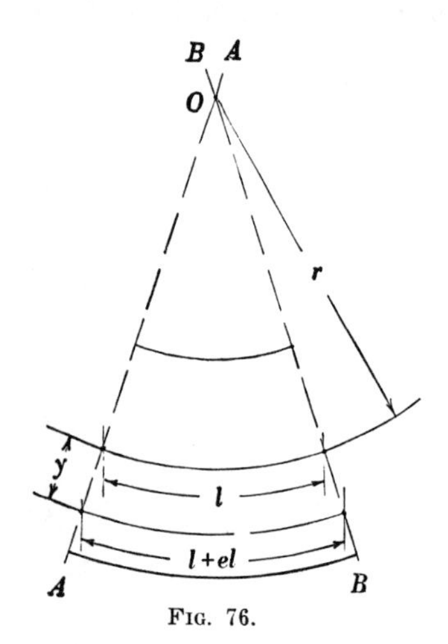

FIG. 76.

$$\frac{l + el}{l} = \frac{r + y}{r}$$

$$1 + e = 1 + \frac{y}{r}$$

and
$$e = \frac{y}{r}$$

The term $1/r$ is a constant, and

$$e \text{ varies as } y$$

We conclude, as a result of the first assumption, that *the strain in any fiber varies directly with the distance of that fiber from the neutral layer.*

This conclusion is equally justified when we consider the fibers above the neutral layer. In that region,

$$\frac{l - el}{l} = \frac{r - y}{r}$$

and
$$e \text{ varies as } y$$

Assumption II. The material obeys Hooke's law, that is, stress is directly proportional to strain.

Since
$$e = \frac{1}{r}y$$

and
$$s = Ee$$

then
$$s = E\frac{1}{r}y = \text{a constant} \times y$$

and
$$s \text{ varies as } y$$

We conclude that *the stress in any fiber is directly proportional to the distance of that fiber from the neutral layer.*

Figure 77 illustrates these relationships. The curve representing the stress–y relationship is a straight line (Fig. 77-a). The curve representing the stress-strain relationship is also linear (Fig. 77-b).

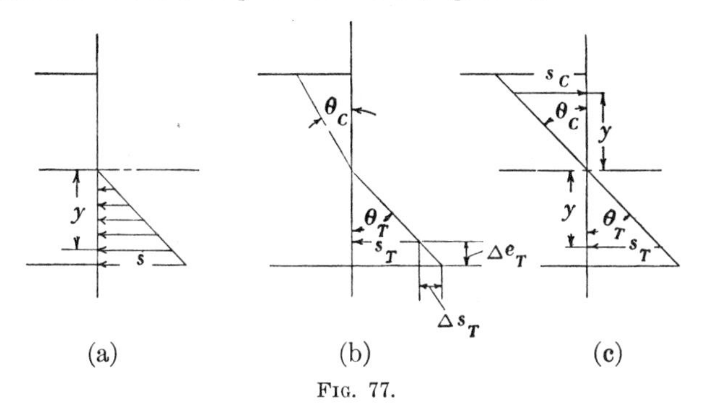

FIG. 77.

It will be noted, in Fig. 77-b, that the angle θ represents, at some scale, the modulus of elasticity, for

$$\theta = \tan^{-1}\left(\frac{\Delta s}{\Delta e} = E\right)$$

In the region of compression θ_C represents the modulus of elasticity in compression, and θ_T represents the modulus of elasticity in tension for the region of tension.

We therefore proceed to make an additional assumption.

Assumption III. The modulus of elasticity in tension is equal to the modulus of elasticity in compression.

Then $\theta_T = \theta_C$, and the line representing the relationship between stress and strain, or between stress and y, is continuous across the entire depth of the beam (Fig. 77-c).

We conclude that *the normal stresses on a cross-sectional area of a beam vary uniformly across the entire section.*

Let us now determine the resultant of this uniformly varying stress.

Figure 78 shows a portion of a beam which has been isolated as a free body. We have just noted that any section of a beam, like A-A, is subjected to a uniformly varying normal stress. (There is also a shearing stress, which we shall consider later.) When, as in this example, the beam is bending downward the uniformly varying normal stress is compressive on the upper portion of section A-A, and tensile on the lower portion. The resultant of the compressive unit stresses is a single force which has been shown as R_C, and the resultant of the tensile unit stresses is, similarly, a single force which is shown as R_T. The free body is in equilibrium, and no other horizontal forces than these two are present, for the limitations of the flexure theory have confined the loading to forces which are perpendicular to the long axis of the beam.

Then
$$R_C = R_T$$

and the resultant of the uniformly varying stress which is formed by these two equal, parallel, and opposite forces is a couple. This couple is one which we have encountered before—it is the "moment of resistance" of Art. 21.

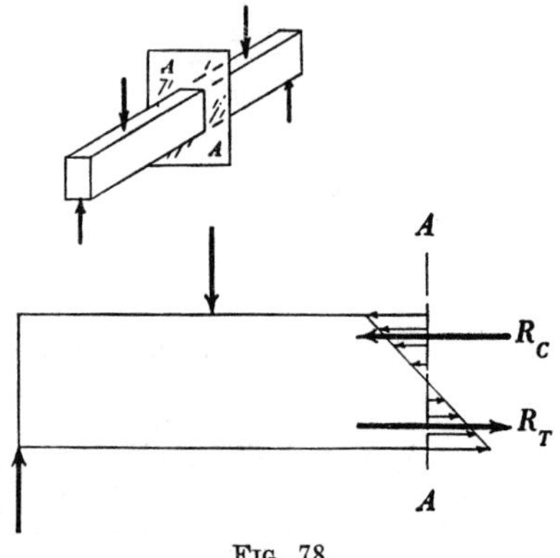

FIG. 78.

Whenever uniformly varying stresses are distributed over a plane surface, as in Fig. 79,

$$s = ky$$

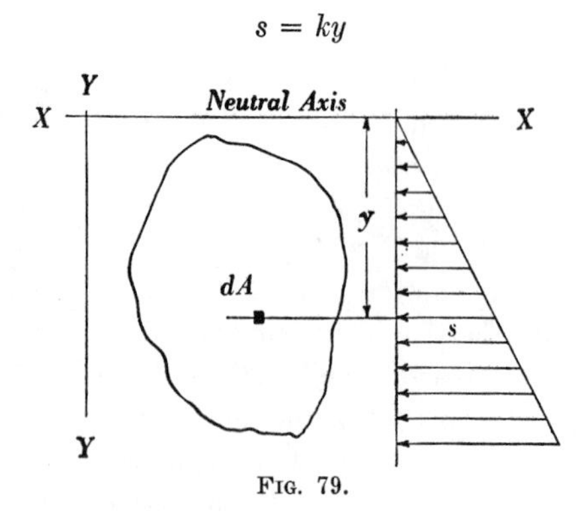

FIG. 79.

where s is the unit stress at distance y from a neutral axis, like the X-X axis shown, where the intensity of stress is zero. k is the constant of proportionality in this uniform variation.

The resultant of the uniformly varying stress on the entire area of Fig. 79 will be

$$R = \int s\,dA = \int ky\,dA = k\int y\,dA = k\,\bar{y}A$$

where $\bar{y}$ is the distance from the neutral axis to the centroid of the area. If the neutral axis passes directly through the centroid of the area, as in Fig. 80, $\bar{y} = 0$, and the resultant of such a uniformly varying stress must be a couple. Conversely, when the resultant of the uniformly varying stress is a couple, the neutral axis is a centroidal axis.

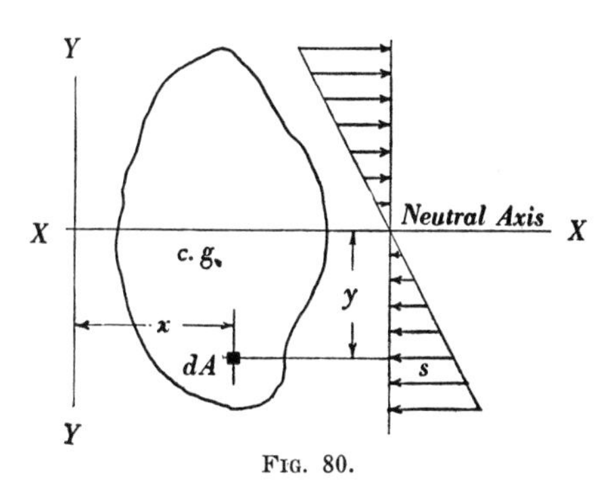

FIG. 80.

We have found, earlier in this article, that the resultant of the uniformly varying normal stresses which act upon the cross-section of a beam is a couple. Then *the neutral axis of a beam passes through its centroid.*

Let us now evaluate the resultant of the uniformly varying stresses of Fig. 80. The force which acts upon any elementary area, dA, is

$$dF = s\,dA = ky\,dA$$

and the moment of this force about the neutral axis is

$$dM = y\,dF = y\,ky\,dA = ky^2\,dA$$

The resultant moment of all such forces about the neutral axis is therefore

$$M_1 = \int ky^2\,dA = k\int y^2\,dA$$

$\int y^2\,dA$ is the second moment, or moment of inertia, I, of the cross-sectional area of the beam about its centroidal axis, and

$$M_1 = kI$$

It will be noted that these uniformly varying stresses also produce moment about any axis which, like Y-Y of Fig. 80, is perpendicular to the neutral axis. For example, the moment of force $s\,dA$ about YY is

$$dM = x\,ky\,dA = k\,xy\,dA$$

The resultant moment about axis YY is

$$M_2 = \int k\,xy\,dA = k\int xy\,dA$$

$\int xy\,dA$ is a second moment of an area which is known as the product of inertia.

A product of inertia of any area about a pair of axes, either of which is an axis of symmetry, is equal to zero.

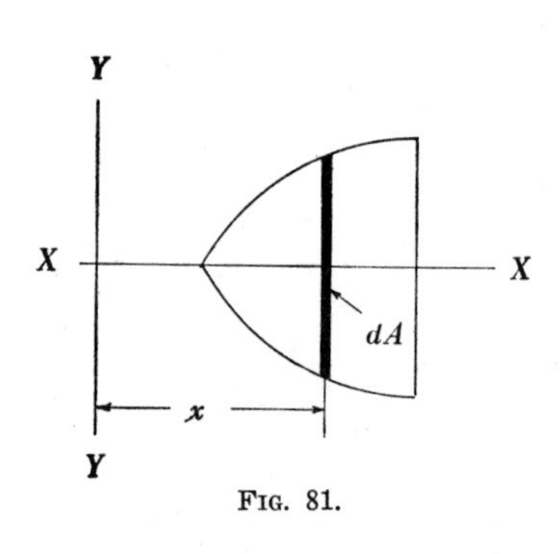

FIG. 81.

The elementary area dA of Fig. 81 has an axis XX, which is an axis of symmetry. Then the product of inertia of dA relative to the X and Y axes is $xy\,dA = x$ times $y\,dA$. $y\,dA$ is the first moment of dA about an axis through its centroid. The first moment of any area about a centroidal axis is zero. Then $xy\,dA = 0$.

The limitations of the flexure theory confine the cross-sectional areas of beams to those having an axis of symmetry in the plane of loading.

Then beam sections are areas in which the product of inertia is zero, and $M_2 = 0$.

M_1 is therefore the resultant of the normal uniformly varying stresses on beam sections. Let us call this resultant M.

Since $$M = kI$$
and $$s = ky$$

$$s = \frac{My}{I} \tag{34}$$

in which s = the normal unit stress on any layer of the beam at distance y from the neutral layer. This is the *bending stress*.

M = the moment of resistance in the beam at the section where the stress is being determined, and

I = the moment of inertia of the entire cross-sectional area of the beam about the neutral axis through the centroid.

In applying this *flexure formula*, the value of bending moment at the section is used in place of the moment of resistance to which it is equal

(Art. 21). The convention which we have already adopted for bending moment establishes the nature of the normal stress—at a section of positive bending moment, the fibers below the neutral layer will be in tension, while those above are in compression.

Illustrative Example I. The beam of Fig. 82 is loaded with two concentrated forces of 1000 lb. and 3000 lb., and a uniformly distributed force of 100 lb./ft.,

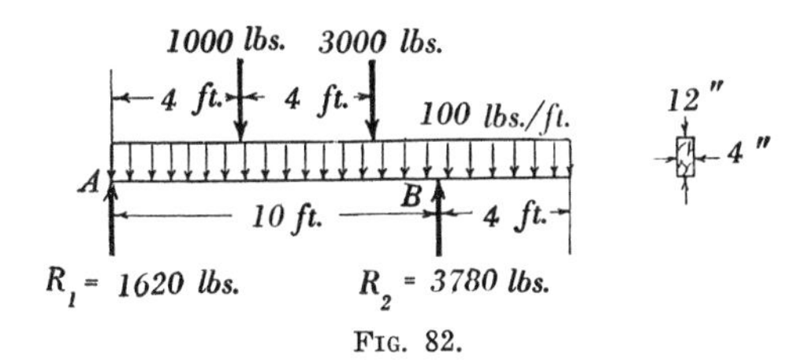

FIG. 82.

which includes the weight of the beam. It is supported by concentrated forces R_1 and R_2. The cross section of the beam is a 4 in. × 12 in. rectangle. We are to determine the maximum bending stress in the beam.

The flexure formula, from equation (34), $s = My/I$ indicates that normal stress varies directly as the product of bending moment and distance y. The moment of inertia, I, is a constant, for the limitations of the flexure theory have confined its application to beams of uniform cross-section.

Then such problems as this demand the determination of, first, the maximum bending moment existing on any section of the beam and, second, the determination of the maximum value of y at that section.

The exploration of the beam by means of a shearing force diagram will reveal the section of maximum bending moment.

We first take moments, about axes at points A and B, to determine the supporting forces R_1 and R_2.

$$(\Sigma M_A = 0) \quad -10R_2 + 1000 \times 4 + 3000 \times 8 + 100 \times 14 \times 7 = 0$$
$$R_2 = 3780 \text{ lb.}$$
$$(\Sigma M_B = 0) \quad +10R_1 - 1000 \times 6 - 3000 \times 2 - 100 \times 14 \times 3 = 0$$
$$R_1 = 1620 \text{ lb.}$$

These supporting forces are checked by applying $\Sigma Y = 0$.

$$+1620 - 1000 - 3000 - 100 \times 14 + 3780 = 0$$

The shearing force diagram may now be plotted (Fig. 83).

In the range of values:

x : 0–4 ft. (from left)

$$V_x = +1620 - 100x$$

x : 4–8 ft. (from left)

$$V_x = +1620 - 100x - 1000 = +620 - 100x$$

$x: 8\text{–}10$ ft. (from left)

$$V_x = +1620 - 100x - 1000 - 3000 = -2380 - 100x$$

$x: 0\text{–}4$ ft. (from right)

$$V_x = +100x$$

The sections **1** and **2** where the shearing force diagram crosses the axis occur as follows:

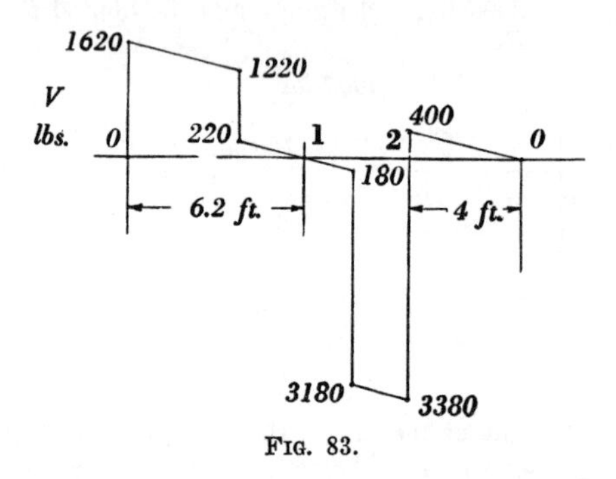

FIG. 83.

Section **1.** Using the equation for shearing force given above for the range of values of x from 4–8 ft. from the left, and setting the value of V_x equal to zero, we have

$$V_x = 0 = +620 - 100x$$
$$x = 6.2 \text{ ft.}$$

Section **2.** Plotting the diagram by entering the beam from the right, the value of shearing force immediately to the right of section **2** is +400 lb., and immediately to the left of the section is −3380 lb. The shearing force diagram therefore crosses the axis at section **2,** 4 ft. from the right.

We have now determined the *location* of each section of maximum bending moment in the beam. Our next move is the evaluation of those moments.

Section **1.** With an axis of moments at section **1,** we add, algebraically, the moments of all of the forces which act upon the portion of the beam to the left of the section.

$$M_1 = +1620 \times 6.2 - 100 \times 6.2 \times 3.1 - 1000 \times 2.2 = +5922 \text{ ft.-lb.}$$

This is the maximum *positive* bending moment in the beam. Its value may be checked by taking moments, about an axis at section **1,** of all of the forces acting on the portion of the beam to the right of the section,

$$M_1 = -100 \times 7.8 \times \frac{7.8}{2} + 3780 \times 3.8 - 3000 \times 1.8 = +5922 \text{ ft.-lb.}$$

Section **2.** With an axis of moments at section **2,** we take the moment of the force acting upon the portion of the beam to the right of the section,

$$M_2 = -100 \times 4 \times 2 = -800 \text{ ft.-lb.}$$

This is the maximum *negative* bending moment in the beam. To check its value, we can take moments, about an axis at section **2**, of all of the forces acting on the portion of the beam to the left of the section,

$$M_2 = +1620 \times 10 - 100 \times 10 \times 5 - 1000 \times 6 - 3000 \times 2 = -800 \text{ ft.-lb.}$$

The greatest bending moment in the beam is, therefore, quantitatively equal to 5922 ft.-lb. Since this bending moment is positive, all fibers which lie below the neutral axis at section **1** will be in tension, while those above the neutral axis will be in compression.

The centroid of the rectangular section is at its geometric center, and the maximum value of y is 6 in. The moment of inertia of the rectangle about its centroidal axis is

$$I = \frac{bh^3}{12} = \frac{4 \times (12)^3}{12} = 576 \text{ in.}$$

Applying equation (34),

$$s = \frac{My}{I} = \frac{5922 \times 12 \times 6}{576} = 740 \text{ psi}$$

The maximum tensile stress at the bottom will be equal to the maximum compressive stress at the top of this beam, for the top and bottom fibers are equidistant from the neutral axis.

Illustrative Example II. The beam shown in Fig. 84 carries a concentrated load of 6000 lb., and a uniformly distributed load of 1000 lb./ft. It is supported by the

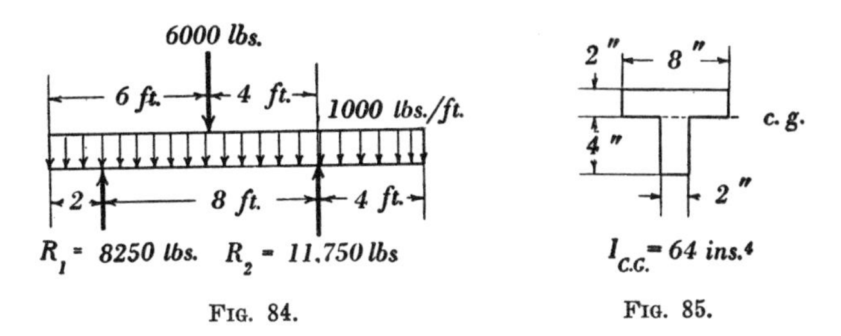

FIG. 84.

FIG. 85.

concentrated forces shown. We are to determine the maximum tensile and compressive bending stresses in the beam. The beam is a T-beam, and its cross-sectional area is shown in Fig. 85.

The shearing force diagram (Fig. 86) is again employed as the exploring device to locate the sections of maximum bending moment.

The maximum bending moments follow:

$$\begin{aligned} \text{Section } \mathbf{1}: M_1 &= -2000 \text{ ft.-lb.} \\ \text{Section } \mathbf{2}: M_2 &= +15{,}000 \text{ ft.-lb.} \\ \text{Section } \mathbf{3}: M_3 &= -8000 \text{ ft.-lb.} \end{aligned}$$

The maximum positive bending moment in the beam is 15,000 ft.-lb., and the maximum negative bending moment is -8000 ft.-lb.

At section **2**, the lower fibers are in tension, and the upper fibers in compression. The cross-section is not symmetrical about the neutral axis, and the maximum bending stresses at this section are therefore unequal. At this section, the maximum bending stresses are, substituting in equation (34),

$$s_T = \frac{15{,}000 \times 12 \times 4}{64} = 11{,}250 \text{ psi}$$

and

$$s_C = \frac{15{,}000 \times 12 \times 2}{64} = 5625 \text{ psi}$$

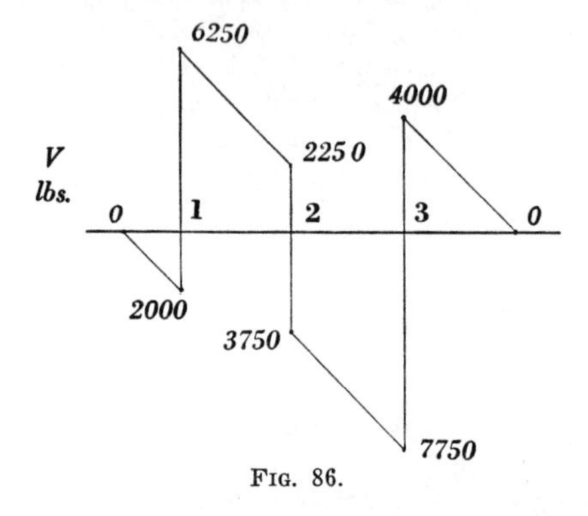

FIG. 86.

At section **3**, the upper fibers are in tension, and the lower fibers in compression. At this section, the bending stresses are, substituting in equation (34),

$$s_T = \frac{8000 \times 12 \times 2}{64} = 3000 \text{ psi}$$

and

$$s_C = \frac{8000 \times 12 \times 4}{64} = 6000 \text{ psi}$$

Then the maximum tensile bending stress is 11,250 psi, and the maximum compressive bending stress is 6000 psi.

26. Section Modulus. The designer is usually concerned with the selection of a proper beam to support announced conditions of loading.

When the choice of material has been made, the physical constants have been fixed, and the allowable bending stresses established.

If we transpose the terms of the flexure formula, equation (34),

$$\frac{I}{y_{\text{max.}}} = \frac{M}{s_{\text{max.}}} \tag{35}$$

In this expression, the quotient on the left side is a specification of the dimensions of the cross-sectional area of a beam. This quotient is known as the *Section Modulus.*

The section modulus, usually symbolized by the letter S, expresses the required beam section when the span and loading of a beam are known, so that the maximum bending moment may be determined, and the allowable bending stress has been fixed by the selection of material.

Before proceeding to illustrate the use of section modulus in design, it will be well for us to examine the nature of variation in this property.

The quotient I/y is very markedly increased by effective distribution of the area available to serve as beam section. When a given area is moved away from the neutral axis, the moment of inertia, I, will increase as the third power of fiber distance y, while the latter varies only linearly.

For example, if we compare the effectiveness of the two-cross-sectional areas of Figs. 87-a and 87-b, we find that for the area of Fig. 87-a,

$$S = \frac{I}{y_{\max.}} = \frac{bh^3/2}{h} = \frac{bh^2}{2}$$

The area of Fig. 87-b will have:

$$S = \frac{I}{y_{\max.}} = \frac{bh^3/6}{h} = \frac{bh^2}{6}$$

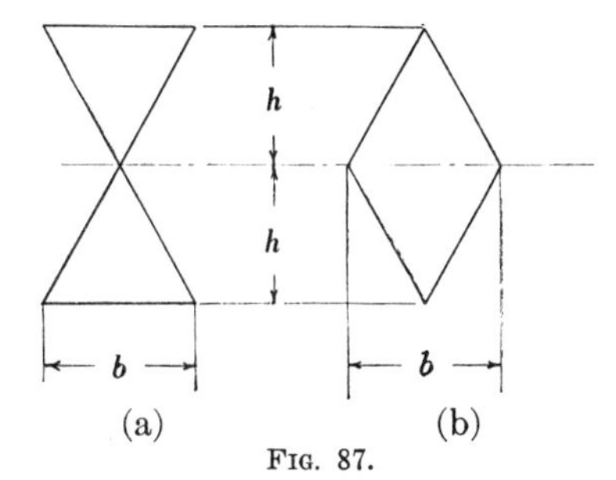

FIG. 87.

The first area yields a section modulus which is three times the second, though, in both cases, the same total amount of area and, hence, of material has been employed.

Such structural shapes as the I-beam of Fig. 88 and the Wide-Flange beam of Fig. 89 illustrate the effectiveness of distributing area so that

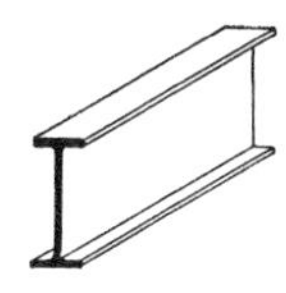
FIG. 88.

FIG. 89.

maximum section modulus is derived. Economy in the use of area is suggested by the following illustration.

Illustrative Example. A beam is subjected to a maximum bending moment of 160,000 ft.-lb. Steel is to be used, at a maximum allowable bending stress of 20,000 psi.

The required section modulus is, by equation (35),

$$S = \frac{160{,}000 \times 12}{20{,}000} = 96 \text{ in.}^3$$

An American Standard I-Beam (see Appendix) 18 in. deep, weighing 65 lb./ft. is necessary to supply this section modulus.

A Wide-Flange beam 18 in. deep, weighing 55 lb/ft., will also satisfactorily carry the loading.

If the cross-section of the beam were to be a rectangle, its sectional modulus would be

$$S = \frac{bh^3/12}{h/2} = \frac{bh^2}{6}$$

If h were made equal to $4b$, whi would be as great a relative value as could properly be tolerated under the limitations of the beam theory,

$$\frac{bh^2}{6} = \frac{b(4b)^2}{6} = 96$$

$$b = 3.3 \text{ in.}$$

$$h = 13.2 \text{ in}$$

This rectangular beam would weigh 148 lb/ft.

The economy of material of sections like the I-beam, and particularly the Wide-Flange beam, when compared with the rectangular section, are convincing proof of the effectiveness of proper area distribution in beam sections.

The Wide-Flange beam used in the previous example presents an advantage over the older section known as the I-beam. In addition, the wide flanges present greater resistance to lateral buckling.

We have, in this discussion of section modulus, considered only the effective distribution of cross-sectional beam area to resist bending stress. The pattern of such distribution must also concern itself with shearing stress, which is discussed in Art. 29.

27. Modulus of Rupture. The criteria of yield point and ultimate strength, which form the background material upon which allowable stresses are based, are discussed in later articles devoted to mechanical properties.* These criteria must be quantitatively evaluated in testing materials laboratories, and the tension test is the predominant evaluating device.

The usual small tensile test specimen is a fair sample of the chemical properties of the material, but may present questionable data in its representation of the physical properties of the material. A more reliable sampling, which could predict behavior with greater accuracy, would demand that the sample be of the same material, size, and form as the service machine or structural part which it represents, and that this full-scale model be subjected to loads identical with those eventually to be faced by the actual part.

Practical considerations usually preclude full-scale testing, and much subsequent investigation has been devoted to the establishment of corre-

*See Chapter X.

lation factors to appraise the degree of similitude between test model and service member.

In establishing allowable bending stresses, compromise between model and member is effected to insure a greater degree of reliability than would be possible if only the results of tests on small tensile specimens were available.

The *modulus of rupture* is a device for establishing such stress criteria.

A beam whose relative dimensions fall within the limitations of the flexure theory is loaded to rupture in bending. The rupture may be evidenced as the opening of a tensile crack at the section of maximum bending moment, or as crushing of the compression fibers at that section.

If the value of applied load at the time of failure is noted, the maximum bending moment in the beam at the time of failure may be computed. If, now, this value of bending moment is introduced in the flexure formula $s = My/I$, and the value of maximum bending stress, $s_{\text{max.}}$, computed, $s_{\text{max.}}$ is called the *modulus of rupture.*

This calculated value is not a true stress in the beam. It is fictitious, but is in error only on the safe side. If we examine the distribution of normal stress on a right section of a beam (Fig. 90), we shall have a basis of comparison between real stress and modulus of rupture.

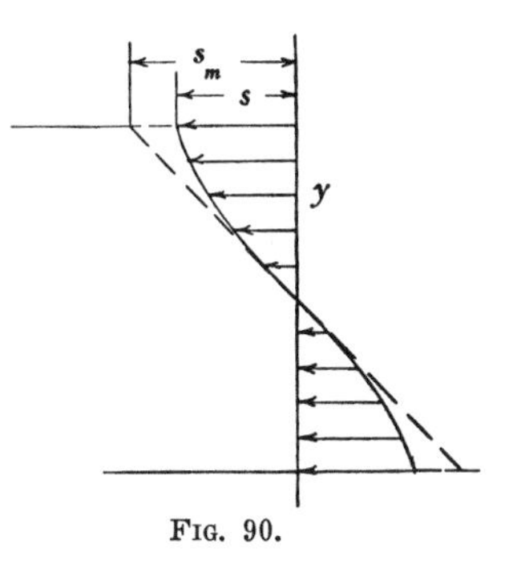

FIG. 90.

When a beam is loaded to the point of rupture, the fibers nearest the neutral axis will not have been stressed beyond the proportional limit; those more remote will have been stressed into the plastic range. The distribution of the actual stresses is illustrated by the solid curve in Fig. 90. The curve of stress vs. y distance is of the same character as the curve of stress vs. strain for the same material. The curve of stress vs. y distance, according to the flexure theory, is shown as a dashed line.

The maximum stress, occurring in the most remote fiber from the neutral axis, will be s, which is the actual stress in this fiber. s is less than s_m, the modulus of rupture. If s_m is used as the basis in the selection of a beam, a stronger beam will be provided than that demanded by the actual stress.

The modulus of rupture is divided by a factor of safety, to fix the allowable stress. This procedure parallels the fixing of allowable stresses when yield point or ultimate strength are used as criteria. In addition to the margin of safety provided by the factor of safety, there is an increment of safety in the difference between actual stress and the modulus of rupture.

Some economy may be introduced in beam design by experimental evaluation of actual bending stresses at the time of rupture. These values are, however, difficult to determine, and the modulus of rupture method, with its simplicity of flexure formula background, offers a satisfactory compromise.

PROBLEMS

Note: Tables of the Rolled Shapes—American Standard steel I-beams, Wide-Flange steel beams, and aluminum I-beams—are given on pages 451–462 of the Appendix. Where beams of these classes are referred to in the following problems, their properties will be found in the tables.

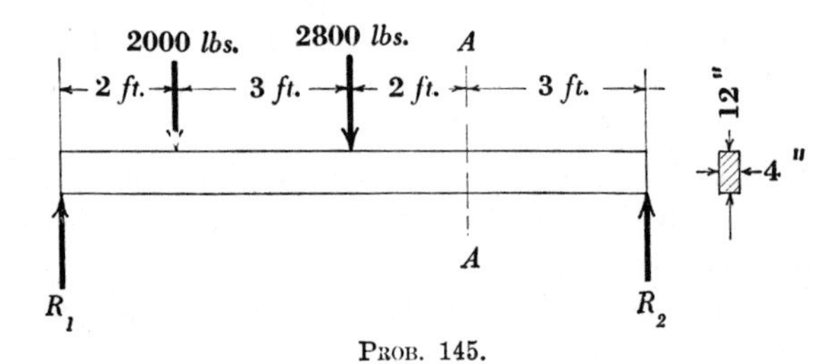

PROB. 145.

145. Determine the bending stress at section *A-A* (a) at the top of the beam, and (b) 2 in. below the neutral axis. *Ans.* a) 675 psi (compression); b) 225 psi (tension).

146. Determine the maximum bending stress in the beam of the preceding problem.

147. A machine weighing 12 tons is supported on two 10-in. × 21-lb./ft. Wide-Flange beams, which are freely supported at their ends. The load is transferred to the beams by four legs, and may be assumed to be concentrated as shown. Determine the maximum bending stress in each beam, assuming that the weight of the beams themselves may be neglected. *Ans.* 16,700 psi.

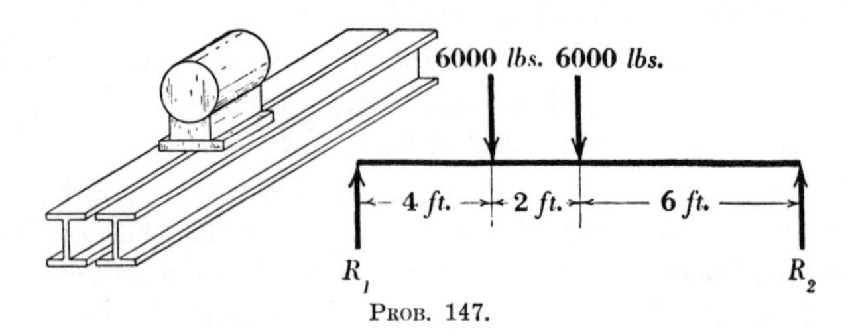

PROB. 147.

148. In the preceding problem, the weight of the beams has been assumed to be negligible. Determine whether this assumption is justified by finding the percentage increase in maximum bending stress when the weight of the beams is considered. *Ans.* 1.26 per cent.

149. A beam is subjected to loads which lie beyond the section shown. The fibers in layer AA' contract 0.02 in., while the fibers in layer BB' stretch 0.03 in. $E = 10^6$ psi. Locate the neutral axis, and determine the maximum bending stress in the beam.

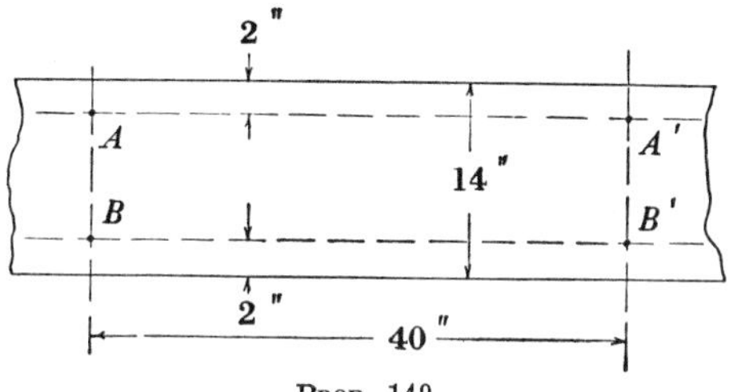

PROB. 149.

150. A 12-in. × 12-in. beam is freely supported at its ends. The beam is made of concrete weighing 144 lb./cu. ft., which has a tensile breaking strength of 300 psi. Determine the maximum span length L which may be used without causing the beam to fail, in tension, under its own weight.

151. The allowable bending stress in both tension and compression is 1200 psi. Determine the maximum allowable uniformly distributed load. *Ans.* 800 lb/ft.

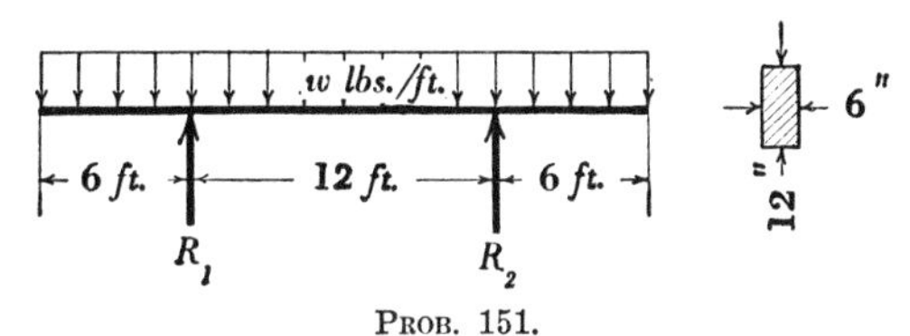

PROB. 151.

152. The maximum allowable bending stress is 1600 psi. Determine the maximum allowable uniformly distributed load.

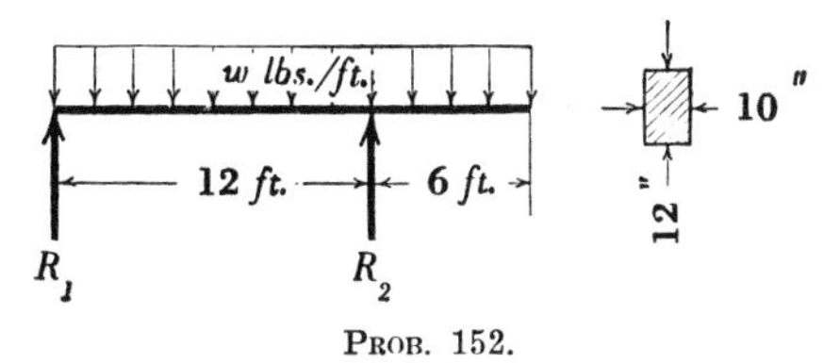

PROB. 152.

153. The cantilever beam consists of two channels, fastened back to back. The channels are 15 in. deep, and for each, $I = 446.2$ in.^{4} Determine the maximum bending stress in the channels.

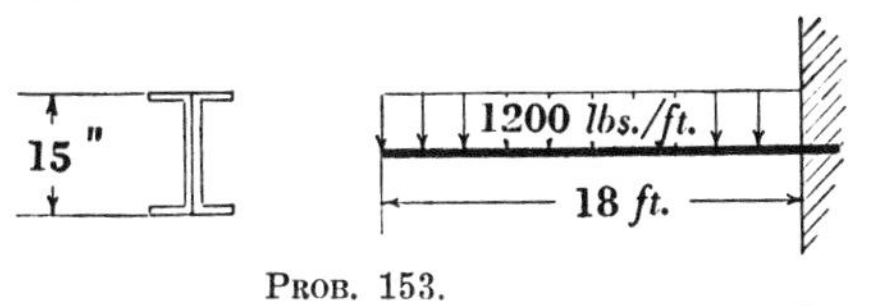

PROB. 153.

154. The beam of Prob. 115 is a 6 in. × 12 in. rectangular beam. Determine the maximum bending stress. *Ans.* 1500 psi.

155. The beam of Prob. 117 is a 4 in. × 12 in. rectangular beam. Determine the maximum bending stress.

156. The beam of Prob. 122 is a 10 in. × 25.4 lb./ft. American Standard steel I-beam. Determine the maximum bending stress in the beam.

157. The beam of Prob. 123 is an aluminum I-beam, 12 in. × 16.01 lb./ft. Determine the maximum bending stress in the beam. *Ans.* 5030 psi.

158. The beam of Prob. 124 is a 2 in. × 6 in. rectangular beam. Determine the maximum bending stress in the beam. *Ans.* 2000 psi.

159. The beam of Prob. 127 is a Wide-Flange steel beam, 10 in. × 29 lb./ft. Determine the maximum bending stress in the beam.

160. The beam is a cylindrical steel shaft, freely supported at its ends. The diameter of the shaft is 2 in., and the maximum allowable bending stress is 16,000 psi. $W_1 = 2W_2$. Determine W_1.

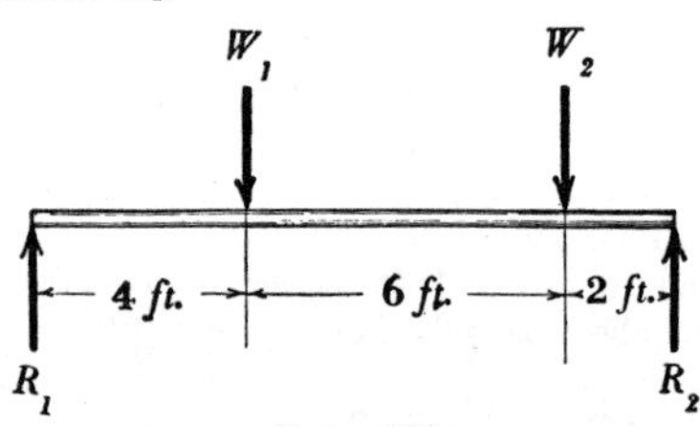

PROB. 160.

161. A beam is loaded as shown. The weight of the beam itself is assumed to be negligible. The allowable bending stress is 20,000 psi. Select the lightest beam which will furnish the required section modulus from the tables in the appendix, using

a) American Standard I-beam with $\bar{X}\bar{X}$ as neutral axis.
b) American Standard I-beam with $\bar{Y}\bar{Y}$ as neutral axis.
c) Wide-Flange beam with $\bar{X}\bar{X}$ as neutral axis.
d) Wide-Flange beam with $\bar{Y}\bar{Y}$ as neutral axis.

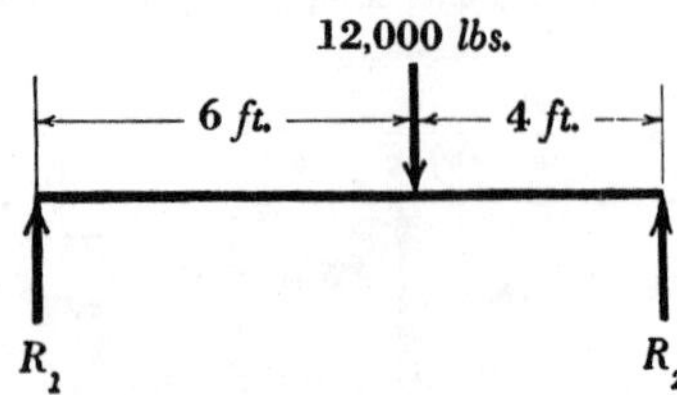

PROB. 161.

162. The cross-section of the beam is an equilateral triangle. The maximum allowable bending stress is 1420 psi. Determine the length of the sides of the triangle. *Ans.* b = 12.5 in.

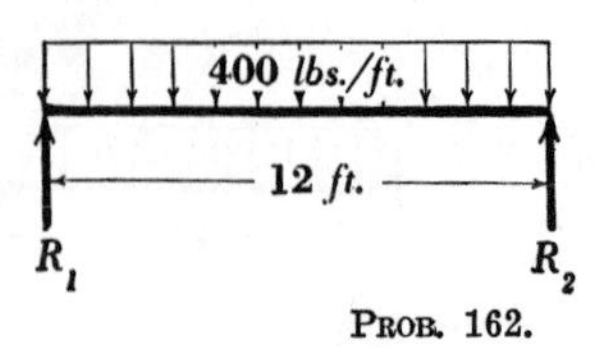

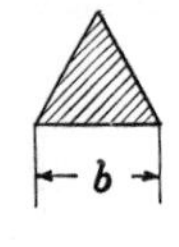

PROB. 162.

163. The left end of the cantilever beam CD is supported by a bar AB fastened to the beam through pin-jointed links, as shown. The bar rests on a platform scale, which indicates a reaction of the scale on bar AB of 900 lb., when CD carries a uniformly distributed load of 300 lb./ft. over its entire length. CD is an aluminum I-beam, 12 in. × 16.01 lb./ft. Determine the maximum bending stress in CD.

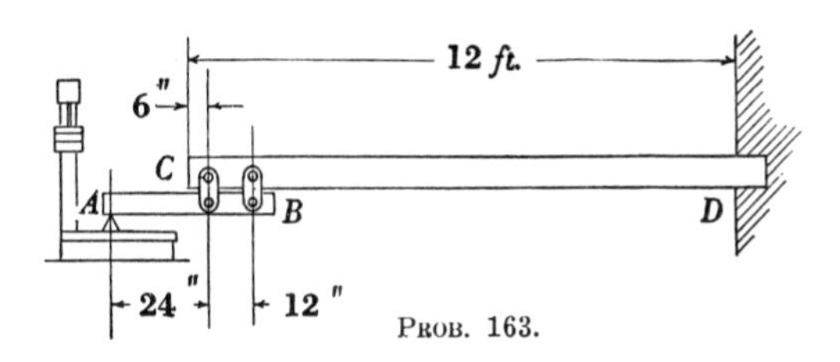

PROB. 163.

164. The maximum allowable bending stress in the beam is 900 psi. Determine the *safe* load W. The beam is fastened to the wall by a pin joint at A.

Ans. $1800 < W < 2700$

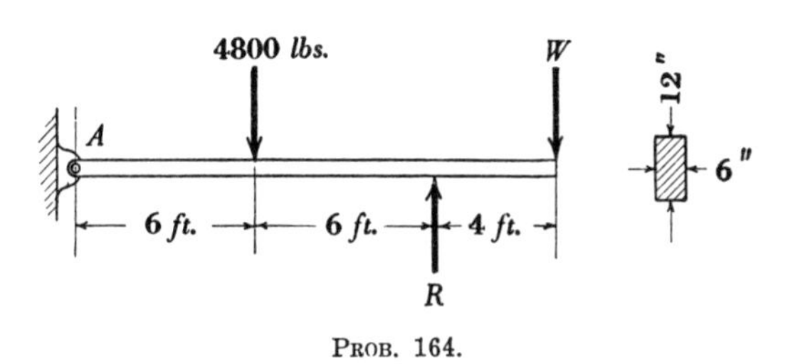

PROB. 164.

165. Determine the maximum tensile and compressive bending stresses.

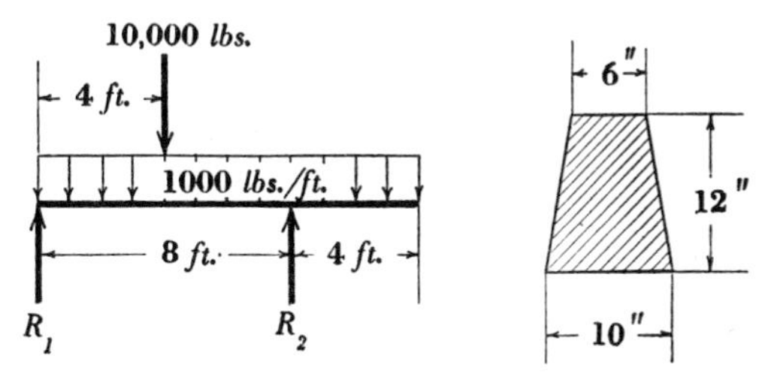

PROB. 165.

166. The beam has a tee-section which is 5 in. deep, with its centroid 1.57 in. from the bottom. $I_{c.g.} = 10.5$ in.[4] Determine (a) the maximum tensile bending stress in the beam and (b) the maximum compressive bending stress. *Ans.* a) 3140 psi; b) 3920 psi.

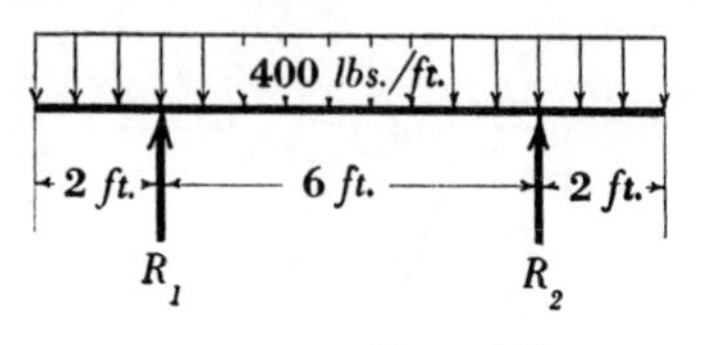

PROB. 166.

167. The maximum allowable tensile bending stress is 4000 psi, and the maximum allowable compressive bending stress is 10,000 psi. Determine the maximum allowable uniformly distributed load which may be placed on the beam.

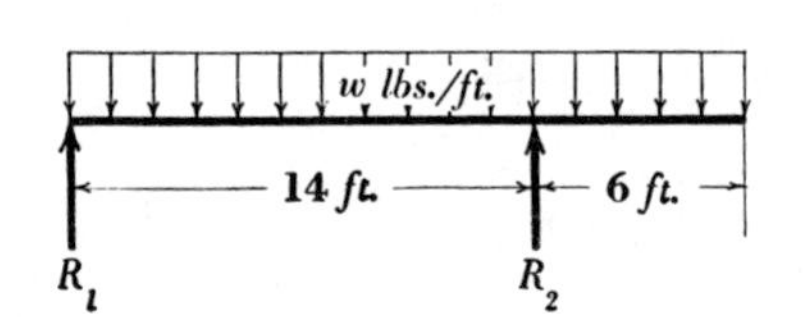

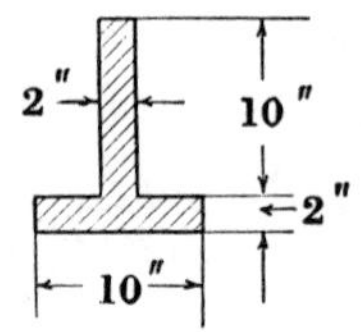

PROB. 167.

168. The tee-beam supports a uniformly distributed load of w lb./ft., a uniformly varying load with a maximum intensity of 800 lb./ft., at mid-span, and two concentrated loads of 1500 lb. each. The maximum allowable tensile bending stress is 6000 psi, and the maximum allowable compressive bending stress is 15,000 psi. Determine the maximum allowable value, w, of the uniformly distributed load. *Ans.* 300 lb./ft.

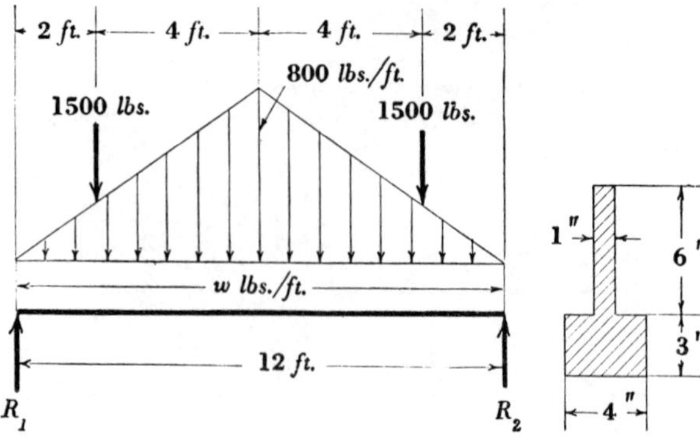

PROB. 168.

169. Beam $ABCD$ is subjected to a uniformly distributed load of 40,000 lb. The beam is supported by a distributed force, which varies uniformly from A to B, is uniform from B to C, and varies uniformly from C to D. Find the section modulus required if the maximum allowable bending stress is 12,000 psi. *Ans.* 36 in.^{3}

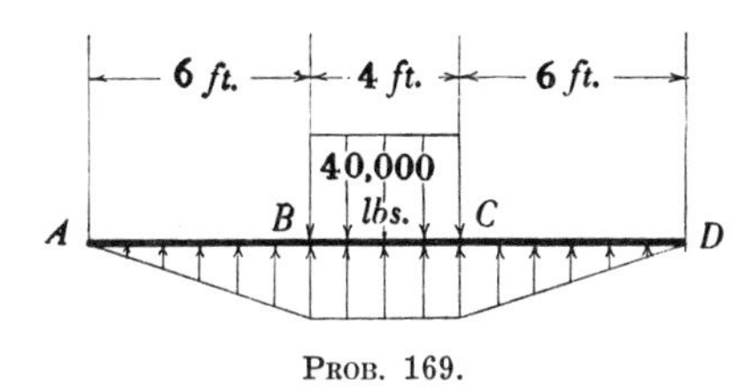

PROB. 169.

170. Find the length of the sides, b, of a square column to carry the indicated loads if the maximum allowable bending stress is 1200 psi. The weight of the column is to be neglected. *Ans.* 6 in.

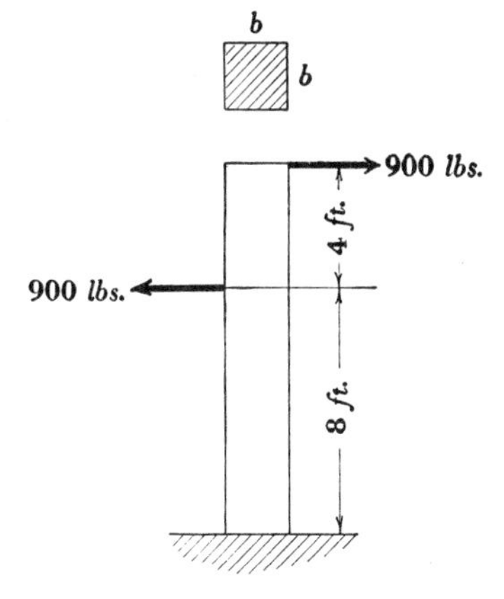

PROB. 170.

171. The maximum allowable bending stress is 1200 psi. Determine the required section modulus, and the dimensions of the rectangular section if $h = 3b$.

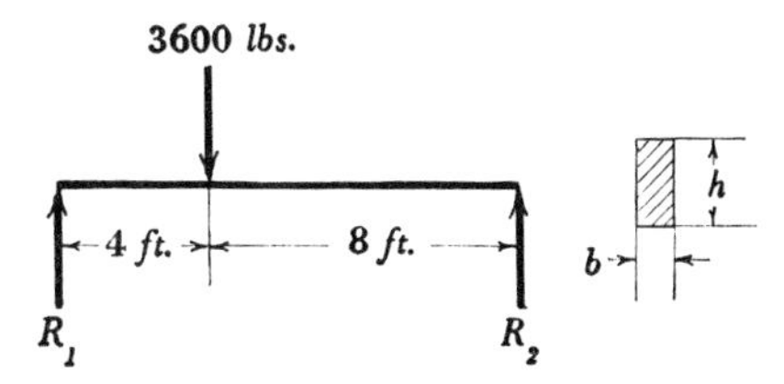

PROB. 171.

172. The drawing shows the plan view of the beams supporting a floor. The load on the floor is 140 lb./sq. ft., including the weight of the flooring and beams. Beam CD is hung from beams GH to support beams EF which, like GH and AB, are the direct floor support. The maximum allowable bending stress is 20,000 psi. Determine the required section modulus for each beam, and select the lightest American Standard steel I-beam from the table in the Appendix.

Ans. AB: 12 in. × 31.8 lb./ft.
CD: 6 in. × 12.5 lb./ft.
EF: 5 in. × 10.0 lb./ft.
GH: 12 in. × 31.8 lb./ft.

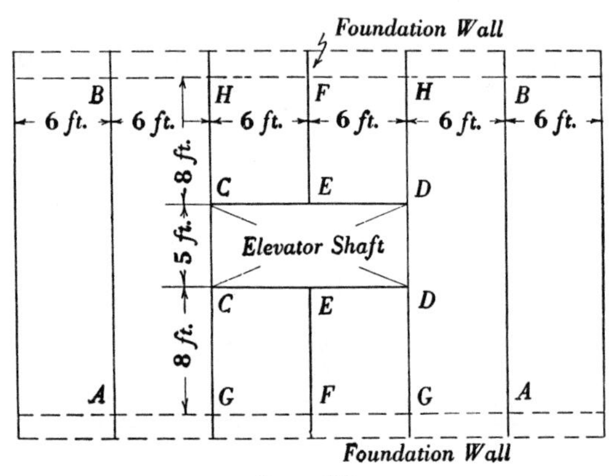

PROB. 172.

173. If Wide-Flange beams are used in the preceding problem, select the proper sizes from the table in the Appendix, and determine the saving in the cost of the steel, assuming that all steel beams cost 6 cents per pound. The calculation should be based upon two beams of each type.

CHAPTER III

Corollary I—The Longitudinal Shear Theory

28. Longitudinal Shear. We have thus far been concerned with the bending stresses which are developed in beams, and their appraisal and evaluation have been the subject of the basic flexure theory.

Other stresses than bending stresses are present and we shall now consider the shearing action and the resulting shearing stresses.

The beam of Fig. 91-a is constructed of several laminations or layers. The several layers are independent and will slide, relative to each other when the beam sags under loading as indicated in Fig. 91-b. If we were to

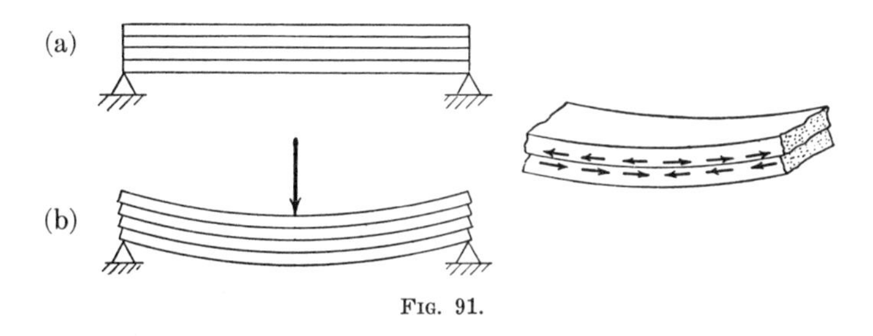

FIG. 91.

restrain the layers from sliding on each other by joining them with a cement or glue, a shearing stress would be set up in the glue. The beams which we shall consider are usually made of one piece rather than of the individual laminations which have been introduced to suggest the presence of shear. Shearing, comparable to that in the glue of the laminated beam, is exerted between the layers of a solid beam. Such shearing stress is called *longitudinal* or *horizontal shear*.

29. The Theory of Longitudinal Shear. The evaluation of longitudinal shear stresses is the function of a corollary of the basic flexure theory known as the *theory of longitudinal shear*.

The beams to which the results of this corollary theory may be applied are confined to those which conform to the limitations of the basic theory, and the assumptions which were made in the development of the flexure theory are held to be valid here.

A free body is isolated from a beam as shown in Fig. 92. The free body is the portion of the beam bounded by sections A-A, B-B, and C-C. A-A and B-B are distance dx apart, and C-C is at distance y_1 from the neutral axis, which is at the centroid of the cross-section.

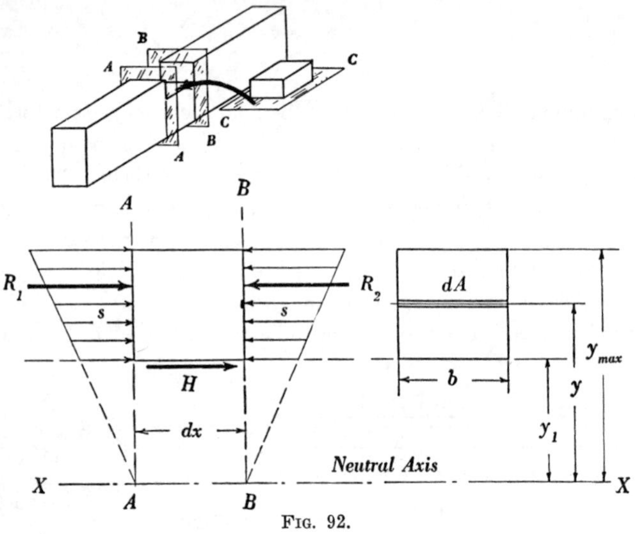

FIG. 92.

The external forces exerted on the free body which are parallel to the longitudinal axis of the beam are shown. These forces are H, the resultant longitudinal shearing force on the bottom face of the body; R_1, the resultant normal force on the left face; and R_2, the resultant normal force on the right face.

The force H is equal to $s_S\, b\, dx$, where s_S is the average unit longitudinal shear stress on the bottom face of the free body, and $b\, dx$ is the area of that face.

If the bending moment in the beam at section A-A is called M, the normal stresses on that face of the body are bending stresses $s = My/I$.

The normal force on an elementary area, dA, will be

$$dF = s\, dA = \frac{My}{I}\, dA$$

and R_1, the resultant of these normal forces will be

$$R_1 = \int dF = \int_{y=y_1}^{y=y_{\text{max.}}} \frac{My}{I}\, dA$$

If the difference between the bending moments at sections A-A and B-B is dM, the bending moment at section B-B is $M + dM$.

Then

$$R_2 = \int_{y=y_1}^{y=y_{max.}} \frac{(M + dM)y}{I} \, dA$$

Now, applying the condition of equilibrium $\Sigma X = 0$ to the free body,

$$+H + R_1 - R_2 = 0$$
$$H = R_2 - R_1$$

Substituting the values given above,

$$s_S \, b \, dx = \int_{y_1}^{y_{max.}} \frac{(M + dM)y \, dA}{I} - \int_{y_1}^{y_{max}} \frac{My \, dA}{I}$$
$$= \frac{dM}{I} \int_{y_1}^{y_{max.}} y \, dA$$

The integral $\int_{y_1}^{y_{max.}} y \, dA$ is the first moment about the neutral axis of the area of the beam's cross-section which lies beyond the level at which we are evaluating longitudinal shear ($y = y_1$). The customary symbol for first moment is Q.

Then $$s_S \, b \, dx = \frac{dM \, Q}{I}$$

and $$s_S = \frac{dM}{dx} \frac{Q}{bI}$$

dM/dx is the first derivative of bending moment with respect to x, which is the vertical shearing force, V (see Art. 22).

Then $$s_S = \frac{VQ}{bI} \qquad \textbf{(36)}$$

This expression evaluates the unit longitudinal shearing stress.

The derivation has rested upon an assumption which we introduced when force H was equated to $s_S \, b \, dx$. Resultant forces equal the product of unit stress times area only when the stress is uniformly distributed over the area.

Longitudinal shear stress is uniformly distributed when the beam width is constant at all levels and varies only slightly when the width of the section is a variable. No error of appreciable magnitude is introduced in this case by the assumption, and the value of longitudinal shear stress given by equation (36) is accepted as the average value over the small area $b\,dx$, whether or not b is constant throughout the depth of the beam.

30. Vertical Shearing Stress. In Art. 20 we noted the presence of vertical shearing force on the right sections of beams. The shearing force V, is the resultant of a system of distributed vertical shearing stresses. We have previously noted, in Art. 3, that unit shear stresses on planes which are mutually perpendicular are equal.

Then, the vertical shear stress on a right section of a beam at any distance y from the neutral axis is numerically equal to the longitudinal shear stress, and may be found by substitution in the equation $s_S = VQ/bI$. The resultant vertical shearing force, V, is therefore

$$V = \int s_S \, dA$$

The variation of vertical shearing stress on a right section of a beam is parabolic. The maximum value will occur at a level which depends upon the nature of the cross-section.

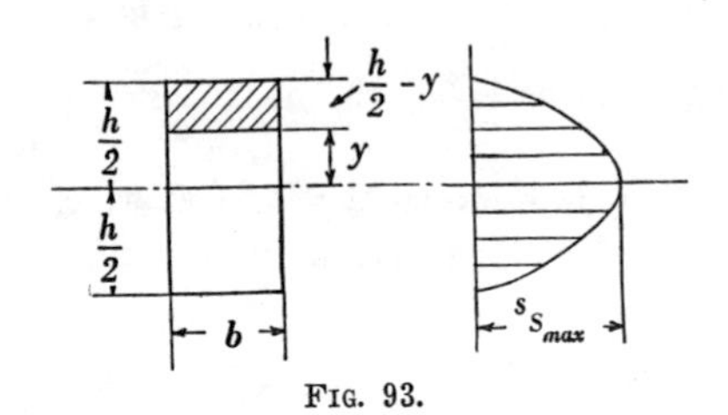

FIG. 93.

For example, Fig. 93 shows a section of a rectangular beam, of width b and height h. The vertical shearing force on the section is V.

The longitudinal (or vertical) shearing stress on any level of the beam at distance y from the neutral axis at the centroid is

$$s_S = \frac{VQ}{bI} = \frac{V\,b\left(\frac{h}{2} - y\right)\left(y + \frac{h}{4} - \frac{y}{2}\right)}{bI}$$

$$= \frac{V(h^2 - 4y^2)}{8I}$$

This general expression shows that the shear stress varies as the second degree of y, and is parabolic. To determine the location of the level at which the shear stress is maximum, we differentiate s_S with respect to y and set the first derivative equal to zero.

$$\frac{ds_S}{dy} = \frac{V}{8I}(0 - 8y) = 0$$

Then $y = 0$, and the maximum shear stress on this rectangular section will occur at the neutral axis, where it will have a value

$$s_S = \frac{Vh^2}{8I} = \frac{Vh^2}{8\,bh^3/12} = \frac{3V}{2bh} = \frac{3V}{2A} \tag{37}$$

where A is the cross-sectional area of the beam.

Other geometric forms of cross-sectional area are admissible under the limitations of the flexure theory. We are restricted only to the use of areas having an axis of symmetry in the plane of loading (except as noted in Art. 54).

The diamond-shaped area of Fig. 94-a will serve to illustrate a different distribution of shear stress. On this type of section, as in all beam sections,

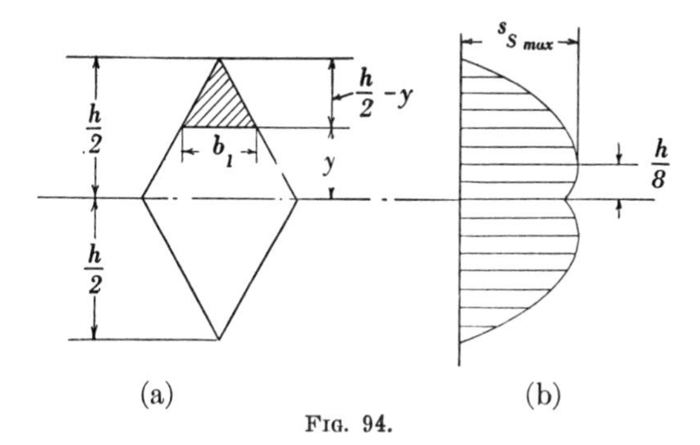

FIG. 94.

the longitudinal shearing stress varies parabolically; in this case, however, the maximum will not occur at the neutral axis.

The longitudinal shear stress at any level y from the neutral axis is

$$s_S = \frac{VQ}{bI} = \frac{V}{b_1 I}\left[\frac{1}{2} b_1 \left(\frac{h}{2} - y\right)\left(y + \frac{h}{6} - \frac{y}{3}\right)\right]$$

$$= \frac{V}{24I}\,[h^2 + 2hy - 8y^2]$$

We observe that the shear stress is again varying parabolically. Differentiation of the shear stress, s_S, with respect to y will yield

$$\frac{ds_S}{dy} = \frac{V}{24I}(2h - 16y) = 0$$

and

$$y = \frac{h}{8}$$

Then the maximum shear stress occurs at a distance $h/8$ above (and below) the neutral axis, as shown in Fig. 94-b.

The distribution of shear stress, s_S, over the beam section of Fig. 95-a is shown in Fig. 95-b.

If each ordinate of this diagram is multiplied by the width of the beam at each level, the resulting diagram of Fig. 95-c shows the nature of distribution of the resultant shearing force on the layers. In this diagram $p = b\, s_S$ is the intensity of shear stress per unit of depth.

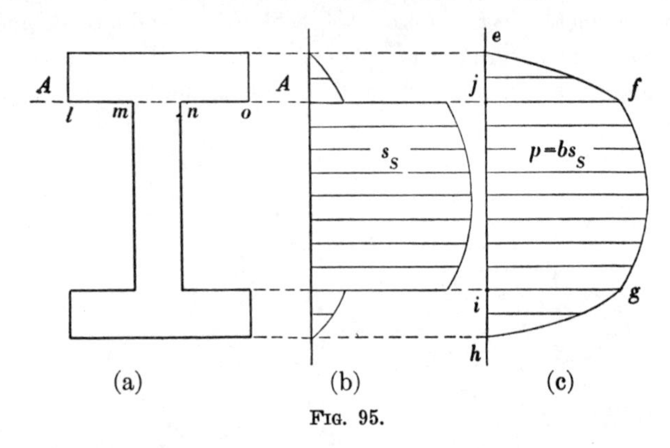

FIG. 95.

The resultant shearing force on the entire cross-sectional area of the beam is

$$V = \int p\, dy = \int s_S\, b\, dy$$

This integral is graphically represented by the total area *efgh*. Area *jfgi* represents the portion of the total shearing force which is carried by the web of the beam section. It is apparent that the major portion of the total shearing force is carried by the web.

In this example, as in all cases of beams of varying width, the assumption has been made that the distribution of shear stress across any horizontal level of the cross-section of a beam is uniform. It will be noted that at the junction of flange and web (section *A*-*A*) there is no development of shear on portions *lm* and *no* for these sections are free of adjacent metal, while section *mn* is subjected to a concentration of shear stress. This concentration is relieved in actual beams by the provision of fillet curves in the corners at *m* and *n*, so that no correction is made in design for the non-uniform distribution.

31. Built-up Beams. When separate pieces are joined to form a beam the sections must be fastened securely if the full strength properties of the beam are to be realized.

A simple case of a "built-up" beam made of separate pieces is shown in Fig. 96. Two timbers are fastened together by a single row of bolts whose axes lie in the central plane of symmetry of the beam. The beam is subjected to a single concentrated load, W, at mid-span and is freely supported at its ends.

Since the bolts prevent the relative sliding of the two members, the load on each bolt is determined by considering the longitudinal shear

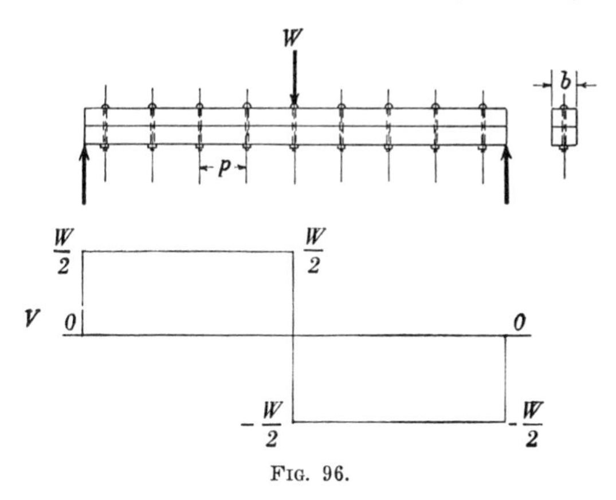

Fig. 96.

stress at the neutral axis which would be developed in a solid beam of the same dimensions.

It is assumed that each bolt is loaded by the resultant shear force acting over the area lying between sections equidistant from adjacent bolts. If p is the pitch, or distance between the bolts, the total load on each bolt is, by equation (11),

$$R = s_S\, A = s_S\, p\, b$$
$$= \frac{VQ}{bI}\, p\, b = \frac{pVQ}{I} \qquad \textbf{(38)}$$

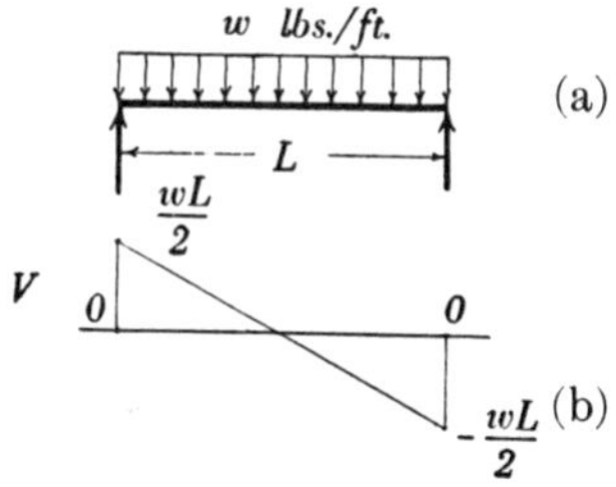

The total shearing force, V, is constant in this beam, and the load on each bolt will be constant if uniform pitch distances are used.

Fig. 97.

When the loading applied to the beam varies in intensity, the shearing force, V, is variable. For example, the uniformly distributed loading of w lb./ft. applied to the beam of Fig. 97-a yields the shearing force diagram of Fig. 97-b. The load per bolt is now a variable, which is maximum at the ends of the beam, and minimum at mid-span. Such variation would make it possible to reduce the number of bolts or to reduce their cross-sectional area in the central portion of the beam. In practice, however, fabrication is simpler and less expensive if uniform pitch and bolts of equal size are used throughout the entire span. In this case, the designer proceeds cautiously on the basis of an engineering philosophy of providing for the worst possible condition of loading. He assigns, to the term V, the maximum vertical shearing force of the shearing force diagram (in this case $V = wL/2$) and has assumed that all bolts have been assigned a design loading as great as, or greater than, any which may actually arise in the completed beam.

Built-up beams are assemblies of available stock structural shapes, like flat plates and angles, which provide large cross-sectional areas when combined—a more economical solution of the problem of building large beams than would be feasible if such sizes were to be built as one unit. In these assemblies, the anchoring of sectional parts to each other necessitates joining by such fasteners as rivets, bolts, or welding.

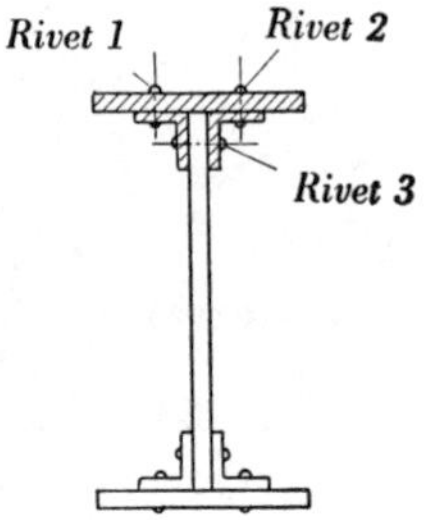

Rivet 1 Rivet 2 Rivet 3

Fig. 98.

The built-up section of Fig. 98 is composed of flat plates used to form the web and flange. These are connected by structural angles.

In the investigation of longitudinal or vertical shear stress, we must identify those portions which tend to slide relative to each other when the beam bends.

The top flange plates will tend to slide relative to the supporting angles, and the total load on rivet 1 or rivet 2 is, by equation (38),

$$R = \frac{pVQ}{2I}$$

The first moment, Q, is the moment of the rectangular cross-section of the flange plate.

To determine the load placed on the web rivet (rivet 3) we must establish the first moment of the sliding portion. Figure 99 will assist us in the determination.

It will be recalled that the derivation of $s_S = VQ/bI$ was based upon the isolation of a free body like that bounded, in this case, by the sections A-A, B-B, and the surface *abc*.

If s_S is the average longitudinal shear stress on *abc*, and l is the length *abc*, the resultant longitudinal shear stress will be

$$s_S\, l\, dx = \frac{dM}{I} \int y\, dA$$

and
$$s_S\, l = \frac{V}{I} \int y\, dA$$

where $\int y\, dA$ is the first moment of area $abcde$ about the neutral axis.

If, as before, a row of bolts is used with pitch distance p, the resultant load per bolt resulting from longitudinal shear will be

$$R = s_S\, p\, l = \frac{pVQ}{I}$$

The curved surface abc may be of any nature and will include the shape shown in Fig. 100, which enables us to deal with web rivet 3 of Fig. 98. We observe that the first moment, Q, in this case is the moment of the shaded area including flange plate and supporting angles. This first moment is, therefore, independent of the level at which rivet 3 is placed.

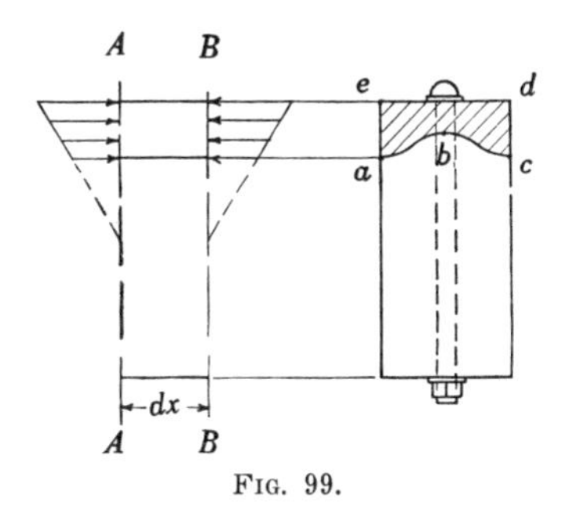

FIG. 99.

Illustrative Example. The built-up beam of Fig. 101 consists of ¾ in. × 14 in. plates as flanges; a ¾ in. × 32 in. plate as web; and four 5 in. × 3½ in. × 9/16 in. angles. The diameter of all rivets is ¾ in. (Area = 0.442 sq. in.) and the allowable unit stresses are $s_C = 19{,}000$ psi; $s_S = 8800$ psi. The span of the beam is 28 ft., and it carries a uniformly distributed load of 5000 lb./ft. We are to determine the pitch of the flange and web rivets.

Computation of I. The moment of inertia, I, of the cross-sectional area is taken, in design, as the moment of inertia of the gross or total area. No deduction is made for rivet holes, except when the reduction of area caused by flange rivet holes is greater than 15 per cent of the total flange area.

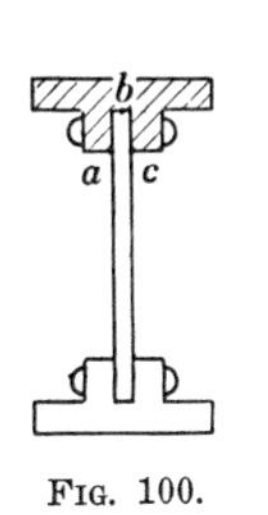

FIG. 100.

Web Plate: $I = \frac{bh^3}{12} = \frac{1}{12} \times \frac{3}{4} \times (32)^3 = 2050 \text{ in.}^4$

Flange Plates: $I = 2\left[\frac{bh^3}{12} + (\bar{y})^2 A\right]$

$$2\left[\frac{14 \times (3/4)^3}{12} + \left(16 + \frac{3}{8}\right)^2 \times \frac{3}{4} \times 14\right]$$

$= 5630 \text{ in.}^4$

Angles: $I = 4[4.40 + (15.07)^2 \times 4.47]$

$= 4080 \text{ in.}^4$

Total: $I = 11{,}760 \text{ in.}^4$

Flange Plate Rivets. The maximum shearing force in the beam is $V = (5000 \times 28)/2 = 70{,}000$ lb.

The first moment of the flange plates about the neutral axis at the center of the beam is

$$Q = 14 \times \frac{3}{4} \times \left(16 + \frac{3}{8}\right) = 172 \text{ in.}^3$$

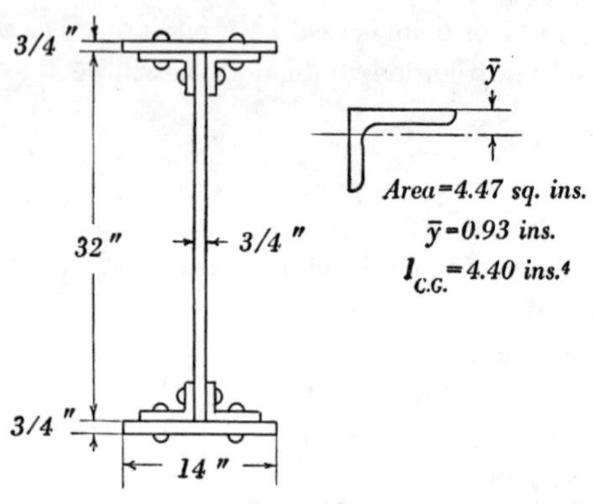

FIG. 101.

The total load on two flange plate rivets is, substituting in equation (38),

$$R = \frac{pVQ}{I} = \frac{p \times 70{,}000 \times 172}{11{,}760} = 1024p \text{ lb.}$$

The resistance to failure by shearing of the two flange plate rivets is, by equation (11),

$$R_S = 2 s_S A = 2 \times 8800 \times 0.442 = 7780 \text{ lb.}$$

and the resistance to failure by crushing (note thickness of angles) is, by equation (12),

$$R_C = 2 s_C d t = 2 \times 19{,}000 \times \frac{3}{4} \times \frac{9}{16} = 16{,}400 \text{ lb.}$$

Equating the total load R to the least resistance R_S,

$$1024p = 7780$$
$$p = 7.6 \text{ in.}$$

This is the required pitch for the flange plate rivets.

Web Plate Rivet. The total load on the rivet used to fasten the web plate to the supporting angles is determined as follows:

$$V = 70{,}000 \text{ lb.}$$

as above. The first moment of the flange plate and angles about the neutral axis at the center of the beam is

$$Q = 14 \times \frac{3}{4} \times \left(16 + \frac{3}{8}\right) + 2(15.07 \times 4.47) = 307 \text{ in.}^3$$

Then, applying equation (38),

$$R = \frac{pVQ}{I} = \frac{p \times 70{,}000 \times 307}{11{,}760} = 1830p \text{ lb.}$$

The web rivets are in double shear. Two cross-sectional areas must be sheared to produce failure. The resistance of these rivets to failure by shearing is, by equation (11),

$$R_S = s_S A = 8800 \times 2 \times 0.442 = 7780 \text{ lb.}$$

and the resistance to failure by crushing is, by equation (12),

$$R_C = s_C\, d\, t = 19{,}000 \times \frac{3}{4} \times \frac{3}{4} = 10{,}700 \text{ lb.}$$

Then
$$1830p = 7780$$
$$p = 4.3 \text{ in.}$$

which is the required pitch for the web rivets. It is customary, in practice, to use the same pitch for flange and web rivets, and the required pitch will be 4.3 in.

PROBLEMS

174. The shearing force at a section of 6 in. × 12 in. wooden beam is 7200 lb. Determine (a) the longitudinal shear stress at 2 in. from the top and (b) the maximum longitudinal shearing stress at the section. *Ans.* (a) 83.3 psi; (b) 150 psi.

175. Determine the longitudinal shearing stress at two points of section *A-A*; point *1* is 2 in. above the centroid of the cross-section, and point *2* is 3 in. below the centroid.

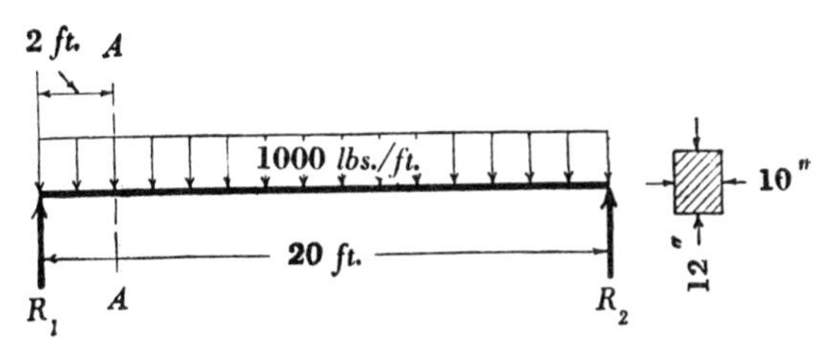

Prob. 175.

176. Determine the maximum longitudinal shearing stress in the beam of the preceding problem. *Ans.* 125 psi.

177. Derive an expression for the maximum longitudinal shearing stress in the symmetrically loaded rectangular beam shown.

$$Ans. \quad \frac{3}{2bh}\frac{(W + wL)}{2}$$

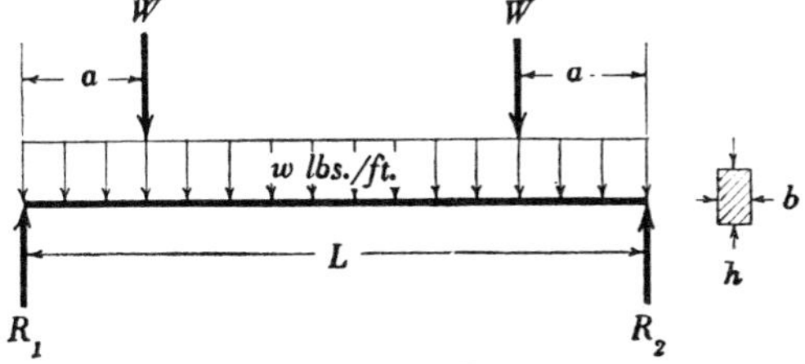

Prob. 177.

178. The total shearing force on the section shown is 9600 lb. Determine the distance y, locating plane A-A on which the longitudinal shearing stress is 120 psi.

Ans. 2.68 in.

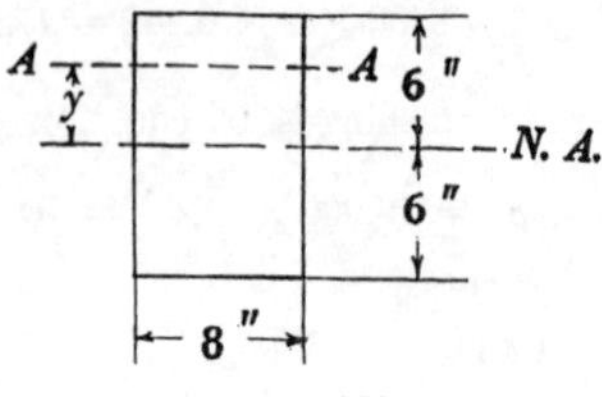

PROB. 178.

179. Make a plot of the longitudinal shearing stresses at 1-in. intervals from top to bottom of the casting shown, which serves as a beam section. The total shearing force at the section is 38,100 lb.

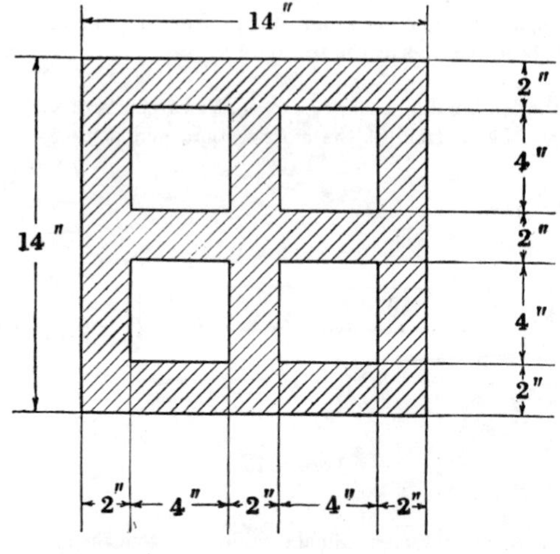

PROB. 179.

180. Determine the maximum longitudinal shearing stress in the beam shown. Plot the shearing stresses at 1-in. intervals from top to bottom at the section of maximum shearing force.

Ans. $s_{S(\max.)} = 300$ psi.

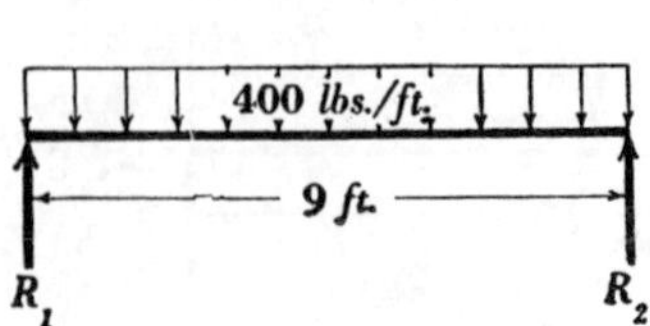

PROB. 180.

181. If the maximum allowable longitudinal shearing stress is 100 psi, determine the maximum allowable uniformly distributed load of w lb./ft.

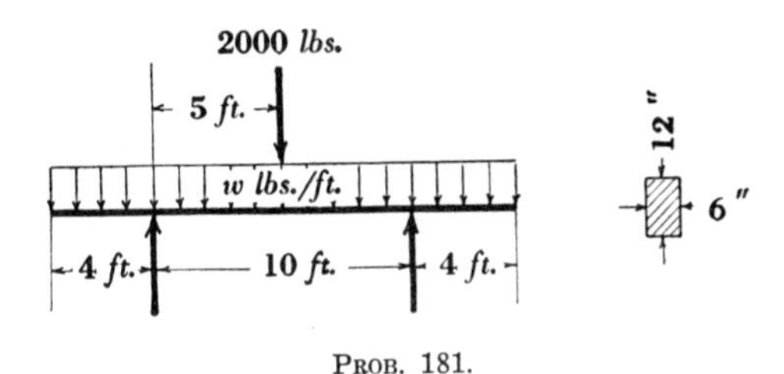

Prob. 181.

182. Determine the maximum longitudinal shearing stress in the beam shown.

Ans. 693 psi.

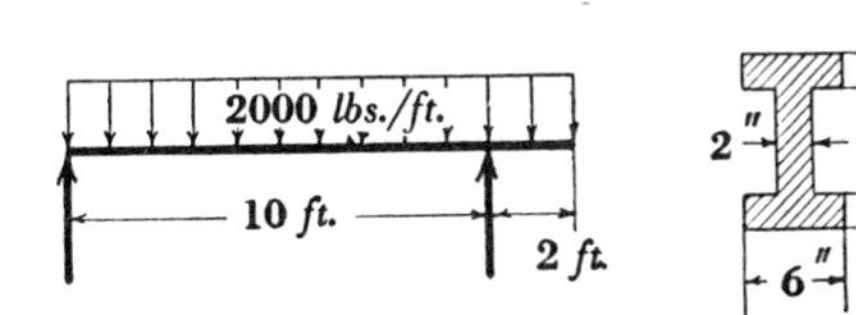

Prob. 182.

183. A uniformly distributed load is carried by a 6 in. × 12 in. rectangular beam. The maximum longitudinal shear stress varies, uniformly, from zero at the right end of the beam, to 75 psi at the left support. The bending moment at the left support is −21,600 ft.-lb. Make a drawing of the beam, showing span, loading, and supporting forces.

184. A 4 in. × 12 in. rectangular beam carries a uniformly distributed load of w lb./ft. over its entire span. The beam is freely supported at its ends. If the maximum allowable bending stress is 1200 psi, and the maximum allowable longitudinal shearing stress is 100 psi, determine the length of the beam. *Ans.* 12 ft.

185. A floor, carrying a load of 100 lb./sq. ft., including the weight of the beams is supported, as shown, by wooden beams which have a span of 20 ft. and are freely supported at their ends. The maximum allowable bending stress in the beams is 1000 psi, and the maximum allowable longitudinal shearing stress is 100 psi. Determine the required breadth, b, of the beams, which are 12 in. deep.

Ans. 10 in.

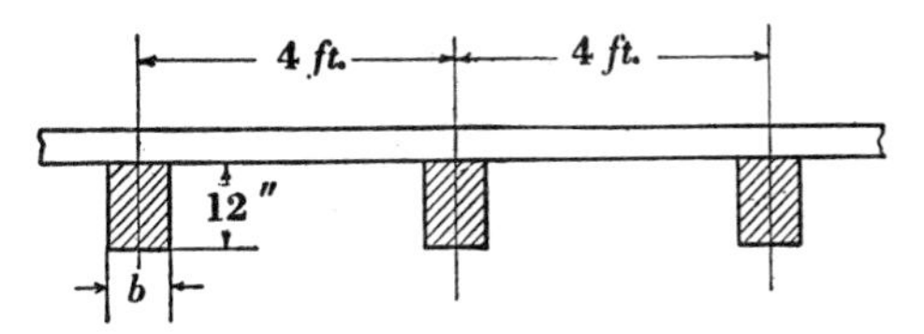

Prob. 185.

186. The beam of Prob. 115 is a 6 in. × 12 in. rectangular wooden beam. Determine the maximum longitudinal shearing stress.

187. The beam of Prob. 125 is a 6 in. × 10 in. timber. Determine the maximum longitudinal shearing stress. *Ans.* 250 psi.

188. A wooden beam is made of three 4 in. × 4 in. timbers glued together as shown. The beam is freely supported at its ends, and has a span of 12 ft. Determine the maximum uniformly distributed load to which the beam may be subjected if the maximum allowable shear stress in the wood is 300 psi, and the maximum allowable stress in the glue is 240 psi.

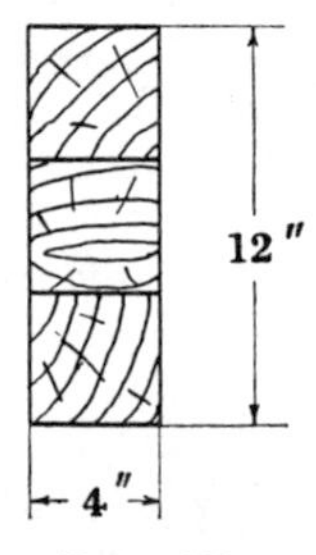

PROB. 188.

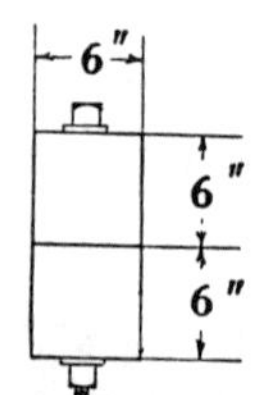

PROB. 189.

189. A beam is made of two 6 in. × 6 in. pieces held together by a single row of bolts. The pitch of the bolts is 8 in., and the allowable shear stress in the bolts is 8800 psi. The cross-sectional area of the bolts is 0.40 sq. in. Determine the maximum uniformly distributed load to which the beam may be subjected if it is freely supported at its ends and has a span of 16 ft. Use gross areas in determining Q and I. *Ans.* 440 lb./ft.

190. Two tee-sections are riveted together to form a beam, as shown. The rivets have a diameter of ¾ in. and a pitch of 5 in. The total shearing force on the section is 10,000 lb. The area of each tee is 4.0 sq. in., the centroid is located at 0.8 in. from the back of the flange, and the moment of inertia of each tee is $I_{c.g.} = 2.7$ in.^{4} Determine the shearing stress in the rivets, and the crushing stress.

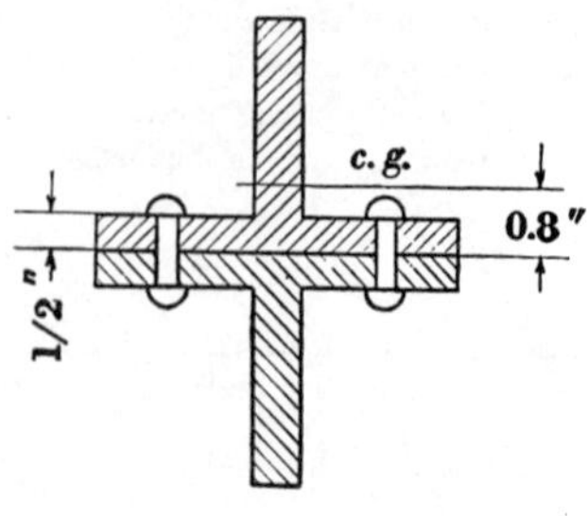

PROB. 190.

191. The beam section is composed of two tees, riveted together as shown. The diameter of the rivets is ½ in. The allowable crushing stress is 20,000 psi, and the allowable shearing stress is 10,000 psi. Determine (a) the proper pitch of the rivets immediately to the right of the left support, and (b) the maximum longitudinal shearing stress in the beam. *Ans.* (a) 5.23 in.; (b) 250 psi.

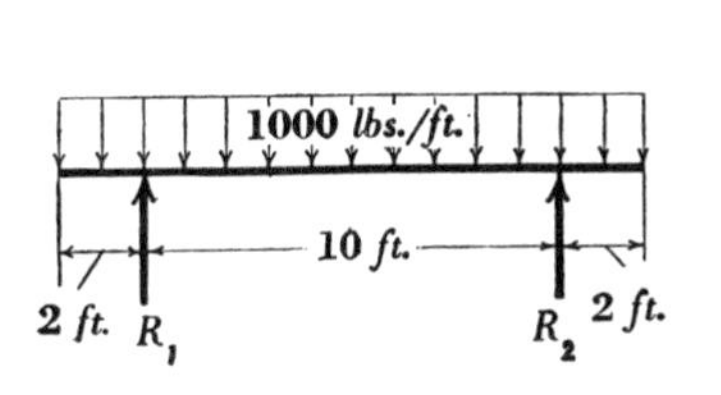

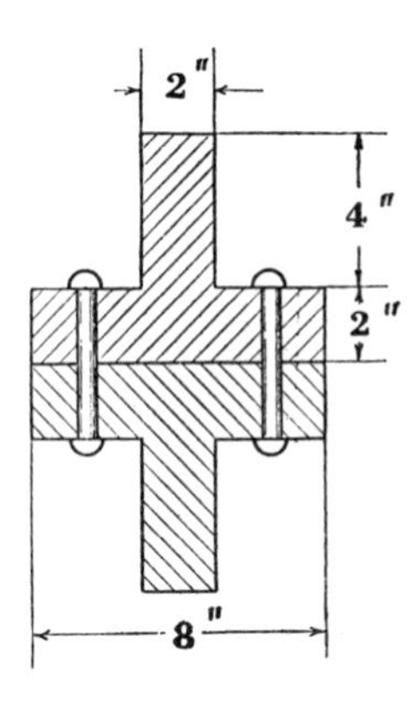

Prob. 191.

192. A built-up beam is composed of two channel sections, as shown. The channels are fastened together with ¾-in. diameter rivets, with a pitch of 4 in. The allowable crushing stress is 15,000 psi, and the allowable shearing stress is 10,000 psi. The area of each channel is 9.0 sq. in., the centroid is located at 1 in. from the base, and $I_{c.g.} = 12 \text{ in.}^4$ for each channel. The beam has a span of 16 ft. and is freely supported at its ends. It carries a concentrated load W at mid-span. Determine the maximum safe value of W, neglecting the weight of the beam itself.

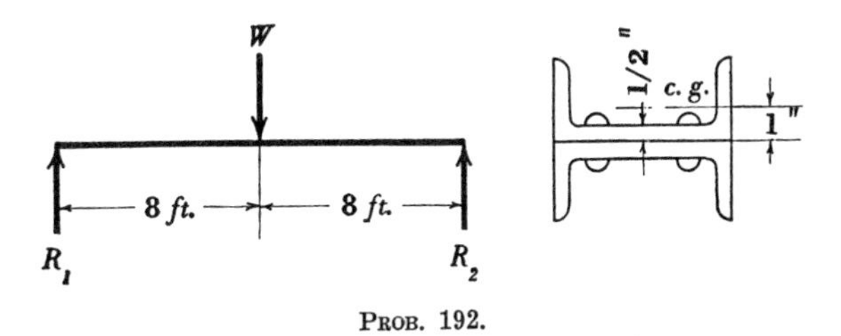

Prob. 192.

193. The built-up beam section is composed of a 1 in. × 20 in. plate, to which flanges (shown shaded) are fastened by rivets. The beam is freely supported at its ends, has a span of 20 ft., and carries a uniformly distributed load of 2000 lb./ft. The diameter of the rivets is ⅞ in. and their pitch is 3 in. Determine the maximum shearing stress in the rivets, and the crushing stress. Use gross areas for Q and I.

Ans. Shearing: 2280 psi; crushing: 3140 psi.

PROB. 193.

194. Determine the length L of the span if the maximum bending stress is 1200 psi, and the maximum longitudinal shearing stress is 100 psi.

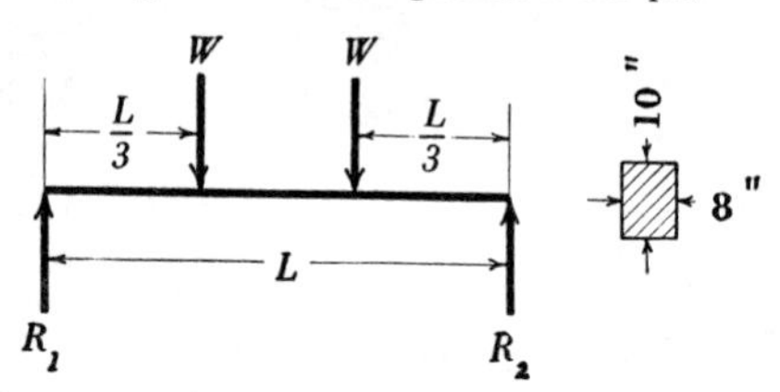

PROB. 194.

195. The total shearing force at the section of a beam is $V = 8960$ lb. Plot a diagram showing the shearing-stress distribution at 1 in. intervals from the top to the bottom of the section, and determine the portion of the total shearing force which is carried by the web.

Ans. 81 per cent.

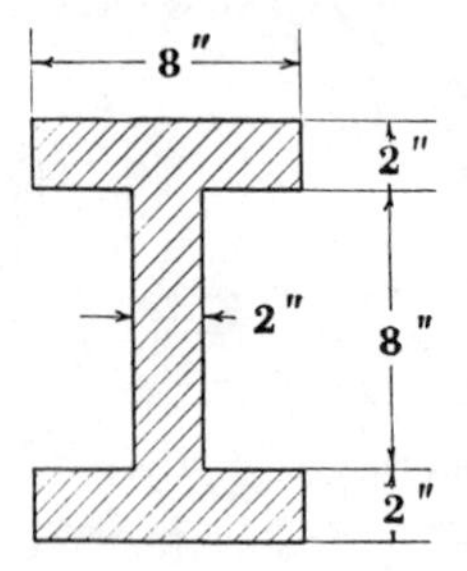

PROB. 195.

CHAPTER IV

Corollary II—The Deflection Theory

32. Deflection Theory. The engineering designer is concerned not only with the bending and shear stresses in beams discussed in the preceding chapters, but with the ability of the loaded beam to resist excessive deformation. The deflection of beams under loads may actually be the governing condition of the design. In structural members, deflections may limit the floor or other loads, even though the beam is not stressed beyond values which lie well within the elastic range. In machine parts, excessive deflection may disturb alignment and prevent the successful operation of the machine.

The deflection theory provides a technique of analysis for evaluating the nature and magnitude of deformation in beams. In addition, the theory provides a tool which enables us to expand analyses of static force systems beyond the limits imposed by the available number of conditions of equilibrium. We shall view the influence of the deflection theory in statically indeterminate cases in later applications.

At present, we shall be interested in deriving the basic deflection equation.

The theory of deflection, like the theory of longitudinal shear, is a corollary of the flexure theory, and the limitations of that theory are assumed to be fulfilled in the development of this theory.

In the discussion of the flexure theory, we found that the neutral layer of a beam passes through the centroid of the cross-sectional area. This layer is indicated by the line A-A of Fig. 102. The limitations of the flexure theory restrict us to the consideration of beams in which the line A-A is straight before the loading is applied.

Loading will cause the beam to bend, and line A-A will become a curve, known as the *elastic curve* of the beam. The vertical deviation, y, of any point of the elastic curve from its original or unloaded position, is the deflection of that point. The slope of the beam at any section is the small angle, θ, whose tangent is dy/dx. Since small angles, measured in radians, are equivalent to their tangents, $\theta = dy/dx$.

To evaluate the deflection y, we borrow the concluding statement of the first assumption of the flexure theory (see page 122).

$$e = \frac{y_1}{r}$$

where e is the strain in any fiber at distance y_1 from the neutral axis, and r is the radius of curvature of that neutral axis (Fig. 102-c).

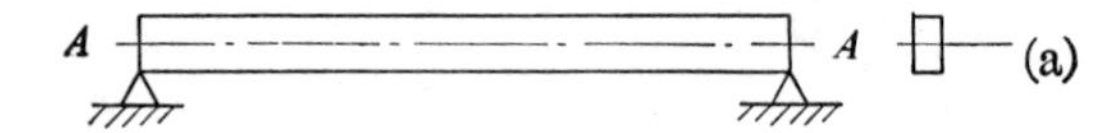

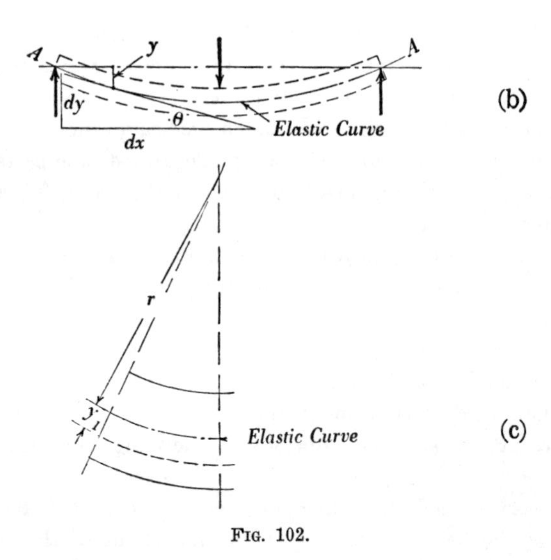

FIG. 102.

From the differential calculus, we take the general expression for all radii of curvature.

$$r = \frac{\left[1 + \left(\frac{dy}{dx}\right)^2\right]^{\frac{3}{2}}}{\frac{d^2y}{dx^2}}$$

Then
$$e = \frac{\frac{d^2y}{dx^2}}{\left[1 + \left(\frac{dy}{dx}\right)^2\right]^{\frac{3}{2}}} y_1$$

dy/dx is the slope of the beam, which is very small, and the term

$(dy/dx)^2$ a higher order of this small quantity is negligible in comparison with the term 1.

Then
$$e = \frac{d^2y}{dx^2} y_1$$

The strain, e, is equal to s/E, where s is the bending stress and E the modulus of elasticity of the material of which the beam is composed.

Bending stress has already been evaluated by the basic theory, as

$$s = \frac{My_1}{I} \quad \text{and} \quad e = \frac{My_1}{EI}$$

Then
$$\frac{My_1}{EI} = \frac{d^2y}{dx^2} y_1$$

and
$$\frac{d^2y}{dx^2} = \frac{M}{EI} \tag{39}$$

This differential equation is the basic deflection formula. It expresses the deflection as a function of bending moment, modulus of elasticity, and moment of inertia, in terms of its second derivative.

The evaluation of slope and deflection in beams is the solution of this basic equation.

The first derivative of deflection y with respect to x, distance along the span of the beam, is *slope* (dy/dx) and is obtained by a first integration of the basic deflection formula. A second integration will yield the *deflection* itself, expressing the relationship of y with respect to x, which is the equation of the elastic curve.

Two methods of integration are employed—analytical integration and graphical or pseudo-graphical integration. Both methods have merit, and we shall consider both. In different types of deflection problems, either may present an advantage, and it is well to have at our command more than one method of attack.

The analytical method will be considered first, because it is the method of integration which is most familiar to engineering students and it will therefore enable us to establish a most effective liaison between the training in mathematics and our present study of the mechanics of materials. In addition, the treatment of the constants which arise as each of the integrations is performed is most clearly illustrated by the analytical method.

33. Analytical Method of Integration.

Simple Beam-Concentrated Load at Mid-span. The beam of Fig. 103

is a simple beam, freely supported at its ends, carrying a single concentrated load, W, at mid-span. The bending moment equation, valid in the first range of loading, is

$$x: 0\text{–}\frac{L}{2}$$

$$M_x = +\frac{W}{2}x$$

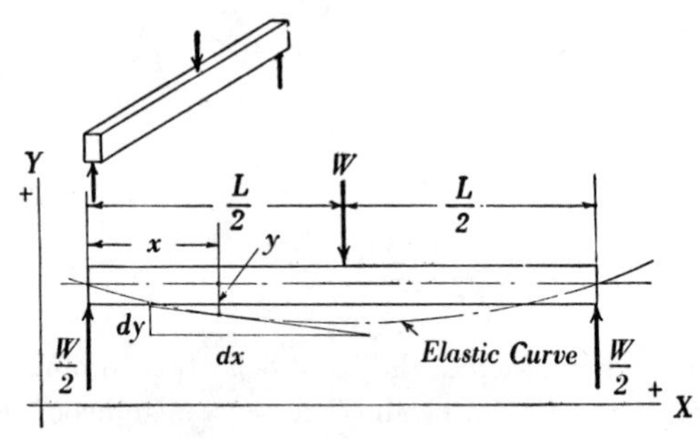

FIG. 103.

The positive sign which has been placed before the bending moment expression is consistent with the conventions already employed in all of our analyses of bending moment.

The deflection of an elastic curve upward from its original or unloaded position will be considered positive, and downward, negative.

The integration will produce these signs if the usual convention for bending moment is employed. Now, applying equation (39),

$$\frac{d^2y}{dx^2} = \frac{M}{EI} = +\frac{Wx}{2EI}$$

A first integration yields

$$\frac{dy}{dx} = \frac{Wx^2}{4EI} + C_1$$

The constant of integration, C_1, may be evaluated by noting that zero slope of the elastic curve will occur at mid-span, for this elastic curve is symmetrical.

When $$x = \frac{L}{2}, \quad \frac{dy}{dx} = 0; \qquad \therefore C_1 = \frac{-WL^2}{16EI}$$

The general equation of slope, valid at any section in the first range of loading, is, therefore,

$$\frac{dy}{dx} = \frac{Wx^2}{4EI} - \frac{WL^2}{16EI}$$

Integrating this equation,

$$y = \frac{Wx^3}{12EI} - \frac{WL^2x}{16EI} + C_2$$

The deflection, y, is zero at the left support.

When $\quad x = 0, \quad y = 0; \qquad \therefore C_2 = 0$

and the general equation of deflection in the first range of loading is

$$y = \frac{Wx^3}{12EI} - \frac{WL^2x}{16EI} \tag{39a}$$

The maximum deflection will occur at mid-span, when $x = L/2$. Then

$$y_{\text{max.}} = \frac{WL^3}{96EI} - \frac{WL^3}{32EI} = -\frac{WL^3}{48EI} \tag{40}$$

The negative sign indicates that this maximum deflection is downward from the unloaded position of the elastic curve.

This expression for deflection is of the form

$$y = k\frac{WL^3}{EI}$$

where W is the total load on the beam and L the span length.

In this case, $k = -1/48$. This coefficient will vary as different types of loading are encountered, but the general form of the expression will remain constant. This constant form permits the adoption of a routine in adjusting the units of any deflection problem.

The only property of a beam which is generally found expressed in *foot* units is the length, or span. The other terms which are factors of the deflection formulae involving units of linear distance are E and I, which are always expressed in *inch* units. The deflection, a small quantity, should also be expressed in inch units. The simplest conversion to insure dimensional balance in the equation is, therefore, the conversion of the span lengths of the beam from **foot to inch units.** Expressions of deflection arise as the result of two successive integrations of bending moment equations. The linear distance, x, of the moment equation has therefore been raised to the third power. In solutions of deflection problems it is only necessary to multiply the form $k\ WL^3/EI$ by $(12)^3$, entering the term L in the foot units characteristic of beam length. E and I are left in their original inch units, and the resulting value of deflection, y, will be in inches.

Illustrative Example. The beam of Fig. 104 carries a concentrated load of 3000 lb., located as shown. Determine the maximum deflection, in inches. $E = 1.2 \times 10^6$ psi. The beam is 4 in. $\times$ 10 in. in cross-section.

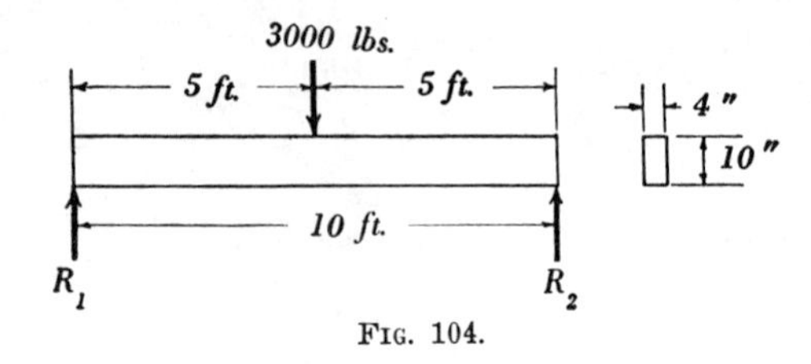

FIG. 104.

Substituting in equation (40),

$$y_{\max.} = -\frac{1}{48}\,\frac{3000 \times (10)^3 \times (12)^3}{1.2 \times 10^6 \times \dfrac{4 \times (10)^3}{12}}$$

$$= -0.27 \text{ in}$$

The constants of integration, which arose in the integration of the above cases of slope and deflection were evaluated simply because inspection of the symmetrical elastic curve revealed known locations of sections of zero slope and zero deflection. Four other cases are frequently encountered in engineering applications. In each of these cases, data for the evaluation of constants may similarly be gleaned from an inspection. These cases follow.

Simple Beam. Uniformly Distributed Load. Figure 105 shows a beam

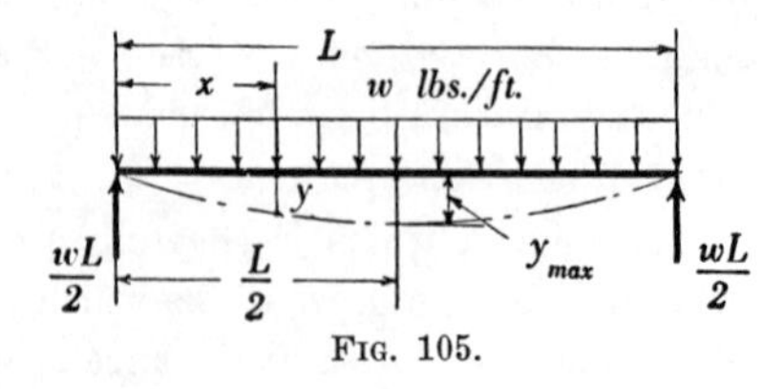

FIG. 105.

of length L, carrying a uniformly distributed load of w lb./ft., which is freely supported at its ends.

$$x : 0\text{–}L$$

$$M_x = +\frac{wLx}{2} - \frac{wx^2}{2}$$

Applying equation (39), $\dfrac{d^2y}{dx^2} = \dfrac{wLx}{2EI} - \dfrac{wx^2}{2EI}$

Integrating, $$\frac{dy}{dx} = \frac{wLx^2}{4EI} - \frac{wx^3}{6EI} + C_1$$

By inspection, when

$$x = \frac{L}{2}, \ \frac{dy}{dx} = 0; \qquad \therefore C_1 = -\frac{wL^3}{24EI}$$

Integrating again,

$$y = \frac{wLx^3}{12EI} - \frac{wx^4}{24EI} - \frac{wL^3x}{24EI} + C_2 \tag{40a}$$

By inspection, when $x = 0, \quad y = 0; \qquad \therefore C_2 = 0$

By inspection, maximum deflection occurs when $x = L/2$, and

$$y_{\text{max.}} = \frac{wL^4}{96EI} - \frac{wL^4}{384EI} - \frac{wL^4}{48EI}$$

$$= -\frac{5}{384}\frac{wL^4}{EI} \tag{41}$$

It will be noted that this expression conforms to the general form of

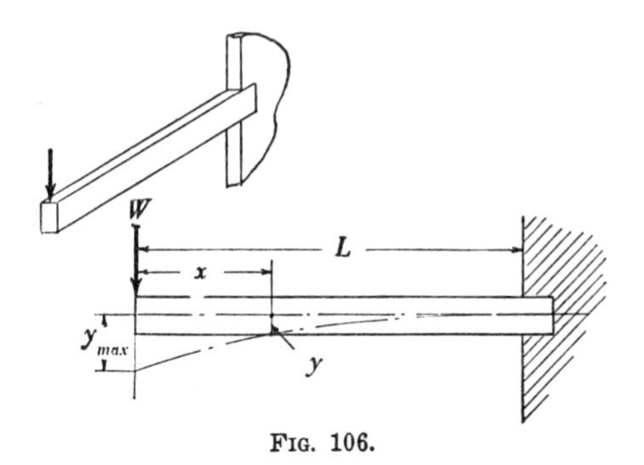

Fig. 106.

the deflection formulae ($y = k\,WL^3/EI$), for the total load $W = wL$.

Cantilever Beam. Single Concentrated Load at Free End. The cantilever beam of Fig. 106 carries a concentrated load, W, at the free end. A cantilever beam is, by definition, rigidly supported at the wall end, and the slope at the wall is zero.

$$x : 0\text{–}L$$

$$M_x = -Wx$$

Applying equation (39),
$$\frac{d^2y}{dx^2} = \frac{-Wx}{EI}$$

$$\frac{dy}{dx} = \frac{-Wx^2}{2EI} + C_1$$

when $x = L,\ \frac{dy}{dx} = 0; \quad \therefore C_1 = +\frac{WL^2}{2EI}$

$$y = -\frac{Wx^3}{6EI} + \frac{WL^2x}{2EI} + C_2$$

when $x = L,\ y = 0; \quad \therefore C_2 = \frac{-WL^3}{3EI}$

Maximum deflection will occur at the free end, when $x = 0$

$$y_{\text{max.}} = -\frac{1}{3}\frac{WL^3}{EI} \tag{42}$$

Cantilever Beam. Uniformly Distributed Load. Figure 107 shows a

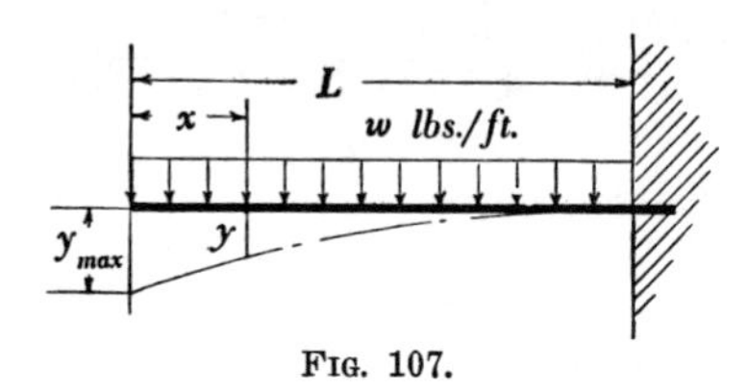

FIG. 107.

cantilever beam, of length L, carrying a uniformly distributed load of w lb./ft.

$$x : 0\text{–}L$$

$$M_x = -\frac{wx^2}{2}$$

Applying equation (39)
$$\frac{d^2y}{dx^2} = -\frac{wx^2}{2EI}$$

$$\frac{dy}{dx} = -\frac{wx^3}{6EI} + C_1$$

when $x = L,\ \frac{dy}{dx} = 0; \quad \therefore C_1 = +\frac{wL^3}{6EI}$

$$y = -\frac{wx^4}{24EI} + \frac{wL^3x}{6EI} + C_2$$

when $x = L,\ y = 0; \quad \therefore C_2 = -\frac{wL^4}{8EI}$

Maximum deflection will occur at the free end, when $x = 0$, and

$$y_{\max.} = -\frac{1}{8}\frac{WL^4}{EI} \tag{43}$$

Cantilever Beam. Couple Applied at Free End. A couple of moment M is applied at the free end of the cantilever beam of Fig. 108. Such a beam

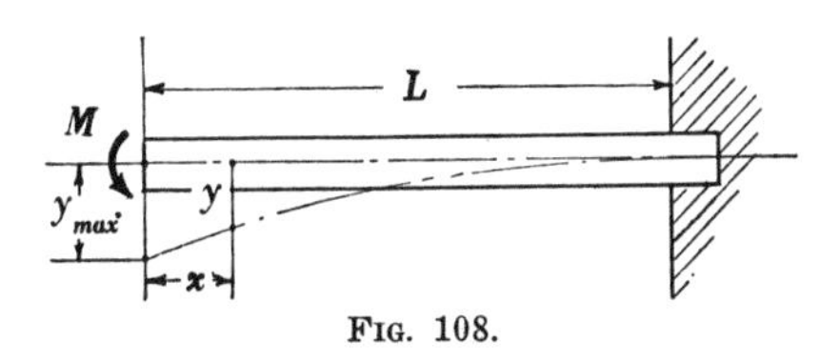

FIG. 108.

has constant bending moment throughout the entire span and is said to be in pure bending.

$$x : 0\text{–}L$$

$$M_x = -M$$

Applying equation (39),

$$\frac{d^2y}{dx^2} = -\frac{M}{EI}$$

$$\frac{dy}{dx} = -\frac{Mx}{EI} + C_1$$

when $x = L,\ \frac{dy}{dx} = 0; \quad \therefore C_1 = +\frac{ML}{EI}$

$$y = -\frac{Mx^2}{2EI} + \frac{MLx}{EI} + C_2$$

wnen $x = L,\ y = 0; \quad \therefore C_2 = -\frac{ML^2}{2EI}$

Maximum deflection will occur at the free end when $x = 0$.

$$y_{\max.} = -\frac{ML^2}{2EI} \tag{44}$$

In each of the preceding examples it has been possible for us to evaluate the constants of integration by means of boundary conditions which were made available by inspection of the elastic curve.

Whenever the elastic curve is symmetrical about its mid-point, inspection of the elastic curve will reveal enough information for evaluation of the constants of integration. For example, in the case of the beam of Fig. 109, the symmetry of the elastic curve presents an opportunity for such evaluation. It is necessary, however, in such an example, to take additional steps in the routine of solution.

The following information is afforded by inspection of the elastic curve. The slope at the center of the beam is zero. Deflection is zero at the supports R_1 and R_2.

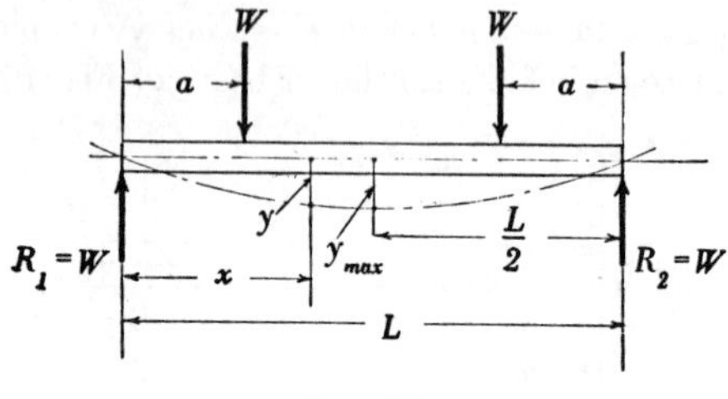

FIG. 109.

The first range of loading includes values of x from 0 to a. In this range the bending moment is

$$M_x = +Wx$$

Applying equation (39) $$\frac{d^2y}{dx^2} = \frac{Wx}{EI}$$

and $$\frac{dy}{dx} = +\frac{Wx^2}{2EI} + C_1 \qquad (1)$$

There is no point of the elastic curve, lying within this range, for which the value of slope is known, and C_1 cannot be evaluated by inspection.

Continuing, we again integrate, and

$$y = +\frac{Wx^3}{6EI} + C_1x + C_2$$

When $$x = 0, \quad y = 0; \qquad \therefore C_2 = 0$$

then $$y = +\frac{Wx^3}{6EI} + C_1x \qquad (2)$$

We now enter the second range of loading, which includes values of x from a to L–a. (The origin of x is being continuously taken from the left end of the beam.)

The general expression for bending moment in the second range is

$$M_x = +Wx - W(x - a) = +Wa$$

Again applying equation (39),

$$\frac{d^2y}{dx^2} = +\frac{Wa}{EI}$$

$$\frac{dy}{dx} = +\frac{Wax}{EI} + C_3$$

In this range of loading, a point of zero slope occurs when $x = L/2$, and $C_3 = -WaL/2EI$.

Then
$$\frac{dy}{dx} = +\frac{Wax}{EI} - \frac{WaL}{2EI} \tag{3}$$

and
$$y = +\frac{Wax^2}{2EI} - \frac{WaLx}{2EI} + C_4 \tag{4}$$

The general equations of slope and deflection now contain two constants of integration, C_1 and C_4.

The junction of the two ranges of loading occurs when $x = a$. At this point, common to both ranges, the value of slope given by equation (1) is identical with the value of the slope given by equation (3).

Then
$$\frac{Wa^2}{2EI} + C_1 = \frac{Wa^2}{EI} - \frac{WaL}{2EI}$$
$$C_1 = \frac{Wa^2}{2EI} - \frac{WaL}{2EI}$$

Similarly, the value of deflection at $x = a$ must be the same whether equation (2) or (4) is used
$$\frac{Wa^3}{6EI} + \frac{Wa^3}{2EI} - \frac{Wa^2L}{2EI} = \frac{Wa^3}{2EI} - \frac{Wa^2L}{2EI} + C_4$$

and
$$C_4 = \frac{Wa^3}{6EI}$$

The final forms of the general equations of the elastic curve are

$$x : 0 - a$$
$$y = \frac{Wx^3}{6EI} + \frac{Wa^2x}{2EI} - \frac{WaLx}{2EI}$$
$$x : a - (L - a)$$
$$y = \frac{Wax^2}{2EI} - \frac{WaLx}{2EI} + \frac{Wa^3}{6EI}$$

The maximum deflection will occur at mid-span, when $x = L/2$.

$$y_{\text{max.}} = \frac{WaL^2}{8EI} - \frac{WaL^2}{4EI} + \frac{Wa^3}{6EI}$$
$$= -\frac{Wa}{24EI}(3L^2 - 4a^2) \tag{45}$$

Non-symmetrical Loading. The technique of associating the equations of slope and deflection at the junction of ranges of loading which was employed in the preceding example is effective, even though a first inspection of the elastic curve may yield little or no information to assist in deter mining the constants of integration.

We note that the simple beam of Fig. 110 carries a single concentrated load, W, which is not located at mid-span. Since the elastic curve of such a beam is not symmetrical, the only information which we may glean by inspection of the elastic curve is the fact that deflection is zero when

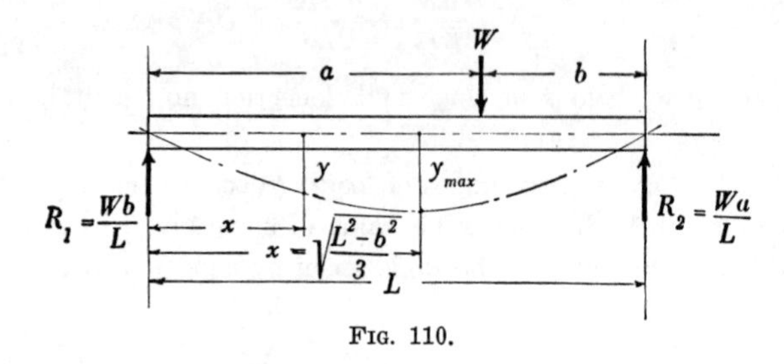

FIG. 110.

$x = 0$ and $x = L$. The maximum deflection will, of course, occur when slope is zero, but the location of that section is not made available by inspection.

In the first range of loading,

$$x : 0 - a$$

$$M_x = +\frac{Wbx}{L}$$

Applying equation (39), $$\frac{d^2y}{dx^2} = +\frac{Wbx}{LEI}$$

$$\frac{dy}{dx} = +\frac{Wbx^2}{2LEI} + C_1 \tag{1}$$

$$y = \frac{Wbx^3}{6LEI} + C_1x + (C_2 = 0) \tag{2}$$

In the second range of loading,

$$x : a - L$$

$$M_x = +\frac{Wbx}{L} - W(x - a)$$

Again, applying equation (39),

$$\frac{d^2y}{dx^2} = +\frac{Wbx}{LEI} - \frac{W(x - a)}{EI}$$

$$\frac{dy}{dx} = +\frac{Wbx^2}{2LEI} - \frac{W(x - a)^2}{2EI} + C_3 \tag{3}$$

$$y = +\frac{Wbx^3}{6LEI} - \frac{W(x - a)^3}{6EI} + C_3x + C_4 \tag{4}$$

when $x = L,\quad y = 0;\qquad C_4 = -\frac{WbL^2}{6EI} + \frac{Wb^3}{6EI} - C_3L$

We now consider the conditions at the junction of the two ranges of loading ($x = a$). The slope given by equation (1) is now identical with that given by equation (3).

$$\frac{Wba^2}{2LEI} + C_1 = \frac{Wba^2}{2LEI} + C_3$$
$$\therefore C_1 = C_3$$

Similarly, the deflection given by equation (2) is identical with that given by equation (4) when $x = a$.

$$\frac{Wba^3}{6LEI} + C_3a = \frac{Wba^3}{6LEI} + C_3a - \frac{WbL^2}{6EI} + \frac{Wb^3}{6EI} - C_3L$$
$$\therefore C_3 = -\frac{WbL}{6EI} + \frac{Wb^3}{6LEI}$$
$$= \frac{Wb}{6LEI}(b^2 - L^2)$$

All constants of integration have now been evaluated. The general equations of slope and deflection in the first range are

$$x : 0 - a,$$
$$\frac{dy}{dx} = \frac{Wb}{6LEI}(3x^2 - L^2 + b^2)$$
$$y = \frac{Wbx}{6LEI}(x^2 - L^2 + b^2)$$

The location of the section at which deflection will be a maximum is determined by finding where the slope is zero.

$$\frac{Wb}{6LEI}(3x^2 - L + b^2) = 0$$
$$3x^2 = L^2 - b^2$$

and

$$x = \sqrt{\frac{L^2 - b^2}{3}}$$

If we introduce this value of x in the general equation of deflection,

$$y_{\text{max.}} = -\frac{Wb}{9\sqrt{3}LEI}(L^2 - b^2)^{\frac{3}{2}} \tag{46}$$

Superposition. We have already employed the technique of superposition (see Art. 15) to obtain a total result by investigation and addition of partial effects. The same technique furnishes an effective method in the solution of many of the problems of deflection.

The validity of superposition may be confirmed by noting that the total bending moment at any section of a beam is the sum of the bending moments at that section caused by the individual forces acting on the beam. If the total bending moment at any section is called M, and the bending moments of individual forces are M_1, M_2, M_3, etc.

$$M = M_1 + M_2 + M_3 + \cdots$$

Then

$$\frac{d^2y}{dx^2} = \left(\frac{d^2y}{dx^2}\right)_1 + \left(\frac{d^2y}{dx^2}\right)_2 + \left(\frac{d^2y}{dx^2}\right)_3 + \cdots$$

and

$$y = y_1 + y_2 + y_3 + \cdots$$

It is frequently simpler to obtain a total deflection by adding the deflections produced by individual loads, instead of laboriously developing a survey through several ranges of loading when many forces are acting.

For example, in the case of such a beam as that shown in Fig. 111-a, the maximum deflection will occur at mid-span.

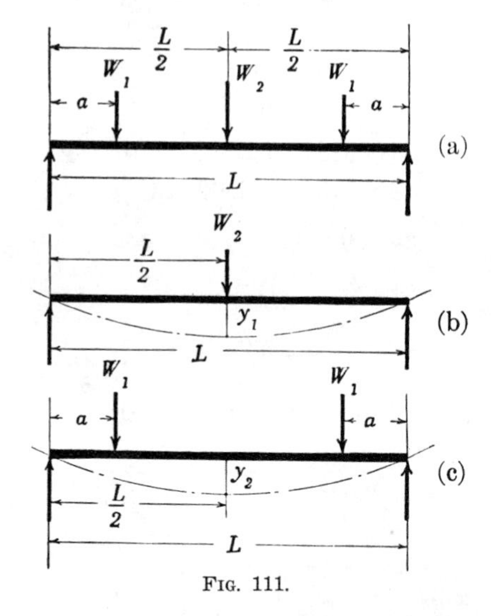

FIG. 111.

If the problem is divided into two stages, we may take advantage of the integration already performed in the preceding paragraphs.

Figure 111-b shows one of the stages of the superposition. The deflection at mid-span due to W_2 is, by equation (40),

$$y_1 = -\frac{1}{48}\frac{W_2L^3}{EI}$$

Figure 111-c shows a second stage of the superposition. The deflection at mid-span resulting from the equal and symmetrical loads W_1 is, by equation (45),

$$y_2 = \frac{-W_1a}{24EI}(3L^2 - 4a^2)$$

The maximum deflection is obtained by superimposing the partial effects, and

$$y_{\max.} = y_1 + y_2 = -\frac{1}{48EI}\left[W_2L^3 + W_1a(6L^2 - 8a^2)\right] \qquad \textbf{(47)}$$

Illustrative Example I. The simple beam of Fig. 112 carries the indicated loads. We are to determine the maximum deflection, and the deflection at 3 ft. from the end.

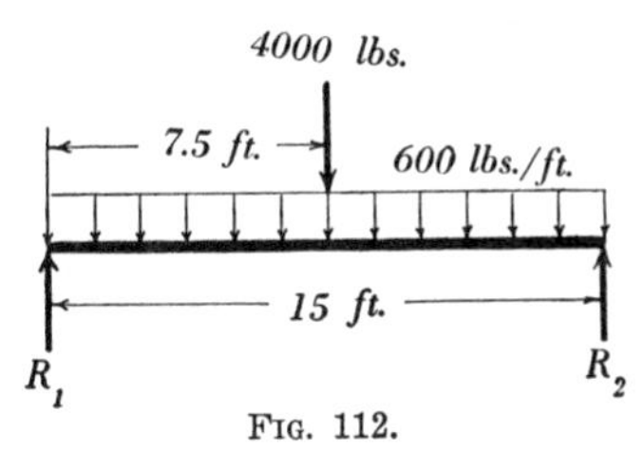

FIG. 112.

The beam is an American Standard I-beam, 8 in. × 23.0 lb./ft., having a moment of inertia about its neutral axis $I = 64.2$ in.^{4} $E = 30 \times 10^6$ psi.

The maximum deflection occurs at mid-span.

Due to the 4000-lb. concentrated load, applying equation (40), we find

$$\begin{aligned} y_1 &= -\frac{1}{48}\frac{WL^3}{EI} \\ &= -\frac{1}{48}\frac{4000 \times (15)^3}{30 \times 10^6 \times 64.2} \times (12)^3 \\ &= -0.252 \text{ in.} \end{aligned}$$

Because of the uniformly distributed load of 600 lb./ft., applying equation (41),

$$\begin{aligned} y_2 &= -\frac{5}{384}\frac{wL^4}{EI} \\ &= -\frac{5}{384 \times 30 \times 10^6 \times 64.2} 600 \times (15)^4 \times (12)^3 \\ &= -0.355 \text{ in.} \end{aligned}$$

The maximum deflection will be

$$y_{\max} = y_1 + y_2 = -0.252 - 0.355 = -0.607 \text{ in.}$$

The deflection at 3 ft. from the left (or right) end may be determined by superposition of the results found by using the general equations of deflection for each of the individual loads.

For the concentrated load of 4000 lb., the general equation [equation (39a)] is

$$\begin{aligned} y &= \frac{Wx^3}{12EI} - \frac{WL^2x}{16EI} \\ &= \frac{Wx}{48EI}(4x^2 - 3L^2) \end{aligned}$$

When $x = 3$ ft.

$$\begin{aligned} y_3 &= \frac{4000 \times 3}{48 \times 30 \times 10^6 \times 64.2}[4(3)^2 - 3(15)^2] \times (12)^3 \\ &= -0.143 \text{ in.} \end{aligned}$$

For the distributed load, the general equation [equation (40a)] is

$$y = \frac{wLx^3}{12EI} - \frac{wx^4}{24EI} - \frac{wL^3x}{24EI}$$
$$= \frac{wx}{24EI}(2Lx^2 - x^3 - L^3)$$

When $x = 3$ ft.

$$y_4 = \frac{600 \times 3}{24 \times 30 \times 10^6 \times 64.2}[(2 \times 15 \times (3)^2 - (3)^3 - (15)^3] \times (12)^3$$
$$= -0.211 \text{ in.}$$

The total deflection at $x = 3$ ft. will be

$$y = y_3 + y_4$$
$$= -0.143 - 0.211 = -0.354 \text{ in.}$$

The problem of determining the deflection when $x = 3$ ft. may also be solved by determining the general expression for bending moment, and integrating.

In this beam,

$$R_1 = \frac{4000}{2} + \frac{600 \times 15}{2} = 6500 \text{ lb.}$$
$$x : 0 - 7.5 \text{ ft.}$$
$$M_x = 6500x - \frac{600x^2}{2} = \frac{EI\,d^2y}{dx^2}$$
$$\frac{dy}{dx} = \frac{1}{EI}\left[3250x^2 - 100x^3\right] + C_1$$

When $x = 7.5$, $\dfrac{dy}{dx} = 0$; $\quad \therefore C_1 = \dfrac{1}{EI}[-3250(7.5)^2 + 100(7.5)^3] = -\dfrac{140{,}625}{EI}$

$$y = \frac{1}{EI}\left[\frac{3250x^3}{3} - \frac{100x^4}{4} - 140{,}625x + (C_2 = 0)\right]$$
$$y_{3\,\text{ft.}} = \frac{1}{30 \times 10^6 \times 64.2}\left[\frac{3250(3)^3}{3} - \frac{100\,(3)^4}{4} - 140{,}625(3)\right] \times (12)^3 = -0.354 \text{ in.}$$

Illustrative Example II. We are to determine the maximum deflection of the cantilever beam (Fig. 113-a). $E = 1.2 \times 10$ psi.

The deflection at the free end resulting from the concentrated load of 1000 lb., if acting alone, will be, by equation (42)

$$y_1 = -\frac{1}{3}\frac{WL^3}{EI}$$
$$= -\frac{1}{3} \times \frac{1000 \times (9)^3}{1.2 \times 10^6 \times 864} \times (12)^3$$
$$= -0.405 \text{ in.}$$

The deflection at the free end resulting from the distributed load, if acting alone, may be obtained by noting that the elastic curve (Fig. 113-b) is parabolic from the wall to the end of the distributed load. It then becomes a straight line, inclined at the slope of the section at the end of the distributed load.

The distance *ab* may be determined by using equation (43).

$$ab = -\frac{1}{8}\frac{wL^4}{EI} = -\frac{1}{8} \times \frac{200 \times (6)^4}{1.2 \times 10^6 \times 864}(12)^3$$
$$= -0.054 \text{ in.}$$

The slope θ_A may be determined by using the general equation of slope given on page 164.

$$\frac{dy}{dx} = -\frac{wx^3}{6EI} + \frac{wL^3}{6EI}$$

$$= 0 + \frac{200 \times (6)^3}{6 \times 1.2 \times 10^6 \times 864} \times (12)^2$$

$$= 0.001 \text{ radians}$$

$$de = -0.001 \times 3 \times 12 = -0.036 \text{ in.}$$

The total deflection at the free end caused by the distributed load is

$$cd = ce + de$$
$$= -0.054 - 0.036 = -0.090 \text{ in.}$$

The total deflection is

$$y = -0.405 - 0.090 = -0.495 \text{ in.}$$

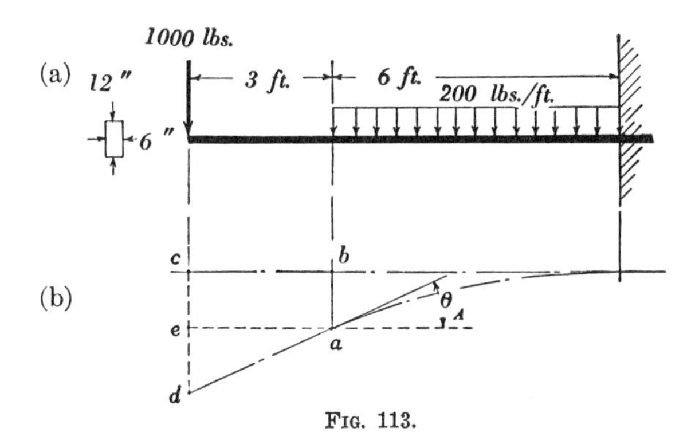

FIG. 113.

34. Deflection Theory As a Tool of Analysis. Statically Indeterminate Cases. We have, thus far, employed the deflection theory to evaluate the slope and deflection—the geometrical properties of the elastic curves of beams.

In addition to such evaluation, the theory of deflection adds an important ally to the conditions of equilibrium and makes possible the solution of many problems which are statically indeterminate.

For example, the cantilever beam of Fig. 114-a is supported by a concentrated force, F, at its right end, in addition to the support furnished by the wall. If we isolate, as a free body, the portion of the beam lying outside of the wall (Fig. 114-b) we find that the system of external forces consists of the couple M_1, the shearing force V_1 at the face of the wall, the force F, and the uniformly distributed load of w lb./ft.

This coplanar system of forces is statically indeterminate, for we have available but two conditions of equilibrium, $\Sigma F = 0$ and $\Sigma M = 0$. Three of the elements of the force system are unknown—M_1, V_1, and F. If we

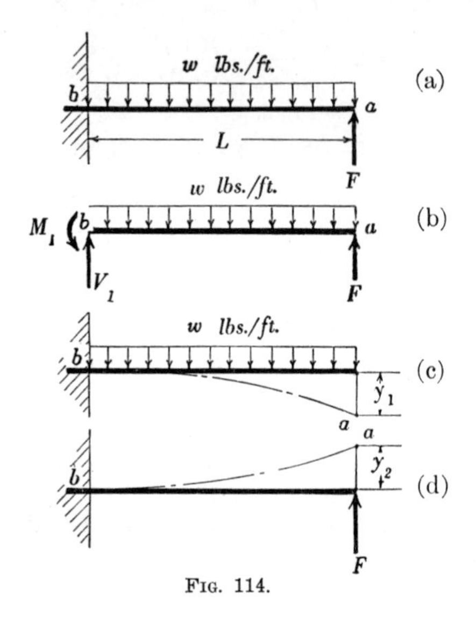

FIG. 114.

add the equation of deflection to the two equations of equilibrium, the problem becomes determinate, for we now have three simultaneous equations at our command.

The relative levels of points a, at which force F is applied, and b, the wall level, will influence the magnitude of F. To illustrate the method of attack, we shall assume that a and b are on the same level.

The technique of superposition is effective here, and as a first stage of loading we shall consider the elastic curve of the beam when only the uniformly distributed load is applied (Fig. 114-c). Under this loading, the deflection of point a downward from point b is, by equation (43),

$$y_1 = -\frac{1}{8}\frac{wL^4}{EI}$$

We now consider the deflection of the cantilever beam when carrying only a single concentrated load F at its free end (Fig. 114-d).

The deflection of point a under this loading will be upward from point b, and will be, applying equation (42)

$$y_2 = +\frac{1}{3}\frac{FL^3}{EI}$$

When both the uniformly distributed load and force F are acting on the beam, point a is to be on the same level as point b, as announced in the original data of the problem.

Then

$$y_1 + y_2 = 0$$

$$-\frac{1}{8}\frac{wL^4}{EI} + \frac{1}{3}\frac{FL^3}{EI} = 0$$

$$F = \frac{3}{8}wL$$

Now that force F has been determined, the shearing force V_1 and the wall or end couple M_1 may be evaluated by applying the conditions of equilibrium.

$$\Sigma F = 0$$

$$+F - wL + V_1 = 0$$

$$V_1 = wL - \frac{3}{8}wL = \frac{5}{8}wL$$

Taking moments about an axis at point b,

$$\Sigma M = 0$$

$$+F \times L - \frac{wL^2}{2} + M_1 = 0$$

$$M_1 = -\frac{3}{8}wL^2 + \frac{wL^2}{2} = \frac{wL^2}{8}$$

Another opportunity for use of the deflection theory in an investigation of a statically indeterminate beam is presented in Fig. 115-a. This beam

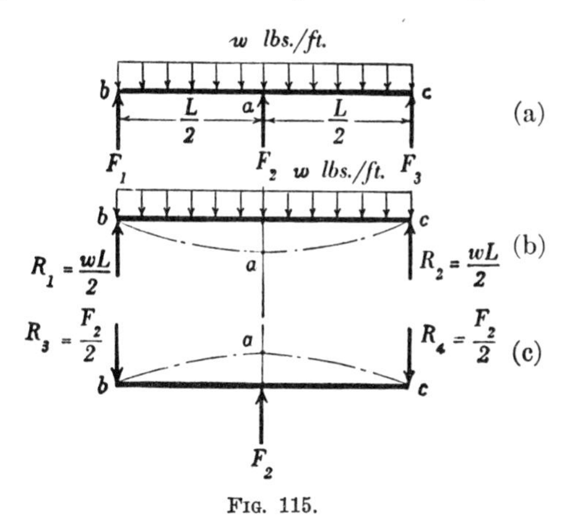

FIG. 115.

carries a uniformly distributed load of w lb./ft. and is supported by the concentrated forces F_1, F_2, and F_3. All three supports are on the same level.

We first consider the beam when loaded with only the uniformly distributed load (Fig. 115-b).

The deflection of point a from the end points b and c will be, by equation (41),

$$y_1 = -\frac{5}{384}\frac{wL^4}{EI}$$

We next consider the beam when loaded with only a single concentrated force, F_2, applied at point a (Fig. 115-c). The deflection of a, relative to points b and c will now be, by equation (40),

$$y_2 = +\frac{1}{48}\frac{F_2L^3}{EI}$$

With points a, b, and c on the same level,

$$y_1 + y_2 = 0$$

$$-\frac{5}{384}\frac{wL^4}{EI} + \frac{1}{48}\frac{F_2L^3}{EI} = 0$$

$$F_2 = \frac{5}{8}wL$$

$$F_1 = F_3 = \frac{3}{16}wL$$

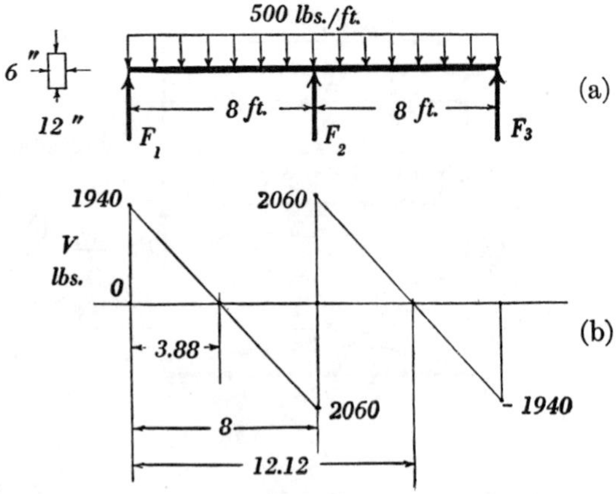

Fig. 116.

Illustrative Example. The beam of Fig. 116-a carries a uniformly distributed load of 500 lb./ft. $E = 1.2 \times 10^6$ psi. When beams are placed in a structure, it is not always possible to maintain exact alignment of the supporting forces, and in this case the support F_2 is applied $\frac{1}{8}$ in. below the level of F_1 and F_3.

We are to determine the maximum bending moment in the beam.

We first apply the deflection theory, using the method of superposition to determine F_2, by equations (40) and (41),

$$+\frac{1}{48}\frac{F_2L^3}{EI} - \frac{5}{384}\frac{wL^4}{EI} = -\frac{1}{8}$$

$$+\frac{F_2(16)^3}{48 \times 1.2 \times 10^6 \times 864} \times (12)^3 - \frac{5 \times 500 \times (16)^4}{384 \times 1.2 \times 10^6 \times 864} \times (12)^3 = -\frac{1}{8}$$

$$F_2 = 4120 \text{ lb.}$$

By taking moments about an axis at the center of the beam, we find

$$\Sigma M = 0 \qquad +8F_1 - 500 \times 8 \times 4 + 500 \times 8 \times 4 - 8F_3 = 0$$

$$\therefore F_1 = F_3$$

Applying $\Sigma F = 0$,

$$2F_1 + 4120 - 500 \times 16 = 0$$

$$F_1 = F_3 = 1940 \text{ lb.}$$

The shearing force diagram (Fig. 116-b) is now plotted to explore the beam for sections of maximum bending moment which will occur when $x = 3.88$ ft., 8 ft., and 12.12 ft. all measured from an origin at the left end of the beam.

$$x = 3.88 \qquad M_1 = 1940 \times 3.88 - \frac{500 \times (3.88)^2}{2}$$

$$= +3764 \text{ ft.-lb.}$$

$$x = 8 \qquad M_2 = 1940 \times 8 - \frac{500 \times (8)^2}{2}$$

$$= -480 \text{ ft.-lb.}$$

$$x = 12.12 \qquad M_3 = +3764 \text{ ft.-lb.}$$

The maximum bending moment in the beam is, therefore, $M = 3764$ ft.-lb.

We shall encounter additional examples of the use of the deflection theory as a tool in the attack on statically indeterminate cases when we consider the moment-area method as an additional technique of solution.

35. Built-in Beams. When beams are supported by walls, or fastened to columns, as indicated in Fig. 117, the system of supporting forces is statically indeterminate. Again, the deflection theory furnishes the equation of the elastic curve to assist the conditions of equilibrium in effecting a solution.

In such cases the nature of the elastic curve at the supports must be known. When the elastic curve is horizontal at the supports ($dy/dx = 0$), the beam is called a *fixed-end* beam. Such a condition demands the provision of a bending moment, M_1, which is great enough to bend the elastic curve at its end so that the slope will be zero.

When the magnitude of the end moment is not large enough to return the elastic curve to a condition of zero slope at the walls, the beam is said to be *partially restrained.* Such a case arises, for example, when a beam is supported by columns which will themselves bend when the beam is loaded (Fig. 118). The elastic curve of the beam will assume a position as shown in the figure, and the slope at the ends of the beam will not be equal to zero.

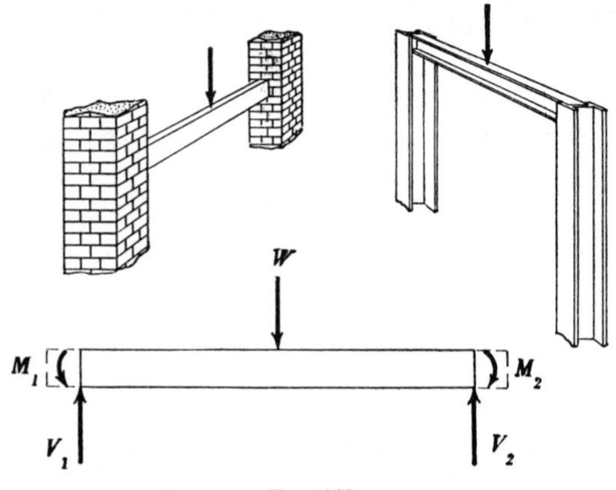

FIG. 117.

The analysis of such cases may be quite complex, particularly when a structure consists of an assembly of several interconnected beams and columns. In such indeterminate structures, designers have recourse to theories of analysis which have as their objective the determination of the pattern of moment distribution. The method of attack most widely accepted was developed by Prof. Hardy Cross. Others have been developed, and may be found in engineering literature devoted to structural analysis. Such cases lie beyond the scope of our present discussion, which will be confined to cases where either the magnitude of the end bending moment or the magnitude of the slope at the end of a single beam is available.

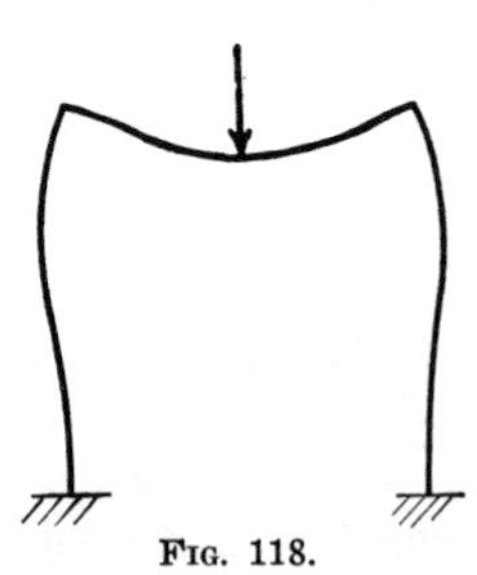

FIG. 118.

We shall first consider the fixed-end beam shown in Fig. 119-a, which is loaded with a uniformly distributed load of w lb./ft. The pattern of bending moment distribution along the beam is to be determined, and an expression for the maximum deflection derived.

Since we are concerned with the portion of the beam lying outside of the walls, a free body is isolated as shown in Fig. 119-b. The external forces acting on this free body comprise the end couples M_1 and M_2, the shearing forces at the face of each wall, V_1 and V_2, and the uniformly distributed load of w lb./ft.

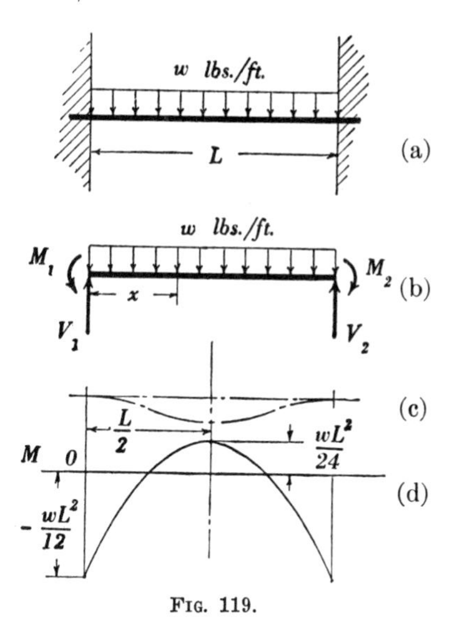

FIG. 119.

The general expression for bending moment at distance x from the left wall is

$$M_x = +V_1x - M_1 - \frac{wx^2}{2}$$

Then, applying equation (39),

$$\frac{d^2y}{dx^2} = \frac{1}{EI}\left(+V_1x - M_1 - \frac{wx^2}{2}\right)$$

$$\frac{dy}{dx} = \frac{1}{EI}\left(+\frac{V_1x^2}{2} - M_1x - \frac{wx^3}{6}\right) + C_1$$

The slope of the beam is zero at $x = 0$ and $x = L$, from the conditions originally set for the problem. We may suspect that in this case of symmetry, V_1 will numerically equal V_2, and M_1 will numerically equal M_2, and that there will be an additional section of slope equal to zero at $x = L/2$. Such an assumption appears to be admissible, but sound engineering philosophy demands that assumptions must be validated by checking, and we shall therefore proceed to evaluate all conditions before drawing conclusions based only upon an assumption that geometrical symmetry insures symmetry in the force system.

When $x = 0, \quad \frac{dy}{dx} = 0 \qquad \therefore C_1 = 0$

When $x = L, \quad \frac{dy}{dx} = 0$

and
$$+\frac{V_1L^2}{2} - M_1L - \frac{wL^3}{6} = 0$$

$$+\frac{V_1L}{2} - M_1 = \frac{wL^2}{6} \tag{1}$$

Integrating the slope equation,

$$y = \frac{1}{EI}\left(\frac{V_1x^3}{6} - \frac{M_1x^2}{2} - \frac{wx^4}{24}\right) + C_2$$

When $x = 0, \quad y = 0 \qquad \therefore C_2 = 0$

When $x = L, \quad y = 0$

and
$$+\frac{V_1L^3}{6} - \frac{M_1L^2}{2} - \frac{wL^4}{24} = 0$$

$$+\frac{V_1L}{3} - \frac{M_1}{1} = \frac{wL^2}{12} \tag{2}$$

Solving equations (1) and (2) simultaneously,

$$V_1 = \frac{wL}{2}$$

and
$$M_1 = \frac{wL^2}{12}$$

The bending moment at the left end is therefore a negative bending moment of magnitude $wL_2/12$, producing, as we suspect from the nature of the elastic curve of Fig. 119-c, tension in the top fibers of the beam. Now, applying the condition of equilibrium $\Sigma F = 0$,

$$+V_1 + V_2 - wL = 0$$

$$V_2 = wL - \frac{wL}{2} = \frac{wL}{2}$$

$$\therefore V_2 = V_1$$

The end shearing forces are, therefore, quantitatively equal, but produce opposite directions of shearing force at sections of the beam.

Substituting the determined values of M_1 and V_1 in the general equation of bending moment,

$$M_x = V_1x - M_1 - \frac{wx^2}{2}$$

When $x = L, \quad M_x = M_2 \qquad M_2 = \frac{wL^2}{2} - \frac{wL^2}{12} - \frac{wL^2}{2} = -\frac{wL^2}{12}$

$$\therefore M_2 = M_1$$

The bending-moment equation for the entire span is

$$M_x = \frac{wLx}{2} - \frac{wL^2}{12} - \frac{wx^2}{2}$$

When $x = L/2$ $\quad M = \frac{wL^2}{4} - \frac{wL^2}{12} - \frac{wL^2}{8} = +\frac{wL^2}{24}$

Let us now check to see whether our assumption that zero slope, and hence, maximum deflection, occur at mid-span, when $x = L/2$.

The general equation of slope is

$$\frac{dy}{dx} = \frac{1}{EI}\left(\frac{V_1x^2}{2} - M_1x - \frac{wx^3}{6}\right)$$

Substituting the values of V_1 and M_1 obtained above when $x = L/2$

$$\frac{dy}{dx} = \frac{1}{EI}\left(\frac{wL}{4}\frac{L^2}{4} - \frac{wL^2}{12}\frac{L}{2} - \frac{w}{6}\frac{L^3}{8}\right)$$

which does equal zero, and the assumption is validated. The deflection will, therefore, be maximum when $x = L/2$. The general equation of deflection is

$$y = \frac{1}{EI}\left(\frac{wLx^3}{12} - \frac{wL^2x^2}{24} - \frac{wx^4}{24}\right)$$

When $x = L/2$

$$y = y_{\max.} = \frac{1}{EI}\left(\frac{wL^4}{96} - \frac{wL^4}{96} - \frac{wL^4}{384}\right) = -\frac{1}{384}\frac{wL^4}{EI} \qquad \textbf{(48)}$$

The results of this investigation reveal the benefits which are to be derived by introducing restraint at the ends of beams, instead of allowing those beams to be freely supported.

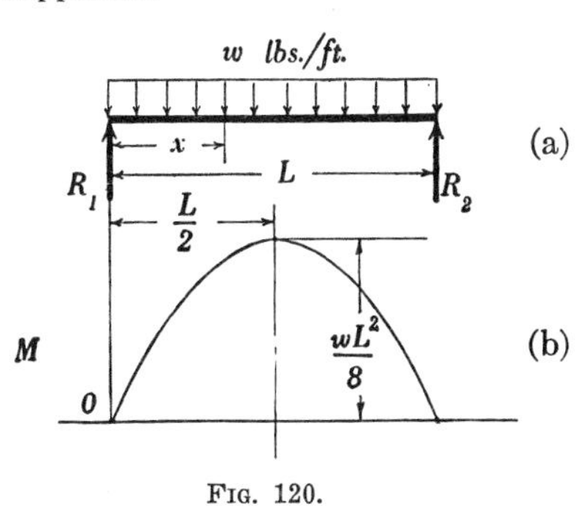

FIG. 120.

The bending moment equation of the *freely* supported beam of Fig. 120-a is

$$M_x = \frac{wL}{2}x - \frac{wx^2}{2} \qquad (3)$$

The bending moment diagram is, therefore, a parabola of the second degree, as shown, having a maximum value $M_{\text{max.}} = wL^2/8$ when $x = L/2$.

The bending moment equation of the *fixed* end beam (Fig. 119) carrying the same loading is

$$M_x = \frac{wLx}{2} - \frac{wx^2}{2} - \frac{wL^2}{12} \tag{4}$$

The maximum negative bending moment in this beam is $M_1 = -wL^2/12$ at the ends when $x = 0$ or L; the maximum positive bending moment is $M_2 = +wL^2/24$ at mid-span when $x = L/2$. The bending moment diagram of this beam is shown in Fig. 119-d.

Comparison of equations (3) and (4) above indicates that both are equations of a parabola of the second degree, and differ only in that equation (4) contains an additional constant term, whose influence is to decrease all ordinates of the parabola by a constant amount. The bending moment curve of the second case is identical in shape with that of the first case, and differs only in that all values of bending moment have been decreased by the same amount ($M_1 = -wL^2/12$). The influence of restraining the ends of a beam by applying end moments is, then, to decrease the magnitude of the maximum bending moment and, in turn, to decrease the value of the required section modulus. It follows that lighter beams may be employed for given loading when the ends are restrained.

The ratio of the required section moduli in the case of two beams, of the same material, same cross-section, and carrying the same uniformly distributed load is

$$\frac{\text{Simple Beam}}{\text{Fixed-end Beam}} = \frac{(I/y)_S}{(I/y)_F} = \frac{M_S}{M_F} = \frac{wL^2/8}{wL^2/12} = \frac{3}{2}$$

The rigid restraint of the fixed-end beam shows a marked advantage over the freedom of the simple beam in the saving of material. The advantage is not usually as great as the above theoretical ratio would indicate, for some yielding of the end supports in an actual structure or machine will take place, and the advantage may be appreciably reduced.

The comparison of the values of maximum deflection in both of the above types of beam further emphasizes the gain which is introduced by end restraint.

The maximum deflection of the fixed-end beam is $y = 1/384(wL^4/EI)$, [equation (48)], while that of the simple beam is $y = 5/384(wL^4/EI)$ [equation (41)], or 5 times as great.

We shall make one additional comparison between the fixed-end and simple beams, confining our investigation in this case, as in the former one, to a symmetrical beam. When non-symmetrical cases arise, the moment-area method, which is discussed in the succeeding articles is usually more efficient than the analytical method, and should be used as the technique of integration.

The beam of Fig. 121-a carries a single concentrated load, W, at mid-span. The beam is fixed at its ends.

The portion of the beam which lies outside the walls has again been selected as a free body (Fig. 121-b) and the system of external forces is shown. The assumption that such symmetry produces symmetry in the distribution of the force system has been validated in the preceding example, where similar conditions were encountered.

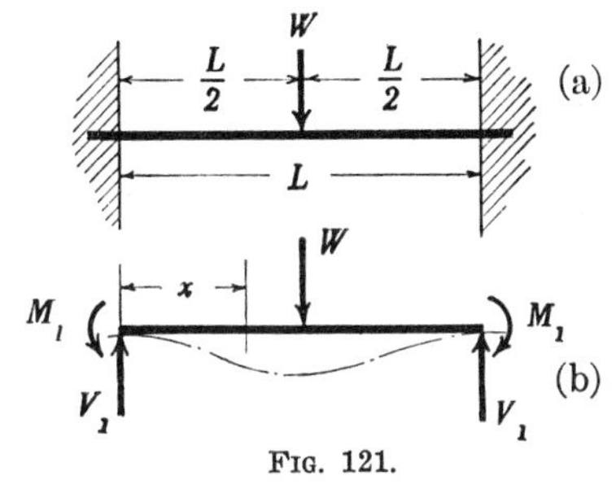

FIG. 121.

Inspection of the elastic curve reveals the following data:

When $x = 0$ $\qquad \dfrac{dy}{dx} = 0$ and $y = 0$

When $x = L/2$ $\qquad \dfrac{dy}{dx} = 0$ and $y = y_{\text{max.}}$

When $x = L$ $\qquad \dfrac{dy}{dx} = 0$ and $y = 0$

The bending moment in the first range of loading is

$$x : 0\text{–}\frac{L}{2}$$

$$M_x = +V_1x - M_1$$

$$= \frac{W}{2}x - M_1$$

Applying equation (39),

$$\frac{d^2y}{dx^2} = \frac{1}{EI}\left(\frac{W}{2}x - M_1\right)$$

$$\frac{dy}{dx} = \frac{1}{EI}\left[\frac{Wx^2}{4} - M_1x\right] + (C_1 = 0)$$

When $x = L/2$, $\qquad \dfrac{dy}{dx} = 0$

then $\qquad \dfrac{WL^2}{16} - \dfrac{M_1L}{2} = 0$

and $\qquad M_1 = -\dfrac{WL}{8}$

The bending moment will be maximum when $x = 0$ or when $x = L/2$.

When $x = L/2$, $$M = \frac{W}{2}\frac{L}{2} - \frac{WL}{8} = +\frac{WL}{8}$$

The maximum bending moment is therefore ½ that of the simple beam.

Integrating the slope equation, we have

$$y = \frac{1}{EI}\left[\frac{Wx^3}{12} - \frac{WL}{16}x^2\right] + (C_2 = 0)$$

when $x = L/2$

$$y = y_{\text{max.}} = \frac{1}{EI}\left[\frac{WL^3}{96} - \frac{WL^3}{64}\right] = -\frac{1}{192}\frac{WL^3}{EI} \tag{49}$$

The maximum deflection is therefore only ¼ that of the simple beam, carrying the same loading [see equation (40)].

Illustrative Example I. The beam shown in Fig. 122 is a 10-in × 54 lb./ft. Wide-Flange steel beam. $E = 30 \times 10^6$ psi. $I = 305.7$ in.^{4} $S = 60.4$ in.^{3} The ends

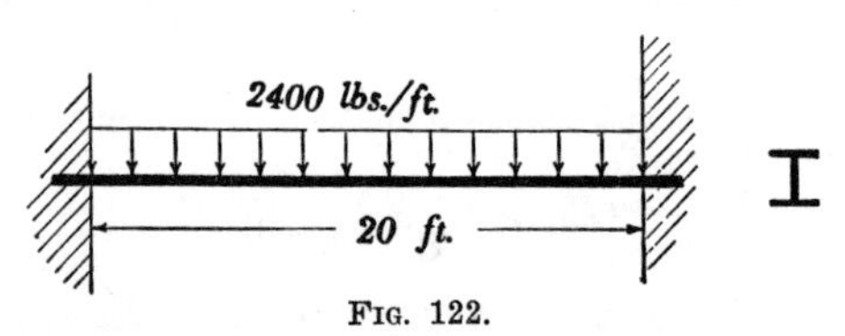

FIG. 122.

are fixed, and the beam carries a uniformly distributed load of 2400 lb./ft., which includes its own weight. The unsupported span length is 20 ft.

The following quantities are to be determined:

a) The maximum bending stress.
b) The maximum deflection.
c) The location of the points of inflection.

a) The maximum bending moment (see page 180) is $M = wL^2/12$.

$$s = \frac{M\,y_{\text{max.}}}{I} = \frac{2400 \times (20)^2 \times 12}{12 \times 60.4} = 15{,}900 \text{ psi}$$

b) The maximum deflection is, by equation (48),

$$y = -\frac{1}{384}\frac{wL^4}{EI}$$
$$= -\frac{1}{384} \times \frac{2400 \times (20)^4}{30 \times 10^6 \times 305.7} \times (12)^3 = -0.189 \text{ in.}$$

c) Points of inflection of the elastic curve will occur when the bending moment is equal to zero.

The bending moment equation for the beam was determined in the preceding article as

$$M_x = \frac{wLx}{2} - \frac{wx^2}{2} - \frac{wL^2}{12}$$

Then $$0 = \frac{2400 \times 20x}{2} - \frac{-2400x^2}{2}\frac{-2400 \times (20)^2}{12}$$

$$x = 10 \pm 5.77 = 15.77 \text{ ft. and } 4.23 \text{ ft.}$$

Illustrative Example II. The beam of Fig. 123 is *partially restrained* at the end walls, by a bending moment of $-18{,}000$ ft.-lb. The beam carries a uniformly distributed load of 600 lb./ft., and a single concentrated load of 6,000 lb. at the central section. $E = 30 \times 10^6$ psi. If the maximum allowable bending stress is 20,000 psi, the required modulus is to be determined and a suitable American

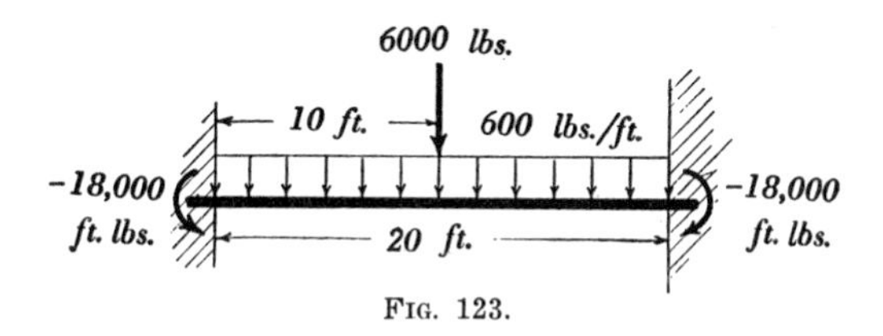

FIG. 123.

Standard I-beam is to be selected. The maximum deflection, and the slope of the beam as it enters the wall, are also to be determined.

By inspection, the following properties of the elastic curve are available:

When $x = 0$, $\quad y = 0$

when $x = L/2$, $\quad \dfrac{dy}{dx} = 0$ and $y = y_{\text{max.}}$

when $x = L$, $\quad y = 0$

x : 0–10 ft.

$$M_x = +9000\,x - \frac{600x^2}{2} - 18{,}000$$

The maximum negative bending moment occurs when $x = 0$, and is $-18{,}000$ ft.-lb. The maximum positive bending moment occurs at $x = 10$, and is $+42\,000$ ft.-lb.

The required section modulus is

$$\frac{I}{y_{\text{max.}}} = \frac{M}{s} = \frac{42{,}000 \times 12}{20{,}000} = 25.2 \text{ in.}^3$$

The lightest American Standard beam satisfying this requirement is (see Appendix) the 10 in. $\times$ 30 lb./ft. beam having a section modulus of 26.7 in.^{3} and a moment of inertia $I = 133.5$ in.^{4}

Now applying equation (39),

$$\frac{d^2y}{dx^2} = \frac{1}{EI}(+9000x - 300x^2 - 18{,}000)$$

$$\frac{dy}{dx} = \frac{1}{EI}\left(+\frac{9000x^2}{2} - \frac{300x^3}{3} - 18{,}000x\right) + C_1$$

When $x = 10$ $\quad \dfrac{dy}{dx} = 0$

and

$$C_1 = \frac{1}{EI}(-4500 \times 100 + 100 \times 1000 + 18{,}000 \times 10)$$

$$= \frac{1}{EI}(-170{,}000)$$

The general equation of slope in the range of loading is

$$\frac{dy}{dx} = \frac{1}{EI}(4500x^2 - 100x^3 - 18{,}000x - 170{,}000)$$

The slope at the wall may be determined by introducing the value $x = 0$ in the general slope equation,

$$\frac{dy}{dx} = -\frac{170{,}000}{30 \times 10^6 \times 133.5} \times (12)^2 = -0.00611 \text{ radians} = -0.35°$$

We have already noted that the section of maximum deflection occurs when $x = L/2$. Integrating the general equation of slope yields

$$y = \frac{1}{EI}(1500x^3 - 25x^4 - 9000x^2 - 170{,}000x) + C_2$$

When $x = 0$, $\quad y = 0$ and $C_2 = 0$

When $x = L/2 = 10$ ft.,

$$y = \frac{1}{EI}(1{,}500{,}000 - 250{,}000 - 900{,}000 - 1{,}700{,}000)$$

$$= -\frac{1{,}350{,}000}{EI}$$

and

$$y_{\text{max.}} = -\frac{1{,}350{,}000}{30 \times 10^6 \times 133.5} \times (12)^3 = -0.582 \text{ in.}$$

36. Integration of $d^2y/dx^2 = M/EI$—Additional Methods. The process of determining slope and deflection has thus far rested upon analytical integration. This technique frequently involves cumbersome expressions or laborious calculations which might be tolerated if the only excuse for alternative methods of investigation were to encourage evasion of labor. When, however, a method of attack may be employed which accomplishes equally valid results and has the attractive advantage of fewer operations in the solution of problems, an altogether worthy purpose is being served—the possibility of error or inaccuracy is reduced in direct proportion to the reduction in the number of steps in the solution.

The methods of integration of the deflection equation which follow present advantages in the solution of deflection problems, particularly when non-symmetrical loading is encountered. We have delayed their introduction until after the more orthodox analytical method had been presented to illustrate fundamentals, particularly with reference to the treatment of constants of integration.

The precautions which have been taken with respect to obtaining information by inspection of the elastic curve, and in the conversion of units to form balanced equations must still be observed. The following methods make use of different techniques, but bring no new basic information to the solution of problems, and are subject to the same limitations and assumptions made when using the analytical method.

37. Moment-Area Method. Slope is the integral of M/EI with respect to x, and deflection is the integral of slope with respect to x. Thus far, we have employed the analytical method of the calculus in effecting these integrations. As in many other engineering fields, graphical or pseudo-graphical methods may be employed when integrating.

Graphical integration always rests upon the premise that the graphical equivalent of an integral is an area. For example, Fig. 124-a is a graph in

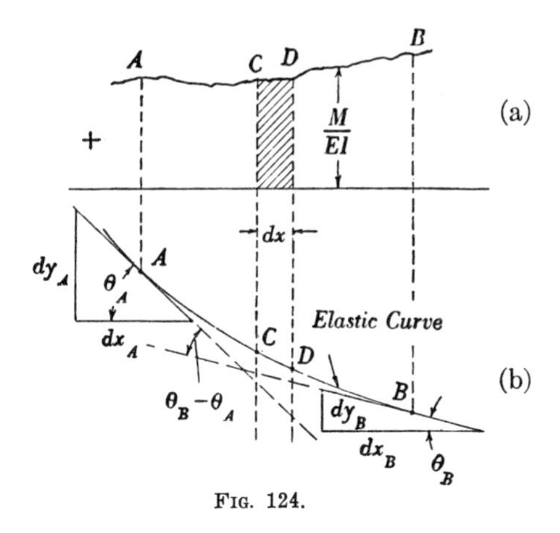

Fig. 124.

which values of M/EI are ordinates, and distances x along the span of a beam are abscissae.

The differential area between sections C and D is a rectangle in which

$$\begin{aligned} \text{area} &= \text{altitude} \times \text{base} \\ &= \frac{M}{EI}\,dx \end{aligned}$$

Any finite area, for example, the area between the sections A and B, is the sum of the differential areas between those limiting sections, and, in this case, is

$$\int_A^B \frac{M\,dx}{EI}$$

The deflection theory has already presented us with the equation

$$\frac{d^2y}{dx^2} = \frac{M}{EI}$$

Then
$$\frac{d(dy/dx)}{dx} = \frac{M}{EI}$$

and
$$d(dy/dx) = \frac{M\,dx}{EI}$$

dy/dx is the slope of the elastic curve at any point, and $d(dy/dx)$ is the change of slope.

Figure 124-b shows the elastic curve of the beam. At section C, the slope is $\left.\frac{dy}{dx}\right|_C$; at section D, the slope is $\left.\frac{dy}{dx}\right|_D$. For very small angles, tangent and angle, expressed in radians, have the same value, and θ_C and θ_D may be substituted for $\left.\frac{dy}{dx}\right|_C$ and $\left.\frac{dy}{dx}\right|_D$, respectively. Similarly, the change of slope between sections C and D, $d(dy/dx)$ may be written $\theta_D - \theta_C$. Then

$$\theta_D - \theta_C = \frac{M\,dx}{EI}$$

and the finite change of slope between sections A and B is

$$\theta_B - \theta_A = \int_A^B \frac{M\,dx}{EI} \tag{50}$$

The integral on the right side of this equation is the area of the M/EI diagram between sections A and B, and we conclude that *the change of slope between two sections of a beam is equal to the area of the M/EI diagram between those two sections.*

Sign System for Slope. The direction of slope, as well as of change of slope, may generally be noted when an elastic curve of the beam is sketched. Very rarely is the system of loading so complex that the nature of the elastic curve cannot be sketched from an inspection of a drawing of the beam with its loading. Such cases do arise, however, and it will be well for us to note the conventional sign system which is operating in this application of the moment-area method.

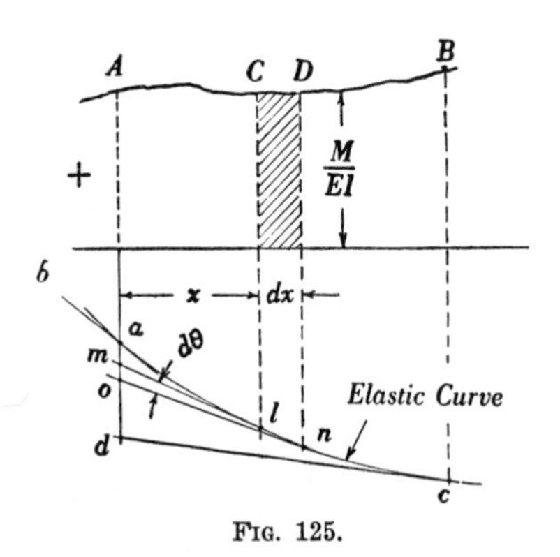

Fig. 125.

The M/EI diagram is always plotted with positive values of M/EI wherever M is positive (tension in the bottom fibers). If the net M/EI area between two sections of a beam is positive, the tangent at the right section will have moved in a positive, or counter-clockwise, direction relative to the tangent at the left section.

Applying this rule to the elastic curve which we are observing in Fig. 124, we note that the area of the M/EI diagram between sections A and B is positive. Then the tangent at B is displaced counter-clockwise relative to the tangent at A, as shown in the figure

Deflection. A similar technique may be employed to determine deflection. The lines ab and cd of Fig. 125 are tangent to the elastic curve of a beam at sections A and B. Lines lm and no are tangent to the elastic curve at sections C and D, which are dx apart, and located at distance x from section A. The values of M/EI are positive between section A and section B.

If $d\theta$ is the differential change of slope from section C to section D,

$$d\theta = \frac{M\,dx}{EI}$$

The distance mo is equal to $d\theta \times x$. (The actual slope of a beam is very small. To observe relationships, the curvature of the elastic curve of the figure has been greatly exaggerated. In reality, $lm = no = x$, so closely that the approximation is permissible.)

Then $$mo = d\theta \times x = \frac{M\,dx}{EI}\,x$$

The product $\frac{M\,dx}{EI}\,x$ is the first moment of the differential area $\frac{M\,dx}{EI}$ about an axis at section A. The element mo is one element of the total distance ad, which is the vertical distance between the tangents to the elastic curve at sections A and B, taken at section A. Just as the shaded area has contributed mo to the vertical distance ad, the remaining differential areas between sections A and B will make contributions, and ad will be their sum. Adding all of these gives us

$$ad = \int_A^B \frac{M\,dx}{EI}\,x \tag{51}$$

We conclude that *the vertical distance between any point of an elastic curve and a tangent to the elastic curve at a second point is equal to the moment of the area of the M/EI diagram between the two sections taken about an axis at the first point.*

Sign System for Vertical Displacements. When the net area of the M/EI diagram between two sections of a beam is positive, the vertical displacement of the point at which moment is taken will be upward relative to the tangent of the point at the other limit of the area.

The two stages of attack on deflection problems, which have been outlined above, are called the *moment-area* method, and were first developed by Otto Mohr, who was also responsible for the Mohr's circle which we have previously discussed.

We should very carefully note that this method does not necessarily yield the actual deflection of one point of the elastic curve from another. It does evaluate the vertical distances between tangents at the two points, which is actual deflection only when the tangent at one point is the horizontal or unloaded position of the elastic curve.

As a first illustration of the application of the moment-area principles outlined above, let us apply the method to the simple beam shown in Fig. 126-a. The maximum deflection of this beam has previously been determined by the analytical method and expressed in equation (40) as

$$y_{\text{max.}} = -\frac{1}{48}\frac{WL^3}{EI}$$

The maximum deflection will occur at $x = L/2$ and is shown in Fig. 126-c as the distance ab. Tangents to the elastic curve have been drawn at sections A and B. The tangent at B, in this symmetrical case, is horizontal.

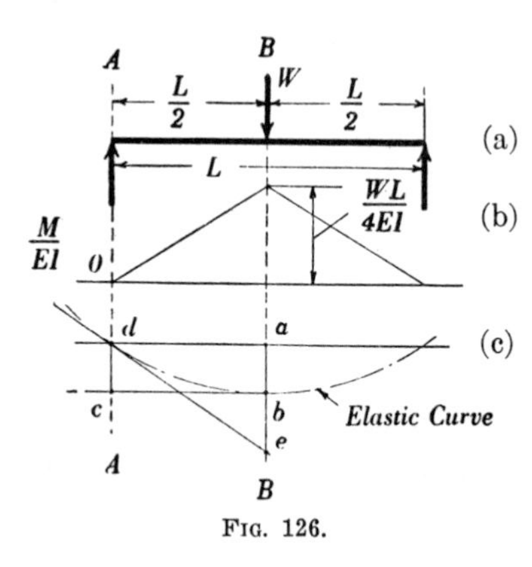

FIG. 126.

We must select an axis about which the moment of the area of the M/EI diagram (Fig. 126-b) will be taken. Either section is available. If an axis is taken at section B, the moment of the area will yield the vertical distance be. If an axis is taken at section A, the moment of the area will yield the vertical distance dc. Since $dc = ab$, this is satisfactory, and the choice of a moment axis at section A is made. Applying equation (51),

$$\Sigma M_A: \qquad dc = \left(\frac{1}{2} \times \frac{L}{2} \times \frac{WL}{4EI}\right)\left(\frac{2}{3} \times \frac{L}{2}\right) = \frac{1}{48}\frac{WL^3}{EI}$$

The area of the M/EI diagram between sections A and B is positive, and, by the sign rule given for vertical displacements, point d is above point c and dc is a downward, or negative, displacement.

Then
$$y_{\text{max.}} = ab = dc = -\frac{1}{48}\frac{WL^3}{EI}$$

a result which is in agreement with equation (40).

The routine which we have followed in applying the moment-area method is an orderly one, and we shall note it here to fix its order. The drawing of the given beam (Fig. 126-a) is first made to initiate the attack on the problem.

We next draw the bending moment diagram and divide its ordinates by the factor EI (Fig. 126-b).

Next, we sketch the elastic curve (Fig. 126-c). While the exact values of deflection are not known, we do know, by inspection, the general geometric pattern of the curve, and now have available a means of exploring the beam to determine the sections at which tangents should be set to enable us to establish the deflection.

The basic technique which we have applied in determining the maximum deflection will serve to obtain the deflections of other points of the elastic curve. In such investigations, however, we may be obliged to apply the method in successive stages. To illustrate such a case, let us determine the deflection of the elastic curve of the beam shown in Fig. 127-a at any distance x from the left support, in the first range of loading.

The moment of the area of the M/EI diagram (Fig. 127-b) between

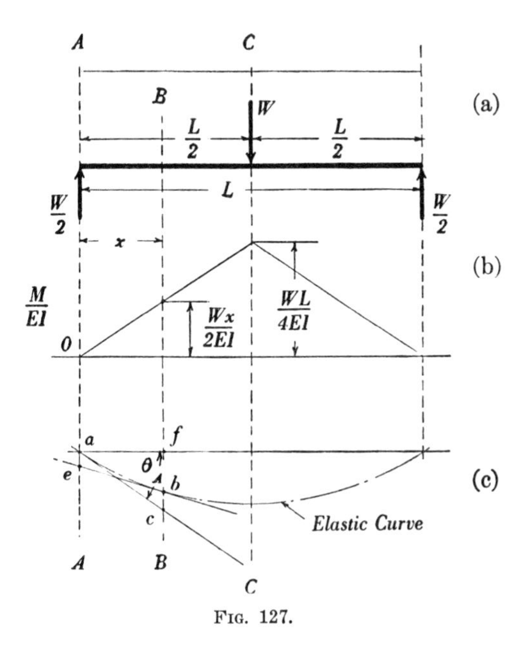

Fig. 127.

sections A and B, taken about an axis at A, will be the vertical distance ae (Fig. 127-c), and the moment of the same area about an axis at B will be bc, for the moment-area method always determines the vertical displacement between tangents. Direct attack by a simple application of the moment-area method therefore fails, and we are obliged to operate in successive stages.

The change of slope between sections A and C is, by equation (50),

$$\theta_C - \theta_A = \int_A^C \frac{M\,dx}{EI}$$

The slope at section C is zero, in this symmetrical elastic curve, and

$$0 - \theta_A = \frac{1}{2} \times \frac{L}{2} \times \frac{WL}{4EI} = \frac{WL^2}{16EI}$$

The area of the M/EI diagram between sections A and C is positive, and by the sign rule for slope the tangent at C will have moved counterclockwise relative to the tangent at A. Then the slope at section A is negative, and

$$\theta_A = -\frac{WL^2}{16EI}$$

θ_A, the initial slope, is a small angle, and is equal to tan θ_A.

$$\text{Distance } fc = x \tan \theta_A = x\left(-\frac{WL^2}{16EI}\right) = -\frac{WL^2x}{16EI}$$

To establish the distance bc, we take the moment of the M/EI diagram lying between sections A and B, about an axis at B. Applying equation (51),

$$\Sigma M_B: \qquad bc = \frac{1}{2}x\frac{Wx}{2EI}\frac{x}{3} = \frac{Wx^3}{12EI}$$

The displacement bc is downward by the rule of signs for vertical displacements. The deflection at x distance from the left support is

$$y_x = fb = fc - bc = -\frac{WL^2x}{16EI} - \left(-\frac{Wx^3}{12EI}\right)$$
$$= \frac{Wx}{48EI}(-3L^2 + 4x^2)$$

The moment-area method is effective when the loads are not distributed symmetrically, and particularly when we deal with concentrated loads which yield the readily evaluated triangular or rectangular areas of the M/EI diagrams. This effectiveness is demonstrated in the illustrative examples which follow.

Illustrative Example I. The beam of Fig. 128 is freely supported at its ends, and carries a single concentrated load, W, which is not at mid-span. The maximum deflection of the beam is to be determined.

The vertical distance between the tangents at sections A and B is determined by applying equation (51), taking moments at section B.

$$\Sigma M_B: \qquad cd = \frac{1}{2} \times a \times \frac{Wba}{LEI} \times \left[\left(b + \frac{a}{3}\right)\right] + \frac{1}{2} \times b \times \frac{Wba}{LEI} \times \frac{2b}{3}$$
$$= \frac{Wba}{6LEI}(3ab + a^2 + 2b^2)$$

The initial slope of the beam at the left support is now determined by dividing cd by the total length L.

$$\theta_A = \frac{cd}{L} = \frac{Wba}{6L^2EI}(3ab + a^2 + 2b^2) \tag{1}$$

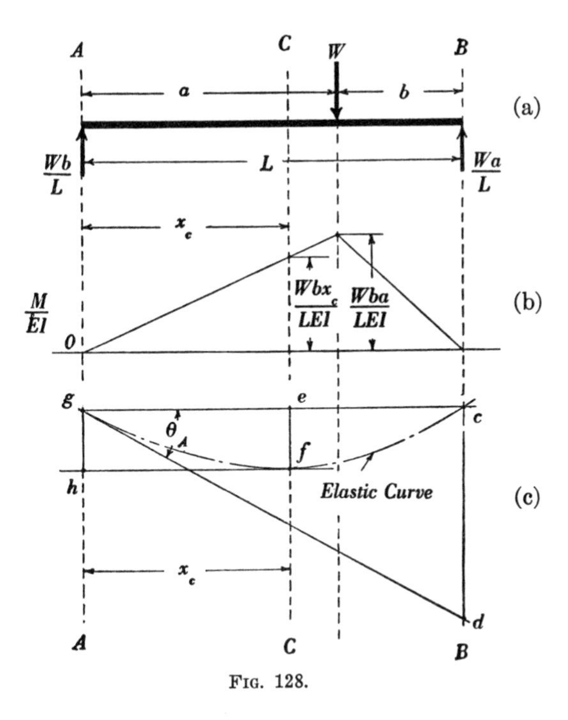

FIG. 128.

x_C is the distance from the left support to the section of zero slope (section C). During this distance the slope must have changed from value θ_A to $\theta_C = 0$. Change of slope is represented by area of the M/EI diagram, and the triangular area between sections A and C must therefore be equated to the value θ_A to evaluate x_C. The area is

$$\theta_A = \frac{1}{2} x_C \frac{Wbx_C}{LEI} \tag{2}$$

Setting the values of θ_A given in equations (1) and (2) equal to each other, we have

$$\frac{Wba}{6L^2EI}(3ab + a^2 + 2b^2) = \frac{Wbx_C^2}{2LEI}$$

$$\frac{a}{3}[(a + 2b)(a + b)] = x_C^2(L) = x_C^2(a + b)$$

and

$$x_C = \left(\frac{a^2 + 2ab}{3}\right)^{\frac{1}{2}} \tag{3}$$

This operation locates the section of zero slope, at which the maximum deflection will occur. The maximum deflection will be determined by taking the moment of the portion of the M/EI diagram lying between sections A and C about an axis at A. Applying equation (51),

$$\Sigma M_A: \qquad gh = \left(\frac{1}{2}x_C \frac{Wbx_C}{LEI}\right)\frac{2}{3}x_C = \frac{Wbx_C{}^3}{3LEI}$$

The vertical displacement gh, and its equivalent, ef, is a downward displacement by the rule of vertical displacements.

Substituting the value of x_C obtained in equation (3) above,

$$y_{\text{max.}} = -\frac{Wb}{3LEI}\left(\frac{a^2 + 2ab}{3}\right)^{\frac{3}{2}}$$

which is in agreement with equation (46). An additional confirming agreement with equation (40) may be noted if we consider the case when the load W is placed at mid-span, and $a = b = L/2$. Substituting these values,

$$y_{\text{max.}} = -\frac{WL}{6LEI}\left[\frac{\left(\frac{L}{2}\right)^2 + 2\left(\frac{L}{2}\right)\left(\frac{L}{2}\right)}{3}\right]^{\frac{3}{2}} = -\frac{WL^3}{48EI}$$

Illustrative Example II. When beams like that of Fig. 129-a are to be investigated to determine slope and deflection, the analytical method of integration will

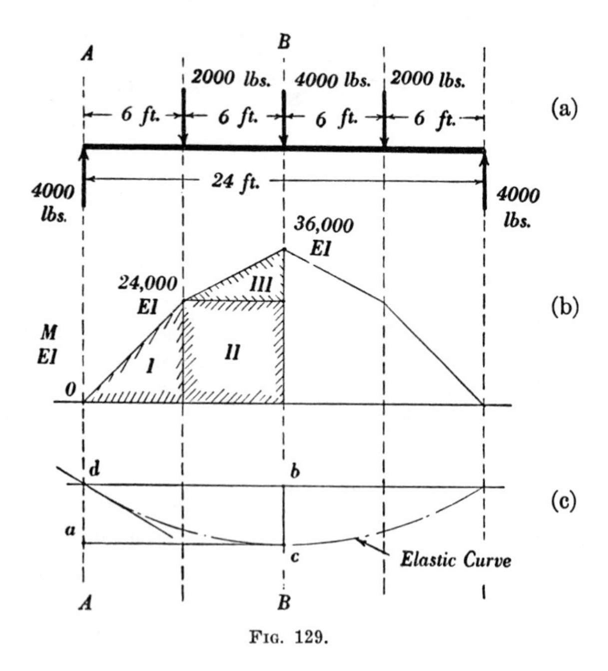

FIG. 129.

require the evaluation of several constants of integration, and the calculations may become somewhat cumbersome. Here the moment-area method of attack will present an advantage.

The beam is a Standard aluminum I-beam, 12 in. $\times$ 17.78 lb./ft. $E = 10.3 \times 10^6$ psi. $I = 304.84$ in.^{4}

The maximum deflection, which will occur at mid-span, is to be determined. The M/EI diagram is shown as Fig. 129-b, and the elastic curve of the beam is shown in Fig. 129-c.

We apply equation (51) as follows: With an axis at A, the moment of areas I, II, and III is

ΣM_A: Area I Area II Area III

$$da = \frac{1}{EI}\left[\left(\frac{1}{2} \times 6 \times 24{,}000 \times 4\right) + (6 \times 24{,}000 \times 9) + \left(\frac{1}{2} \times 12{,}000 \times 6 \times 10\right)\right]$$

$$= \frac{1{,}944{,}000}{EI}$$

da is a downward deflection by the rule of vertical displacements, as is $bc = da$.

Then
$$y_{\max.} = -\frac{1{,}944{,}000}{10.3 \times 10^6 \times 304.84} \times (12)^3$$
$$= -1.07 \text{ in.}$$

Distributed Forces. The moment-area method need not be confined to beams carrying concentrated forces as loads. When distributed loading is encountered, the method is valid, for there has been no qualifying factor

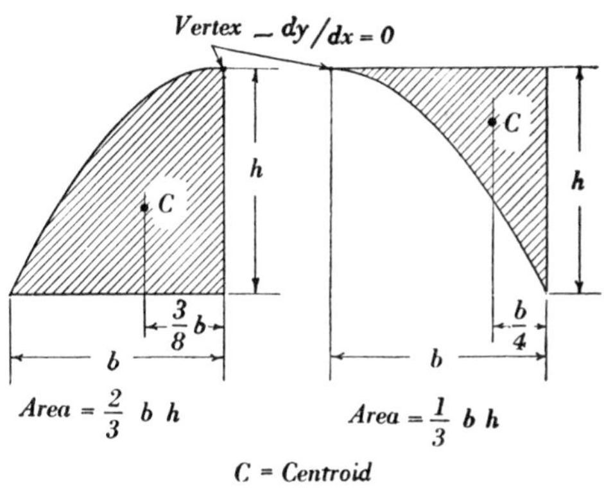

FIG. 130.

in its derivation other than the limitations which govern the basic flexure theory.

The moment-area method has a disadvantage when the beam loading is of any nature requiring analytical integration to determine the M/EI curve. In such cases it is most efficient to continue the analytical integration through its successive steps to evaluate slope and deflection.

The most common type of beam loading, however, consists of uniformly distributed or constant-intensity forces. Such loading produces bending moment diagrams which are simple parabolas, and the moment-area method may be applied effectively.

Two areas, bounded by parabolas of the second degree, are shown in Fig. 130. The magnitude of the area, and the location of the centroid, is given for each case.

With this information, we may apply the moment-area method to a beam (Fig. 131-a) which is freely supported at its ends, and carries a uniformly distributed load of w lb./ft.

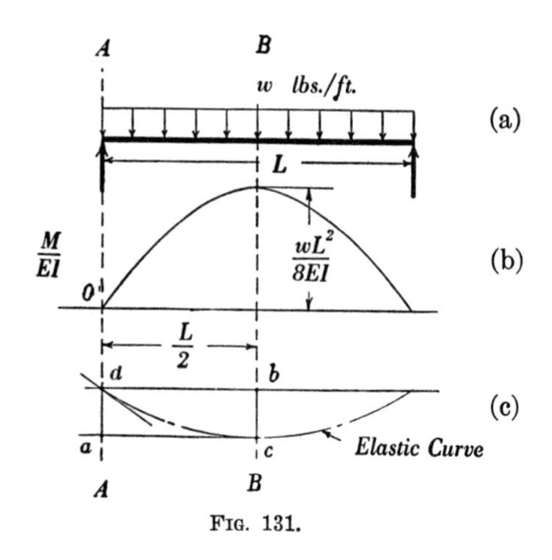

FIG. 131.

The bending moment equation is

$$M_x = +\frac{wL}{2}x - \frac{wx^2}{2}$$

The parabolic M/EI diagram is shown in Fig. 131-b, and its maximum value is $wL^2/8EI$, at mid-span.

The elastic curve is shown as Fig. 131-c. Applying equation (51),

$$\Sigma M_A: \qquad da = \frac{2}{3} \times \frac{L}{2} \times \frac{wL^2}{8EI} \times \frac{5}{8} \times \frac{L}{2} = \frac{5}{384}\frac{wL^4}{EI}$$

The area of the M/EI diagram between sections A and B is positive, and, by the sign rule for vertical displacements, point d will lie above point a, and vertical displacement da is downward. Then

$$y_{\text{max.}} = bc = da = -\frac{5}{384}\frac{wL^4}{EI}$$

which agrees with equation (41).

The cantilever beam of Fig. 132-a carries a uniformly distributed load of w lb./ft. The M/EI diagram is shown in Fig. 132-b, and the elastic curve in Fig. 132-c. Applying equation (51), taking moments at section A,

$$\Sigma M_A: \qquad ab = \frac{1}{3} \times L \times \frac{wL^2}{2EI} \times \frac{3}{4} \times L = \frac{1}{8}\frac{wL^4}{EI}$$

The area of the M/EI diagram between sections A and B is negative, and point b of the elastic curve will lie below point a.

Then $$y_{\text{max.}} = -\frac{1}{8}\frac{wL^4}{EI}$$

which is consistent with equation (43), derived by analytical integration.

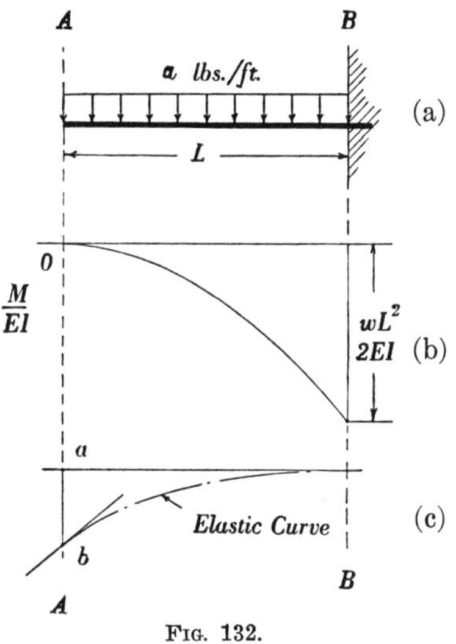

FIG. 132.

Illustrative Example I. The beam of Fig. 133-a carries a single concentrated force of 2000 lb. The beam is supported on knife edges at sections A and B. Figure 133-b shows the isolation of the beam as a free body; Fig. 133-c is the M/EI diagram; and Fig. 133-d is the elastic curve. $E = 30 \times 10^6$ psi. $I = 33.6$ in.^{4}

The deflection of the beam at its free end (section C) is to be determined. To apply equation (51) effectively, we must set tangents cautiously. If we set a tangent to the elastic curve at section B, the tangent will be bd. The deflection which we seek to evaluate will be

$$y = cd + de$$

cd may now be determined by noting that the triangles cdf and abf are similar, and

$$\frac{cd}{ab} = \frac{6}{8} \qquad cd = \frac{3}{4}ab$$

To evaluate ab, we shall now apply equation (51), taking moments at section A of the portion of the M/EI diagram lying between sections A and B.

$$\Sigma M_A: \qquad ab = \frac{1}{2} \times 8 \times \frac{12{,}000}{EI} \times \frac{2}{3} \times 8 = \frac{256{,}000}{EI}$$

The area of the M/EI diagram lying between sections A and B is negative—point a will lie below point b, and vertical displacement ab is an upward displacement. Line cd is on the opposite side of the line ca, and cd is, therefore, a negative displacement.

$$cd = -\frac{3}{4}ab = -\frac{3}{4} \times \frac{256{,}000}{EI} = -\frac{192{,}000}{EI}$$

We have yet to determine the distance de. This may be done by another application of equation (51), taking moments, at section C, of the portion of the M/EI diagram which lies between sections C and B.

$$\Sigma M_C: \qquad de = \frac{1}{2} \times 6 \times \frac{12{,}000}{EI} \times \frac{2}{3} \times 6 = \frac{144{,}000}{EI}$$

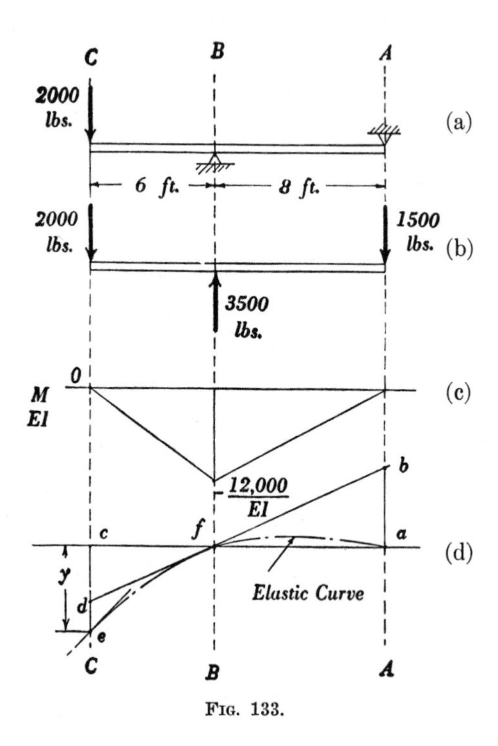

FIG. 133.

The M/EI area is negative, and by the rule of signs for vertical displacements, de is a downward deflection.

The total deflection at section C will be

$$y = cd + de = -\frac{192{,}000}{EI} - \frac{144{,}000}{EI} = -\frac{336{,}000}{EI}$$

$$= -\frac{336{,}000}{30 \times (10)^6 \times 33.6} \times (12)^3$$

$$= -0.576 \text{ in.}$$

Illustrative Example II. The cantilever beam of Fig. 134-a is loaded as shown. $E = 30 \times 10^6$ psi. $I = 36.2$ in.^{6} We are to determine the maximum deflection, as well as the deflection at 6 ft. from the wall end of the beam.

When several loads are present, there may be advantage in using the method of superposition—determining the deflection caused by each of the loads when acting alone, and adding these individual deflections to find the total deflection. In the moment-area method, the individual stages of the process are represented by individual M/EI diagrams. To afford an opportunity of comparing the use of individual and combined diagrams, we shall employ both methods as illustrations, using the individual-diagram method in this illustrative example, and the combined-diagram method in the following illustrative example.

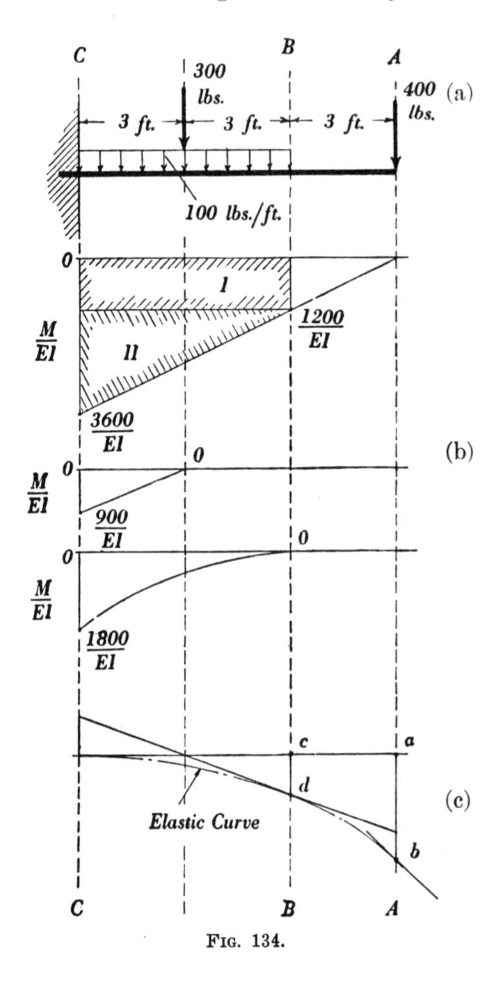

FIG. 134.

The individual M/EI diagram for each of the loads is shown in Fig. 134-b. These have been plotted proceeding from the right end of the beam toward the left. The elastic curve of the beam is shown in Fig. 134-c.

We now apply equation (51), taking moments at section A of each of the individual M/EI diagrams. The vertical displacement at A resulting from each load is:

ΣM_A: 400-lb. load: $\frac{1}{2} \times 9 \times \frac{3600}{EI} \times 6 = \frac{97{,}200}{EI}$

300-lb. load: $\frac{1}{2} \times 3 \times \frac{900}{EI} \times 8 = \frac{10{,}800}{EI}$

100 lb./ft. load: $\frac{1}{3} \times 6 \times \frac{1800}{EI} \times 7.5 = \frac{27{,}000}{EI}$

Total vertical displacement (ab):

$$\frac{97{,}200 + 10{,}800 + 27{,}000}{EI} = \frac{135{,}000}{EI}$$

ab is a downward deflection, for the net area between sections A and C is negative, and point b will lie below point a. Then,

$$y_{\text{max.}} = ab = -\frac{135{,}000}{30 \times (10)^6 \times 36.2} \times (12)^3 = -0.215 \text{ in}$$

The deflection at 6 ft. from the left end is vertical distance cd (Fig. 134-c) which may be found by again applying equation (51), taking moments at section B of the M/EI diagrams between sections B and C.

ΣM_B: 400-lb. load: Area I. $6 \times \frac{1200}{EI} \times 3 = \frac{21{,}600}{EI}$

Area II. $\frac{1}{2} \times 6 \times \frac{2400}{EI} \times 4 = \frac{28{,}800}{EI}$

300-lb. load: $\frac{1}{2} \times 3 \times \frac{900}{EI} \times 5 = \frac{6750}{EI}$

100-lb./ft. load: $\frac{1}{3} \times 6 \times \frac{1800}{EI} \times 4.5 = \frac{16{,}200}{EI}$

Total vertical displacement (cd):

$$\frac{21{,}600 + 28{,}800 + 6750 + 16{,}200}{EI} = \frac{73{,}350}{EI}$$

and
$$y_{6\text{ ft.}} = -\frac{73{,}350}{30 \times (10)^6 \times 36.2} \times (12)^3 = -0.117 \text{ in.}$$

Illustrative Example III. The beam of Fig. 135-a carries a uniformly distributed load of 600 lb./ft. on the overhang, and is supported on knife edges at sections A and B. The maximum deflection in each range of loading is to be determined. The beam is a 4 in. $\times$ 12-in. timber, with $E = 1.2 \times 10^6$ psi.

In the preceding illustrative example, the individual-diagram method was employed. In this example we shall make use of the total or combined M/EI diagram, which is shown in Fig. 135-c. Figure 135-d shows the elastic curve of the beam.

To determine the maximum deflection in the overhanging range, we apply equation (51) in the manner which was discussed in Illustrative Example I, making use of the similar triangles *cdf* and *abf*.

$$\Sigma M_A: \quad ab: \ \frac{1}{2} \times 9 \times \frac{10{,}800}{EI} \times 6 = \frac{291{,}600}{EI}$$

by proportion,

$$cd: \ \frac{6}{9} \times \frac{291{,}600}{EI} = \frac{194{,}400}{EI}$$

$$de: \ \frac{1}{3} \times 6 \times \frac{10{,}800}{EI} \times 4.5 = \frac{97{,}200}{EI}$$

$$ce = cd + de = \frac{194{,}400}{EI} + \frac{97{,}200}{EI} = \frac{291{,}600}{EI}$$

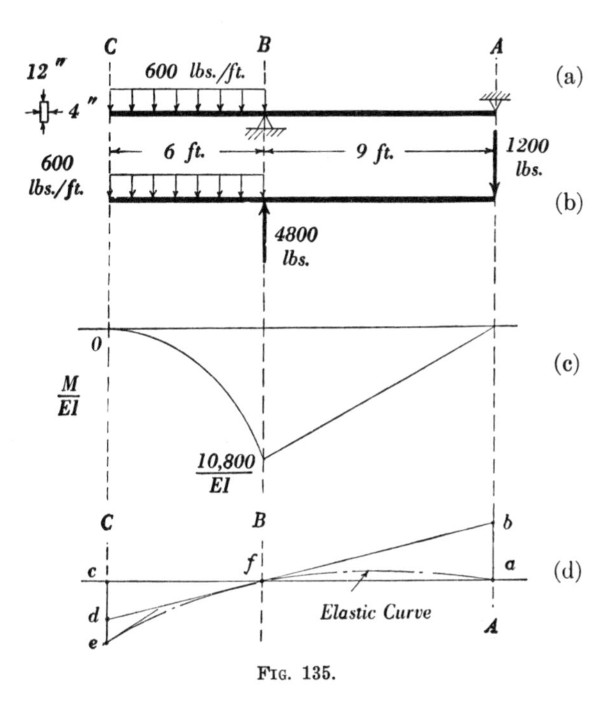

FIG. 135.

By the rule of signs for vertical displacements *ce* is a downward deflection, and the maximum deflection in the overhang range is

$$y_{\text{max.}} = -\frac{291{,}600}{1.2 \times 10^6 \times 576} \times (12)^3 = -0.729 \text{ in.}$$

Before we can determine the maximum deflection in the range of loading between sections A and B (Figs. 135 and 136) we must determine the location of the section of zero slope (section D) at which maximum deflection will occur.

This location will be available when we apply equation (50), which evaluates change of slope as area of the M/EI diagram. The slope at section B, which is shown in Fig. 136-b as θ_B, may be determined from the data made available in our preceding deflection survey (Fig. 135).

$$\theta_B = \frac{ab}{9} = \frac{291{,}600}{9EI} = \frac{32{,}400}{EI}$$

Applying equation (50) $\quad \theta_B - \theta_D = \theta_B - 0 = \int_D^B \frac{M\,dx}{EI}$

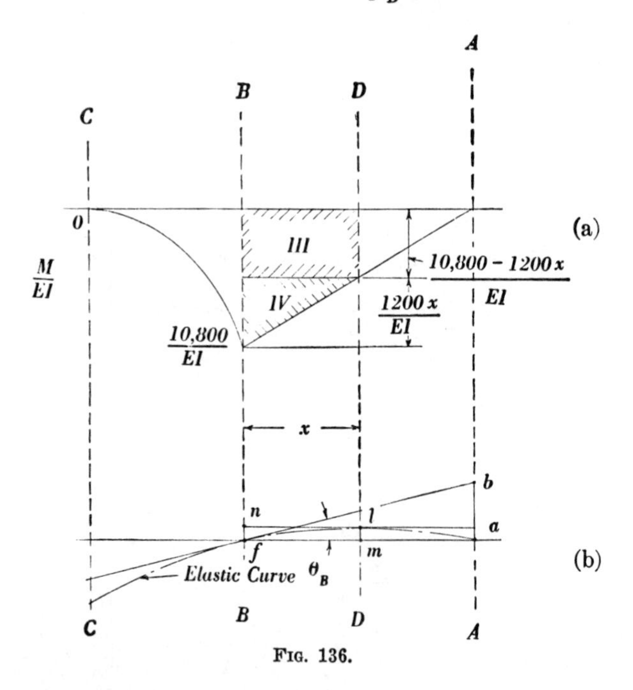

FIG. 136.

The area of the M/EI diagram between sections B and D (see Fig. 136) is

Area III. $\quad \dfrac{(10{,}800 - 1200x)x}{EI} = \dfrac{10{,}800x - 1200x^2}{EI}$

Area IV. $\quad \dfrac{1}{2} \times \dfrac{1200x^2}{EI} = \dfrac{600x^2}{EI}$

Total Area: $\quad \dfrac{10{,}800x - 600x^2}{EI}$

Then $\quad \dfrac{32{,}400}{EI} = \dfrac{10{,}800x - 600x^2}{EI}$

Solving, $\quad x = 3.80$ ft.

Now we apply equation (51) to determine the deflection at section D, which will be the maximum deflection in this range of loading. Taking moments about an axis at section B of the M/EI area between sections B and D yields

$$\Sigma M_B: \quad nf = \frac{(10{,}800 - 1200 \times 3.80)}{EI} \times 3.80 \times \frac{3.80}{2} + \frac{1}{2} \times 1200 \times 3.80 \times 3.80 \times \frac{3.80}{3}$$

$$= \frac{56{,}000}{EI}$$

The area of the M/EI diagram between the sections is negative, and point f will lie below point n. fn is, therefore, an upward deflection, and, in this range,

$$y_{\text{max.}} = lm = fn = \frac{56{,}000 \times (12)^3}{1.2 \times 10 \times 576} = +0.140 \text{ in.}$$

38. Statically Indeterminate Cases by Moment-Area Method. We have already noted the value of the deflection theory as an aid to the conditions of equilibrium in the solution of statically indeterminate problems. Article

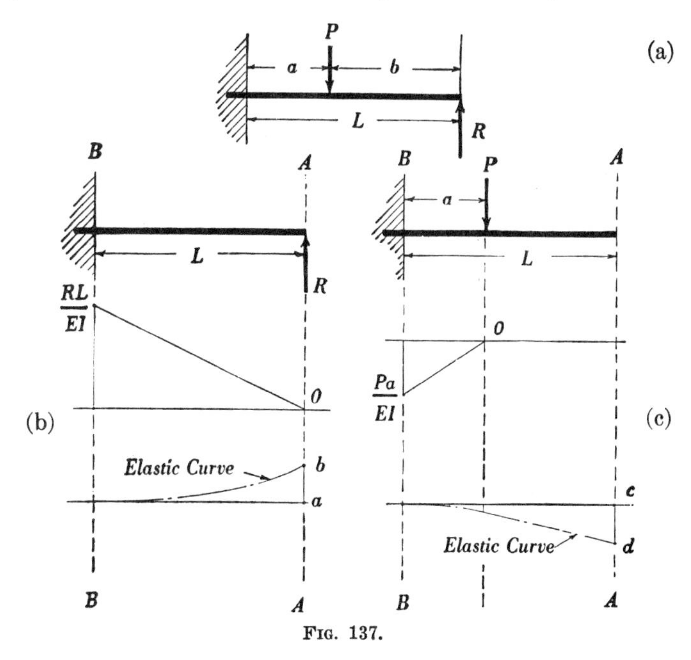

FIG. 137.

34 considered the use of the analytical integration in such problems. Two cases of statically indeterminate beams will be discussed here to illustrate the use of the moment-area method.

The cantilever beam of Fig. 137-a is supported by a reaction R in addition to the wall support. R is applied on the same level as the wall. To evaluate such design factors as bending stress, or longitudinal shear stress, force R must be determined.

The individual M/EI diagrams and elastic curves, produced by each of the loads when acting alone, are shown as Fig. 137-b and 137-c. When the beam is subjected to force R alone (Fig. 137-b), the deflection of the right end will be, by equation (51),

$$\Sigma M_A: \qquad ab = \frac{1}{2} \times L \times \frac{RL}{EI} \times \frac{2}{3}L = \frac{RL^3}{3EI} \qquad \text{(upward)}$$

When load P acts alone (Fig. 137-c) the deflection of the right end will be, by equation (51),

$$\Sigma M_A: \; cd = \frac{1}{2} \times a \times \frac{Pa}{EI} \times \left(L - \frac{a}{3}\right) = \frac{Pa^2}{6EI}(3L - a) \qquad \text{(downward)}$$

The total deflection of the right end with both loads acting is fixed as zero by the data of the given problem;

therefore
$$\frac{RL^3}{3EI} = \frac{Pa^2}{6EI}(3L - a)$$

and
$$R = \frac{Pa^2}{2L^3}(3L - a)$$

Another example of a statically indeterminate case is that of the built-in beam, *fixed* at both ends, which is illustrated in Fig. 138-a. The beam, isolated from the supporting walls as a free body, is shown in Fig. 138-b. M_1 is the end or wall moment. V_1 is the shearing force at the face of the wall.

$$V_1 = \frac{W}{2} + \frac{wL}{2}$$

M_1 is to be evaluated.

Individual M/EI diagrams are shown in Fig. 138-c, and represent the three sources of bending moment, proceeding from the left end of the beam. The elastic curve, shown in Fig. 138-d, presents the following data by inspection: Slope is equal to zero when $x = 0$ (section A); when $x = L/2$ (section B); and when $x = L$ (section C).

Equation (50) tells us that change of slope between sections is equivalent to area of the M/EI diagrams. Then the total area of these individual diagrams between sections A and B must be equal to zero.

Load V_1: Area I. $\frac{1}{2} \times \frac{L}{2} \times \left(\frac{WL}{4EI} + \frac{wL^2}{4EI}\right) = \frac{L^2}{16EI}(W + wL)$

Load M_1: Area II. $-\frac{M_1 L}{2EI}$

Load-w lb./ft.: Area III. $-\frac{1}{3} \times \frac{L}{2} \times \frac{wL^2}{8EI} = -\frac{wL^3}{48EI}$

Tne sum of these areas is

$$\frac{L^2}{16EI}(W + wL) - \frac{M_1 L}{2EI} - \frac{wL^3}{48EI} = 0$$

$$M_1 = \frac{WL}{8} + \frac{wL^2}{12}$$

Then M_1 is a negative bending moment of magnitude

$$\left(\frac{WL}{8} + \frac{wL^2}{12}\right)$$

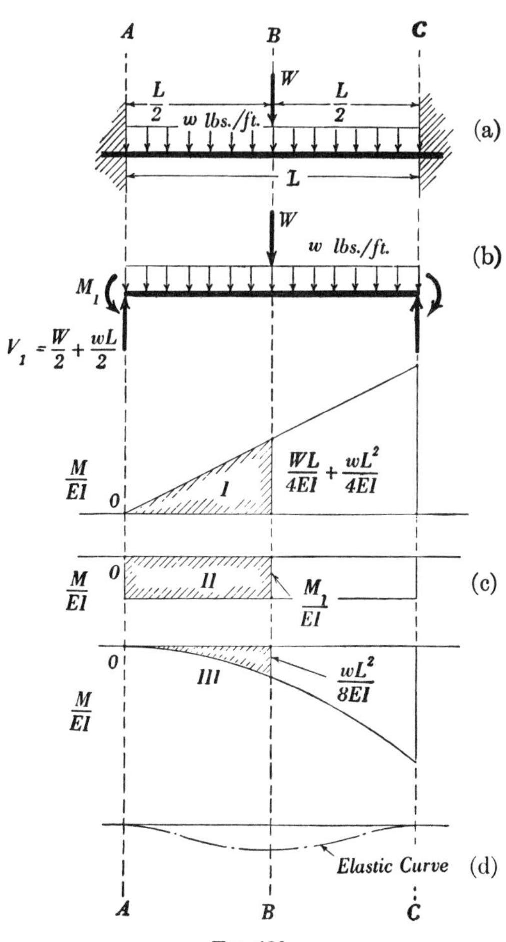

FIG. 138.

Illustrative Example I (Fig. 139-a). The beam carries a uniformly distributed load of 300 lb./ft. and is supported by forces F_1, F_2, and F_3. All supports are on the same level. F_1, F_2, and F_3 are to be determined. The method of superposition will be used, and the two stages of loading, with their accompanying M/EI diagrams and elastic curves, are shown in Figs. 139-b and 139-c.

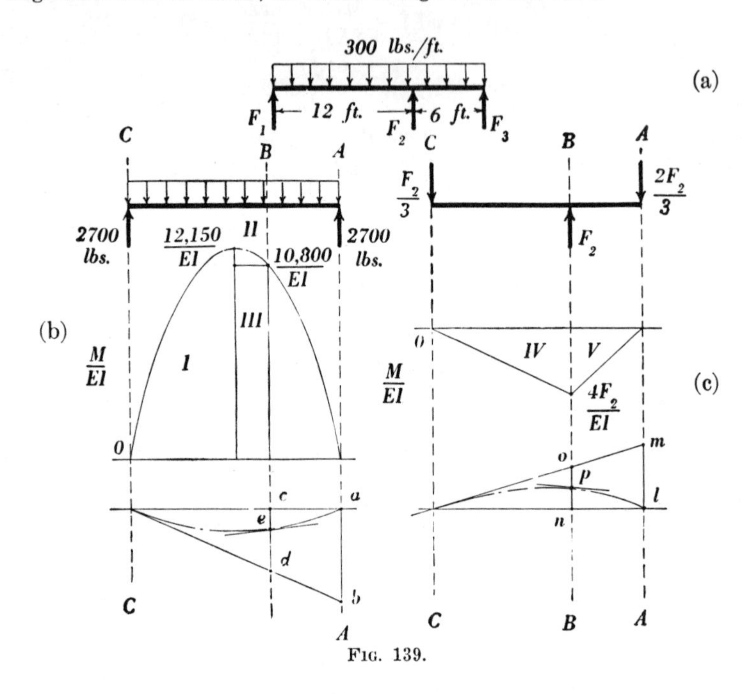

FIG. 139.

For the first stage of loading (Fig. 139-b), applying equation (51),

$$\Sigma M_A: \qquad ab = \frac{2}{3} \times 18 \times \frac{12{,}150}{EI} \times 9 = \frac{1{,}312{,}200}{EI}$$

by proportion

$$cd = \frac{12}{18} \times \frac{1{,}312{,}200}{EI} = \frac{874{,}800}{EI}$$

Again applying equation (51), taking moments at section B,

$$\Sigma M_B: \quad \text{Area I.} \quad \frac{2}{3} \times 9 \times \frac{12{,}150}{EI} \times 6.375 = \frac{464{,}740}{EI}$$

$$\text{Area II.} \quad \frac{2}{3} \times 3 \times \frac{1350}{EI} \times 1.875 = \frac{5060}{EI}$$

$$\text{Area III.} \quad 3 \times \frac{10{,}800}{EI} \times 1.5 = \frac{48{,}600}{EI}$$

$$\text{Total:} \qquad de = \frac{464{,}740}{EI} + \frac{5060}{EI} + \frac{48{,}600}{EI} = \frac{518{,}400}{EI}$$

$$ce = cd - de = \frac{874{,}800}{EI} - \frac{518{,}400}{EI} = \frac{356{,}400}{EI}$$

ce will be the downward deflection at section B when only the uniformly distributed load is acting.

We now consider the effect of F_2 when it is acting alone (Fig. 139-c). Applying equation (51),

$$\Sigma M_A: \quad \text{Area IV.} \qquad \frac{1}{2} \times 12 \times \frac{4F_2}{EI} \times 10 = \frac{240F_2}{EI}$$

$$\text{Area V.} \qquad \frac{1}{2} \times 6 \times \frac{4F_2}{EI} \times 4 = \frac{48F_2}{EI}$$

$$lm = \frac{240F_2}{EI} + \frac{48F_2}{EI} = \frac{288F_2}{EI}$$

by proportion,

$$no = \frac{12}{18} \times \frac{288F_2}{EI} = \frac{192F_2}{EI}$$

Again applying equation (51)

$$\Sigma M_B: \quad \text{Area IV.} \qquad \frac{1}{2} \times 12 \times \frac{4F_2}{EI} \times 4 = \frac{96F_2}{EI}$$

$$op = \frac{96F_2}{EI}$$

$$np = no - op = \frac{192F_2}{EI} - \frac{96F_2}{EI} = \frac{96F_2}{EI}$$

np is the upward deflection at section B when only supporting force F_2 is acting.

Since all supports are on the same level, the net deflection at section B with all loads acting, is zero.

$$\frac{96F_2}{EI} = \frac{356{,}400}{EI}$$

and

$$F_2 = 3712 \text{ lb.}$$

Applying the conditions of equilibrium to the entire beam taken as a free body (Fig. 139-a),

$$\Sigma M_C = 0: \qquad -18F_3 - 12 \times 3712 + 300 \times 18 \times 9 = 0$$

$$F_3 = 225 \text{ lb.}$$

$$\Sigma M_A = 0: \qquad +18F_1 + 6 \times 3712 - 300 \times 18 \times 9 = 0$$

$$F_1 = 1463 \text{ lb.}$$

Illustrative Example II. The cantilever beam of Fig. 140 carries a single concentrated force of 1000 lb. and is supported by force R at the right end. The right end is $\frac{1}{8}$ in. below the wall end. The beam is an aluminum beam, with $E = 10.3 \times 10^6$ psi, and $I = 134.81$ in.^{4} We are to determine the magnitude of R.

The elastic curves and the M/EI diagrams for each of the forces, when acting alone, are shown in Figs. 140-b and 140-c. Applying equation (51),

$$\Sigma M_A: \qquad ab = \frac{1}{2} \times 9 \times \frac{9R}{EI} \times 6 = \frac{243R}{EI}$$

$$cd = -\frac{1}{2} \times 6 \times \frac{6000}{EI} \times 7 = -\frac{126{,}000}{EI}$$

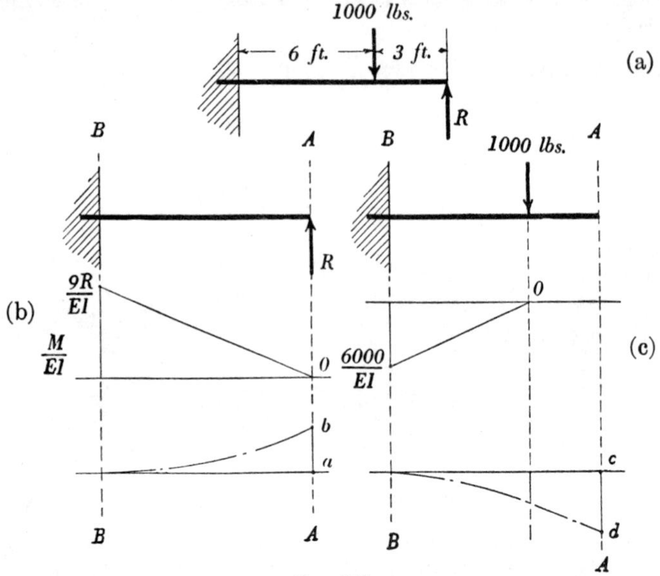

FIG. 140.

Since the net deflection of the beam at section A, when both forces are acting, is $-\frac{1}{8}$ in.

$$ab - cd = -\frac{1}{8}$$

$$(243R - 126{,}000) \times \frac{(12)^3}{10.3 \times 10^6 \times 134.81} = -\frac{1}{8}$$

and

$$R = 105 \text{ lb.}$$

39. Alternative Methods for Determining Slope and Deflection. The solutions of problems of deflection which have thus far been discussed have been concerned with techniques of integration of the basic differential equation of the elastic curve.

In many cases the routine of calculation may be simplified through the use of techniques which arise as corollaries of the preceding method. Two of these alternatives will be discussed in the following articles.

40. The Cantilever-Beam Technique. The cantilever beam is distinguished by the presence of zero slope at the wall. Whenever the location of a section of zero slope is known in a beam, that beam may be divided into portions, with the section of zero slope forming the dividing section, and the resulting divisions treated as cantilever beams. This method offers a simplification in that we can take advantage of the equations (42) and (43) to accomplish the solution rather than developing new equations, by integration, in each case.

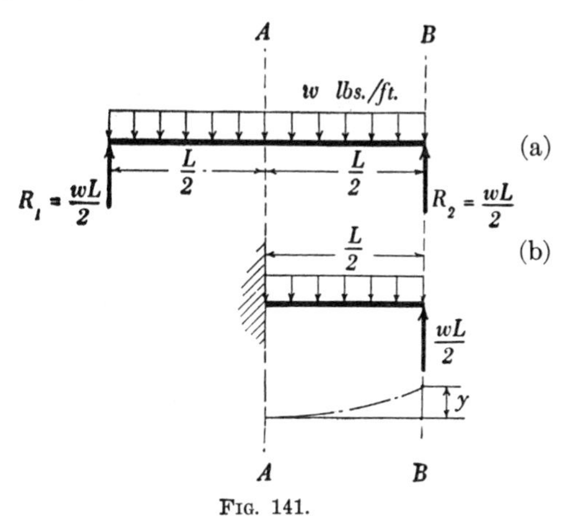

FIG. 141.

For example, the simple beam of Fig. 141-a is subjected to a uniformly distributed load of w lb./ft. The concentrated supporting forces are $R_1 = R_2 = wL/2$. The maximum deflection is to be determined by the cantilever beam method.

The central section of the beam (section A) is a section of zero slope.

The portion of the beam lying to the right of section A is shown in Fig. 141-b. It is equivalent to a cantilever beam of length $L/2$, carrying a uniformly distributed load. We may assume that the section at A is stationary, and serves the same purpose as the wall at the end of a cantilever beam.

The deflection of section B relative to section A will be

$$y = +\frac{1}{3}\frac{R_2(L/2)^3}{EI} - \frac{1}{8}\frac{w(L/2)^4}{EI}$$

$$= \frac{5}{384}\frac{wL^4}{EI}$$

Other beams, including those which are statically indeterminate, which present readily available sections of zero slope may be similarly analyzed.

For example, the built-in beam of Fig. 142-a has fixed ends and carries a uniformly distributed load. The couples M at the end of such a beam are statically indeterminate but may be evaluated by applying the cantilever-beam technique. The beam is treated as a cantilever beam, loaded

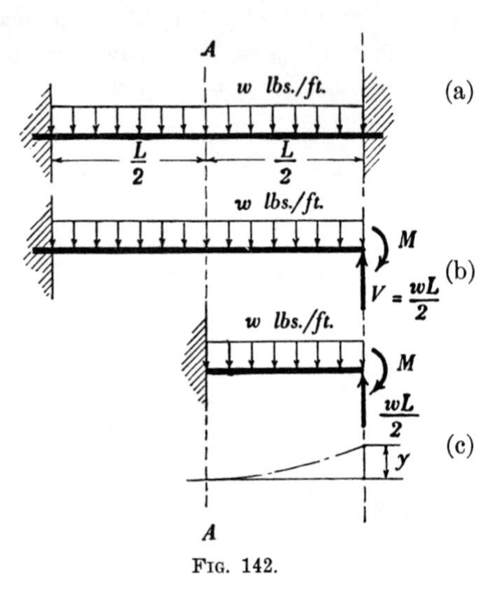

FIG. 142.

as shown in Fig. 142-b. The force system at the right end includes the shearing force at the face of the wall ($V = wL/2$) and the wall couple M.

The deflection at the right end of such a beam is the sum of the deflections caused by the individual loads. If this deflection is called y,

$$y = \underset{\text{Equation (42)}}{\frac{1}{3}\left(\frac{wL}{2}\right)\frac{L^3}{EI}} - \underset{\text{Equation (43)}}{\frac{1}{8}\frac{wL^4}{EI}} - \underset{\text{Equation (44)}}{\frac{ML^2}{2EI}}$$

Since the total deflection is zero, $M = -wL^2/12$.

With M determined, the cantilever-beam technique may again be employed to evaluate the maximum deflection which, we note by inspection, will occur at section A, the central section (Fig. 142-c).

$$y_{\text{max.}} = \frac{1}{EI}\Bigg[\underset{\text{Equation (42)}}{\frac{1}{3}\left(\frac{wL}{2}\right)\left(\frac{L}{2}\right)^3} - \underset{\text{Equation (43)}}{\frac{1}{8}w\left(\frac{L}{2}\right)^4} - \underset{\text{Equation (44)}}{\frac{1}{2}\left(\frac{wL^2}{12}\right)\left(\frac{L}{2}\right)^2}\Bigg]$$

$$= \frac{1}{384}\frac{wL^4}{EI}$$

Illustrative Example I (Fig. 143-a). The beam which we have already considered in Illustrative Example II, on page 207 (Fig. 140) furnishes an additional opportunity for us to apply the cantilever-beam technique in the analysis of a deflection problem.

We shall divide the loading into two stages, and employ the method of superposition of these stages to accomplish the final result, which is the determination of the statically indeterminate force R.

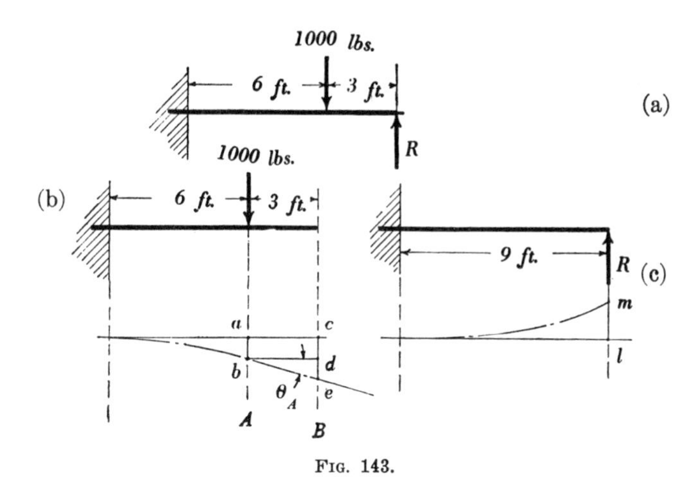

FIG. 143.

Figure 143-b shows the first stage. The total deflection of the right end of the beam, when only the 1000-lb. load is acting, is composed of two segments, cd and de. By equation (42),

$$cd = ab = -\frac{1000 \times (6)^3}{3EI} = -\frac{72{,}000}{EI}$$

The unloaded portion of the beam lying between sections A and B will be a straight line, 3 ft. long, having a slope equal to θ_A.

$$\theta_A = \frac{WL^2}{2EI} = \frac{1000 \times (6)^2}{2EI} \qquad \text{(see page 219)}$$

and

$$de = \theta_A \times 3 = -\frac{54{,}000}{EI}$$

Then

$$ce = cd + de = \frac{-72{,}000 - 54{,}000}{EI} = -\frac{126{,}000}{EI}$$

We now consider, as the second stage of superposition, the beam of Fig. 143-c. The elastic curve of this beam will have its maximum deflection at the right end, where it will be, by equation (42),

$$lm = \frac{R \times (9)^3}{3EI} = \frac{243R}{EI}$$

The total deflection of the right end of the beam when both loads are acting will be

$$ce + lm = \frac{-126{,}000 + 243R}{EI}$$

Then

$$\frac{(-126{,}000 + 243R) \times (12)^3}{10.3 \times 10^6 \times 134.81} = -\frac{1}{8}$$

and

$$R = 105 \text{ lb.}$$

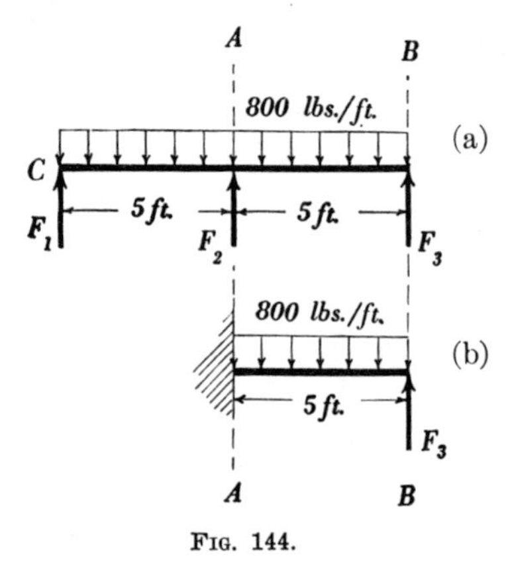

FIG. 144.

Illustrative Example II (Fig. 144-a). The supporting forces F_1, F_2, and F_3 are to be determined, using the cantilever-beam method. All supports are on the same level. The beam is symmetrical about the central section A.

The right half of the beam, isolated as a free body, is shown in Fig. 144-b. The deflection of section B relative to section A is

Equation (42) *Equation* (43)

$$y = \frac{1}{3}\frac{F_3(5)^3}{EI} - \frac{1}{8}\frac{800(5)^4}{EI} = 0$$

$$F_3 = 1500 \text{ lb.}$$

F_1 and F_2 may now be determined by statics, using the conditions of equilibrium on the entire beam (Fig. 144-a).

$\Sigma M_C = 0$

$$+800 \times 10 \times 5 - 1500 \times 10 - F_2 \times 5 = 0$$
$$F_2 = 5000 \text{ lb.}$$

$\Sigma M_B = 0$

$$-800 \times 10 \times 5 + 5000 \times 5 + F_1 \times 10 = 0$$
$$F_1 = 1500 \text{ lb.}$$

41. Point of Inflection Method. The fixed end beam shown in Fig. 145-a has its points of inflection at $x = 4.23$ and 15.77 ft. from the left end of the beam. (These locations were determined in Illustrative Example I on page 184.) Since there is no bending moment at points of inflection, the beam is equivalent, in the behavior of its elastic curve, to the series of three beams shown in Fig. 145-c. $E = 30 \times 10^6$ psi. $I = 305.7$ in.^{4}

The section to the left of the first point of inflection is a cantilever beam, fixed at its left end, and carrying a uniformly distributed load of 2400 lb./ft., as well as a force V at its right end, where V is the shearing force in the original beam at the point of inflection.

The central portion is a simple beam, carrying a uniformly distributed load of 2400 lb./ft., and supported at its ends by forces V.

The right portion is a cantilever beam, equivalent in dimensions and loading to the left portion.

The shearing force V may be evaluated by considering the simple beam, which is the central portion.

$$V = \frac{2400 \times (15.77 - 4.23)}{2} = 13{,}850 \text{ lb.}$$

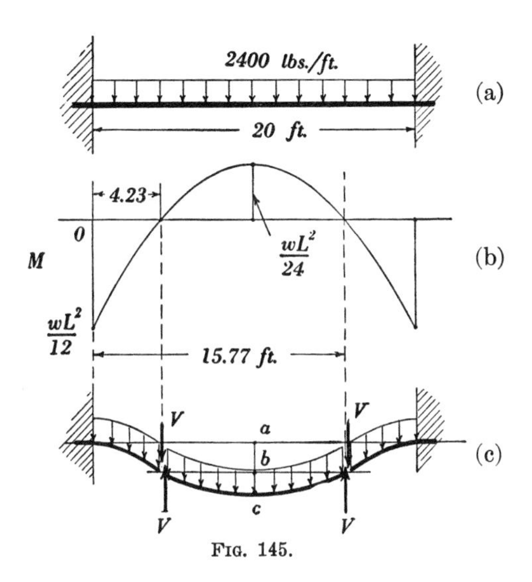

FIG. 145.

The deflection ab of the point of inflection is now determined by applying equations (42) and (43) to the left portion of the beam

$$\begin{aligned} ab &= -\left(\frac{1}{3}\frac{VL^3}{EI} + \frac{1}{8}\frac{wL^4}{EI}\right) \\ &= -\frac{1}{30 \times 10^6 \times 305.7}\left[\frac{1}{3} \times 13{,}850 \times (4.23)^3 + \frac{1}{8} \times 2400 \times (4.23)^4\right] \times (12)^3 \\ &= -0.084 \text{ in.} \end{aligned}$$

The deflection bc will be the maximum deflection of the simple beam which forms the central portion. Applying equation (41),

$$\begin{aligned} bc &= -\frac{5}{384}\frac{wL^4}{EI} \\ &= -\frac{5}{384}\frac{2400 \times (11.54)^4}{30 \times 10^6 \times 305.7} \times (12)^3 \\ &= -0.105 \text{ in.} \end{aligned}$$

The total deflection, $y_{max.}$, will be

$$ac = ab + bc = -0.084 - 0.105 = -0.189 \text{ in.}$$

This value is in agreement with that obtained by using the analytical method of integration on page 184.

42. The Conjugate-Beam Method is an application of the moment-area method which has already been discussed in Art. 37. Like the basic method of which it is an auxiliary, it was the product of the fertile mind of Otto Mohr.

In the moment-area method we found that the change of slope of a

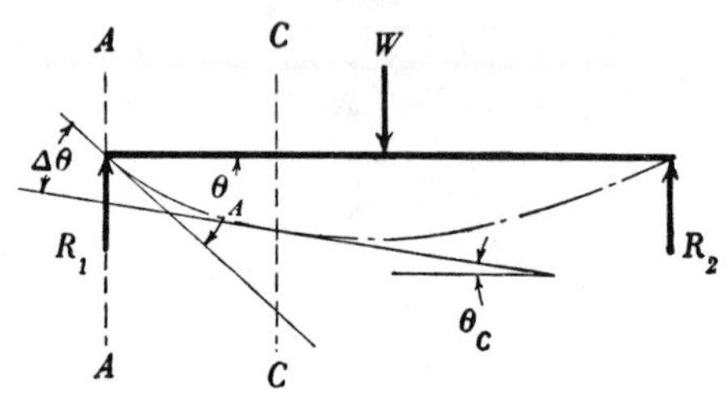

FIG. 146.

beam between two sections is the area of the M/EI diagram between those sections.

Then, in Fig. 146, by applying equation (50),

$$\Delta\theta = \theta_C - \theta_A = \int_A^C \frac{M\,dx}{EI}$$

where $\int_A^C \frac{M\,dx}{EI}$ is the area of the M/EI diagram between the limiting sections A and C.

The slope at any section C may be obtained by transposing the terms of the basic expression thus:

$$\theta_C = \int_A^C \frac{M\,dx}{EI} + \theta_A \qquad (1)$$

or the slope at any section C of a beam is equal to the area of the M/EI diagram between sections A and C, plus the initial slope at A, θ_A.

In this transposed form, the *conjugate-beam method* is used to determine slope. The constant, θ_A, is added to the area of the M/EI diagram by a technique which exactly parallels the path in which shearing force in a beam is determined (Art. 20).

Figure 147 illustrates the method of investigating shearing force which is directly analogous to the treatment of slope in the conjugate-beam method.

If we isolate the portion of the beam to the left of section A (Fig. 147-b) and assume that the only force acting on that body is the uniformly distributed load, the shearing force at section A will be $-wx$. The curve representing this shearing force is the sloping straight line of Fig. 147-b.

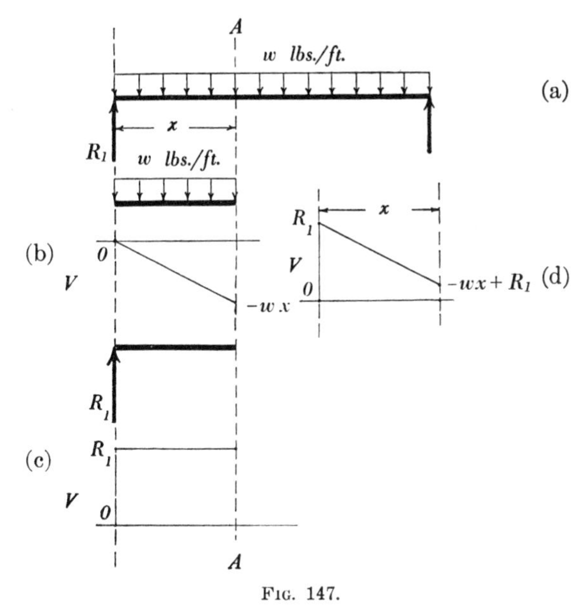

FIG. 147.

If only the supporting force R_1 were acting on the beam, the shearing force throughout the length x would be R_1. The horizontal line representing this shearing force is shown as Fig. 147-c. The effect of the supporting force R_1 is to add a constant of magnitude R_1 to each ordinate of the curve of Fig. 147-b, and the combined shearing force diagram appears as Fig. 147-d.

The constant θ_A of equation (1) above can be introduced into an M/EI diagram in identical fashion.

If a fictitious beam were to carry a loading, which is the M/EI diagram, it would appear as in Fig. 148. The slope at any section like C could then be determined just as we have determined the shearing force in a real beam. Just as

$$V_x = -wx + R_1$$

$$\theta_C = \int_A^C \frac{M\,dx}{EI} + \theta_A$$

The slope of the fictitious beam at section C is the "shearing force" at section C in this imaginary beam. The support at A is not a force, but represents θ_A, the initial slope, and its presence properly introduces the constant θ_A. The area of the M/EI diagram is not force, but serves to introduce the change of slope.

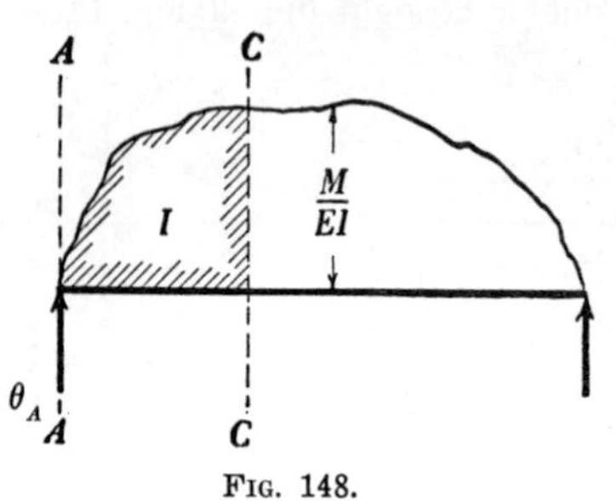

FIG. 148.

Repeating the process used above in discussing shearing force, Fig. 148 shows the change of slope from section A to section C as area I. The slope at section C will be

$$\theta_C = \theta_A - \text{Area } I$$

Such a fictitious beam as that which we have used in the demonstration is called a *conjugate beam.*

The technique of replacing the real beam by a conjugate beam carrying as its loading the M/EI diagram of the real beam can also be used to determine deflection. Once again, we take advantage of the analogy between conjugate and real beam properties.

Bending moment in a real beam is the integral of shearing force. Deflection is the integral of slope and is, therefore, the "bending moment" in a conjugate beam.

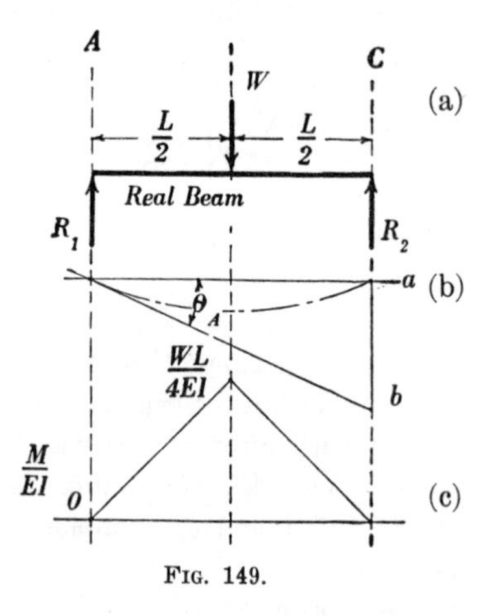

FIG. 149.

To illustrate these principles, we turn to Fig. 149. Figure 149-a shows a real beam, carrying a single concentrated force, W, at mid-span. The beam is freely supported at its ends. The elastic curve of the real beam is shown as Fig. 149-b, and its M/EI diagram is shown as Fig. 149-c.

The initial slope, θ_A, may be determined as in any application of the moment-area method.

$$\Sigma M_C: \quad ab = \left(\frac{1}{2} \times \frac{L}{2} \times \frac{WL}{4EI} \times \frac{2}{3}L\right) + \left(\frac{1}{2} \times \frac{L}{2} \times \frac{WL}{4EI} \times \frac{L}{3}\right)$$

$$= \frac{WL^3}{16EI}$$

$$\theta_A = \frac{ab}{L} = \frac{WL^2}{16EI}$$

The conjugate beam is shown in Fig. 150. The "shearing force" in this beam, representing slope, at distance x will be

$$\theta_x = \frac{WL^2}{16EI} - \frac{1}{2}x\frac{x}{L/2}\frac{WL}{4EI}$$
$$= \frac{WL^2}{16EI} - \frac{Wx^2}{4EI}$$

The "bending moment" in the conjugate beam, representing deflection, at distance x, will be

$$y_x = \frac{WL^2}{16EI}x - \left(\frac{1}{2}x\frac{x}{L/2}\frac{WL}{4EI}\right)\frac{x}{3}$$
$$= \frac{WL^2x}{16EI} - \frac{Wx^3}{12EI}$$

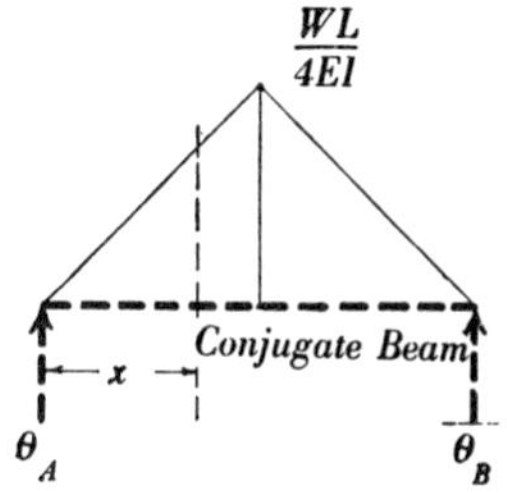

Fig. 150.

Note that the expressions derived above have been used to establish the magnitude of the slope and deflection—the direction may be observed from the elastic curve of the real beam.

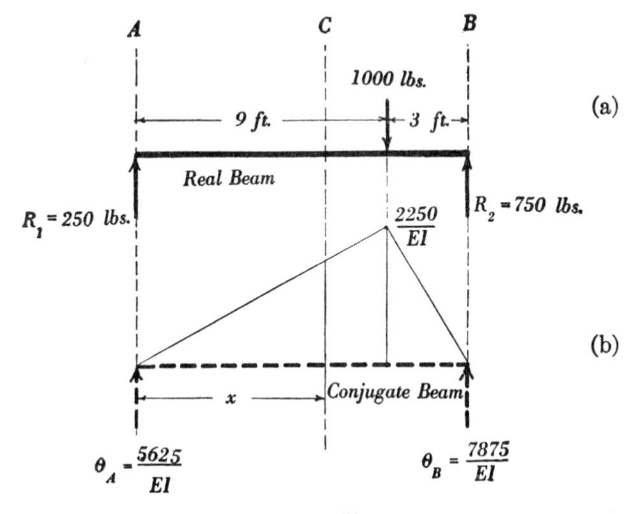

Fig. 151.

Illustrative Example I (Fig. 151-a). The simple beam carries a concentrated load of 1000 lb. $E = 10^6$ psi. $I = 288$ in.^{4} The maximum deflection is to be determined.

The real beam is in equilibrium, and the supporting forces are evaluated by using the conditions of equilibrium.

$\Sigma M_A = 0$: $\quad -R_2 \times 12 + 1000 \times 9 = 0 \quad R_2 = 750$ lb.
$\Sigma M_B = 0$: $\quad +R_1 \times 12 - 1000 \times 3 = 0 \quad R_1 = 250$ lb.
Check: $\quad \Sigma Y = 0; \quad +250 - 1000 + 750 = 0$

The M/EI diagram is plotted as loading of a conjugate beam (Fig. 151-b) supported by initial slope θ_A and final slope θ_B. This loading of a conjugate beam, together with its supports, forms a system in equilibrium, and we may apply the conditions of equilibrium to evaluate θ_A and θ_B.

$$\Sigma M_A = 0: \; -\theta_B \times 12 + \frac{1}{2} \times 9 \times \frac{2250}{EI} \times 6 + \frac{1}{2} \times 3 \times \frac{2250}{EI} \times 10 = 0$$

$$\theta_B = \frac{7875}{EI}$$

$$\Sigma M_B = 0: \; +\theta_A \times 12 - \frac{1}{2} \times 3 \times \frac{2250}{EI} \times 2 - \frac{1}{2} \times 9 \times \frac{2250}{EI} \times 6 = 0$$

$$\theta_A = \frac{5625}{EI}$$

Check: $\Sigma Y = 0; \quad +\dfrac{5625}{EI} - \dfrac{1}{2} \times 9 \times \dfrac{2250}{EI} - \dfrac{1}{2} \times 3 \times \dfrac{2250}{EI} + \dfrac{7875}{EI} = 0$

Maximum deflection will occur at the section of zero slope (section C) located at distance x from the left support, which is where the "shearing force" of the conjugate beam is equal to zero.

Then
$$+\frac{5625}{EI} - \frac{1}{2} x \frac{x}{9} \frac{2250}{EI} = 0$$

$$x = 6.71 \text{ ft.}$$

The deflection at section C is evaluated as the "bending moment" of the conjugate beam at C.

$$y_{\text{max.}} = \frac{1}{EI}\left(+5625 \times 6.71 - \frac{1}{2} \times 6.71 \times 250 \times 6.71 \times \frac{6.71}{3}\right)$$

$$= \frac{25{,}160}{EI} = \frac{25{,}160 \times (12)^3}{10^6 \times 288}$$

$$= 0.151 \text{ in.}$$

43. Summary of Deflection Formulas.

Case	Beam	Description	Max. Slope	Max. Deflection
1.	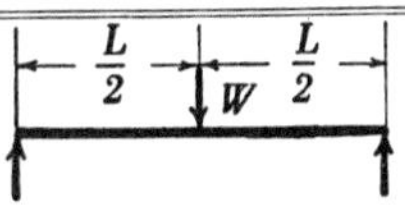	Simple Beam—Concentrated Load at Mid-Span	$\frac{WL^2}{16EI}$	$\frac{WL^3}{48EI}$
2.	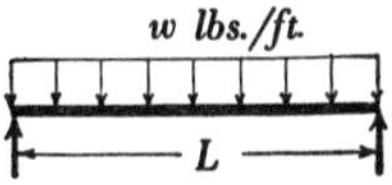	Simple Beam—Uniformly Distributed Load	$\frac{wL^3}{24EI}$	$\frac{5}{384}\frac{wL^4}{EI}$
3.	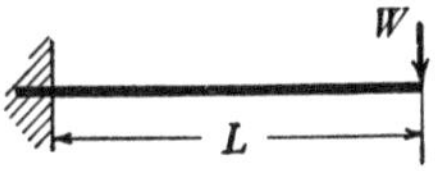	Cantilever—Concentrated Load at Free End	$\frac{WL^2}{2EI}$	$\frac{1}{3}\frac{WL^3}{EI}$
4.	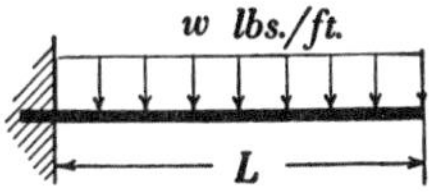	Cantilever—Uniformly Distributed Load	$\frac{wL^3}{6EI}$	$\frac{1}{8}\frac{wL^4}{EI}$
5.	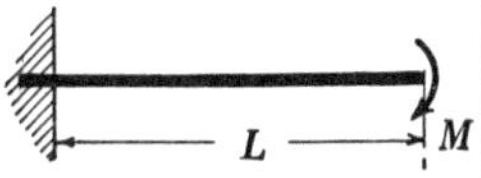	Cantilever—Couple at Free End	$\frac{ML}{EI}$	$\frac{ML^2}{2EI}$
6.	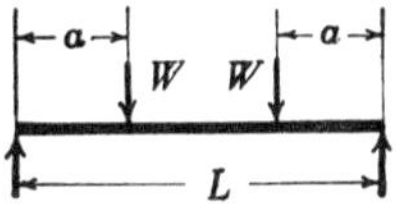	Simple Beam—Two Equal Symmetrical Concentrated Loads	$\frac{Wa}{2EI}(a-L)$	$\frac{Wa}{24EI}(3L^2-4a^2)$
7.	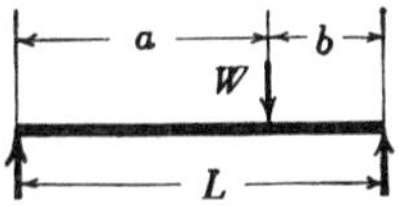	Simple Beam—Non-Symmetrical Concentrated Load	$\frac{Wab(2L-b)}{6LEI}$	$\frac{Wb(L^2-b^2)^{\frac{3}{2}}}{9\sqrt{3}LEI}$
8.	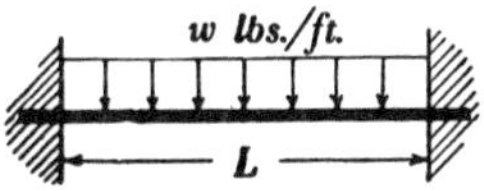	Fixed End—Uniformly Distributed Load	—	$\frac{wL^4}{384EI}$
9.	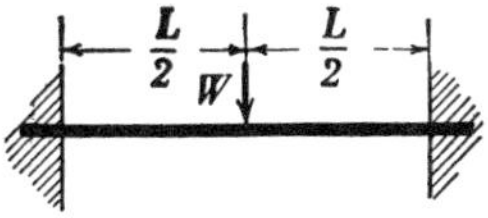	Fixed End—Concentrated Load at Mid-Span	—	$\frac{WL^3}{192EI}$
10.	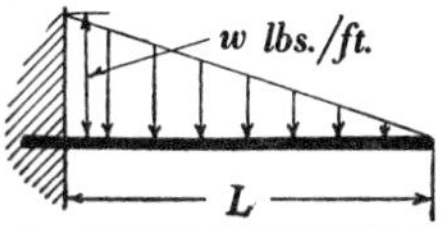	Cantilever—Uniformly Varying Load	$\frac{wL^3}{24EI}$	$\frac{wL^4}{30EI}$

PROBLEMS

Note: The following problems are concerned with the subject of deflection. Any of the methods discussed in Arts. 32–42, inclusive, may be employed as the method of attack, or training in attack upon such problems may be enhanced by employing one method as an original solution, and another as means of checking the first. Problems 196–235, inclusive, consider beams which are statically determinate, Probs. 236–258, inclusive, deal with statically indeterminate cases, and Probs. 259–262, inclusive, are devoted to review problems involving bending and longitudinal shear stresses as well as deflection.

The value of modulus of elasticity, E, for each material should be taken from the table on page 79. The moment of inertia, $I_{N.A.}$, for the structural shapes will be found in the tables of the Appendix.

196. The beam carries a single concentrated load of 8000 lb. at mid-span. Determine the maximum deflection. $I_{N.A.} = 500$ in.,^{4} $E = 1.2 \times 10^6$ psi. *Ans.* −0.829 in.

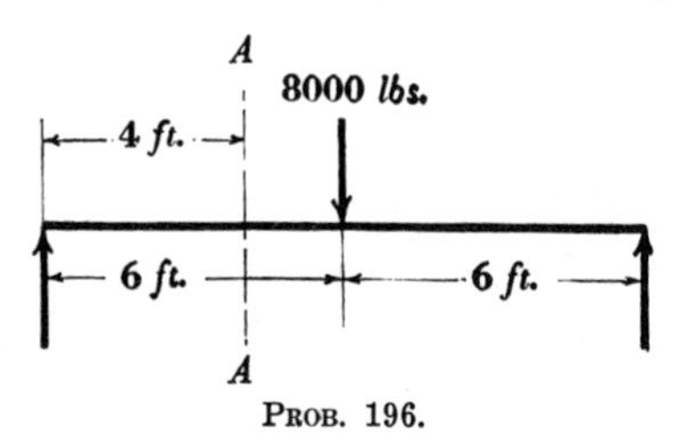

PROB. 196.

197. Determine the deflection at section A–A of the beam of Prob. 196. *Ans.* −0.707 in.

198. The beam is an American Standard steel I-beam, 10 in. × 40 lb./ft. Determine the maximum slope and the maximum deflection.

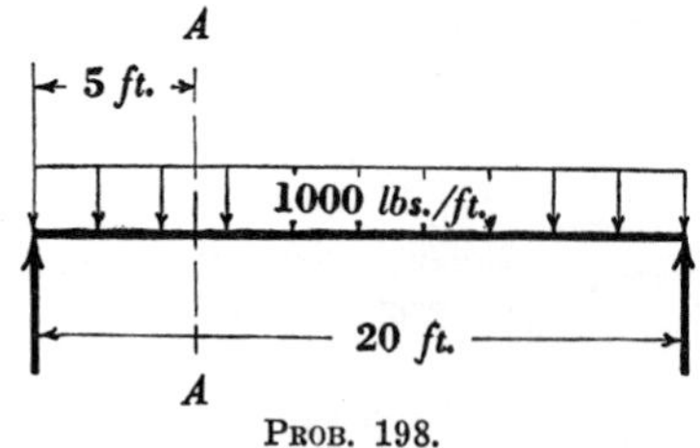

PROB. 198.

199. Determine the slope and deflection at section A–A of the beam of Prob. 198.

200. Determine the deflection at 3 ft. from the end of the beam. $E = 1.2 \times 10^6$ psi. *Ans.* −0.186 in.

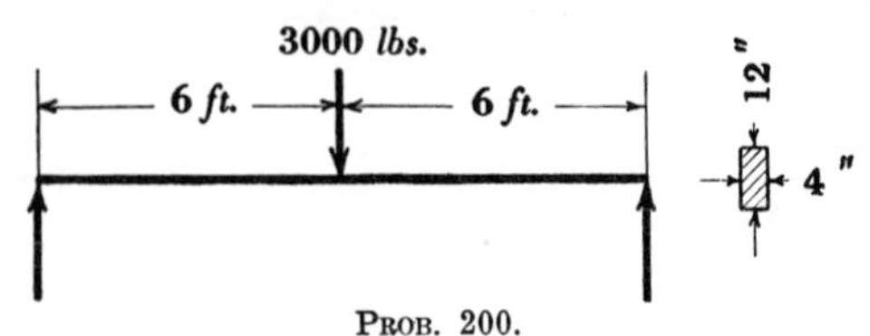

PROB. 200.

201. The beam shown has a modulus of elasticity, $E = 1.2 \times 10^6$ psi. Determine the following:
a) The maximum deflection.
b) The maximum slope.
c) The deflection at 3 ft. from the end of the beam.
d) The slope at 3 ft. from the end of the beam.

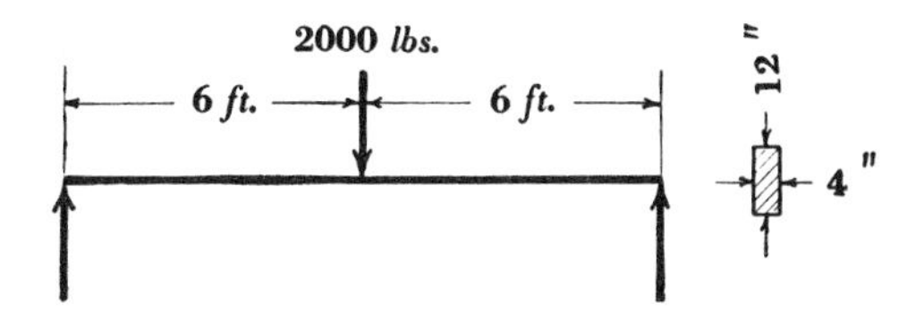

PROB. 201.

202. The beam shown is an American Standard steel I-beam, 10 in. × 30 lb./ft. The maximum allowable deflection, according to the City Building Code, is Span/360. Neglecting the weight of the beam itself, determine the maximum allowable concentrated load W which may be placed at mid-span. *Ans.* 11,450 lb

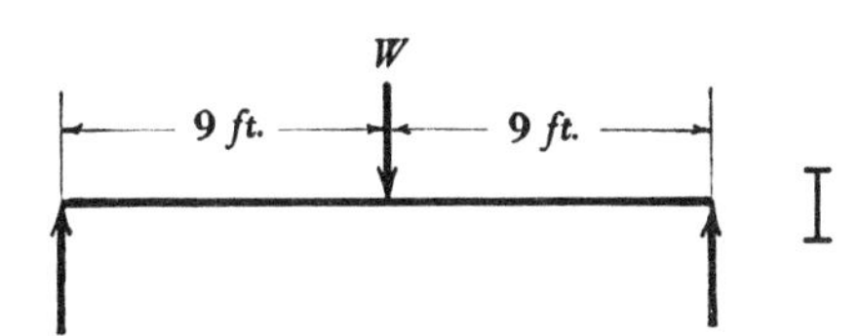

PROB. 202.

203. Determine the maximum allowable load W in Prob. 202 if the weight of the beam itself is considered. *Ans.* 11,100 lb.

204. A 12 in. deep steel beam is subjected to the maximum uniformly distributed load permitted by an allowable bending stress of 20,000 psi. The beam is freely supported at its ends, and the length of span is 16 ft. Determine the maximum deflection of the beam when carrying this maximum permissible load. *Ans.* −0.427 in.

205. A steel beam AB is subjected to a system of loads. The general equations of deflection in the ranges of loading shown are:

x:0–6; $EIy = 750x^3 - 25x^4 - 55{,}800x$
x:6–12; $EIy = 750x^3 - 25x^4 - 500(x - 6)^3 - 55{,}800x$
x:12–16; $EIy = -100(16 - x)^3 - 25(16 - x)^4 - 30{,}200x - 349{,}600$

Make a drawing of the beam showing all loads and supporting forces.

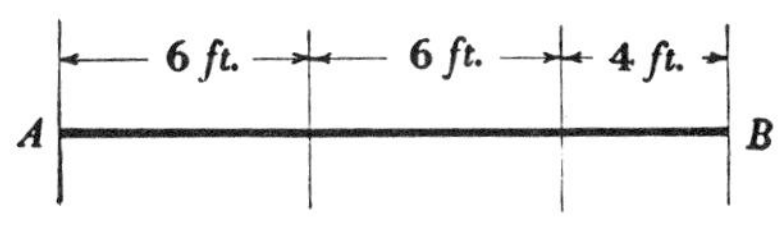

PROB. 205.

206. The beam is a Wide-Flange steel beam, 10 in. $\times$ 77 lb./ft. Determine the maximum deflection. The weight of the beam itself has been included in the uniformly distributed load of 1000 lb./ft. *Ans.* -0.473 in.

207. The beam is a Wide-Flange steel beam, 18 in. $\times$ 50 lb./ft. Determine the maximum deflection.

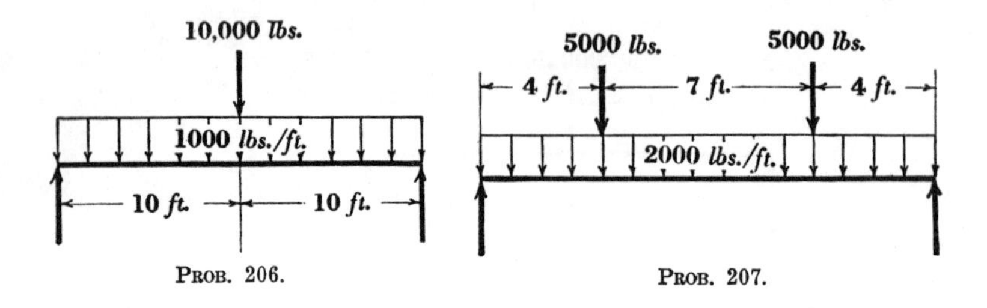

PROB. 206. PROB. 207.

208. A cantilever beam has a 6 in. $\times$ 12 in. rectangular cross-section. The span is 12 ft., and $E = 10^6$ psi. The beam is subjected to a single concentrated load of 1200 lb., applied at the free end. Determine the maximum slope and the maximum deflection.

209. A cantilever beam has an 8 in. $\times$ 12 in. rectangular cross-section. The span is 10 ft., and $E = 1.2 \times 10^6$ psi. If the beam carries a uniformly distributed load of 150 lb./ft., determine the maximum slope and the maximum deflection.

Ans. 0.0026 radians; -0.234 in.

210. Determine the slope and the deflection at 5 ft. from the free end of the cantilever beam of Prob. 209.

211. Determine the maximum deflection. $E = 10^6$ psi.

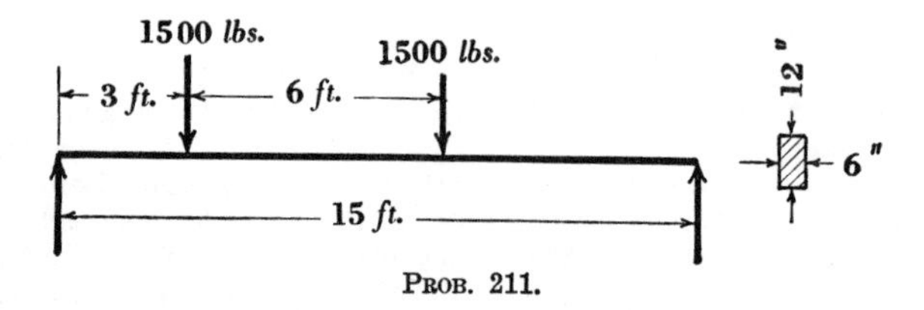

PROB. 211.

212. Determine the maximum deflection. $E = 2 \times 10^6$ psi. *Ans.* -1.00 in.

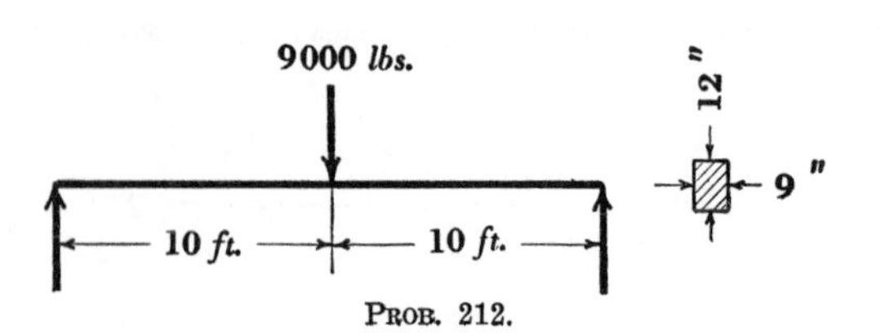

PROB. 212.

213. The beam is a 12 in. × 17.78 lb./ft. aluminum I-beam. Determine the deflection under the 1000 lb. loads, and the maximum deflection. Neglect the weight of the beam. *Ans.* −0.119 in.; −0.145 in.

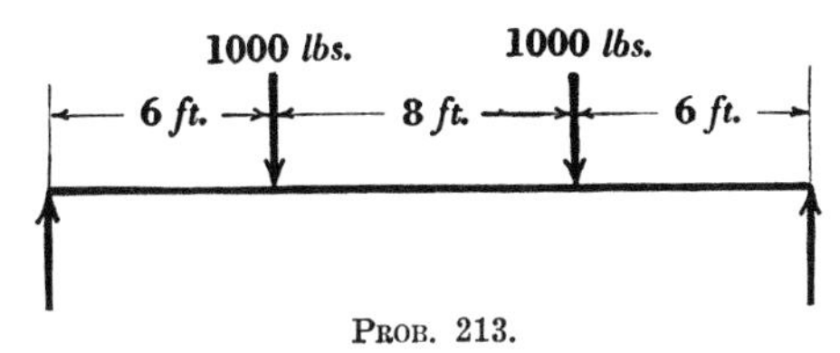

PROB. 213.

214. Derive an expression for the maximum deflection in each range of loading.

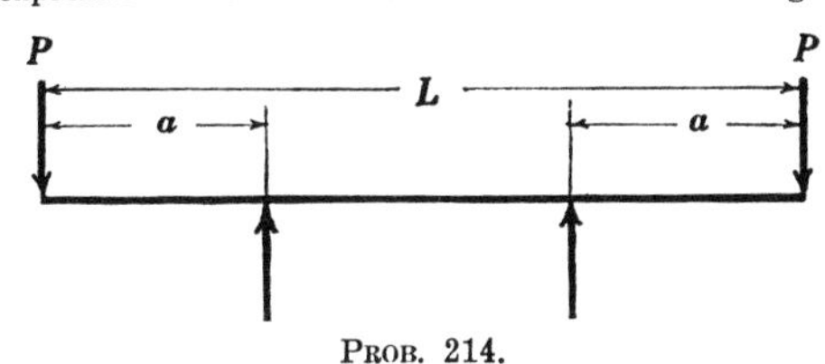

PROB. 214.

215. Determine the maximum deflection in each range of loading. $E = 10^6$ psi.

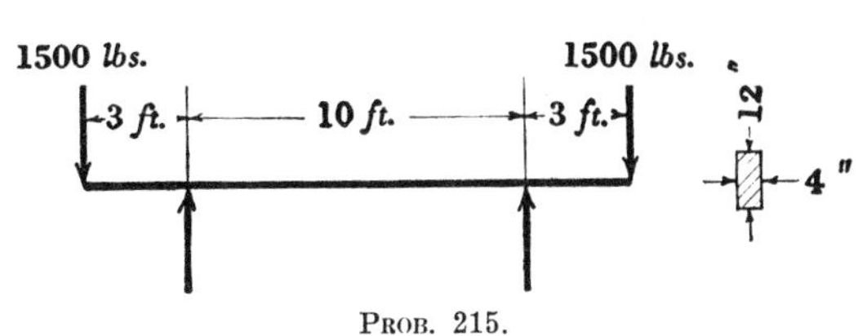

PROB. 215.

216. Determine the length of overhang in Prob. 215, all other data remaining unchanged, which will make the maximum deflection in the central section equal in magnitude to the deflection at the ends. *Ans.* 2.18 ft.

217. The aluminum I-beam is supported on knife edges at A and B. $I = 167.5$ in.^{4} Determine the deflection at the right end. *Ans.* −0.10 in.

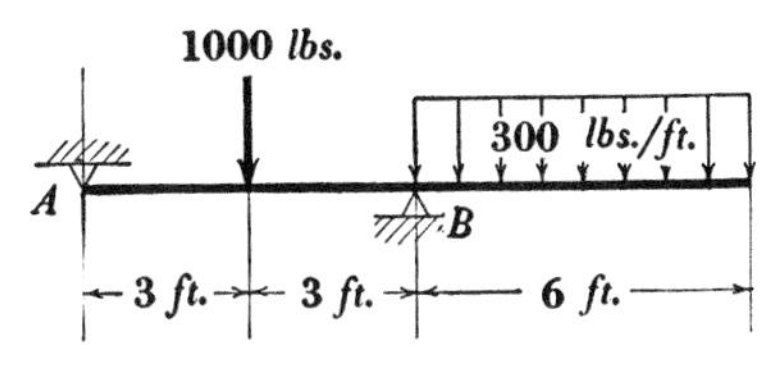

PROB. 217.

218. Determine the deflection at the center of the middle span. $E = 10^6$ psi.

219. Determine the deflection of the cantilever beam at the free end and at 3 ft. from the free end. The beam is a Wide-Flange steel beam, 14 in. × 38 lb./ft.

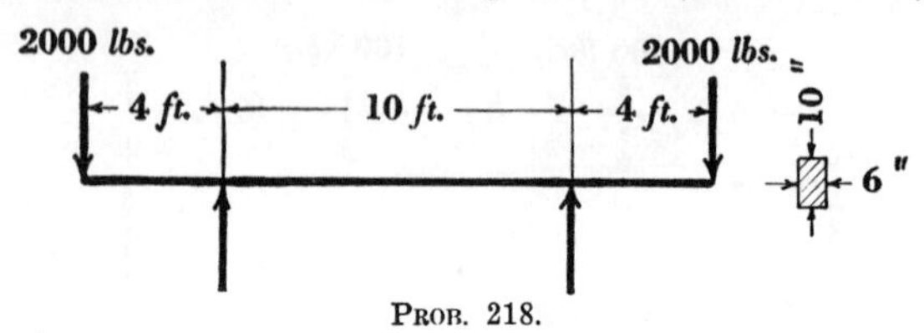

PROB. 218.

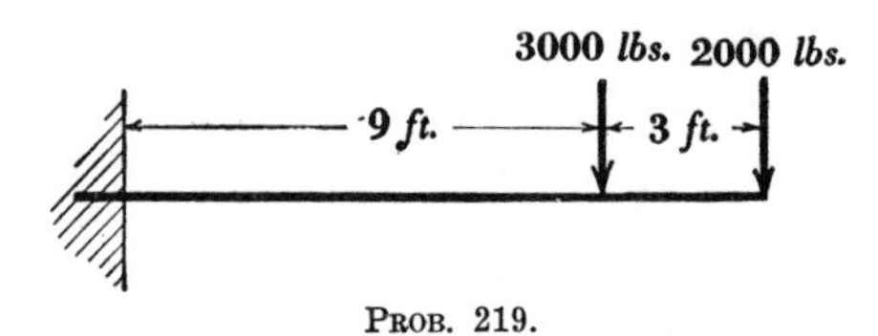

PROB. 219.

220. The beam is an American Standard steel beam, 10 in. × 40 lb./ft. Determine the maximum slope and the maximum deflection. *Ans.* 0.00287 radians; −0.11 in.

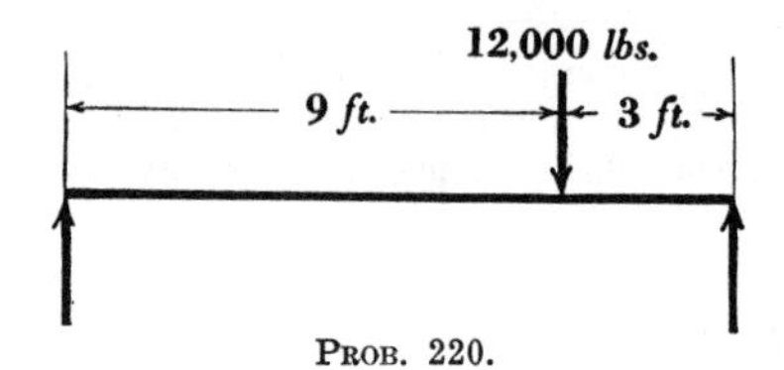

PROB. 220.

221. Determine the deflection of the free end C. $E = 8 \times 10^5$ psi. *Ans.* −0.36 in

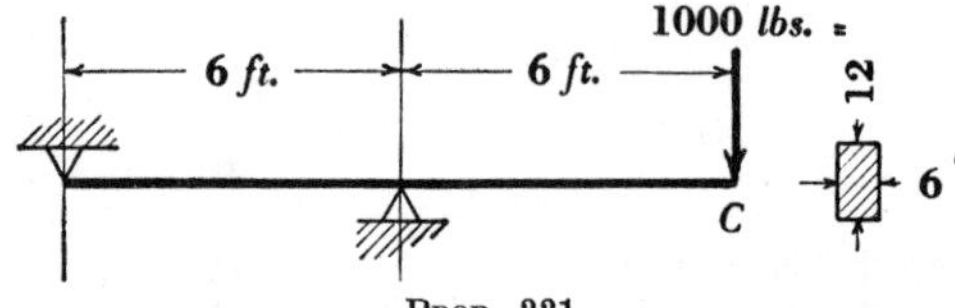

PROB. 221.

222. The beam is an aluminum beam with $I = 600$ in.^{4} Determine the maximum deflection.

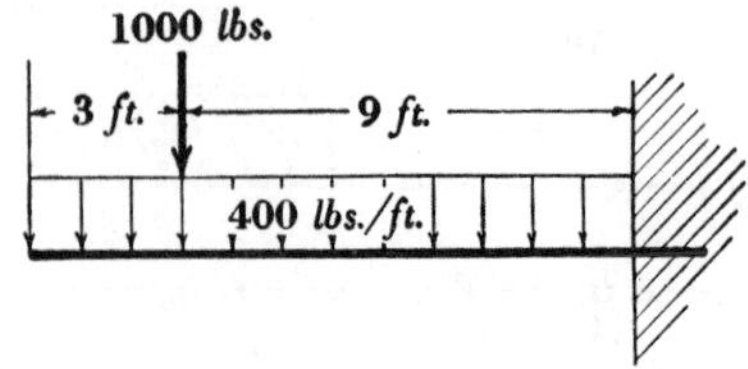

PROB. 222.

223. The beam is an American Standard steel I-beam, 15 in. × 60.8 lb./ft. Determine the maximum slope and the maximum deflection.

224. The beam is a steel beam, with $I = 400$ in.^{4} Determine the deflection under each load.

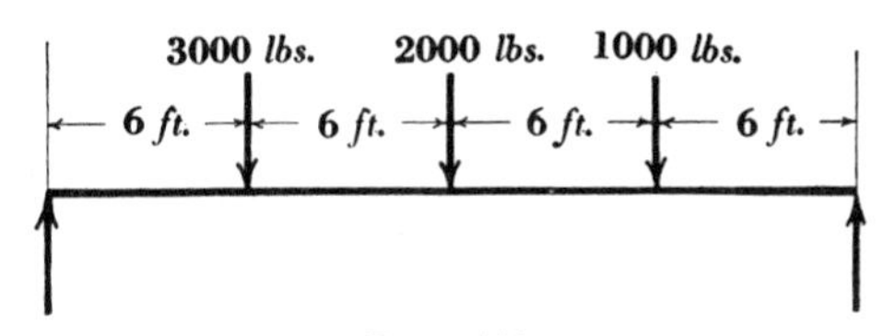

Prob. 223.

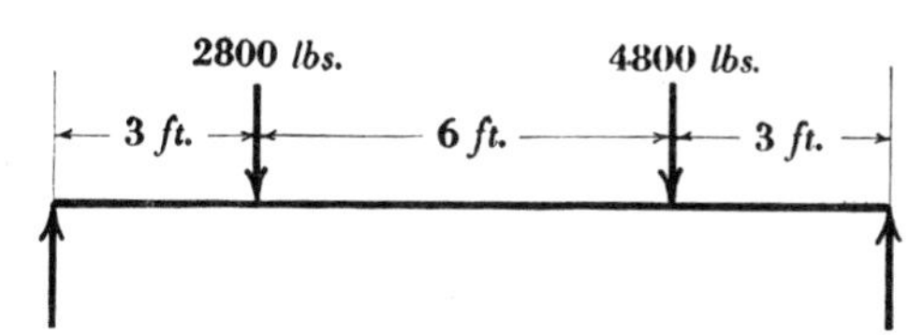

Prob. 224.

225. The beam is a steel beam, with $I = 57.6$ in.^{4} Determine the maximum deflection.

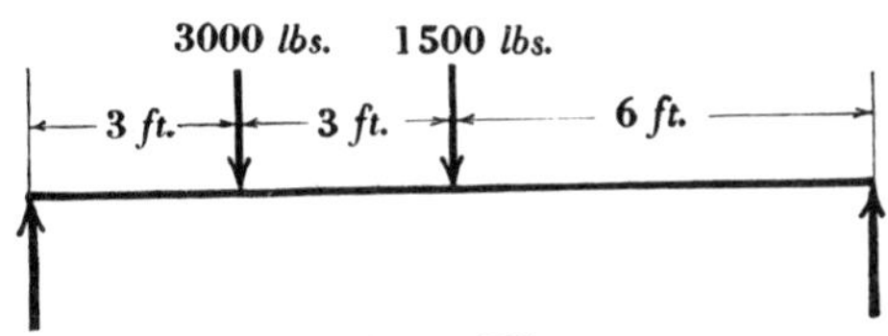

Prob. 225.

226. The steel beam is supported on knife edges at A and B. $I = 120.6$ in.^{4} Determine the deflection at the right end. *Ans.* -0.068 in.

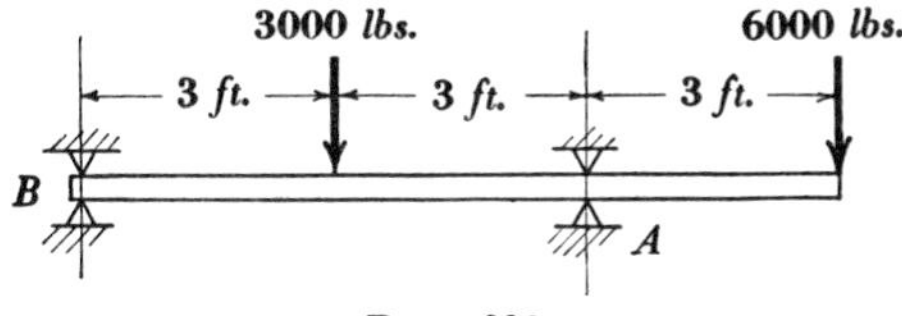

Prob. 226.

227. Locate the section of the beam of Prob. 226 at which the maximum upward deflection will occur. *Ans.* 3.73 ft. (from B)

228. The beam is supported on knife edges at A and B and loaded by a couple M applied at C. Derive an expression for the deflection at C.

Ans. $\frac{M}{6EI}(-3L^2 + 4aL - a^2)$.

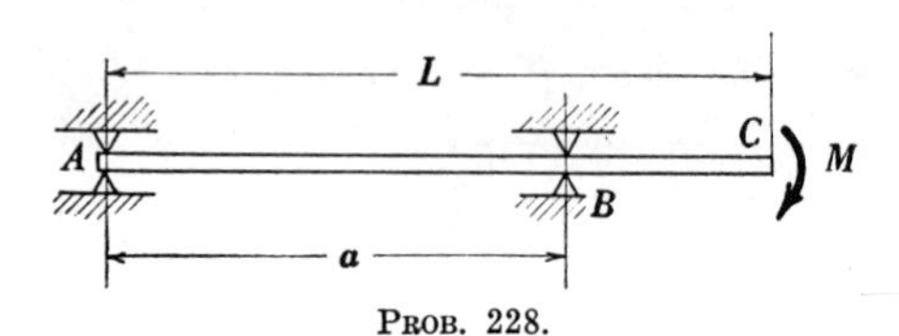

PROB. 228.

229. Determine the deflection at the right end, in terms of P, L, E, and I.

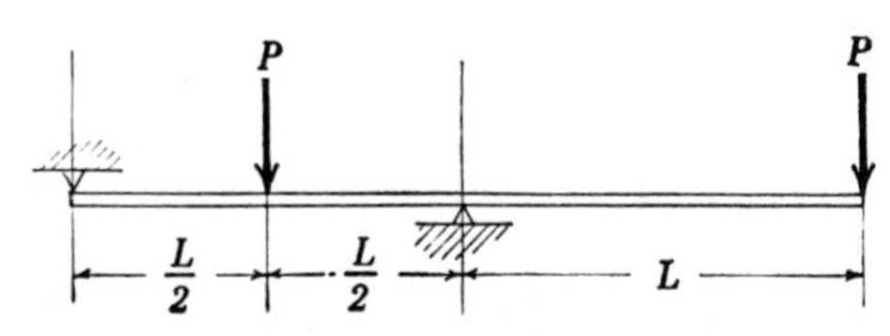

PROB. 229.

230. The beam CD is 6 in. wide and 12 in deep. The bending moment diagram is shown. The bending moment varies uniformly from zero at the ends to 12,000 ft.-lb. at A and B. $E = 1.2 \times 10^6$ psi. If the deflection is zero at A and B, find the deflection at the center and at the ends of the beam.

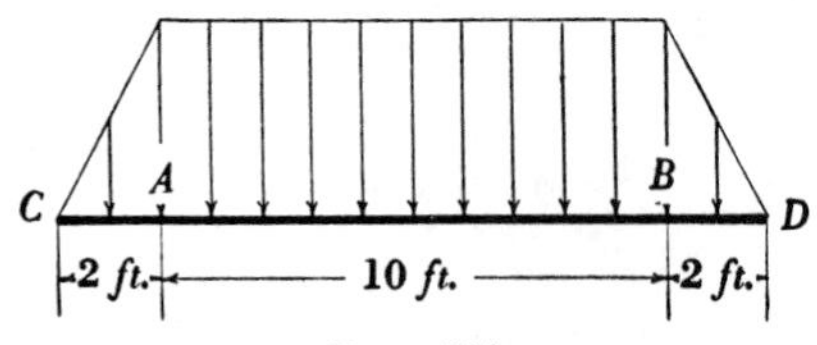

PROB. 230.

231. The steel cantilever beam is loaded by a uniformly varying force, which varies from 200 lb./ft. at A to 500 lb./ft. at B. $I = 300$ in.^{4} Determine the maximum deflection.

Ans. -0.209 in.

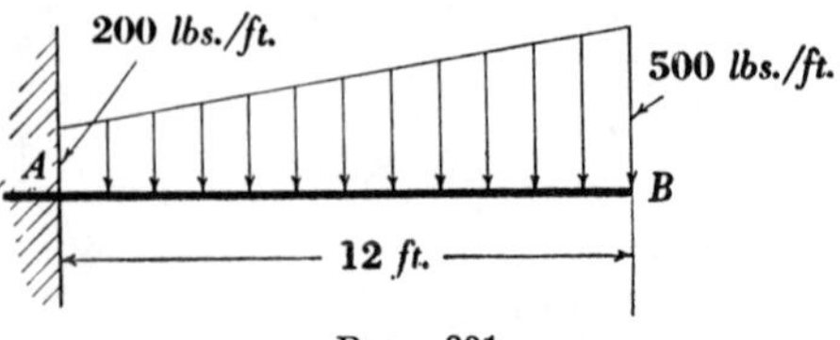

PROB. 231.

232. Determine the slope and deflection at 3 ft. from the left end of the beam. The beam is steel, and $I = 216$ in.^{4} *Ans.* 0.0017 radians; 0.073 in.

233. Determine the uniformly distributed load of w lb./ft. if the deflection at the right end of the beam must not exceed 0.368 in. $E = 10^6$ psi. $I = 432$ in.^{4}

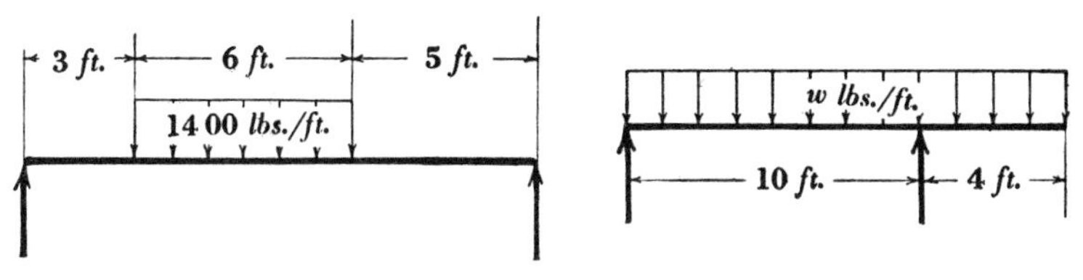

PROB. 232. PROB. 233.

234. Determine the maximum deflection in the first range of loading from the left end of the beam of Prob. 233 if $w = 1000$ lb./ft.

235. The beam carries a uniformly varying load, which varies from an intensity of zero at the left end to 3000 lb./ft. at the right end. The beam is steel, and $I =$ 172.8 in.^{4} Determine the maximum deflection. *Ans.* -0.135 in.

STATICALLY INDETERMINATE CASES

236. The beam is built into the end walls with fixed ends. $E = 1.2 \times 10^6$ psi. $I = 144$ in.^{4} Determine the maximum deflection and the maximum bending moment.
Ans. $y_{max.} = 0.288$ in.; $M_{max.} = -5400$ ft.-lb.

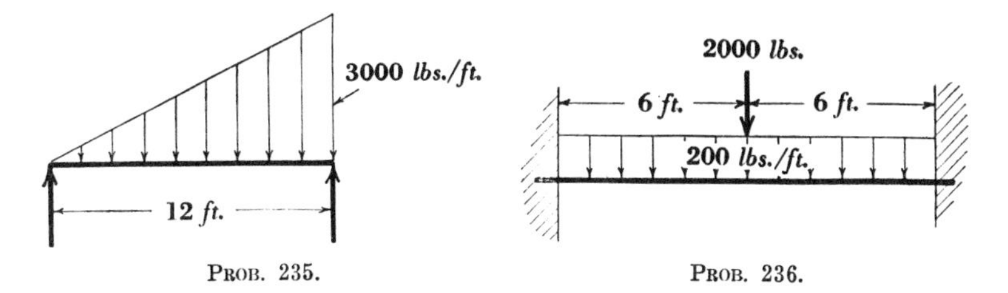

PROB. 235. PROB. 236.

237. The beam is an American Standard steel I-beam, 7 in. × 17.5 lb./ft. The ends are fixed. Determine the following:

a) Maximum positive bending moment.
b) Maximum negative bending moment.
c) Maximum deflection.

Ans. a) 6000 ft.-lb.; b) 12,000 ft.-lb.; c) -0.08 in.

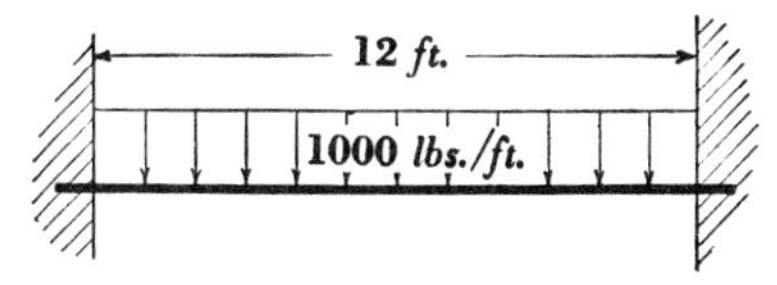

PROB. 237.

238. The beam is partially restrained at the end walls by bending moments $M_1 = -30{,}000$ ft.-lb. $E = 30 \times 10^6$ psi; $I = 216$ in.^{4} Determine the maximum deflection.

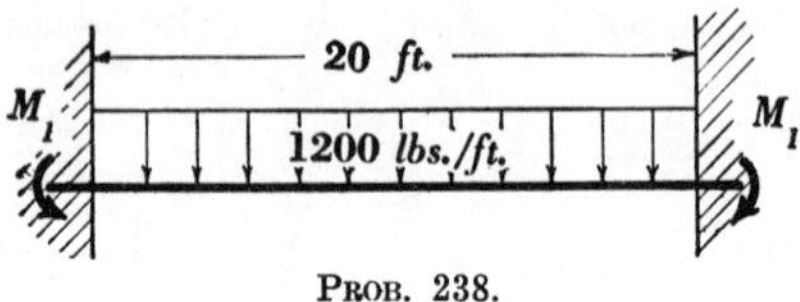

PROB. 238.

239. A 12 in. × 17.78 lb./ft. aluminum beam is supported by columns as shown. The columns exert a partial restraint on the beam which is $M_1 = -3000$ ft.-lb. Determine the deflection at 3 ft. from the left end. *Ans.* −0.024 in.

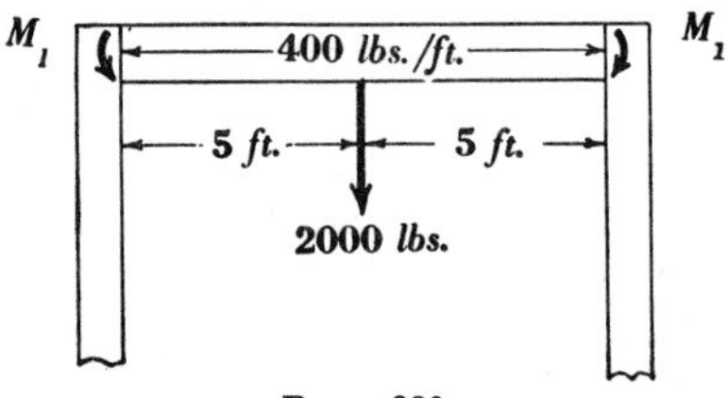

PROB. 239.

240. The 10 in. wide × 12 in. deep beam carries a uniformly varying load which varies from zero at the wall ends to 1200 lb./ft. at the center. The beam is partially restrained at its ends by couples $M_1 = -8000$ ft.-lb. Determine the maximum deflection. $E = 10^6$ psi. *Ans.* −0.076 in.

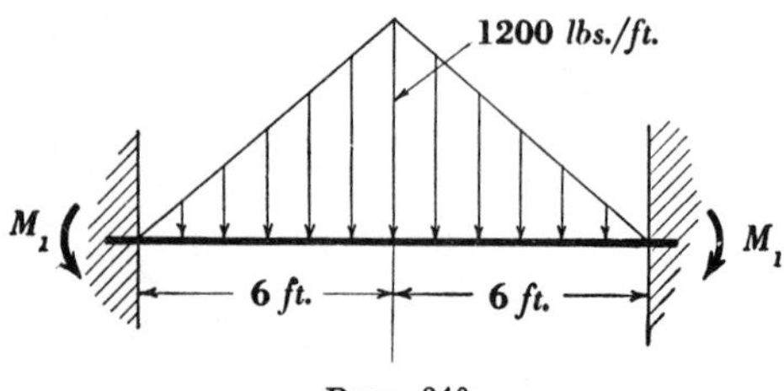

PROB. 240.

241. The beam is built into the walls with fixed ends. Determine V_1, V_2, M_1, and M_2.

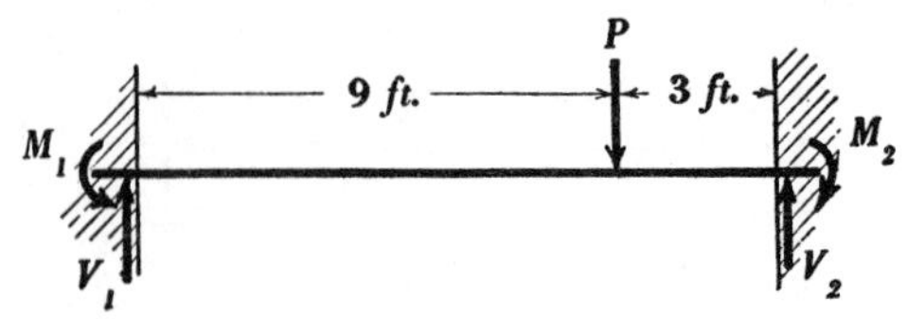

PROB. 241.

242. Determine the maximum deflection of the beam of the preceding problem.

Ans. $-\dfrac{4.86P}{EI}$

243. All of the supporting forces are applied at the same level. Determine the supporting forces R_1, R_2, R_3.

244. In Prob. 243, determine the supporting forces if R_2 is applied at 1/16 in. below the level of R_1 and R_3, using the following data: $W = 3000$ lb.; $a = 3$ ft.; $E = 1.2 \times 10^6$ psi; the beam section is a 12 in. square.

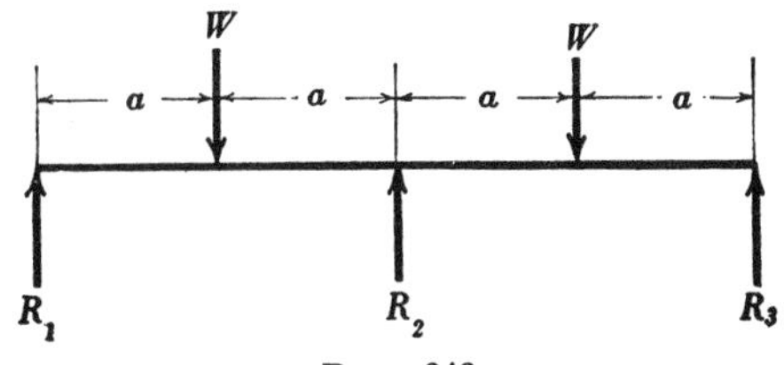

PROB. 243.

245. The three supports are applied at the same level. Determine the supporting forces R_1, R_2, and R_3. *Ans.* $R_1 = R_3 = 4500$ lb.; $R_2 = 15{,}000$ lb.

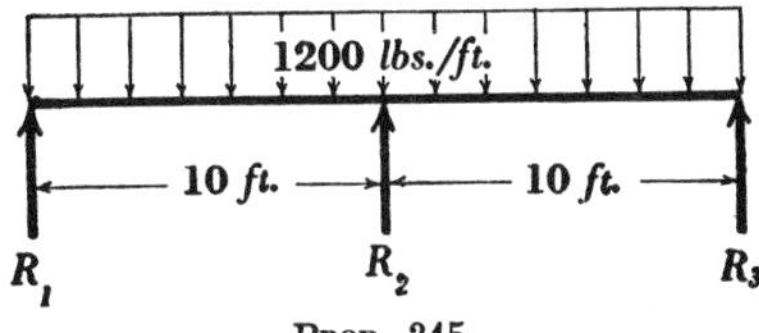

PROB. 245.

246. In Prob. 245, determine the supporting forces and the maximum bending moment in the beam, using the following data: R_2 is applied 1/4 in. below the level of R_1 and R_3; $E = 1.2 \times 10^6$ psi; the beam has a rectangular cross-section which is 10 in. wide by 12 in. deep.

247. The beam is supported on knife edges at A, B, and C. All supports are on the same level. Determine the maximum bending moment in the beam. *Ans.* 4130 ft.-lb.

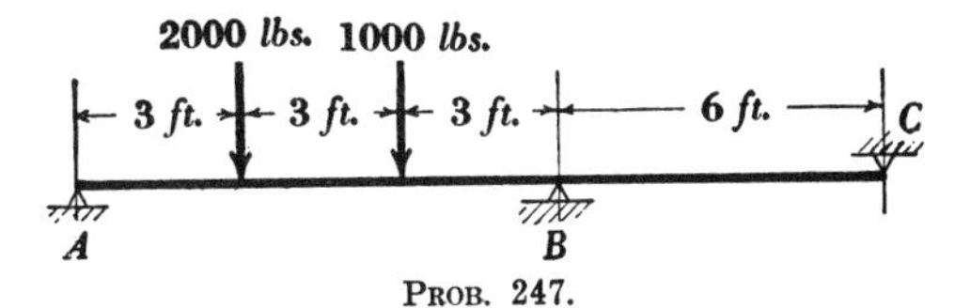

PROB. 247.

248. All supports are on the same level. Determine the supporting forces R_1, R_2, and R_3.

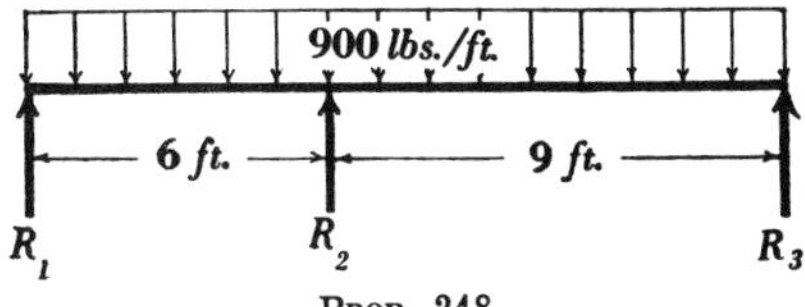

PROB. 248.

249. The beam is supported by the wall, where it is fixed-ended, and on knife edges at A and B. Determine the maximum bending moment in the beam if all supports are applied at the same level.

250. The cantilever beam shown is supported by a force R applied on the same level as the wall support. Determine the maximum positive and maximum negative bending moments in the beam.

Ans. $M_{\text{max.}}$ (positive) = 1700 ft.-lb.; $M_{\text{max.}}$ (negative) = 6400 ft.-lb.

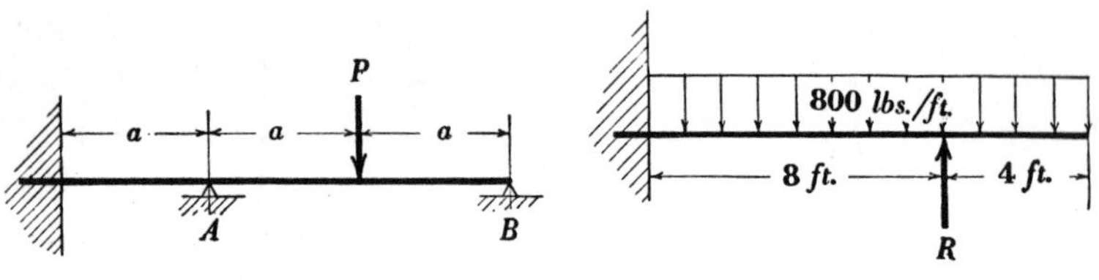

PROB. 249. PROB. 250.

251. The Tee-beam shown is built into a wall (fixed end) and supported by force R_1. The supports are on the same level. The beam carries a uniformly distributed load of w lb. per ft. The moment of inertia of the beam about its neutral axis is $I = 250$ in.[4] The maximum allowable bending stress in tension is $s_T = 3000$ psi, and the maximum allowable bending stress in compression is $s_C = 8000$ psi. Determine the maximum allowable load. *Ans.* 1540 lb./ft.

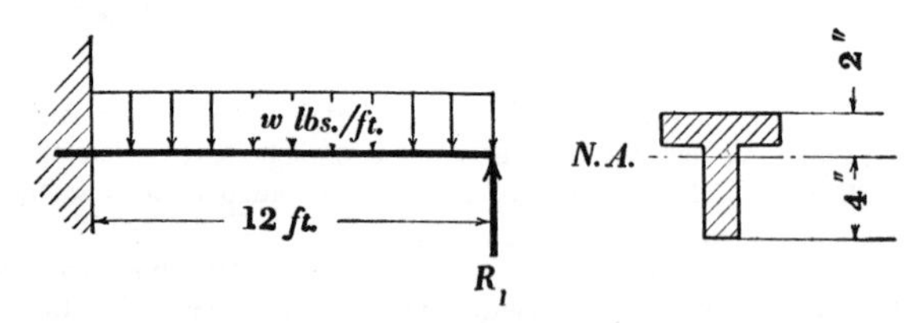

PROB. 251.

252. The beam is built in at A (fixed end) and freely supported at B. The support at B is applied ¼ in. below the level at A. $E = 30 \times 10^6$ psi; $I = 108$ in.[4] Determine the deflection under the 10,000 lb. load. *Ans.* -0.214 in.

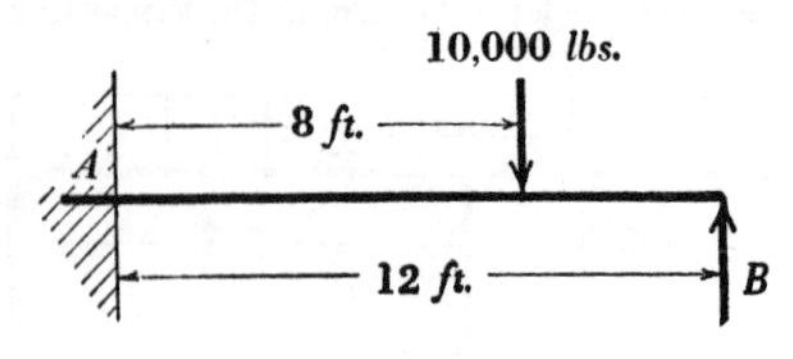

PROB. 252.

253. Two beams, each 10 ft. long, of identical material and cross-section are supported as shown. Beam AB is a cantilever beam, carrying a uniformly distributed load of 1000 lb./ft., freely supported on beam CD. Beam CD is freely supported at its ends. $E = 10^6$ psi; $I = 100$ in.^{4} Determine the deflection at B.

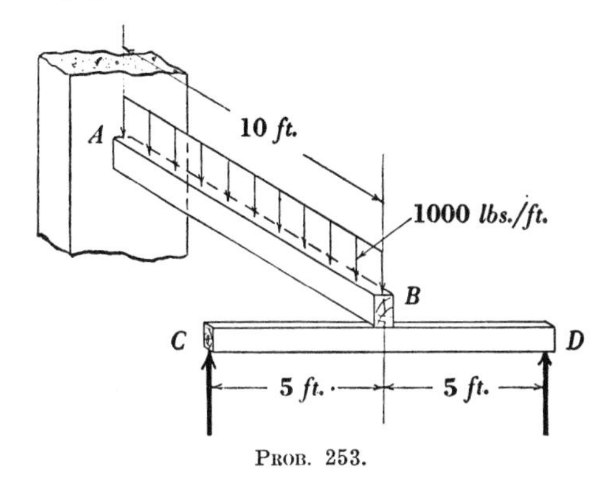

PROB. 253.

254. The cantilever beam is built in at end A (fixed end) and elastically supported by a spring at end B. The beam is loaded by a single concentrated force P applied at mid-span as shown. Determine the force exerted by the beam on the spring, using the following data:

$E = 30 \times 10^6$ psi.
$I_{N.A.} = 100$ in.^{4}
$L = 8.5$ ft.
$P = 3200$ lb.
k = spring constant = 9000 lb./in. *Ans* 515 lb.

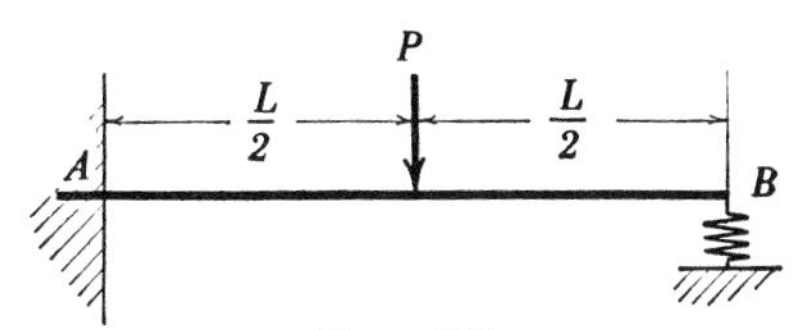

PROB. 254.

255. The beam is freely supported at A and B and rests on a spring at C. $E = 30 \times 10^6$ psi; $I = 200$ in.^{4}; the spring constant is $k = 60{,}000$ lb./in. Determine the force exerted by the beam on the spring.

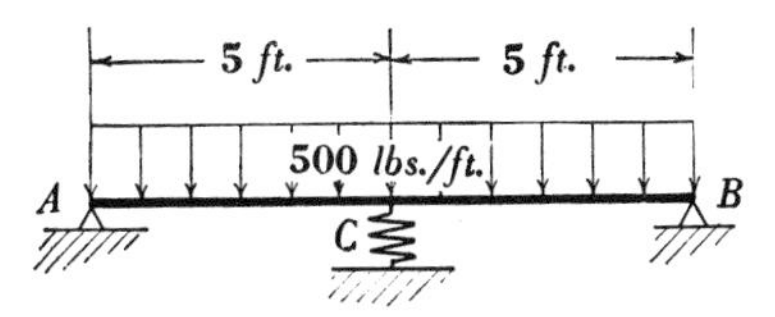

PROB. 255.

256. The steel beam CD is built into a wall (fixed end) at D. $I_{N.A.} = 1000$ in.[4] The steel rod AB has a cross-sectional area of ½ sq. in. Points D, B, and C were on the same horizontal level before loading. When the beam is loaded by a force of 1000 lb. at C, determine the unit stress in rod AB and the deflection of the beam at C.
Ans. 2540 psi; −0.02 in.

257. The steel cantilever beam AB is built in (fixed end) at B, and held in position by steel rod CD. Points A, C, and B are on the same horizontal level before the load of 4000 lb. is applied. Determine the unit stress in rod CD when the load is applied The moment of inertia of the beam is $I_{N.A.} = 100$ in.[4], and the cross-sectional area of CD is 0.20 sq. in.

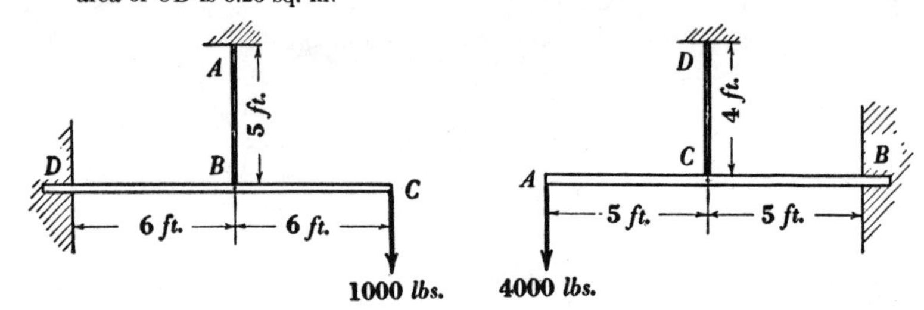

PROB. 256. PROB. 257.

258. In the structure shown, beams AB and CDE are built in (fixed end) at the wall. The bar BD is fastened by pin joints to the two beams. Before loading, beams AB and CDE are horizontal, and bar BD is vertical. The cross-sectional area of BD is 0.1 sq. in.; the moment of inertia of beams AB and CDE is $I_{N.A.} = 20$ in.[4]; the modulus of elasticity of all members is $E = 30 \times 10^6$ psi. When the two loads of 500 lb. are applied, determine the unit stress in member BD. *Ans.* 3550 psi.

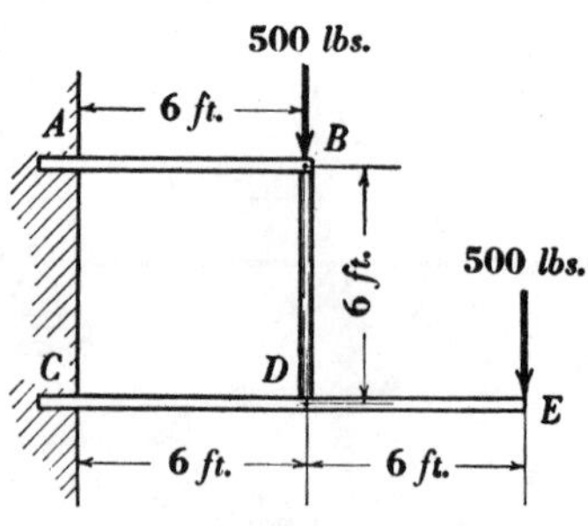

PROB. 258.

259. A simple beam, freely supported at its ends, having a span of 12 ft. is loaded with a single concentrated load W at mid-span. Determine the maximum value of W that may be applied to the beam under the following conditions. The beam has a rectangular cross-section, 6 in. wide and 12 in. deep.
Maximum allowable bending stress: 1000 psi.
Maximum allowable longitudinal shear stress: 100 psi.
Maximum allowable deflection: Span/400
$E = 1.2 \times 10^6$ psi. *Ans.* 4000 lb.

260. A cantilever beam, 9 ft. long, carries a single concentrated load W at the free end. The beam is a 12 in. deep I-beam, having a moment of inertia $I_{N.A.} = 400$ in.^{4} $E = 30 \times 10^6$ psi. Determine the maximum allowable value of W under the following conditions:
Maximum allowable bending stress: 20,000 psi.
Maximum allowable deflection: Span/400.

261. A simple beam, freely supported at its ends, carries a uniformly distributed load of w lb./ft. The span is 12 ft., and the beam has a rectangular cross-section 6 in. wide by 12 in. deep. $E = 1.2 \times 10^6$ psi. Determine the maximum allowable value of w under the following conditions:
Maximum allowable bending stress: 1000 psi.
Maximum allowable longitudinal shear stress: 100 psi.
Maximum allowable deflection: Span/400.

262. A cantilever beam carrying a uniformly distributed load of w lb./ft. has a span of 10 ft. The beam has a rectangular cross-section 4 in. wide by 10 in. deep. $E = 10^6$ psi. Determine the maximum allowable value of w under the following conditions:
Maximum allowable bending stress: 1200 psi.
Maximum allowable longitudinal shear stress: 135 psi
Maximum allowable deflection: Span/300. *Ans.* 62 lb./ft.

44. Deflection of Beams of Varying Cross-Section. The theory of deflection, upon which we have based our work, is a corollary of the flexure theory. The beams which we may explore for slope or deflection are, therefore, confined to those which satisfy the limitations of the flexure theory. Included in those limitations is the demand that the beam must be of uniform cross-section.

The machine shaft of Fig. 152-a is composed of three cylindrical sections which vary in size, but not in general geometric characteristics. In such cases, it has been found that no error of appreciable magnitude is introduced when deflection is predicted through the use of the deflection theory.

When the moment of inertia, I, is not constant, the M/EI diagram is an efficient means of solution which can readily be adapted to recognize the influence of the different moments of inertia.

Let us examine the method of adjustment of the M/EI diagram, assuming a specific relationship of the moments of inertia of the different sections, $I_2 = 4I$, where I is the moment of inertia of the smaller section, and I_2 is the moment of inertia of the larger section. The maximum deflection of the shaft is to be determined when the shaft is subjected to a single concentrated weight, W, at mid-span. The weight of the shaft is assumed to be of negligible magnitude in comparison to W.

The bending-moment diagram is shown as Fig. 152-b.

If, now, we construct the M/EI diagram, its ordinates will be affected by the moment of inertia of each section.

For the first range of loading ($x : 0$–a) the diagram is a straight line. The equation of the M/EI curve is $M/EI = Wx/2EI$. The maximum value of M/EI in this range occurs just to the left of the junction ($x = a$).

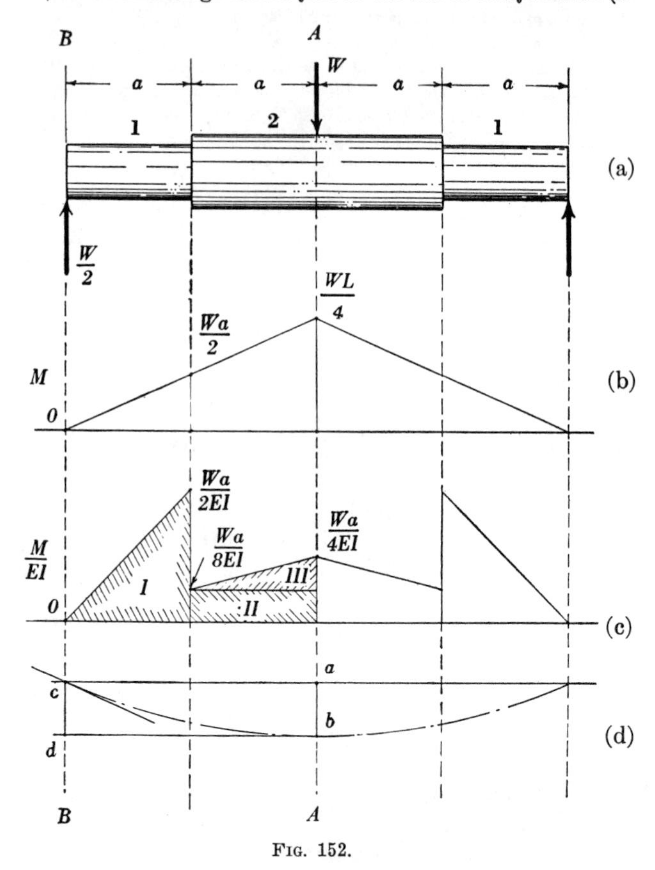

FIG. 152.

This maximum value will be (see Fig. 152-c)

$$\frac{M}{EI} = \frac{Wa}{2EI}$$

Immediately to the right of the junction, the value of bending moment is $Wa/2$, and the value of M/EI will be

$$\frac{M}{EI} = \frac{Wa}{2EI_2} = \frac{Wa}{8EI}$$

The M/EI curve will, therefore, drop vertically to one fourth of its previous value, as indicated in Fig. 152-c.

In the second range of loading $(x : a–2a)$ the equation of bending moment will be $M = Wx/2$; and the value of M/EI will be

$$\frac{M}{EI} = \frac{Wx}{2EI_2} = \frac{Wx}{8EI}$$

The maximum value will occur at the central section (section A) and will be

$$\frac{M}{EI} = \frac{W \times 2a}{8EI} = \frac{Wa}{4EI}$$

The remainder of the M/EI diagram will be symmetrical about section A. The elastic curve is shown as Fig. 152-d.

The maximum deflection will occur at section A, and will be equal to vertical distance $ab = cd$. Applying equation (51),

$$\Sigma M_B: \quad \text{Area I:} \quad \frac{1}{2} \times a \times \frac{Wa}{2EI} \times \frac{2}{3}a = \frac{Wa^3}{6EI}$$

$$\text{Area II:} \quad a \times \frac{Wa}{8EI} \times \frac{3}{2}a = \frac{3}{16}\frac{Wa^3}{EI}$$

$$\text{Area III:} \quad \frac{1}{2} \times a \times \frac{Wa}{8EI} \times \frac{5}{3}a = \frac{5}{48}\frac{Wa^3}{EI}$$

$$y_{\text{max.}} = cd = \frac{Wa^3}{EI}\left(\frac{1}{6} + \frac{3}{16} + \frac{5}{48}\right) = \frac{11}{24}\frac{Wa^3}{EI} = \frac{11}{1536}\frac{WL^3}{EI}$$

A shaft of the same material, length, and loading, having a uniform cross-section with moment of inertia I would have a maximum deflection,

$$y_{\text{max.}} = \frac{1}{48}\frac{WL^3}{EI}$$

The first shaft will weigh 1½ times the second, but will have a maximum deflection which is only $^{11}/_{32}$ as great, justifying the use of the extra material where conditions of alignment are dependent upon the stiffness of the loaded member.

PROBLEMS

263. The cylindrical bar, made of aluminum, serves as a cantilever beam to support the 400-lb. load at its free end. Section **1** has a diameter of 1 in., and section **2** has a diameter of 2 in. Determine the maximum deflection. *Ans.* 0.66 in.

264. The cantilever beam shown is a triangular plate. Determine the maximum deflection when load P is applied at the free end. *Ans.* $-PL^3/2EI_{\max}$.

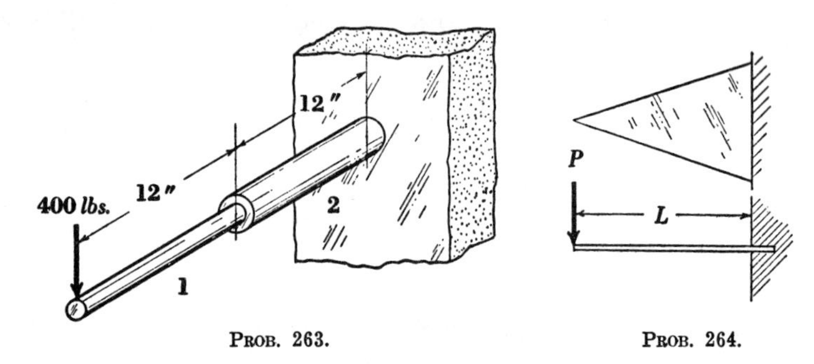

PROB. 263. PROB. 264.

265. The two-step steel shaft is freely supported at its ends and carries a concentrated load of 500 lb. at the junction of the sections. Determine the maximum slope and the maximum deflection.

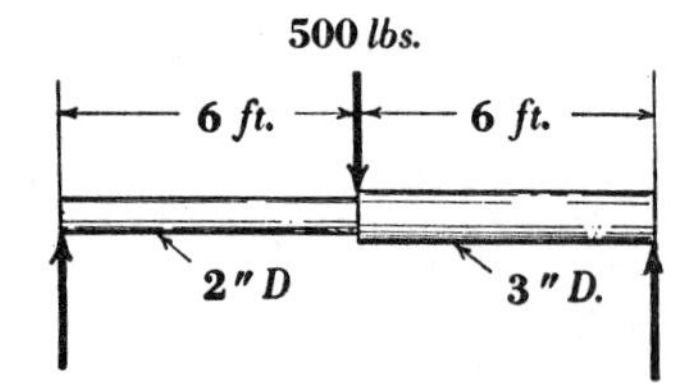

PROB. 265.

266. The prismatic steel bar is freely supported at its ends, and supports the indicated load of 700 lb. Determine the deflection under the 700-lb. load. Sections **1** and **3** are 2 in. square, and section **2** is 3 in. square. *Ans.* −0.067 in.

267. Determine the maximum deflection of the bar of Prob. 266.

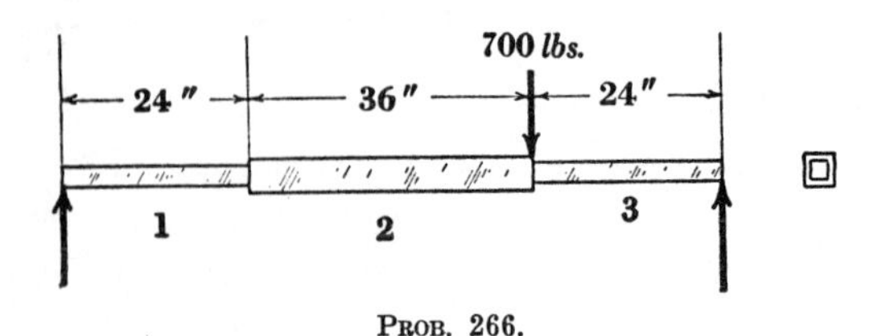

PROB. 266.

268. Determine the maximum slope of the steel beam shown. The end sections have a 2 in. diameter, and the central section has a 3 in. diameter. $a = 1.5$ ft.

Ans. 0.0115 radians.

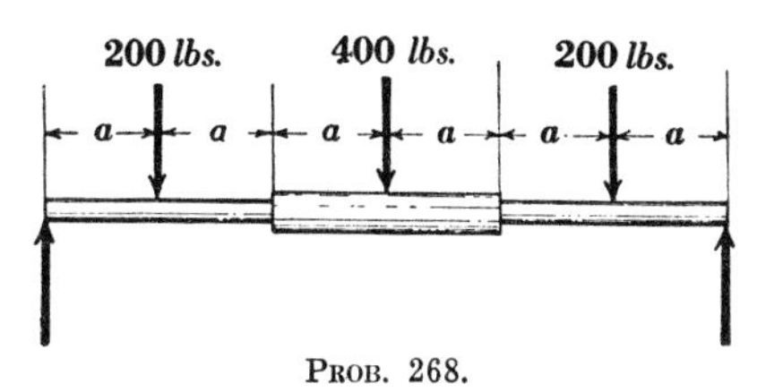

PROB. 268.

269. Determine the maximum deflection of the beam of Prob. 268. *Ans.* 0.31 in.

45. Continuous Beams. The Three-Moment Equation. *Distributed Forces.* Many of the beams which are used in structures are continuous over three or more supporting forces.

We have already noted the fact that beams which are placed upon three supporting forces are statically indeterminate. The theory of deflection has been used to increase the number of available equations by its addition to the conditions of equilibrium—and, in the case of the beam on three supports, such an addition makes the problem of evaluating the supporting forces a determinate one.

When the beam is continuous over more than three supports, the same consideration of slope and deflection may be used to determine the supporting forces.

We shall confine ourselves, in this discussion, to only those beams which conform to the limitations of the flexure theory.

A continuous beam is shown in Fig. 153. All supports are on the same level.

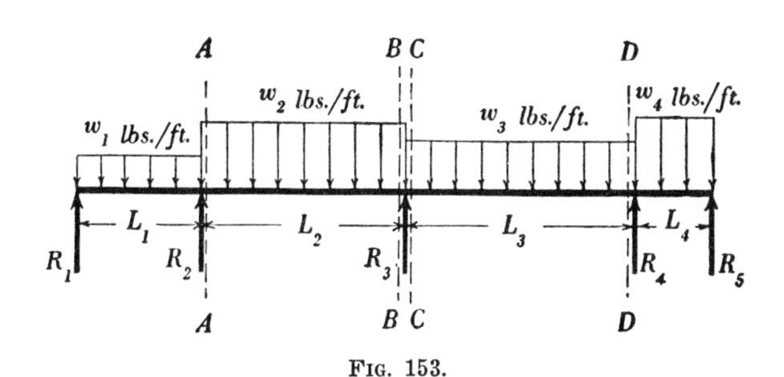

FIG. 153.

As in all of the problems of mechanics, successful solution is dependent upon the proper isolation of a free body. We shall first consider, for example, the portion of the beam lying between sections *A-A* and *B-B*. Section *A-A* is taken immediately to the right of supporting force R_2 and section *B-B* immediately to the left of supporting force R_3.

The isolated free body appears in Fig. 154-a. V_A and V_B represent the shearing forces, M_A and M_B, the bending moments at sections A and B, respectively.

To attack the problem of evaluation of the moments, we have at our command the conditions of equilibrium $\Sigma F = 0$ and $\Sigma M = 0$. In addition, we may apply the slope and deflection relationships furnished by deflection theory. These may make use of integration by either the analytical or moment-area methods. The latter leads to greater simplicity, and will be employed.

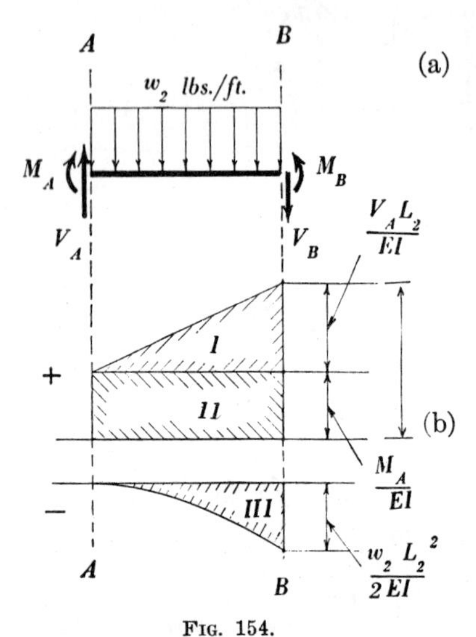

FIG. 154.

The M/EI diagrams for the free body of Fig. 154-a, taken from an origin at section A-A and proceeding to the right have been plotted as Fig. 154-b. The positive and negative areas have been plotted separately.

At section B, the net value of M/EI is

$$\frac{M_B}{EI} = +\frac{V_A L_2}{EI} + \frac{M_A}{EI} - \frac{w_2 L_2^2}{2EI}$$

Since E and I are constant throughout the beam, these factors will vanish from each side of the equation.

Then
$$V_A L_2 = +M_B - M_A + \frac{w_2 L_2^2}{2} \tag{1}$$

We now repeat this routine to explore the region of the beam between sections C and D of Fig. 153. Section C is taken immediately to the right of R_3 and section D immediately to the left of R_4. The free body is shown in Fig. 155-a. The net value of M/EI at section C is

$$\frac{M_C}{EI} = +\frac{V_D L_3}{EI} + \frac{M_D}{EI} - \frac{w_3 L_3^2}{2EI}$$

and
$$V_D L_3 = +M_C - M_D + \frac{w_3 L_3^2}{2} \tag{2}$$

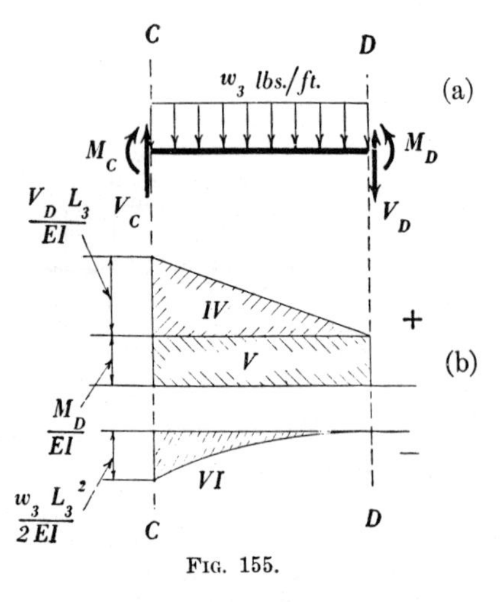

FIG. 155.

We are now prepared to consider deflection relationships.

The elastic curve of the continuous beam between sections A and D is shown in Fig. 156. The line db is the tangent to the curve at R_3 and ab is the vertical displacement between this tangent and a tangent to the curve at section D. The vertical displacement between the tangent db and a tangent to the curve at section A is cd. The M/EI diagrams for the two ranges of loading are combined in Fig. 157.

From the geometry of Fig. 156, we note that triangles abe and cde are similar, and

$$\frac{cd}{L_2} = \frac{ab}{L_3} \tag{3}$$

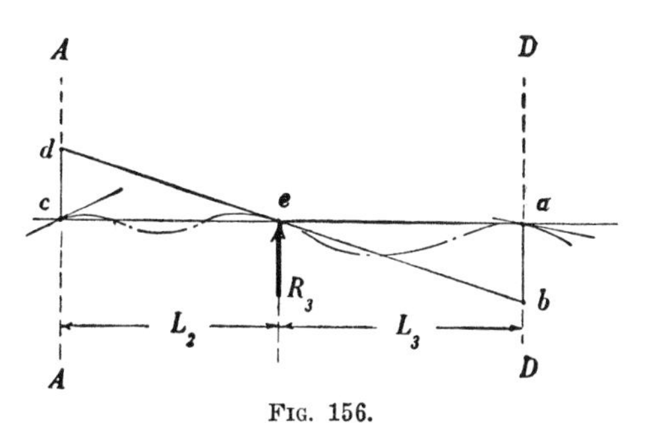

Fig. 156.

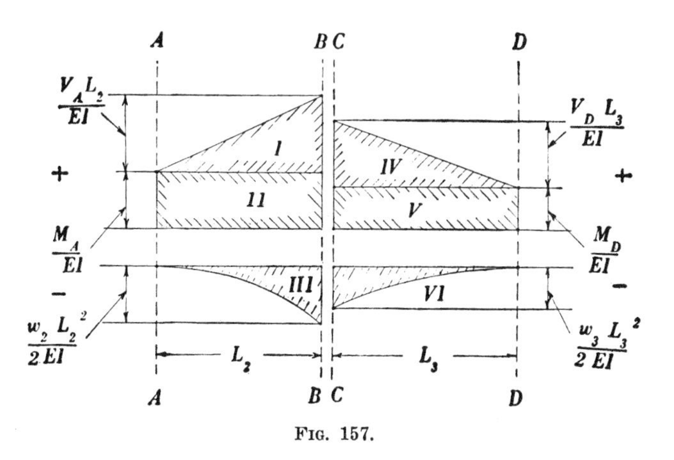

Fig. 157.

Both vertical displacements may be evaluated by applying equation (51) as follows (Fig. 157):

ΣM_A: Area I. $\quad \frac{1}{2} \times L_2 \times \frac{V_A L_2}{EI} \times \frac{2}{3} \times L_2 = +\frac{V_A L_2^3}{3EI}$

Area II. $\quad \frac{M_A}{EI} \times L_2 \times \frac{L_2}{2} = +\frac{M_A L_2^2}{2EI}$

Area III. $\quad -\frac{1}{3} \times L_2 \times \frac{w_2 L_2^2}{2EI} \times \frac{3}{4} \times L_2 = -\frac{w_2 L_2^4}{8EI}$

Net Area. $\quad cd = +\frac{V_A L_2^3}{3EI} + \frac{M_A L_2^2}{2EI} - \frac{w_2 L_2^4}{8EI} \quad (4)$

Taking moments at section D,

$$\Sigma M_D:\quad \text{Area IV.}\quad \frac{1}{2}\times L_3\times\frac{V_DL_3}{EI}\times\frac{2}{3}\times L_3 = +\frac{V_DL_3^3}{3EI}$$

$$\text{Area V.}\quad \frac{M_D}{EI}\times L_3\times\frac{L_3}{2} = +\frac{M_DL_3^2}{2EI}$$

$$\text{Area VI.}\quad -\frac{1}{3}\times L_3\times\frac{w_3L_3^2}{2EI}\times\frac{3}{4}\times L_3 = -\frac{w_3L_3^4}{8EI}$$

$$\text{Net Area.}\quad ab = +\frac{V_DL_3^3}{3EI}+\frac{M_DL_3^2}{2EI}-\frac{w_3L_3^4}{8EI} \tag{5}$$

Substituting these values for cd and ab in equation (3) above, and removing the constant values of E and I from both sides of the equation,

$$+\frac{V_AL_2^2}{3}+\frac{M_AL_2}{2}-\frac{w_2L_2^3}{8} = -\left(\frac{V_DL_3^2}{3}+\frac{M_DL_3}{2}-\frac{w_3L_3^3}{8}\right)$$

[The values of cd and ab given in equations (4) and (5) are quantitative. Qualitatively, these displacements are opposed in direction, and opposite signs have, therefore, been assigned to them.]

Now, introducing the values of V_AL_2 and V_DL_3 given in equations (1) and (2) above, we have,

$$+\frac{M_BL_2}{3}-\frac{M_AL_2}{3}+\frac{w_2L_2^3}{6}+\frac{M_AL_2}{2}-\frac{w_2L_2^3}{8} =$$
$$-\frac{M_CL_3}{3}+\frac{M_DL_3}{3}-\frac{w_3L_3^3}{6}-\frac{M_DL_3}{2}+\frac{w_3L_3^3}{8}$$

Gathering like terms to simplify the equation yields

$$+\frac{M_AL_2}{6}+\frac{M_BL_2}{3}+\frac{M_CL_3}{3}+\frac{M_DL_3}{6} = -\frac{w_2L_2^3}{24}-\frac{w_3L_3^3}{24}$$

M_B and M_C are equal, for both represent the bending moment in the beam at R_3.

$$\text{Then}\quad \mathbf{M_AL_2 + 2M_B(L_2+L_3) + M_DL_3 = -\frac{w_2L_2^3}{4} - \frac{w_3L_3^3}{4}} \tag{52}$$

This equation, expressing the relationship of the bending moments at three successive sections of the continuous beam in terms of the loading and span lengths is called the *three-moment equation.* Together with the conditions of equilibrium, it may be used to make the problem of the continuous beam determinate. Its application will be demonstrated in the following example.

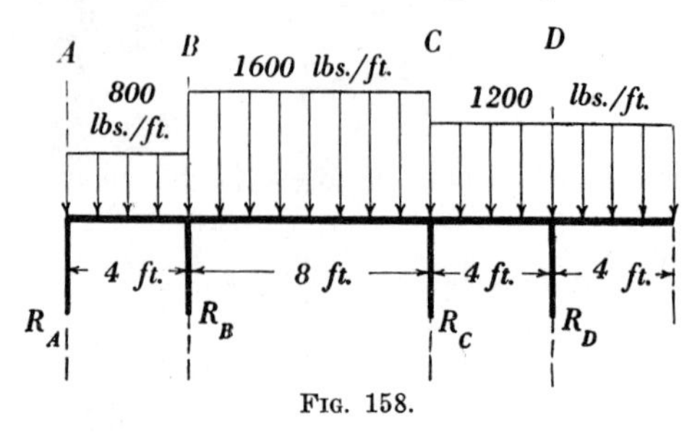

FIG. 158.

Illustrative Example I. The continuous beam shown in Fig. 158 is to be investigated to determine

a) The supporting forces (all supports are on the same level).
b) The maximum bending moment in the beam.

Part a) Equation (52) is first applied to the two ranges of loading lying between sections A and C.

$$0 + 2M_B(4+8) + M_C \times 8 = -\frac{800 \times (4)^3}{4} - \frac{1600 \times (8)^3}{4}$$

$$24M_B + 8M_C = -12{,}800 - 204{,}800 = -217{,}600 \qquad (1)$$

We now apply equation (52) to the two ranges of loading which lie between sections B and D. The bending moment at section D is $M_D = -1200 \times 4 \times 2 = -9600$ ft.-lb.

$$M_B \times 8 + 2M_C(8+4) - 9600 \times 4 = -\frac{1600 \times (8)^3}{4} - \frac{1200 \times (4)^3}{4}$$

$$8M_B + 24M_C = -204{,}800 - 19{,}200 + 38{,}400 = -185\,600 \qquad (2)$$

Equations (1) and (2) are simultaneous, and contain but two unknowns, M_B and M_C. Solving simultaneously,

$$M_B = -7300 \text{ ft.-lb.}$$
$$M_C = -5300 \text{ ft.-lb.}$$

The bending moments at all supports are now evaluated, and the supporting forces may be determined.

The bending moment at section B, obtained by taking moments of all of the external forces acting on the portion of the beam to the left of B is

ΣM_B:
$$R_A \times 4 - 800 \times 4 \times 2 = -7300$$
$$R_A = -225 \text{ lb.} \qquad \text{(downward)}$$

This operation is repeated, establishing the bending moment at section C is

ΣM_C:
$$-225 \times 12 - 800 \times 4 \times 10 + R_B \times 8 - 1600 \times 8 \times 4 = -5300$$
$$R_B = +10{,}075 \text{ lb.} \qquad \text{(upward)}$$

We now establish the bending moment at section C by proceeding from the right end of the beam.

ΣM_C:
$$+R_D \times 4 - 1200 \times 8 \times 4 = -5300$$
$$R_D = +8275 \text{ lb.} \qquad \text{(upward)}$$

Finally, the force R_C is evaluated by taking moments at section B of all of the external forces to the right of that section,

ΣM_B:
$$+8275 \times 12 + R_C \times 8 - 1200 \times 8 \times 12 - 1600 \times 8 \times 4 = -7300$$
$$R_C = +7475 \text{ lb.} \qquad \text{(upward)}$$

Checking such results is good engineering procedure. Since the entire continuous beam is a free body in equilibrium, $\Sigma F = 0$.
The sum of the upward forces is

$$F_U = +10{,}075 + 7475 + 8275 = +25{,}825$$

The sum of the downward forces is

$$F_D = -225 - (800 \times 4) - (1600 \times 8) - (1200 \times 8) = -25{,}825$$

Then F_U balances F_D, and the results are confirmed.

Part b) The investigation of maximum bending moment in the continuous beam may now be pursued as in any other beam. We first plot the shearing-force diagram to explore all ranges of loading for potential sections of maximum bending moment. The shearing force diagram is shown in Fig. 159. It crosses the zero axis at sections B, C, and D, and, in addition, at sections E and F.

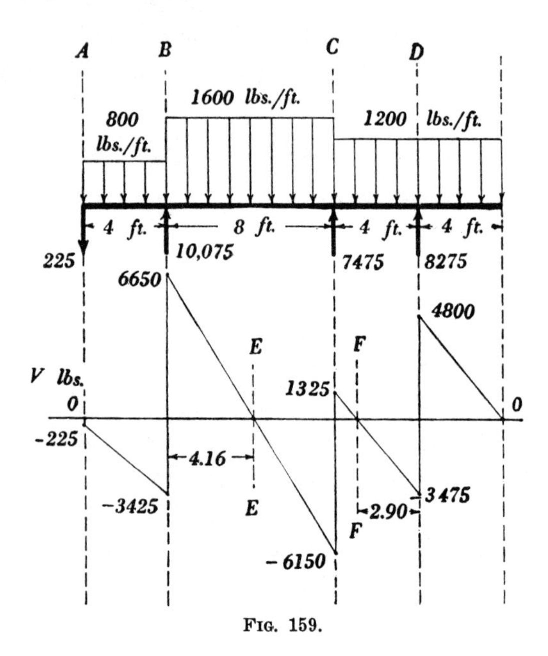

FIG. 159.

The bending moments at the first three sections have been determined in Part a) and are

$$M_B = -7300 \text{ ft.-lb.}$$
$$M_C = -5300$$
$$M_D = -9600$$

Section E is located at 4.16 ft. (6650/1600) to the right of section B and

$$M_E = -225 \times 8.16 - 3200 \times 6.16 + 10{,}075 \times 4.16 - 1600 \times 4.16 \times 2.08 = +6520 \text{ ft.-lb.}$$

Section F is located at 2.90 ft. (3475/1200) to the left of section D

$$M_F = -1200 \times 6.90 \times 3.45 + 8275 \times 2.90 = -4570 \text{ ft.-lb.}$$

Then the maximum *negative* bending moment in the beam is $M_D = -9600$ ft.-lb., and the maximum *positive* bending moment is $M_E = +6520$ ft.-lb.

Illustrative Example II. When a continuous beam is restrained so that its ends are *fixed* as in Fig. 160, the three-moment method may be employed to effect a solution. Here we employ the device of adding two imaginary ranges of loading,

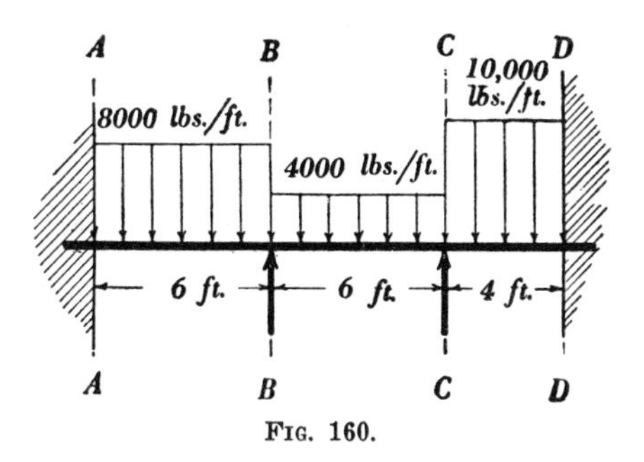

FIG. 160.

as indicated in Fig. 161, with $L_1 = L_2 = 0$. Such a device enables us to apply equation (52) as follows.

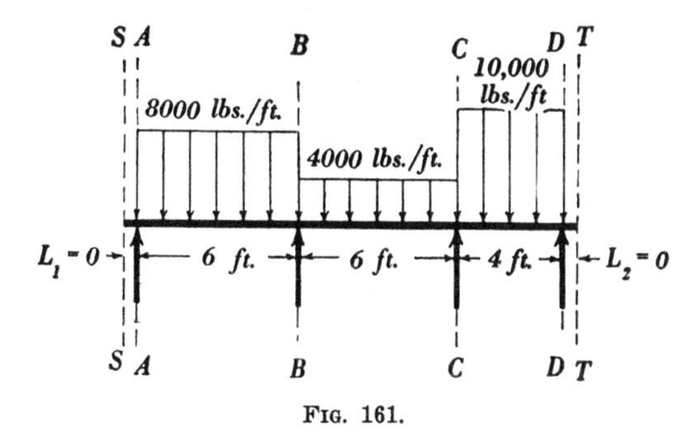

FIG. 161.

Applying equation (52) at section A,

$$M_S \times 0 + 2M_A(0 + 6) + M_B \times 6 = 0 - \frac{8000 \times (6)^3}{4}$$

$$12M_A + 6M_B = -432{,}000 \tag{1}$$

Applying equation (52) at section B,

$$M_A \times 6 + 2M_B(6 + 6) + M_C \times 6 = -\frac{8000 \times (6)^3}{4} - \frac{4000 \times (6)^3}{4}$$

$$6M_A + 24M_B + 6M_C = -648{,}000 \tag{2}$$

Applying equation (52) at section C,

$$M_B \times 6 + 2M_C(6 + 4) + M_D \times 4 = -\frac{4000 \times (6)^3}{4} - \frac{10{,}000 \times (4)^3}{4}$$

$$6M_B + 20M_C + 4M_D = -376{,}000 \tag{3}$$

Finally, applying equation (52) at section D,

$$M_C \times 4 + 2M_D(4 + 0) + M_T \times 0 = -\frac{10{,}000 \times (4)^3}{4} - 0$$

$$4M_C + 8M_D = -160{,}000 \tag{4}$$

Equations (1), (2), (3), and (4) may be solved simultaneously to yield

$$\begin{aligned} M_A &= -27{,}230 \text{ ft.-lb.} \\ M_B &= -17{,}530 \\ M_C &= -10{,}600 \\ M_D &= -14{,}700 \end{aligned}$$

Concentrated Forces. The application of the moment-area method to the determination of bending moments in continuous beams need not be confined to cases of uniformly distributed loading.

We shall explore one case involving concentrated loads to demonstrate the derivation of an applicable three-moment equation. The continuous beam of Fig.

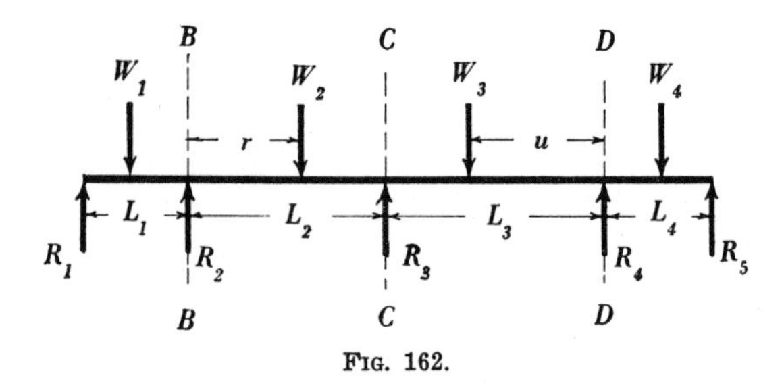

FIG. 162.

162 carries a single concentrated load in each span. All supports are on the same level, and the beam conforms to the limitations of the flexure theory, so that E and I are constant throughout the entire length of the beam.

As in the preceding case, we isolate a free body so that we may properly appraise the force system. The free body selected and shown in Fig. 163 is the

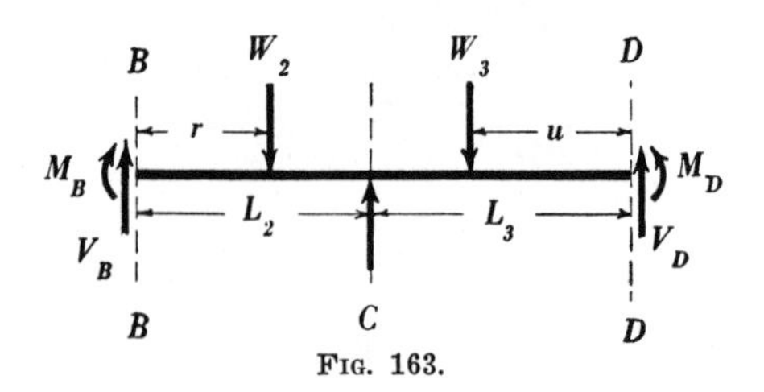

FIG. 163.

portion of the beam lying between sections B and D. Section B is taken immediately to the right of supporting force R_2, and section D immediately to the left of R_4.

We noted, in the preceding example, that the terms E and I, which are constants, vanish from the resulting equations, and need not be introduced in this derivation. The M diagrams have, therefore, been shown in Fig. 164 to serve in

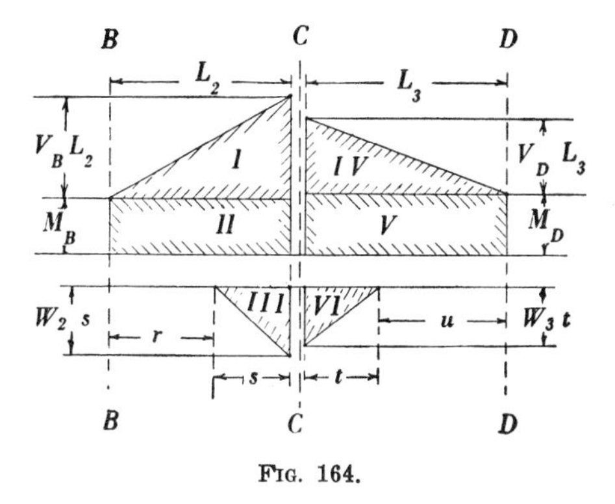

FIG. 164.

the same capacity as the usual M/EI diagrams. The elastic curve is shown in Fig. 165.

We first apply equation (51), modified by the omission of the EI factor in all

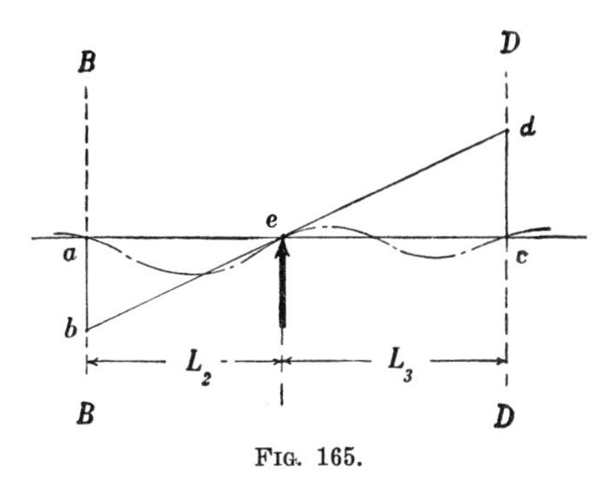

FIG. 165.

denominators, to determine displacement ab of Fig. 165. Taking moments of the areas of Fig. 164 at section B,

$$\Sigma M_B: \quad \text{Area I.} \quad \frac{1}{2} \times L_2 \times V_B L_2 \times \frac{2}{3} \times L_2 = +\frac{V_B L_2^3}{3EI}$$

$$\text{Area II.} \quad M_B \times L_2 \times \frac{L_2}{2} = +\frac{M_B L_2^2}{2}$$

$$\text{Area III.} \quad -\frac{1}{2} \times s \times W_2 s \times \left(r + \frac{2s}{3}\right) = -\frac{W_2 s^2}{6}(3r + 2s)$$

$$\text{Net Area.} \quad ab = \frac{V_B L_2^3}{3} + \frac{M_B L_2^2}{2} - \frac{W_2 s^2}{6}(3r + 2s)$$

The moment at section C is

$$M_C = V_B L_2 + M_B - W_2\, s$$

and

$$V_B L_2 = M_C - M_B + W_2\, s$$

Substituting this value of $V_B L_2$ in the equation for ab given above,

$$ab = \frac{M_C L_2^2}{3} - \frac{M_B L_2^2}{3} + \frac{W_2\, s\, L_2^2}{3} + \frac{M_B L_2^2}{2} - \frac{W_2\, s^2}{6}(3r + 2s) \tag{1}$$

Similarly, by taking moments at section D of areas **IV**, **V**, and **VI**, we obtain

$$cd = \frac{M_C L_3^2}{3} - \frac{M_D L_3^2}{3} + \frac{W_3\, t L_3^2}{3} + \frac{M_D L_3^2}{2} - \frac{W_3\, t^2}{6}(3u + 2t) \tag{2}$$

The triangles abe and cde of Fig. 165 are similar, and displacements ab and cd are of opposite sign. Then

$$\frac{ab}{L_2} = -\frac{cd}{L_3} \tag{3}$$

Substituting the values of ab and cd in equation (3) which were given in equations (1) and (2), and simplifying the resulting expression yields

$$M_B L_2 + 2M_C(L_2 + L_3) + M_D L_3 = -\frac{W_2 r}{L_2}(L_2^2 - r^2) - \frac{W_3 u}{L_3}(L_3^2 - u^2) \tag{53}$$

This is the three-moment equation which is applicable to a continuous beam carrying a single concentrated load in each span.

Illustrative Example. The continuous beam of Fig. 166 carries the concentrated loads shown. All supports are on the same level. We are to determine the following:

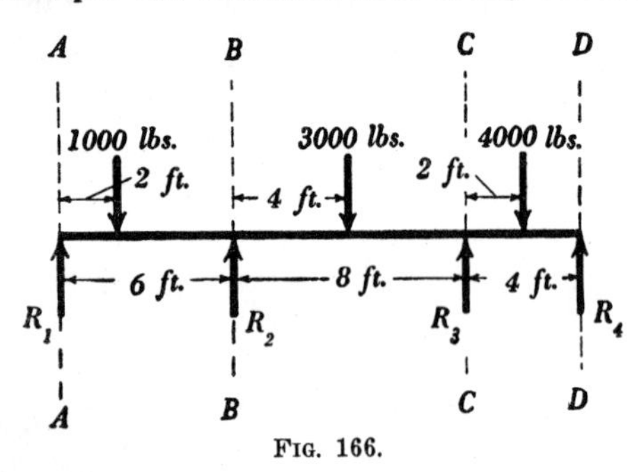

FIG. 166.

a) The bending moment at each support.
b) The supporting forces.
c) The maximum positive and negative bending moments.

Part a) We first apply equation (53) to the portion of the beam lying between sections A and C.

$$0 \times 6 + 2M_B(6 + 8) + M_C \times 8 = -\frac{1000 \times 2}{6}[(6)^2 - (2)^2] - \frac{3000 \times 4}{8}[(8)^2 - (4)^2]$$

$$28M_B + 8M_C = -82{,}760 \tag{1}$$

In the range bounded by sections B and D, equation (53) yields

$$M_B \times 8 + 2M_C(8 + 4) + 0 \times 4 =$$

$$-\frac{3000 \times 4}{8}[(8)^2 - (4)^2] - \frac{4000 \times 2}{4}[(4)^2 - (2)^2]$$

$$8M_B + 24M_C = -96{,}000 \qquad (2)$$

Solving equations (1) and (2) simultaneously,

$$M_B = -2000 \text{ ft.-lb.}$$
$$M_C = -3333 \text{ ft.-lb.}$$

Part b) The supporting forces are determined by writing the equations for bending moment at sections B and C, entering the beam at the left end.

ΣM_B: $$+6R_1 - 1000 \times 4 = -2000$$
$$R_1 = 333 \text{ lb.} \quad \text{(upward)}$$

ΣM_C: $$14 \times 333 - 1000 \times 12 + R_2 \times 8 - 3000 \times 4 = -3333$$
$$R_2 = 2000 \text{ lb.} \quad \text{(upward)}$$

Now, entering the beam at the right end, the bending moments at sections C and B are

ΣM_C: $$4R_4 - 4000 \times 2 = -3333$$
$$R_4 = 1167 \text{ lb.} \quad \text{(upward)}$$

ΣM_B: $$12 \times 1167 - 4000 \times 10 - 3000 \times 4 + R_3 \times 8 = -2000$$
$$R_3 = 4500 \text{ lb.} \quad \text{(upward)}$$

Checking, the sum of the upward forces is

$$F_U = +333 + 2000 + 4500 + 1167 = +8000$$

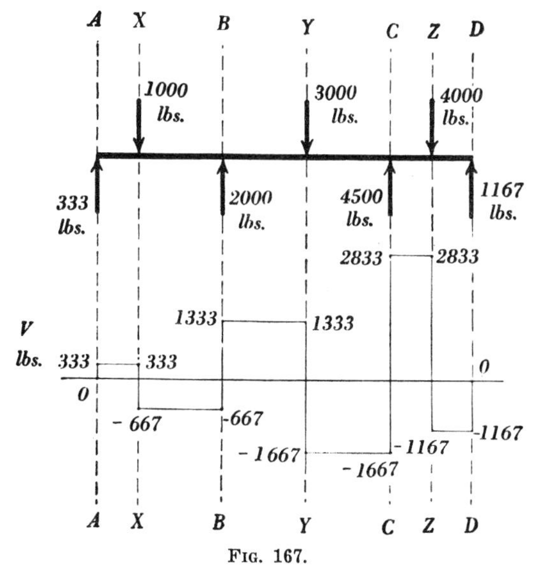

FIG. 167.

and the sum of the downward forces is

$$F_D = -1000 - 3000 - 4000 = -8000$$

Part c) The shearing-force diagram is shown in Fig. 167. The potential locations of maximum bending moment occur wherever the shearing-force curve crosses the axis.

At section B, $M_B = -2000$ ft.-lb.
At section C, $M_C = -3333$
At section X, $M_X = +666$
At section Y, $M_Y = +3333$
At section Z, $M_Z = +2333$

The maximum positive bending moment is, therefore, $M_C = +3333$ ft.-lb., and the maximum negative bending moment is $M_Y = -3333$ ft.-lb.

PROBLEMS

270. All supports of the continuous beam shown are on the same level. Determine the supporting forces.

Ans. $R_1 = +\ 106$ lb.
$R_2 = +2908$
$R_3 = +2596$
$R_4 = -\ \ 49$
$R_5 = +\ 342$

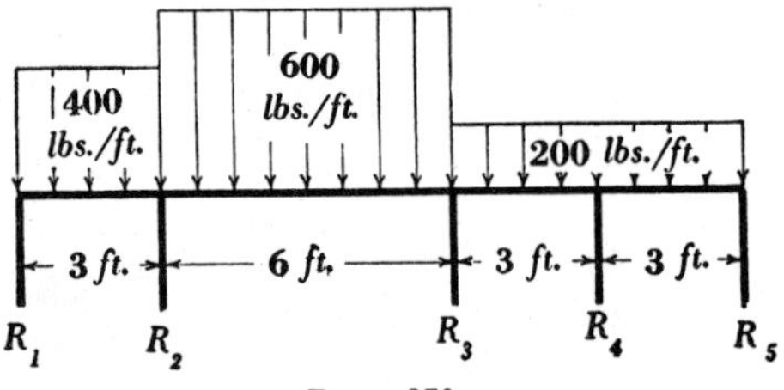

PROB. 270.

271. Determine the maximum shearing force and the maximum positive and negative bending moments for the beam of Prob. 270.

272. Determine the supporting forces and the maximum shearing force in the continuous beam shown. All supports are on the same level. $a = 3$ ft.

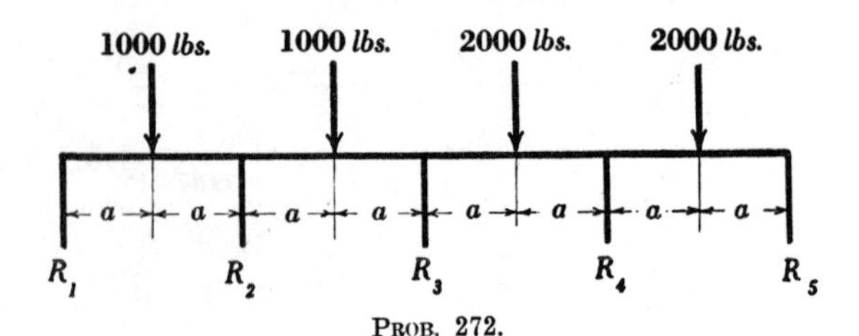

PROB. 272.

273. Determine (a) the maximum positive bending moment and (b) the maximum negative bending moment for the beam of Prob. 272. *Ans.* a) 1995 ft.-lb.
b) 2010 ft.-lb.

274. All supports are on the same level. Determine the supporting forces.

275. For the beam of Prob. 274 determine the maximum shearing force, and the maximum positive and negative bending moments.

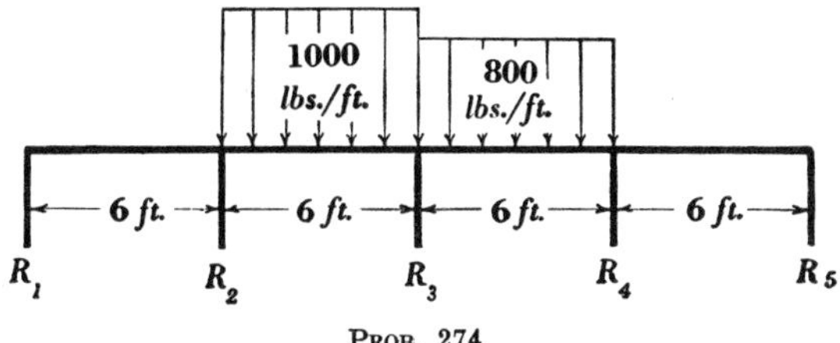

Prob. 274.

276. All supports of the continuous beam shown are on the same level. The ends of the beam are fixed. Determine the maximum shearing force in the beam.
Ans. 4200 lb.

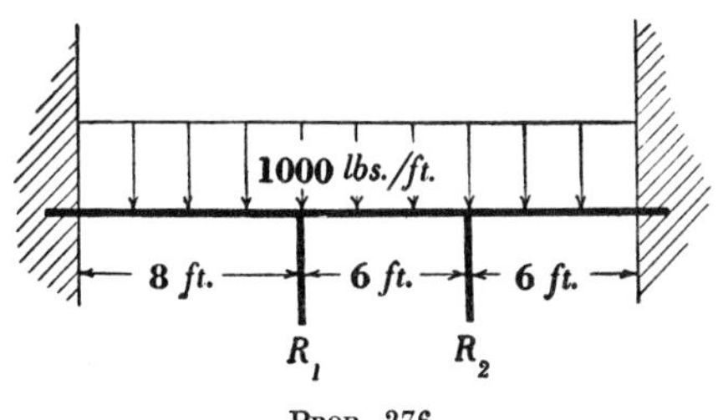

Prob. 276.

277. For the continuous beam of Prob. 276, determine (a) the maximum positive bending moment, and (b) the maximum negative bending moment.
Ans. a) 2950 ft.-lb.
b) 5870 ft.-lb.

278. The continuous beam has fixed ends. Determine the maximum positive and maximum negative bending moments.

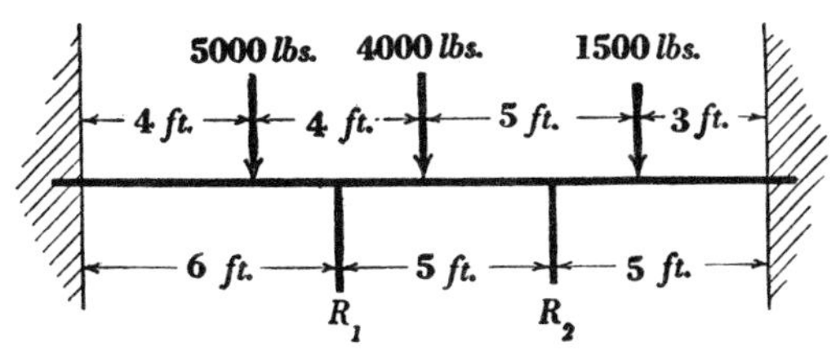

Prob. 278.

CHAPTER V

Violations of the Limitations of the Flexure Theory

46. Review of Limitations. The basic flexure theory, together with its corollaries, the longitudinal shear and deflection theories, are valid only when applied to beams whose properties fall within the imposed limitations. The assumptions which were made in the derivations can be verified only when those beam properties are properly within the range of limitations.

We shall not always encounter beams which may be described as "flexure theory" beams, and this chapter is devoted to suggesting the methods of attack which are employed when the limitations of the flexure theory are violated.

Before we proceed to a discussion of such violations, it will be well to review the nature of the limitations. These were concerned (see Art. 25) with the geometry of the beam, its material, and the pattern of loading.

Listing these in the order in which they were discussed in the flexure theory, the limitations are:

1) The beam must be straight.
2) The cross-section must be uniform.
3) The beam must be made of homogeneous material.
4) The relative dimensions must be considered.
5) All forces must lie in a single plane.
6) The plane of loading must cut every cross-section symmetrically.
7) All loads must be acting normal to the longitudinal axis.

We shall, in the individual articles which follow, concern ourselves with a violation of each of these conditions. Such a rigid separation is not always found in engineering applications. When we have established a command of the nature of attack with which we can meet the challenge of each violation, we shall have firm bases which may be built upon each other when multiple violations of basic theory arise within one application.

47. Axial and Bending Components. The supporting arm of Fig. 168-a is not straight. A load of P is supported, as shown. To discover the nature of the normal stress on a typical section (A-A) of the straight portion of the beam, we isolate, as a free body, the portion of the beam illustrated in Fig. 168-b.

This free body is in equilibrium. Then the force system acting on

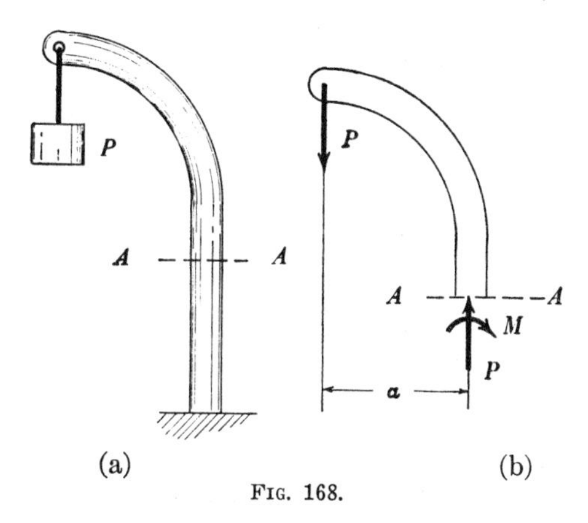

Fig. 168.

section A-A must consist of an upward force P, which may be assumed to act at the centroid, and a clockwise moment $M = P \times a$.

It is usually assumed that the force P will set up a uniformly distributed normal stress, s_1, on the section, and

$$s_1 = \frac{P}{A}$$

The couple M is a moment of resistance and a bending stress s_2 will be superimposed on s_1. By equation (34),

$$s_2 = \frac{My}{I}$$

The combination of these two normal stresses will be

$$s_N = s_1 + s_2 = \frac{P}{A} \pm \frac{My}{I} \qquad \textbf{(54)}$$

The addition is an algebraic one, for s_1 may be either tensile or compressive across the entire section while s_2 will be tensile on one side of the neutral axis and compressive on the other side.

This type of attack is of questionable merit, for we have assumed both a uniform distribution of s_1 and a flexure-theory or linear distribution of s_2. In defense of this method, empirical observations will show that when the radius of curvature of the curved portion is very great, reasonably accurate results are obtained by its use.

When, however, the radius of curvature decreases, the accuracy of this equation in predicting stress is also decreasing, and a more refined method of attack must be obtained. Before proceeding to derive such a method, let us determine the stress at the section A-A if we apply equation (54), which is given above to the open link, shown in Fig. 169-a. The cross-section of the link is a rectangle, as indicated.

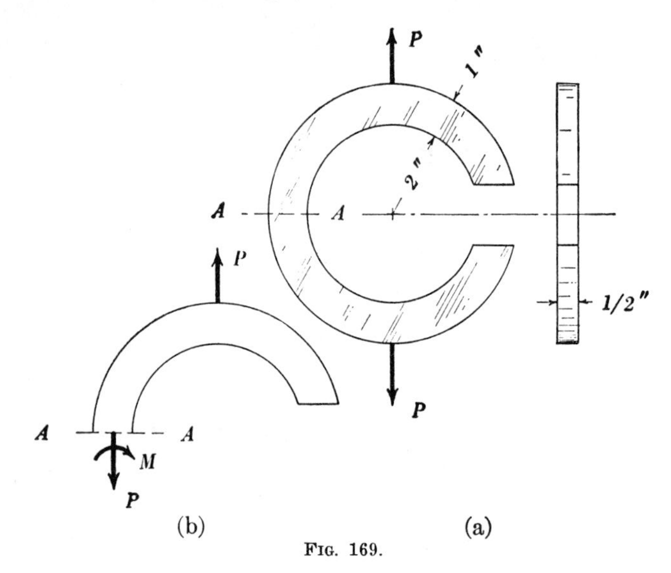

FIG. 169.

The isolation of the half-link as a free body is shown in Fig. 169-b. As a result of the axial loading, P,

$$s_1 = \frac{P}{A} = \frac{P}{0.5 \times 1} = 2P$$

which is tensile across the entire section.

The bending moment at A-A will be $M = P \times 2.5$, and, applying the flexure equation (34),

$$s_2 = \frac{P \times 2.5 \times 0.5}{0.5 \times (1)^3/12} = 30P$$

which is tensile at the inner surface, and compressive at the outer surface.

The total normal stress at the inner surface will be

$$s_I = s_1 + s_2 = 2P + 30P = 32P \qquad \text{(tension)}$$

and the total normal stress at the outer surface will be

$$s_O = s_1 - s_2 = 2P - 30P = 28P \qquad \text{(compression)}$$

It should be observed that the neutral axis, which is always defined as the locus of the points of zero stress will have been displaced to the left of the centroid of the section, as indicated in Fig. 170. The amount of displacement is d. Since at the neutral axis the tensile stress resulting from

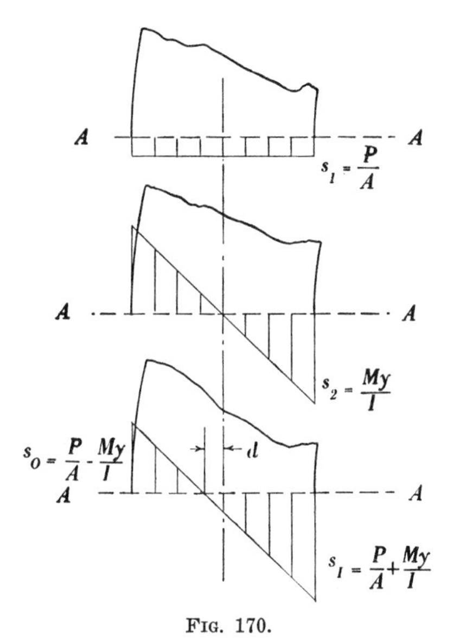

FIG. 170.

the axial loading must be exactly balanced by the compressive stress caused by bending,

$$\frac{P}{A} = \frac{Md}{I}$$

$$2P = \frac{P \times 2.5 \times d}{0.5 \times (1)^3/12}$$

and

$$d = 1/30 \text{ in.}$$

Oblique Loads. The final limitation of the flexure theory restricted the forces applied to the beam to those which are normal to the longitudinal axis of the beam.

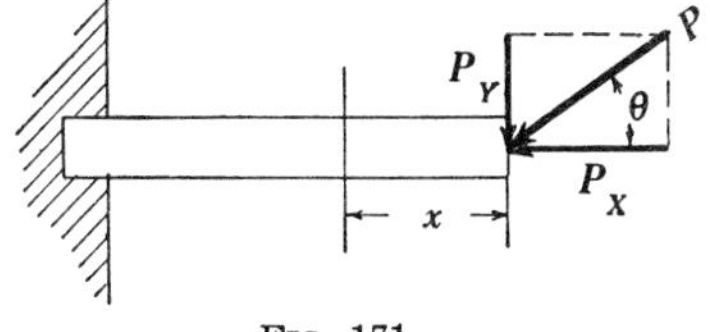

FIG. 171.

When oblique loads, like the force P of Fig. 171, are encountered, the equivalent system of components, $P_X = P \cos \theta$ and $P_Y = P \sin \theta$ may be substituted. The substitution of these components reduces the original oblique loading, precluded by the limitations of the flexure theory to (1) an axial loading, which will set up a normal stress on any right section of the beam.

$$s_A = \frac{P \cos \theta}{A}$$

and (2) a bending loading which is admissible under the limitations of the beam theory, and causes bending stress

$$s_B = \frac{My}{I} = \frac{(P \sin \theta\, x)y}{I}$$

Illustrative Example. The beam AB of Fig. 172 is supported by a pin joint at A, and a cable CD. The beam is loaded as shown. The maximum normal stress on

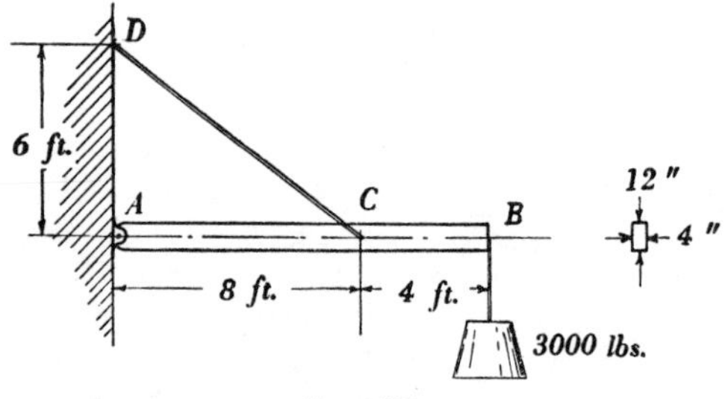

FIG. 172.

a right section of the beam is to be determined. The beam is 4 in. wide by 12 in. deep.

The beam has been shown as an isolated free body in Fig. 173-a. Applying the condition of equilibrium,

$$\Sigma M_A = 0 \qquad -F_{CD} \times \frac{6}{10} \times 8 + 3000 \times 12 = 0$$

$$F_{CD} = 7500 \text{ lb.}$$

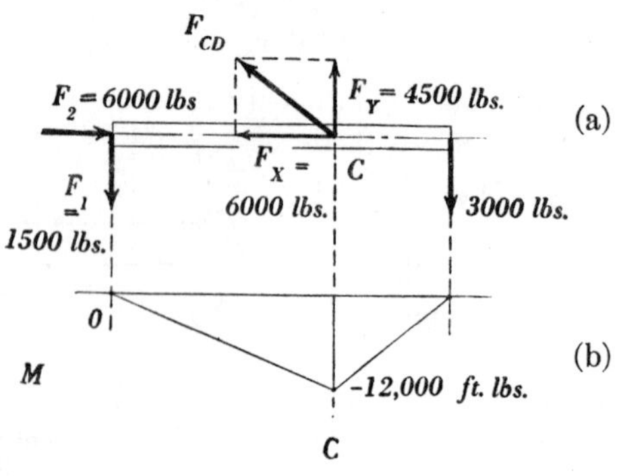

FIG. 173.

The vertical component of F_{CD} is

$$F_Y = 7500 \times \frac{6}{10} = 4500 \text{ lb.}$$

and the horizontal component of F_{CD} is

$$F_X = 7500 \times \frac{8}{10} = 6000 \text{ lb.}$$

$$\Sigma X = 0; \quad -6000 + F_2 = 0 \quad F_2 = 6000 \text{ lb.}$$

$$\Sigma Y = 0; \quad -3000 + 4500 - F_1 = 0 \quad F_1 = 1500 \text{ lb.}$$

The bending moment diagram for the beam is shown in Fig. 173-b. In the range of loading from $x = 0$ to $x = 8$ ft. (origin at left end) the normal stress on a right section produced by the axial loading will be

$$s_A = \frac{6000}{4 \times 12} = 125 \text{ psi (compression)}$$

In this range of loading, the maximum bending stress will occur at section C, and will be, by equation (34),

$$s_B = \frac{12{,}000 \times 12 \times 6}{4 \times (12)^3 / 12} = 1500 \text{ psi (compression in bottom fibers.)}$$

The maximum normal stress on a right section of the beam will, therefore, occur in the fibers at the bottom of the beam, immediately to the left of section C, and will be

$$s_N = s_A + s_B = 125 + 1500 = 1625 \text{ psi (compression)}$$

PROBLEMS

279. The 3600 lb. loads are applied on the central axis of the beam, which also supports a uniformly distributed load of 75 lb./ft. Determine the maximum normal stress on a right section of the beam. *Ans.* 550 psi (tension).

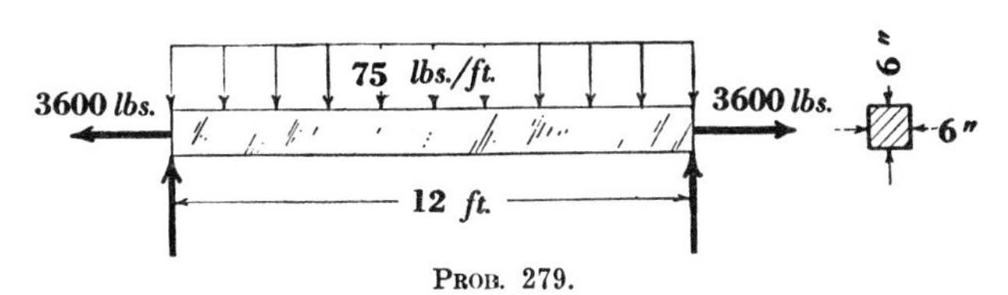

PROB. 279.

280. The support shown has a circular cross-section of 2 in. diameter. Determine the maximum normal stress on section A-A.

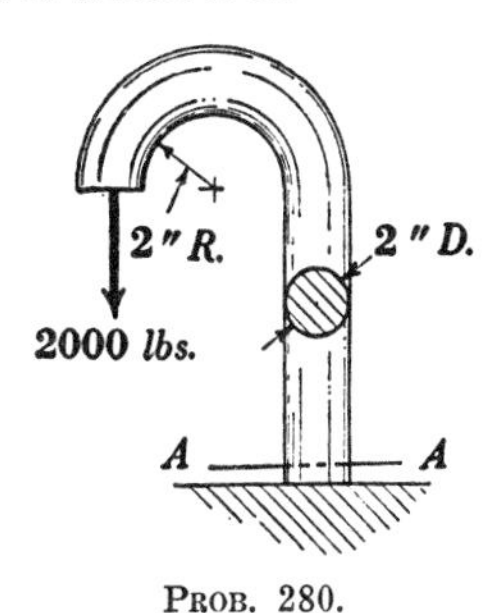

PROB. 280.

281. The forces P are applied at the center of the end faces. Determine the maximum allowable value of P if the maximum normal stress on any right section of the bar must not exceed 7000 psi. Neglect the effect of stress concentration.

Ans. 12,000 lb.

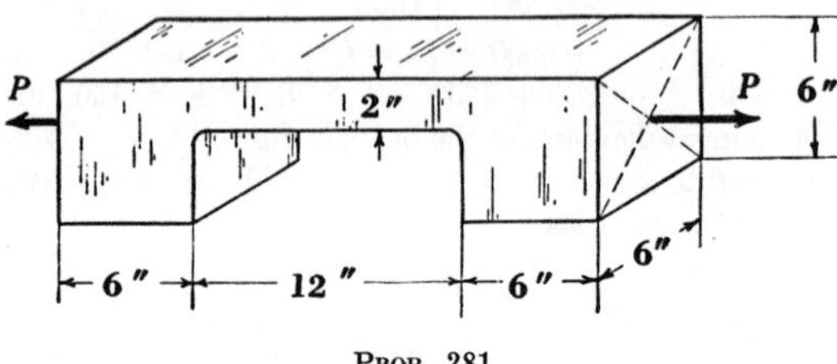

PROB. 281.

282. A connecting rod (not shown) applies a thrust of 400 lb. to the crankpin. Determine the maximum normal stress on a right section of crank AB.

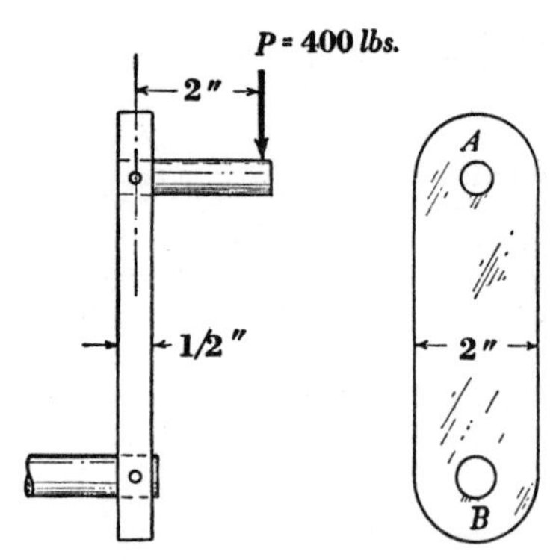

PROB. 282.

283. An oblique load P is applied at the top surface of the beam, which is supported by a pin joint at A and rests on a knife edge at B. Determine the maximum load P if the maximum normal stress on a right section of the beam must not exceed 1200 psi.

Ans. 5760 lb.

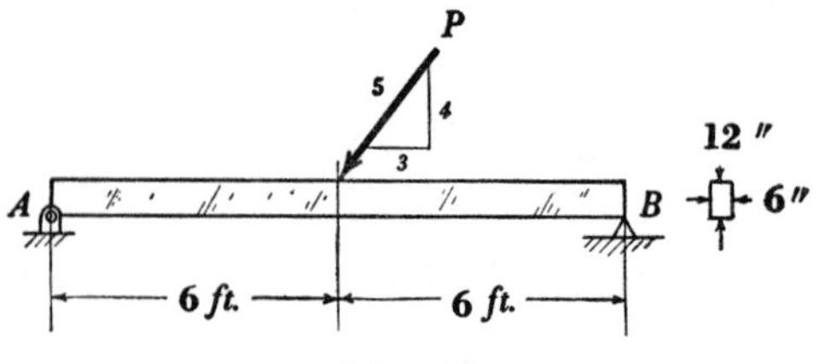

PROB. 283.

284. If force $P = 140{,}000$ lb., determine the maximum normal stress on section A-A of the machine frame shown.

285. Determine the maximum normal stress on a right section of the beam, which is supported by a pin joint at A and rests on a knife edge at B. *Ans.* 1070 psi.

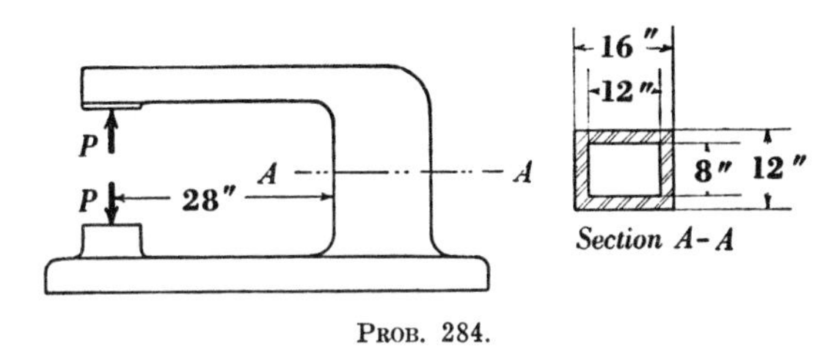

PROB. 284.

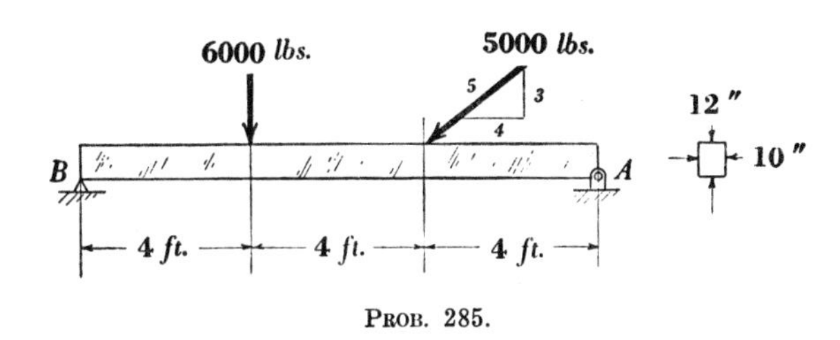

PROB. 285.

286. The beam shown is supported on a roller at A, and by a pin joint at B. The 2400 lb. load is vertical, and the 1200 lb. load is horizontal, and applied 1 ft. above the centroid of the section. Determine the maximum normal stress on a right section of the beam.

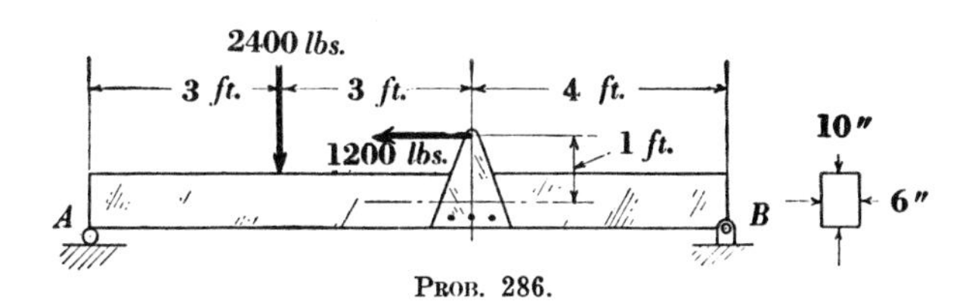

PROB. 286.

287. The beam is supported by a roller at A and a pin joint at B applied at the bottom of the beam. The 1000 lb. load is vertical, and the 3200 lb. load is horizontal and applied 6 in. above the top surface of the beam. Determine the maximum normal stress on a right section of the beam. *Ans.* 533 psi.

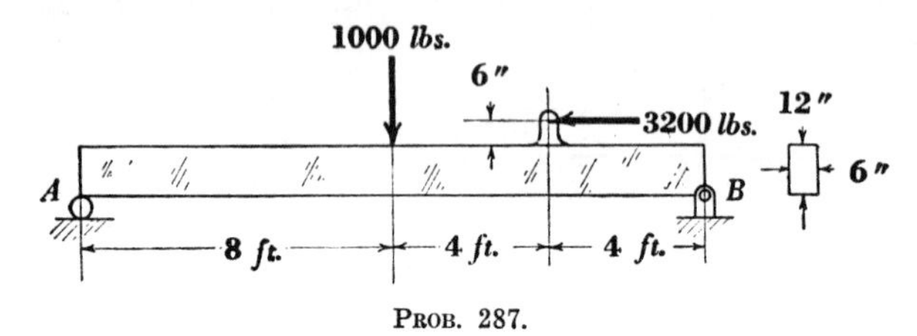

PROB. 287.

288. The beam is supported on a roller at A and a pin joint at B. The beam is a 10 in. deep Wide-Flange beam, with $I = 120.6$ in.^{4}, and $A = 6.77$ sq. in. Determine the maximum normal stress on a right section of the beam.

Ans. 6960 psi (compression).

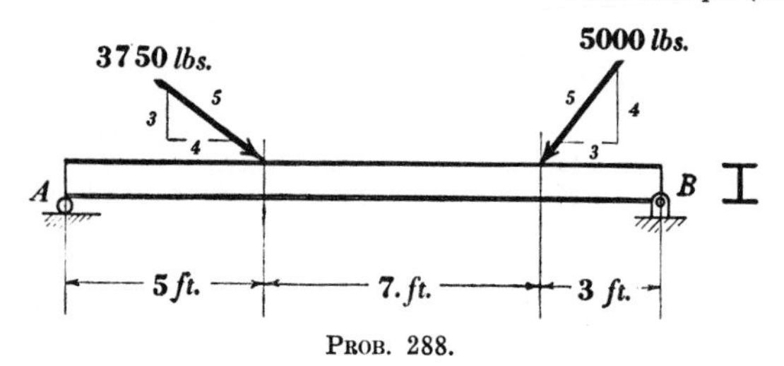

PROB. 288.

289. A 12 in. × 31.8-lb./ft. I-beam AB supports a uniformly distributed vertical load (including its own weight) of w lb./ft. The beam is supported on a knife edge at A, which exerts a horizontal force, and by a pin joint at B. Both supports act on the center line of the beam. If the maximum allowable normal stress on a right section is 10,000 psi, determine the maximum allowable value of w.

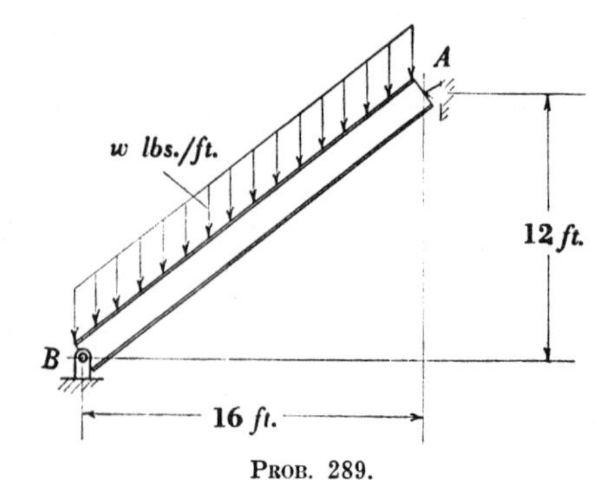

PROB. 289.

290. A 4 in. × 12 in. beam, *AB*, is supported on a pin joint at *A*, and held in position by a tie rod *CD*. All loads are applied at the center line of the beam. Determine the maximum normal stress on a right section of the beam.

Ans. 690 psi (compression).

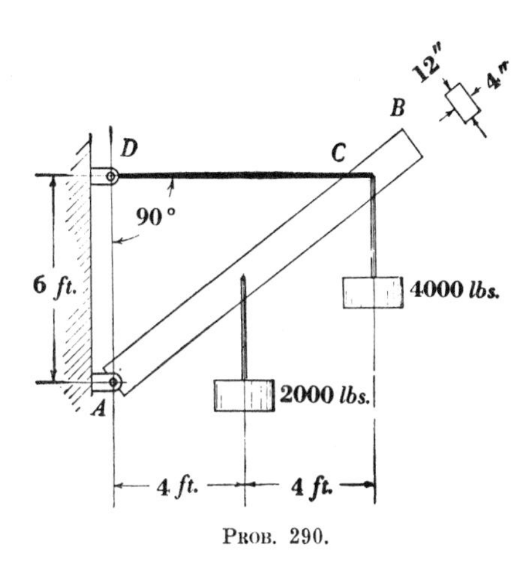

Prob. 290.

291. A wooden post, 6 in. × 10 in., securely fastened to the ground, supports a bar *AB* loaded as shown. The post also carries the two loads indicated at its upper end. Determine the maximum normal stress on a right section of the post.

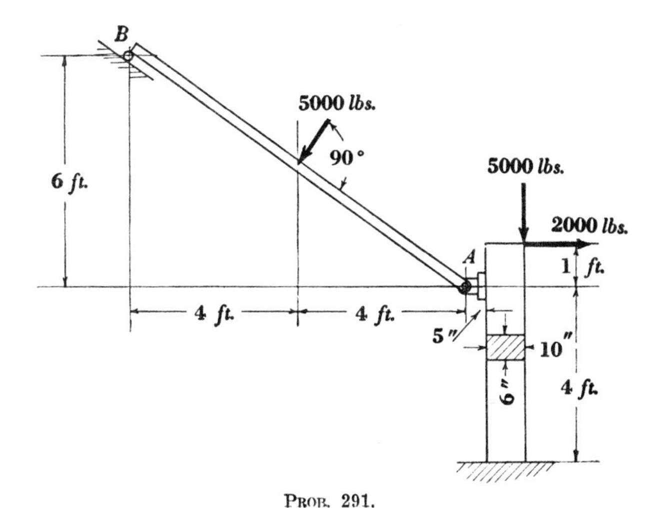

Prob. 291.

292. Determine the maximum normal stress on a right section of the beam, which is supported on a pin joint at A, and rests on a roller at C. The beam is a 12 in. I-beam, with $I = 268.9$ in.^{4}, and $A = 11.84$ sq. in. In addition to the loads shown, the beam carries a uniformly distributed load of 600 lb./ft., including its own weight, for its entire length. *Ans.* 9660 psi (compression).

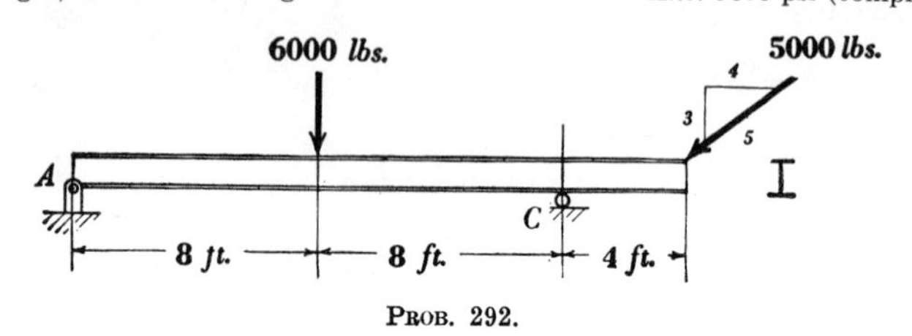

PROB. 292.

293. The beam AB is a 5 in. × 14.75 lb./ft. American Standard I-beam. It is supported by a pin joint at A and held in position by cable BC. All forces are applied along the central axis of the beam. Determine the maximum normal stress on a right section of the beam.

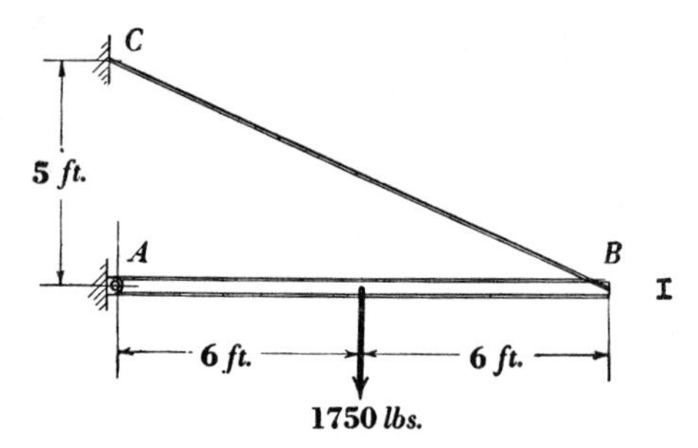

PROB. 293.

294. The 4 in. × 10 in. rectangular beam AC is supported by a pin joint at A, and held in position by cable BD. All forces are applied to the beam along its central axis. If the maximum allowable normal stress on a right section is 1400 psi determine the maximum value of load W. *Ans.* 930 lb.

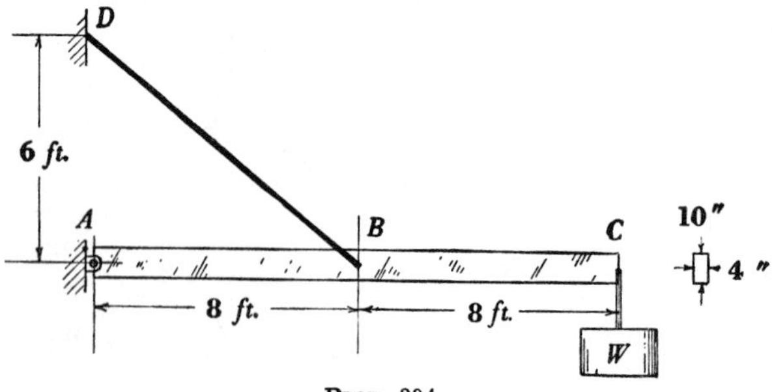

PROB. 294.

295. Beam AD is pinned to the wall at A, and supported by brace BC. The beam carries a uniformly distributed load (including its own weight) of 500 lb/ft., and a concentrated load of 8000 lb. applied at D. All concentrated forces act along the central axis of the beam. Joints A, B, and C are pin joints. Determine the maximum normal stress on a right section of the beam. *Ans.* 3320 psi (tension).

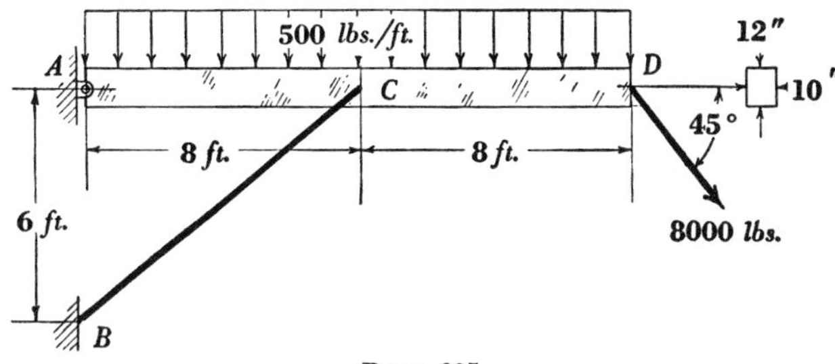

Prob. 295.

296. The truss is subjected to a system of vertical loads F, each equal to 1000 lb. The loads are spaced at equal distances apart. If members AB and BC are rectangular timbers 6 in. × 10 in., determine the maximum normal stress on a right section of AB and BC. All joints are pinned. *Ans.* AB: 505 psi (compression); BC: 460 psi (compression).

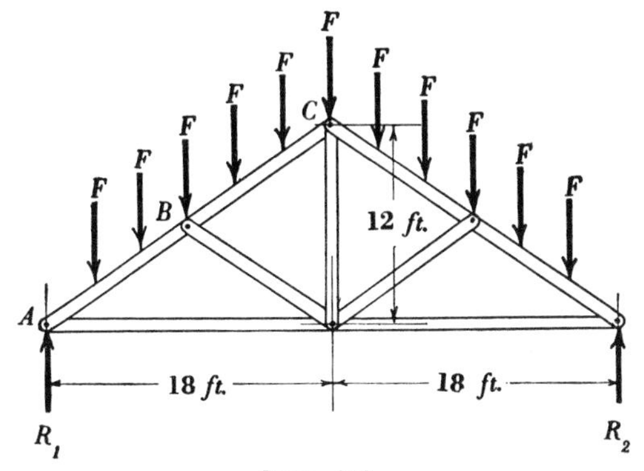

Prob. 296.

48. The Curved Beam. The combination of P/A and My/I discussed in the preceding article rests upon assumptions of very questionable merit. We recall that the derivation of My/I was based upon the limitation that the beam was straight, as well as an assumption that right sections of the beam remained planes when the beam was loaded. In that event, the neutral axis was found to lie at the centroid of the cross-section.

When the curvature of an unloaded beam is marked, prediction of normal stress by the flexure theory is not reliable. Figure 174 shows a portion of a curved beam. In this case, as in the straight beam, we may accept with confidence the assumption that plane radial sections, like A-A and B-B, remain plane surfaces. Our confidence is based upon laboratory testing, which has proved experimentally that the assumption is a valid one. Then A-A and B-B will converge. The total deformation

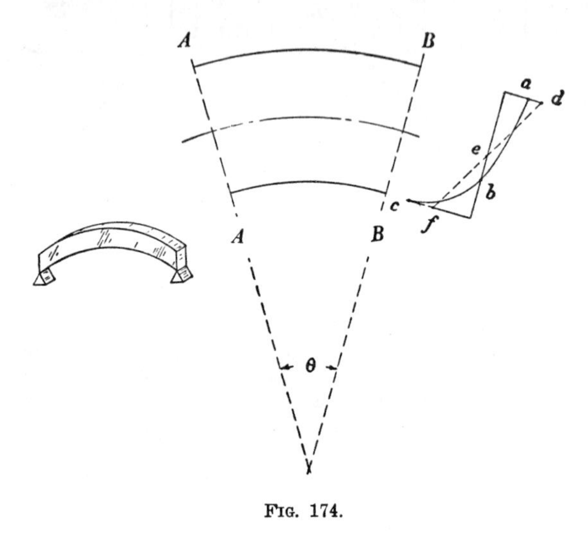

FIG. 174.

of the fibers will vary, when the beam is loaded, as their respective distances from some neutral fiber. The strains, or unit deformations, will not vary uniformly. The total deformation in any fiber will be

$$\delta = eL$$

where e is the strain in a fiber and L the original length of that fiber. The original lengths are not the same, for each is an arc subtending angle θ. Then the unit strains will vary with both δ and L which means that the strains are not varying linearly. The actual pattern of the strains is shown as the curve *abc* and it differs from the strain pattern of beams conforming to the flexure theory, which is shown as the dashed straight line *def*. The point e represents the neutral axis of the flexure-theory beam, while b is the location of the neutral axis of the curved beam. Point e lies at the centroid of the section, but point b is displaced toward the center of curvature.

To properly appraise the development of stress in the curved beam, we must recognize this displacement of the neutral axis from the centroid of the cross-section.

Figure 175 shows a free body which has been isolated from a curved beam. The radial sections *A-A* and *B-B* are neighboring sections and their included angle is $d\theta$. The outer radius is r_0 and the inner radius is r_i.

When bending moment M is applied, section *B-B* will rotate through some angle $d\alpha$. Somewhere in the free body there is a fiber which will remain undeformed. This is the neutral fiber which is shown as *nf*,

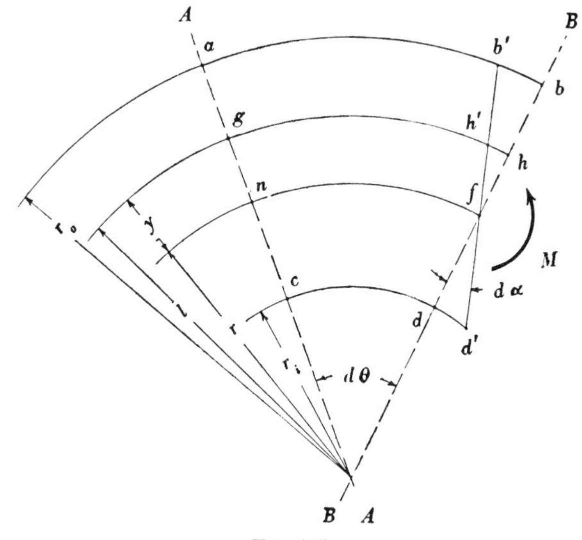

FIG. 175.

and the section *B-B* will rotate about point *f*. The radius of curvature of *nf* is called r. A fiber *cd* at the inner surface will be stretched to length *cd'*, while a fiber at the outer surface, *ab*, will be compressed to length *ab'*.

Any fiber, like *gh*, which is located at radial distance y from the neutral fiber and l from the center of curvature will undergo a total deformation $hh' = y\, d\alpha$. The strain in this typical fiber will be

$$e = \frac{y\, d\alpha}{l\, d\theta}$$

and the stress in this typical fiber will be

$$s = E\, e = \frac{E\, y\, d\alpha}{l\, d\theta}$$

This is a proper basic expression for the normal stress on the radial sections of a curved beam, but it is not very effective in its present form, for r and $d\alpha/d\theta$ are not directly available in a given beam. We must, therefore, evaluate those two terms.

The resultant of the normal stresses acting on a section like B-B is a couple, for this resultant must balance the bending moment. In order that the resultant may be a couple, the sum of the tensile and compressive forces acting on the section must be zero, and

$$\int s\,dA = \int \frac{E\,y\,d\alpha\,dA}{l\,d\theta} = 0$$

$d\alpha/d\theta$ is the same for all fibers across the section, and the constants E and $d\alpha/d\theta$ may be placed outside of the integral sign. Then

$$E\frac{d\alpha}{d\theta}\int \frac{y\,dA}{l} = 0$$

Since E and $d\alpha/d\theta$ are not zero,

$$\int \frac{y\,dA}{l} = 0 \qquad (55)$$

The force $s\,dA$ acting upon each elementary area of the section has a moment $y\,s\,dA$ about the neutral axis and the sum of all of these moments must be equal to M.

$$\int s\,y\,dA = \int \frac{E\,y^2\,d\alpha\,dA}{l\,d\theta} = E\frac{d\alpha}{d\theta}\int \frac{y^2\,dA}{l} = M \qquad (56)$$

We can now locate the neutral axis.

The integral of equation (56) may be transformed as follows:

$$\int \frac{y^2\,dA}{l} = \int \frac{y^2\,dA}{(y+r)} = \int \left(\frac{y^2 + ry - ry}{(y+r)}\right) dA =$$

$$\int \frac{y(y+r)dA}{(y+r)} - r\int \frac{y\,dA}{l} \qquad (57)$$

From equation (55) $\int \frac{y\,dA}{l} = 0$, and equation (57) becomes

$$\int \frac{y^2\,dA}{l} = \int y\,dA$$

$\int y\,dA$ is the first moment of the cross-sectional area about the neutral axis, and may be written $\bar{y}A$, where $\bar{y}$ is the radial distance from the neutral axis to the centroid of the cross-sectional area.

Equation (56) may now be written

$$E\frac{d\alpha}{d\theta}A\bar{y} = M \qquad \text{and} \qquad \frac{E d\alpha}{d\theta} = \frac{M}{A\bar{y}}$$

Since $$s = \frac{E\,y\,d\alpha}{l\,d\theta},\quad \frac{E\,d\alpha}{d\,\theta} = \frac{s\,l}{y}$$

then $$\frac{s\,l}{y} = \frac{M}{A\bar{y}}$$

and $$s = \frac{My}{l\,A\bar{y}} = \frac{My}{(r+y)A\bar{y}} \qquad (58)$$

The radius of curvature of the neutral surface, r, may be evaluated as follows:

From equation (55)
$$\int \frac{y\,dA}{l} = 0$$

then
$$\int \frac{(l-r)dA}{l} = \int dA - r\int \frac{dA}{l} = 0$$

and
$$r = \frac{A}{\displaystyle\int \frac{dA}{l}} \tag{59}$$

Equations (58) and (59) equip us with tools which make it possible to determine the normal stress in a curved beam. Equation (59) serves to determine the location of the neutral axis in terms of the properties of any given cross-section. Equation (58) will then serve to determine the normal stress at any distance y from the neutral axis.

Illustrative Example. To illustrate the application of the equations just derived, we shall again consider the open link of Fig. 176, which was investigated in the preceding article (see Fig. 169). We first evaluate r, the distance from the center of curvature to the neutral axis, by applying equation (59).

$$r = \frac{A}{\displaystyle\int \frac{dA}{l}}$$

$$= \frac{1 \times 0.5}{\displaystyle\int_{l=2}^{l=3} \frac{0.5dl}{l}} = \frac{1}{\log_e \left(\frac{3}{2}\right)} = \frac{1}{0.4055} = 2.466 \text{ in.}$$

The locations of the neutral axis (ab), centroidal axis (cc), inner and outer surfaces of the link section are shown in Fig. 176.

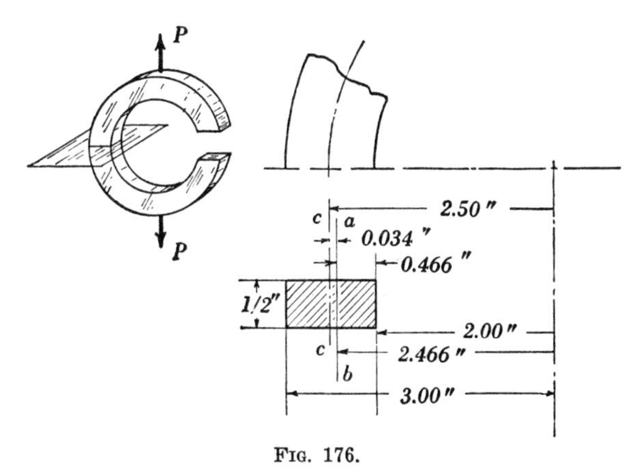

Fig. 176.

The bending stress at the inner surface ($y = -0.466$) will now be found by applying equation (58),

$$s_1 = \frac{My}{(r + y)A\bar{y}} = \frac{P \times 2.5 \times 0.466}{(2.466 - 0.466)0.5 \times 1 \times 0.034}$$
$$= 34.29P \text{ (tension)}$$

There is also an axial stress at the inner surface (and across the entire section) which is

$$s_2 = \frac{P}{A} = \frac{P}{0.5 \times 1} = 2P \text{ (tension)}$$

The total normal stress on the section at its inner surface is

$$s_I = s_1 + s_2 = (34.27 + 2)P = 36.27P \text{ (tension)}$$

The bending stress at the outer surface ($y = +0.534$) is, by equation (58),

$$s_3 = \frac{P \times 2.5 \times 0.534}{(2.466 + 0.534)0.5 \times 1 \times 0.034}$$
$$= 26.18P \text{ (compression)}$$

The net normal stress on the section at its outer surface will be

$$s_O = s_3 + s_2 = (26.18 - 2)P = 24.18P \text{ (compression)}$$

We should now compare these stresses, evaluated by means of the curved beam theory as expressed in equations (58) and (59), with the less accurate use of $P/A + My/I$, discussed in the preceding article. In the latter case, we found that the net stress at the inner surface was $32P$ (tension), while the net stress at the inner surface, according to the curved-beam theory, is 36.27/32, or 1.13 times as great, and the stress at the outer surface is 24.18/28, or 0.86 times as great. These differences are sufficiently great to warrant the use of the curved beam theory when the unloaded beam seriously violates the first limitation of the flexure theory.

PROBLEMS

Note: In curved-beam problems, the calculations should be carried through with greater accuracy than that afforded by the slide rule.

297. Axis *A-A* is the center of curvature of a bent bar of the 1 in. × 2 in. cross-section shown. Determine the distance from the centroid of the section to the neutral axis of the curved bar *Ans.* 0.085 in.

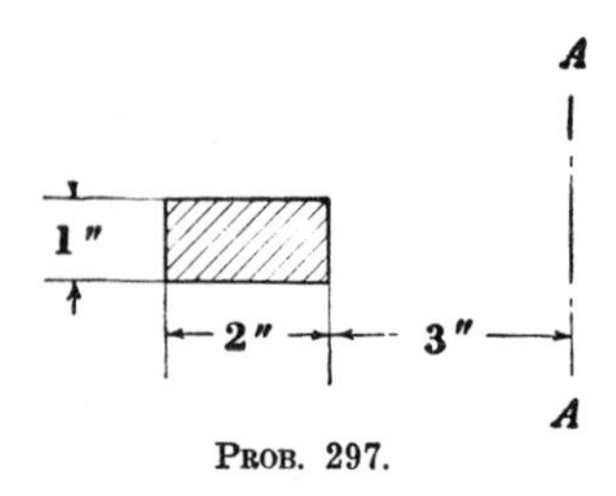

PROB. 297.

298. For the curved bar of Prob. 297, determine the ratio of the stress at the inner surface to the stress at the outer surface if the bar is subjected to pure bending.

Ans. 1.41.

299. The open link shown is made of a 1-in. square bar. Determine the normal stress at the inner surface of section A-A when load $P = 600$ lb.

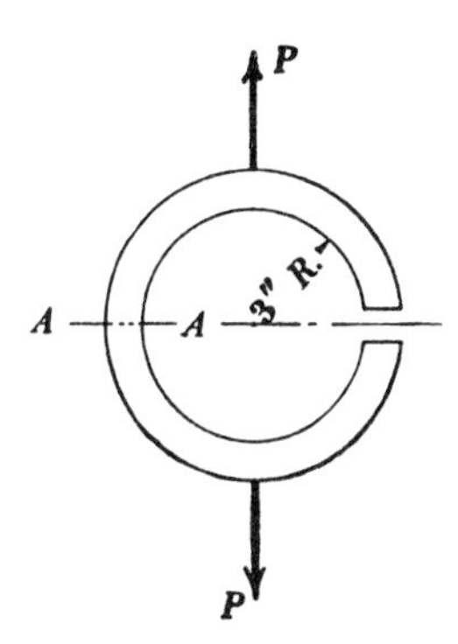

PROB. 299.

300. Determine the normal stress at the outer surface of section A-A of the open link of Prob. 299.

301. Determine the stress at the inner surface of section A-A of the machine frame shown when a load $P = 3600$ lb. is applied. *Ans.* 3870 psi.

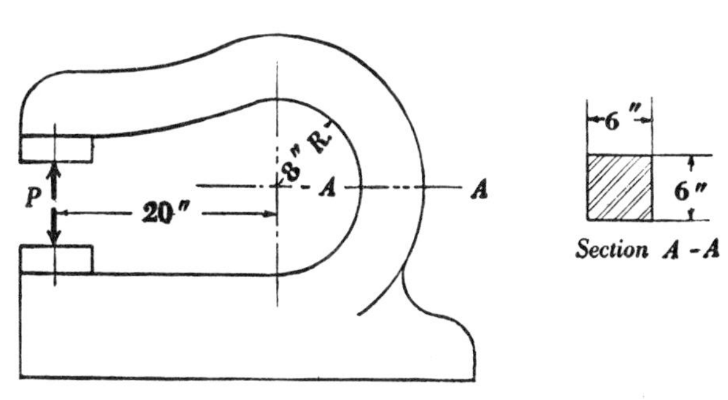

PROB. 301.

302. If $P = 8000$ lb. determine the normal stresses at the inner and outer surfaces of section A-A of the support.

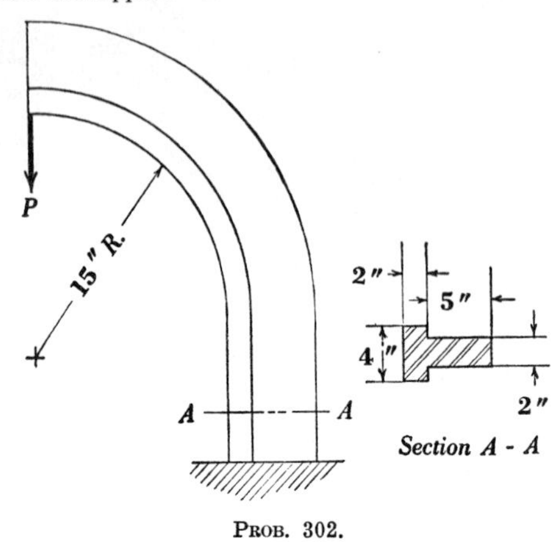

PROB. 302.

49. Beams of Varying Cross-Section.

Although the flexure theory is properly limited to beams which have the same cross-section throughout the entire span, an exact solution for beams of variable cross-section will not invalidate the flexure formula [equation (34)]. This expression will still yield results which are sufficiently reliable to serve as a design basis, provided that the other limitations have not been violated.

Then $s = My/I$ approximately holds for beams of varying cross-section, and the bending stresses at any section are determined by considering the bending moment and the section modulus of the particular section.

A beam of *uniform strength*—that is, a beam in which the maximum bending stress is the same at each section—will have a varying section, for

$$s_{\text{max.}} = \text{constant} = \frac{My_{\text{max.}}}{I}$$

and, with M varying, $y_{\text{max.}}/I$ must vary.

For example, in the case of the beam shown in Fig. 177-a, which is rectangular, the bending moment varies uniformly during the first range of loading, and is constant in the second range, as shown in Fig. 177-b.

In order that the beam may be of uniform strength, the section modulus of the beam must vary with the bending moment.

The section modulus of a rectangular beam is

$$\frac{I}{y_{\text{max.}}} = \frac{\dfrac{bh^3}{12}}{\dfrac{h}{2}} = \frac{bh^2}{6}$$

and such a varying modulus may be obtained by varying either b, or h, or both.

The simplest design would consist of maintaining constant depth, h, and varying the breadth, b, uniformly from zero at the end of the beam to

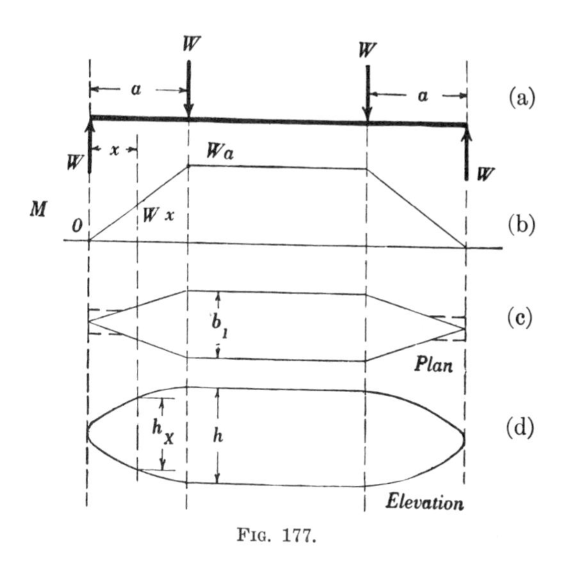

Fig. 177.

b_1 at the beginning of the second range. b_1 will be constant in the second range. The plan view of such a beam is shown in Fig. 177-c. The ends of the beam would have, in theory, breadth $b = 0$, for, at the end sections, the bending moment $M = 0$. However, immediately to the right of the left support, the beam section must be of sufficient size to withstand the shearing force caused by the left support and the section must be given finite width, as indicated by the dotted lines.

If, instead of varying the breadth of the beam, we elect to vary the depth, h, we should note that once again

$$s_{\text{max.}} = \text{constant} = \frac{My_{\text{max.}}}{I} = M \times \frac{6}{bh^2}$$

In the first range of loading from the left,

$$M = Wx$$

If the depth required in the central section, which has a constant bending moment, is h, substitution in the flexure formula will yield the proper value of h.

$$s = \frac{W\,a\,h/2}{bh^3/12} = \frac{6\,W\,a}{bh^2}$$

and

$$h^2 = \frac{6\,W\,a}{s\,b}$$

The required depth, h_X, at any section located at distance x from the left end may be found by applying the flexure formula in that range.

$$s = \frac{W\,x\,(h_X/2)}{b\,(h_X)^3/12}$$

and

$$(h_X)^2 = \frac{6Wx}{s\,b}$$

Then

$$\frac{(h_X)^2}{h^2} = \frac{6\,W\,x/s\,b}{6\,W\,a/s\,b} = \frac{x}{a}$$

and

$$(h_X)^2 = \frac{x}{a}\,h^2$$

The depth of the beam in the first range will therefore vary parabolically from zero at the left end to a maximum at the end of the first range. The depth will be constant in the second range and will diminish parabolically to zero in the last range of loading. As in the previous case, provision must be made at the end sections for resistance to the shearing force. Figure 177-d shows the elevation of the beam.

Illustrative Example. The cantilever beam (Fig. 178) is to have a rectangular section with the breadth, b, held constant, and the depth, h_x, varying to provide uniform strength. The allowable bending stress is 1500 psi. We are to determine the depth of the beam at the wall, $h_1 = 3b$, and to derive an equation for values of h has a function of span distance. The equation of shearing stress and the maximum deflection of the beam are also to be determined. $E = 10^6$ psi.

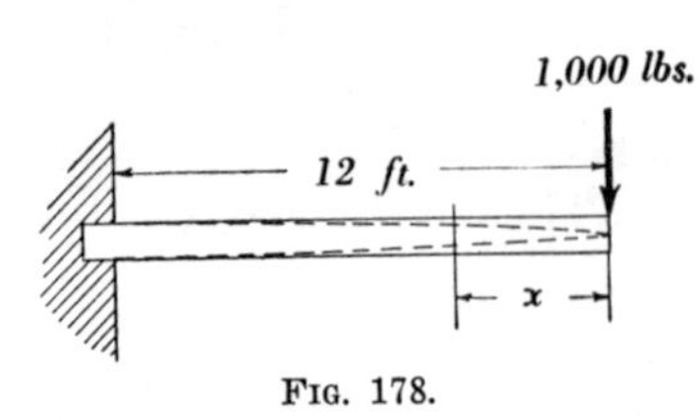

FIG. 178.

The depth of the beam at the wall, h_1, will be determined by applying the flexure formula.

$$s = 1500 = \frac{1000 \times 12 \times 12 \times \dfrac{h_1}{2}}{\dfrac{h_1}{3} \times \dfrac{(h_1)^3}{12}}$$

$$h_1 = 12 \text{ in.} \qquad b = 4 \text{ in.}$$

The bending moment at x ft. from the right or free end is

$$M_X = -1000x$$

and
$$s = 1500 = \frac{1000x \times 12 \times h_X/2}{4(h_X)^3/12} = \frac{18{,}000x}{(h_X)^2}$$

$$(h_X)^2 = 12x$$

where h_X is the depth of the beam in inches and x the distance from the free end in feet.

The maximum shearing stress will occur at the neutral axis, as in all rectangular beams, and

$$s_S = \frac{VQ}{bI} = \frac{1000 \times 4 \times \left(\frac{h_X}{2}\right) \times \left(\frac{h_X}{4}\right)}{4 \times 4 \times \frac{(h_X)^3}{12}} = \frac{375}{h_X}$$

Since $(h_X)^2 = 12x$, h_X will diminish in value as x approaches zero. Then, since h_X appears in the denominator, the shearing stress will rise in value as we approach the free end of the beam. The uniform-strength beam designed for bending stress cannot, therefore, be permitted to have zero cross-sectional area at the free end, but must be designed to resist the shearing force.

The maximum deflection may be obtained by applying equation (39) and integrating

$$\frac{d^2y}{dx^2} = \frac{M}{EI} = \frac{-1000x}{E \times 4 \times (h_X)^3/12} = \frac{-3000x}{E(12x)^{\frac{3}{2}}} = \frac{-250x^{-\frac{1}{2}}}{E(12)^{\frac{1}{2}}}$$

$$\frac{dy}{dx} = \frac{-250(x)^{\frac{1}{2}}}{E(12)^{\frac{1}{2}}} \times \frac{2}{1} + C_1$$

When $x = 12$,
$$\frac{dy}{dx} = 0; \qquad \therefore C_1 = +\frac{500}{E}$$

$$y = \frac{-500(x)^{\frac{3}{2}}}{E(12)^{\frac{1}{2}}} \times \frac{2}{3} + \frac{500x}{E} + C_2$$

When $x = 12$, $y = 0$

$$\therefore C_2 = +\frac{500(12)^{\frac{3}{2}}}{E(12)^{\frac{1}{2}}} \times \frac{2}{3} - \frac{500 \times 12}{E} = -\frac{2000}{E}$$

When $x = 0$,
$$y = y_{max.} = -\frac{2000}{10^6} \times (12)^3 = -3.456 \text{ in.}$$

The deflection of a 4 in. × 12 in. beam of constant cross-section, carrying the same loading, would be

$$y_{max.} = -\frac{1}{3} \times \frac{1000 \times (12)^3}{10^6 \times 4 \times (12)^3/12} \times (12)^3 = -1.728 \text{ in.}$$

The uniform-strength beam, therefore, lacks the stiffness of the beam of uniform cross-section, and has a maximum deflection which is twice as great as that of the latter.

Another method of determining deflections when the beam is of varying cross-section has already been discussed in Art. 44.

50. Beams of Different Materials. The Transformed Section. The engineer frequently finds that beams composed of more than one material present advantages. Such partnerships of materials united to form *composite* beams are used to derive benefit from combination of the most desirable properties of each of the contributing materials.

The flexure-theory limitations preclude investigation of bending stresses in such beams through the use of the flexure formula, for we are restricted by those limitations to beams of homogeneous material.

We shall, however, find it possible to determine an equivalent beam section, assumed to be made of a single material, which will have the same strength properties as those of the original composite beam. The flexure formula [equation (34)] may then be applied as we explore the bending stress.

Figure 179 shows a cross-section of a beam which is composed of two materials. Plates A are made of the same material, and core B is made of

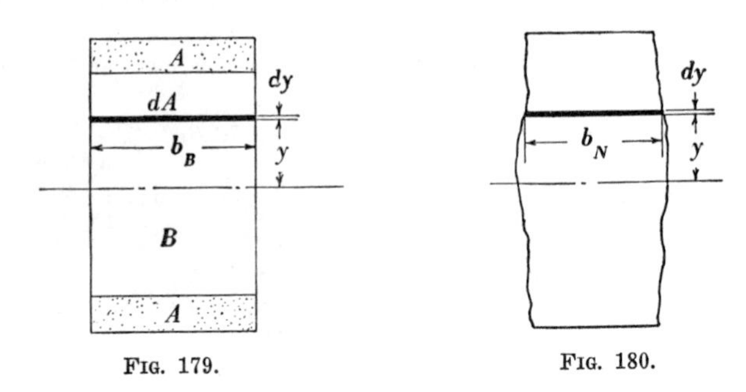

FIG. 179. FIG. 180.

a different material. The plates are fastened to the core so that they cannot move relative to it.

The force which acts on an elementary area of the core, dA, will be

$$dF_B = s_B\,dA = s_B b_B\,dy$$

s_B is the bending stress in the material of core B, and b_B is the width of the core at distance y from a neutral axis.

$$s_B b_B\,dy = E_B e_B b_B\,dy$$

where E_B is the modulus of elasticity of the core material and e_B is the strain at distance y from a neutral axis.

The moment of force dF_B about the neutral axis is $dF_B \times y$, and the total moment of resistance is $M = \int (dF_B \times y)$.

Figure 180 shows a cross-section of a beam of different material than core B. The new cross-section will satisfactorily replace that of Fig. 179 without disturbing the total moment of resistance if at each level y from the neutral axis, a force equal to dF_B may be applied. In the new, or transformed, section, the force acting at distance y from the neutral axis is

$$dF_N = s_N b_N \, dy = E_N e_N b_N \, dy$$

Then, in order that $dF_N = dF_B$, the following relationship must be established

$$E_B e_B b_B \, dy = E_N e_N b_N \, dy$$

The two sections—that of the original beam, and that of the new or transformed beam—must be made equivalent in one other respect. If the flexure formula is to be applied, we must recall that it rested upon an assumption that plane sections remain planes, and strain therefore varies uniformly from the neutral axis. The strain at any level must be the same in the original or transformed section.

Then $$e_B = e_N \quad \text{and} \quad E_B b_B = E_N b_N \tag{60}$$

If we provide a width b_N in the transformed section which is equal to $E_B b_B / E_N$, the section will be equivalent to the original section in its ability to support the same moment of resistance.

Let us next note the relationship between the actual stresses on the original section, and the fictitious stresses on the transformed section.

Since $$s_B b_B \, dy = s_N b_N \, dy$$

$$\frac{s_B}{s_N} = \frac{b_N}{b_B} = \frac{E_B}{E_N} \tag{61}$$

This device of transformation may be employed to analyze the bending stresses in the composite beam of Fig. 179. Both materials A and B may be transformed into a third material to represent the transformed section. It is unnecessary to make such a complete transformation, for we have had as our objective the use of the flexure theory in preparing to analyze composite beams. That theory demands only that the entire cross-section of a beam be made of one material, and the transformation may be made in terms of either of the existing materials, A or B.

For example, the beam of Fig. 181-a is composed of a wooden beam, B, which has been reinforced by two steel plates, A. The modulus of elasticity of the wood is $E_W = 1.5 \times 10^6$ psi; that of the steel is $E_S = 30 \times 10^6$ psi. The section has been subjected to a bending moment $M = 50{,}000$ ft.-lb., and we are to determine the maximum bending stress in each material.

The transformation of the composite section into an all-steel section is shown in Fig. 181-b.

Since $$\frac{E_B}{E_A} = \frac{1.5 \times 10^6}{30 \times 10^6} = \frac{1}{20}$$

the width of steel which will properly replace the wooden portion of the beam is, by equation (61),

$$b = \frac{1}{20} \times 6 = 0.3 \text{ in.}$$

This transformed section (Fig. 181-b) consists of one material, and the flexure formula may now be used to determine the bending stresses.

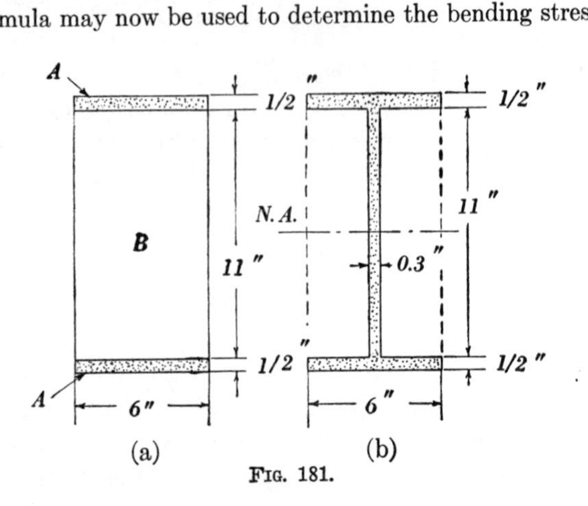

FIG. 181.

The moment of inertia of the all-steel, or transformed, section about the neutral axis at its centroid is

$$I = \frac{6 \times (12)^3}{12} - \frac{5.7 \times (11)^3}{12} = 232 \text{ in.}^4$$

The maximum bending stress on the transformed section will occur at the extreme fibers, where it will be

$$s = \frac{50{,}000 \times 12 \times 6}{232} = 15{,}520 \text{ psi}$$

Since the actual material at the extreme fibers is steel, which has not been disturbed by the transformation, this stress is the actual maximum bending stress in the steel.

The maximum bending stress in the wood will be found by first determining the stress in the transformed section at the layer which is 5.5 in. from the neutral axis. This level represents the location of the most remote wooden fiber. At this level, the stress in the steel will be

$$s_1 = \frac{50{,}000 \times 12 \times 5.5}{232} = 14{,}220 \text{ psi}$$

This fictitious stress must be translated, or "re-transformed" to present the actual stress in wood. The relationship between stress in the transformed material and stress in the actual material is the same as that of their respective moduli of elasticity, and, applying equation (61),

$$s_{\text{wood}} = \frac{1}{20} \quad s_1 = \frac{1}{20} \times 14{,}220 = 711 \text{ psi}$$

Deflection of Composite Beams. The curvature of any beam in bending results from the changes in length of the several fibers comprising the beam. We have, in the process of transforming beam sections, maintained the same change in the length of fibers at each level, whether we were considering the original material or the transformed equivalent. Then the deflections of the two beams—original and transformed—will be the same, and deflections in composite beams may be determined by using the expressions already derived in the chapter devoted to the deflection theory.

The adjustment in the case of the composite beams occurs in the EI factor of each deflection. In the illustrative example which follows, an application of this principle is made to illustrate the adjustment.

Illustrative Example. The Engelmann spruce timber A of Fig. 182-a has an allowable bending stress $s_W = 600$ psi, and a modulus of elasticity $E = 8 \times 10^5$ psi. It is reinforced with a plate of Douglas fir B, having an allowable bending

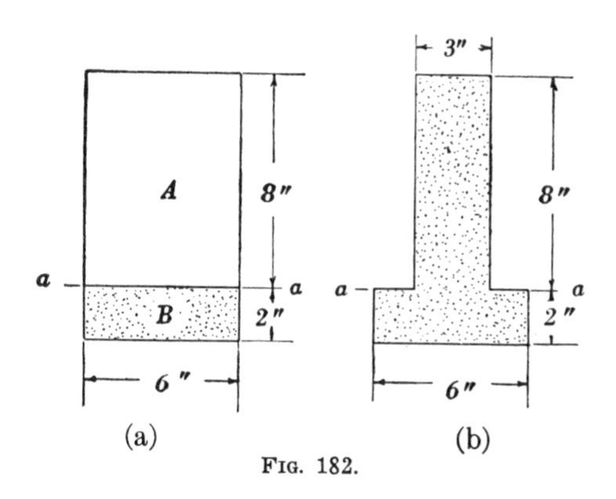

FIG. 182.

stress $s_W = 1700$ psi and $E = 1.6 \times 10^6$ psi. The two sections are glued together. The span of the beam is 16 ft., and it is freely supported at its ends. We are to determine the following:

a) The maximum allowable concentrated load, W, which may be placed at mid-span.
b) The maximum shear stress in the glue.
c) The maximum deflection of the beam when it is supporting load W.

The transformed section of the beam is shown in Fig. 182-b. The original beam has been transformed into an all-fir beam, and the resulting cross-section is tee-shaped, having a "web" width of

$$b = \frac{0.8 \times 10^6 \times 6}{1.6 \times 10^6} = 3 \text{ in.} \qquad \text{(Equation 61)}$$

The neutral axis passes through the centroid of the transformed section at distance $\bar{y}$ from the base.

$$\bar{y} = \frac{6 \times 2 \times 1 + 3 \times 8 \times 6}{6 \times 2 + 3 \times 8} = 4.33 \text{ in.}$$

The moment of inertia of the transformed section about the neutral axis is

$$I = \frac{6 \times (2)^3}{12} + (3.33)^2 \times 6 \times 2 + \frac{3 \times (8)^3}{12} + (1.67)^2 \times 3 \times 8$$
$$= 332 \text{ in.}^4$$

The permissible maximum bending moment must be based upon a consideration of the strength properties of both materials. If the fir governs in fixing the maximum bending moment,

$$s_W = 1700 = \frac{M \times 4.33}{332}$$

and

$$M = 130{,}250 \text{ in.-lb.}$$

If the spruce governs, the most stressed fiber is at the top of the beam. The stress in the transformed section at that level is

$$s = \frac{M \times 5.67}{332} \quad \text{and} \quad M = 58.6\, s$$

Since the allowable bending stress for spruce is $s_W = 600$ psi, the corresponding value of s in the transformed section will be

$$s = 600 \times \frac{1.6 \times 10^6}{0.8 \times 10^6} = 1200 \text{ psi}$$

Then

$$M = 58.6 \times 1200 = 70\,320 \text{ in.-lb.}$$

The least of the two possible values of bending moment must be selected, ($M =$ 70,320 in.-lb.) or the allowable stress in one of the two materials will be excessive.

a) A single concentrated load, W, at mid-span will produce a maximum bending moment in the beam, $M = WL/4$, and

$$70{,}320 = \frac{W \times 16}{4} \times 12$$
$$W = 1465 \text{ lb.}$$

b) The glue which is used to fasten the sections together is applied at section a-a of Fig. 182.

The maximum shearing force in the beam when the load of 1465 lb. is applied is $V = 732.5$ lb.

The shear stress in the glue may be determined by considering the level of the beam immediately below section a-a. The material at this level in the transformed section is the same as that of the original beam. The stress is longitudinal shear, and, applying equation (36),

$$s_S = \frac{VQ}{bI} = \frac{732.5 \times 2 \times 6 \times 3.33}{6 \times 332}$$
$$= 14.7 \text{ psi}$$

This value of stress may be checked by considering the level of the beam immediately above section *a-a*. The material is now "transformed" material and the stress is

$$s_S = \frac{VQ}{bI} = \frac{732.5 \times 2 \times 6 \times 3.33}{3 \times 332}$$
$$= 29.4 \text{ psi}$$

This value must be adjusted to represent the original material, and

$$s_S = \frac{29.4 \times 0.8 \times 10^6}{1.6 \times 10^6} = 14.7 \text{ psi}$$

c) The maximum deflection of a simple beam carrying a single concentrated load at mid-span is, by equation (40),

$$y_{\text{max.}} = -\frac{1}{48}\frac{WL^3}{EI}$$

Then, in this case, using the transformed section,

$$y_{\text{max.}} = -\frac{1}{48} \times \frac{1465 \times (16)^3}{1.6 \times 10^6 \times 332} \times (12)^3$$
$$= -0.41 \text{ in.}$$

Since checking is always sound engineering procedure, it is well that we have available a second approach to the determination of this deflection. If, instead of transforming the composite beam to an all-fir section, the transformation is made

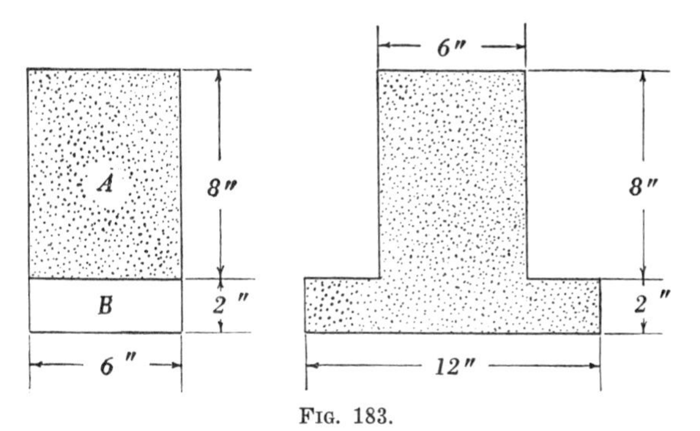

Fig. 183.

to all spruce as the single material, the transformed section will appear as in Fig. 183. The neutral axis of this section will lie at level $\bar{y} = 4.33$ in. from the base, and the moment of inertia of this equivalent section about the neutral axis will be $I = 664$ in.^{4}

The maximum deflection will be

$$y_{\text{max.}} = -\frac{1}{48}\ \frac{1465 \times (16)^3}{8 \times 10^5 \times 664} = -0.41 \text{ in.}$$

PROBLEMS

Note: The values of modulus of elasticity, E, for the materials used in the following composite-beam problems will be found in Table II, on page 79.

303. The beam whose cross-section is shown is composed of steel plates, A, fastened to a brass core, B. The bending moment at the section is 10,000 ft.-lb. Determine the maximum bending stress in each material. *Ans.* A: 7830 psi; B: 2610 psi.

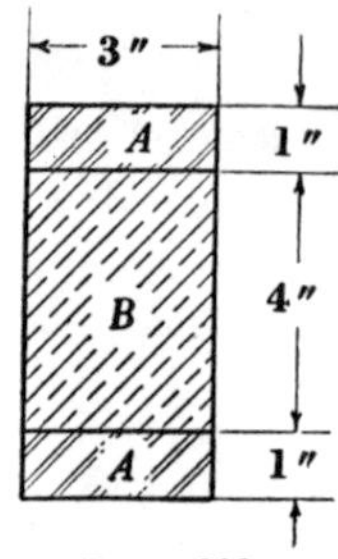

PROB. 303.

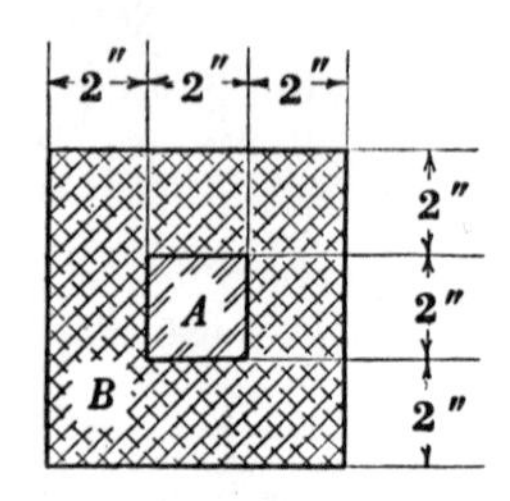

PROB. 305.

304. If the composite beam of Prob. 303 is composed of a brass core, B, and aluminum plates, A, of the same dimensions, determine the maximum bending stress in each material when the bending moment at the section is 10,000 ft.-lb.

305. In an experimental machine part, steel bar, A, is embedded in an aluminum casing, B, to form the composite-beam section shown. When the section is subjected to a bending moment of 20,000 ft.-lb. determine the maximum bending stress in the aluminum. *Ans.* 6510 psi.

306. In the composite-beam section shown, material A is aluminum, material B is brass, and material C is steel. If the section is subjected to a bending moment of 40,000 ft.-lb., determine the maximum bending stress in each material.
Ans. A: 2260 psi; B: 2390 psi; C: 5910 psi.

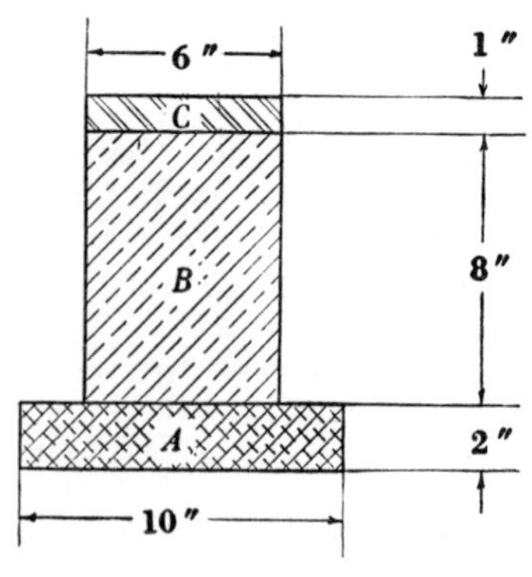

PROB. 306.

307. The composite-beam section shown is composed of a timber core, A, reinforced by steel plates, B. The modulus of elasticity of the timber is 2×10^6 psi; that of the steel is 30×10^6 psi. The maximum allowable bending stress in the timber is 600 psi; in the steel, 18,000 psi.

If the beam is freely supported at its ends and carries a uniformly distributed load of w lb./ft., determine the maximum allowable value of w. Span = 12 ft.

Ans. 980 lb./ft.

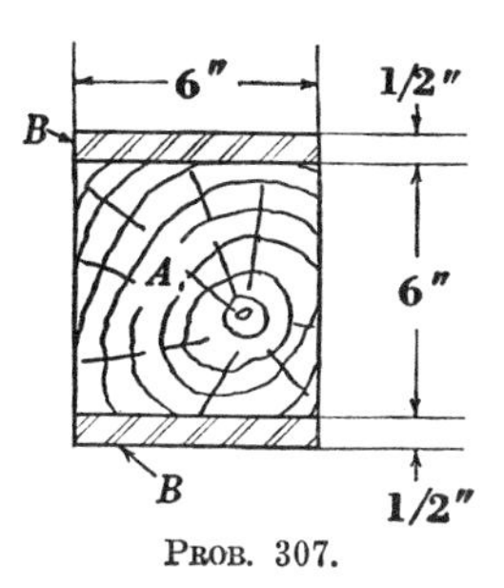

PROB. 307.

308. A composite beam is made of a soft pine timber, A, and plywood boards, B, glued to the pine timber at the top and bottom. The beam is freely supported at its ends and carries a concentrated load of 500 lb. at mid-span, as shown. The modulus of elasticity of the soft pine is 10^6 psi; that of the plywood is 2×10^6 psi. Determine:

a) The maximum bending stress in the plywood. *Ans.* a) 444 psi;
b) The maximum bending stress in the soft pine. b) 167 psi;
c) The maximum longitudinal shear stress in the glue. c) 6.5 psi.

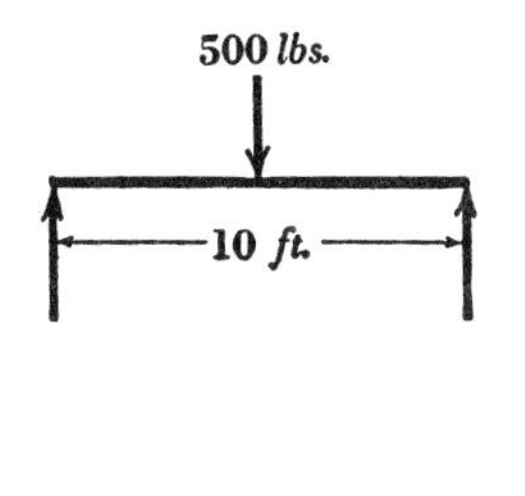

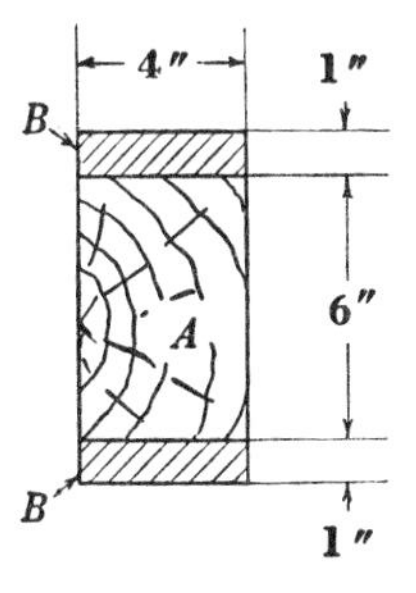

PROB. 308.

309. Determine the maximum bending stress in each material if the section of a composite beam shown is subjected to a bending moment of 5000 ft.-lb. The modulus of elasticity of material A is 30×10^6 psi; that of B is 2×10^6 psi.

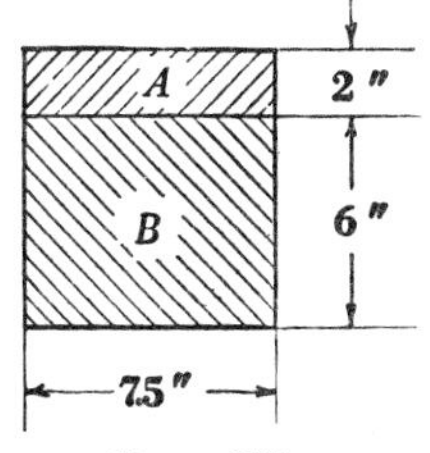

PROB. 309.

310. If the allowable bending stresses for the materials of the preceding problem are 8000 psi for material A and 1500 psi for material B, determine the maximum bending moment to which the section may be subjected.

311. A bimetallic strip is composed of a brass strip, A, 0.50 in. wide by 0.10 in. deep, and a steel strip, B, of the same dimensions, to which the brass strip is brazed. In a machine element, the strip is freely supported at its ends and loaded by a concentrated force $P = 20$ lb. Determine the maximum bending stress in each material. *Ans.* A: 2540 psi; B: 3640 psi.

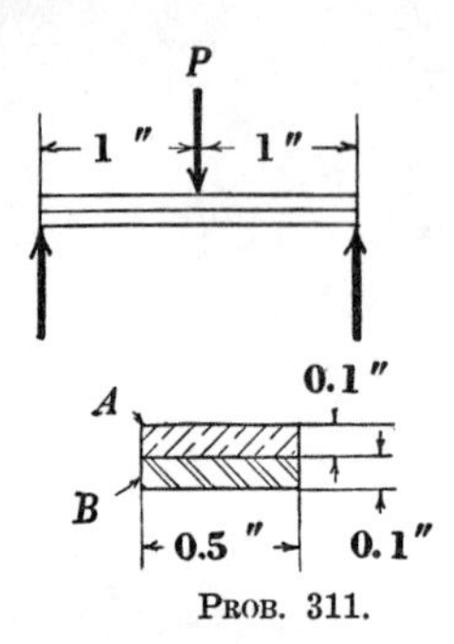

PROB. 311.

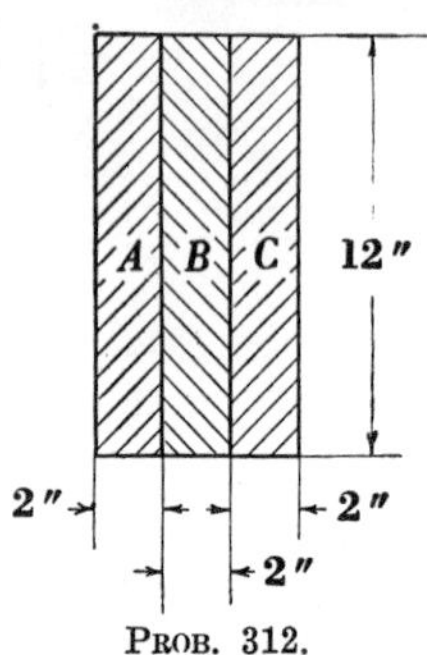

PROB. 312.

312. The composite beam is composed of three plies as shown, having the following properties:

Section	E—psi	*Allowable bending stress*—psi
A	12×10^6	900
B	15×10^6	1200
C	24×10^6	1800

Determine the maximum bending moment which may be applied to the section.

313. The section of a composite beam shown is subjected to a bending moment of 3000 ft.-lb. Determine the maximum bending stress in each material. $E_A = 12 \times 10^6$ psi; $E_B = 18 \times 10^6$ psi; $E_C = 30 \times 10^6$ psi. *Ans.* A: 1560 psi; B: 1040 psi; C: 2600 psi.

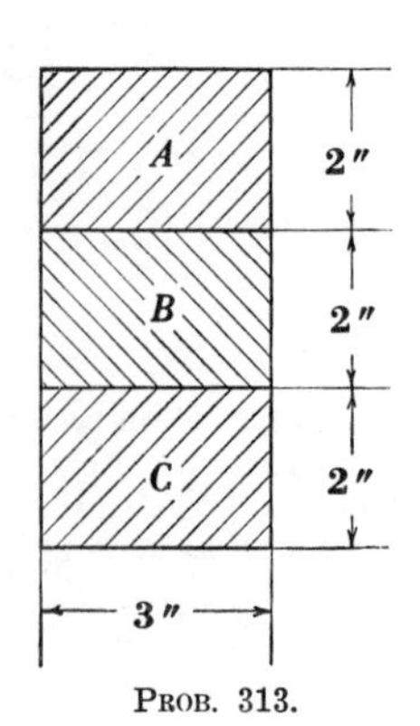

PROB. 313.

314. An aluminum tee-beam is reinforced, as shown, by two wooden 2 in. × 4 in. beams. The beam is freely supported at points A and B and carries a load which varies, uniformly, from zero at C to w lb./ft. at B. The modulus of elasticity of the wood is 10^6 psi, and its maximum allowable stress is 600 psi; the modulus of elasticity of the aluminum is 10.3×10^6 psi, and its maximum allowable stress is 8000 psi. Determine the maximum value of w.

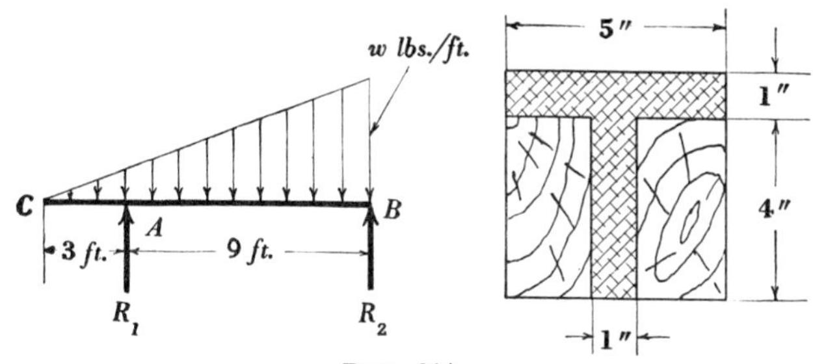

PROB. 314.

315. A wooden beam, of the cross-section shown in Prob. 308, is composed of a core, A, having a modulus of elasticity of 10^6 psi and allowable bending stress of 600 psi; and plywood plates, B, having a modulus of elasticity of 2×10^6 psi and allowable bending stress of 1200 psi. The beam is freely supported at its ends and carries a single concentrated load W at mid-span. Span = 12 ft. In order that the advantage of this beam over a beam 4 in. wide by 8 in. deep, made entirely of material A, may be demonstrated, determine the following:

a) The maximum value of W for the composite beam. *Ans.* a) 1125 lb.;

b) The maximum value of W for the one-material beam. b) 710 lb.

316. A composite beam is made by bolting a steel channel to a wooden plank, as shown. The beam is 10 ft. long, is freely supported at its ends, and carries a uniformly distributed load of 800 lb./ft. The pitch of the bolts is 12 in. The channel is made of steel, with $E = 30 \times 10^6$ psi. It has a cross-sectional area $A = 3$ sq. in., and moment of inertia about its centroid $I_{c.g.} = 0.87$ in.^{4} The centroid of the channel is 0.5 in. from the back of the channel web. The wood has a modulus of elasticity, $E = 1.5 \times 10^6$ psi.

Determine a) the thickness t of the wooden plank which will cause the neutral axis of the composite section to lie at the junction of the steel and the wood and b) the maximum shearing stress in the bolts, if they each have a cross-sectional area of 0.5 sq. in.

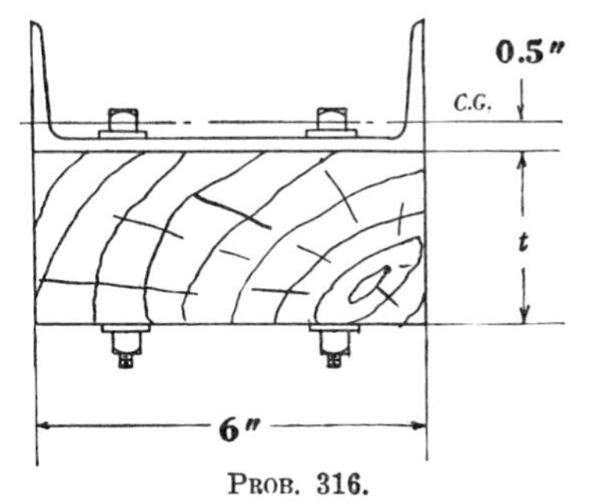

PROB. 316.

317. The cross-section of a composite beam is shown. It consists of a rectangular beam of material *B*, in which square rods of material *A* have been imbedded. $E_A = 30 \times 10^6$ psi. $E_B = 15 \times 10^6$ psi. If the section is subjected to a bending moment of 11,900 ft.-lb., determine the maximum bending stress in each material.

Ans. *A*: 4800 psi; *B*: 2400 psi.

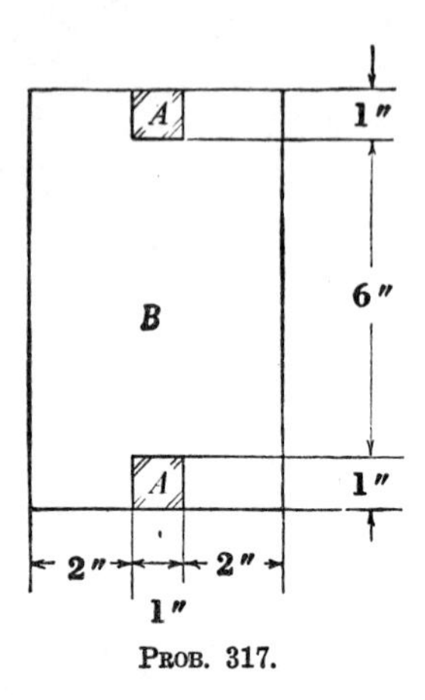

PROB. 317.

318. A composite beam is made of brass and steel as shown. The upper portion is steel and the lower portion is brass. The beam is used to distribute a single concentrated load *P* *uniformly* along its entire span of 60 in. The maximum allowable stress in the brass is 10,000 psi, and the maximum allowable stress in the steel is 20,000 spi. Determine the maximum allowable value of force *P*. *Ans.* 26,700 lb.

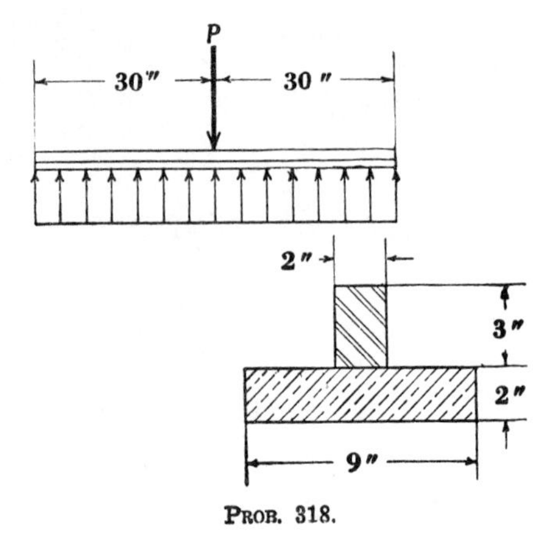

PROB. 318.

Reinforced Concrete. Courtesy Portland Cement Association

51. Reinforced Concrete. Transformed Section. Another example of the effective use of the transformed-section technique discussed in the previous article arises in the analysis of reinforced concrete.

Concrete is comparatively cheap, possesses excellent strength properties in compression, and is capable of acting as a fireproofing agent. It also presents the disadvantage of low tensile strength. Steel, while relatively expensive, has high tensile strength. The two materials form one of the most effective partnerships which have ever been introduced in the use of engineering materials.

Reinforced-concrete beams consist of basic concrete beams with steel rods embedded in the region of tensile stress. The combination is most efficient, for the compressive stresses are resisted by the concrete and the tensile stresses by steel. The cost of the composite beam is very much lower than that of a steel beam. In addition, the embedding of the steel rods takes advantage of the insulating property of the concrete, and the steel is protected from damage caused by fire.

Figure 184-a shows the cross-section of a reinforced-concrete beam at a section of positive bending moment. The black circles indicate the embedded steel rods

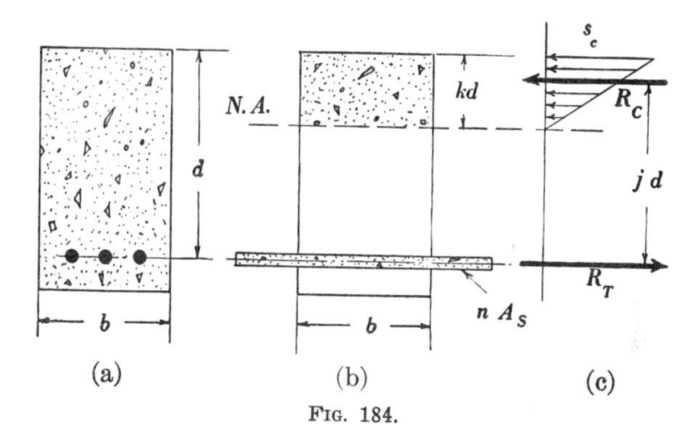

FIG. 184.

which are provided to resist the tension, while the concrete resists compression. It is customary, in the design of such beams, to make the assumption that all of the tension is resisted by the steel, despite the fact that there is a large area of concrete exposed to tension. It is also assumed that the concrete obeys Hooke's law, which is not quite true. To compensate for the variation a lower value of modulus of elasticity is usually assigned to the concrete than the value which would be obtained from compression tests.

The value of the ratio of moduli of elasticity usually employed in effecting the transformation of steel area into equivalent area of concrete is

$$n = \frac{E_S}{E_C} = 15$$

and

$$\frac{A_C}{A_S} = \frac{15}{1}$$

where A_C is the area of concrete representing transformation from A_S, the area of the original steel.

The transformed section is shown as Fig. 184-b. This is transformation into an all-concrete section, and lower shaded area is the area of concrete replacing the steel, which is $A_C = nA_S$.

The location of the neutral axis is determined by equating the first moments of the shaded areas of Fig. 184-b.

$$b \times kd \times \frac{kd}{2} = nA_S(d - kd)$$

It will be noted that the depth of the beam is taken as d, the distance from the top of the beam to the level of the steel rods. The concrete area below the rod level serves as fireproofing, but is not credited in determining stress properties.

The ratio of the area of steel to the area of concrete is called the *steel percentage* and is symbolized as p, where

$$p = \frac{A_S}{bd}$$

Then

$$\frac{b\,k^2\,d^2}{2} = n\,p\,b\,d\,(d - kd)$$

and

$$k = \sqrt{2pn + (pn)^2} - pn \tag{62}$$

If the maximum compressive stress in the concrete is s_C, the resultant compressive force above the neutral axis (Fig. 184-c) is

$$R_C = \frac{1}{2} \times s_C \times b \times kd = \frac{s_C\,b\,k\,d}{2}$$

and the total moment of resistance in the beam as far as the concrete is concerned will be

$$M_1 = \frac{s_C\,b\,kd}{2} \times j\,d = \frac{s_C\,b\,j\,k\,d^2}{2} \tag{63}$$

where jd is the moment arm of the couple formed by R_C and R_T. (R_T is the resultant tensile force exerted by the steel).

Since the resultant compressive force, R_C, will act at a distance $kd/3$ from the top of the beam,

$$jd = d - \frac{kd}{3}$$

and

$$j = 1 - \frac{k}{3} \tag{64}$$

When the allowable compressive stress of concrete is inserted in equation (63), we will have determined the maximum bending moment which the beam section will resist, assuming that the strength property of the concrete governs. It is quite as possible that the allowable tensile stress of the steel may be the governing control. In that event, the total moment of resistance of the beam section will be

$$M_2 = R_T\,j\,d = s_T\,A_S\,j\,d \tag{65}$$

where s_T is the allowable tensile stress of the steel rods.

In determining the safe bending moment in a beam of given dimensions, both M_1 and M_2 must be checked, the lesser of the two being the safe bending moment.

When a beam is to be designed to support a given bending moment, the equations are used to fix the dimensions of the concrete and the amount of steel area which is required. Other considerations than the bending stress are vital to such design—shear and diagonal tension, bond stress and anchorage of the embedded steel also play a part. Such design is beyond the scope of the present discussion, which has only been intended to offer an additional example of the technique of transforming sectional areas of composite beams.

Illustrative Example. A concrete beam, of the dimensions shown in Fig. 185-a is reinforced with steel rods. $n = 15$. The maximum allowable stresses for the steel and concrete are $s_S = 18{,}000$ psi, and $s_C = 600$ psi, respectively.

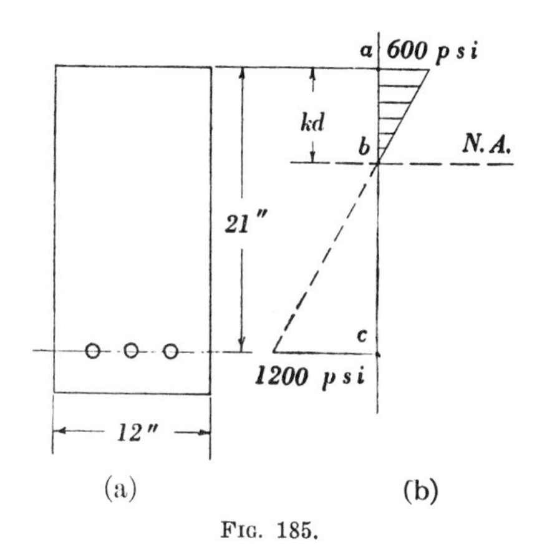

FIG. 185.

We are to determine the amount of steel area which must be used for *balanced reinforcement*, which is the utilization of both materials at their maximum allowable stresses for greatest efficiency.

We are also to determine the maximum bending moment which may be safely applied to the section.

The stress diagram of Fig. 185-b indicates the variation of stress across the transformed, all-concrete section. The stress at the top will be $s_C = 600$ psi. The stress at the level of the steel will be $18{,}000/n = 1200$ psi in the transformed section.

Then the neutral axis must be located at point b, with

$$\frac{ab}{bc} = \frac{600}{1200}$$

$$ab + bc = 21$$

$$ab = 7 \text{ in.} \qquad bc = 14 \text{ in.}$$

Since $ab = 7$ in. $= kd$, k must be $\frac{1}{3}$.

Then, by equation (64), $$j = 1 - \frac{k}{3} = \frac{8}{9}$$

M_1 [equation (63)] is the allowable moment when the concrete governs, and M_2 [equation (65)] the corresponding moment when steel governs. For balanced reinforcement,

$$M_1 = M_2$$

$$\frac{s_C\, b\, j\, k\, d^2}{2} = s_T\, A_S\, j\, d$$

$$s_C\, b\, k\, d = 2\, s_T\, A_S$$

$$600 \times 12 \times \frac{1}{3} \times 21 = 2 \times 18{,}000 \times A_S$$

$$A_S = 1.4 \text{ sq. in.}$$

The maximum bending moment may now be determined. According to equation (63),

$$M_1 = \frac{s_C\, b\, j\, k\, d^2}{2}$$

$$= \frac{600 \times 12 \times 8/9 \times 1/3 \times (21)^2}{2}$$

$$= 470{,}400 \text{ in.-lb.}$$

The maximum bending moment may be checked in terms of the steel. From equation (65),

$$M_2 = s_T\, A_S\, j\, d = 18{,}000 \times 1.4 \times \frac{8}{9} \times 21$$
$$= 470{,}400 \text{ in.-lb.}$$

PROBLEMS

319. A reinforced-concrete beam carries a uniformly distributed load of 500 lb./ft. The span is 16 ft., and the beam may be assumed to be freely supported at its ends. $b = 10$ in.; $d = 12$ in.; $n = 15$. There are two reinforcing rods, each ¾ in. square. Determine the maximum stress in the concrete and the maximum stress in the steel. *Ans.* Concrete: 760 psi: Steel: 16,500 psi.

320. A reinforced-concrete beam is subjected to a maximum bending moment of 450,000 in.-lb. Determine the maximum stress in each material if $b = 12$ in.; $d = 24$ in.; $n = 15$; and $A_S = 1.5$ sq. in.

321. Determine the maximum bending moment to which a reinforced-concrete beam may be subjected if $b = 10$ in.; $d = 18$ in.; $n = 15$; and $A_S = 1$ sq. in. The allowable stress in the concrete is 600 psi, and the allowable stress in the steel is 18,000 psi. *Ans.* 24,000 ft.-lb.

322. A reinforced-concrete beam supports a load of 400 lb./ft., uniformly distributed over a span of 16 ft. Assume that the beam is freely supported at its ends. $b = 10$ in.; $d = 12$ in.; $n = 15$. The allowable stress in the concrete is 600 psi. Determine a) the required area of steel, and b) the stress in the steel. *Ans.* a) 1.15 sq. in. b) 12,900 psi.

323. A reinforced-concrete beam is subjected to a maximum bending moment of 45,000 ft.-lb. $b = 15$; $d = 25$; $n = 15$. The allowable stress in the concrete is 500 psi. Determine a) the required area of steel, and b) the maximum stress in the steel.

52. Violations of Relative Dimensions. Deflection Produced by Shearing Force. The limitations of the flexure theory provided that the length–depth–breadth relationship in the beam be of such nature that the assumptions which were made would be proper, and might be confirmed when the beam was built and subjected to test.

In general, no serious disturbance of the theory is encountered when the dimensional limitations are violated, except in two noteworthy cases. When a beam is loaded axially, it is in effect a column. When the length to cross-sectional dimensional ratio is very great, buckling may become the source of failure. Such a feature will be discussed later, in the articles devoted to column action. Buckling is also a menace in transverse loading if the length–width ratio is excessive.

When the depth-length ratio is quite large—that is, when a beam has a short span and a relatively deep cross-section—an action will result in which we can no longer claim that the assumptions of the deflection theory are valid. The deflection theory has concerned itself only with the deflection resulting from bending moment. In short deep beams, the deflection will be due not only to bending moment, but shearing force. In the cantilever beam of Fig. 186 the loading will cause deflection of the beam. The shearing force will cause adjacent sections of the beam to slide along each other, as indicated by the isolated free body of Fig. 186-b, which is a small prism of length dx att he neutral axis of the beam.

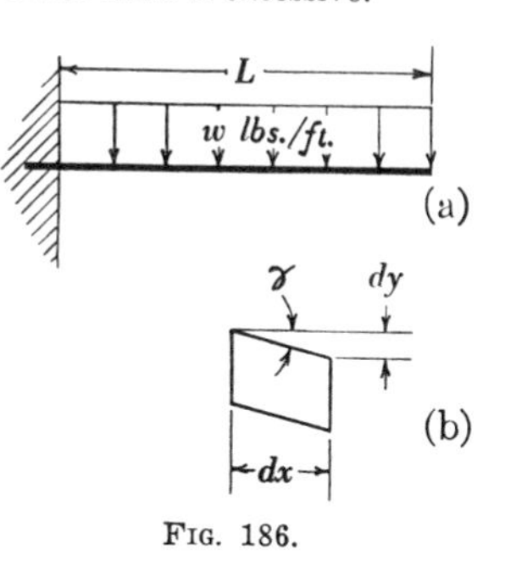

Fig. 186.

The deflection of the right side of the prism, relative to the left side, will be dy.

$$dy = \gamma \, dx$$

γ is the shearing strain discussed in Arts. 14 and 16, and is equal to s_S/G.

Then
$$dy = \frac{s_S \, dx}{G}$$

and
$$\frac{dy}{dx} = \frac{s_S}{G}$$

The slope of the elastic curve at any section due to shearing force is dy/dx. s_S may be expressed in terms of the average stress over the section as

$$s_S = f\left(\frac{V}{A}\right)$$

where f is a constant factor dependent upon the form of the beam cross section, V is the vertical shearing force, and A is the area of the cross-section.

$$\frac{d^2y}{dx^2} = \frac{d\left(\frac{s_S}{G}\right)}{dx} = \left(\frac{f}{A\,G}\frac{dV}{dx}\right)$$

If V can be expressed as a function of x, the equation may be integrated to evaluate the deflection produced by shearing force.

To illustrate the possibilities of integration, let us examine the cantilever beam of Fig. 186 which has a rectangular cross-section. In this cantilever beam, $V = -wx$, and $dV/dx = -w$.

Then
$$\frac{d^2y}{dx^2} = -\frac{f\,w}{A\,G}$$
$$\frac{dy}{dx} = -\frac{f\,w\,x}{A\,G} + C_1$$

When $x = L$
$$\frac{dy}{dx} = 0; \qquad \therefore C_1 = +\frac{f\,w\,L}{A\,G}$$
$$y = -\frac{f\,w\,x^2}{2A\,G} + \frac{f\,w\,L\,x}{A\,G} + C_2$$

When $x = L$ $\qquad y = 0;$
$$\therefore C_2 = +\frac{f\,w\,L^2}{2A\,G} - \frac{f\,w\,L^2}{A\,G} = -\frac{f\,w\,L^2}{2A\,G}$$

The maximum deflection will occur when $x = 0$, and will be

$$y_S = -\frac{f\,w\,L^2}{2A\,G}$$

In a rectangular beam the maximum longitudinal shear stress is equal to 1.5 times the average shear stress, which would be V/A, assuming uniform distribution. Then, for a rectangular beam, $f = 1.5$, and

$$y_S = -\frac{3wL^2}{4AG}$$

The maximum deflection, in such a beam, resulting from bending moment, is

$$y_B = -\frac{wL^4}{8EI}$$

The total deflection, caused by both shearing force and bending moment, will be

$$y_{\max.} = y_S + y_B = -\frac{3wL^2}{4AG} - \frac{wL^4}{8EI}$$

For a rectangle, $A = 12I/h^2$. If the ratio of G to E is 2/5,

$$y_{\max.} = -\frac{15\,w\,L^2\,h^2}{96EI} - \frac{wL^4}{8EI}$$
$$= -\frac{wL^4}{8EI}\left(\frac{5h^2}{4L^2} + 1\right)$$

The form of the equation indicates that the portion of the total deflection which is due to shearing force increases parabolically with the depth to length ratio (h/L) of the beam.

When the ratio $h/L = 1/10$, which is within the limitations of the flexure theory, the deflection caused by the shearing force will be only 1/80 of the deflection produced by bending moment. When, however, the ratio is doubled $(h/L = 1/5)$, the shearing-force deflection will increase to 1/20 that of the bending moment.

53. Loads Not in a Single Plane. The beam shown in Fig. 187-a carries loads P_1 and P_2, which are not confined to a single plane, and the beam therefore violates the limitations of the basic flexure theory. The beam is freely supported at its ends.

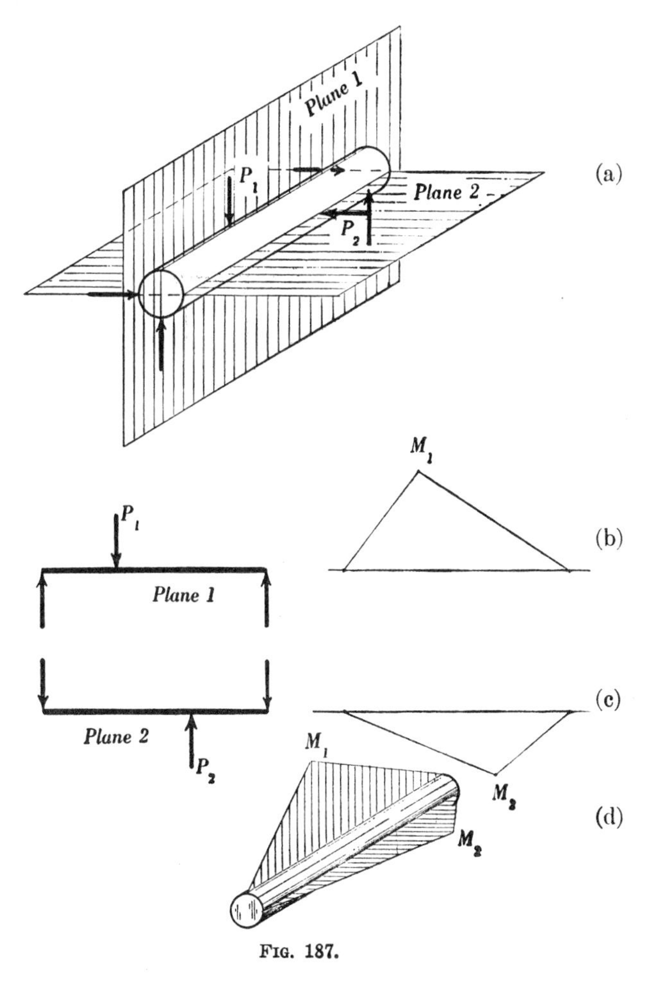

FIG. 187.

If the loading is divided into two stages, each stage will be capable of being individually treated by the flexure theory. The stages may then be combined to determine the total effect.

As a first stage in this treatment by superposition, we may imagine load P_2 to be removed from the beam. The remaining loading, comprising load P_1 and its supporting forces, lies in a single plane, which is indicated in the figure as plane 1. The beam, loaded in this manner, is shown in Fig. 187-b, together with its bending moment diagram. All bending stresses in the beam resulting from this load alone may now be determined by the flexure theory.

A similar analysis of the beam, when load P_1 is removed, and the loading consists of P_2 and its supporting forces, all lying in plane 2 is shown in Fig. 187-c.

Both bending moment diagrams, superimposed on the beam, are indicated in Fig. 187-d and show the component bending moments arising from the loading in planes 1 and 2 to which the beam is subjected when both loads are acting. These component moments are vector quantities, and may be added to determine the resultant bending moment at any section of the beam.

Illustrative Example I. The cylindrical beam of Fig. 188-a has a diameter of 4 in. Load $P_1 = 2000$ lb. lies in a vertical plane which passes through the centroid

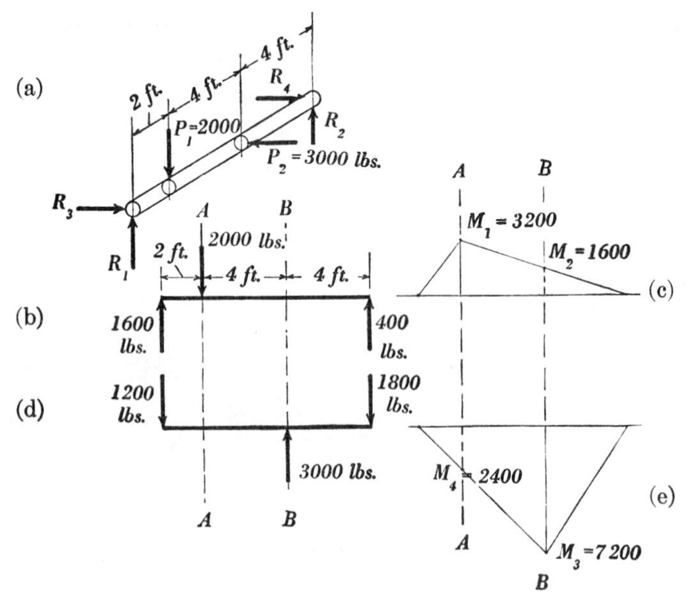

FIG. 188.

of the beam. Load $P_2 = 3000$ lb. lies in a horizontal plane which also passes through the centroid of the cross-section. The maximum bending moment and maximum bending stress in the beam are to be determined.

Figure 188-b shows the analysis of the beam when P_2 is assumed to have been removed. The supporting forces R_1 and R_2 have been determined by applying the conditions of equilibrium to the entire beam as a free body. The bending moment which results from this loading is shown as the bending moment diagram (Fig. 188-c). The maximum bending moment produced by this loading will occur at section A, and will be $M_1 = 3200$ ft.-lb. The bending moment at section B resulting from this loading will be $M_2 = 1600$ ft.-lb.

We now consider the beam as shown in Fig. 188-d with P_1 removed, and load P_2 acting. The bending moment diagram under this loading is shown in Fig. 188-e. The maximum bending moment caused by this loading will arise at section B, and will be $M_3 = 7200$ ft.-lb. The bending moment at section A, produced by this loading, will be $M_4 = 2400$ ft.-lb.

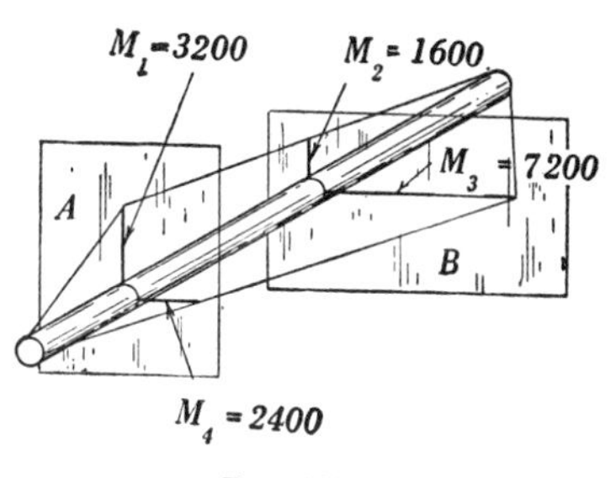

Fig. 189.

Both bending moment diagrams are shown in position on the beam in Fig. 189.

These bending moments lie in planes which are perpendicular to each other. At section A, the resultant bending moment will be

$$M_A = \sqrt{(M_1)^2 + (M_4)^2} = \sqrt{(3200)^2 + (2400)^2}$$
$$= 4000 \text{ ft.-lb.}$$

At section B, the resultant bending moment will be

$$M_B = \sqrt{(M_3)^2 + (M_2)^2} = \sqrt{(7200)^2 + (1600)^2}$$
$$= 7376 \text{ ft.-lb.}$$

Both of the component bending moments are varying linearly, and their vector sum will, therefore, vary linearly with x, the distance along the beam. A linear variation appears, graphically, as a straight line. The curve representing the resultant bending moment must, in this case, be a straight line which has a value of zero at the ends of the beam, rises in value in the first and last ranges of loading, and is a straight line in the middle range. Such a curve can only have a maximum value at either section A or B. Then the maximum bending moment in the entire beam is $M_B = 7376$ ft.-lb.

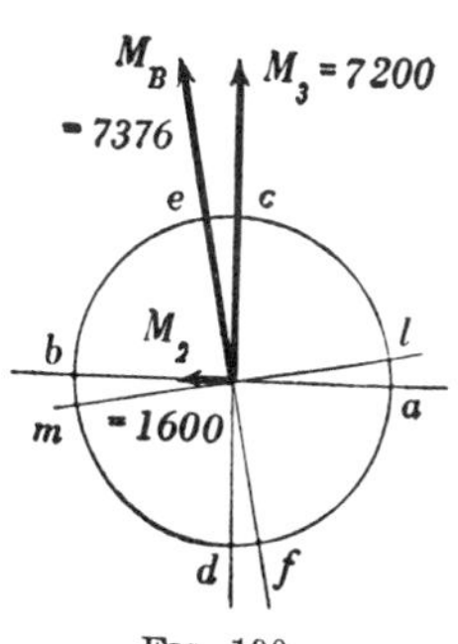

Fig. 190.

Figure 190 illustrates the location of the neutral axis at section B. It will be recalled that moments are vector quantities. The vector representing such quantities is erected perpendicular to the plane of the couple with the right-hand screw convention employed to indicate the sense of the vector—that is, if one views the vector from the origin looking toward the terminus, indicated by the arrow-head, one is witnessing clockwise rotation.

The couple M_2 produces bending about the horizontal axis ab. The moment acts in a vertical plane, and produces tension in the fibers of the beam which lie below *ab*. Viewed from the right of the section the moment is clockwise. Vector M_2 represents this bending moment.

M_3 produces bending about the vertical axis *cd*. The moment acts in a horizontal plane, and produces tension in the fibers of the beam which lie to the left of *cd*. Viewed from the top of the section, the moment is counter-clockwise. Vector M_3 represents this bending moment.

M_B, the resultant vector, will be inclined as shown. This vector represents bending in an inclined plane, perpendicular to vector M_B, with the neutral axis at *ef*, and with tension in all fibers which are downward and to the left of *ef*. There will be compression in all fibers upward and to the right of *ef*. The most stressed fibers will be those at *l* and *m*, which lie at the greatest distance from neutral axis *ef*. The stress in the fiber at *l* will be, by equation (34),

$$s = \frac{My}{I} = \frac{7376 \times 12 \times 2}{\pi \times (2)^4/4}$$

$$= 14{,}100 \text{ psi (compression)}$$

while at *m*, $$s = 14{,}100 \text{ psi (tension)}$$

Illustrative Example II. The beam which we have investigated in the preceding example was cylindrical. When the cross-sectional area of the beam is a circle, the neutral axis is always a diameter of the circle. The section modulus of the circular section, $I/y_{\text{max.}}$ will be constant, regardless of the inclination of the diameter serving as neutral axis. The foregoing exploration of bending stress was, therefore, concerned only with the variation of bending moment. When we consider the rectangular sections which are illustrated in Fig. 191, we find that axes 1–1 and 2–2 are axes of symmetry. Loading in planes containing axes 1–1 and 2–2 is therefore admissible under the limitations of the flexure theory.

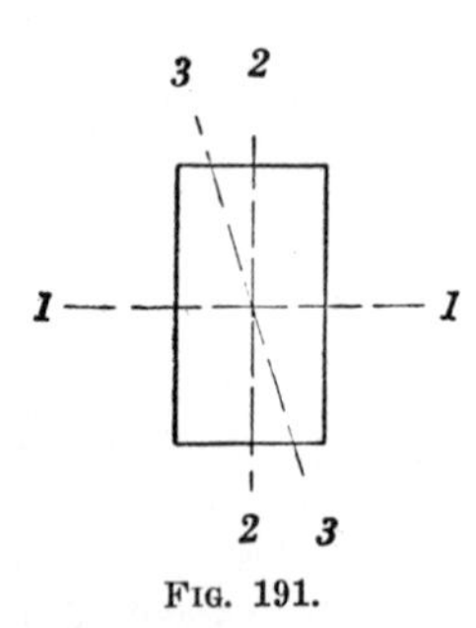

FIG. 191.

Axis 3–3, representing any other axes than those which are axes of symmetry, may become a neutral axis when loading such as that of Example I is applied. In this case, since axis 3–3 is not an axis of symmetry, the flexure theory cannot be applied directly. We can again, however, use the method of superposition, applying it to bending stresses rather than bending moments.

The beam of Fig. 192-a carries loading which is identical with that of Example I (see Fig. 188). The maximum bending moment, as a result of load P_1, when acting alone, will again occur at section A, and will be $M_1 = 3200$ ft.-lb. The bending moment at section B, produced by P_1, will be $M_2 = 1600$ ft.-lb. When load P_2 acts alone, the maximum bending moment occurs at section B, and is $M_3 = 7200$ ft.-lb. The bending moment at section A resulting from P_2 is $M_4 = 2400$ ft.-lb.

Section A is shown in Fig. 192-b. Bending moment M_1 will cause bending about the horizontal neutral axis 1–1, and the maximum bending stresses at this section due to M_1 will be in those fibers which lie in the lines *ef* and *gh*. The bending stresses at those levels will be, by equation (34),

$$s = \frac{My}{I} = \frac{3200 \times 12 \times 4}{3 \times (8)^3/12} = 1200 \text{ psi}$$

Fibers in *ef* will be in compression, fibers in *gh* in tension.

We now consider the bending action at this section A, which is caused by M_4. This bending has as its neutral axis the vertical axis 2–2. The maximum bending

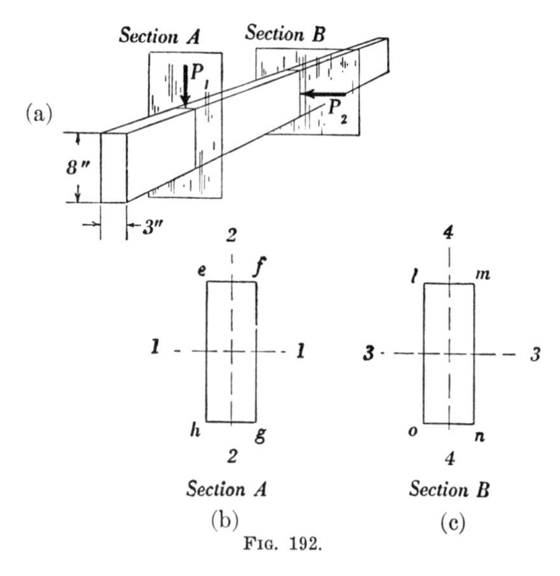

Fig. 192.

stresses, due to M_4, will occur in the fibers which lie in lines *fg* and *eh*. Their magnitude will be, by equation (34),

$$s = \frac{2400 \times 12 \times 1.5}{8 \times (3)^3/12} = 2400 \text{ psi}$$

The stress in all fibers in *fg* will be 2400 psi (compression), and that in all fibers in *eh* will be 2400 psi (tension).

A fiber at corner f may now be considered. When both loads are acting, this fiber receives a normal stress of 1200 psi (compression) from bending moment M_1, and a normal stress of 2400 psi (compression from bending moment M_4. The total normal stress on the section at corner f will be 3600 psi (compression). The total normal stress on the section at corner h will be 3600 psi (tension). These stresses are the maximum normal stresses on section A of the beam.

Section B must now be explored (Fig.192-c) for it is at that section that the only other possibility of maximum normal stress in this beam is encountered. At corner m, the normal stress produced by the bending moment M_2 is, by equation (34),

$$s = \frac{1600 \times 12 \times 4}{3 \times (8)^3/12} = 600 \text{ psi (compression)}$$

and the normal stress due to bending moment M_3 is, by equation (34),

$$s = \frac{7200 \times 12 \times 1.5}{8 \times (3)^3/12} = 7200 \text{ psi (compression)}$$

The total normal stress on section B at corner m is $s = 600 + 7200 = 7800$ psi (compression). Then this stress is the maximum compressive normal stress on any right section of the beam. The maximum tensile stress will occur at corner o of section B, and will be 7800 psi.

The neutral axis at any section, like A, may be determined by locating the fibers of zero stress, for neutral axes are loci of points of zero stress.

At section A, which is shown again in Fig. 193, the bending about axis 1–1 will induce normal stresses.

According to equation (34), $s_1 = \dfrac{3200 \times 12 \times y_a}{3 \times (8)^3/12} = 300y_a$

where y_a is the distance to any fiber, measured normal to axis 1–1. These stresses will be compressive in the region above axis 1–1, and tensile in the region below.

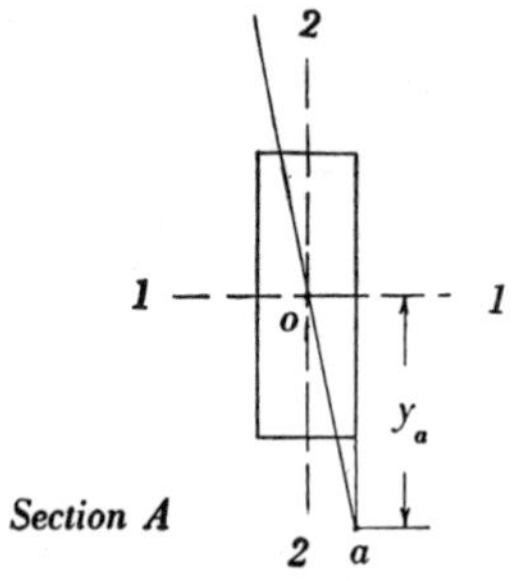

At this section of the beam, the bending about axis 2–2 will induce normal stresses.

From equation (34), $s_2 = \dfrac{2400 \times 12 \times y_b}{8 \times (3)^3/12} = 1600y_b$

where y_b is the distance to any fiber, measured normal to axis 2–2. These stresses will be compressive in the region to the right of axis 2–2, and tensile in the region to the left.

Section A

FIG. 193.

The central point o of section A is the location of one unstressed fiber. The location of a second unstressed fiber may be determined by noting that all other fibers receive stress from bending moments M_1 and M_4 and that, in those fibers, a compressive stress must balance a tensile stress to obtain a resultant which is zero.

Along the right face of the section such a point is a, located at distance y_a from axis 1–1. Point a lies in the region of tension resulting from M_1 and compression resulting from M_4.

At a,

$$s_1 = s_2$$
$$300y_a = 1600 \times 1.5$$
$$y_a = 8.0 \text{ in.}$$

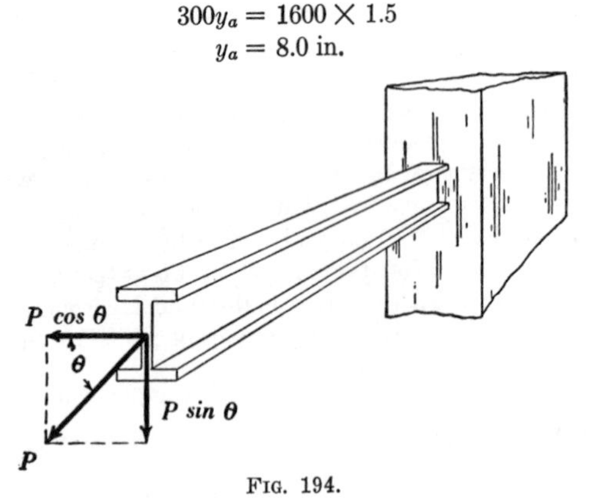

FIG. 194.

Points o and a determine the neutral axis, for the stress variation is linear, and the neutral axis must be a straight line.

When an *oblique* load P is placed upon a beam whose cross-section has axes of symmetry, as in Fig. 194, it may be resolved into components $P \sin \theta$ and $P \cos \theta$, parallel to the axes of symmetry, and the method of attack becomes that which has been discussed above, provided that the oblique load passes through the centroid of the section. When the line of action of the load does not pass through the shear center of the section, the beam will be twisted (Art. 55). When the cross-section of the beam has no axis of symmetry, or the load is placed in a plane which does not contain an axis of symmetry, other methods of attack must be employed. The following two articles are devoted to a consideration of such loading.

PROBLEMS

324. The cylindrical beam is freely supported at its ends, and loaded with a vertical force of 4000 lb. at A and a horizontal force of 2000 lb. at B. The diameter of the beam is 4 in. Determine the maximum normal stress on a right section of the beam.
Ans. 18,600 psi.

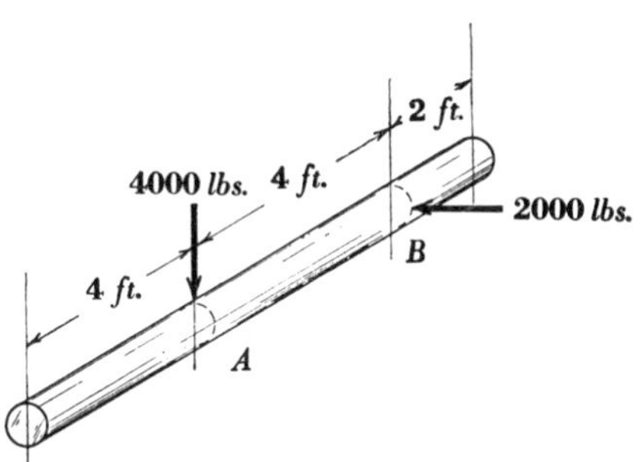

Prob. 324.

325. The cylindrical beam is freely supported at its ends, and loaded with a vertical force of 4000 lb. at A and a horizontal force of 3000 lb. at B. If the maximum allowable normal stress on a right section of the beam is 20,000 psi, determine the required diameter of the beam.

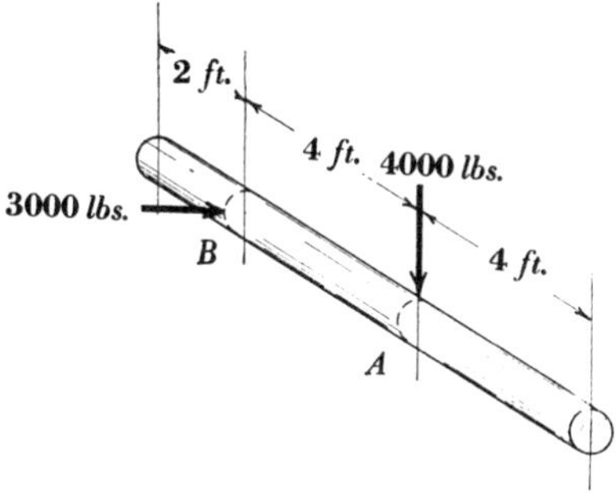

Prob. 325.

326. The 6 in. × 8 in. beam is freely supported at its ends. Two 4000-lb. loads, one vertical and one horizontal, are applied as shown. The lines of action of the forces pass through the central axis of the beam. Determine the maximum normal stress on a right section of the beam. *Ans.* 2600 psi.

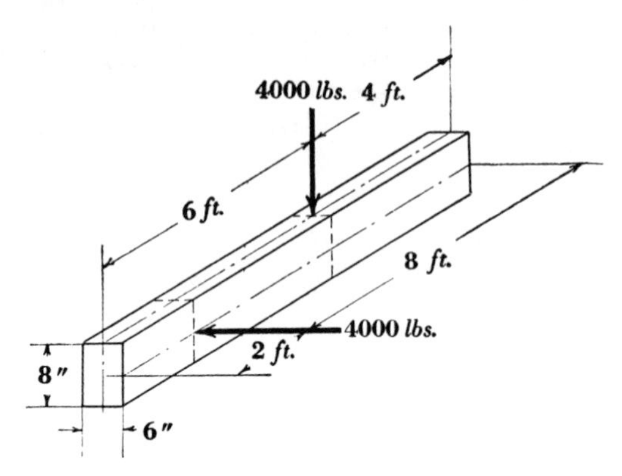

PROB. 326.

327. The 6 in. × 12 in. beam is freely supported at its ends and loaded with a vertical force of 3000 lb. and a horizontal force of W lbs. If the maximum allowable normal stress on a right section of the beam is 1200 psi, determine the maximum value of W.

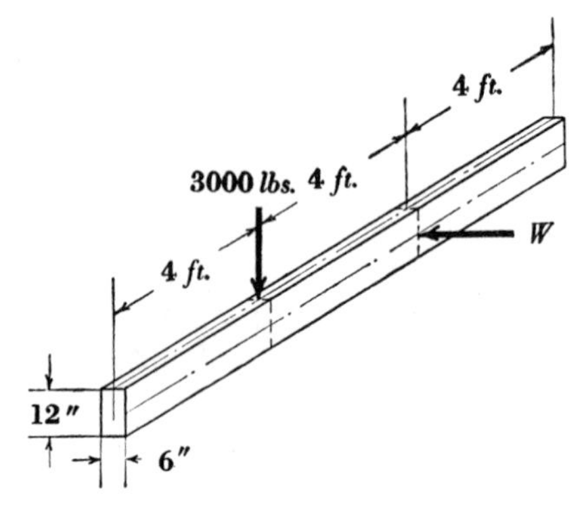

PROB. 327.

328. The cylindrical beam is freely supported at its ends and subjected to a vertical load of 3000 lb. and a horizontal load of W lb. If the maximum allowable normal stress on a right section of the beam is 18,000 psi, determine the maximum load W.

Ans. 4460 lb.

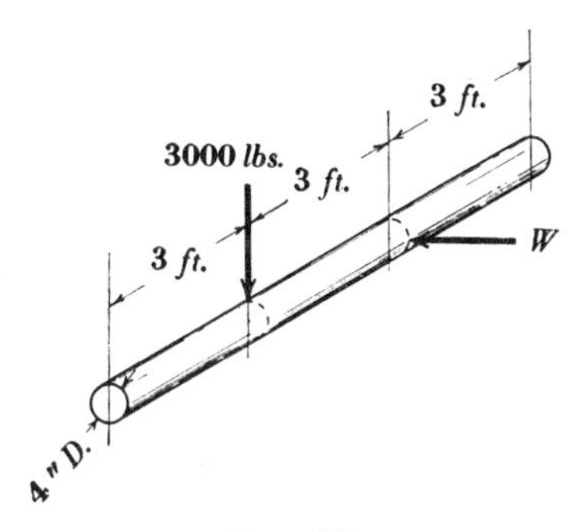

PROB. 328.

329. The 10 in. × 12 in. beam is freely supported at its ends and loaded with the three vertical and two horizontal loads shown. All loads act through the central axis of the beam. Determine the maximum normal stress on a right section of the beam.

Ans. 1800 psi.

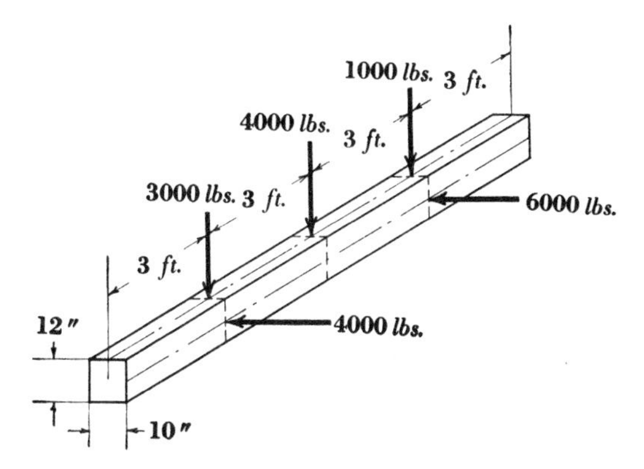

PROB. 329.

330. The indicated loads lie in planes which are perpendicular to the central axis of the hollow cylindrical beam. The 1000-lb. load is inclined at 30° with the vertical, and the 3000-lb. load at 45° with the vertical. The line of action of the loads passes through the center of the beam. The outer diameter of the cross-section is four-thirds the inner diameter. If the maximum allowable normal stress on a right section of the beam is 20,000 psi, determine the required outside diameter.

Ans. 5.58 in.

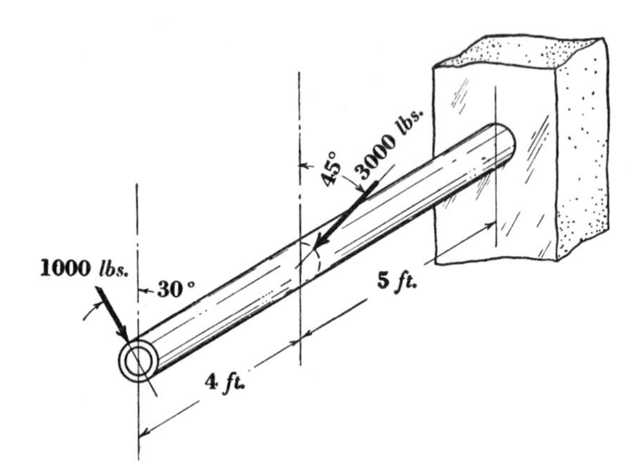

PROB. 330.

331. The cylindrical beam is freely supported at its ends. Diameter = 2 in. $W_1 = 2W_2$ If the maximum allowable normal stress on a right section is 20,000 psi, determine W_1.

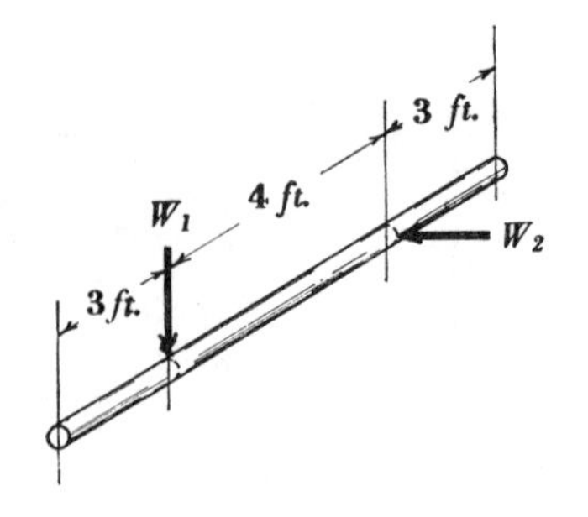

PROB. 331.

332. The rectangular beam is freely supported at its ends and loaded by a vertical force of 2000 lb. and a horizontal force of 1200 lb. If the maximum normal stress on a right section of the beam must not exceed 800 psi, determine the minimum breadth of the beam, b. *Ans.* 4.57 in.

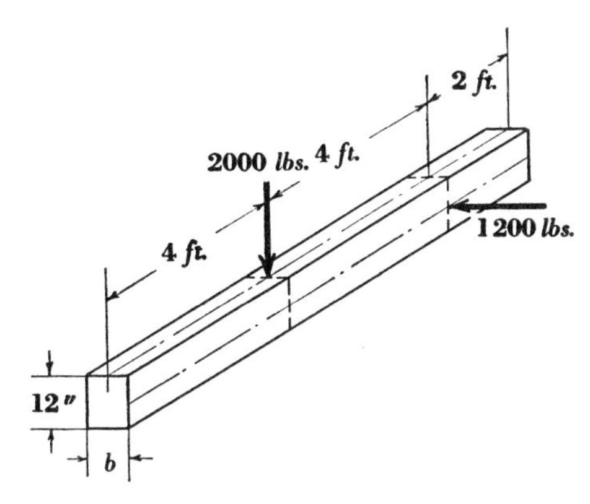

Prob. 332.

333. The rectangular beam is freely supported at sections A and B and loaded with the two indicated vertical loads and one horizontal load. All forces pass through the central axis of the beam. Determine the maximum normal stress on a right section of the beam.

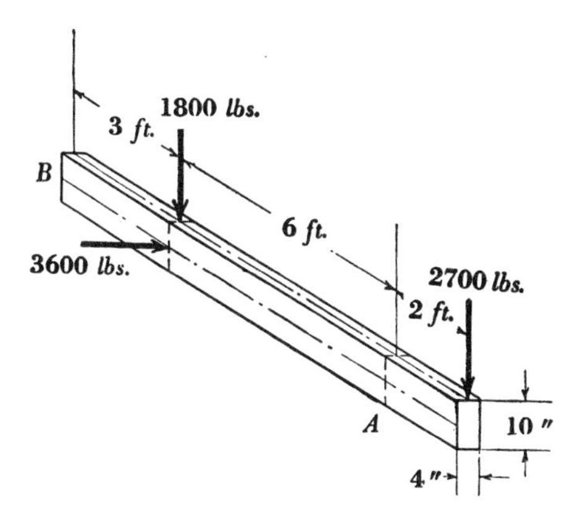

Prob. 333.

334. The cylindrical beam is loaded with two forces, one vertical and the other inclined at 30° with the vertical. The beam is freely supported at its ends. Determine the maximum bending moment in the beam. *Ans.* 7100 ft.-lb.

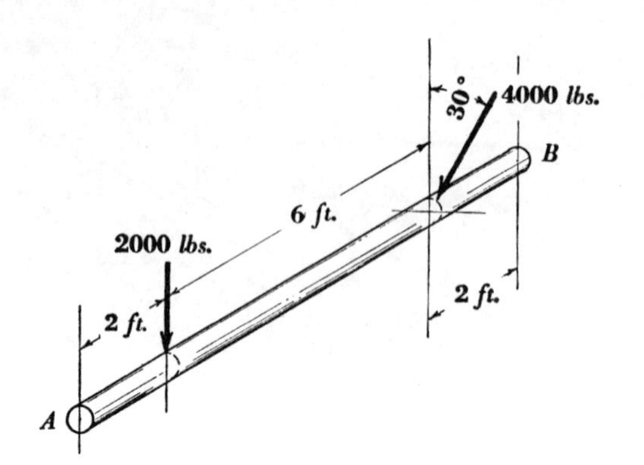

PROB. 334.

335. The cylindrical beam is freely supported at sections *A* and *B*. The loads are all in planes perpendicular to the central axis of the beam. Determine the maximum bending moment in the beam. *Ans.* 13,560 ft.-lb.

336. If the normal stress on any right section of the beam of Prob. 335 must not exceed 20,000 psi, determine the minimum diameter which the beam must have. *Ans.* 4.36 in.

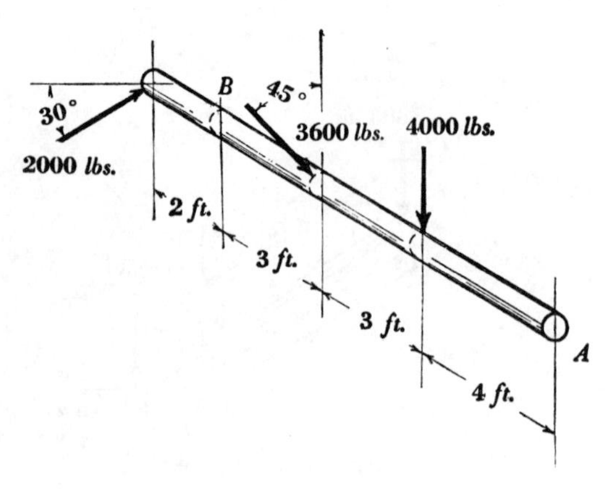

PROB. 335.

337. The cylindrical beam is freely supported at sections A and B. All loads lie in planes perpendicular to the central axis of the beam. Determine the maximum bending moment in the beam.

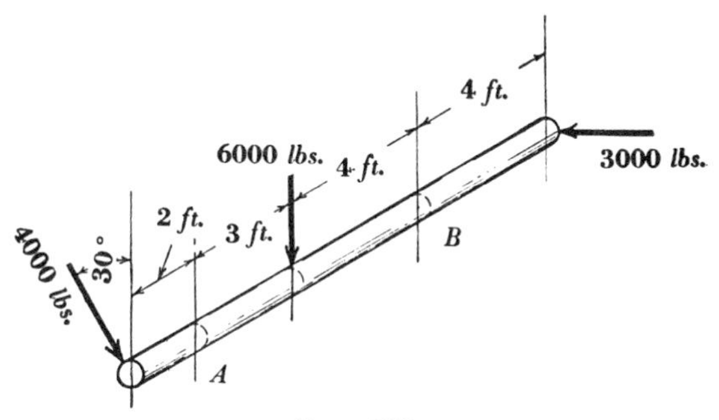

PROB. 337.

338. If the normal stress on any right section of the beam of Prob. 337 must not exceed 18,000 psi, determine the minimum required diameter of the beam.

339 The 6 in. × 12 in. rectangular beam carries vertical loading, consisting of the 2400 lb. concentrated load and a uniformly distributed load (including its own weight) of 200 lb./ft., and a concentrated horizontal load of 1200 lb. The beam is freely supported at its ends. Locate the section at which the normal stress on a right section is maximum. *Ans.* 9.5 ft. from left end.

340. Determine the maximum normal stress for the beam of Prob. 339.

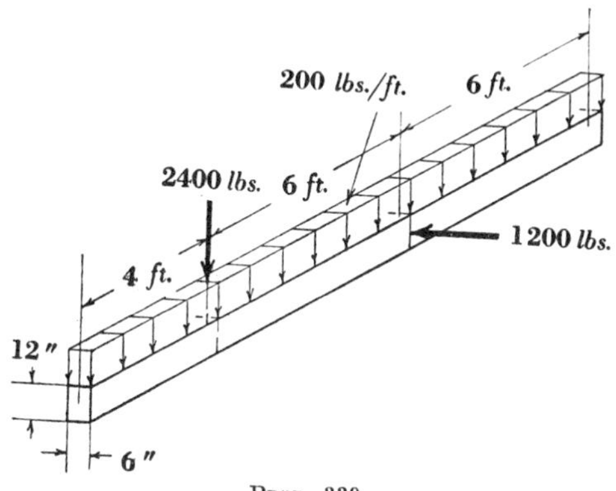

PROB. 339.

54. Unsymmetrical Bending. Through every point in a plane area an axis may be passed about which the moment of inertia of the area is a maximum; perpendicular to that axis, there will be a second axis about which the moment of inertia of the area is a minimum (see Art. 91). These two axes are called the principal axes of inertia for the given point. When the principal axes are those of the centroid, they are called principal centroidal axes. The product of inertia of an area relative to a pair of principal axes is zero (Art. 91). Axes of symmetry of areas are always principal axes of inertia.

These properties of areas are usually discussed in the courses in Statics and Dynamics which, in the educational career of the engineering student, have preceded this course in the mechanics of materials. They are reviewed in Chapter XI of this textbook which discusses the necessary formulas for locating principal axes of inertia, and for evaluating principal moments of inertia of the areas commonly used in beam sections.

In the basic flexure theory we found that the resultant of the normal stresses acting on right sections of a beam is a couple, called the moment of resistance. We also noted (Art. 25) that whenever the resultant of a uniformly varying stress is a couple, the neutral axis will pass through the centroid.

If we review the conditions which prevail when such a couple is present, we shall have at our command a more general theory of bending than that which the flexure theory affords.

Figure 195 shows an area of any shape upon which a uniformly varying stress is acting. The neutral axis passes through centroid C, and the

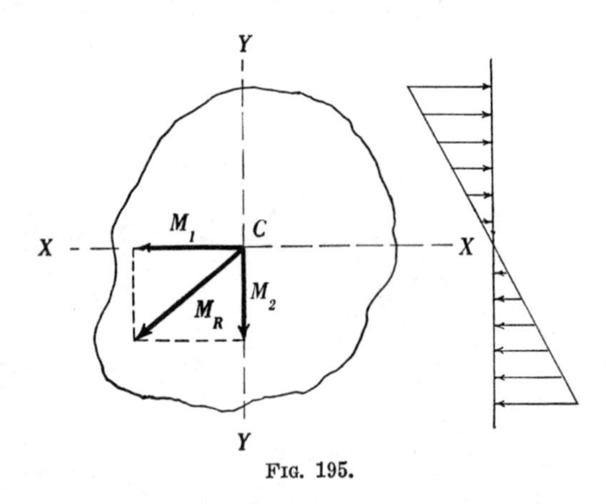

FIG. 195.

resultant of the stress is therefore a couple. In Art. 25 such a resultant was discussed in detail, and we noted that

$$M_1 = \int ky^2\,dA = kI_{XX}$$

and

$$M_2 = \int kxy\,dA = kI_{XY}$$

Now I_{XY} is the product of inertia of the area relative to axes X-X and Y-Y. When X-X and Y-Y are principal axes of inertia, whether they are axes of symmetry or not, the product of inertia, I_{XY} will equal zero.

Then
$$M_R = \sqrt{(kI_{XX})^2 + (kI_{XY})^2} = kI_{XX}$$

and the bending stress will be, as in Art. 25,

$$s = \frac{My}{I}$$

For this reason the flexure formula may be applied when the plane of loading does not contain an axis of symmetry but does pass through the centroid of the section.

We shall now consider some examples of unsymmetrical bending, to explore the routine of analysis which must be employed when the plane of loading does not contain a principal centroidal axis.

The beam of Fig. 196 has a plane of loading which is oblique to the principal centroidal axes of the area X-X and Y-Y. The forces which lie

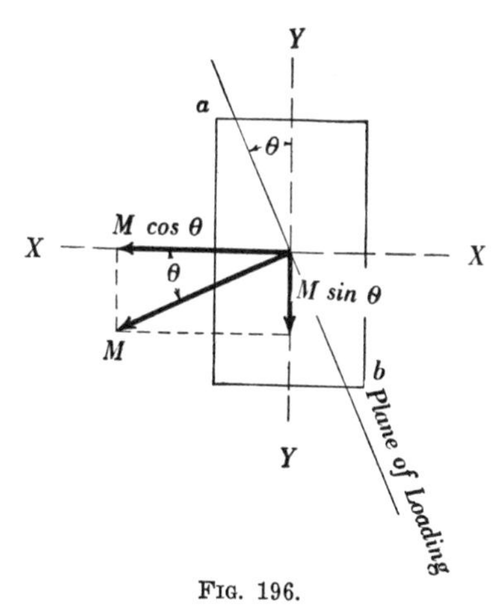

Fig. 196.

in the plane of loading will produce a bending moment, M, which lies in the plane of loading. This moment has been shown as a vector, using the convention for moment which is described in the preceding article, and vector M appears perpendicular to the plane of loading.

M may be resolved into component moments $M \cos \theta$, which produces bending about the axis X-X, and $M \sin \theta$, which produces bending about axis Y-Y. The maximum normal stresses produced by the component moments will occur at corners a and b, and may be obtained by superposition, as in the preceding article.

This maximum normal stress will be

$$s = \frac{M \cos \theta}{S_{XX}} + \frac{M \sin \theta}{S_{YY}}$$

where S_{XX} is the section modulus of the beam section about axis X-X, and S_{YY} is the section modulus about axis Y-Y.

When θ is zero, we have, as maximum normal stress

$$s = \frac{M \cos \theta}{S_{XX}} = \frac{M\,y}{I_{XX}}$$

as in all flexure theory cases.

When the plane of loading is displaced from axis Y-Y, there will be a serious increase in the magnitude of the normal stress, even though the displacement may be small. This very marked effect may be noted in the actual case which follows.

Illustrative Example I. A 20 in. × 65.4 lb./ft. American Standard I-beam (Fig. 197) has section moduli $S_{XX} = 116.9$ in.³ and $S_{YY} = 8.9$ in.³

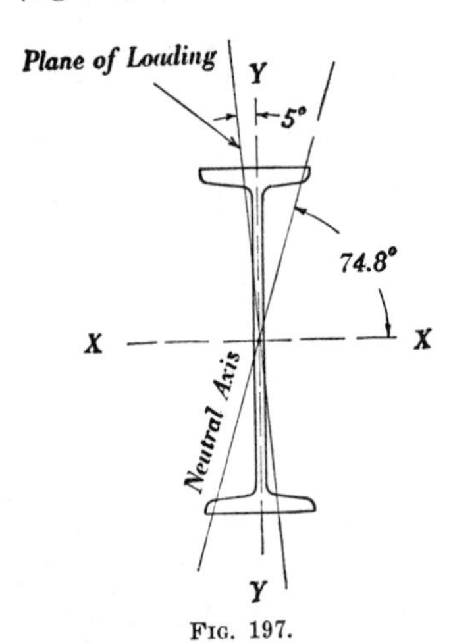

Fig. 197.

If the plane of loading makes an angle of 5° with Y-Y, the maximum normal stress on the section will be

$$\begin{aligned} s &= \frac{M \cos \theta}{S_{XX}} + \frac{M \sin \theta}{S_{YY}} \\ &= \frac{M \times 0.9962}{116.9} + \frac{M \times 0.0872}{8.9} \\ &= 0.01832M \end{aligned}$$

If the plane of loading had contained axis Y-Y, the value of θ would have been zero, and the maximum normal stress would have been

$$s = \frac{My}{I} = \frac{M}{116.9} = 0.00855M$$

The displacement of the plane of loading through an angle of only 5° has had a marked influence on the maximum normal stress, which has a value of 2.14 times the corresponding stress of the undisplaced plane of loading.

Displacement of the Neutral Axis in Unsymmetrical Bending. The resultant bending moment, M, shown vectorially in Fig. 198, has been resolved into moments causing bending about principal centroidal axes. The component moments are $M \cos \theta$, which causes bending about principal centroidal axis X-X, and $M \sin \theta$, which causes bending about principal centroidal axis Y-Y.

A neutral axis of a beam section is a locus of points at which there is zero normal stress. The centroid of the section, point C, is one such point.

If we are to locate the neutral axis—a straight line—we must establish the location of a second point, like a, which is a point of zero stress. There is bending in this beam about axis X-X, which will produce a compressive

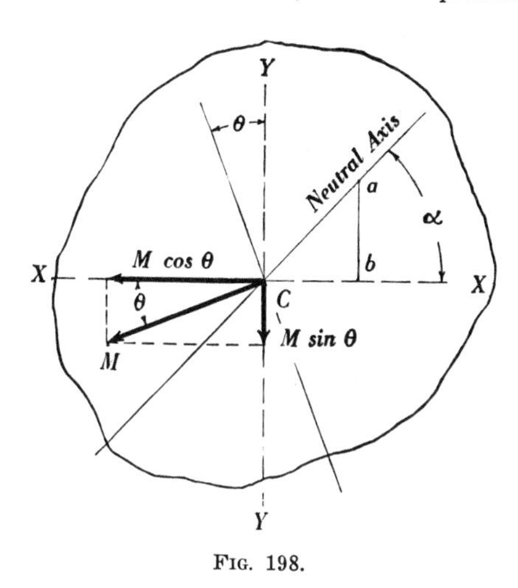

FIG. 198.

stress at point a, and bending about axis Y-Y which will produce a tensile stress at a. If the net stress at a is to be zero, the compressive stress must balance the tensile stress.

The compressive stress at point a due to moment $M \cos \theta$ is

$$s_C = \frac{M \cos \theta \times ab}{I_{XX}} \tag{66}$$

and the tensile stress at a resulting from moment $M \sin \theta$ is

$$s_T = \frac{M \sin \theta \times Cb}{I_{YY}} \tag{67}$$

When balance is effected,

$$s_C = s_T$$

Applying equations (66) and (67),

$$\frac{M \cos \theta \times ab}{I_{XX}} = \frac{M \sin \theta \times Cb}{I_{YY}}$$

Then

$$\frac{ab}{Cb} = \frac{\text{M} \sin \theta \times I_{XX}}{M \cos \theta \times I_{YY}} = \frac{I_{XX}}{I_{YY}} \tan \theta$$

$$\frac{ab}{Cb} = \tan \alpha$$

$$\tan \alpha = \frac{I_{XX}}{I_{YY}} \tan \theta \tag{68}$$

The neutral axis, it will be noted, is not perpendicular to the plane of loading but is a function of the principal moments of inertia and the angle of displacement of the plane of loading.

We have already observed the change in the magnitude of the maximum normal stress which arises when the plane of loading is displaced. Let us now observe the change in location of the neutral axis.

Illustrative Example II. The 20 in. × 65.4 lb./ft. I-beam used as illustration is subjected to the same loading conditions as in Illustrative Example I. For this beam section, $I_{XX} = 1169.5$ in.^{4} and $I_{YY} = 27.9$ in.^{4}.

If the plane of loading contains axis Y-Y (Fig. 197), the neutral axis coincides with axis X-X.

When the plane of loading is shifted through the angle of 5°, the neutral axis will shift through an angle in accordance with the equation just derived, and, by equation (68),

$$\tan \alpha = \frac{I_{XX}}{I_{YY}} \tan \theta$$

$$= \frac{1169.5}{27.9} \times 0.0875 = 3.668$$

and

$$\alpha = 74.8°$$

PROBLEMS

341. A bending moment of 3000 ft.-lb. is applied to the 4 in. × 10 in. section in the indicated plane of loading. Determine the maximum bending stress on the section.

Ans. 1000 psi.

342. Determine the angle through which the neutral axis of the beam section of Prob. 341 is displaced when the plane of loading is shifted from axis Y-Y to the position indicated.

Ans. 68.2°.

343. The angle between the Y-Y axis and the plane of loading is indicated as θ. Determine the maximum bending stress in the cantilever beam when a) $\theta = 0°$; b) $\theta = 10°$; $\theta = 20°$.

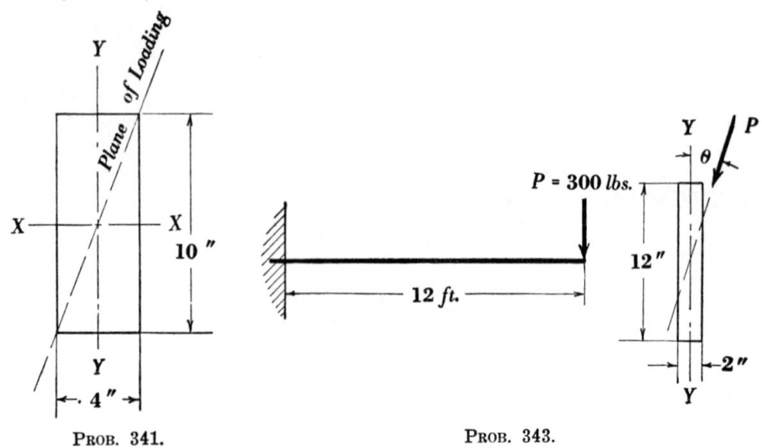

PROB. 341. PROB. 343.

344. Determine the displacement of the neutral axis of the beam of Prob. 343 when $\theta = 10°$.

345. The Z-section shown is subjected to a positive bending moment of 10,000 ft.-lb. in the Y-Y plane. Determine the bending stress at corner A. Axes X-X and Y-Y pass through the centroid. *Ans.* 310 psi (tension).

346. Determine the bending stress at corner B and C of the beam section of Prob. 345 for the same conditions of loading.

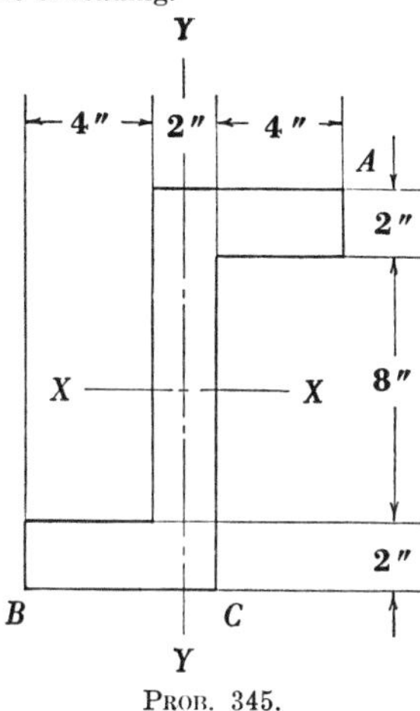

PROB. 345.

347. The indicated loads are applied at the free end of a cantilever beam. Span = 14 ft. All loads pass through the shear center, so that there is no tendency for the beam to twist. (See Art. 55) Determine the maximum tensile and compressive bending stresses in the beam. *Ans.* s_T = 12,100 psi; s_C = 14,200 psi.

348. The loads shown are applied at the free end of a cantilever beam which has a span of 15 ft. All loads pass through the shear center of the beam. The beam is a 14 in. × 84 lb./ft. Wide-Flange beam, and the weight of the beam itself is to be considered. Determine the maximum bending stress in the beam.

349. Determine the inclination of the neutral axis of the beam of Prob. 348 at the section of maximum bending moment.

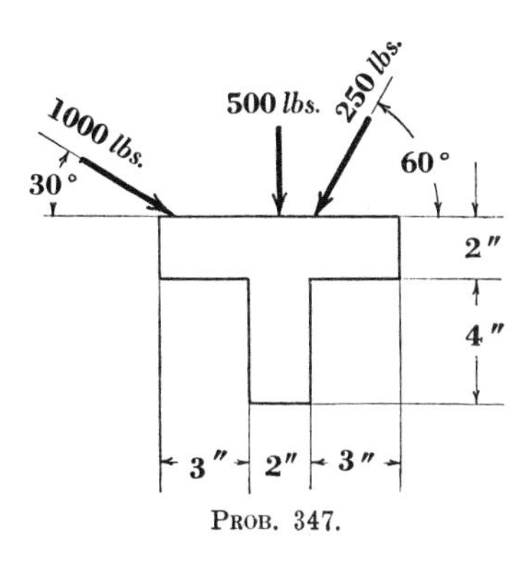

PROB. 347.

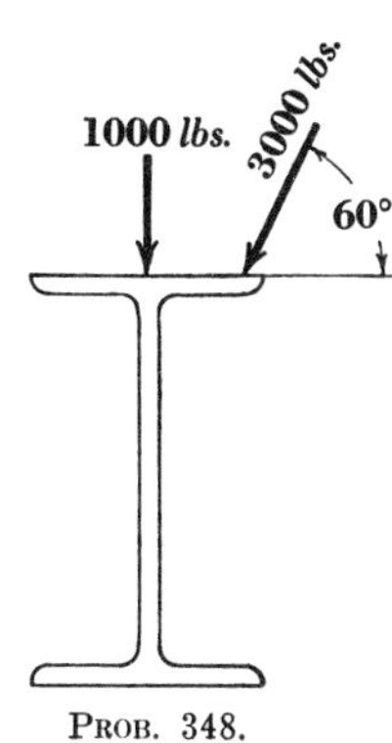

PROB. 348.

350. A cantilever beam is reinforced with cables exerting the forces indicated. All loads are placed in planes perpendicular to the long axis of the beam, and the resultant load in any plane passes through the shear center of the section. The channel is a 15 in. American Standard channel, with $S_X = 57.2$ in.^{3}, and $S_Y = 4.1$ in.^{3}. Determine the maximum bending stress in the channel. *Ans.* 16,200 psi.

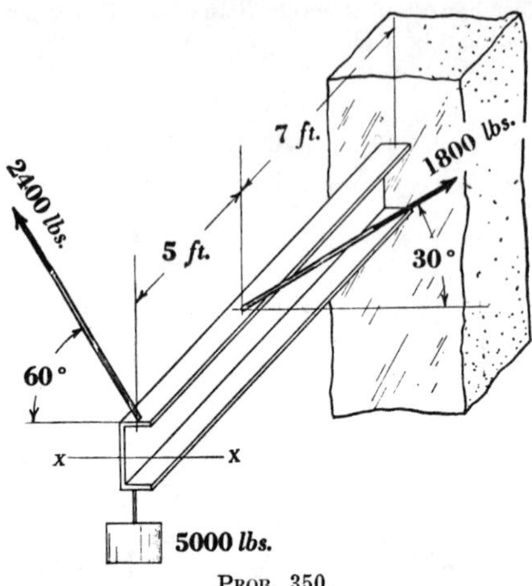

PROB. 350.

351. A 15 in. channel is used as a supporting purlin for roof timbers. The slope of the roof is 1:3.5. Each purlin is 16 ft. long and supports a uniformly distributed vertical load of 400 lb./ft. The resultant load passes through the shear center of the channel section. Assuming that the purlins are freely supported at their ends, determine the maximum bending stress. For the channel section $S_X = 41.7$ in.^{3} and $S_Y = 3.2$ in.^{3} *Ans.* 16,700 psi.

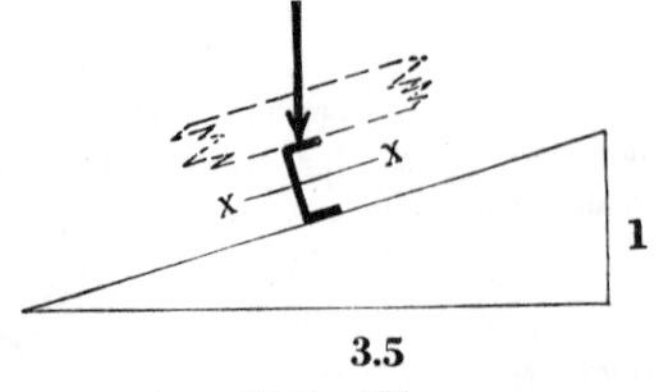

PROB. 351.

55. The Shear Center. Most of the structural shapes which are commonly employed as beam sections have areas which possess at least one axis of symmetry. We have already noted, in the discussion of the flexure theory, the influence of loading which is applied in a plane which includes the axis of symmetry of the cross-section. In addition, the preceding article has been devoted to cases of unsymmetrical bending which arise when the plane of loading does not contain an axis of symmetry. In each of those cases it is assumed that plane right sections of the beam do not rotate, relative to each other, about the long axis of the beam. Experience bears witness to the validity of the assumption. There is, therefore, no need to consider the possibility of twisting in the beam, and only bending has been of primary importance.

Cases do arise, however, in which the loading is so placed that right sections of a beam will tend to rotate about the longitudinal axis.

The channel section beam of Fig. 199-a carries loads which are perpendicular to the long axis of the beam. However, the plane of loading does

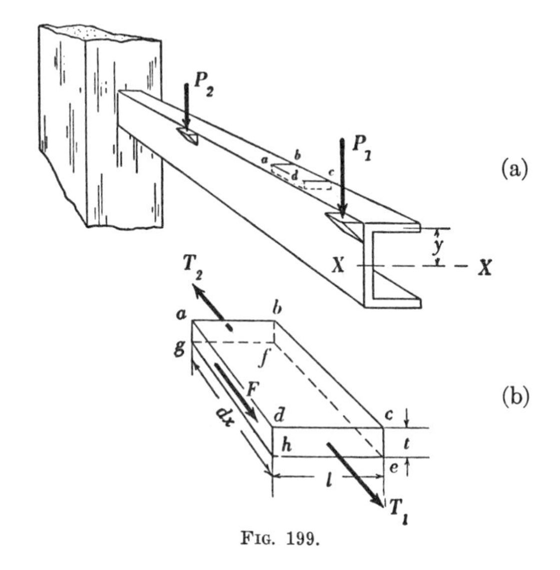

Fig. 199.

not contain the axis of symmetry of the channel section, and the limitations of the flexure theory have been violated. There is no very apparent feature of the loading which would suggest to us that twisting is present and that there is any tendency for the several right sections to rotate about the longitudinal axis. Experience with the use of these sections, however, does indicate that such action takes place, and we shall investigate such sections to establish an understanding of their characteristics.

A very short portion of the flange of the channel section (shown as *abcd* of Fig. 199-a) has been isolated in Fig. 199-b, which shows an enlarged view. Only forces which are parallel to the long axis of the beam have been shown.

There is a bending moment at section *cehd*, and a greater bending moment at section *abfg*. These bending moments are negative, and this flange must be in tension. The tensile stresses on face *cehd* will have a resultant, which is the tensile force T_1. Similarly, the face *abfg* will be acted upon by a greater tensile force T_2. The free body is in equilibrium and some force must act upon it, in addition to T_1 and T_2 to maintain the balance. Such a force can only be supplied by the remainder of the flange from which the isolated free body has been taken, and must be force F, a shearing force acting upon face *adhg*. Then

$$F = T_2 - T_1$$

If we assume that the shearing stress, s_S, on the face *adhg* is uniformly distributed,

$$F = s_S \, dx \, t$$

where t is the thickness of the flange.

If the bending moment at face *cehd* is called M, and the greater bending moment at face *abfg* is called $M + dM$, we shall be able to evaluate the difference between forces T_2 and T_1.

An approximate value of the normal stresses on the faces where T_2 and T_1 act may be obtained by assuming that since the flange is rather thin in comparison with its distance from the centroid of the channel, the normal stress is uniformly distributed, and

$$T_2 = \frac{(M + dM)\, y\, t\, l}{I_{XX}}$$

where t is the thickness, l the width of the flange, and y is the distance from the centroid of the section to the center of the flange.

Similarly,

$$T_1 = \frac{M\, y\, t\, l}{I_{XX}}$$

and

$$F = s_S \, dx \, t = \frac{dM\, y\, t\, l}{I_{XX}}$$

whence

$$s_S = \frac{dM}{dx} \frac{y\, l}{I_{XX}} = \frac{V\, y\, l}{I_{XX}}$$

Shear stresses on planes which are mutually perpendicular are equal; then the shear stress on the face *cehd* at corner *dh* will have this same value, and will vary uniformly to a value of zero at the outer corner *ce*. The average shear stress on face *cehd* will therefore be one-half of the maximum value at corner *dh*, and will be

$$\text{average } s_S = \frac{V\, y\, l}{2I_{XX}}$$

All that we have said concerning the shear stresses on the upper flange of the channel will be true of the lower flange, except that those on the lower flange will be oppositely directed.

The shear stresses on faces *cehd* and *abfg* will have as their resultant a force

$$F_F = \frac{V\,y\,l}{2I_{XX}}\,t\,l = \frac{V\,y\,t\,l^2}{2I_{XX}}$$

These shear forces are shown in position on the upper and lower flanges in Fig. 200-a. Since the shear forces on the upper and lower flanges are equal

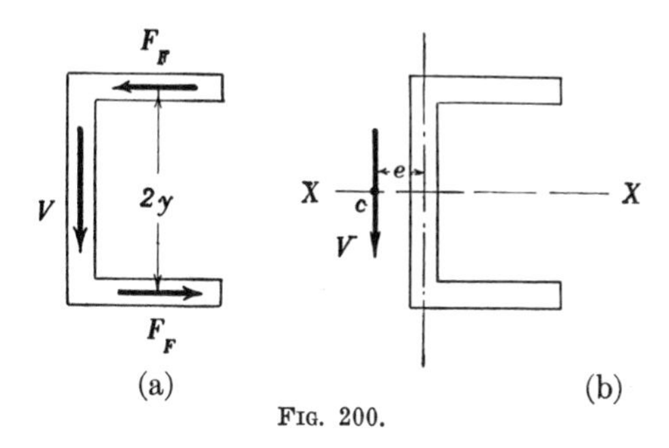

FIG. 200.

in magnitude and opposed in direction, their resultant will be a couple of magnitude

$$M = \frac{V\,y\,t\,l^2}{2I_{XX}} \times 2y = \frac{V\,y^2\,t\,l^2}{I_{XX}}$$

In addition to the flange shear forces, the channel web has acting upon it a shearing force V, which may be assumed to act along the center line of the comparatively thin web. (In the case of the beam of Fig. 199, $V = P_1$.) This force is also shown in Fig. 200-a. The entire system of shearing forces acting on the section comprises force V and couple M. This system is equivalent to a force V, applied at a distance e (see Fig. 200-b) from the center of the web, where

$$e = \frac{M}{V} = \frac{V\,y^2\,t\,l^2}{V I_{XX}} = \frac{y^2\,t\,l^2}{I_{XX}} \qquad \textbf{(69)}$$

The point of application of V is shown in Fig. 200-b as point c. If the plane of loading contains point c, there will be no tendency for the channel section to twist, for the resultant shear force will pass through point c and no twisting moment will be produced. The center c is called the *shear center*, or *center of twist*, of the beam section. When such members as channel sections are used as beams, the designer can prevent twisting of the beam about its longitudinal axis by placing the plane of loading so that it will pass through the shear center.

Illustrative Example I. The 12 in. × 25 lb./ft. American Standard channel shown in Fig. 201 has $I_{XX} = 143.5$ in.^{4} y is approximately 6 in.; $l = 3$ in.; average $t = \frac{1}{2}$ in. The location of the shear center is to be determined. Applying equation (69), we find that

$$e = \frac{(6)^2 \times \frac{1}{2} \times (3)^2}{143.5} = 1.13 \text{ in.}$$

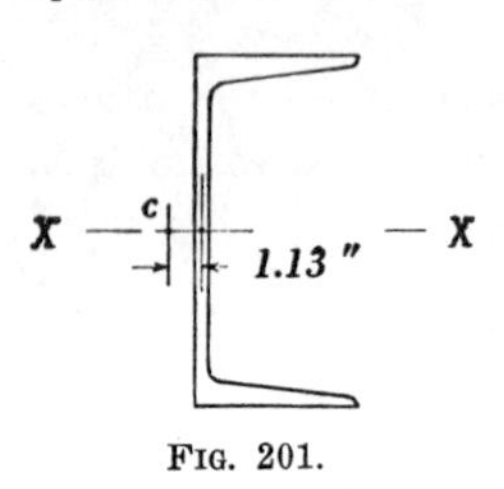

FIG. 201.

If the plane of loading passes through point c, there will be no twisting of the loaded beam.

Illustrative Example II. The tee-section of Fig. 202 has a shear center through which the plane of loading must be passed if the successive right sections of the beam are not to rotate relative to each other. We shall make use of an additional method of attack in this problem to suggest the presence and approximate location of such a center.

The beam (Fig. 202-a) carries a uniformly distributed load, which is distributed over the surfaces ab and fg. The total section may be considered to be made of two

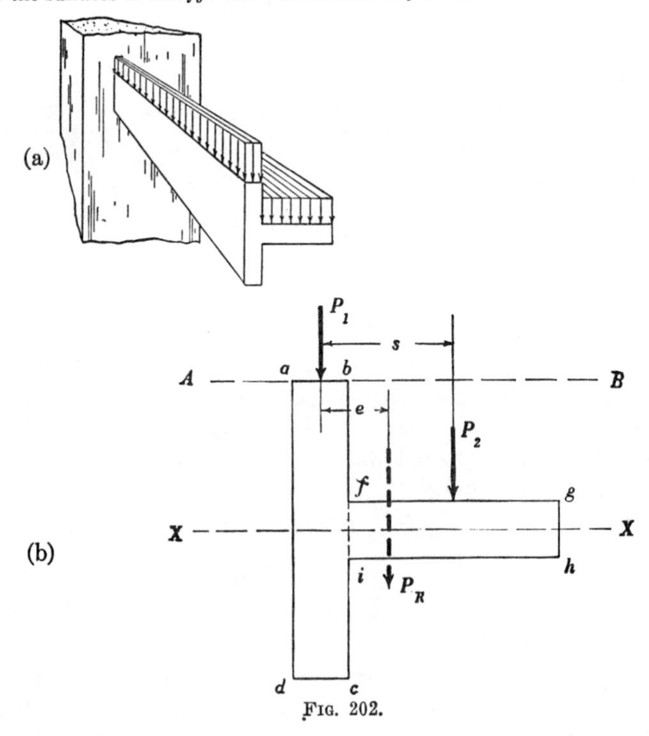

FIG. 202.

rectangular sections $abcd$ and $fghi$, which are indicated in Fig. 202-b. P_1 is the resultant load on ab, and P_2 is the resultant load on fg. The resultant of P_1 and P_2 is indicated as force P_R.

If the section is not to rotate about the long axis of the beam, the deflection of every point of the cross-sectional area from a horizontal axis, like AB, must be the same.

Let us first consider the deflection of a rectangular beam of cross-section *abcd* under the influence of load P_1. This deflection will be

$$y = \frac{P_1 k}{I_1}$$

where k is a constant which includes the span length, the coefficient of the appropriate deflection expression, and the modulus of elasticity of the beam material. I_1 is the moment of inertia of section *abcd* about axis X-X.

If we now consider section *fghi*, the deflection is

$$y = \frac{P_2 k}{I_2}$$

where I_2 is the moment of inertia of section *fghi* about X-X.

If the deflection of the entire section under the influence of P_R is considered,

$$y = \frac{P_R k}{I}$$

where I is the moment of inertia of the entire section about X-X.

The constant k is the same for all sections and we intend to have the deflection of all sections the same, so that there will be no twisting. Then

$$\frac{P_1}{I_1} = \frac{P_2}{I_2} = \frac{P_R}{I} \qquad \text{and} \qquad P_2 = \frac{I_2}{I} \times P_R$$

Since P_R is the resultant of P_1 and P_2,

$$P_R e = P_2 s = \frac{I_2 P_R s}{I}$$

and

$$e = \frac{I_2 s}{I} \tag{70}$$

If I_2 is very small relative to I, which will be true if the web of the tee is short relative to the height of the flange, the distance e will be very nearly zero, and the shear center will lie approximately on the center line of the flange.

The location of the shear center of the tee beam of Fig. 203 is determined as follows:

$$I_2 = \frac{5.5 \times (0.5)^3}{12} = 0.057 \text{ in.}^4$$

where I_2 is the moment of inertia of the web.

$$I = 0.057 + \frac{0.5 \times (6)^3}{12} = 9.057 \text{ in.}^4$$

where I is the moment of inertia of the entire section.

$$s = 0.25 + 2.75 = 3.00 \text{ in.}$$

and, by equation (70), $e = \dfrac{0.057}{9.057} \times 3.00 = 0.019$ in.

This solution indicates that the shear center of a tee beam, or an angle section which is also composed of two approximate rectangles, will lie very near the intersection of the center lines of the rectangles; the deviation is so slight that it need not be considered in the usual cases of design employing such shapes.

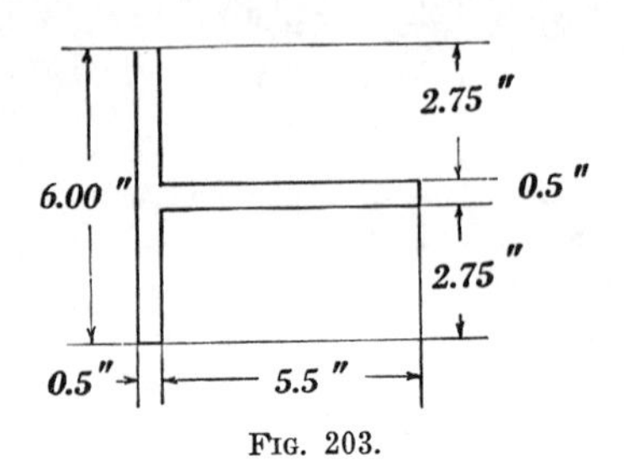

FIG. 203.

PROBLEMS

352. Locate the shear center of a 15 in. × 50 lb./ft. American Standard channel. $I_X = 401.4$ in.^{4}; $y = 7.2$ in.; $l = 3.75$ in.; $t = 0.625$ in. *Ans.* $e = 1.13$ in.

353. Locate the shear center of a 13 in. × 50 lb./ft. shipbuilding channel. $I_X = 312.9$ in.^{4}; $y = 6.20$ in.; $l = 4\frac{3}{8}$ in.; $t = 0.625$ in.

354. The beam section carries a uniformly distributed load. Locate the shear center. *Ans.* $e = 0.6$ in.

355. Locate the shear center of the section shown which is subjected to a load distributed uniformly over the entire top surface.

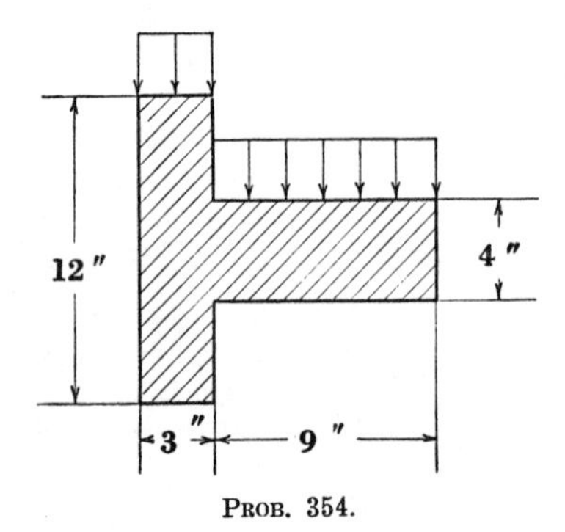

PROB. 354.

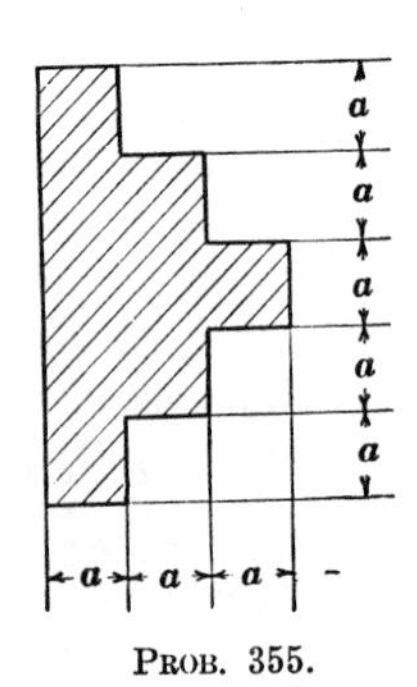

PROB. 355.

CHAPTER VI

Torsion

56. The Torsion Theory. Many machine parts are subjected to twisting or torsion as they transmit power. A line or propeller shaft undergoes twisting as it rotates, conducting power from a motor or an engine to the driven units. Structural members are also frequently subjected to torsion: the loads placed upon a floor area that is supported on joists which are, in turn, fastened to an end girder may set up torsion in the girder.

When a body, like the shaft of Fig. 204, is loaded by a twisting moment, M_T, torsional shear stresses will be developed parallel to the surfaces of sections like S. The evaluation of such shear stress is the responsibility of the theory of torsion.

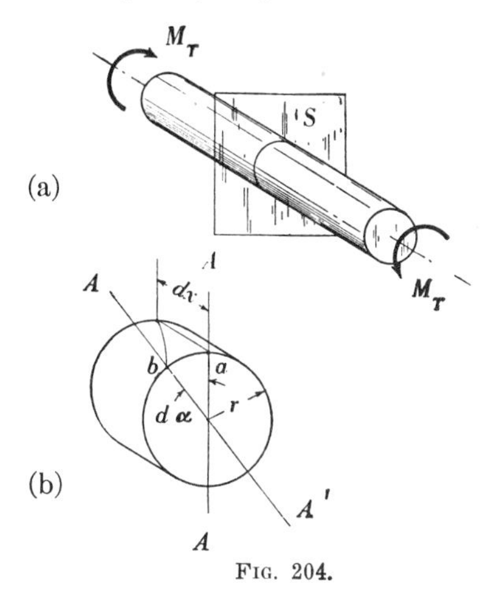

FIG. 204.

As we enter the consideration of a theory which will be valid in determining torsional shear stress, we are compelled, as in the other theories of stress analysis, to acknowledge limitations. The shape of the cross-sectional area of the loaded body plays an important role in the distribution of the shear stress. In this type of stress behavior, all loaded bodies having cross-sectional areas other than circular ones exhibit characteristics that are more complex than those which may be determined through the medium of one basic and simple theory.

We find, too, that it is impossible to produce, physically, pure twisting without introducing other sources of stress. If, for example, a shaft is mounted horizontally, it must be supported on bearings and its own weight will be the source of bending stress, for the shaft will now possess the characteristics of a beam. If the drive contains a pulley-and-belt assembly, the belt tensions will furnish a source of bending as well as twisting action.

If the shaft is mounted vertically, as in hydroelectric turbo-generator drives, its own weight will be a source of axial stress.

To derive a theory which may be a simple and fundamental tool, we shall confine our present interest to the cylindrical shaft of homogeneous material. We shall, in addition, limit our consideration to the shear stress which is induced by twisting moment alone. The consideration of the inevitable combination of this stress with bending or axial stresses will be left to later articles in which combined loading will be investigated. We shall also limit the theory to cases in which the shear stress varies as the shear strain.

In addition to restricting the application of the theory to those shafts which conform to the above limitations, we shall make two basic assumptions. These assumptions are admissible because experimental evidence has assured us of their validity. When such shafts are designed and built, their behavior agrees very closely with the predictions of the torsion theory.

Assumption I. The sections of the shaft which are perpendicular to the longitudinal axis remain plane surfaces when the shaft is twisted.

Assumption II. All diameters of the cross-section remain straight diametral lines when the shaft is twisted.

The cross-sectional surfaces remain, according to these assumptions, plane surfaces at constant distance from each other after loading.

The shaft of Fig. 204 is subjected to equal and oppositely directed twisting moments, M_T, at its ends. To investigate the torsional shear stresses in the shaft we shall isolate the short cylinder of length dx shown in Fig. 204-b. When the twisting moment is applied, diameter A-A will rotate relative to a diameter at the other end of the cylinder through an angle $d\alpha$ to position A'-A'. Point a of the front surface will move through the arc distance $ab = r\, d\alpha$ where r is the radial distance of point a from the center of the shaft.

The shearing strain, which was defined in Art. 14, will be

$$\gamma = \frac{r\, d\alpha}{dx}$$

Any other fiber, at distance ρ from the center will have as its shearing strain

$$\gamma_1 = \frac{\rho\, d\alpha}{dx} \tag{1}$$

and the shearing strains in all fibers will be directly proportional to the distances of the fibers from the center of the shaft. The angle $d\alpha$ is called the *angle of twist*, and $d\alpha/dx$ is the angle of twist per unit of length of the shaft.

Since we have assumed that shear stress is proportional to shear strain

$$s_S = G\gamma_1 \tag{2}$$

in which G is the constant of proportionality, called the modulus of elasticity in shear or the *modulus of rigidity*. Like the comparable modulus of elasticity in tension or compression, its units are pounds per square inch. (See Art. 16.)

If we now combine equations (1) and (2),

$$s_S = \frac{G\,\rho\,d\alpha}{dx}$$

The angle of twist, $d\alpha$, is proportional to the length, and $d\alpha/dx$ is a constant which will be symbolized as θ.

Then

$$\boldsymbol{s_S = G\,\rho\,\theta} \tag{71}$$

The torsional shear stress varies, therefore, directly as the distance ρ from the center of the shaft, and is maximum at the outer surface. If the radius of the shaft is r,

$$\boldsymbol{s_S = G\,r\,\theta} \tag{72}$$

This equation expresses the shear stress as a function of the modulus of rigidity, radial distance, and angle of twist. In most of the problems of engineering we shall require the services of an equation which will express the torsional shear stress as a function of the applied twisting moment.

The torsional shear stress on an elementary area dA of a loaded shaft (Fig. 205) is s_S, and the shearing force on the elementary area, dA, is

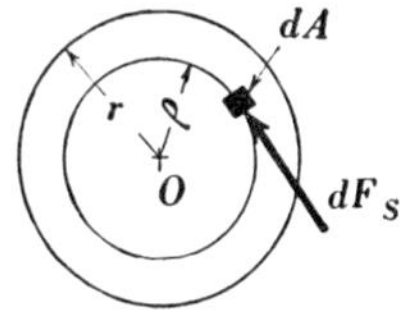

FIG. 205.

$$dF_S = s_S\,dA = G\,\rho\,\theta\,dA$$

The moment of shearing force dF_S about the longitudinal axis of the shaft, O, is

$$dM = dF_S\,\rho = s_S\,dA\,\rho = G\,\rho^2\,\theta\,dA$$

The total twisting moment on the section will be

$$M_T = \int dM = \int G\rho^2\,\theta\,dA = G\theta \int_{\rho=0}^{\rho=r} \rho^2\,dA = G\,\theta\,I_P$$

where I_P is the polar moment of inertia of the circular cross-sectional area about an axis at its center ($I_P = \pi r^4/2$).

From equation (71),

$$\theta = \frac{s_S}{G\,\rho}$$

and

$$M_T = \frac{s_S\,I_P}{\rho}$$

or

$$s_S = \frac{M_T\,\rho}{I_P} \tag{73}$$

It will be noted that this expression for torsional shear stress as a function of twisting moment is directly analogous to the flexure formula for bending stress produced by the bending moment $s = M\,y/I$ [equation (34)].

The angle of twist may also be expressed in terms of the twisting moment. The angle of twist per unit of length is θ. Then the total angle of twist in a length of shaft L is

$$\Theta = \theta L$$

From equation (71) $\theta = s_S/G\rho$ and from equation (73) $s_S = M_T\rho/I_P$.

Then

$$\Theta = \frac{M_T\,\rho\,L}{I_P\,\rho G} = \frac{M_T\,L}{I_P\,G} \tag{74}$$

This expression for angular deformation is analogous to the expression for axial deformation $\delta = PL/AE$ (see equation 30).

Hollow Cylindrical Shcft. The assumptions which have been made in the development of the torsion theory apply with equal validity to the hollow cylindrical shaft. Since the torsional shear stresses vary uniformly from the center of the shaft to the outer surface, the region at the core of the shaft is subjected to the lowest stresses. It follows that the material of the central region is not being used efficiently. The hollow shaft provides a more efficient cross-sectional area—the greatest amount of material is placed in the region of greatest stress.

The shearing force on an elementary area will again be

$$dF_S = s_S\,dA = G\,\rho\,\theta\,dA$$

and its moment about the axis will be

$$dM = G\,\theta\,\rho^2\,dA$$

Then

$$M_T = \int dM = G\theta \int \rho^2\,dA = G\,\theta\,I_P$$

The limits of the integral will be $\rho = r_i$ and $\rho = r_o$, where r_i and r_o are the inner and outer radii of the shaft, respectively.

Then

$$s_S = \frac{M_T\,\rho}{I_P} = \frac{2M_T\,\rho}{\pi(r_o^4 - r_i^4)} \tag{75}$$

The amount of power transmitted by a shaft is usually expressed in horsepower. To determine the twisting moment, M_T, in a loaded shaft we may convert as follows:

$$\text{h.p.} = \frac{M_T \, \omega}{33{,}000}$$

where M_T is the twisting moment in foot-pounds and ω is the angular speed of the shaft in radians per minute.

Illustrative Example I. The motor of Fig. 206 delivers 80 h.p. at 120 r.p.m. to the shaft. This power drives two machines, located at sections A and B, respec-

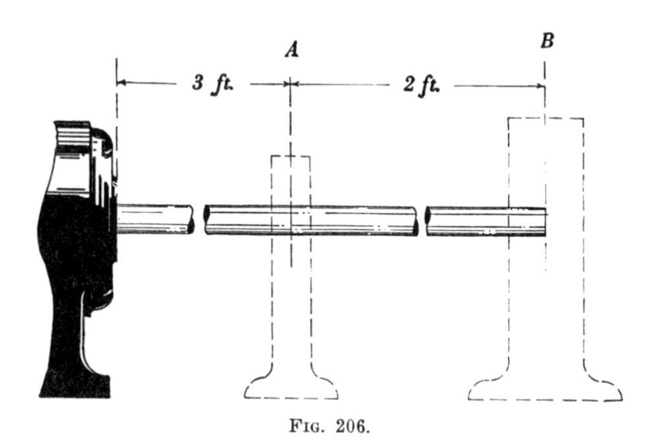

FIG. 206.

tively. 20 h.p. is used to drive the unit at A, and 60 h.p. the unit at B. Diameter of shaft = 3 in., $G = 12 \times 10^6$ psi.

We are to determine the maximum shear stress produced by torsion in each section of the shaft, and the total angle of twist of the shaft.

The twisting moment in the first range of loading from the motor will be

$$M_T = \frac{80 \times 33{,}000}{120 \times 2\pi} = 3500 \text{ ft.-lb.}$$

Applying equation (73),

$$s_{S(\text{max.})} = \frac{3500 \times 12 \times 1.5}{\pi (1.5)^4/2} = 7920 \text{ psi}$$

The angle of twist in this range will be, by equation (74),

$$\Theta_1 = \frac{M_T L}{G I_P} = \frac{3500 \times 12 \times 3 \times 12}{12 \times 10^6 \times \pi (1.5)^4/2}$$
$$= 0.0158 \text{ radians} = 0.905 \text{ degs.}$$

In the second range of loading the magnitude of power transmitted is 60 h.p. Then, in this range,

$$M_T = \frac{60 \times 33{,}000}{120 \times 2\pi} = 2625 \text{ ft.-lb.}$$

Applying equation (73),

$$s_{S(\text{max.})} = \frac{2625 \times 12 \times 1.5}{\pi(1.5)^4/2} = 5940 \text{ psi}$$

In this range, the angle of twist is, by equation (74),

$$\Theta_2 = \frac{2625 \times 12 \times 2 \times 12}{12 \times 10^6 \times \pi(1.5)^4/2}$$
$$= 0.00792 \text{ radians} = 0.453 \text{ degs.}$$

The total angle of twist in the shaft will be

$$\Theta = \Theta_1 + \Theta_2 = 0.905 + 0.453 = 1.358 \text{ degs.}$$

Illustrative Example II. The efficiency of the hollow shaft in reduction of weight has been suggested in the preceding article. Two shafts of equal length, one hollow and one solid, are to be subjected to the same twisting moment. They are made of the same material, and the allowable torsional shear stress, s_S, is the same for both shafts.

We are to determine the ratio of the weights of the two shafts if the inner radius (r_i) of the hollow shaft is two-thirds of the outer radius(r_o).

In the hollow shaft, substituting in equation (75), we find that

$$s_S = \frac{M_T r_o}{\frac{\pi(r_o^4 - r_i^4)}{2}} = \frac{M_T r_o^2}{\pi\left[r_o^4 - \left(\frac{2}{3}r_o\right)^4\right]} = \frac{2M_T}{\pi \times \frac{65}{81} r_o^3}$$

In the solid shaft, by equation (73),

$$s_S = \frac{M_T\, r}{I_P} = \frac{2M_T}{\pi r^3}$$

Then

$$\frac{2M_T}{\pi \frac{65}{81}(r_o)^3} = \frac{2M_T}{\pi r^3}$$

$$\frac{65}{81}(r_o)^3 = r^3$$

The radius of the solid shaft is equal to $\sqrt[3]{65/81}$ times the outer radius of the hollow shaft.

The weights of the two shafts are directly proportional to the magnitudes of their cross-sectional areas. The area of the hollow shaft is

$$A_H = \pi(r_o^2 - r_i^2) = \pi \times \frac{5}{9} r_o^2$$

and the area of the solid shaft is

$$A_S = \pi r^2 = \pi\left(\frac{65}{81} r_o\right)^{\frac{2}{3}}$$

The ratio of the weights of the shafts will be

$$\frac{A_H}{A_S} = \frac{\frac{5}{9}\pi r_o^2}{\pi r^2} = \frac{5}{9} \times \frac{1}{\left(\frac{65}{81}\right)^{\frac{2}{3}}} = 0.65$$

The hollow shaft will therefore reduce the weight very appreciably—a marked advantage in such applications as aircraft structures, where refinement of design through reduction of weight is essential. The cost of machining, however, may offset such an advantage in cases where the shaft weight is not a significant factor.

Illustrative Example III. The torsion theory, like the deflection theory, may be used to furnish assistance in some problems which are statically indeterminate. For example, the shaft of Fig. 207 is supported rigidly at its ends and subjected to

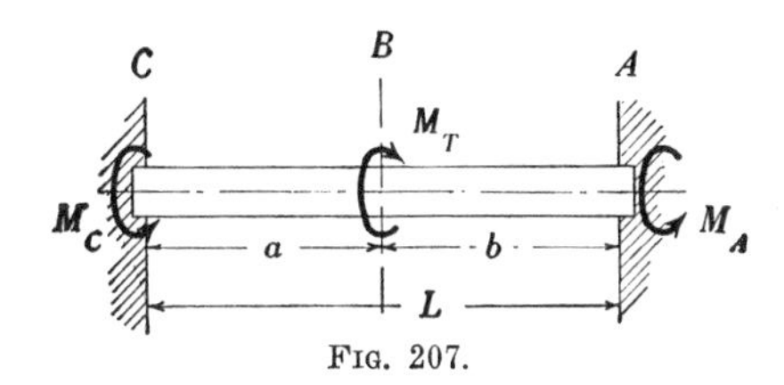

FIG. 207.

a twisting moment, M_T, applied at section B. The conditions of equilibrium will not suffice to determine the distribution of twisting moment into the two portions of the shaft for only one condition is available, $\Sigma M = 0$. From this equation,

$$M_T = M_A + M_C \tag{1}$$

If we isolate, as a free body, the portion of the shaft which lies between sections A and B, the twisting moment in this portion is M_A. A diameter of the cross-section at B will rotate, relative to a fixed diameter at A through an angle of twist

$$\Theta_1 = \frac{M_A\, b}{GI_P}$$

Similarly, if the portion of the shaft between sections B and C is isolated, the twisting moment in this portion is M_C. According to equation (74), a diameter at section B will rotate, relative to a fixed diameter at C, through an angle of twist

$$\Theta_2 = \frac{M_C\, a}{GI_P}$$

Since Θ_1 and Θ_2 must be equal when the shaft as a whole is considered,

$$\frac{M_A\, b}{GI_P} = \frac{M_C\, a}{GI_P}$$

and

$$\frac{M_A}{M_C} = \frac{a}{b} \tag{2}$$

Solving equation (1) and (2) simultaneously,

$$M_A = \frac{M_T\, a}{L} \quad \text{and} \quad M_C = \frac{M_T\, b}{L}$$

57. Torsional Modulus of Rupture. Torsional deformation under twisting moment is very similar in its behavior to the relationship which we have already observed between axial loading and linear deformation in bars subjected to tension. When a shaft of ductile steel, for example, is subjected to a gradually increasing twisting moment, the stress–strain curve follows the same pattern as the corresponding curve of the tensile-test specimen.* Both curves are straight lines as far as the proportional limit. The stress beyond which there is a permanent set in torsion is called the elastic limit in torsion, and a yield point will appear in torsion just as it does in tension. This yield point is not as marked, however, in the torsional case, for the inner fibers and outer fibers of the shaft are not equally stressed, and the latter will yield sooner than those subjected to the lower stresses of the interior. In a hollow shaft, the stresses are more nearly uniform, and the analogy with the tensile stress-strain pattern is more direct.

We have based the derivation of the expression for torsional shear stress upon an assumption that no stress beyond the elastic limit was induced in the shaft. When twisting moments are of such magnitude that stresses greater than the elastic limit arise, the use of the derived expression is open to criticism. However, comparison of the behavior of shafts of different size or material is frequently based upon the torsional shear expression, even though the stresses at the outer surface may have values greatly in excess of the elastic limit. When M_T is the twisting moment at rupture of the shaft and r is the outer radius,

$$s_S = \frac{M_T\, r}{I_P}$$

becomes the *torsional modulus of rupture*. This is a fictitious stress, comparable to the bending modulus of rupture in beams (Art. 27). The modulus of rupture is a convenient measure, for it is readily determined and is satisfactory because it is used only as a relative measure when comparing shafts similarly loaded.

58. Non-Circular Sections. The theory which we have employed in evaluating the stress and angular deformation due to torsion has been limited to cylindrical bodies.

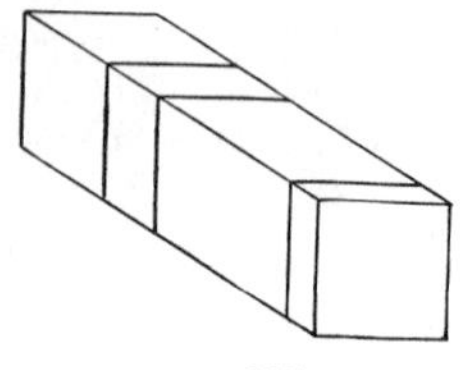

Fig. 208.

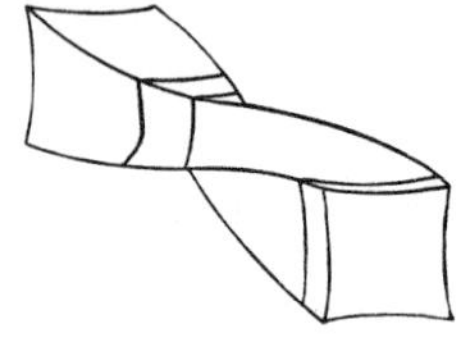

Fig. 209.

Other shapes of cross-section present a very different pattern of stress distribution. If, for example, straight lines perpendicular to the long axis of a rectangular rubber bar are drawn on the faces of the rubber, as in Fig. 208, and the bar is twisted, the lines will become curved, as in Fig. 209,

*See Art. 77.

indicating that the right sections of the bar, which are plane surfaces before loading, become warped surfaces when the bar is twisted. The mathematical analysis of such stress distribution is complex and design formulas are employed which were originally deduced by Saint-Venant. The formulas of Saint-Venant for two cross-sectional areas of shafts subjected to torsion follow.

Elliptical Section. If a is the semimajor axis of the ellipse, and b is the semiminor axis, the maximum torsional shear stress will be

$$s_S = \frac{2M_T}{\pi\, a\, b^2} \tag{76}$$

This maximum stress will occur at the ends of the minor axis

The angle of twist in an elliptical shaft of length L will be

$$\Theta = \frac{(a^2 + b^2)M_T L}{\pi a^3\, b^3\, G} \tag{77}$$

Rectangular Section. If a is the length of the longer side, and b is the length of the shorter side, the maximum torsional shear stress will be

$$s_S = M_T\left[\left(\frac{3}{ab^2} + \frac{9}{5a^2b}\right)\right] \tag{78}$$

This maximum stress will occur at the center of the longer side.

The angle of twist in a rectangular shaft of length L will be approximately

$$\Theta = \frac{10(a^2 + b^2)M_T L}{3\, a^2\, b^2\, G} \tag{79}$$

More recent investigators have made use of experimental techniques in studying the effect of torsion on other cross-sectional areas than the circle. One such device is the membrane analogy. In this experiment, a soap-film membrane is stretched over a hole in a closed vessel. The hole has a contour which is identical with that of the cross-section of the shaft under investigation. The film is deformed by air pressure and assumes a shape from which the shear stress distribution may be determined. The elevation at different points of the film is measured, and lines of the same elevation, called contour lines, are plotted. A mathematical analysis of the contour of the film can then be made to establish the nature of the stress distribution. The slope of the soap film is proportional to the shear stress, and its volume proportional to the twisting moment. Such experimental techniques and the analysis of the results lie beyond our present scope, but suggest the possibilities of meeting a challenge by laboratory exploration when mathematical analysis either fails or must be assisted by experiment.

59. Thin-walled Sections in Torsion. In addition to machine shafting, which is subjected to torsion as it transmits power, structural members are frequently subjected to twisting. In aircraft structures, for example, thin-walled sections which may be subjected to torsion in flight, are encountered. The wall may be of uniform or varying thickness. The distribution of the torsional shear stress over the comparatively short extent of wall is much more nearly uniform than in the case of the solid shaft, as has already been suggested in our discussion of the hollow shaft.

If the wall thickness is small in comparison with other dimensions of the shell, and no sharp corners or other sudden changes in the character of the outline shape are encountered, which might give rise to stress concentration, the following theory gives results which are reasonably consistent with the experimental evidence.

The section of a thin-walled shell shown in Fig. 210 is subjected to a twisting moment M_T. Torsional shear stresses will be induced on the wall

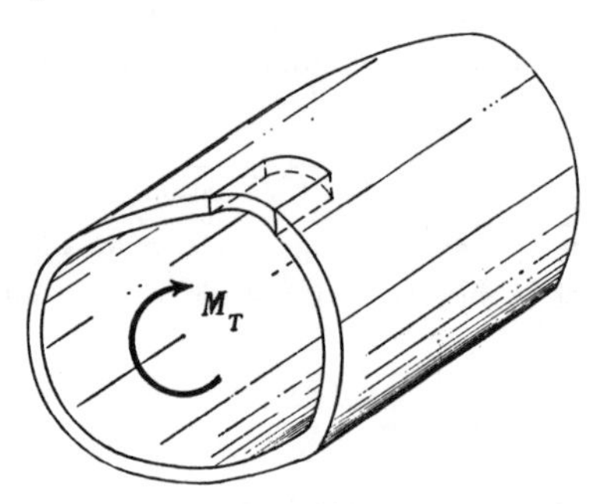

FIG. 210.

cross-sectional area. The torsional shear stress on the surface at any section of the shell is s_S and the thickness of the wall at that section is t. The total shear force per unit of length of circumference at any section, sometimes called the *shear flow*, is

$$q = s_S t$$

If we isolate a small prism as a free body (Fig. 211), the shear forces on the faces will be F_1, F_2, F_3, and F_4.

$$F_2 = s_2 t_2 \, dx$$

where $s_2 t_2$ is the shear flow on face *cefd*.

Similarly, $$F_4 = s_4 t_1 \, dx$$

where $s_4 t_1$ is the shear flow on face *abhg*.

From the conditions of equilibrium for the free body,

$$F_2 = F_4$$

and

$$s_2 t_2 \, dx = s_4 t_1 \, dx$$

whence

$$s_2 t_2 = s_4 t_1$$

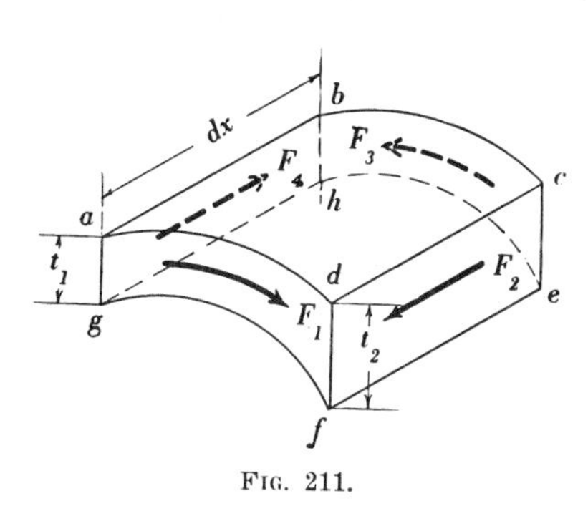

FIG. 211.

The product $s_2 t_2$ is the value of q at corner df of the prism, and $s_4 t_1$ is the value of q at corner ag. The shear flow is, then, the same on face $adfg$ at each of its corners. Then the term q is a constant around the perimeter of the shell, whether the wall thickness is constant or variable.

To evaluate the shear stress in terms of the twisting moment, we turn to Fig. 212.

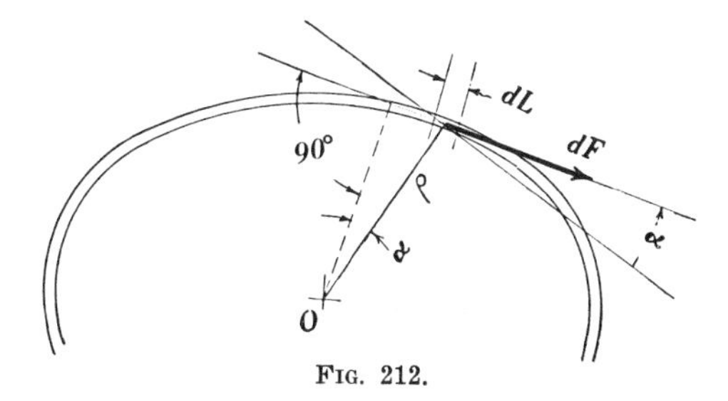

FIG. 212.

The shearing force on the face of an element of the wall of length dL is dF, located at distance ρ from the axis of the shell, point O.

$$dF = q \, dL$$

and the moment of force dF about an axis at O is

$$dM = dF \, \rho \cos \alpha = q \, dL \, \rho \cos \alpha$$

The resultant moment, which must be equal to the applied twisting moment, is

$$\int dM = \int q\,dL\,\rho\cos\alpha = q\int dL\,\rho\cos\alpha = M_T$$

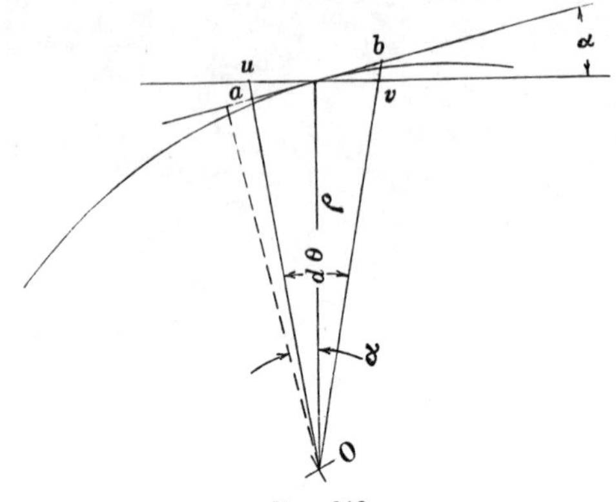

FIG. 213.

The integration may be performed if we consider the relationships indicated in Fig. 213. ab represents the elementary length dL of Fig. 212.

$$uv = ab\cos\alpha = dL\cos\alpha$$

$$uv = \rho\,d\theta$$

$$dL = \frac{\rho\,d\theta}{\cos\alpha}$$

Then $$M_T = q\int d\mathrm{L}\,\rho\cos\alpha = q\int\frac{\rho\,d\theta}{\cos\alpha}\rho\cos\alpha = q\int\rho^2\,d\theta$$

The area of triangle uOv is

$$dA = \frac{1}{2}(\rho\,d\theta)\rho = \frac{\rho^2\,d\theta}{2}$$

and $$\int dA = \int\frac{\rho^2\,d\theta}{2}$$

$\int dA$ is the entire area A enclosed by the shell and

$$M_T = 2qA$$

But q is always equal to $s_S t$, where s_S is the torsional shear stress at a section of the wall and t is the thickness of the wall at that section.

Then $$M_T = 2\,s_S\,t\,A$$

$$s_S = \frac{M_T}{2\,t\,A} \tag{80}$$

This torsional shear stress is not the only source of possible failure in a thin-walled section. The compressive stresses which are induced on oblique sections of the shell wall are of serious concern for they may cause buckling of the shell. Such induced stress has already been discussed in the articles devoted to stress at a point in Chapter I and will again be referred to in the discussion of combined loading in Chapter VIII.

Illustrative Example. The thin-walled hollow section of Fig. 214 is subjected to a twisting moment $M_T = 6000$ ft.-lb. The thickness of the wall is $t = 1/8$ in. The torsional shear stress in the wall is to be determined. The area enclosed by the shell is

$$A = \pi\left(4\frac{7}{8}\right)^2 + 9\frac{3}{4} \times 15 = 220 \text{ sq. in.}$$

Applying equation (80),

$$s_S = \frac{6000 \times 12}{2 \times \frac{1}{8} \times 220} = 1300 \text{ psi}$$

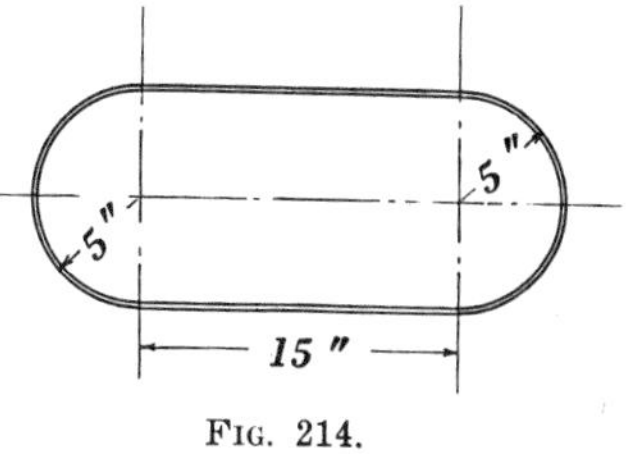

FIG. 214.

60. Helical Springs.

Helical, or coiled, springs are formed by wrapping a wire or rod of uniform cross-section around a cylinder. A fixed distance between the successive coils is maintained, so that the axis of the wire forms a helix. When the distance between the coils is small, the spring is called a *close-coiled spring*, and, in the consideration of stress in the wire, the torsion theory may be applied.

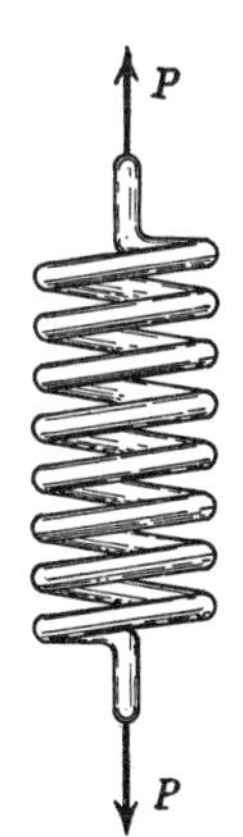

FIG. 215.

Figure 215 shows a close-coiled spring of circular cross-section which is subjected to axial loading by the end tensile force P. In Fig. 216-a a portion of the spring has been isolated, and we note that the cut section must have acting upon it a force equal to P, and a couple, M, for the free body is in equilibrium. P and M must lie in the same vertical plane. $M = Pr$, where r is the radius of the spring.

A view of the spring wire at the cut section has been taken from the right and is shown in Fig. 216-b. The couple M, acting in the vertical plane, has been shown as a vector, and is resolved into two components, M_B and M_T, which lie in planes which are tangential and normal to the helix, respectively.

The couple M_B tends to cause bending of the isolated portion of the spring wire, and M_T is acting so as to cause twisting. The angle θ is the angle of inclination of the helix with any plane perpendicular to the axis of the coil.

$$M_B = M \sin \theta \qquad \text{and} \qquad M_T = M \cos \theta$$

When the spring is close-coiled, the angle θ is very small, and M_B is negligible. Then M_T will approximately equal M.

Figure 216-c shows a similar resolution of force P into components, P_N and P_S, which are causing normal and shearing components of stress, respectively, on the cut section.

$$P_N = P \sin \theta \qquad \text{and} \qquad P_S = P \cos \theta$$

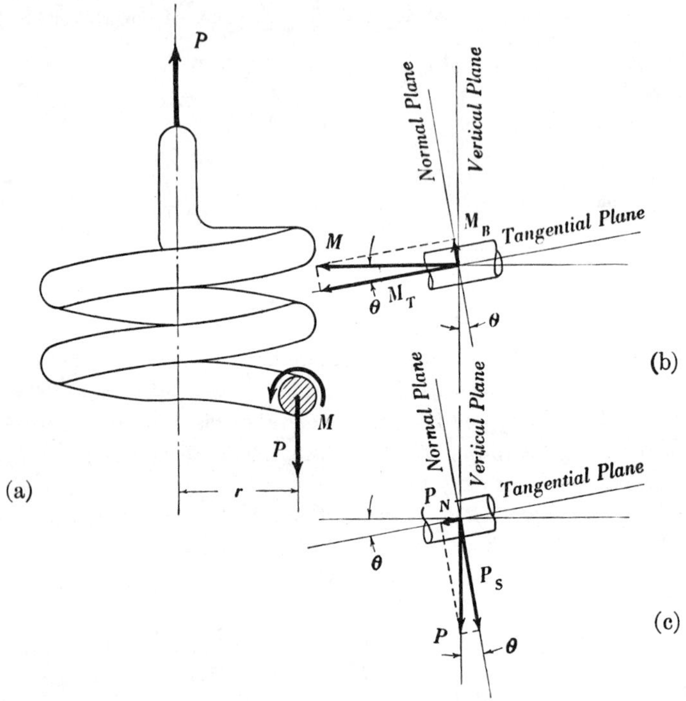

FIG. 216.

For the close-coiled spring, P_N is negligible, and P_S is approximately equal to P.

In a close-coiled spring, then, the only sources of stress which need be considered are force P and couple M. Both cause shearing stress on the cut section. The shearing stress due to P is assumed to be uniformly distributed, and is

$$s_1 = \frac{P}{A}$$

where A is the area of the cross-section of the wire.

The shearing stress due to M will be a torsional shear stress

$$s_2 = \frac{Me}{I_P}$$

where e is the radius of the spring wire, and I_P the polar moment of inertia of the cross-section.

The total stress will be

$$s_S = s_1 + s_2 = \frac{P}{A} + \frac{Me}{I_P} \tag{81}$$

The distribution of this shear stress across the circular cross-section is shown in Fig. 217. It will be noted that the stress on the inner side of the coil is maximum and, in practice, springs will begin to fail on the inner side.

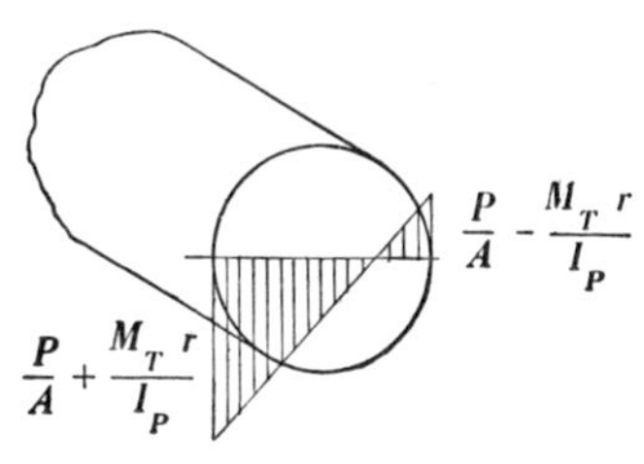

Fig. 217.

The equation for shear stress which has just been derived has rested upon assumptions which are only approximately true, and more exact treatment will be found in the engineering literature.*

The deformation of the close-coiled spring may be determined, with reasonable accuracy through the use of the torsion theory. Figure 218 shows a small element of the spring wire isolated as a free body of length

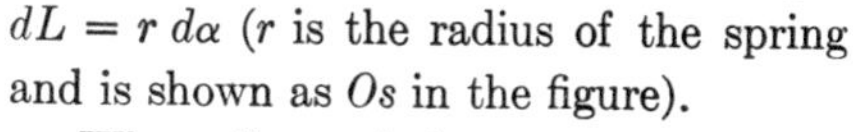

$dL = r\,d\alpha$ (r is the radius of the spring and is shown as Os in the figure).

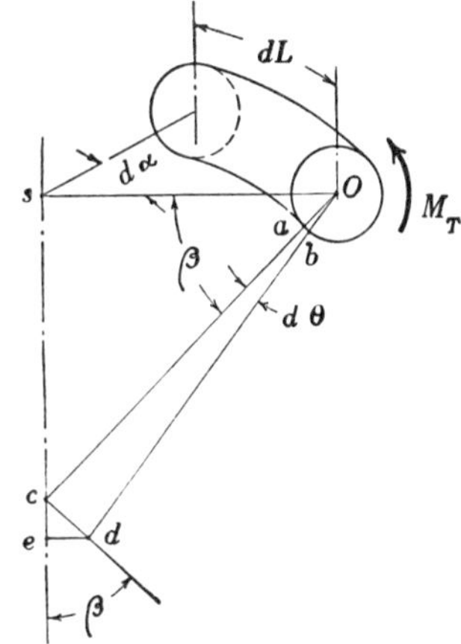

Fig. 218.

When the twisting moment M_T is applied, radius Oa of the cross-section will rotate to position Ob. The point of application of force P (point c) will be lowered through a vertical distance ce.

$$ce = Oc\,d\theta \cos\beta = Oc\,d\theta\frac{r}{Oc} = d\theta\, r$$

$d\theta$ is the angle of twist of the small element in a length dL.

$$d\theta = \frac{M_T\,dL}{GI_P}$$

$$ce = \frac{M_T\,dL}{GI_P}r = \frac{P\,r\,dL}{GI_P}r$$

$$= \frac{P\,r^3\,d\alpha}{GI_P}$$

The vertical distance ce is the contribution which the element of length dL makes to the total vertical displacement of the point of application of force P, and that total will be

$$\delta = \int \frac{Pr^3\,d\alpha}{GI_P} = \frac{Pr^3}{GI_P}\int d\alpha$$

*See Wahl: *Mechanical Springs*, Penton Publishing Co., 1944.

$\int d\alpha$ is the total angular distance, in radians, around the circumference of the helix which must be $2\pi n$, where n is the number of complete turns.

Then
$$\delta = \frac{2\pi P r^3 n}{GI_P} \tag{82}$$

The horizontal displacement de will be zero for each complete revolution, and δ is the actual displacement of the bottom of the spring.

Illustrative Example. A close-coiled spring having 16 coils ($G = 12 \times 10^6$ psi, maximum allowable shear stress, $s_S = 10{,}000$ psi) is subjected to a tensile load P. The diameter of the spring is 4 in., and the diameter of the spring wire is ¾ in. The maximum allowable load P, and the deformation of the spring at that load are to be determined.

Applying equation (81),

$$s_S = 10{,}000 = \frac{P}{\pi(3/8)^2} + \frac{P \times 2 \times 3/8}{\frac{\pi(3/8)^4}{2}}$$

$$= 2.26P + 24.1P = 26.36P$$

$$P = 379 \text{ lb.}$$

Applying equation (82),

$$\delta = \frac{2\pi \times 379 \times (2)^3 \times 16}{12 \times 10^6 \times \pi(3/8)^4/2} = 0.818 \text{ in.}$$

PROBLEMS

Note: In the torsion problems which follow, the values of G, the modulus of rigidity given in Table IV below, should be used.

TABLE IV. MODULUS OF RIGIDITY

Material	G
Steel	12×10^6 psi
Cast iron, gray	6×10^6
Aluminum	4×10^6
Brass	5×10^6
Copper	6×10^6

356. What twisting moment will induce a torsional shear stress of 10,000 psi in a shaft which has a 4 in. diameter? *Ans.* 10,470 ft.-lb.

357. If the shaft of Prob. 356 is 10 ft. long and is made of steel, determine the total angle of twist. *Ans.* 2.86°.

358. The shaft of Prob. 356 is to transmit 300 h.p. at 360 r.p.m. Determine the maximum torsional shear stress.

359. A steel shaft is to be designed so that the maximum torsional shear stress will be 8000 psi., and the maximum angle of twist per foot of length will be 0.25°. Determine the required diameter of the shaft. *Ans.* 3.66 in.

360. A solid bronze shaft, 2 in. diameter and 22 in long, was subjected to torsion. The test showed that an increase in twisting moment from 2000 in.-lb. to 6940 in.-lb caused an increase in angle of twist of 0.72°. Determine the modulus of rigidity of the bronze.

361. Two shafts, of the same material and same weight per unit of length, are subjected to twisting. One shaft is solid; the other is hollow, with its inside diameter equal to three-quarters of the outside diameter.

Determine the ratio of the maximum twisting moment which may be applied to the hollow shaft to the maximum twisting moment which may be applied to the solid shaft. *Ans.* 2.37

362. A pulley is keyed to a solid shaft having a 4 in. diameter. The moment of inertia of the pulley and shaft about the axis of the shaft is 30,000 lb. ft.^{2} Determine the maximum torsional shear stress in the shaft when a twisting moment is applied to the pulley which gives it an angular speed of 300 r.p.m. in 10 sec., starting from rest.

363. Determine the maximum permissible twisting moment which may be applied to a hollow shaft, 16 in. outside diameter and 10 in. inside diameter, if the maximum allowable torsional shear stress of the material is 8000 psi. *Ans.* 454,200 ft.-lb.

364. If the shaft of Prob. 363 is made of steel, determine the angle of twist in a length of 10 ft.

365. A hollow steel shaft, 16 in. outside diameter and 12 in. inside diameter, transmits 12,000 h.p. with a maximum torsional shear stress of 7000 psi. Determine the speed of the shaft. *Ans.* 196 r.p.m.

366. The two-stage steel shaft is held rigidly at its ends as shown. The diameter of section **1** is 4 in. and the diameter of section **2** is 2 in. Determine the maximum torsional shear stress in each section of the shaft when the twisting moment of 10,000 ft.-lb. is applied. *Ans.* Section **1**: 9250 psi; **2**: 2320 psi.

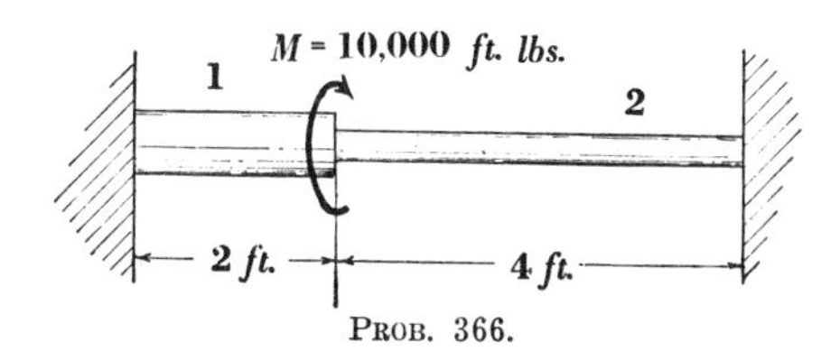

Prob. 366.

367. 60 h.p. is delivered to pulley *A*. 20 h.p. leaves the assembly at pulley *B*, and the remaining 40 h.p. at pulley *C*. The speed of the shaft is 600 r.p.m. The diameter of the steel shaft is 1½ in. Determine a) the maximum torsional shear stress in the shaft and b) the angle of twist, in degrees, between pulleys *A* and *C*.

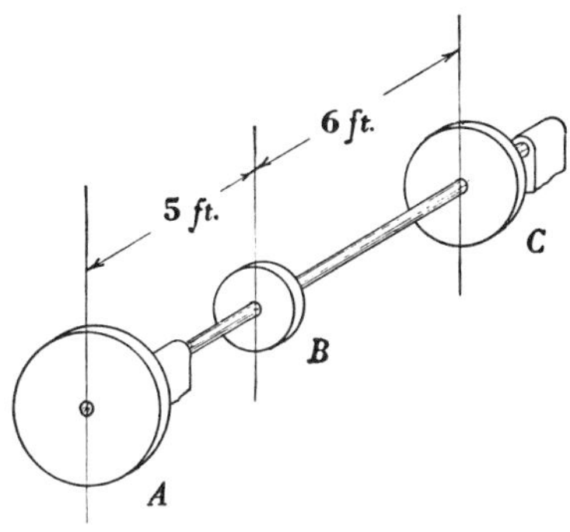

Prob. 367.

368. The shaft has a diameter of 2 in. and is held rigidly at its ends. Section **1** is made of aluminum; section **2** of copper; section **3** of steel, and the three sections are fastened securely to each other. Determine the twisting moment in each section when $M_1 = 1200$ ft.-lb. and $M_2 = 1600$ ft.-lb. are applied.

Ans. Section **1**: 626 ft.-lb.; **2**: 574 ft.-lb.; **3**: 2174 ft.-lb.

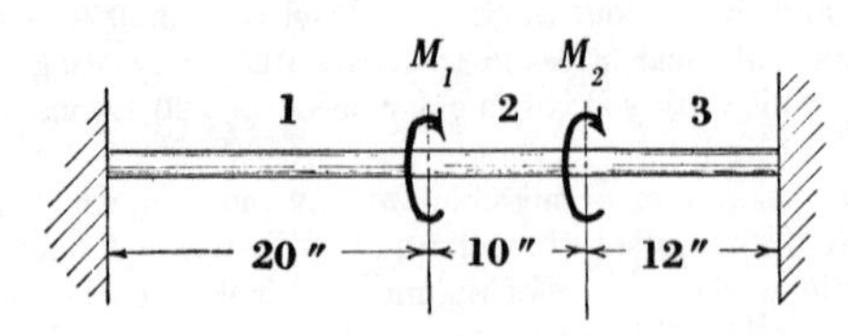

PROB. 368.

369. Determine the maximum torsional shear stress in each section of the shaft of Prob. 368.

370. A motor at M drives an automatic press at P, through the indicated train of gears. The motor supplies 200 h.p. at 1100 r.p.m. All shafts are made of steel. The pitch diameters of the gears are: A, 15 in.; B, 5 in.; C, 10 in.; D, 5 in. Diameter of shafts: M-A: 2 in.; B-C: 1.5 in.; D-P: 1.25 in. Determine

a) The maximum torsional shear stress in each shaft.
b) The total angle of twist from motor to press.

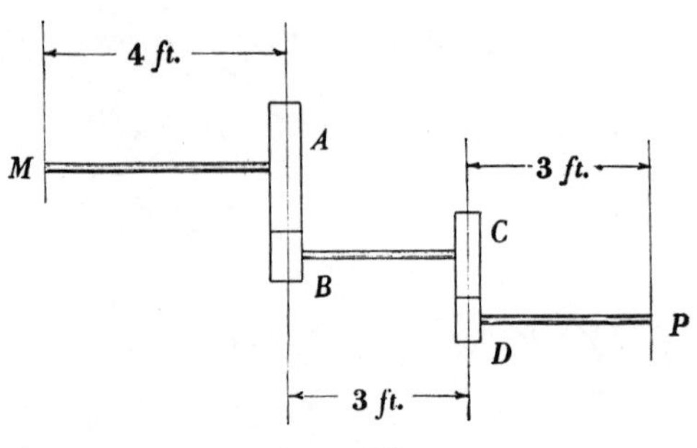

PROB. 370.

371. Pulleys A, B, and C are joined by solid steel shafting. The torque applied at the driving pulley A is $M_1 = 3540$ ft.-lb.; the torque delivered at pulley B is $M_2 = 2150$ ft.-lb.; and the torque delivered at pulley C is $M_3 = 1390$ ft.-lb. The maximum allowable torsional shear stress in the shafting is 8000 psi. Determine

a) The required diameters of the shafts in each section.

b) The angle of twist between pulleys A and C.

Ans. a) Diameter A-B = 3.00 in. Diameter B-C = 2.20 in.; b) 1.38°

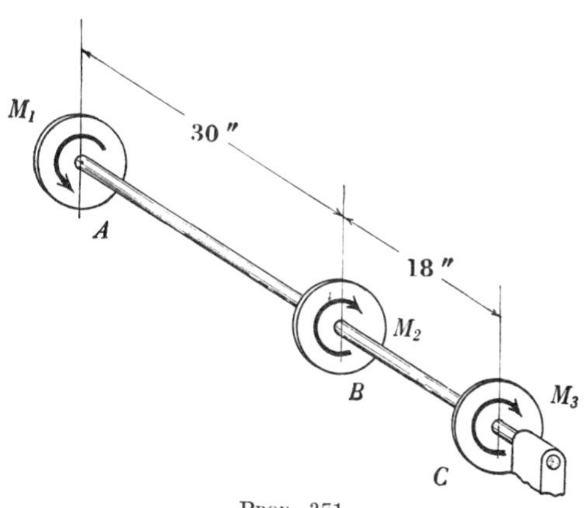

PROB. 371.

372. A solid shaft has a 2 in. diameter. If the maximum allowable torsional shear stress is 8000 psi, determine

a) The maximum twisting moment which may be applied to the shaft.

b) The percentage of weight reduction and the percentage of permissible twisting moment reduction, if a 1 in.-diameter concentric hole is bored in the shaft.

Ans. a) 1050 ft.-lb.; b) 25 per cent; 6.25 per cent

373. The main shaft, S, transmits 1500 h.p. at 2700 r.p.m. The diameter of the shaft is 2.4 in. Determine

a) The maximum torsional shear stress in the shaft.

b) The linear displacements of points at the tip of the propeller which is caused by the twisting of the main shaft. Assume that the propeller blades and small connecting shaft are rigid. The diameter of the propeller is 10 ft. and the gears reduce the speed of the propeller to 1000 r.p.m.

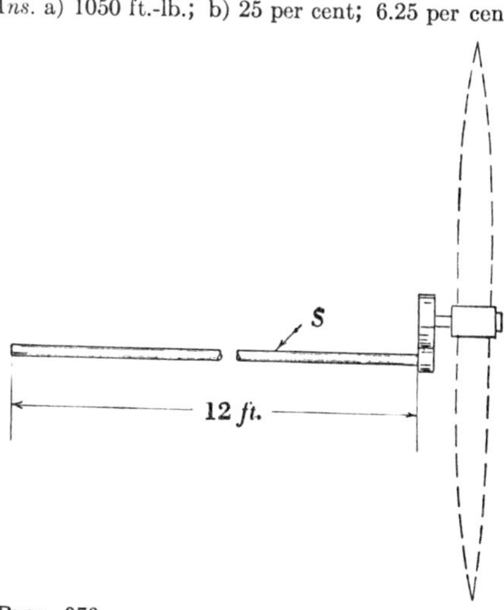

PROB. 373.

374. A machine drive consists of a disk D which drives a roller R by frictional contact. The shaft S is to be made of steel in which the torsional shear stress must not exceed 6000 psi. Determine the required diameter of S if the normal pressure between the disk D and roller R is 2000 lb., and the coefficient of friction is $\mu = 0.25$. The diameter of the roller is 8 in. *Ans.* 1.19 in.

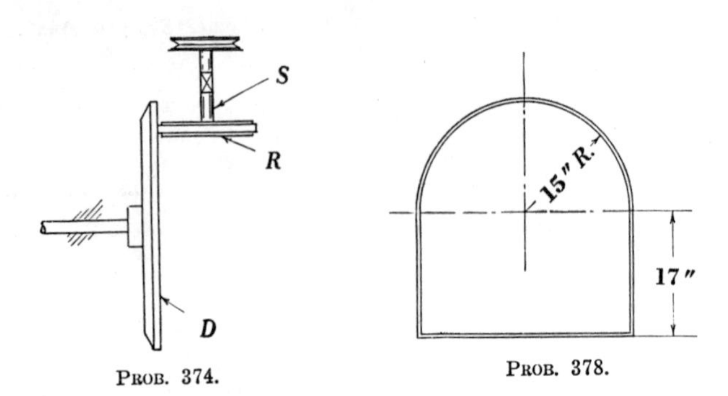

PROB. 374. PROB. 378.

375. A cast iron cylindrical bar, 2 in. in diameter, is subjected to a twisting moment. The maximum allowable tensile stress for the material is 3000 psi. Determine the maximum twisting moment which may be applied if only torsional shear stress is considered. *Ans.* 4720 in.-lb.

376. If a twisting moment of 400 ft.-lb. is applied to a steel bar, 2 in. in diameter, and the factor of safety based on the tensile strength of the material must be 10, determine the minimum tensile strength which the steel must have.

377. A thin hollow cylinder, having a diameter of 20 in. and a wall thickness of ⅛ in. is subjected to a twisting moment of 5000 ft.-lb. Determine the torsional shear stress in the wall. *Ans.* 764 psi.

378. If the torsional shear stress in the wall of the thin shell shown is not to exceed 600 psi, determine the maximum twisting moment which may be applied. The thickness of the wall is 0.1 in.

379. A close-coiled steel spring has 20 coils. The diameter of the spring is 6 in. and the diameter of the spring wire is 1 in. If a load of 1000 lb. is placed on the spring, determine the maximum shearing stress on the transverse section of the wire. *Ans.* 16,600 psi.

380. Determine the deflection of the spring of Prob. 379. *Ans.* 2.88 in.

381. If the spring described in Prob. 379 deflects 1 in. when a load P is applied, determine the magnitude of P.

382. A close-coiled helical spring is made of ½-in.-diameter wire. There are 12 turns, and the wire was wound on a 3-in.-diameter core. Determine the maximum load which may be placed on the spring if the allowable shear stress is 9000 psi.

383. Determine the deflection of the spring of Prob. 382 if a load of 100 lb. is placed on the spring and the material is copper.

CHAPTER VII

Column Theory

61. Columns. When, as in the case of the loaded bodies shown in Fig. 219, the loading acts parallel to the long axis, the members are placed in compression. If the member is long relative to the dimensions of the cross-section, it is called a *column*; if relatively short, it becomes a *compression block* or *strut*. This distinction in nomenclature is hardly important, but the influence of the difference between longitudinal and lateral dimensions produces effects which are so serious that we must investigate them with caution.

The influence of the dimensional relationship reveals itself when we consider the action of the loading force P in the two cases. The comparatively short block of Fig. 219 will fail by crushing or by shearing action on the planes of maximum shear. The long, slender column, however, will fail by bending, or buckling. This tendency may be noted if we examine the action which is suggested in Fig. 220. If a load which may have been intended to have its resultant act directly along the axis of the column is, as is usually true, slightly displaced from the central axis, a bending moment is set up in the column. We know,

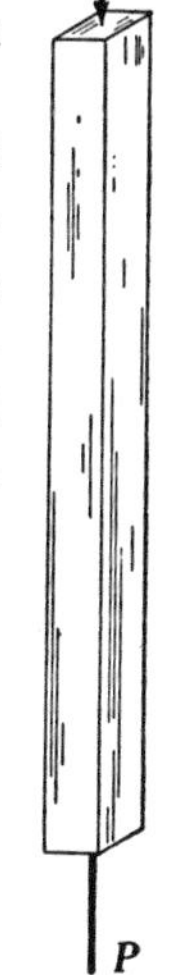

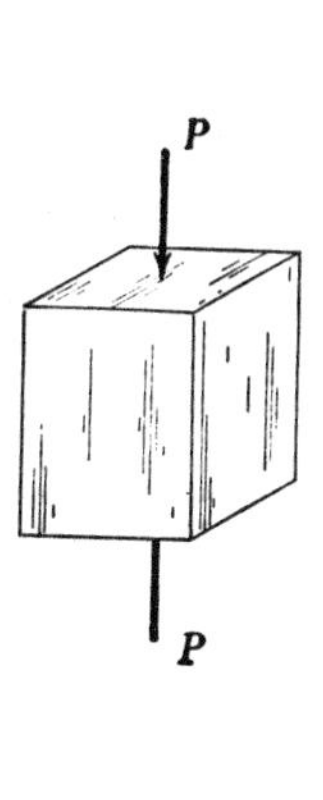

Fig. 219

Fig. 220.

from our previous discussions, that the bending moment will cause a deflection, x, at any section like A-A. The deflection will increase the moment arm of the bending moment and, in turn, the deflection, so that a growing and vicious circle of events will tend to cause extreme deflection, or collapse by *buckling*.

The introduction of bending moment need not be caused by an initial displacement of the line of action of the resultant load. Man does not produce in building structures, or in manufacturing the elements of structures like the rolled structural shapes, solids which are geometrically perfect. Lack of homogeneity is present in all material, as are deviations from the perfection of geometric lines. Initial stresses may also be present, which will cause deformation of the members. All of these departures from the ideal solid will tend to induce the bending moments which lead to eventual buckling.

The exact limit of dimensional relationship, which distinguishes the compression block (in which we need not fear buckling) from the column, can no more be assigned with certainty than can the limiting dimensional relationship of beams in the flexure theory or the wall–diameter ratio in the theory of the thin hollow cylinder. As in those cases, there is a limiting range, rather than an absolute limiting value, in which the validity of any theory may be questionable. It is usually true that a compression member may be considered a compression block—that is, free of buckling tendency when the length is not greater than ten times the least lateral dimension.

Since it is the relationship of dimensions which plays the most important role in the determination of column action, a ratio has been established which is used in all theories of column action, and which will sensitively reflect the relationship between longitudinal and lateral dimensions. This is the *slenderness ratio*, L/r, in which L represents the unsupported length of the column and r is the minimum radius of gyration of the cross-sectional area about a centroidal axis. The radius of gyration of an area is $\sqrt{I/A}$ and is therefore influenced not only by the amount of area but by the distribution of that area as reflected in the moment of inertia. When buckling occurs, a column will generally fail by bending about the axis yielding the least radius of gyration.

The classical theory which deals with column action was formulated by Euler, and is discussed in the following article. The succeeding articles are devoted to other design theories, which summarize the empirical data gathered by many observers, and expressed in the form of designers' equations.

62. Euler Column Theory. We start with the assumption that the direct compressive stress is negligible in the column and that the column must never be subjected to a load greater than that which would initiate the buckling action. Such a load is called the *critical load.*

The theory of bending action, first propounded by Euler, a Swiss mathematician of the eighteenth century, is restricted to columns which are governed by the following limitations:

1) The material is homogeneous and isotropic.
2) The cross-section of the column is uniform throughout its entire length.
3) The maximum stress is below the elastic limit of the material, which obeys Hooke's law.

We shall find that the results will be affected materially by the conditions under which loads are applied at the ends of the column. For example, a column which is fixed at its lower end and is free to bend elsewhere will yield different results than one which may pivot, such as one supported by pin joints. We shall, therefore, consider the end conditions individually. In each case, it will be our objective to determine the value of the critical load.

Case I. A Column Fixed at One End and Free to Bend at the Other (Fig. 221). A load P is applied at the centroid of the cross-section and is assumed to remain vertical. The method of attack upon the problem of buckling consists of displacing P, as shown, through a small distance a. The column is now subjected to bending moment, which causes deflection. If there is to be no buckling, the deflection must be very small—so small, in fact, that the total length of the column when bent is approximately equal to its original, or unloaded, length. The value of P which will just maintain this very small deflection, a, is the maximum load which may be applied without causing excessive deflection, or buckling. This maximum value of P is the critical load, which is evaluated in the following derivation.

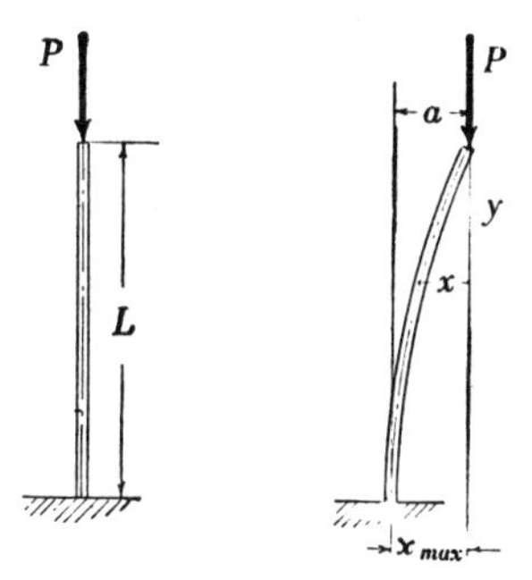

Fig. 221.

When the load P is applied, the bending moment at any distance, y, from the origin at the top of the column is

$$M = -Px$$

Applying equation (39), $$\frac{d^2x}{dy^2} = \frac{M}{EI} = \frac{-Px}{EI}$$

or $$\frac{d\left(\frac{dx}{dy}\right)}{dy} = \frac{-Px}{EI}$$

Multiplying both sides of the equation by dx,

$$\frac{dx}{dy}\,d\left(\frac{dx}{dy}\right) = \frac{-Px\,dx}{EI}$$

Integrating,

$$\frac{\left(\frac{dx}{dy}\right)^2}{2} = \frac{-Px^2}{2EI} + C_1$$

When $y = L$, $\qquad \frac{dx}{dy} = 0 \qquad$ and $\qquad x = x_{max.} = a$

Then $\qquad C_1 = \frac{Pa^2}{2EI}$

and $\qquad \frac{dx}{dy} = \sqrt{\frac{-Px^2}{EI} + \frac{Pa^2}{EI}} = \sqrt{\frac{P}{EI}}\ \sqrt{a^2 - x^2}$

If we now separate the variables,

$$\frac{dx}{\sqrt{a^2 - x^2}} = \sqrt{\frac{P}{EI}}\,dy$$

Now, integrating,

$$\sin^{-1}\frac{x}{a} = \sqrt{\frac{P}{EI}}\,y + C_2$$

When $y = 0$, $\qquad x = 0 \qquad$ and $\qquad C_2 = 0$

Then $\qquad \sin^{-1}\frac{x}{a} = \sqrt{\frac{P}{EI}}\,y$

and $\qquad \sin\sqrt{\frac{P}{EI}}\,y = \frac{x}{a}$

$$x = a\sin\sqrt{\frac{P}{EI}}\,y$$

This is the equation of the elastic curve of the column, in terms of the maximum deflection, and we note that the curve is a sine curve.

When $x = x_{max.} = a$, $\qquad y = L$

$$\frac{x_{max.}}{a} = 1 = \sin\sqrt{\frac{P}{EI}}L$$

$$\sin\sqrt{\frac{PL^2}{EI}} = 1$$

$$\sqrt{\frac{PL^2}{EI}} = \frac{\pi}{2} \text{ or } \frac{3\pi}{2} \text{ or } \frac{5\pi}{2} \cdots$$

Since we are determining the least value of P which will cause buckling,

$$\sqrt{\frac{PL^2}{EI}} = \frac{\pi}{2}; \quad \frac{PL^2}{EI} = \frac{\pi^2}{4}$$

and

$$\mathbf{P = \frac{\pi^2 EI}{4L^2}} \tag{83}$$

This is the value of P which will just maintain the deflection a, holding the sine curve in balance to form the elastic curve of the beam, and is therefore the critical load. It should be noted that this is an *ultimate*, not an allowable load.

Case II. Column Fixed at Both Ends (Fig. 222). If the ends of the column are rigidly restrained, the tangents to the elastic curve at both ends will be vertical. This condition is fulfilled by the presence of the indicated end couples. The elastic curve will be symmetrical about the central axis 0 − 0. There will be points of inflection in such a column at sections A and B, located at the quarter points, as shown.

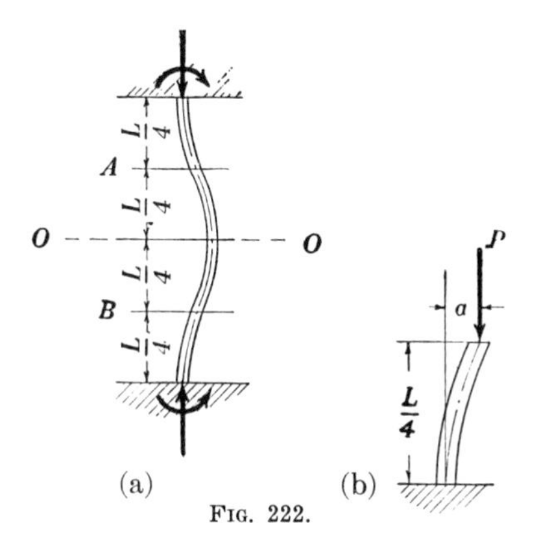

Fig. 222.

The bottom quarter of the column is shown, isolated as a free body in Fig. 222-b. The deflection of the point of inflection from the central axis is called a. This short column is equivalent, in its loading, to the column discussed in case I, and will behave in identical fashion to that column.

Applying the results of the previous derivation as expressed in equation (83) to a column of length $L/4$, we find, upon substituting $L/4$ for the term L of that equation, that the critical load is now

$$P = \frac{\pi^2 EI}{4(L/4)^2}$$

$$= \mathbf{\frac{4\pi^2 EI}{L^2}} \tag{84}$$

Case III. Column Free to Rotate at Both Ends (Fig. 223). The column is now supported at its ends by rounded ends, or frictionless pin joints, and the tangents to the elastic curve at the ends are free to turn in any direction.

The elastic curve will be symmetrical about the central level O-O. If the top half of the column is isolated as a free body (Fig. 223-b), we note that we have a column length $L/2$ possessing the qualifications of that of equation (83). Now the critical load will be

$$P = \frac{\pi^2 EI}{4(L/2)^2} = \frac{\pi^2 EI}{L^2} \tag{85}$$

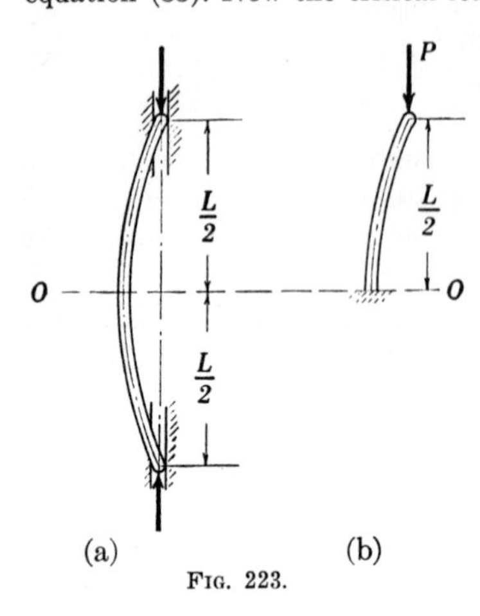

FIG. 223.

Case IV. Column with One End Fixed and One End Free to Rotate (Fig. 224). While the top of the column is free to rotate, it is restrained from moving sideways by the indicated horizontal force. In this case, the point of inflection lies at section A-A, located at distance y_1, which is approximately equal to $L/3$, from the bottom, or fixed, end.

The isolated free body, shown in Fig. 224-b, is therefore a fixed-end column approximately $L/3$ long. Applying equation (83), the critical load is

$$P = \frac{\pi^2 EI}{4(L/3)^2} = \frac{9}{4}\frac{\pi^2 EI}{L^2} \quad \text{approximately} \tag{86}$$

When columns are designed on the basis of the Euler equations derived above and subjected to test loading, it is found that the experimental results are consistent with the values given by the equations for slenderness ratios which are greater than a certain limiting value. Let us now determine the limiting value which bounds the range of usefulness of the equations.

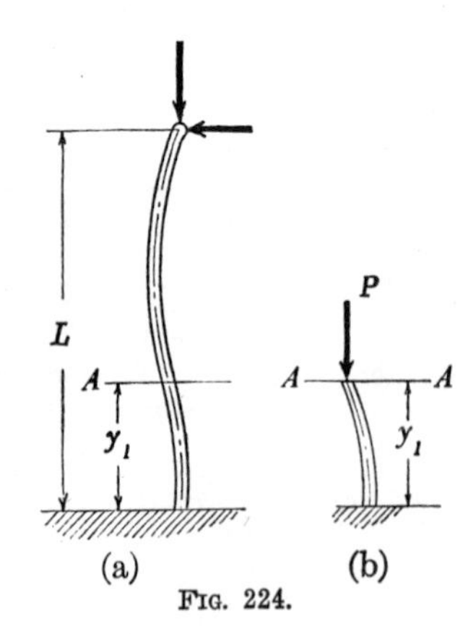

FIG. 224.

In the following discussion the critical stress, $s_{CR.}$, is used. This is defined as the quotient obtained by dividing the critical load P, obtained in any of the above cases, by the cross-sectional area of the column A, or

$$s_{CR.} = \frac{P}{A}$$

In deriving the Euler equations we have assumed that the material obeyed Hooke's law. The limiting value of stress is, therefore, the proportional limit, $s_{P.L.}$, and that limit is the maximum permissible value of $s_{CR.}$

For the case represented by equation (83), the critical load is

$$P = \frac{\pi^2 EI}{4L^2}$$

Then

$$s_{CR.} = s_{P.L.} = \frac{P}{A} = \frac{\pi^2 EI}{4L^2 A}$$

Since the radius of gyration $r = \sqrt{\frac{I}{A}}$

$$s_{P.L.} = \frac{\pi^2 E r^2}{4L^2}$$

$$\frac{L^2}{r^2} = \frac{\pi^2 E}{4\, s_{P.L.}}$$

and

$$\frac{L}{r} = \sqrt{\frac{\pi^2 E}{4\, s_{P.L.}}} = \frac{\pi}{2}\sqrt{\frac{E}{s_{P.L.}}}$$

This is the limiting, or lowest, value of slenderness ratio for which equation (83) may be used.

In a steel column, fixed at one end and free to bend at the other, having a proportional limit $s_{P.L.} = 30{,}000$ psi, and a modulus of elasticity $E = 30 \times 10^6$ psi, the limit of slenderness ratio will be

$$\frac{L}{r} = \frac{\pi}{2}\sqrt{\frac{E}{s_{P.L.}}} = \frac{\pi}{2}\sqrt{\frac{30 \times 10^6}{30 \times 10^3}} = 49.6$$

For columns which have pin-jointed ends we use equation (85), and

$$P = \frac{\pi^2 EI}{L^2}$$

Then

$$s_{CR.} = s_{P.L.} = \frac{P}{A} = \frac{\pi^2 EI}{L^2 A}$$

and

$$\frac{L}{r} = \pi\sqrt{\frac{E}{s_{P.L.}}}$$

If we again introduce the values of $s_{P.L.} = 30{,}000$ psi and $E = 30 \times 10^6$ psi, the limiting value of slenderness ratio is

$$\frac{L}{r} = \pi\sqrt{\frac{E}{s_{P.L.}}} = \pi\sqrt{\frac{30 \times 10^6}{30 \times 10^3}} = 99.2$$

The influence of slenderness ratio may be noted in Fig. 225, in which the critical stress P/A is plotted against slenderness ratio in a pin-ended column made of steel.

The slenderness ratio may be controlled in design by adjusting the radius of gyration for a column of fixed length. The most efficient use of the material, as in the case of beams, demands that cross-sectional areas be made of such shape that the greatest moment of inertia is realized. In the beam, the axis about which bending will take place can generally be predicted, and the material is arranged to yield the greatest moment of inertia about that axis.

In the column, buckling usually takes place about the axis having the least moment of inertia and least radius of gyration. A column should be

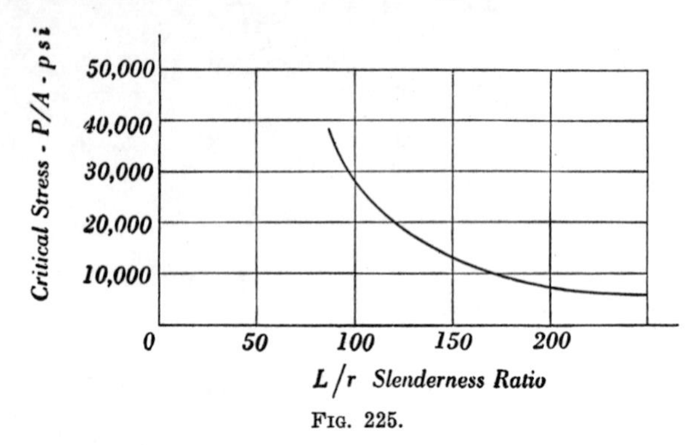

FIG. 225.

equally strong in all directions and, in design, cross-sectional areas are employed which yield uniform radii of gyration about all axes. The hollow cylinder is the most efficient of all cross-sectional areas in columns.

63. Additional Column Design Bases. A great deal of attention has been devoted to the complex behavior of column action. Most of our present design is based upon empirical or pseudo-rational approaches that have resulted in equations which are satisfactory in that they afford the designer a working technique of attack. These equations rest, for the most part, upon the fitting of an equation to the results of a large number of experimental tests. They involve liberal factors of safety, recognize the menace of increase in slenderness ratio, and may be used with confidence because of the extensive amount of actual observation of which they are the formulated expression.

These empirical formulas are grouped into two basic classifications—straight-line equations, and parabolic equations.

Straight-Line Equations. This group of equations assumes that the relation between the critical stress in the column and the slenderness ratio may be expressed with a reasonable degree of accuracy in the form

$$s_{\text{CR.}} = C_1 - C_2\frac{L}{r}$$

in which $s_{\text{CR.}}$ is the critical stress, or normal stress, on the right section of the column, which must not be exceeded; C_1 and C_2 are constants dependent upon the physical properties of the material, and L/r is the slenderness ratio, with L the unsupported length of the column and r the least radius of gyration of the column section.

The straight-line formula arose from observation, particularly by Johnson in 1884, that plotted test results indicated that failure of columns obeyed Euler's equation for large slenderness ratios, and followed a straight-line tangent to Euler's curve for small slenderness ratios.

Various building codes and organizations have established constants which may be used in the straight-line type of formula.

The most widely used of these formulas for steel columns is that of the Chicago Building Code.

$$s_W = 16{,}000 - 70\frac{L}{r} \tag{87}$$

in which s_W is the working or design stress, rather than the critical stress. This formula may be used for column slenderness ratios greater than 30 and less than 120 for main load-carrying members, and slenderness ratios as high as 150 for secondary, or lateral-bracing, members. For slenderness ratios below 30, $s_W = 14{,}000$ psi is to be used.

The straight-line formula also finds use in designs employing other materials than steel.

For example, in designing columns made of aluminum alloys the Structural Handbook of the A'uminum Company of America gives a formula for each aluminum alloy. Two typical examples follow. These are expressed in terms of the "effective slenderness ratio" KL/r, in which the term K is a term introduced to reflect the different end conditions. $K = 0.5$ for columns which have both ends fixed; $K = 0.7$ when one end is fixed and the other pinned; $K = 1.0$ when both ends are pinned; and $K = 2.0$ when one end is fixed and the other end free.

Two of the most widely used aluminum alloys are 14S and 61S. Their properties vary with the heat treatment to which they are subjected.

Straight-line formulas in these cases are used for slenderness ratios below certain values, and parabolic formulas above those values. In the following table, s represents the ultimate column strength, and must be reduced by a suitable factor of safety.

TABLE V

Aluminum Alloy	*Straight-line Formula*	*Maximum Effective Slenderness Ratio*
14S–T4	$s = 43{,}800 - 350\ KL/r$	83
14S–T6	$s = 78{,}000 - 830\ KL/r$	63
61S–T4	$s = 23{,}200 - 134\ KL/r$	109
61S–T6	$s = 48{,}000 - 400\ KL/r$	77

Parabolic Equations. The parabolic formulas, in the case of steel columns, have quite generally superseded the straight-line formulas. Such equations were first proposed by Gordon and Rankine, Scottish engineers of the nineteenth century. The derivation of the Gordon-Rankine formula has a pseudo-rational basis, which follows.

If P is the maximum permissible load which may be placed upon a column, s_W the working or allowable stress, e the maximum deflection of the column under load P, y the distance from the neutral axis to the extreme or outside fiber of the section, and A the cross-sectional area, we substitute, in equation (54), as follows

$$s_W = \frac{P}{A} + \frac{P\,e\,y}{I}$$

The moment of inertia, I, is equal to Ar^2, in which the least radius of gyration, r, is used, and

$$s_W = \frac{P}{A} + \frac{P\,e\,y}{Ar^2} = \frac{P}{A}\left(1 + \frac{e\,y}{r^2}\right)$$

e is unknown, and the assumption is made that it will vary with L^2/y, which is only approximately true. Then

$$e = \frac{cL^2}{y}$$

where c is the constant of proportionality between e and L^2/y.

Now, substituting this value of e,

$$s_W = \frac{P}{A}\left(1 + \frac{cL^2}{r^2}\right) \tag{88}$$

With equation (88) as a background, a number of current formulas have been developed. Some typical ones are given in Table VI to illustrate their form.

A somewhat different form is that of Alcoa, which recommends, for all aluminum alloys, in columns having slenderness ratios greater than those given in Table V on page 343 the following equation:

$$s = \frac{102 \times 10^6}{(KL/r)^2} \tag{98}$$

The value of stress, s, given in this equation is the *ultimate stress*. The values of K which are to be used are those given for the straight-line aluminum-column formulas on page 343.

Timber Columns (rectangular section). The U.S. Forest Products Laboratory, in collaboration with such engineering groups as A.S.T.M.,

TABLE VI. PARABOLIC FORMULAS FOR STRUCTURAL STEEL COLUMNS

Source		*Slenderness Ratio Limits*	s_w, psi	*Eq. No.*
New York City Building Code		$60 < \frac{L}{r} < 120$	$\dfrac{18{,}000}{1 + \frac{1}{18{,}000}\frac{L^2}{r^2}}$	**(89)**
New York City Building Code		$\frac{L}{r} < 60$	15,000	
A.I.S.C.		$\frac{L}{r} < 120$	$17{,}000 - 0.485\frac{L^2}{r^2}$	**(90)**
A.I.S.C.		$120 < \frac{L}{r} < 200$	Use Equation (89)	
A.S.C.E. (high-strength steels)			$\dfrac{24{,}000}{1 + \frac{1}{9000}\frac{L^2}{r^2}}$	**(91)**
A.S.S.H.O.	Riveted ends		$15{,}000 - \frac{1}{4}\frac{L^2}{r^2}$	**(92)**
	Pinned ends		$15{,}000 - \frac{1}{3}\frac{L^2}{r^2}$	**(93)**
A.R.A (structural steel)	Riveted ends		$17{,}000 - 0.35\frac{L^2}{r^2}$	**(94)**
	Pinned ends		$17{,}000 - 0.47\frac{L^2}{r^2}$	**(95)**
A.R.A. (high-strength steel)	Riveted ends		$20{,}000 - 0.46\frac{L^2}{r^2}$	**(96)**
	Pinned ends		$20{,}000 - 0.61\frac{L^2}{r^2}$	**(97)**

has developed standards (ASTM, 1937, D245–37) in which design bases for wooden columns are given.

Short Columns (those whose unsupported length, L, is not more than 11 times the least cross-sectional dimension, d). Allowable unit stresses are given directly in the tables developed by the Forest Products Laboratory, and Table VII gives some of these values for the most commonly used timbers.

TABLE VII. STRUCTURAL TIMBER

	Allowable Comp. Stress, Parallel to Grain, psi	*Modulus of Elasticity E, psi* $\times 10^{-6}$
Ash, white	1400	1.5
Birch	1400	1.6
Cypress	1300	1.2
Fir, Douglas	1400	1.6
Hemlock, Eastern	870	1.1
Maple, hard	1400	1.6
Oak	1300	1.5
Pine, Southern Longleaf	1350	1.6
Redwood	1300	1.2
Spruce, Eastern	975	1.2

Intermediate-length Columns (ratio of unsupported length to least dimension, L/d, is greater than 10). Equation (99), which follows is a parabolic-type formula of the fourth power, which is recommended. The allowable unit stress is

$$s_W = s\left[1 - \frac{1}{3}\left(\frac{L}{Kd}\right)^4\right] \tag{99}$$

where s is the allowable unit compressive stress, parallel to the grain, as given in the table, and K is given in the following expression:

$$K = \frac{\pi}{2}\sqrt{\frac{E}{6s}}$$

where E is the modulus of elasticity of the timber in bending. Equation (99) is to be used in columns having a ratio L/d greater than 10, and less than the value of L/d which makes $s_W = 2s/3$. This value occurs when $L/d = K$.

Long Columns (those which have a slenderness ratio L/d which is greater than K and less than 50. The upper limiting value in any rectangular wooden column is 50). Equation (100), which follows, is an Euler-type formula [equation (33)] in which a factor of safety of 3 has been introduced.

$$s_W = \frac{\pi^2 E}{36L^2/d^2} \tag{100}$$

The timbers used in structural practice vary greatly in their properties, with such factors as their grade and moisture conditions. The value of allowable stresses discussed above should, therefore, be used with caution and are intended only to indicate the design basis of wooden columns. The ASTM specifications quoted should be consulted for more detailed information.

PROBLEMS

384–390, inclusive. In each case, determine the slenderness ratio of a column of the indicated cross-section and unsupported length L.

384. A tee-section of the indicated dimensions. $L = 10$ ft. *Ans.* 73.1.

385. A 2 in. × 4 in. rectangle. $L = 4$ ft.

386. An angle section of the indicated dimensions. $L = 9$ ft. *Ans.* 103.

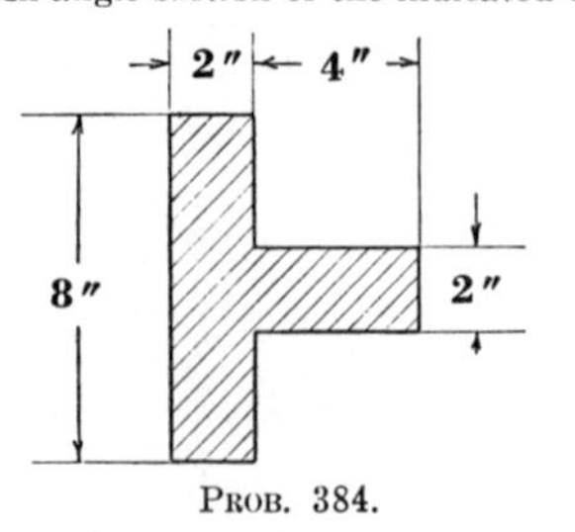

PROB. 384.

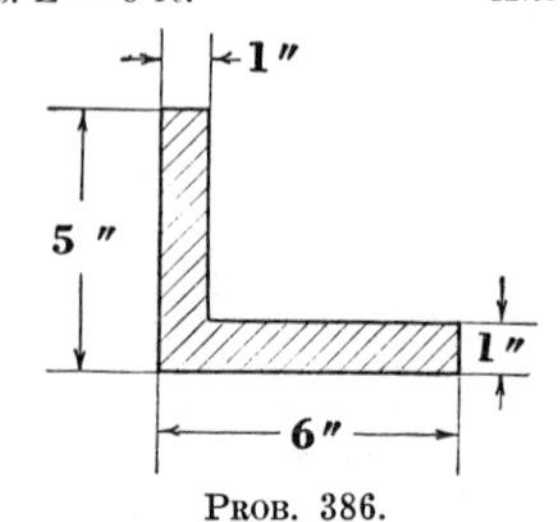

PROB. 386.

387. A 3-in. diameter circle. $L = 6$ ft.

388. A hollow circle, 20 in. outside diameter, 16 in. inside diameter. $L = 12$ ft.

389. An 18 in. × 96 lb./ft. Wide-Flange beam. $L = 18$ ft. *Ans.* 79.7.

390. A 12 in. × 50 lb./ft. American Standard I-beam. $L = 15$ ft.

391. If two triangles of the indicated dimensions are used as a column section, determine the distance a such that the column section will have the same slenderness ration about axes X-X and Y-Y.

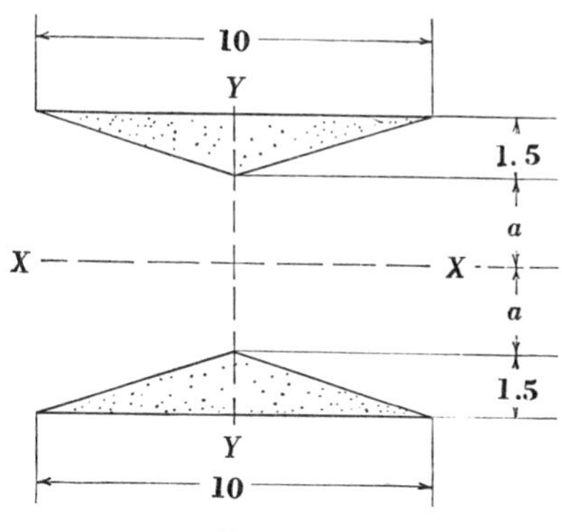

Prob. 391.

392. A 14 in. × 30 lb./ft. Wide-Flange steel column is fixed at one end and is free to bend at the other. $L = 15$ ft. Determine the critical load P, using Euler's formula. *Ans.* 40,000 lb.

393. If the column of Prob. 392 has both ends fixed, determine the critical load P, using Euler's formula.

394. If the column of Prob. 392 is supported by pin joints at both ends, determine the critical load P, using Euler's formula.

395. Determine the minimum slenderness ratio for which Euler's formula may be used in a column which is pinned at both ends. The column is made of steel which has a proportional limit of 36,000 psi. *Ans.* 90.6.

396. Determine the minimum length of a 12 in. × 50 lb./ft. Wide-Flange steel column, having both ends fixed, for which Euler's formula may be used. The proportional limit of the steel is 30,000 psi. *Ans.* 32.4 ft.

397. Select the lightest Wide-Flange section for a column which is fixed at one end and free to bend at the other, when an axial load of 90,000 lb. is applied. The factor of safety is to be 4. The unsupported length of the column is 20 ft. Use Euler formula. *Ans.* 18 in. × 124 lb./ft.

398. If the column of Prob. 397 is fixed at both ends, select the lightest Wide-Flange section which may be used under the same conditions to note the effect of end restraint in saving of steel.

399. A 12 in. × 50 lb./ft. Wide-Flange steel column is 18 ft. long. Determine the maximum axial load which may be placed on the column using the Chicago Building Code formula [equation (87)]. *Ans.* 122,000 lb.

400. Determine the maximum axial load which may be placed on the column of Prob. 399 if (a) the New York Building Code formula is used, (b) the A.I.S.C. formula is used.

401. An aluminum column, made of 14S–T4 alloy, has both ends fixed. The column is an 8 in. × 7.30 lb./ft. standard I-beam. If the factor of safety is to be 2, determine the maximum allowable axial load. Length = 10 ft. *Ans.* 53,900 lb.

402. If the length of the aluminum column of Prob. 401 is increased to 15 ft. determine the maximum allowable load. *Ans.* 24,900 lb.

403. If an axial load of 45,000 lb. is placed on an aluminum column made of 14S–T4 alloy, determine the factor of safety. The column is 12 ft. long, and is made of an 8 in. × 11.04 lb./ft. Wide-Flange beam. Both ends are pinned.

404. A steel column section consists of four 4 × 4 × ½-in. angles, riveted together as shown. The length of the column is 20 ft. Using the A.I.S.C. formula, determine the safe axial load with a factor of safety of 1.8. (See Table XII—Appendix for angle properties.)

PROB. 404.

405. An aluminum machine part is a rectangular prism, 1 in. × 2 in. × 10 in. long. The part has both ends pinned and is subjected to column action. The alloy is 61S–T6. If the factor of safety is to be 10, determine the maximum axial thrust to which the part may be subjected. *Ans.* 6830 lb.

406. If the length of the aluminum machine part of Prob 405 is increased to 24 in. determine the maximum axial thrust.

407. A 4 in. × 6 in. oak timber, 8 ft. long, is used as a column. Determine the allowable unit stress in the column. *Ans.* 714 psi.

408. Determine the maximum load which may be placed on a Douglas fir column, 4 in. × 4 in. × 10 ft. long.

64. Eccentrically Loaded Columns. The occurrence of eccentric, rather than axial, loading on columns is encountered frequently in practice. This type of loading may be intentional, as when supporting brackets fastened to the column carry the loads. Or the eccentricity may be present without any intent on the part of the designer—in fact, some unavoidable eccentricity is probably always present. Initial kinks or bends, initial stress, lack of homogeneity in the material, combine to effect a condition which is equivalent to eccentricity of loading.

A short column, eccentrically loaded, is shown in Fig. 226-a. The load P is eccentric to both principal centroidal axes 1–1 and 2–2. The resolution of P into a force and a pair of couples is indicated in Fig. 226-b. P has been resolved into the equivalent system—a force P passing through the centroid, a couple Pe_2 which causes bending about axis 2–2, and a couple Pe_1 which causes bending about axis 1–1.

The normal stress on a right section of the column may be determined by superposition, that is, by considering the individual normal stresses and adding them to obtain the combined effect.

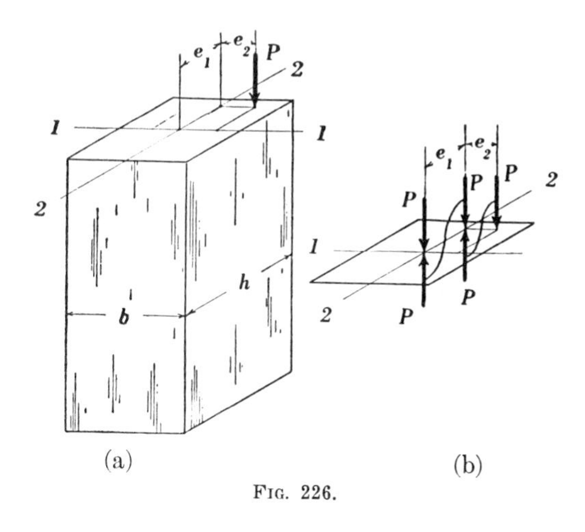

FIG. 226.

We first consider the normal stress s_1 due to the axial force P,

$$s_1 = \frac{P}{A}$$

which will be a compressive stress.

Since axes 1–1 and 2–2 are principal axes, the maximum bending stress resulting from bending moment Pe_2 will be

$$s_2 = \frac{P\,e_2\,b/2}{I_{2-2}}$$

which will be compressive in all fibers to the right of axis 2–2 and tensile in all fibers to the left of the axis.

Similarly, the maximum bending stress caused by bending moment Pe_1 will be

$$s_3 = \frac{P\,e_1\,h/2}{I_{1-1}}$$

which will be compressive in all fibers behind axis 1–1 and tensile in all fibers in front of the axis.

For proper addition of these normal stresses, Fig. 227 indicates the state of stress in each of the corner fibers. The maximum normal stress will be that which is present in the corner fiber nearest the load that has received compression from each of the three sources. The stress in that fiber will be

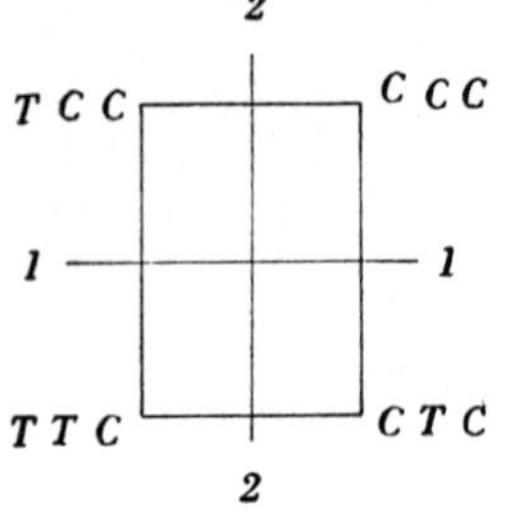

FIG. 227.

$$s_{\text{TOTAL}} = s_1 + s_2 + s_3 = \frac{P}{A} + \frac{P\,e_2\,b}{2I_{2-2}} + \frac{P\,e_1\,h}{2I_{1-1}} \qquad (101)$$

The *neutral* axis of the section may be located by noting that it is a locus of the points of zero stress.

Fibers lying in axis 2–2 (Fig. 226) will receive a stress from the axial load P and from the bending moment Pe_1. They will not be stressed by the bending moment Pe_2, for the axis 2–2 is the neutral axis of bending when only bending moment Pe_2 is considered. Then one point of the neutral axis of the column may be located by determining where the compressive stress P/A is balanced by the tensile stress resulting from bending about axis 1–1. This will be point m of Fig. 228. If the distance from centroid c to point m is called y,

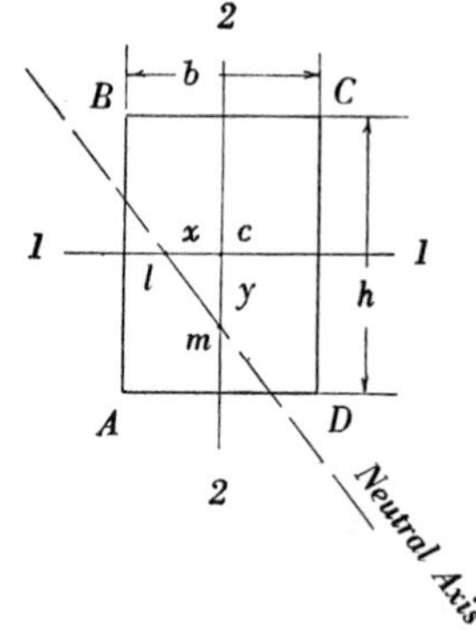

FIG. 228.

$$\frac{P}{A} = \frac{P\,e_1\,y}{I_{1-1}}$$

and

$$y = \frac{I_{1-1}}{A\,e_1} = \frac{(r_{1-1})^2}{e_1} \qquad (102)$$

where r_{1-1} is the radius of gyration relative to axis 1–1.

Point l, another point on the neutral axis, will be located at distance x from c. Now x may be determined by noting that we are again seeking a point of zero stress, and that the compressive stress P/A must now be balanced by tensile stress caused by bending about axis 2–2.

$$\frac{P}{A} = \frac{P\,e_2\,x}{I_{2-2}}$$

and

$$x = \frac{I_{2-2}}{A\,e_2} = \frac{(r_{2-2})^2}{e_2} \qquad (103)$$

where r_{2-2} is the radius of gyration relative to axis 2–2.

Since the normal stresses are uniformly varying, the neutral axis will be a straight line, passing through points l and m.

Illustrative Example. The rectangular short column shown in Fig. 229 is subjected to vertical loads of 1000 and 3000 lb., located at points *a* and *b*, respectively. We are to determine a) the maximum normal stress on a right section of the column and b) the location of the neutral axis. The weight of the column itself is assumed to be negligible.

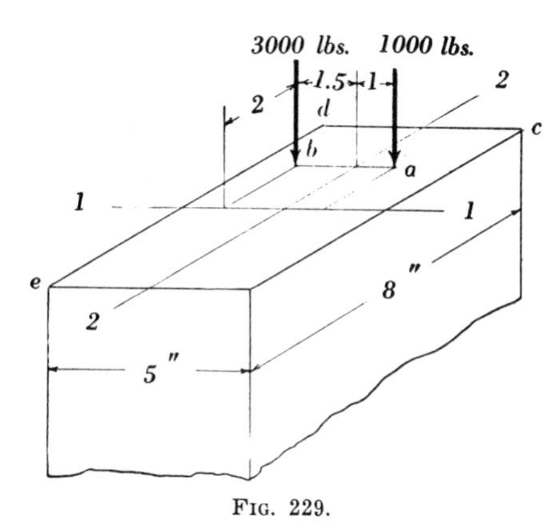

Fig. 229.

Part a) The axial stress will be

$$s_1 = \frac{P}{A} = \frac{3000 + 1000}{40} = 100 \text{ psi (compression)}$$

The bending moment which causes bending about axis 1–1 will be

$$M_1 = 3000 \times 2 + 1000 \times 2 = 8000 \text{ in.-lb.}$$

and the maximum bending stress caused by M_1 will be

$$s_2 = \frac{8000 \times 4}{5 \times (8)^3/12}$$
$$= 150 \text{ psi (compression in fibers in } cd)$$

The moment which causes bending about axis 2–2 will be

$$M_2 = 3000 \times 1.5 - 1000 \times 1 = 3500 \text{ in.-lb.}$$

and the maximum bending stress produced by M_2 will be

$$s_3 = \frac{3500 \times 2.5}{8 \times (5)^3/12}$$
$$= 105 \text{ psi (compression in fibers in } de)$$

The maximum normal stress will occur at corner d, where its value will be

$$s = s_1 + s_2 + s_3 = 100 + 150 + 105$$
$$= 355 \text{ psi (compression)}$$

Part b) The neutral axis will be located by determining its intersection with axes 1–1 and 2–2.

Axis 1–1. $$s_1 = \frac{P}{A} = 100 \text{ psi (compression)}$$

In fibers which lie to the right of axis 2–2 the bending stress resulting from M_2 will be tensile, and will have magnitude

$$s_2 = \frac{3500x}{8 \times (5)^3/12} = 42x$$

Axis 1–1 is the neutral axis of bending caused by M_1, and

$$s_1 = s_2$$
$$100 = 42x$$
$$x = 2.38 \text{ in.}$$

Axis 2–2. $$s_1 = \frac{P}{A} = 100 \text{ psi (compression)}$$

In fibers which lie in front of axis 1–1, the bending stress produced by M_1 will be tensile, and will have a magnitude of

$$s_3 = \frac{8000y}{5 \times (8)^3/12} = 37.5y$$

Then $$37.5y = 100$$
$$y = 2.67 \text{ in.}$$

The neutral axis is shown in Fig. 230.

The region of the area of Figs. 226 and 228 which lies upward and to the right of the neutral axis will be in compression, while the region to the left and downward will be in tension. The corner of the rectangular section indicated as A (Fig. 228) is the most remote fiber from the neutral axis in the tension region, and the stress at A will be the maximum tensile stress on the area. In the design of such compression members as columns, a condition frequently imposed on the design, demands that no fiber of the section be left in tension.

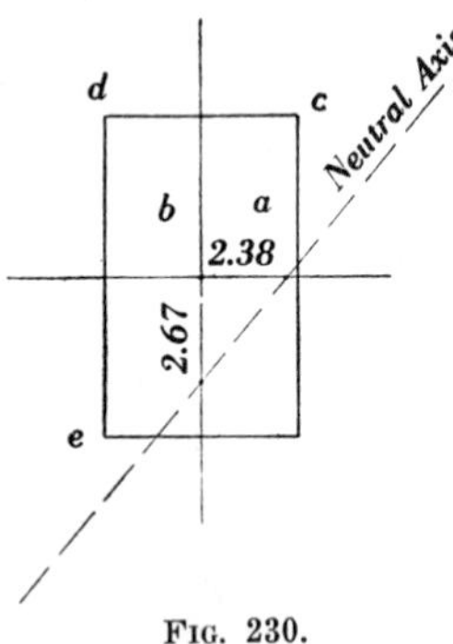

FIG. 230.

This condition will be satisfied if the sum of the tensile stresses at corner A (Fig. 228) is made equal to the compressive direct stress P/A.

Then $$\frac{P}{A} = \frac{P\,e_2 b/2}{h\,b^3/12} + \frac{P\,e_1 h/2}{b\,h^3/12}$$
$$= \frac{6P\,e_2}{h\,b^2} + \frac{6P\,e_1}{b\,h^2}$$

The area is equal to bh, and

$$\frac{P}{A} = \frac{6Pe_2}{Ab} + \frac{6Pe_1}{Ah}$$

or $$1 = \frac{6e_2}{b} + \frac{6e_1}{h}$$

This is the equation of a straight line which intersects axis 1–1 at $e_1 = h/6$ and $e_2 = b/6$ (Fig. 231). e_1 and e_2 are the eccentric distances from axes 1–1 and 2–2, respectively, to the resultant load. If, then, the resultant load is placed within the shaded triangle *ghi*, there will be no tensile stress in any fiber of the section.

The same considerations may be used to insure that no tensile stress will arise at corners *B*, *C*, and *D*. If the eccentric load is placed within the rhombus comprising the four triangles like *ghi*, there will be no tensile stress in any fiber. The shaded area is called the *kern* or kernel of the column section.

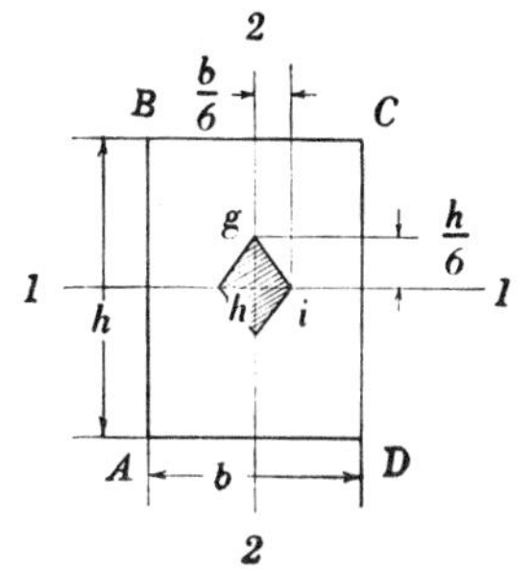

Fig. 231.

The diamond-shaped area which we have just found to be the kern will apply only to a rectangular section; other column sections will have kerns of different shapes.

We have, in this discussion of the short columns under eccentric loading, depended upon the flexure theory to furnish the evaluation of bending stress. As the slenderness ratio increases, buckling failure becomes imminent, and column-action theory must be recognized.

A typical designer's method of attack consists of superimposing direct stress P/A upon column action by introducing column formulas in appraising the bending stress. For example, any eccentric load P may be resolved into an axial force at the centroid and a resultant bending moment $P \times e$, where e is the eccentricity of the load from the centroid.

The column action is recognized by modifying equation (89) as follows:

$$\frac{P}{A} = \frac{s}{1 + \frac{1}{18{,}000}\frac{L^2}{r^2}}$$

Then

$$s = \frac{P}{A} + \frac{P}{A}\left(\frac{1}{18{,}000}\frac{L^2}{r^2}\right)$$

The first term is the direct stress and the second term is the column action. The equation is now further modified, in eccentric loading, to account for the bending stress due to moment $P\,e$, by adding the $M\,y/\,I$ term of equation (34), and

$$s = \frac{P}{A} + \frac{P}{A}\left(\frac{1}{18{,}000}\frac{L^2}{r^2}\right) + \frac{P\,e\,y}{A\,r_0^2}$$

In the third term, y is the distance from the centroidal axis perpendicular to eccentricity e to the most remote fiber, and r_0 is the radius of gyration of the cross-sectional area relative to that axis. The quotient P/A is common to all terms, and

$$s = \frac{P}{A}\left(1 + \frac{1}{18{,}000}\frac{L^2}{r^2} + \frac{ey}{r_0^2}\right) \tag{104}$$

Illustrative Example. Determine the maximum stress in an eccentrically loaded column when supporting a load of 80,000 lb. as shown in Fig. 232. The load is placed upon the Y-Y axis at a distance of 5 in. from axis X-X. The column is a 14 in. $\times$ 43-lb./ft. Wide-Flange section, having the following properties: $A = 12.65$

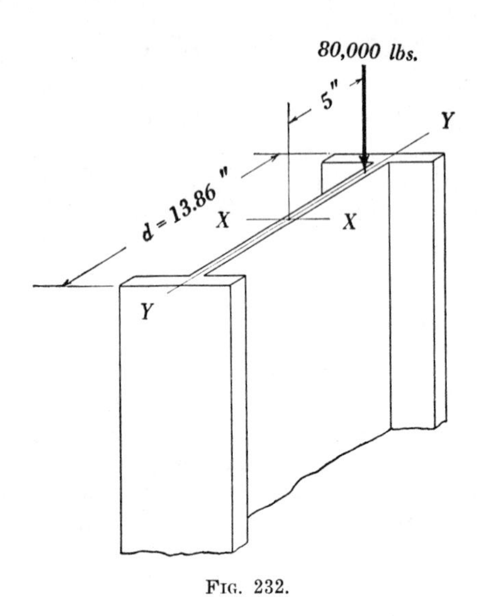

FIG. 232.

in.^{2}, $d = 13.68$ in., $r_{X-X} = 5.82$ in., $r_{Y-Y} = 1.89$ in. The unsupported length of the column is 20 ft.

$$\frac{P}{A} = \frac{80{,}000}{12.65} = 6324 \text{ psi}$$

$$\frac{L^2}{r^2} = \left(\frac{20 \times 12}{1.89}\right)^2 = 16{,}130$$

$$e = 5 \text{ in.}$$

$$y = \frac{13.68}{2} = 6.84 \text{ in.}$$

Applying equation (104),

$$s = \frac{P}{A}\left(1 + \frac{1}{18{,}000}\frac{L^2}{r^2} + \frac{ey}{r_o^2}\right) = 6324\left(1 + \frac{16{,}130}{18{,}000} + \frac{5 \times 6.84}{(5.82)^2}\right)$$

$$= 6324\ (1 + 0.9 + 1.01)$$

$$= 18{,}400 \text{ psi}$$

PROBLEMS

409. The short strut shown is subjected to an eccentric load $P = 45{,}000$ lb. placed on axis 2–2 at 2 in. from the centroid of the section. Determine the following:
a) The maximum normal stress on a right section.
b) The location of the neutral axis.

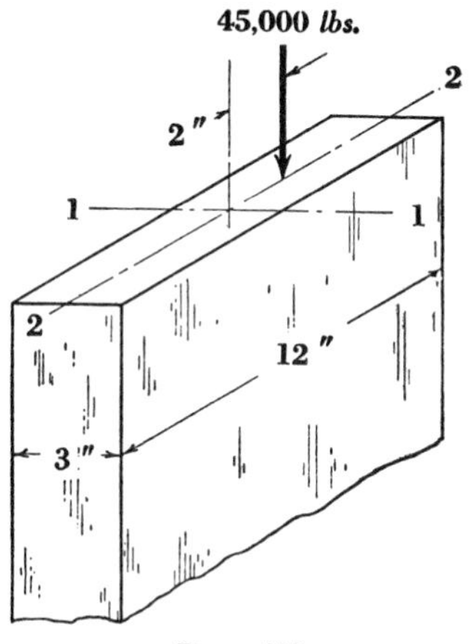

Prob. 409.

410. If the maximum allowable normal stress on a right section of the short column is 10,000 psi, determine the maximum allowable load P. *Ans.* 55,600 lb.

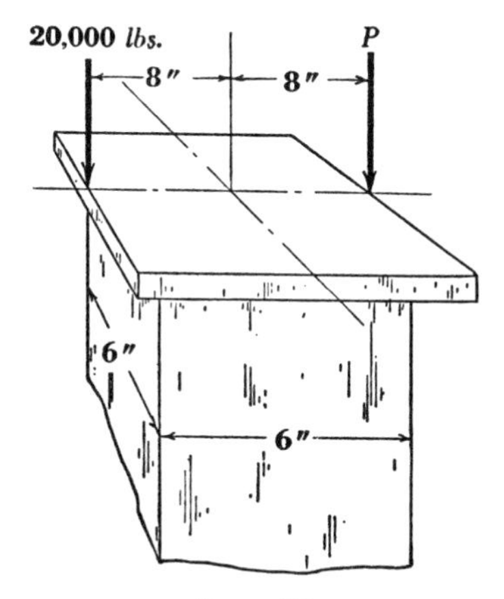

Prob. 410.

411. A short column supports the indicated loads on brackets. The column is a 12 in. × 65 lb./ft. Wide-Flange section. Determine the maximum normal stress on a right section. *Ans.* 11,060 psi.

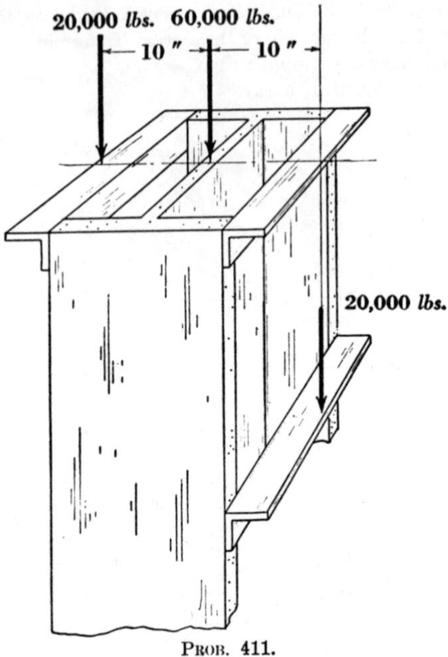

PROB. 411.

412. Locate the neutral axis of the column of Prob. 411 at the section of maximum normal stress.

413. Determine the maximum normal stress on a right section of the column shown. *Ans.* 600 psi (compression)

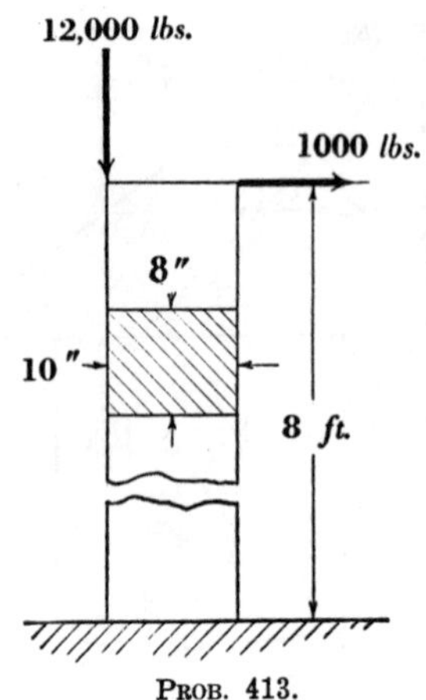

PROB. 413.

414. The area of the column is 10 sq. in. $I_{1-1} = 120$ in.[4] If the allowable normal stress on a right section is 12,000 psi, find the maximum allowable value of force F.

415. Determine the maximum normal stress on a right section, in terms of the eccentric load P. *Ans.* 0.047 P (compression).

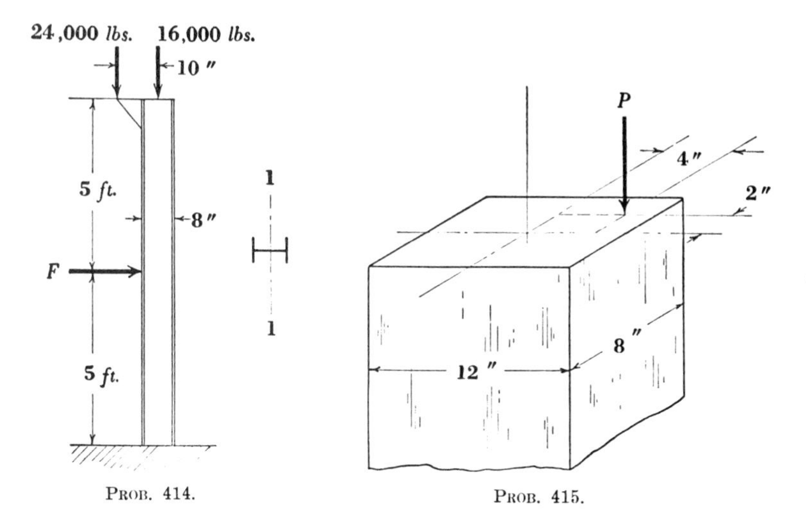

PROB. 414. PROB. 415.

416. Locate the neutral axis of the column section of Prob. 415.

417. The column is loaded by a vertical force P, applied at point a, and by a vertical force of 16,000 lb. applied at the centroid of the section. If the maximum normal stress on a right section of the column is 3000 psi, determine the magnitude of force P. *Ans.* 45,700 lb.

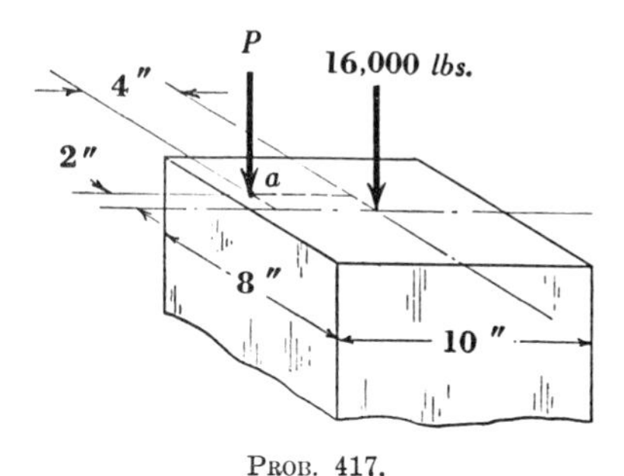

PROB. 417.

418. Locate the neutral axis of the column of Prob. 417, when the maximum allowable load P is applied.

419. A short steel strut of the cross-section shown is subjected to a load of 90,000 lb. acting through point c parallel to the axis of the strut. Find the maximum normal stress on a right section.

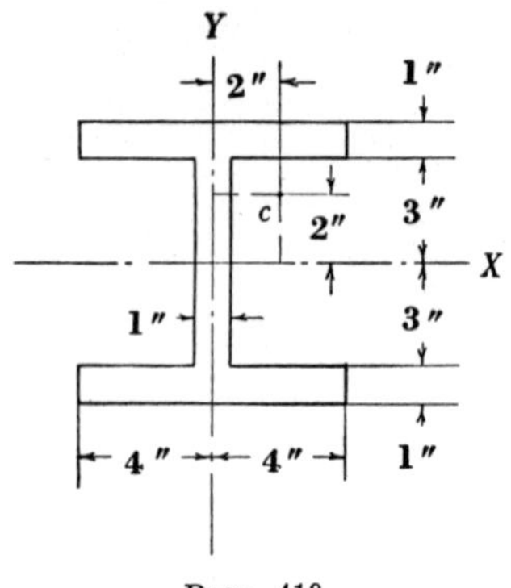

PROB. 419.

420. The column shown is made of an 18 in. × 60 lb./ft. American Standard I-beam. The loading consists of a vertical force of 25,000 lb. and a horizontal force of 5000 lb. Determine the maximum normal stress on a right section.

Ans. 10,600 psi (compression).

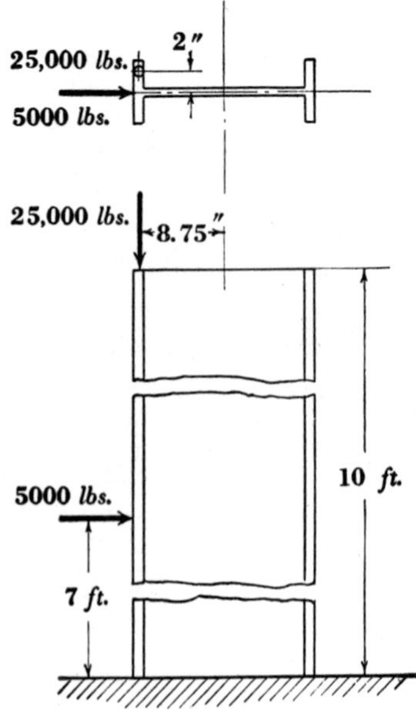

PROB. 420.

65. The Secant Formula. While the empirical formulas which we have discussed in the preceding article form the basis of most column design, a more correct analysis, from the standpoint of theory, is available and, despite the fact that it is awkward to apply in design, is gaining in favor. Our primary emphasis, in a text which like this one is devoted to the study of the fundamentals of mechanics of materials, should be placed upon the theoretical backgrounds rather than upon the techniques and procedures of the practical designer. It will therefore be proper for us to proceed with the derivation of the "secant formula" to observe its rational development, whether or not it furnishes a convenient design routine.

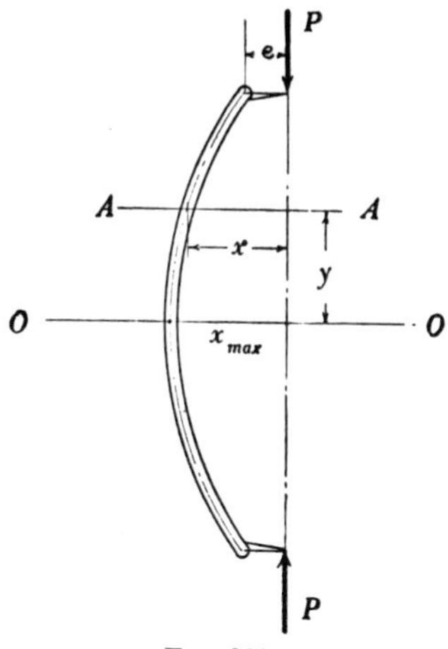

FIG. 233.

Figure 233 shows a round-ended column carrying an eccentric load, P. The eccentricity of the load from the axis of the column is e.

The bending moment at any section (such as A-A) will be

$$M = -Px$$

and

$$\frac{d^2x}{dy^2} = \frac{M}{EI} = -\frac{Px}{EI}$$

We shall employ the same methods of integration which furnished the method of attack leading to the Euler formula.

$$\frac{dx\, d\left(\frac{dx}{dy}\right)}{dy} = -\frac{Px}{EI}\, dx$$

Integrating,

$$\frac{1}{2}\left(\frac{dx}{dy}\right)^2 = -\frac{Px^2}{2EI} + C_1$$

When $y = 0$, $\qquad \frac{dx}{dy} = 0 \qquad$ and $\qquad x = x_{\text{max.}}$

$$C_1 = \frac{P(x_{\text{max.}})^2}{2EI}$$

$$\left(\frac{dx}{dy}\right)^2 = -\frac{Px^2}{EI} + \frac{P(x_{\text{max.}})^2}{EI}$$

$$\frac{dx}{dy} = \sqrt{\frac{P}{EI}}\sqrt{(x_{\text{max.}})^2 - x^2}$$

Separating the variables,

$$\frac{dx}{\sqrt{(x_{\max.})^2 - x^2}} = \sqrt{\frac{P}{EI}}\, dy$$

Integrating,

$$\sin^{-1} \frac{x}{x_{\max.}} = \sqrt{\frac{P}{EI}}\, y + C_2$$

When $y = 0$, $x = x_{\max.}$

and
$$C_2 = \sin^{-1}\left(\frac{x_{\max.}}{x_{\max.}} = 1\right) = \frac{\pi}{2}$$

Then
$$\sin^{-1} \frac{x}{x_{\max.}} = \sqrt{\frac{P}{EI}}\, y + \frac{\pi}{2}$$

$$\sin\left(\sqrt{\frac{P}{EI}}\, y + \frac{\pi}{2}\right) = \frac{x}{x_{\max.}}$$

When $y = \frac{L}{2}$, $x = e$

$$\sin\left(\sqrt{\frac{P}{EI}}\, \frac{L}{2} + \frac{\pi}{2}\right) = \frac{e}{x_{\max.}}$$

$$\cos \sqrt{\frac{PL^2}{4EI}} = \frac{e}{x_{\max.}}$$

and
$$x_{\max.} = e \sec \sqrt{\frac{PL^2}{4EI}}$$

The maximum stress in an eccentrically loaded column (Arts. 47 and 64) is

$$s = \frac{P}{A} + \frac{My}{I}$$

The maximum bending moment in this column occurs at the central section 0–0 when $x = x_{\max.}$, and

$$M = P\, x_{\max.} = Pe \sec \sqrt{\frac{PL^2}{4EI}}$$

Then
$$s = \frac{P}{A} + \frac{Pe \sec \sqrt{\frac{PL^2}{4EAr^2}}\, y}{Ar^2}$$

and
$$s = \frac{P}{A}\left(1 + \frac{ey}{r^2} \sec \frac{L}{r} \sqrt{\frac{P}{4EA}}\right)$$

or
$$\frac{P}{A} = \frac{s}{1 + \frac{ey}{r^2} \sec \frac{L}{r} \sqrt{\frac{P}{4EA}}} \qquad \textbf{(105)}$$

This is the *secant formula*. If affords an expression for the maximum stress, s, caused by a load P of eccentricity e, in terms of the area of the cross-section A, the radius of gyration r, the distance from the centroid to the extreme fiber y, the modulus of elasticity of the material E, and the unsupported length of the column L.

When a given load P is placed upon a given column of known cross-section, length, and material, the only unknown is the maximum stress, s, which may be found by substituting. In design, however, the properties of the column cross-section are the objective, and are not known at the start. A trial-and-error solution must therefore be employed when the secant formula is used.

CHAPTER VIII

Combined Loading

66. Introduction. Many of the elements of machines or of structures are bodies which are loaded by more than one type of loading. A shaft, for example, may transmit power as it rotates, and is subjected to twisting. The shaft must be supported in bearings, and the source of power may be gears or belt drives, which apply transverse forces, so that the shaft is also exposed to beam loading. The vertical shaft of a hydroelectric turbo-generator is subjected to torsion, but also to axial thrust.

As we face such cases of combinations of loading, the method of attack will usually become another example of superposition. We shall appraise the total loading, separating it into its component parts. Each of the components will be one with which we are familiar from our earlier work—the beam action of a shaft supported on bearings will be a problem to be faced with the flexure theory as a tool, and the twisting will properly be confronted with the torsion theory. With those theories we shall evaluate the stresses for which each of the sources of loading is responsible. We shall then combine these individual stresses to determine resultant stresses.

Before proceeding to those cases in which the loading is attributable to more than one source, we shall review the method of attack upon stresses on the different planes which may be passed through a point of a loaded body, and thus establish our basic method of attack.

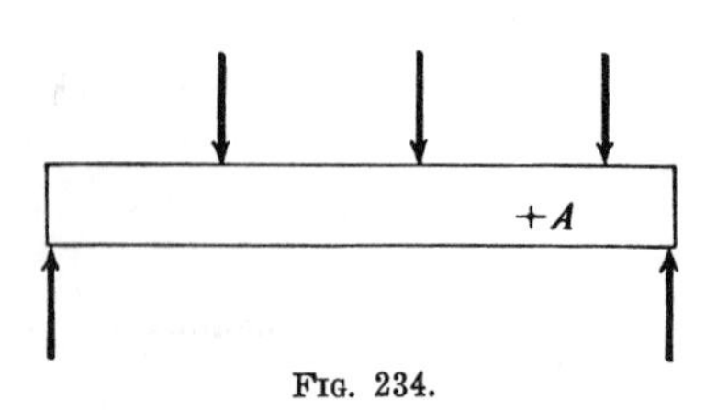

FIG. 234.

Principal Stresses in Bending. The beam shown in Fig. 234 conforms to the limitations of the flexure theory. At any point (such as A) there will be a bending stress, which has already been expressed in equation (34) as

$$s_X = \frac{My}{I}$$

and a longitudinal shear stress, expressed in equation (36) as

$$s_{XY} = \frac{VQ}{bI}$$

The value of s_Y in a beam is of significance only when the particle upon which it acts is located directly under a load. At all other locations, this normal stress on the Y-planes of particles is of negligible magnitude.

Figure 235-a shows a magnification of point A of Fig. 234 where it is

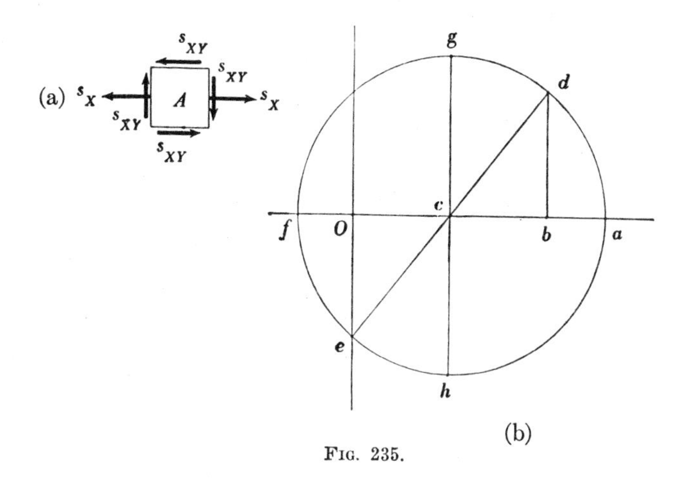

FIG. 235.

presented as a small prism of finite dimensions in order to show the stresses on its faces.

On all of the oblique planes which may be passed through point A perpendicular to the plane of the drawing, there will be resultant stresses and these resultant stresses will have normal and shearing components. In Chapter I we have considered the techniques of evaluation of such stresses by either analytical methods or by Mohr's cricle. A Mohr's circle for point A of this loaded beam is presented in Fig. 235-b. On the Mohr's circle, the distances are

$$Ob = s_X = \frac{My}{I}$$

$$bd = s_{XY} = \frac{VQ}{bI}$$

$$Oe = -s_{XY} = -\frac{VQ}{bI}$$

The maximum normal stress on any inclined plane through point A will be the principal stress Oa; the minimum normal stress will be the principal stress Of; and the maximum shearing stress will be the radius cg or ch.

These stresses indicate that at any point in a beam, loaded as demanded by the limitations of the flexure theory, there will be stresses on inclined planes which may be greater than the bending and longitudinal shear stresses. In practical beam design, the bending and longitudinal shear stresses are the criteria used as design bases, and we have employed the beam as an example only to suggest the presence of other and quantitatively greater stresses. In the cases of combined loading, which will be considered in the following articles, the presence of these greater stresses is recognized in setting the design criteria.

Illustrative Example. The simple rectangular beam shown in Fig. 236 carries a uniformly distributed load of 2880 lb./ft. The principal stresses, and the location

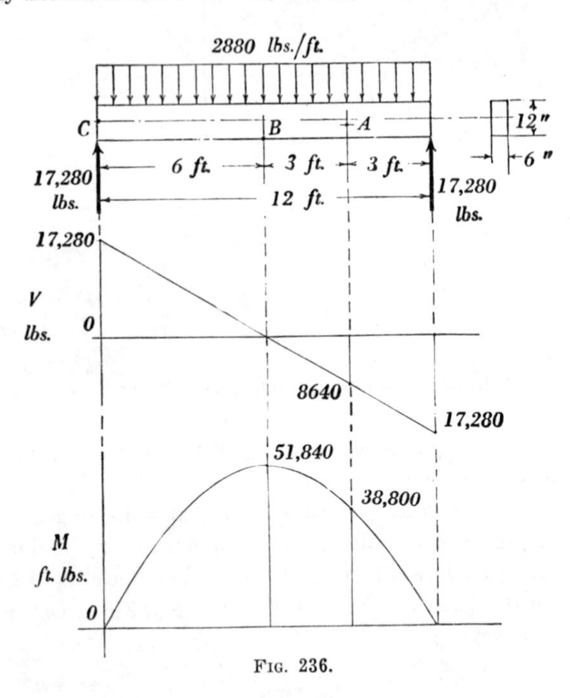

FIG. 236.

of the principal planes of stress for points A, B, and C are to be determined. We are also to determine the maximum shear stress at each of those points.

Point A. This point is located 1 in. below the neutral axis, at a section 3 ft. from the right end.

By equation (34),
$$s_X = \frac{My}{I} = \frac{38{,}880 \times 12 \times 1}{6 \times (12)^3/12}$$
$$= 540 \text{ psi (tension)}$$

By equation (36),
$$s_{XY} = \frac{VQ}{bI} = \frac{8640 \times 5 \times 6 \times 3.5}{6 \times 6 \times (12)^3/12}$$
$$= 175 \text{ psi (negative on the } X \text{ plane)}$$

A small prism (Fig. 237-a) indicates the presence of these stresses. A Mohr's circle for point A appears in Fig. 237-b. $Oa = s_X = 540$; $ab = s_{XY} = -175$; $Od = -s_{XY} = +175$.

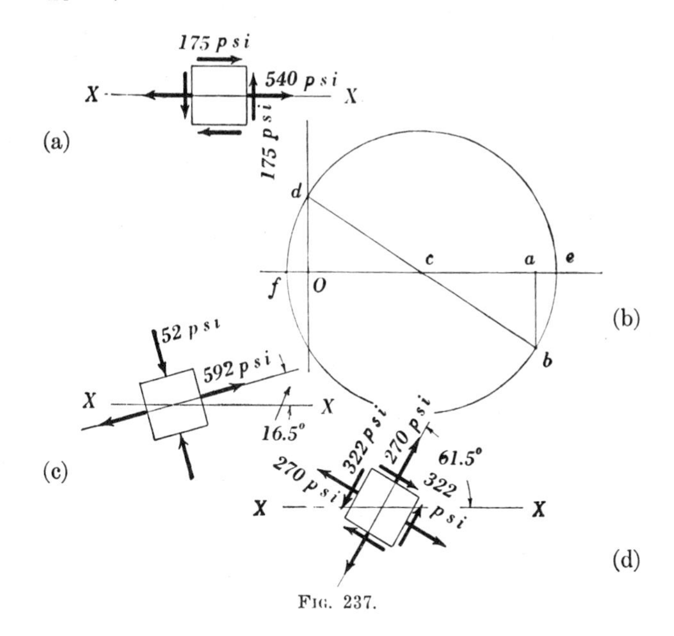

FIG. 237.

The radius of the circle is

$$R = \sqrt{\left(\frac{540}{2}\right)^2 + (175)^2} = 322$$

Then the principal stresses are

$$Oe = s_1 = 270 + 322 = 592 \text{ psi (tension)}$$
$$Of = s_2 = 270 - 322 = -52 \text{ psi (compression)}$$

The location of the principal planes for this point is determined as follows.

$$\angle bca = 2\theta = \tan^{-1}\frac{175}{270} = 33°$$
$$\theta = 16.5°$$

The location of the principal planes, and the principal stresses are shown in Fig. 237-c.

The maximum shear stress, which will occur on the planes which make an angle of 45°, with the principal planes, is the radius of the Mohr's circle, $s_S = 322$ psi (Fig. 237-d).

Point B. This point lies in the bottom fiber of the beam at the central section where the bending moment $M = M_{\text{max.}} = 51{,}840$ ft.-lb., and the shearing force is $V = 0$.

The normal stress on the X-plane through point B is, by equation (34),

$$s_X = \frac{51{,}840 \times 12 \times 6}{6 \times (12)^3/12} = 4320 \text{ psi (tension)}$$

and by equation (36) $\qquad s_{XY} = 0$

Figure 238-a shows the isolated prism, and Fig. 238-b is the Mohr's circle for point B. At this point, the X- and Y-planes are the principal planes, and $Oa = s_X = 4320$ psi is the maximum normal stress. The minimum normal stress is zero.

The maximum shear stress is

$$cl \text{ or } cm = \frac{4320}{2} = 2160 \text{ psi}$$

occurring on planes inclined at 45° with the X- and Y-planes (Fig. 238-c).

Point C. This point lies in the neutral axis at the end of the beam, immediately to the right of the support, and the bending moment is $M = 0$, while the shearing force is $V = V_{\text{max.}} = 17{,}280$ lb.

The normal and shear stresses on the X- and Y-planes at point C are, by equation (34)

$$s_X = \frac{My}{I} = 0$$

and, by equation (36) $\quad s_{XY} = \dfrac{VQ}{bI} = \dfrac{17{,}280 \times 6 \times 6 \times 3}{6 \times 6 \times (12)^3/12}$

$$= 360 \text{ psi (positive on the } X\text{-plane)}$$

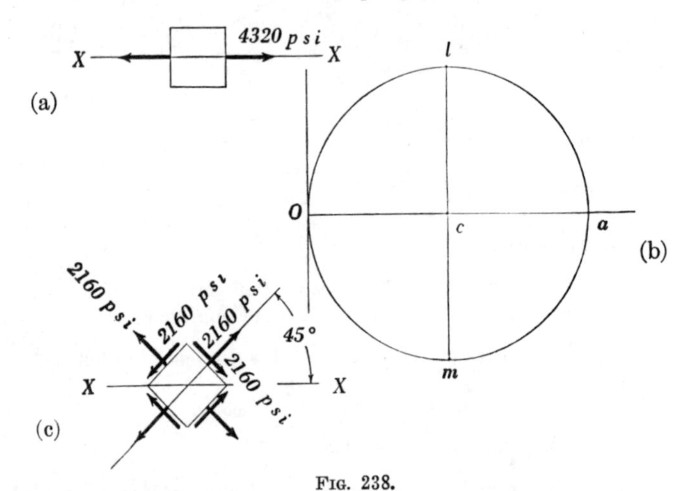

Fig. 238.

The prism representing point C is shown in Fig. 239-a, and the Mohr's circle will be that shown in Fig. 239-b. The principal stresses will be

$$Oc = s_1 = 360 \text{ psi (tension)}$$
$$Od = s_2 = 360 \text{ psi (compression)}$$

Oa respresents the X-plane; Ob the Y-plane.

The principal planes are determined by noting that

$$\angle aOc = 2\theta = 90°$$
$$\theta = 45°$$

Figure 239-c shows the principal planes and principal stresses. The maximum shear stress will be $Oa = Ob = 360$ psi.

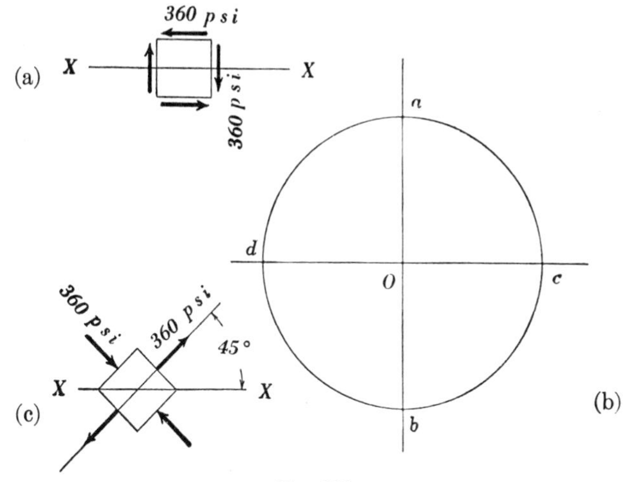

FIG. 239.

67. Torsional and Axial Loading. In many practical applications of machine shafting, the shaft is subjected to loading from two sources: the twisting caused by the transmission of torsional moment, and an axial force, such as the thrust of a propeller or an axial pull when a weight is placed on a vertical shaft.

The shaft of Fig. 240 is subjected to an axial load, P, and a twisting moment, M_T.

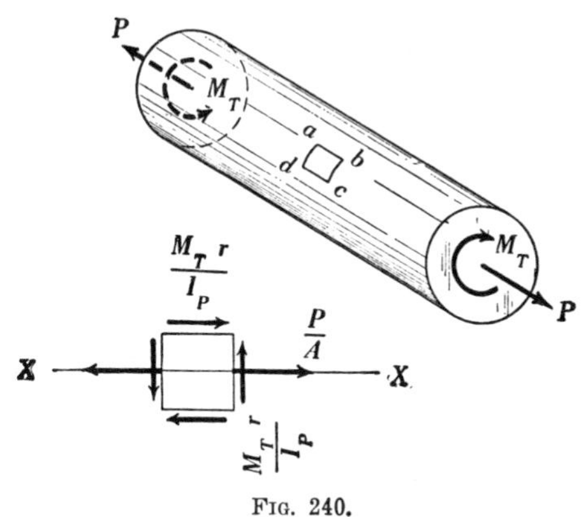

FIG. 240.

The determination of the maximum normal and shear stresses at the surface of the shaft may be accomplished by isolating a small prism *abcd* as a free body, as shown. This free body may be isolated in any portion of the shaft, all of which faces uniform conditions of loading.

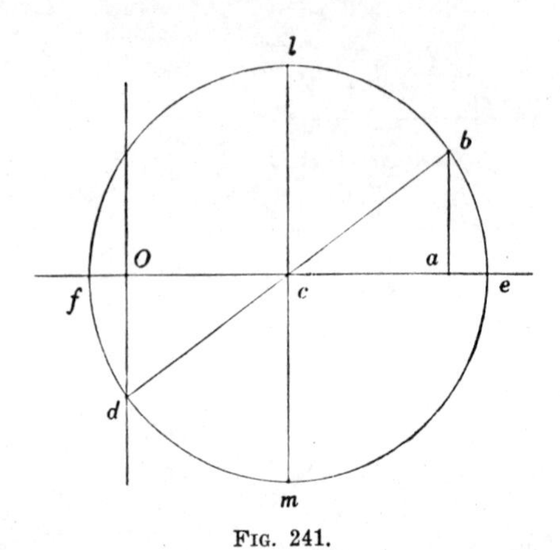

FIG. 241.

The Mohr's circle (Fig. 241) is drawn, using the following values:

$$Oa = s_X = \frac{P}{A}$$

$$ab = s_{XY} = \frac{M_T r}{I_P}$$

$$Od = -s_{XY} = -\frac{M_T r}{I_P}$$

The maximum normal stress will be

$$Oe = Oc + (ce = cb)$$

$$= \frac{s_X}{2} + \sqrt{\left(\frac{s_X}{2}\right)^2 + (s_{XY})^2}$$

and the maximum shear stress will be

$$cl \text{ or } cm = cb \tag{1}$$

The maximum shear stress is of greatest concern, for such shafting is usually designed in accordance with the maximum shear theory (Art. 69). When the axial load is compressive, we are faced with the problem which is common to all compression members or columns, that is, the problem of possible collapse by buckling. This possibility is recognized, in design, by modifying the allowable value of the normal stress $s_X = P/A$ in accordance with the recommendations which were formulated in the Design Code of

Transmission Shafting of the A.S.M.E. In that code it is suggested that the maximum shear value, given in equation (1) above, be expressed as

$$s_{S(\text{max.})} = \sqrt{\left(f\frac{P}{A}\right)^2 + \left(\frac{M_T r}{I_P}\right)^2}$$

where f is a factor which recognizes the buckling tendency of this compression member by assuming that the shaft is a column having a slenderness ratio, L/r, where L is the unsupported length of the shaft, and r the radius of gyration of the circular cross-section about its centroidal axis. (For a circle, the radius of gyration, r, in terms of the radius of the circle, r_c, is

$$r = \sqrt{\frac{I}{A}} = \sqrt{\frac{\pi r_c^4}{4\pi r_c^2}} = \frac{r_c}{2}$$

A straight-line column formula is employed to evaluate f, as follows:

$$f = \frac{16{,}000}{16{,}000 - 69.3\ L/r}$$

68. Torsion and Bending. Most of the rotating shafts which are used to transmit power are subjected to twisting and bending. The twisting is due

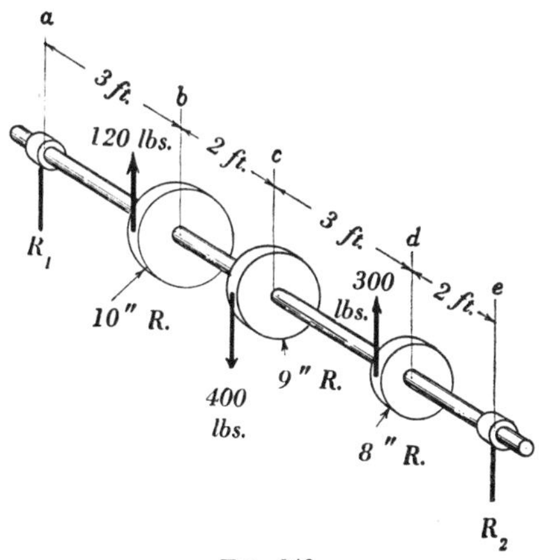

FIG. 242.

to the transmitted torsional moment, and the bending is due to the weight of the shaft, the weights and belt pulls of pulley and belt drives, or the thrust of gears or cranks.

The loading of such shafts may be separated into the two contributing parts—twisting and bending. The torsion theory is applied to determine the torsional shear stress, and the flexure theory to evaluate the bending stress.

The shaft of Fig. 242 is typical of such cases. The loading consists of vertical forces of 120, 400, and 300 lb. All of these forces are applied at the circumferences of pulleys which are mounted at sections *b*, *c*, and *d*, respectively. The diameter of the shaft is 2 in., and it is supported on bearings at *a* and *e*. The bearing reactions are sufficiently localized so that they may be represented by concentrated forces. The weight of the shaft and pulleys may be neglected.

The loading of Fig. 242 may be resolved into the equivalent force system shown in Fig. 243 by resolving each of the original forces into a force at

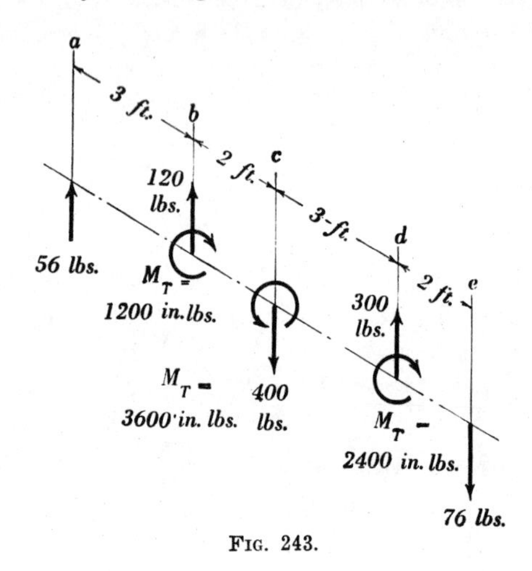

FIG. 243.

the central axis of the shaft and a moment. This resolution divides the problem into two stages—the system of moments at the pulleys is responsible for the twisting of the shaft, and the forces at the axis form a transverse system of forces on a beam which serve to produce bending stress.

There will be twisting in the range of loading from *b* to *c*, and from *c* to *d*. In the range from *b* to *c*, M_T = 1200 in.-lb., and from *c* to *d*, M_T = 2400 in.-lb. These torsional moments are constant throughout their respective ranges.

The bending moment diagram for the system of transverse forces is shown in Fig. 244. The maximum bending moment is M_B = 520 ft.-lb.

At the section of the shaft immediately to the right of section *c*, the torsional shear stress, s_{XY}, and the bending stress, s_X, will both be maximum. They will have the following values:
According to equation (73),

$$s_{XY} = \frac{M_T r}{I_P} = \frac{2400 \times 1}{\pi(1)^4/2} = 1530 \text{ psi}$$

and, by equation (34),

$$s_X = \frac{M_B\, r}{I} = \frac{520 \times 12 \times 1}{\pi(1)^4/4} = 7950 \text{ psi}$$

The bending stress will be tensile in the bottom fibers of the shaft.

Figure 245-a is a view, taken from the bottom of the shaft, of a small prism immediately to the right of section c at the outside fibers. The Mohr's

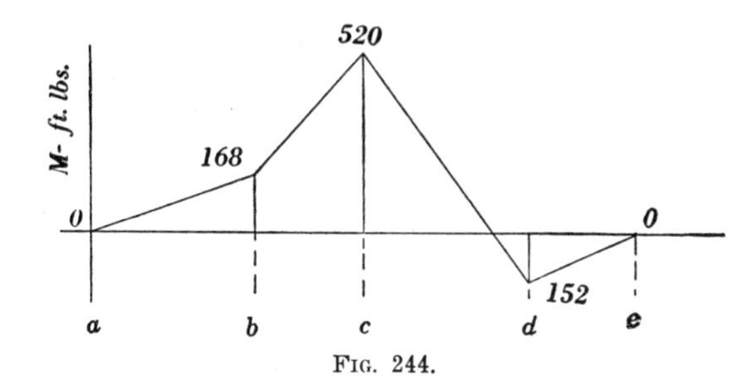

FIG. 244.

circle (Fig. 245-b) may now be used to investigate the maximum normal and shear stresses. $Oa = s_X = 7950$; $ab = s_{XY} = -1530$; $Od = -s_{XY} = +1530$. The principal stresses are

$$Oe = Oc + \text{radius } (cb = ce)$$

$$= 3975 + (\sqrt{(3975)^2 + (1530)^2} = 4260) = 8235 \text{ psi (tension)}$$

and

$$Of = 3975 - 4260 = -285 \text{ psi (compression)}$$

The maximum shear stress is the radius of the Mohr's circle $cl = cm = cb$

$$s_{S\,(\text{max.})} = 4260 \text{ psi}$$

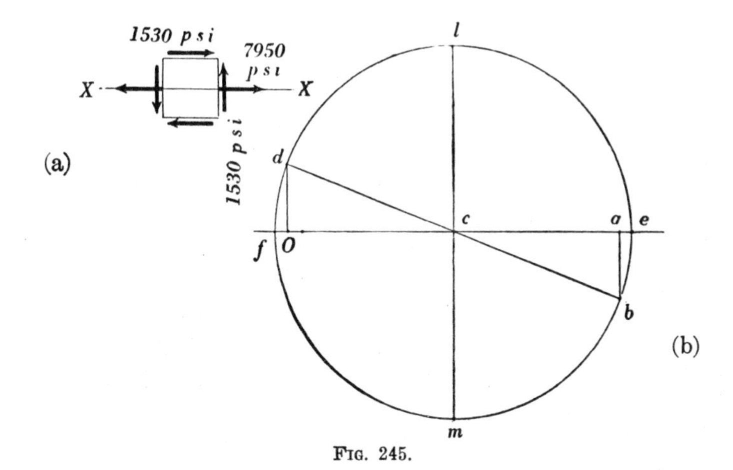

FIG. 245.

There is an additional shear stress in the shaft which has not yet been considered. When any beam is subjected to bending, there will be a longitudinal shear stress, $s = VQ/bI$ [equation (36)]. This shear stress will be zero at the outside fibers of the shaft, which were considered in the preceding analysis. The longitudinal shear stress will increase toward the center of the shaft. At the same time, however, the torsional shear stress and the bending stress, both of which are maximum at the outside fiber, will decrease as the center is approached. In addition, the magnitude of the longitudinal shear stress is relatively small when compared with the other two stresses. The previous analysis, which neglected the longitudinal shear stress and concerned itself only with the torsional shear stress and the bending stress, will therefore be found to be correct in all engineering applications of shafting.

Another feature of interest to the designer is the reversal of the bending stress as the shaft rotates. The fibers at the bottom of the shaft just discussed are in tension, while fibers at the top are in compression. When the shaft turns through an angle of 180°, the fibers which were previously at the bottom will now be at the top, and there will have been a complete reversal of the nature of the bending stress. In addition, the rate at which the loads are applied will materially affect the development of stress in the shaft, and must be recognized in design. We shall later, in the articles devoted to fatigue and to the suddenly applied load, concern ourselves with some of the features of these forms of loading. These discussions, however, will, in common with all of our points of interest in this text, be concerned with the fundamentals of behavior of loaded bodies, rather than with details of practical design. The reader is referred, for factors of adjustment covering reversed bending and shock loading in shafts to the Code for Design of Transmission of the American Society of Mechanical Engineers.

69. Theories of Failure. The study of the mechanics of materials which we have thus far pursued has devoted itself, very largely, to investigating the manner in which stress is induced in loaded bodies. We have assumed that all loads were gradually applied, and that the loaded bodies were in equilibrium under the influence of the force system. In addition, we have been concerned with the deformation of the loaded bodies.

Engineers, equipped with basic knowledge concerning the development of stress in bodies, can apply this knowledge to the design of machines and of structures only when they have available criteria which will establish allowable values of stress. The selection of these strengths, or allowable stresses, is a field of investigation which engineers have long explored, and with which they are still greatly preoccupied. The complexities of the behavior of materials in response to loading have led, most naturally, to differences of interpretation and of opinion. It is most improbable that one theory concerning the nature of failure can ever be entirely reasonable, and therefore be universally acceptable. Such simplification would be possible only if the materials which man manufactures or nature supplies were ideal in their properties and our knowledge of their exact behavior perfect. While search and research continuously add to our store of such knowledge, we never attain a state of such understanding. The production of new materials constantly demands knowledge of their unique properties. In addition, the uses to which both new and old materials are put ever pose additional problems—for example, information concerning materials which has been gleaned by testing at room temperatures may have little validity when those materials are employed in applications where extremely high or low temperatures may be encountered.

Since machines must be built and structures erected whether man's knowledge of the materials he will use is perfect or imperfect, there must be some basis from which to initiate a design attack and, at present, four *theories of failure* are in active service as design bases.

The failures of materials occur, as the loads placed upon bodies are increased, in manners which may be grouped in two broad classifications. Ductile materials will usually fail by yielding when the elastic range is passed, and the deformation of the body becomes permanent. Failure of a brittle material, in general, consists of a rupture, or fracture, of the material. The line of demarcation between ductile and brittle materials is not an exact one and, as we have noted in other cases of classification, no exact boundary may be closely defined. The ordinary mild steels are examples of ductile materials, while cast iron is the prototype of the brittle ones. The properties of ductility and brittleness are discussed in the chapter devoted to mechanical properties of materials.

Most of the values of the strength of materials are determined by laboratory testing of a loaded cylinder or prism of the material, and the usual approach to fixing allowable stresses consists of setting such test results as criteria. The interpretation of the test and the assignment of appropriate values is then faced by using a *theory of strength.*

Maximum Stress Theory. This theory, also known as *Rankine's* theory, is the oldest of the strength theories. It maintains that the maximum principal stress should be used as the standard of the behavior of the material.

We have already noted, in our discussions of plane or two-dimensional stress, the presence of two principal stresses at any point of a loaded body. The numerically greater of these two stresses, according to this theory, should be equated to the yield-point stress for ductile materials and to the ultimate stress for brittle materials. Expressed in equation form,

$$s_{\text{max.}} = s_{\text{Y.P.}} \text{ for ductile materials} \quad (106)$$

$$s_{\text{max.}} = s_{\text{ULT.}} \text{ for brittle materials} \quad (106a)$$

The results of tests indicate that the theory is fairly reliable in the case of brittle materials. In the case of ductile materials, however, it is not reliable, for it fails to recognize the possibility of the shearing action which causes slipping on planes inclined at 45° with the principal planes, where maximum shearing stress occurs.

Maximum Strain Theory. This theory was propounded by the French mathematician, Saint-Venant.

In a loaded body, we have noted (Art. 14) that the unit deformation in the direction of the greatest principal stress, s_1, when both principal stresses are tensile, will be

$$e_1 = \frac{s_1}{E} - \frac{\mu s_2}{E}$$

where e_1 is the strain in the direction of principal axis 1, and s_1 is the stress in the direction of that principal axis, while s_2 is the other principal stress, and μ is Poisson's ratio.

This strain, or unit deformation, is equated, in the use of this theory, to the maximum strain in a tensile test specimen at the yield point, or

$$\frac{s_{\text{Y.P.}}}{E} = \frac{s_1}{E} - \frac{\mu s_2}{E} \quad (107)$$

This theory is losing in favor with designers because experimental proving tests show that it is inaccurate.

Maximum Shear Theory. This is the theory which currently enjoys the greatest favor, particularly with machine designers, for the evidence of experimental tests agrees with its predictions most closely, and because it is a simple and convenient tool for the designer.

The theory assumes that yielding of the material begins when the maximum shear stress in the loaded body is equal to the maximum shear stress in the material at yield point when that material is subjected to the simple axial tension test. The maximum shear stress is the radius of the Mohr's circle of Fig. 246, in which Oa is the tensile stress at yield point.

$$s_{S(\text{max.})} = \frac{Oa}{2} = \frac{s_{\text{Y.P.}}}{2} \quad (108)$$

Deformation Energy Theory. Some investigators, in their search for a plausible theory of failure for ductile materials, have focused their attention upon the strain energy which is stored in the loaded body. Von Mises and Hencky have proposed, after extensive investigation of failures involving the general three-dimensional state of stress, the following equation, which summarizes the results of their observations. The equation has been shown by the experimental evidence to be extremely promising in predicting the behavior of ductile materials, and it is gaining in favor with engineering designers.

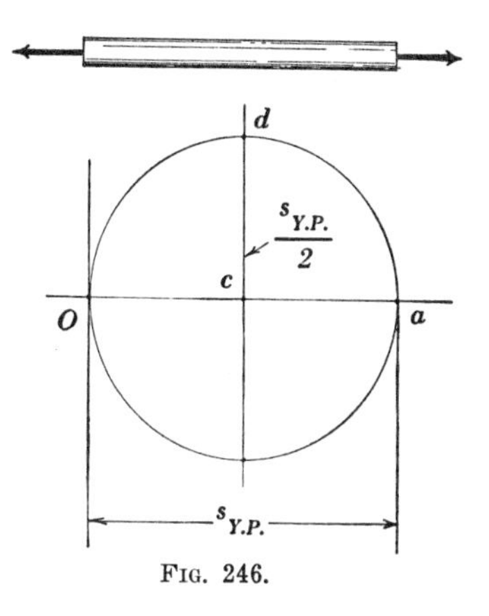

FIG. 246.

The general three-dimensional stress condition is shown in Fig. 247. The general equation of the theory is

$$\sqrt{(s_1 - s_2)^2 + (s_2 - s_3)^2 + (s_3 - s_1)^2} = \sqrt{2}s_{Y.P.}$$

where s_1, s_2, and s_3 are the principal stresses.

In the two-dimensional stress cases with which we are concerned in this text, $s_3 = 0$, and the equation takes the form

$$s_1^2 + s_2^2 - s_1 s_2 = (s_{Y.P.})^2 \qquad \textbf{(109)}$$

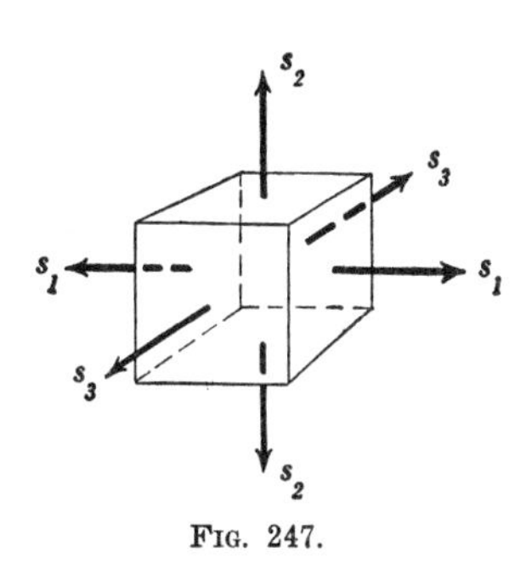

FIG. 247.

Illustrative Example I. A cylindrical shaft is subjected to a maximum bending moment of 2000 ft.-lb., and a twisting moment of 3000 ft.-lb. A specimen of the material has been found, in the tensile test, to have a yield point $s_{Y.P.} = 54{,}000$ psi. The factor of safety is to be 3.

We are to determine the diameter of the shaft using the following:

a) The maximum stress theory.
b) The maximum shear theory.
c) The deformation energy theory.

The maximum bending stress in the shaft is, by equation (34),

$$s_B = \frac{2000 \times 12 \times r}{\pi r^4/4} = \frac{30{,}570}{r^3}$$

The maximum torsional shear stress is, by equation (73),

$$s_S = \frac{3000 \times 12 \times r}{\pi r^4/2} = \frac{22{,}930}{r^3}$$

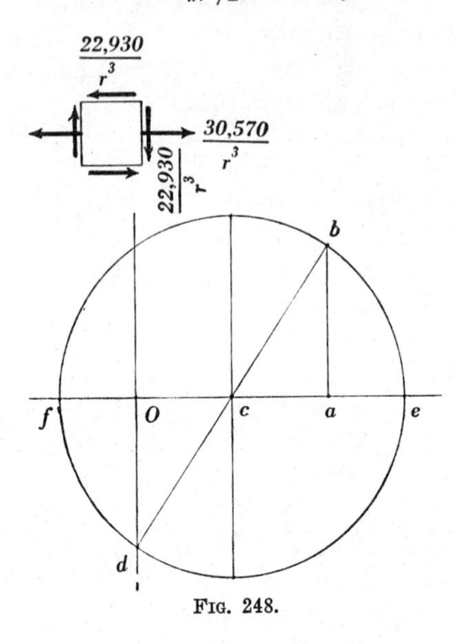

Fig. 248.

a) Using Mohr's circle (Fig. 248) with $Oa = 30{,}570/r^3$; $ab = 22{,}930/r^3$; $Od = -22{,}930/r^3$, the maximum principal stress will be

$$Oe = Oc + \text{radius } cb$$

$$= \frac{30{,}570}{2r^3} + \sqrt{\left(\frac{30{,}570}{2r^3}\right)^2 + \left(\frac{22{,}930}{r^3}\right)^2}$$

$$= \frac{30{,}570}{2r^3} + \frac{27{,}560}{r^3}$$

$$= \frac{42{,}845}{r^3}$$

This maximum principal stress is now equated to the allowable stress determined in the tensile test, which is, according to equation (106),

$$s_{\text{max.}} = \frac{s_{\text{Y.P.}}}{\text{F.S.}} = \frac{54{,}000}{3} = 18{,}000$$

Then
$$18{,}000 = \frac{42{,}845}{r^3}$$

and
$$r = \sqrt[3]{\frac{42{,}845}{18{,}000}} = 1.34 \text{ in.}$$

$$\text{Diameter} = 2.68 \text{ in.}$$

b) The allowable shear stress, according to the maximum shear theory, is by equation (108),

$$s_{\text{max.}} = \frac{s_{\text{Y.P.}}}{2\text{F.S.}} = \frac{54{,}000}{2 \times 3} = 9000$$

The radius of the Mohr's circle, obtained in Part a) is $27{,}560/r^3$.

Then
$$9000 = \frac{27{,}560}{r^3}$$

$$r = \sqrt[3]{\frac{27{,}560}{9000}} = 1.45 \text{ in.}$$

$$\text{Diameter} = 2.90 \text{ in.}$$

c) The Von Mises-Hencky equation [equation (109)] is used, with the values of the principal stresses taken from Part a) as

$$s_1 = Oe = \frac{42{,}845}{r^3} \text{ (tension)}$$

$$s_2 = Of = \frac{12{,}275}{r^3} \text{ (compression)}$$

$$s_1^2 + s_2^2 - s_1 s_2 = \left(\frac{s_{\text{Y.P.}}}{\text{F.S.}}\right)^2$$

$$\left(\frac{42{,}845}{r^3}\right)^2 + \left(\frac{12{,}275}{r^3}\right)^2 - \left(+\frac{42{,}845}{r^3}\right) \times \left(-\frac{12{,}275}{r^3}\right) = (18{,}000)^2$$

$$r = \sqrt[3]{\frac{50{,}130}{18{,}000}} = 1.41 \text{ in.}$$

$$\text{Diameter} = 2.82 \text{ in.}$$

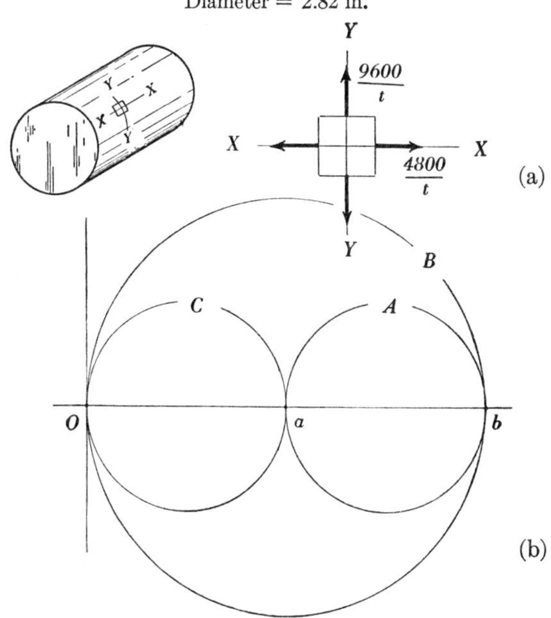

FIG. 249.

Illustrative Example II. A cylindrical tank is subjected to an internal pressure of 400 psi. The diameter of the tank is 4 ft. The stress at yield point in a tensile-test specimen of the wall material is 50,000 psi. The factor of safety is to be 4.

We are to determine the minimum wall thickness using the maximum shear theory.

The stresses which must be considered are the hoop and end tensions (Art. 9). The stress in the radial direction is negligible. If we isolate, as a free body, the prism indicated in Fig. 249-a, the stresses s_X and s_Y are the end and hoop tensions, respectively.

Substituting in equation (10),

$$s_X = \frac{pr}{2t} = \frac{400 \times 2 \times 12}{2t} = \frac{4800}{t} = Oa \text{ (Fig. 249-b)}$$

Substituting in equation (9),

$$s_Y = \frac{pr}{t} = \frac{9600}{t} = Ob \text{ (Fig. 249-b)}$$

Since both of these principal stresses are tensile, three possible values of maximum shear stress must be considered (see page 28). The Mohr's circles A, B, and C (Fig. 249-b) reveal that the greatest shear stress is the radius of circle B, which is

$$s_{S(\text{max.})} = \frac{9600}{2t} = \frac{4800}{t}$$

The allowable shear stress is by equation (108),

$$s_S = \frac{s_{Y.P.}}{2\text{F.S.}} = \frac{50{,}000}{2 \times 4} = 6250 \text{ psi}$$

Then

$$\frac{4800}{t} = 6250$$

$$t = \frac{4800}{6250} = 0.768 \text{ in.}$$

PROBLEMS

421. Determine the principal stresses at point a, which is 2 in. above the centroidal axis of the beam. *Ans.* 314 psi (tension) at $-12°$; 14 psi (compression) at 78°.

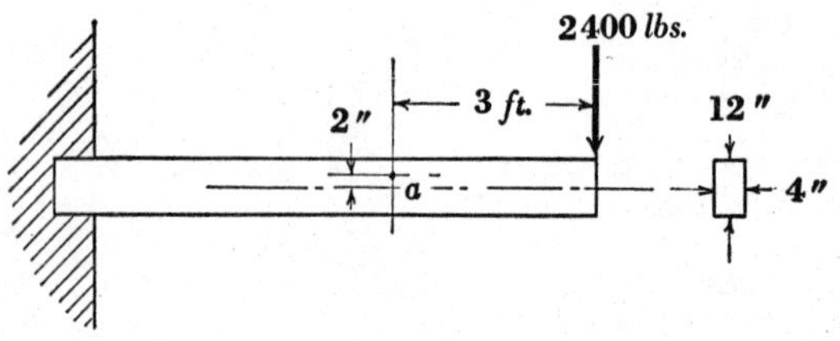

PROB. 421.

422. Determine the principal stresses at point a, which is 2 in. below the centroidal axis of the beam.

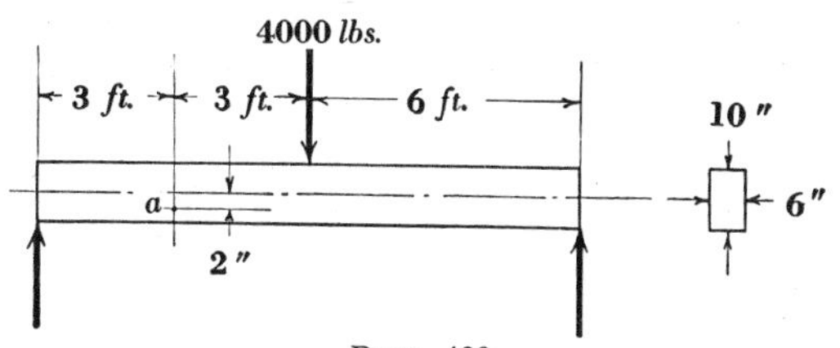

PROB. 422.

423. If the maximum principal stress at point a, which is 2 in. below the centroidal axis of the beam, is 300 psi, determine the magnitude of load W. *Ans.* 5370 lb.

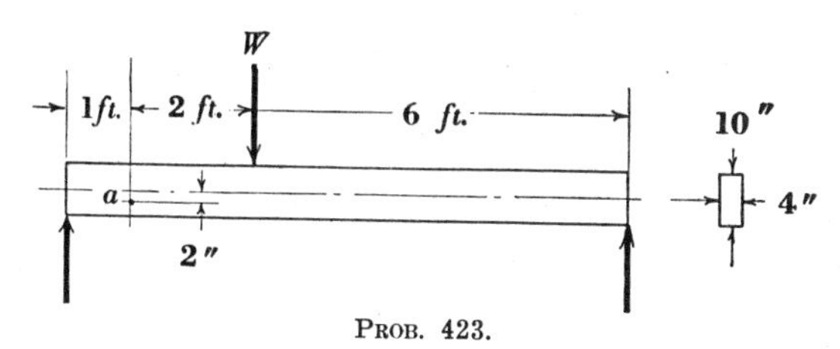

PROB. 423.

424. Determine the principal stresses at point a, which is 1 in. above the centroidal axis.

425. For the beam of Prob. 424, determine the principal stresses at a point located 1 in. above the centroidal axis at the wall section.

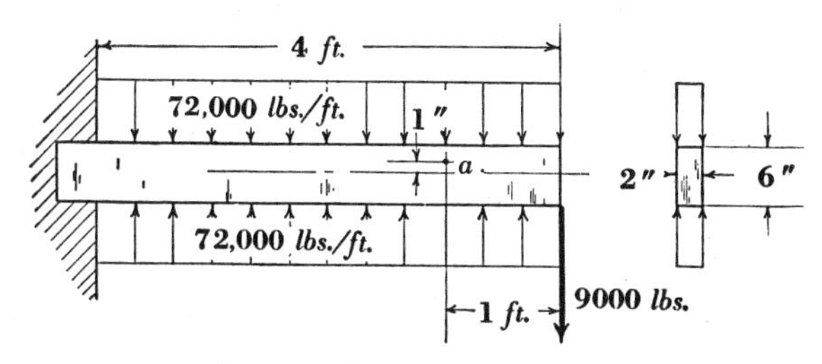

PROB. 424.

426. A 2 in.-diameter shaft is subjected to an axial thrust of 14,400 lb. and a twisting moment of 400 ft.-lb. Determine the maximum normal and maximum shear stresses in the shaft. *Ans.* $s_N = 6110$ psi; $s_S = 3820$ psi.

427. Determine the diameter of a shaft which is to be subjected to an axial thrust of 20,000 lb. and a twisting moment of 1200 ft.-lb., if the maximum allowable shear stress is 6000 psi.

428. A solid steel shaft, 2 in. in diameter, is held rigidly against rotation by end clamps. The shaft is loaded by a twisting moment $M_T = 20{,}000$ in-lb. and by the end axial thrust $P = 30{,}000$ lb. Determine the maximum shear stress in the shaft.
Ans. 9750 psi.

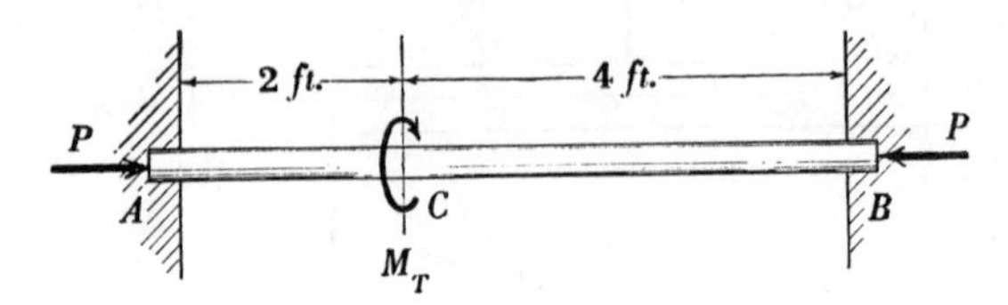

PROB. 428.

429. A torsional pendulum consists of a rod R, 0.2 in. in diameter by 20 in. long, clamped at the top and supporting a disk D weighing 188.5 lb. at the bottom. Find the largest angle θ through which the disk can be twisted and then released to oscillate if the maximum allowable shear stress in the rod is 9000 psi. $G = 12 \times 10^6$ psi.
Ans. 8.1°.

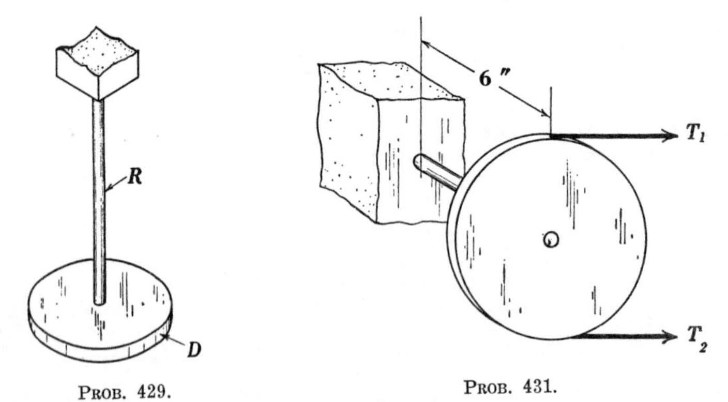

PROB. 429. PROB. 431.

430. A ship propeller shaft has an outside diameter of 8 in. and an inside diameter of 7 in. The shaft transmits 400 h.p. at 120 r.p.m. The end thrust of the screw is 40,000 lb. Neglecting bending stresses, determine the maximum principal stress and the maximum shear stress in the shaft.

431. In the overhanging pulley drive shown, the pulley weighs 100 lb. Horizontal belt pulls T_1 and T_2 transmit 5 h.p. at 600 r.p.m. to the shaft. $T_1 = 3T_2$. Determine the minimum diameter of the shaft if the maximum allowable shearing stress of the material is 6000 psi. Diameter of pulley = 24 in.
Ans. 0.94 in.

432. The horizontal shaft, 2 in. in diameter, is driven by a torque of 3200 in.-lb. The power is transmitted through pulleys P_1 and P_2 to two machines, each of which has a torque requirement of 1600 in.-lb. The shaft is supported by bearings at A and B. Diameter P_1 = 10 in.; diameter P_2 = 20 in. Neglecting the weight of the pulleys, determine the maximum shear stress in the shaft. *Ans.* 6450 psi.

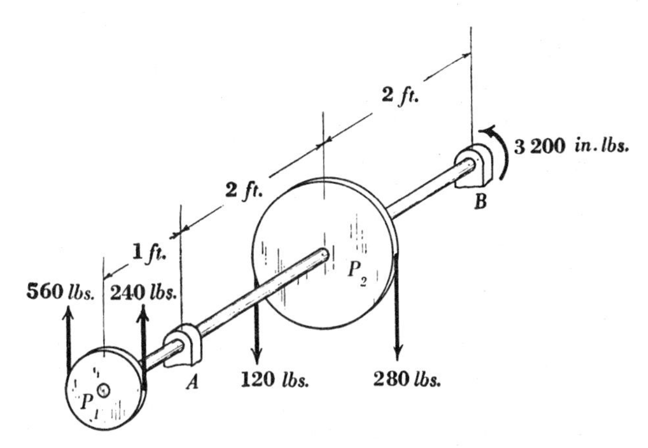

Prob. 432.

433. Pinion P transmits 100 h.p. to gear G. Speed of G = 600 r.p.m. Pitch diameter of G = 21 in. The shaft S is supported in bearings at A and B. The maximum allowable shear stress in the shaft is 8000 psi, and the maximum normal stress is 12,000 psi. Determine the required diameter of shaft S.

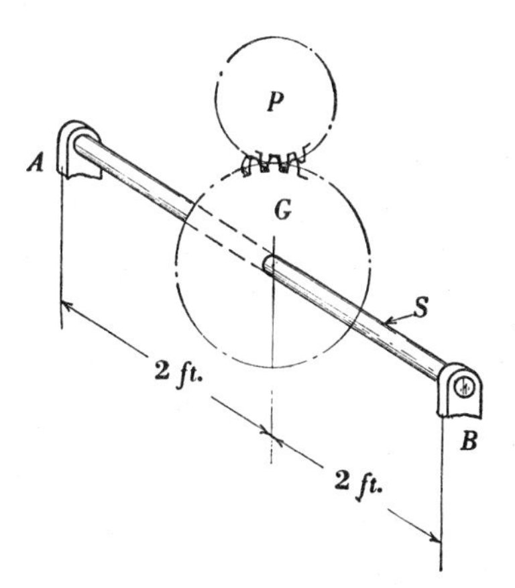

Prob. 433.

434. An overhanging bracket consists of a solid cylindrical shaft, 2 in. in diameter with an overhanging arm. The bracket is loaded with a 1000 lb. force, parallel to the X-axis, as shown. Point c lies on the diameter parallel to the X-axis and 20 in. beyond the line of action of the 1000-lb. force. Determine the principal stresses at point c. *Ans.* $s_{max.}$ = 27,900 psi (compression); $s_{max.}$ = 1500 psi (tension).

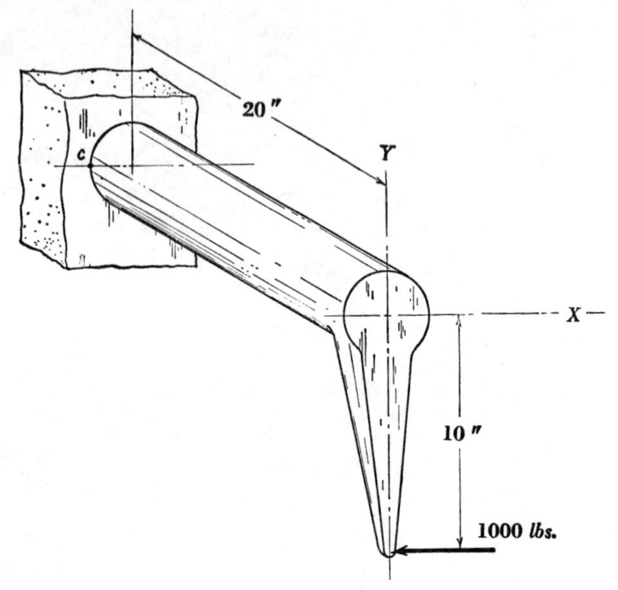

PROB. 434.

435. Find the maximum force P which may be applied to the end of the wrench handle under the following conditions. Diameter of shaft = 2 in. $s_{Y.P.}$ = 30,000 psi. Factor of safety = 6. Use the maximum shear theory. *Ans.* 73.2 lb.

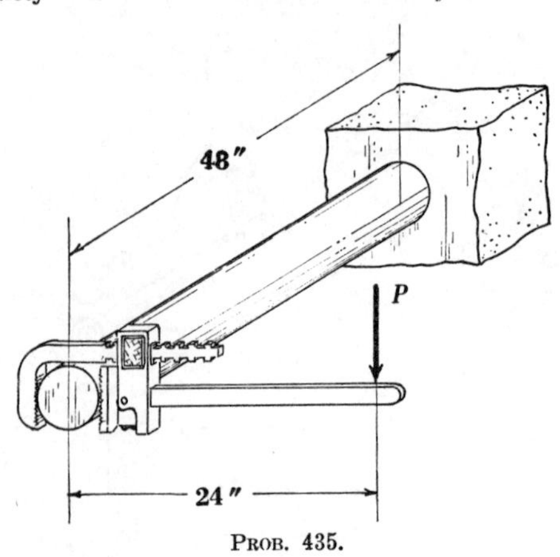

PROB. 435.

436. At 300 r.p.m., 15 h.p. is delivered to the shaft at pulley C, and leaves at pulley D. Diameter $C = 10$ in.; diameter $D = 20$ in. Forces F_1 and F_2 are tangent to the pulleys. F_1 is horizontal and F_2 is vertical. The shaft has a 2 in. diameter and is supported in bearings at A and B. Determine the maximum principal stress in the shaft.

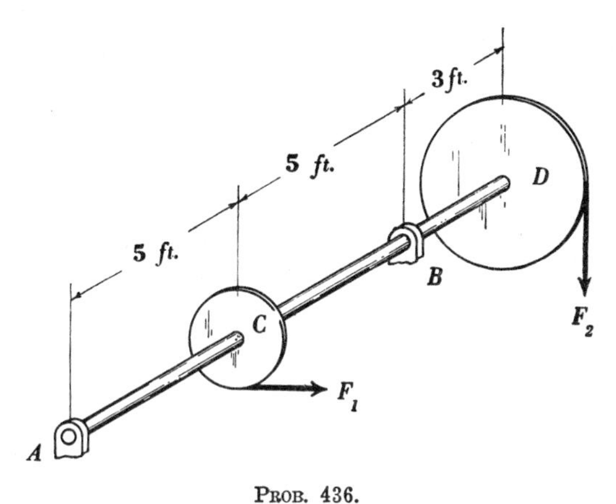

PROB. 436.

437. If pulley C of Prob. 436 weighs 60 lb., and pulley D weighs 80 lb., determine the maximum principal stress in the shaft.

438. Determine the maximum shear stress in the shaft of Prob. 436. *Ans.* 12,700 psi.

439. The diameter of pulley P_1 is 12 in., and the diameter of pulley P_2 is 10 in. The diameter of the shaft is 2 in. Neglecting the weight of pulleys and shaft, determine the maximum shear stress in the shaft.

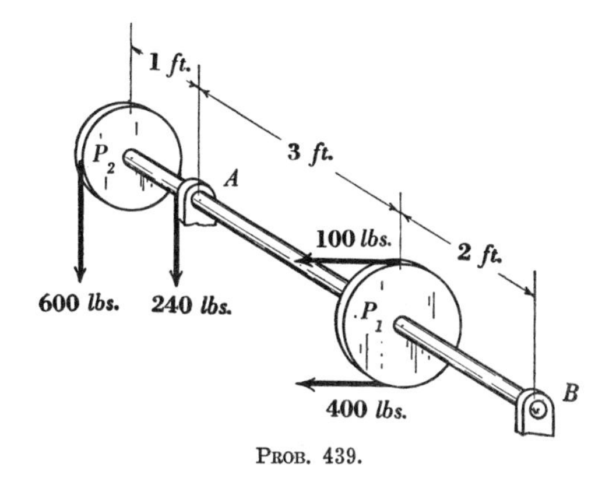

PROB. 439.

440. If each of the pulleys of Prob. 439 weighs 100 lb., determine the maximum principal stress in the shaft.

441. The shaft of Prob. 439 is supported in bearings at A and B. Determine the minimum yield point of the material which must be used if the factor of safety is to be 3, using the maximum shear theory. Neglect the weight of the pulleys and shaft.
Ans. 39,100 psi.

442. A cylindrical shaft is subjected to a maximum bending moment of 1200 ft.-lb., and a constant twisting moment of 2400 ft.-lb. The material of which the shaft is made has a yield point, in tension, of 36,000 psi. Determine the minimum diameter of the shaft, with a factor of safety of 4, using the maximum stress theory.
Ans. 2.98 in.

443. Determine the minimum diameter of the shaft of Prob. 442 if the maximum shear theory is used.

444. Determine the minimum diameter of the shaft of Prob. 442 if the deformation-energy theory is used.

445. A cylindrical shaft, 2 in. diameter, is subjected to a bending moment of 900 ft.-lb. and a twisting moment of 900 ft.-lb. Determine the factor of safety, if the yield point of the material, in tension, is 40,000 psi. Use the maximum stress theory.

446. Determine the factor of safety of the shaft of Prob. 445, using the maximum shear theory.

447. Determine the factor of safety of the shaft of Prob. 445, using the deformation-energy theory.

448. A horizontal force $P = 200$ lb. is applied to the pulley, which has a diameter of 4 ft. The shaft has a diameter of 2 in. and is made of steel which has a yield point, in tension, of 30,000 psi. Neglecting the weight of the pulley, determine the factor of safety, using the maximum shear theory. *Ans.* 2.19.

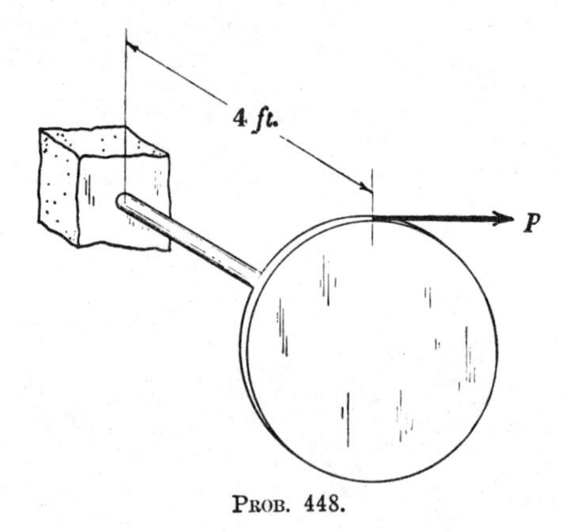

PROB. 448.

449. Determine the factor of safety of the shaft of Prob. 448 if the weight of the pulley is 400 lb. *Ans.* 1.07.

450. If the diameter of the shaft of Prob. 448 is changed to 2.4 in. determine the percentage increase in the factor of safety, and the percentage increase in weight of the shaft.

451. Determine the diameter of the shaft of Prob. 448 which will double its factor of safety. Use maximum shear theory.

452. Determine the factor of safety of the shaft of Prob. 449, using the deformation-energy theory.

453. All loads are applied at the center of the shaft. $M_T = 1440$ ft.-lb. Forces F_1 and F_2 are applied in planes which are perpendicular to the long axis of the shaft. Force F_1 is 866 lb. inclined at an angle of 30° with the vertical. Force F_2 is 172 lb. and is horizontal. The yield point of the material of the shaft is 36,000 psi, in tension. The shaft is freely supported at its ends. Determine the radius required if the factor of safety of the shaft is to be 2, using the maximum shear theory.

Ans. 1.2 in.

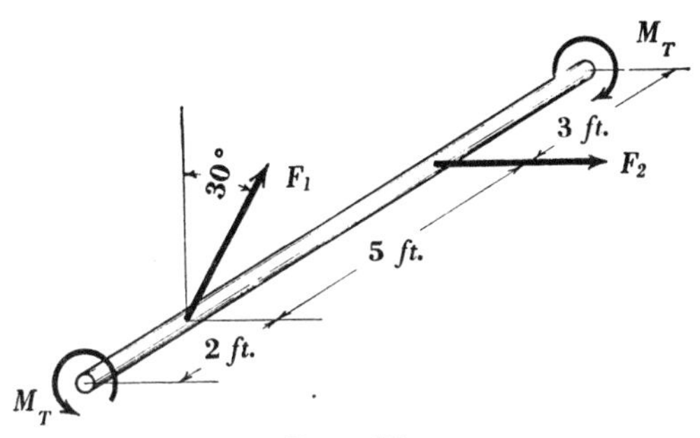

PROB. 453.

454. Determine the diameter of the shaft required for the loading of Prob. 453 which will raise the factor of safety to 5, using the maximum shear theory.

455. The drawing shows the tail wheel assembly of an airplane. The vertical supporting force exerted by the ground is 6000 lb. The most critical loading condition occurs when the hollow strut S cannot swivel and the tail is sliding sideways (perpendicular to the plane of the drawing). Determine the factor of safety of the hollow strut, using the maximum shear theory. The outside diameter of the strut is 6 in., and the inside diameter is 5 in. The coefficient of friction of the tire on the ground is 0.4, and the yield point of the strut material in tension is 60,000 psi.

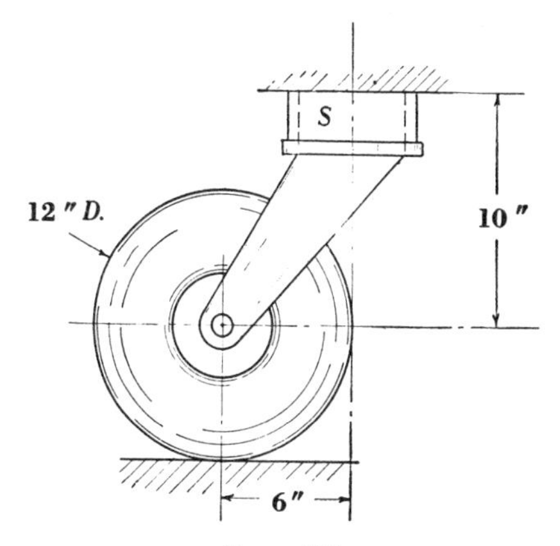

PROB. 455.

456. The shaft is freely supported at A and B. Pulley P_1 has a diameter of 14 in. and weighs 280 lb. Pulley P_2 has a diameter of 12 in. and weighs 160 lb. The shaft has a diameter of 2 in. and the yield point of the material in tension is 15,000 psi. Determine the factor of safety of the shaft, using the maximum shear theory.

Ans. 9.9.

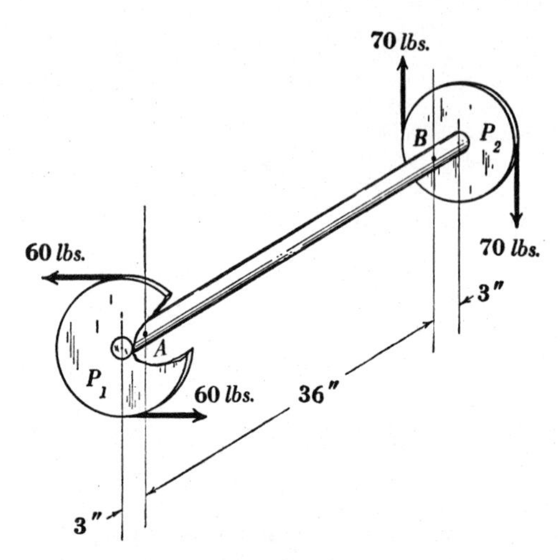

PROB. 456.

457. Determine the factor of safety of the shaft of Prob. 456, using the deformation-energy theory.

458. Determine the diameter which is required for the shaft of Prob. 456 if the twisting moment is increased to 150 ft.-lb. and the factor of safety is to be 10, using the maximum shear theory.

459. A solid cylindrical shaft is made of material having a yield point, in tension, of 12,000 psi. The shaft is subjected to a bending moment of 4000 ft.-lb. and a twisting moment of 5000 ft.-lb. Determine the minimum diameter of the shaft using (a) the maximum stress theory and (b) the maximum shear theory.

Ans. (a) 3.76 in.; (b) 4.02 in.

460. If a 4 in. diameter shaft is used for the loading condition of Prob. 459 and material is used which has a yield point in tension of 30,000 psi, determine the factor of safety. Use the deformation-energy theory. *Ans.* 2.67.

461. A solid shaft is made of steel having a yield point of 50,000 psi. The shaft is subjected to a bending moment of 6000 ft.-lb. and a twisting moment of 7200 ft.-lb. Determine the required diameter of the shaft for a factor of safety of 1.8 using the maximum shear theory.

462. Determine the required diameter of the shaft of Prob. 461 if the deformation-energy theory is used.

463. If a 3 in.-diameter shaft is used for the loading conditions of Prob. 461, determine the factor of safety using the maximum shear theory.

464. An element of metal has a yield point of 20,000 psi, in tension. If the element is loaded so that the indicated stresses are induced, determine the factor of safety, using the maximum shear theory. *Ans.* 1.6.

465. If the deformation-energy is applied in the case of the element of Prob. 464, determine the factor of safety. *Ans.*1 .8.

466. A shaft, 4 in. in diameter, is subjected to an axial tensile force of 12 tons, a bending moment of 8000 ft.-lb., and a twisting moment of 10,000 ft.-lb. Find the maximum normal and shearing stresses in the shaft. *Ans.* $s_N = 21{,}450$ psi; $s_S = 12{,}850$ psi.

467. Determine the minimum yield point which a material must have to be safely used in the shaft of Prob. 466 if the factor of safety is to be 2.5, using the maximum shear theory.

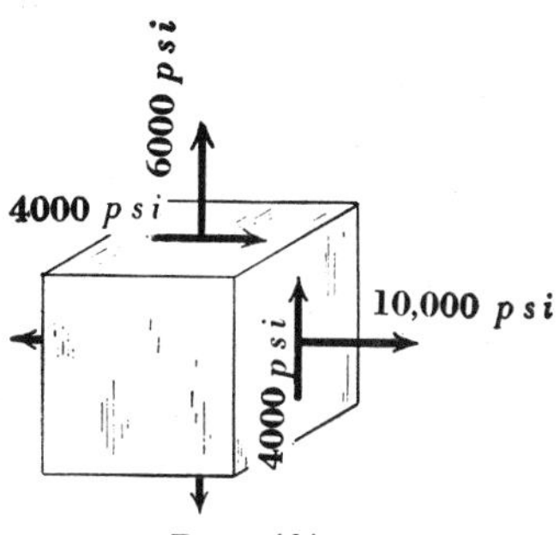

PROB. 464.

468. A horizontal hollow shaft, 8 in. outside diameter by 7 in. inside diameter, 16 ft. long, is subjected to an end thrust of 19,000 lb. and a twisting moment of 6000 ft.-lb. The shaft weighs 100 lb./ft. and is freely supported at its ends. Determine the factor of safety if the material has a yield point of 30,000 psi. Use the maximum shear theory. *Ans.* 6.13.

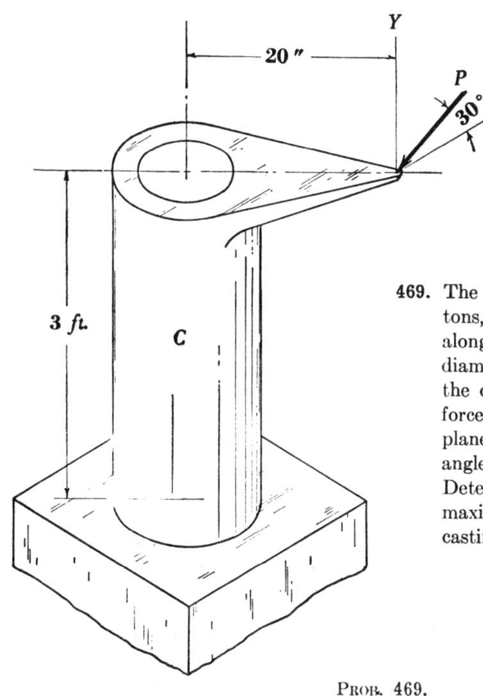

469. The weight of the casting C is 4 tons, which may be assumed to act along the central axis. The inside diameter of the casting is 8 in. and the outside diameter is 12 in. The force $P = 20$ tons lies in a vertical plane X-Y and is inclined at an angle of 30° with the horizontal. Determine the maximum normal and maximum shearing stresses in the casting.

PROB. 469.

470. If the cast material of Prob. 469 has a yield point of 20,000 psi in tension, determine the factor of safety, using the maximum shear theory. *Ans.* 1.77.

471. The block weighing 300 lb. is supported by an arm, which in turn is held in position by the hollow pipe S. The inside diameter of the pipe is 5 in. and the outside diameter is 6 in. The pipe weighs 30 lb./ft. Determine the maximum shear stress in the pipe when the load of 400 lb. (horizontal) is applied. *Ans.* 4120 psi.

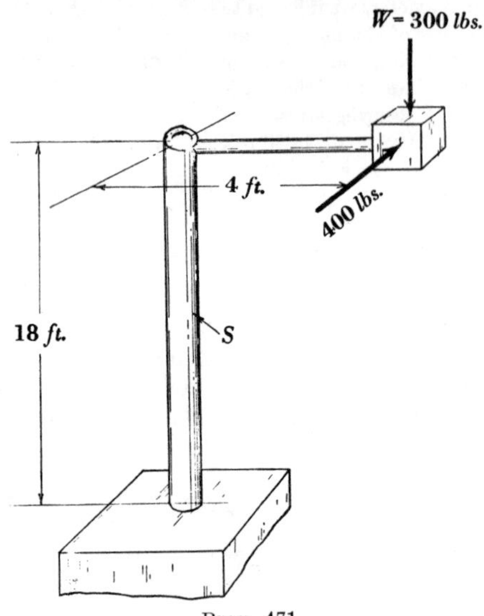

PROB. 471.

472. If the 400 lb. load of Prob. 471 is increased to 600 lb. determine the maximum principal stress in the hollow pipe S.

473. Determine the maximum shear stress in the hollow pipe of Prob. 471 when the load of 400 lb. is increased to 600 lb

474. A thin hollow tube, T, is subjected to an internal pressure of 200 psi. The diameter of the tube is 8 in.; the thickness of the wall is ¼ in. At the same time an axial load $P = 6800$ lb. and a twisting moment $M_T = 2000$ ft.-lb. are applied. Determine the maximum principal stress in the wall of the tube. *Ans.* 3560 psi.

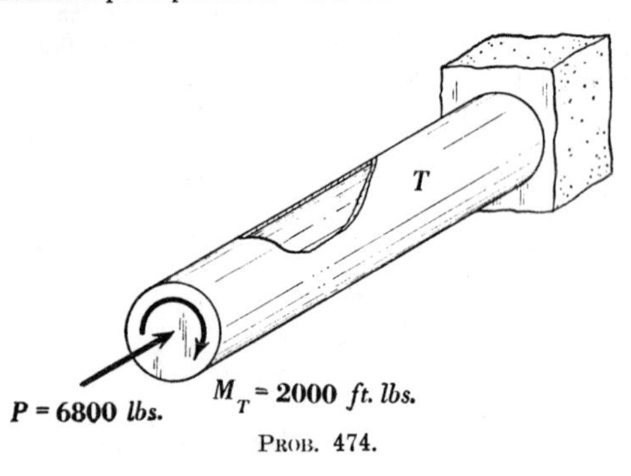

PROB. 474.

475. Determine the maximum shear stress in the tube of Prob. 475. *Ans.* 1780 psi.

476. If the tube of Prob. 474 is made of a material which has a yield point, in tension, of 18,000 psi determine the factor of safety. Use the maximum shear theory.

477. A 2 ft. bar *ab* is inserted through holes in the top and bottom of the thin tube *T*. The bar lies in the vertical *X*-*Y* plane, and is inclined at an angle of 30° with the *Y*-axis. The bar is welded to the tube and the ends of the tube are sealed.

Two horizontal forces F_1 and F_2 of 3800 lb. each, parallel to the *X*-axis, and two horizontal forces F_3 and F_4 of 500 lb. each, parallel to the *Z*-axis, are applied as shown.

The pressure inside the tube *T* is 100 psi. The diameter of the tube is 6 in. and the wall thickness is 0.1 in. The tube is made of steel, with a yield point in tension of 30,000 psi.

Determine the factor of safety of the tube, using the maximum shear theory. *Ans.* 3.54.

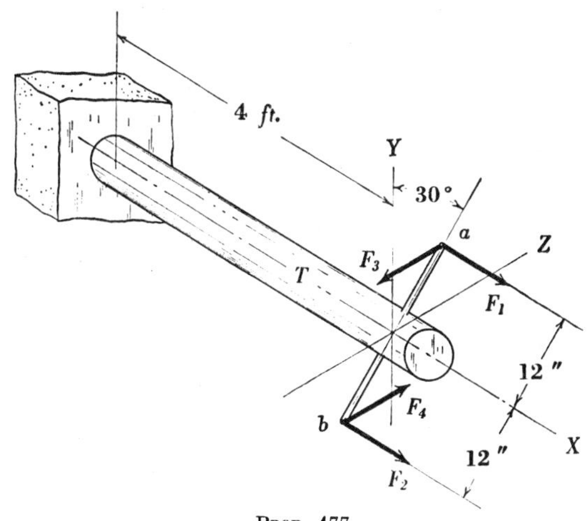

PROB. 477.

CHAPTER IX

Elastic Strain Energy

70. Elastic Strain Energy. When a body is loaded by forces which deform it, work has been done by those forces during the displacement of their points or regions of application. This work is stored as energy in the loaded body while the external forces are present, and will be released when the forces are removed. If the body is elastic, and no permanent deformation has been caused by the loading forces, the stored energy will be completely released. Such stored energy is called the *potential energy of elastic deformation*, or, more simply, the elastic *strain energy.* The property of a material which enables it to serve as a reservoir for the storage of energy is called its *resilience.*

Energy considerations furnish a powerful ally in attacking many of the complex problems of mechanics, and we shall, in the following articles establish a working basis for such attacks by noting the manner in which elastic strain energy is appraised and evaluated. We shall then have prepared ourselves for those theorems of mechanics such as the theorem of Castigliano, which make use of energy considerations.

71. Strain Energy in Axial Loading. When an axial force F is applied to a prism so that the stress remains within the elastic range, the work done by the force will equal the strain energy which is stored in the body, provided that the load is gradually applied. If we assume that there was no initial stress in the body and that the stress varies directly as the strain, the average force will be $F/2$, and the total elongation of the prism will be $\delta = eL$. The strain energy will be

$$U = \frac{F}{2} e\,L = \frac{sA}{2}\frac{s}{E} L = \frac{s^2 AL}{2E} \tag{110}$$

The volume of the prism is $V = AL$, and

$$U = \frac{s^2 V}{2E}$$

The amount of energy which can be absorbed by a loaded body if the maximum stress is not to be excessive, is therefore a function of the volume and the modulus of elasticity of the given material. A material which has a high elastic limit and a low modulus of elasticity is capable of absorbing a large amount of elastic strain energy in a given volume. When machine or structural parts are subjected to shock or impact loading, this property of high resilience may become the factor which governs the choice of material.

The amount of strain energy *per unit of volume* that will be stored in a given material when stressed to its elastic limit is called the *modulus of resilience.* We may obtain some idea of the ability of different materials to absorb such energy by noting the values of their moduli of resilience.

$$\text{Modulus of Resilience} = \frac{s^2}{2E} \tag{111}$$

where s is the elastic limit and E is the modulus of elasticity. The values of elastic limit given in the table below are average values—they will vary with the method of manufacture, heat treatment, and alloying of the material, and are intended only to indicate the influence of elastic limit and modulus of elasticity on the modulus of resilience.

TABLE VIII

Material	*Elastic Limit psi*	*Modulus of Elasticity, psi*	*Modulus of Resilience, in.-lbs./cu. in.*
Low-carbon steel	30,000	30×10^6	15
High-carbon steel	80,000	30×10^6	107
Malleable cast iron	25,000	23×10^6	14
Aluminum, hard drawn	25,000	10.3×10^6	30
Common rolled brass	25,000	14×10^6	22
Wood (oak)	9,500	1.7×10^6	53

72. Falling Weight. Suddenly Applied Load. The collar A, whose weight is W (Fig. 250), is allowed to drop through distance h. It will strike the stop B and continue to fall through an additional distance δ, elongating the rod.

Assuming that the rod is perfectly elastic, and stop B inelastic, the kinetic energy which the falling collar possesses will be transferred to the rod, where it will be stored as strain energy. The energy supplied by the falling weight is

$$U = W(h + \delta)$$

and the energy in the rod will be

$$W(h + \delta) = \frac{1}{2} s A \delta$$

Then the stress in the rod at the instant of greatest elongation is

$$s = \frac{2W(h + \delta)}{A\delta} \tag{112}$$

It has been assumed that all of the work done by the falling weight in this ideal case is available for transfer to the rod. Actually, a small amount of the energy supplied in the case of real bodies will be dissipated, and the actual elongation will be less than that noted above.

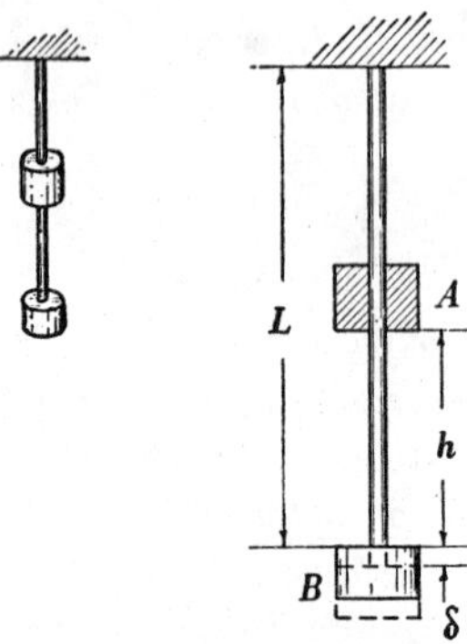

FIG. 250.

When a load is suddenly applied to a body like the rod of our example—that is, when all of the load W is assumed to be placed instantaneously at the bottom of the rod, the term h of equation (112) is equal to zero, and

$$s = \frac{2W}{A}$$

If the load W were to be applied gradually, as has been the case in all of the static loads we have already discussed, the stress in the rod would be

$$s = \frac{W}{A}$$

which is only one-half as great as the stress induced by the suddenly applied load.

The static or gradually applied load is always balanced by the force of resistance of the rod. During this state of equilibrium, a weight W will elongate the rod a distance δ. The suddenly applied load, on the other hand differs in that as it elongates the rod through a distance δ, the force of resistance is increasing as the weight is falling. When the force in the rod just equals W, the elongation will be δ. At this instant, however, the falling weight will have kinetic energy, and it will continue to fall until its velocity becomes equal to zero. This additional deformation, during which the kinetic energy of the falling weight is transferred to strain energy in the rod will also be equal to δ. If the total elongation of the rod when subjected to the action of the suddenly applied load is called δ_S, then

$$\delta_S = 2\delta$$

and a suddenly applied load produces an elongation which is twice that of the static load.

73. Strain Energy in Torsion. The work done by a gradually applied couple or torque, as it rotates a body, is $M\theta/2$, where M is the moment and θ the angular displacement. If the body is elastic, the strain energy which will be stored in the rotating body is equal to the work done by the couple.

If the loaded body is a cylindrical shaft which conforms to the limitations of the torsion theory, the angular displacement is the angle of twist, $M_T L/GI_P$ (see Art. 56), and

$$U = \frac{M_T{}^2 L}{2GI_P} \tag{113}$$

The maximum torsional shear stress in such a shaft is, by equation (73),

$$s_S = \frac{M_T\, r}{I_P} \qquad \text{and} \qquad M_T = \frac{s_S\, I_P}{r}$$

Then

$$U = \frac{s_S{}^2\, I_P{}^2}{2\, r^2}\,\frac{L}{GI_P}$$

$$= \frac{s_S{}^2\, I_P\, L}{2\, r^2 G} \tag{1}$$

But

$$I_P = A\rho^2$$

where ρ is the radius of gyration of the cross-section of the shaft relative to its diameter. The polar moment of inertia of a circular section is $\pi r^4/2$ and its area is πr^2.

Then

$$I_P = \frac{\pi r^4}{2}; \qquad A = \pi r^2$$

and

$$\rho^2 = \frac{r^2}{2}$$

Substituting in equation (1)

$$U = \frac{s_S{}^2\, I_P\, L}{2\, r^2 G} = \frac{s_S{}^2\, A\, \rho^2\, L}{4\, \rho^2\, G} = \frac{s_S{}^2 A\, L}{4G}$$

$$= \frac{s_S{}^2 V}{4\, G} \tag{114}$$

where V is the volume of the shaft. The *modulus of torsional resilience*, like its counterpart in axial loading, is the amount of strain energy which may be stored in a unit volume of a shaft subjected to twisting, when the shaft is stressed to its torsional elastic limit.

$$\text{Torsional Modulus of Resilience} = \frac{s_S{}^2}{4G} \tag{115}$$

where s_S is the elastic limit in torsion, and G is the modulus of rigidity.

74. Strain Energy in Bending. When the transverse loads to which we are limited in the flexure theory are gradually applied, each load does an amount of work

$$U = \frac{Py}{2}$$

where y is the deflection of the point of application of a concentrated load P. This work, stored in the beam as potential energy, is available for complete release if the material is elastic.

For example, a simple beam, freely supported at its ends, and carrying a single concentrated load P at mid-span will have a deflection under the load which is, by equation (40),

$$y = \frac{1}{48}\frac{PL^3}{EI}$$

and the strain energy in the beam will be

$$U = \frac{1}{96}\frac{P^2L^3}{EI}$$

When the beam carries a distributed load, as in Fig. 251, the deflection caused by an elementary load $w\,dx$ will be y, and the strain energy due to that load will be

$$dU = \frac{(w\,dx)y}{2}$$

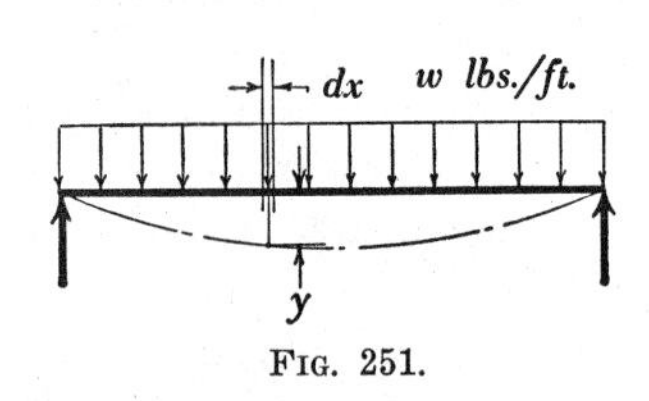

Fig. 251.

The total strain energy in the beam will be

$$U = \int\frac{(w\,dx)y}{2}$$

To accomplish the integration, y must be expressed in terms of x. We can develop a general method of attack by considering the elementary portion of the beam of Fig. 252 which lies between beam sections A-A and B-B.

The change of slope between A-A and B-B is $d\theta$. If the bending moment at the elementary section is M, the work done in changing the slope will be $\frac{1}{2}M\,d\theta$, assuming that the load is gradually applied.

$$d\theta = \frac{ds}{r}$$

where r is the radius of curvature of the elastic curve at the section which we are investigating. We have already found, in the deflection theory, that

$$\frac{1}{r} = \frac{M}{EI}$$

and the strain energy of the elementary section will be

$$\frac{M\,d\theta}{2} = \frac{M\,ds}{2r} = \frac{M^2\,ds}{2EI}$$

which is very nearly equal to

$$\frac{M^2\,dx}{2EI}$$

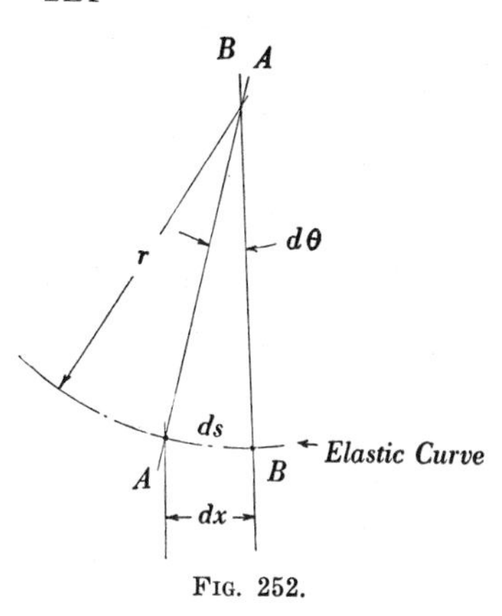

Fig. 252.

The strain energy in the entire beam may now be determined by adding the energies in its several elementary sections, and

$$U = \int \frac{M^2\,dx}{2EI} \qquad \textbf{(116)}$$

We have assumed, in this derivation, that all of the strain energy in the beam is that which is produced by the bending moment, and that the amount of energy for which the shearing force is responsible is negligible. This is approximately true except when, as in the case of a very short and relatively deep beam, the deflection resulting from shearing is of appreciable magnitude. The deflection of such a beam has been considered in Art. 52.

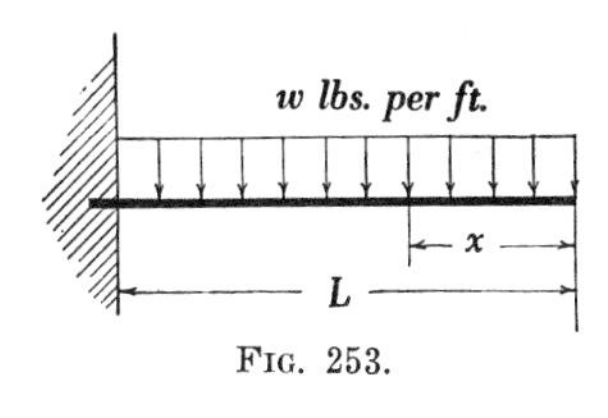

Fig. 253.

Illustrative Example. A cantilever beam (Fig. 253) carries a uniformly distributed load of w lb./ft. The elastic strain energy in the beam is to be determined.

By equation (116), $\quad U = \int \frac{M^2\,dx}{2EI}$

The bending moment in the beam is most readily established by considering the origin of x at the right or free end.

$$M = -\frac{wx^2}{2}$$

Then

$$U = \int_{x=0}^{x=L} -\frac{w^2 x^4\,dx}{8EI}$$

$$= -\frac{w^2L^5}{40EI}$$

In terms of the maximum deflection, the strain energy is

$$U = -\frac{wL}{5} \times \left(-\frac{1}{8}\frac{wL^4}{EI}\right) = \frac{1}{5} w\,L\,y_{\text{max.}}$$

75. Strain Energy in Combined Loading. When a member is subjected to combinations of forces or couples, or both, the total energy which will be stored in the loaded member will be the algebraic sum of the work done by each of the loads, for energy is a scalar quantity. We shall again assume that the material is elastic and that all loads are gradually applied.

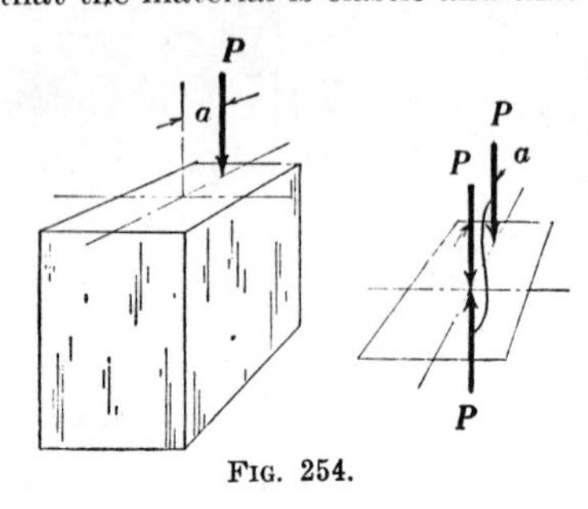

FIG. 254.

The method of attack upon the total strain energy is one of superposition; we determine the strain energy from each source or load, and add to obtain the combined effect.

For example, if a load P is applied to a compression block as shown in Fig. 254, the loading is equivalent to an axial load P, and a bending moment $M = Pa$.

The strain energy from the axial load is, by equation (110),

$$U_A = \frac{P^2L}{2AE}$$

The strain energy from the bending moment is, substituting in equation (116),

$$U_B = \frac{P^2\,a^2L}{2EI}$$

The total strain energy is

$$\begin{aligned} U &= U_A + U_B \\ &= \frac{P^2L}{2AE} + \frac{P^2\,a^2L}{2EI} \\ &= \frac{P^2L}{2E}\left(\frac{1}{A} + \frac{a^2}{I}\right) \end{aligned}$$

Illustrative Example. A propeller shaft is subjected to a twisting moment $M_T = 1000$ ft.-lb., and a constant bending moment, $M_B = 1200$ ft.-lb. The shaft is 5 ft. long, and has 2 in. diameter. $E = 30 \times 10^6$ psi; $G = 12 \times 10^6$ psi. The total strain energy in the shaft is to be determined.

From the torsion equation (73),

$$s_S = \frac{M_T\,r}{I_P} = \frac{1000 \times 12 \times 1}{\pi \times (1)^4/2} = 7640 \text{ psi}$$

Using equation (114),

$$\begin{aligned} U_T = \frac{s_S{}^2V}{4G} &= \frac{(7640)^2(\pi \times 1)(5 \times 12)}{4 \times 12 \times 10^6} \\ &= 229 \text{ in.-lb.} \end{aligned}$$

Using equation (116),

$$\begin{aligned} U_B = \frac{M_B{}^2L}{2\,EI} &= \frac{(1200 \times 12)^2 \times 5 \times 12}{2 \times 30 \times 10^6 \times (\pi \times 1)^4/4} \\ &= 264 \text{ in.-lb.} \end{aligned}$$

$$U = U_T + U_B = 229 + 264 = 493 \text{ in.-lb.}$$

PROBLEMS

478. A steel rod has a cross-sectional area of 2 sq. in. and a length of 4 ft. Determine the strain energy in the rod when an axial load of 20,000 lb. is applied.
Ans. 160 in.-lb.

479. How much strain energy is stored in a cylindrical aluminum rod, 2 in. in diameter, 6 ft. long, when an axial load of 15,000 lb. is applied?

480. A steel rod has a cross-sectional area of 4 sq. in. The strain energy in the rod is 560 in.-lb. when the unit stress is 12,000 psi. Determine the length of the rod.
Ans. 4.86 ft.

481. Determine the modulus of resilience of an alloy having a modulus of elasticity $E = 18 \times 10^6$ psi and an elastic limit of 12,000 psi. *Ans.* 4 in.-lb./cu. in.

482. Determine the modulus of resilience of a material having a modulus of elasticity $E = 10^6$ psi, and an elastic limit of 1200 psi.

483. The modulus of resilience of a material is 150 in.-lb./cu. in. The modulus of elasticity of the material is $E = 12 \times 10^6$ psi. If a bar of the material has a cross-sectional area of 1.6 sq. in., what axial load may be safely applied if the factor of safety, based on the elastic limit, is to be 4? *Ans.* 24,000 lb.

484. A straight steel bar, 10 ft. long, has a rectangular cross-section which varies uniformly from 1 by 2 in. at one end to 1 by 4 in. at the other end. Determine the strain energy in the bar when it is subjected to an axial load of 30,000 lb.

485. Rods A and B are made of brass and rod C of aluminum. Area A = area B = 1 sq. in.; area C = 1.2 sq. in. Determine the amount of strain energy stored in each rod when load P = 24,000 lb. is applied.

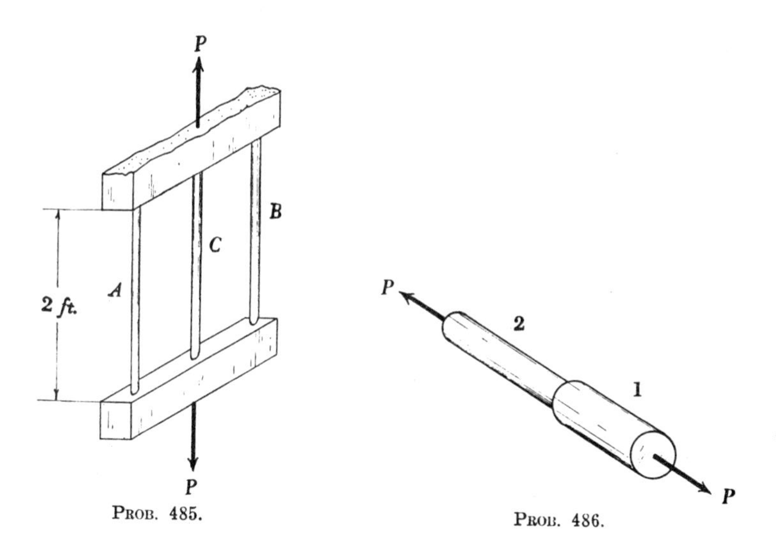

Prob. 485.

Prob. 486.

486. What load P may be applied to the shaft if the modulus of resilience of the materials must not be exceeded? Section **1** is made of low-carbon steel and has a cross-sectional area of 2 sq. in.; section **2** is made of malleable cast iron and has a cross-sectional area of 1 sq. in. Use values given in Table VIII. *Ans.* 25,400 lb.

487. The cross-sectional area of steel rod A is 4 sq. in. The collar C is allowed to drop from a height of 1 ft. to strike the inelastic stop S at the end of the rod. If the maximum allowable tensile stress in the rod is 12,000 psi, determine the maximum safe weight of collar C. *Ans.* 47.9 lb.

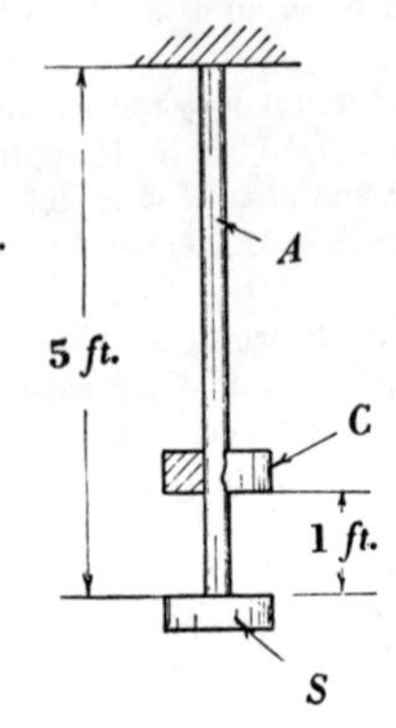

PROB. 487.

488. Determine the gradually applied load which may be placed on the steel rod of Prob. 487 without exceeding the same allowable tensile stress. *Ans.* 48,000 lb.

489. If the collar C of Prob. 487 is dropped from a distance of 3 in., what is the maximum safe weight of C for the same allowable stress?

490. What weight W may be safely dropped through a distance of 5 in. to strike a block of aluminum alloy, 2 by 2 by 5 in. tall, without causing a stress greater than the elastic limit of 25,000 psi? $E = 10.3 \times 10^6$ psi.

491. If the material of Prob. 490 is changed to malleable cast iron, having an elastic limit of 25,000 psi, and $E = 23 \times 10^6$ psi, determine the safe weight.

492. If the material of Prob. 490 is changed to high-carbon steel, having an elastic limit of 80,000 psi, and $E = 30 \times 10^6$ psi, determine the safe weight.

493. Determine the minimum dimensions of a cube of steel, having an elastic limit of 30,000 psi, and $E = 30 \times 10^6$ psi, to absorb, without permanent distortion, the energy of a weight of 200 lb. dropped from a height of 6 in. above the top of the cube. *Ans.* 4.31 in.

494. A steel shaft, 4 in. in diameter, length = 5 ft., is subjected to a twisting moment at its ends which produces a maximum torsional shear stress of 10,000 psi. Determine the strain energy in torsion. $G = 12 \times 10^6$ psi. *Ans.* 1570 in.-lb.

495. Determine the strain energy stored in a hollow steel shaft, 6 in. outside diameter and 4 in. inside diameter, when the maximum torsional shear stress is 8000 psi. Length = 10 ft.

496. Determine the strain energy in a solid steel shaft of the same outside diameter, length, and maximum torsional shear stress as the hollow shaft of Prob. 495.

497. Find the modulus of torsional resilience of a steel having an elastic limit in torsion of 36,000 psi. $G = 12 \times 10^6$ psi. *Ans..* 27 in.-lb./cu. in.

498. Determine the modulus of torsional resilience of a high-carbon steel having an elastic limit in torsion of 48,000 psi. $G = 12 \times 10^6$ psi.

499. A 2 in. diameter steel shaft transmits 30 h.p. at 600 r.p.m. The length of the shaft if 16 ft. $G = 12 \times 10^6$ psi. Determine the amount of strain energy stored in the shaft. *Ans.* 50.6 in.-lb.

500. Determine the strain energy of bending stored in the cantilever beam when load $P = 3600$ lb. is applied. $E = 1.2 \times 10^6$ psi. *Ans.* 9330 in.-lb.

501. The beam is an American Standard steel I-beam, 12 in. × 35 lb./ft. Determine the strain energy of bending under the indicated load.

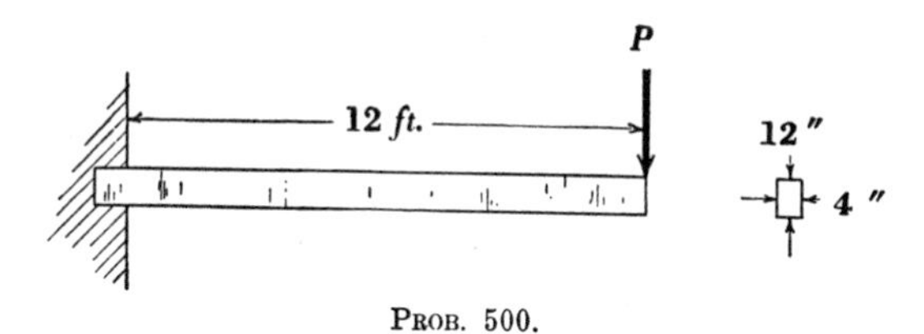

Prob. 500.

502. The beam is an 8 in. × 31 lb./ft. Wide-Flange steel beam. Determine the total strain energy of bending under the indicated loads. *Ans.* 245 in.-lb.

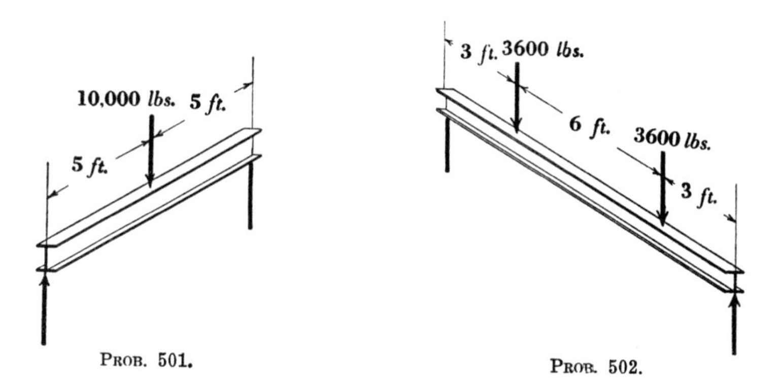

Prob. 501. Prob. 502.

503. Determine the strain energy of bending of the beam under the indicated load. $E = 1.2 \times 10^6$ psi.

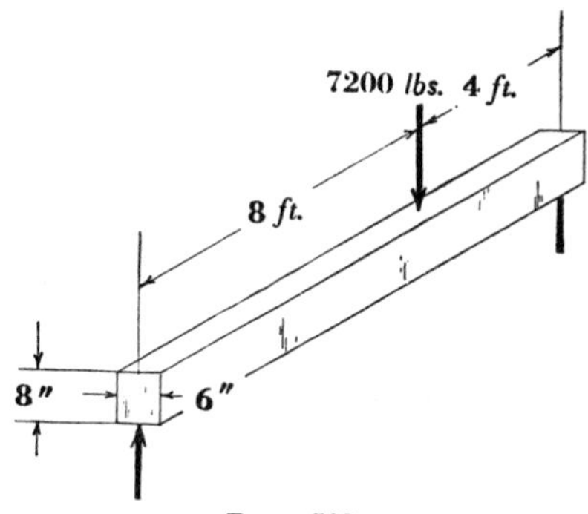

Prob. 503.

504. The beam is a 12 in. × 31.8-lb./ft. American Standard steel I-beam. Determine the total strain energy of bending under the indicated loads.

505. A cantilever beam carries a uniformly distributed load of 300 lb./ft., including its own weight. The beam is 9 ft. long and has a rectangular cross-section, 8 in. wide and 12 in. deep. $E = 1.6 \times 10^6$ psi. Determine the strain energy of bending in the beam. *Ans.* 125 in.-lb.

506. A rectangular beam, 6 in. wide and 9 in. deep, carries a uniformly distributed load of w lb./ft. The beam is freely supported at its ends and has a length of 12 ft. $E = 1.2 \times 10^6$ psi. If the strain energy of bending under this load is 575 in.-lb. determine the value of w. *Ans.* 375 lb./ft.

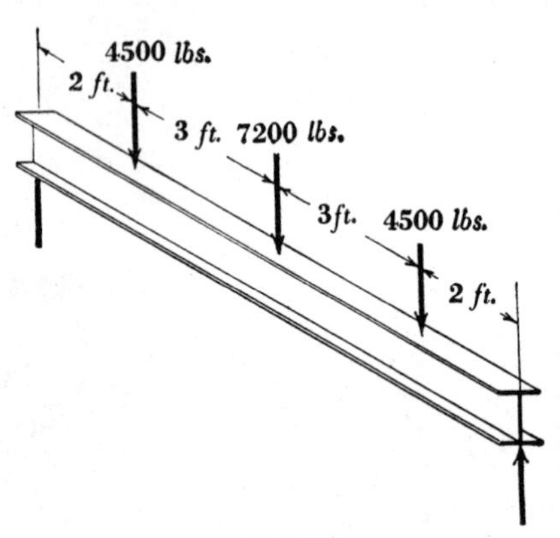

PROB. 504.

507. A cantilever beam carries a uniformly distributed load of 100 lb./ft. which includes its own weight, and a concentrated load of 400 lb. as shown. $E = 1.6 \times 10^6$ psi. Determine the strain energy of bending in the beam.

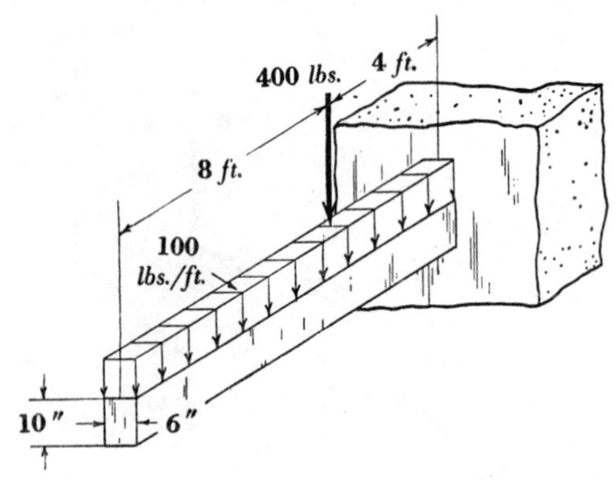

PROB. 507.

508. The beam is supported by a pin joint at A and held in position by cable BC. All loads are applied along the central axis of the beam. $E = 1.2 \times 10^6$ psi. Determine the total strain energy in the beam when load $W = 1200$ lb. is applied.

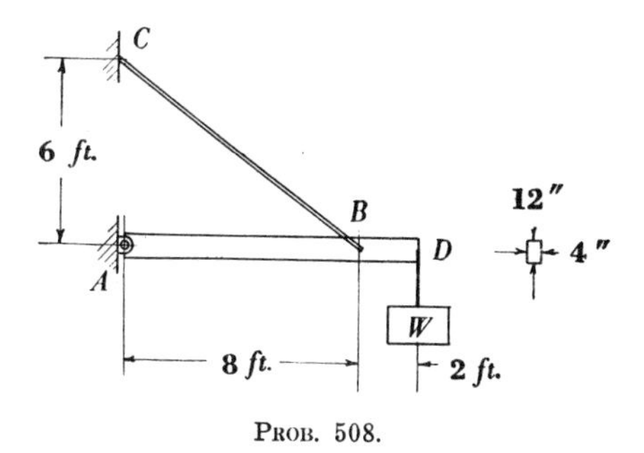

PROB. 508.

509. The steel shaft has a diameter of 2 in. $G = 12 \times 10^6$ psi. $E = 30 \times 10^6$ psi. The diameter of pulley P_1 is 12 in. and the diameter of pulley P_2 is 18 in. Determine the total strain energy in the shaft, neglecting the weight of the pulleys and shaft.

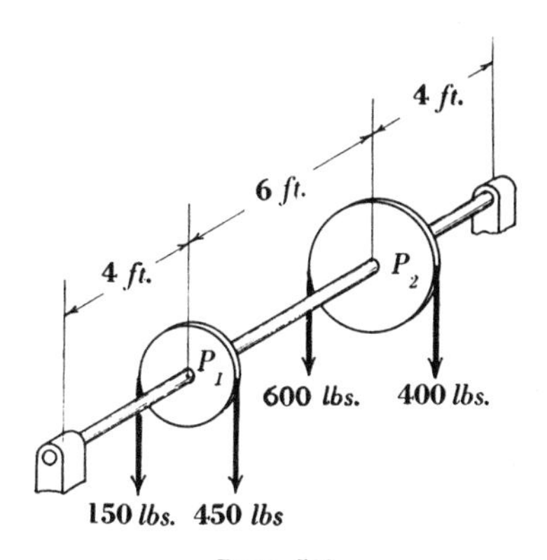

PROB. 509.

CHAPTER X

Mechanical Properties of Materials

76. Mechanical Properties. In studying the fundamentals of the mechanics of materials, we are primarily concerned with the behavior of loaded bodies. Here, unlike the studies which were pursued in the field of elementary statics, we cannot build trusses of geometric lines, or pursue the conditions of equilibrium upon idealized bodies which are assumed to be rigid, or built of nondeformable materials.

The nature of the material comprising the free bodies which we isolate for study does have an influence upon the behavior of those bodies. It is, therefore, necessary that the engineering student be equipped with an awareness of some of the properties of the actual bodies with which he is concerned. More thorough training lies in the province of courses devoted to engineering materials, and to their chemical and physical properties, but we shall, in this chapter, discuss those major characteristics which play a direct part in the mechanics problem when the engineering materials are used as elements of machines or of structures, and which are therefore commonly grouped as the *mechanical properties.*

Our discussion will confine itself to those properties which are the basis of current engineering design practice. That field of endeavor is affected as the intensive investigations of the research laboratory yield greater knowledge. Design practice can benefit in approaching an objective of greater economy in the use of materials as it accepts the revelations of the researchers. It takes time, however, before the pressure of the necessity for improved efficiency makes itself felt to the extent that designers will abandon the comfortable security of familiar method, and design practice usually lags behind the most recent discoveries of the experimental laboratory.

An example of recent advance toward greater mastery of the properties of materials has been the development of the science of metallography which concerns itself with the structure of the metals. Microscopic observation and X-ray examination are responsible for a growing literature of the structure and of its relationship to strain and to fracture of loaded bodies. It appears, from such studies, that deformation of the loaded bodies is very intimately associated with the crystal structure. Metals consist of an aggregate of individual crystalline grains. Fracture may consist of slip at the boundaries of the grains, or it may be caused by fracture of the grains themselves, or of yielding along planes of cleavage of the individual crystals. Little of this developing body of information has, as yet, affected current design procedures. As the collection of additional evidence continues, design will be influenced, probably in the evolution of more accurate theories of strength than those which are at present employed (see Art. 69).

77. The Tension Test. The most widely used means of seeking knowledge of the mechanical properties of materials is the tension test, and we can define and illustrate the influence of many of those properties by observing the data which are collected in the course of such a test.

In this test, a specimen of the material is machined into the form of a cylinder. The dimensions of the test piece are fixed by standardization, so that the results of the test may be universally understood, no matter where, or by whom, the test is conducted. Other conditions of the test, like the rate of deformation and the temperature of the surrounding medium are also standardized, notably by such groups as the American Society for Testing Materials. The specimen is mounted between the jaws of a tensile testing machine, which is simply a device for stretching the specimen at a controlled rate. The resistance which the specimen offers to being stretched, and the linear deformations are measured by sensitive instrumentation.

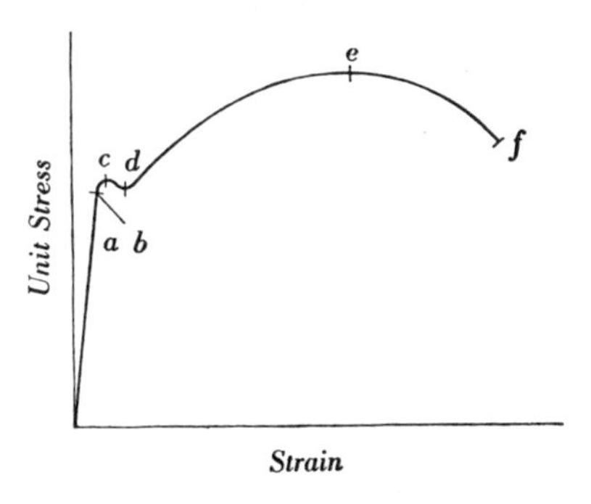

FIG. 255.

The force of resistance divided by the original cross-sectional area of the specimen is the apparent unit stress in the specimen.* The strain is the total deformation divided by the original length.

If the stresses in the specimen are plotted as ordinates of a graph, with the accompanying strains as abscissae, a number of the mechanical properties are graphically revealed. Figure 255 shows such a stress–strain diagram for a mild-steel specimen.

When load is applied and gradually increased, the specimen is stretched and the stresses at various loads, in such a material, are found to be in a linear relationship with the strains. If the load is removed, the specimen

*The distinction between this apparent stress and the true stress is discussed in Art. 7.

will return to its original shape and size. If additional loads are imposed and then removed, we find that the specimen continues to return to its original shape and size until a limiting load is reached. The unit stress at this limiting load is called the *elastic limit* of the material. At this load, the material ceases to remain unaffected, and when greater load is applied, it will have been permanently set, or distorted.

When a bar is stretched, as in tensile testing, the structure of the material is probably changed, as in any manner of "working" the material. Some permanent distortion may have been introduced even though the applied loads are small. Imperfections in the material may be the scene of stress concentration, and relief of such concentration may have occurred by yielding in those localities. We shall later, in the discussion of repeated loading, note the influence of such local conditions. The order of magnitude of such permanent distortion in a test specimen submitted to only a gradually applied load is so minute that materials are assumed to suffer no permanent deformation until they are stressed beyond the elastic limit.

The values of stress below the elastic limit are called the *elastic range*. When the elastic limit is passed, the material is permanently deformed—it has "flowed" or become plastic, and the range of stress values above the elastic limit is therefore called the *plastic range*.

Point b of Fig. 255 shows the location of the elastic limit. At approximately the same value of stress, we find another limiting value—point a—called the *proportional limit*. This unit stress, while very nearly equal in magnitude to the elastic limit, is based upon a different concept of mechanical properties.

In many materials—this is true of the steel described in the graph of Fig. 255—the material obeys Hooke's law in the elastic range. Stress is proportional to strain, and the portion of the curve which indicates this range is a straight line. The maximum value of unit stress—the upper limit of the straight line (point a)—is the proportional limit. Not all materials possess such a limit. Many materials, notably those which are brittle, like cast iron and concrete, do not follow a linear relationship in their stress–strain curves.

If the load is increased so that the development of stress is carried into the plastic range, the deformation will increase until a point like c of Fig. 255 is reached. At this stress, marked deformation—frequently so marked that it can be noted by the naked eye—takes place. This stress is called the *yield point*. The yield point, particularly in the case of ductile materials, is taken as the criterion upon which some theories of strength and standards of allowable stresses are based, as we have noted in Art. 69.

As the yield point is reached, the marked deformation takes place even though the load may be decreased. Points of the curve are values of stress that represent the resistance which the specimen is offering to being deformed. This resistance may decrease at the yield point, as indicated by the dip in the curve between points c and d, while the elongation continues. c and d are then referred to as the upper and lower limits of the yield point, respectively. Testing techniques and variables influence the upper limit more seriously than the lower limit, and the latter is the more reliable measure of yield point.

When the load is increased beyond the yield point, the typical pattern of stress values is represented by the portion of the curve between points d and e. e is the greatest value of the resistance, expressed as a unit stress, and is called the *ultimate strength* of the material. This value furnishes a measure of the greatest resistance which the specimen can offer to failure by tension, but actual fracture does not usually occur at this point. The specimen continues to deform, as indicated by the portion of the curve between points e and f. In this extreme portion of the plastic range, marked deformation is not confined to the longitudinal direction, but is exhibited in the form of marked reduction of the cross-sectional area, and the test piece assumes the shape shown in Fig. 256. The distortion, or narrowing, of the specimen is called "necking." This portion of the curve, lying between points e and f gives an indication of the *ductility* of the material, which is defined as its ability to deform in the plastic range without actually rupturing. This property is, naturally, of concern when the part which is to be made must be fashioned by metal-working, as in the drawing of wire. The amount of reduction of cross-sectional area in the necking region before rupture is an additional indication of ductility.

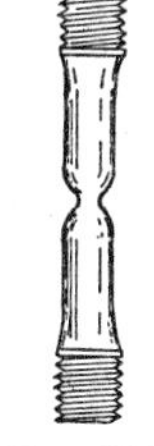
FIG. 256.

The description of a material as ductile is commonly accepted, primarily because mild steels, which are the prototype of the ductile materials, exhibit the plastic behavior which we have noted above, but only when axially loaded by a gradually applied load at room temperatures. At elevated temperatures, which have become an area of serious concern as materials are demanded for use in gas turbines and other recent developments, the distinction between ductile and brittle materials is not sharp and may even vanish. A material which is ductile at room temperatures may fail as a brittle one does when the temperature is elevated. The state of stress may also act to erase the distinction, for a material which may be ductile under axial tensile stress may behave like a brittle one when tensile stresses acting in three mutually perpendicular directions are encountered.

The property of *brittleness*, as commonly defined, is the inverse concept to ductility. If the portion of the stress–strain diagram of Fig. 255 which lies between points e and f is shorter, the material is said to be more brittle. Similarly, if there is little or no reduction of area, or necking, before rupture, the material is more brittle. Brittleness is, then, a relative term.* Cast iron is the prominent example of a brittle material. Figure 257 shows the stress–strain diagram for a specimen of cast iron submitted to a tension test at room temperature. It will be noted that the ultimate strength (point a) is the stress at which fracture actually occurs.

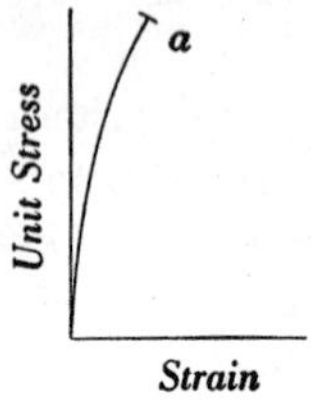

Fig. 257.

We have, earlier in the text, defined the *modulus of elasticity* as the constant of proportionality between stress and strain in the elastic range. Such a modulus may be determined by means of the stress–strain diagram of the tension test for a material which obeys Hooke's law. The slope of the curve in the elastic range is a measure of the modulus of elasticity, for we note that $\tan\theta = \Delta s/\Delta e = E$ (Fig. 258). *Stiffness* is the mechanical property which defines the ability of a material to resist deformation in the elastic range. If a material requires a large increase in loading to produce a given deformation, it will have a large value of $\tan\theta = \Delta s/\Delta e = E$. Conversely, if a material has a low value of modulus of elasticity it will lack stiffness, and a small increase in loading will produce a large deformation.

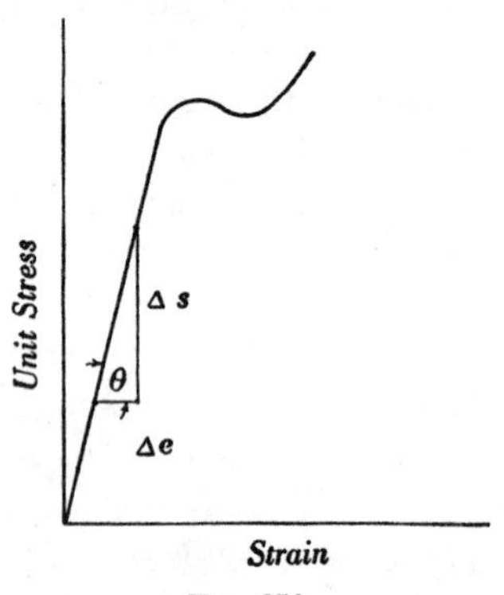

Fig. 258.

Another mechanical property which plays a part in the designer's selection of materials is *toughness*, or the ability to absorb large amounts of energy without rupturing. The supporting arms of a car bumper are an example of a machine part where such a property is of great value. The ability of a loaded body to absorb energy is noted in testing through the determination of its modulus of resilience, which has already been defined in Art. 71. The present consideration of the stress–strain diagram of the tension test furnishes another opportunity of noting the relationships involved in resilience. Figure 259 shows a modification of the stress–strain diagram. In this case, total resistance, P, has been plotted as ordinate, and total elongation, δ, serves as abscissa. The work done in stressing the

*For a more detailed discussion the reader is referred to "Working Stresses"—C. R. Soderberg: *Handbook of Experimental Stress Analysis*, Wiley, 1951.

body to the proportional limit, located at point b, is represented by the triangle abc, and is

$$W = \frac{1}{2} P \delta$$

in which P and δ are the values of load and deformation at the proportional limit. This amount of work, provided that the elastic limit has not been exceeded, is stored as strain energy in the material. Since there will be no permanent deformation of the material within these limits, all of this potential energy will be recovered when the load is removed. Expressed in terms of stress and strain

$$W = U = \frac{1}{2} \; P \delta = \frac{1}{2} s \, A \, eL$$

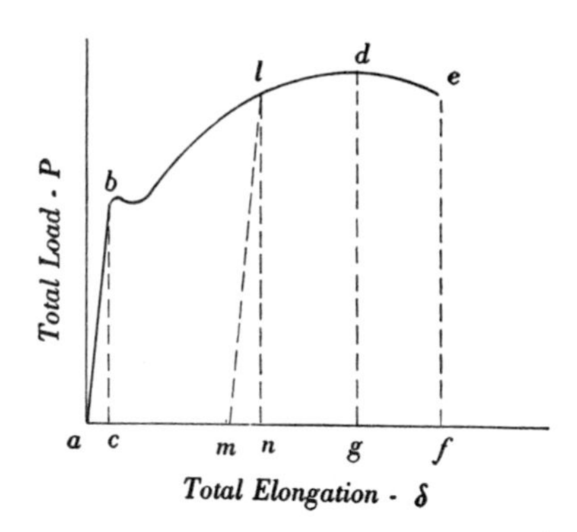

FIG. 259.

When the material is stressed into the plastic range, the total work done in loading the material to rupture will be the area $abdef$, which is approximately equal to

$$af \frac{bc + dg}{2}$$

or

$$W = \delta \frac{P_U + P_Y}{2}$$

in which W is the total work, δ the total deformation to rupture, P_U the load at the ultimate strength, and P_Y the load at yield point. This area represents the amount of work done in loading the body to rupture; much of the corresponding energy has been dissipated in the form of heat and in deforming the body, and only a small portion can be recovered. The amount of energy which may be recovered when the body is loaded to a point in the plastic range, like l, is represented by the area lmn. When the load represented by point l is removed, the specimen, which has, at the instant of removal, a total deformation an, will contract only as far as point m, representing the permanent set. Since area lmn is but a small part of area $abln$, which represents the total work done in stretching the bar to deformation n, only a correspondingly small part of the work done may be recovered.

The area $abdef$ represents the total amount of energy absorbed by the material to the point of rupture, and therefore indicates the toughness of the material.

The tensile test serves as a convenient and inexpensive medium for evaluating most of the mechanical properties of materials, particularly the ductile ones like mild steel. The results of such a test are not absolute, but they do serve the designer satisfactorily, even though he is forced to proceed on a relative basis, in the absence of absolute values. The apparent values which are yielded are somewhat fictitious as we have noted in the discussion of true stress (Art. 7), but they have served us in illustrating the concepts of elastic limit, yield point, ultimate strength, and modulus of elasticity. This vocabulary of the terms and concepts is qualitatively valid when the loading produces compression or shear. The values of the properties may, however, be very different, quantitatively, than those observed under tensile loading.

Another property of the engineering materials is of interest to the designer. This is the *hardness*, which is the resistance of the material to plastic deformation by indentation. This value is determined by pressing a small indenter, spherical or pyramidal in shape, into the surface of the material. The size of the impressions made under identical conditions for different materials gives a relative comparison of their respective hardnesses. Some correlation between hardness and tensile strength has been noted by observers.

Materials Which Do Not Obey Hooke's Law. There are many materials which do not exhibit the straight-line relationship between stress and strain in the elastic range. Such materials manifest the curved-line relationship which was shown in Fig. 257. There is, in such cases, no marked elastic limit, and no definite yield point, nor has the modulus of elasticity significance as a constant of proportionality. Since designers have developed many of their current techniques upon these concepts of mechanical property, arbitrary rules have been adopted to fix values for these materials which are analogous to those which we have illustrated in the case of the mild-steel specimen. These apparent values are fixed by arbitrary definitions which seek to standardize practice.

The *initial* slope of the stress–strain curve of Fig. 260 is On. If any horizontal line like abc be drawn, a distance bc equal to one-half of ab may be laid out. A line dcO will make an angle with the vertical axis 50 per cent greater than that of line On. If st be drawn parallel to dcO tangent to the curve at point u, the ordinate uv will represent a unit stress value at which the material is deforming at a rate which is 50 per cent greater than it was at the start. Such an increase of rate of deformation may be accepted as an indication of very marked deformation, or evidence that the material has definitely entered its plastic range. The factor of 50 per cent increase, while resulting from arbitrary choice, has been found empirically to be a satisfactory criterion in many cases where the nature of the material, or the lack of sufficiently sensitive testing technique or instrumentation, make exact observation of the boundary between the elastic and plastic ranges difficult. The value of stress, which is represented by the ordinate

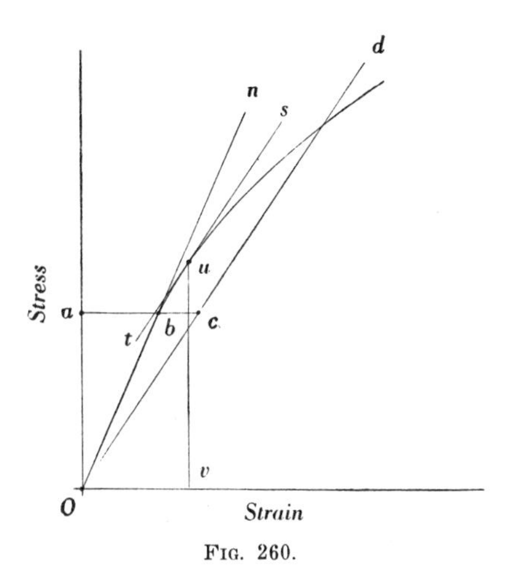

FIG. 260.

uv, is called Johnson's apparent elastic limit, and is employed by designers in the same manner as the elastic limit noted in the tension test of the ductile materials, which do obey Hooke's law.

Another example of an arbitrary compromise, fixed by convention, is the *apparent yield strength*. This property is analogous to the yield point of ductile materials and is intended to serve the same purpose in design. In the determination of the apparent yield strength, the beginning of yielding or plastic flow is defined as the stress at which the permanent set reaches a specified value. One commonly employed value of such deformation is a strain equal to 0.002 in./in. In applying this device to a stress–strain curve of a material a line *ab* (Fig. 261) is drawn from point *a*, parallel to the initial slope of the curve (*Od*). The intersection of this line with the curve establishes a point *b*, whose ordinate *bc* is taken as the apparent yield strength.

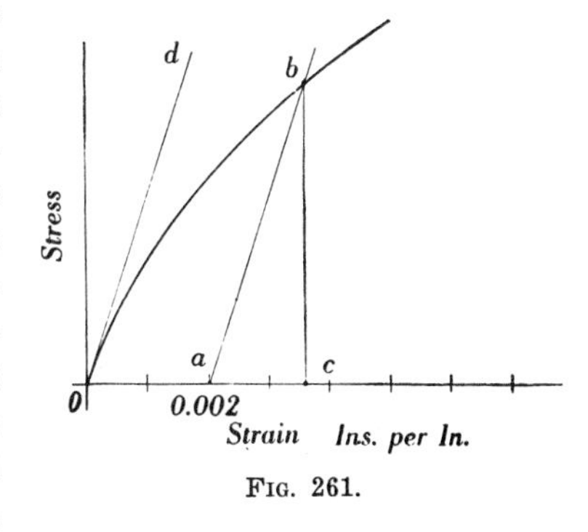

FIG. 261.

When the stress–strain curve is of the nature shown in Fig. 262, the significance of modulus of elasticity as a constant of proportionality is lost. The slope of the curve is ever variable, and angle θ whose tangent is $\Delta s/\Delta e$ can represent modulus of elasticity only instantaneously. In order that the designer may have available a convenient factor which will play the role of modulus of elasticity, the Johnson apparent elastic limit (Fig. 260) may be determined and the quotient obtained by dividing that stress by the corresponding strain employed as an *apparent* modulus of elasticity, sometimes called the *secant modulus.*

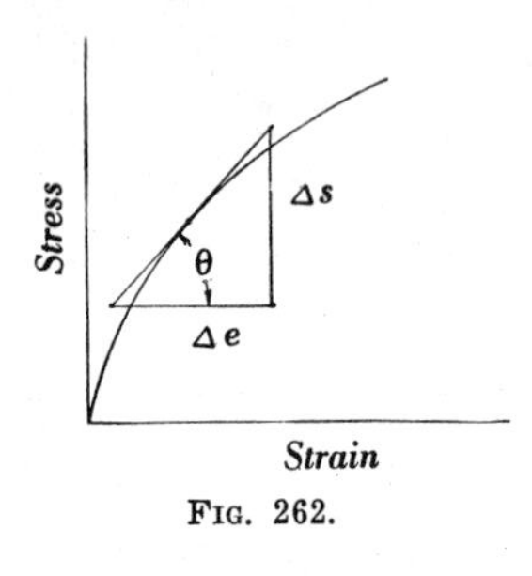

FIG. 262.

78. Additional Mechanical Properties. Other mechanical properties of materials are of interest to the engineering designer, in addition to the most common ones which were discussed in the preceding article. Interest in materials follows the development of new engineering applications, which may be properly served only when new materials or additional knowledge of the properties of old ones becomes available. Among other developments the progress of the chemical industries, the development of pressure vessels as well as steam and gas turbines focused attention upon the necessity of obtaining information concerning the mechanical properties of materials when used at elevated temperatures.

It has long been known that materials may exhibit a gradual flow or change in dimension when subjected to a constant load over a period of time.. This phenomenon is known as *creep.* Some soft metals (like lead) may creep at normal temperatures. This property, however, becomes critical in materials like steel when temperatures are elevated, and there is a viscous flow of the material caused by the temperature rise. The flow is resisted by the strain hardening of the material below a critical temperature. Beyond that temperature the strain hardening apparently does not balance the flow, and excessive creep, which is objectionable, is encountered.

The yield point and ultimate strength of materials subjected to tension at elevated temperatures are also affected. Creep, however, is the property which is of greatest concern, for it may take place at elevated temperature even though the stresses are held to values within the elastic range.

Creep tests are conducted by maintaining constant tensile stress in a specimen which is surrounded by a constant-temperature chamber. The axial strain is read periodically, and the curve of axial strain vs. time plotted.

Such curves are of the form illustrated in Fig. 263. The region of the curve between points b and c is a region of constant slope, de/dt, which is called the *creep rate*. It is this region which represents the usable lifetime of the material, and excessive slope or rate of deformation indicates that the material is unsuitable for its destined application.

The permissible strength of the material at elevated temperature is announced as the *creep strength*, which is defined as the maximum unit stress which may be developed in the material during a specified time without causing more than a specified deformation. The period of time and the rate of deformation vary with the type of service for which the material is intended.*

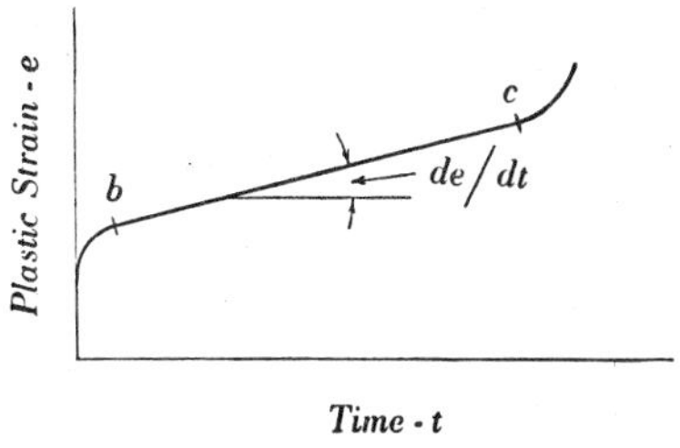

Plastic Strain - e

b

c

de/dt

Time - t

FIG. 263.

When bolts are used to fasten the flanges of joints together, the creep effect will act to decrease the tightness of the joint at elevated temperatures. In this case, the total deformation—the sum of the elastic and plastic deformations—remains constant, and the effect of the decreasing tensile stress in the bolt, which is called *relaxation* of stress, must be considered. There has been some investigation of this phenomenon, and some empirical test data are available.

79. Repeated Loading. Fatigue. In all of the preceding discussions of the behavior of bodies under stress, we have been concerned with the influence of static loads which were gradually applied to the body. Such loads are usually found in the structural members of buildings. In the moving parts of machines, however, we encounter loads which are responsible for repetitions or fluctuations of the stress values. Such stresses may vary, repeatedly, many millions of times in the service of the member and, unlike the static loads, may actually determine its effective life.

A shaft carrying the armature of an electric motor is, in reality, a beam to which the weight of the armature is applied, with the end bearings supplying the supporting forces. As this beam rotates, fibers which are at one instant at the bottom and in tension will during the next instant move to the top which is a region of compression. This complete reversal of the nature of the stress takes place repeatedly as the shaft continues to

*See C. R. Soderberg: "Interpretation of Creep Tests for Machine Design," *Trans. A.S.M.E.* (Nov. 1936); also papers on Creep: *Proc. Fifth Int. Congress for Applied Mechanics*, Wiley (1938).

rotate. If the motor is running at a constant speed of 1800 r.p.m., there will be 2,592,000 reversals of stress in only 24 hours.

In some cases of repeated stress, as in the connecting rod of an automobile where pressure acts upon the driving piston, the stress may not change in its nature—the connecting rod of the engine is always in compression—but will fluctuate between maximum and minimum values of the same nature of stress.

More machine parts fail from the effect of this factor of repetition of loading than from any other cause. Such a failure is called a *fatigue* failure, a name given to the phenomenon when it was believed, improperly, that the repeated loading caused gradual change in the crystalline structure of the material. Fatigue has been the object of much investigation in recent times, and it is now known that the failure results from the development of localized stress in some region of the member which is different in its nature than in other sections. Neither nature nor man produces the ideal material—all materials are neither perfectly homogeneous nor perfectly isotropic. When materials are fabricated into machine or structural parts, they are never geometrically ideal. All loaded bodies contain some discontinuities—these may be flaws or other irregularities in the material itself, or they may be geometric faults introduced when the material is fashioned into a machine part.

We have already noted, in the article devoted to stress concentration, the fact that when a hole is drilled in a bar of steel and the bar is loaded, there will be greater stresses at the surface of the hole than in the remainder of the bar. Even though such a flaw in material as is represented by the drilled hole may be very tiny, the stress concentration at its boundaries may be of sufficient magnitude to cause a fracture of the neighboring material, and the small hole or flaw will spread. Eventually the resisting area within the body may be reduced, and the unit stress values increased until there is a sudden fracture of the machine part. Such gradual or progressive fracture may be occurring in a part while the accompanying deformations are confined to the interior of the part and are not discernible when the part is viewed externally. The serious nature of such progressive fracture is evident when we realize that the properties of yield point and of ultimate strength are determined by assuming, as in the tensile test, that such stresses are uniformly distributed, and are therefore only average values. When used as design bases, those properties have failed to recognize the possibility of greater stresses in the process of averaging. A more sensitive approach to the use of materials demands that they be tested to ascertain to what degree the potentiality of failure by progressive fracture is present.

Such tests, called fatigue tests, are performed by submitting specimens of the material to repeated or cyclic stresses. The loading is applied either mechanically or magnetically. The nature of the stress–time (or number of cycles of loading) relationship is typified in Fig. 264. The mean stress is s_m, which is the average of the maximum stress, $s_{max.}$, and the minimum

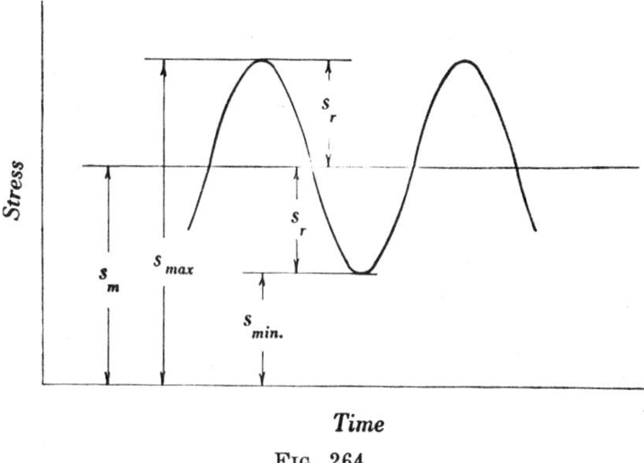

FIG. 264.

stress, $s_{min.}$. This mean stress may be made equal to zero, or to any desired positive or negative value.

$$s_m = \frac{s_{max.} + s_{min.}}{2}$$

The range of stress is the algebraic difference between $s_{max.}$ and $s_{min.}$.

Any actual stress, represented by an ordinate of the diagram, may be considered to be made up of a static or steady stress, s_m, to which there is added a fluctuating stress that varies between positive and negative maximum values, s_r.

$$s_r = \frac{s_{max.} - s_{min.}}{2}$$

The term *reversed* or *alternating* stress is applied to the case where s_m is zero, and the stress reverses completely from tension to compression. When the stresses vary in one direction from zero to $s_{max.}$, the value of s_m is $s_{max.}/2$, and such stress is described as *pulsating.*

The alternating stress exposes the material to the most severe test of fatigue properties, and loading which produces such stress has been most frequently used in investigations. A rotating beam, from which is suspended a fixed weight, is the apparatus that is used for complete reversal of the stress. This equipment possesses the disadvantage of stressing only the extreme fiber to maximum stress, while axial loading offers the advantage of exposing the entire cross-section, but is more difficult to apply.

In a fatigue test, several specimens are exposed to loading, and the number of repetitions of stress or cycles to failure is recorded. The load is reduced for each successive test specimen, and data are collected which

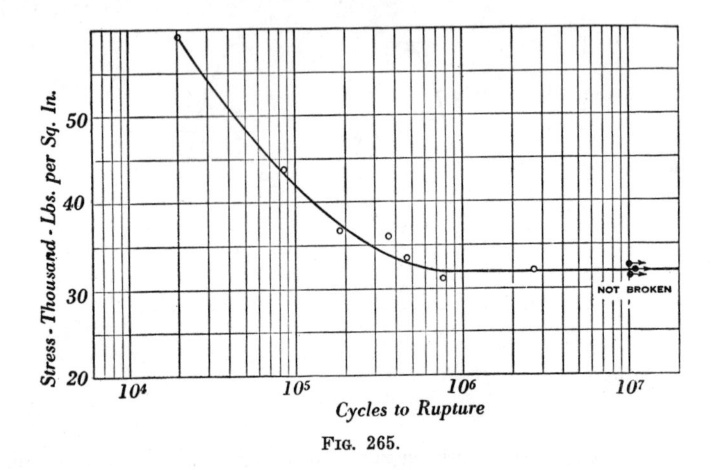

FIG. 265.

may be plotted as shown in Fig. 265. Ordinates are stresses, s, and abscissae are numbers of cycles to rupture, N. The curve is called an sN. diagram. For convenience it is usually plotted, as shown, in semilogarithmic coordinates. The sN. curve will eventually become horizontal as the value of applied load, and hence of induced stress, is decreased. The ordinate of the horizontal line is called the *endurance limit* of the material and defined as the unit stress which may be repeated an indefinitely great number of times without causing failure.* The endurance limit of the material of Fig. 265 is 32,000 psi.

The establishment of endurance limits for many metals by tests has presented a survey of fatigue properties which is an apparent oversimplification. Such results are far more sensitive to variation in apparently similar materials than are such mechanical properties as the yield point or ultimate strength. The medium in which the specimen is tested, the size and finish of the machined test specimen, play a part in the determination of the endurance limit, and the designer should be aware of the test conditions and of how closely they approximate the conditions under which the part which he is designing will be used.

*See *Prevention of Fatigue of Metals*, Wiley (1941).

Few conclusions may be drawn which presently indicate correlation between endurance limit and other mechanical properties. One which seems to be confirmed by present information is a ratio of endurance limit to tensile strength of between 0.4 and 0.6, valid only in the case of ferrous metals, particularly mild steel. The endurance limit must be considered, however, whenever a part is to be subjected to repeated stress.

Attempts to express relationship between repeated and static stress for the guidance of designers have appeared in several different forms. The method of Soderberg* consists of plotting a graph like that shown in Fig. 266 in which ordinates are the amplitude of the varying stress, s_r, and abscissae the steady or mean stress, s_m.

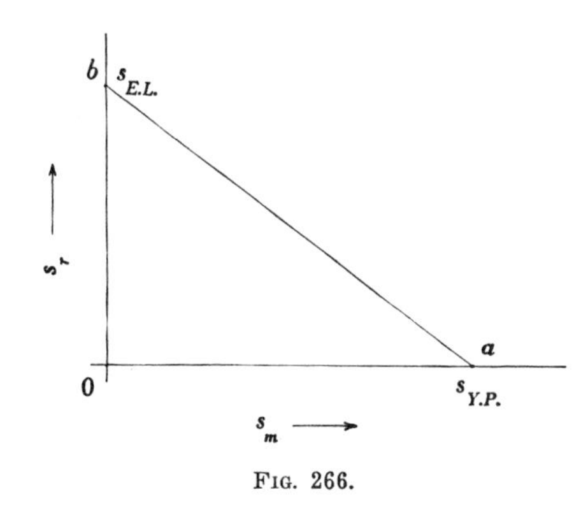

FIG. 266.

The yield point of the material is a, as determined in the static tension test ($s_r = 0$). This point represents failure under steady stress, for yielding of the material destroys its usefulness.

The endurance limit of the material for completely reversed stress is b, and $s_m = 0$.

Points a and b therefore represent limiting stresses. If they are connected by a straight line ab, it is assumed that stresses which lie within the triangle aOb are criteria which may be employed in determining working stresses. While the phenomenon of fatigue, as has previously been noted, is complex, the Soderberg criterion enables the designer to interpret test data on a given material with confidence, for the experimental evidence available does indicate that all cases of failure fall beyond the boundary line ab.

*See *Trans. A.S.M.E*, App. Mech. Div., Vol. 1, No. 3, 1933-APM-55-16

The equation of the limiting line may be determined by noting that in the similar triangles adc and aOb of Fig. 267

$$\frac{s_{Y.P.} - s_m}{s_{Y.P.}} = \frac{s_r}{s_{E.L.}}$$

where $s_{Y.P.}$ is the yield point stress, $s_{E.L.}$ the endurance limit, s_m the steady or static stress, and s_r the varying stress.

Then
$$\frac{s_r}{s_{E.L.}} + \frac{s_m}{s_{Y.P.}} = 1 \qquad (117)$$

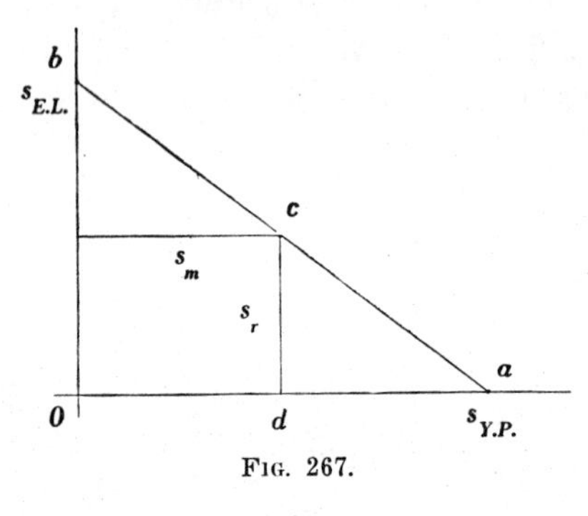

FIG. 267.

This limiting range may be reduced by introducing factors of safety, n_1 and n_2, applied to the terms $s_{E.L.}$ and $s_{Y.P.}$, respectively as in Fig. 268. The equation of the limiting range will now be

$$\frac{s_r}{\dfrac{s_{E.L.}}{n_1}} + \frac{s_m}{\dfrac{s_{Y.P.}}{n_2}} = 1 \qquad (118)$$

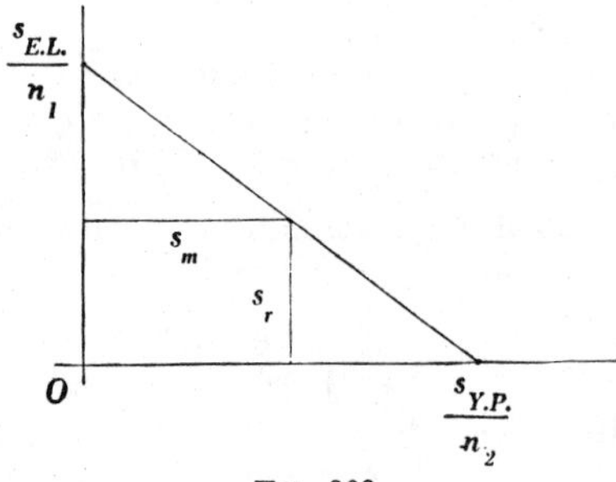

FIG. 268.

When the same factor of safety, n, is applied to both endurance limit and yield point, the limiting equation becomes

$$\frac{s_r}{s_{E.L.}} + \frac{s_m}{s_{Y.P.}} = \frac{1}{n}$$

Illustrative Example. The tensile stress in a machine part varies from 10,000 to 18,000 psi. The material has the following properties: $s_{E.L.} = 30{,}000$ psi; $s_{Y.P.} = 45{,}000$ psi. The factor of safety, based on the endurance limit is to be determined when the factor of safety, based on the yield point, is to be 2.

$$s_r = \frac{s_{max.} - s_{min.}}{2} = \frac{18{,}000 - 10{,}000}{2} = 4000$$

$$s_m = \frac{s_{max.} + s_{min.}}{2} = \frac{18{,}000 + 10{,}000}{2} = 14{,}000$$

Substituting in equation (118),

$$\frac{4000}{30{,}000/n_1} + \frac{14{,}000}{45{,}000/2} = 1$$

and

$$n_1 = 2.83$$

CHAPTER XI

Additional Uses of Mohr's Circle

80. Introduction. We have already found that the circle of Otto Mohr is a very valuable ally in the problems of mechanics which deal with stress at a point.

This circle presents a technique of solution of an equation of a particular form and may be used very effectively whenever an equation of that form arises. Its use is, therefore, not confined to the relationship of stresses. In fact, two additional situations are encountered in Mechanics where this basic form expresses relationship. These are

1) the relationship between the moments and products of inertia at a point of an area or body, and
2) the relationship of the strains at a point of a loaded body.

The following articles are devoted to a discussion of the manner in which Mohr's circle may be applied in these two cases.

We shall first explore the application of Mohr's circle to moments and products of inertia (the *mathematical* properties of areas) and later note its influence in a consideration of plane strain.

MATHEMATICAL PROPERTIES OF AREAS

The following articles consider those properties of areas which play a part in the Mechanics of Materials. These properties are usually discussed

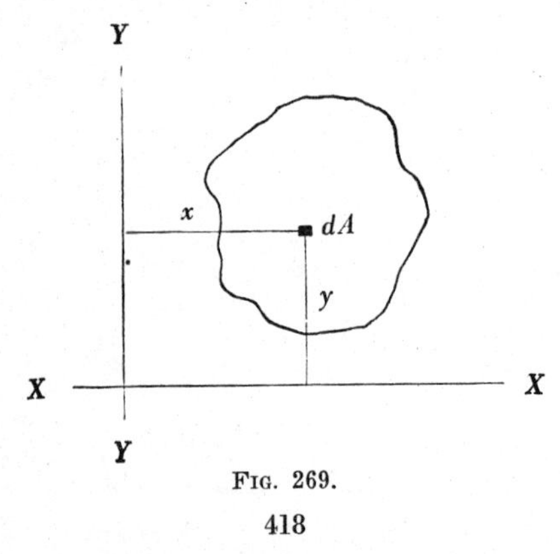

FIG. 269.

in the preceding courses in Statics and Dynamics, but will be reviewed here in sufficient detail to insure that the application of Mohr's circle may rest upon a firm foundation.

81. First Moment. The *first* or statical moment of an elementary area, dA, relative to a given axis, is defined as the product of the area and the distance from the area to the axis.

In Fig. 269 the coordinates of the area dA relative to axes X-X and Y-Y are y and x, respectively. Then, by the definition, the first moment of dA relative to axis X-X is $y\,dA$, and its first moment relative to axis Y-Y is $x\,dA$. The first moment (usually symbolized as Q) of the indicated finite area, relative to X-X, will be the sum of all of the elementary first moments $y\,dA$, or

$$Q_{X-X} = \int y\,dA \qquad \textbf{(119)}$$

and the first moment of the finite area, relative to Y-Y will be

$$Q_{Y-Y} = \int x\,dA \qquad \textbf{(120)}$$

Since a first moment is the product of three linear distances, its units will be inches³ or feet³.

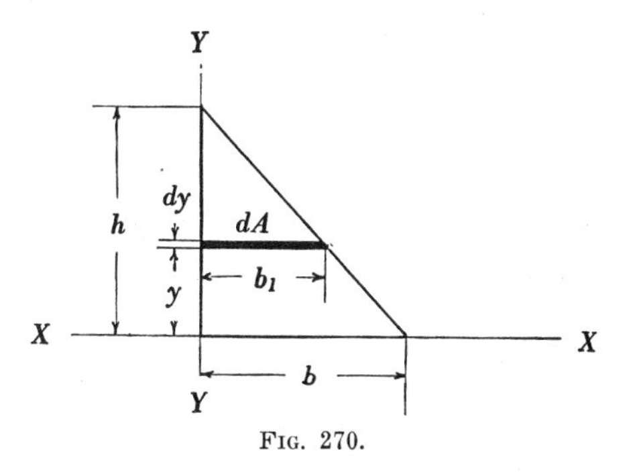

FIG. 270.

Illustrative Example. The first moment of the triangle of Fig. 270 relative to its base is, applying equation (119),

$$Q_{X-X} = \int y\,dA = \int b_1\,y\,dy = \int_{y=0}^{y=h} \frac{h-y}{h}\,b\,y\,dy$$
$$= \frac{bh^2}{6}$$

82. Centroid. The *centroid* of an area is defined as the point of application of the resultant of a uniformly distributed force acting on the area.

A plate of uniform material, whose density per unit volume is δ, and of uniform depth, t, is shown in Fig. 271. The centroid of the bottom area of the plate may be located by considering the system of parallel forces acting

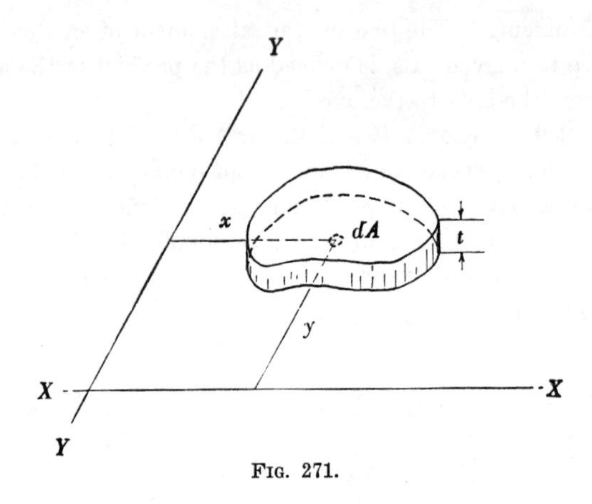

FIG. 271.

on that bottom area. The force which acts on the elementary area dA is typical of the parallel forces, and is

$$dF = \delta\, t\, dA$$

and the total force acting on the bottom area of the plate is the sum

$$R = \int dF = \int \delta\, t\, dA = \delta\, t \int dA$$

The moment of dF about the Y-Y axis is

$$dM = x\, dF$$

and the sum of the moments of all of the forces acting on the bottom area relative to the Y-Y axis is

$$M_{Y-Y} = \int dM = \int \delta\, t\, dA\, x = \delta\, t \int x\, dA$$

The point of application of the resultant force, R, will be located at distance $\bar{x}$ from Y-Y, and

$$\bar{x} = \frac{M_{Y-Y}}{R} = \frac{\delta\, t \int x\, dA}{\delta\, t \int dA} = \frac{\int x\, dA}{\int dA} \tag{121}$$

Similarly, the distance from the X-X axis to the point of application of the resultant force will be

$$\bar{y} = \frac{\int y\, dA}{\int dA} \tag{122}$$

Equations (121) and (122) are the basic equations which are used in locating the centroid of any given area. It will be noted that the numerator in each case is the first moment which was discussed in the preceding article.

Illustrative Example. The triangle of Fig. 270 has base b and height h. The distance from the base to the centroid is to be determined.

Applying equation (122),

$$\bar{y} = \frac{\int y\,dA}{dA} = \frac{Q_{X-X}}{A}$$

From the illustrative example of Art. 81,

$$Q_{X-X} = \frac{bh^2}{6}$$

Then

$$\bar{y} = \frac{bh^2/6}{bh/2} = \frac{h}{3}$$

83. Formulas for Centroids of Plane Areas. (Fig. 272. In each case, point C is the centroid.)

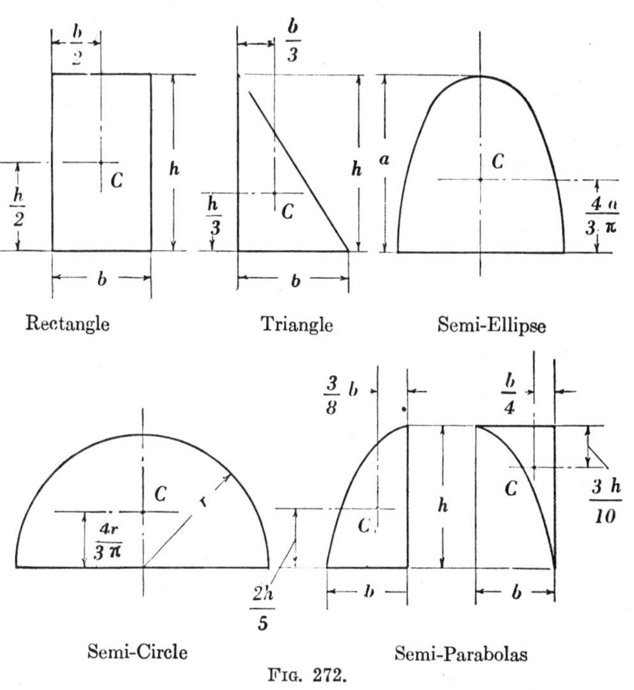

Fig. 272.

84. Centroids of Composite Areas. In locating the centroid of an area such as those used in beams and similar structural shapes, we find that these cross-sections are generally composed of finite areas, each of which is one of those given in the preceding article. The location of the centroids of the individual areas is available from the formulas given in that article. The centroid of the composite area is determined by the equations

$$\bar{x} = \frac{\Sigma Ax}{A} \tag{123}$$

$$\bar{y} = \frac{\Sigma Ay}{A} \tag{124}$$

in which ΣAx is the sum of the first moments of the individual areas about axis Y-Y, and ΣAy is the sum of the first moments of the individual areas about axis X-X, while A is the total area.

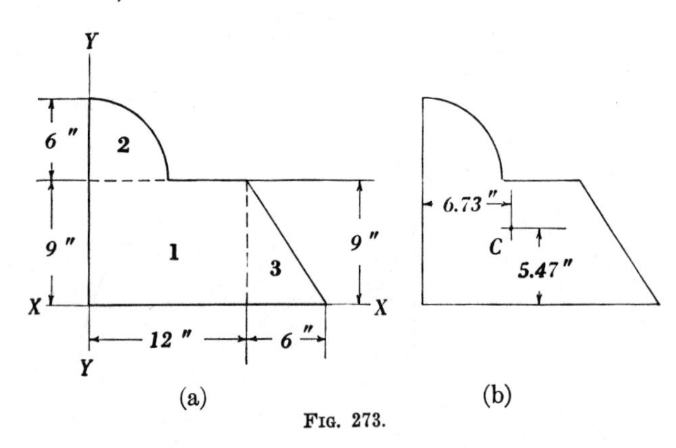

FIG. 273.

Illustrative Example. The area shown in Fig. 273-a has been divided into the individual common areas comprising the total area.

Area **1** is a 12- by 9-in. rectangle.
Area **2** is a quarter-circle having a 6-in. radius.
Area **3** is a 6- by 9-in. triangle.

The centroid of each of these common geometrical shapes is given in Art. 83.

The distance from the base, X-X, to the centroid of the total area will be found by substitution in equation (124).

$$\bar{y} = \frac{\Sigma Ay}{A} = \frac{Ay\ (\text{Area 1}) + Ay\ (\text{Area 2}) + Ay\ (\text{Area 3})}{A\ (\text{Area 1}) + A\ (\text{Area 2}) + A\ (\text{Area 3})}$$

$$= \frac{12 \times 9 \times 4.5 + \frac{\pi(6)^2}{4}\left(9 + \frac{4 \times 6}{3\pi}\right) + \frac{9 \times 6}{2} \times 3}{12 \times 9 + \frac{\pi(3)^2}{4} + \frac{9 \times 6}{2}}$$

$$= 5.47 \text{ in.}$$

The distance from Y-Y to the centroid of the total area will be, by equation (123),

$$\bar{x} = \frac{\Sigma Ax}{A} = \frac{9 \times 12 \times 6 + \frac{\pi(6)^2}{4} \times \frac{4 \times 6}{3\pi} + \frac{9 \times 6}{2} \times 14}{9 \times 12 + \frac{\pi(6)^2}{4} + \frac{9 \times 6}{2}}$$

$$= 6.73 \text{ in.}$$

The location of the centroid determined above is shown in Fig. 273-b.

PROBLEMS

510. Determine the first moment of the indicated area about the X-axis. *Ans.* 123 in.^{3}

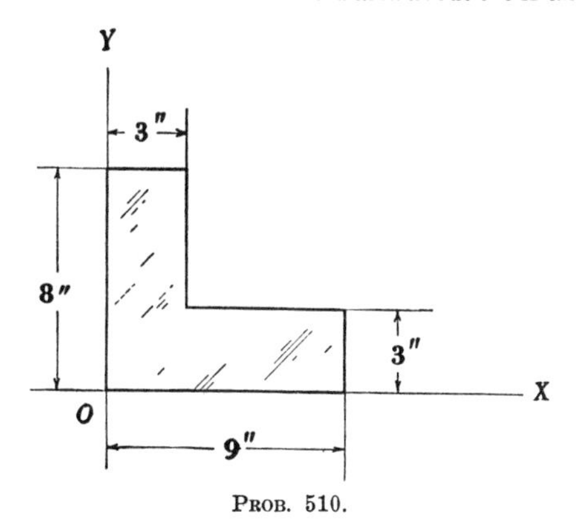

PROB. 510.

511. Determine the first moment of the area of Prob. 510 about the Y-axis.

512. Locate the centroid of the area of Prob. 510. *Ans.* 3.43 in.; 2.93 in.

513. Locate the centroid of the indicated area. *Ans.* 4.28 in.; 0.84 in.

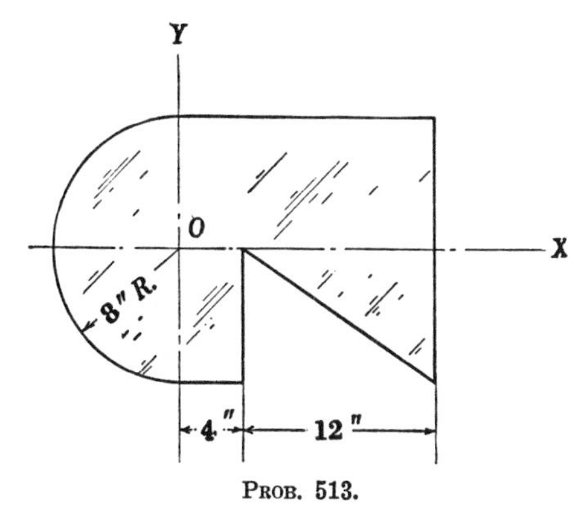

PROB. 513.

514. Locate the centroid of the indicated area.

515. Locate the centroid of the indicated area. *Ans.* −2.67 in.; −3.00 in.

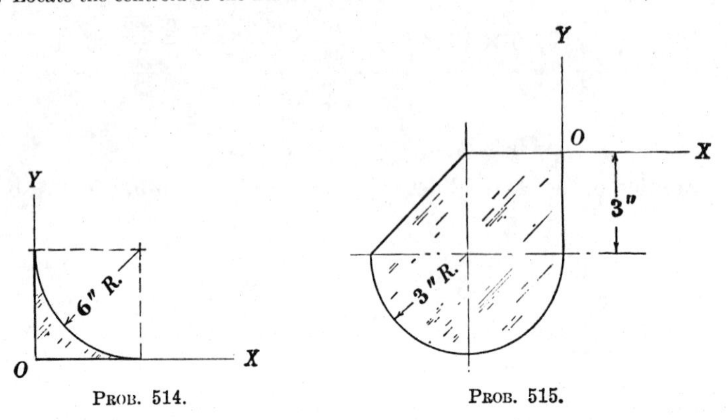

PROB. 514. PROB. 515.

85. Second Moment of Plane Areas. Moment of Inertia. The *second moment* of an elementary area, dA, relative to a given axis is defined as the product of the area and the square of the distance between the area

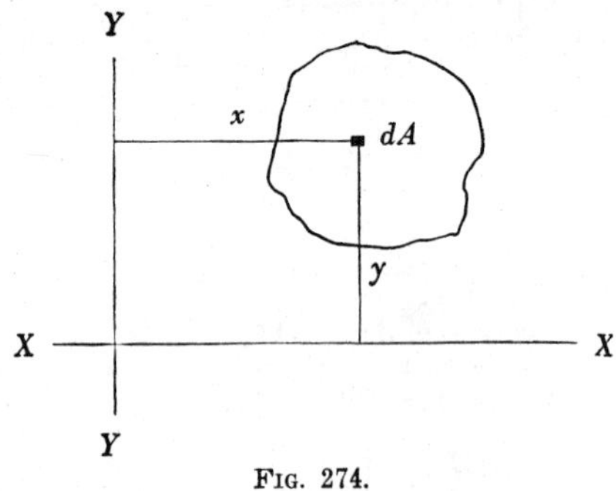

FIG. 274.

and the given axis. For example, the second moment, or *moment of inertia*, of the area dA of Fig. 274 relative to axis X-X is

$$dI_{X-X} = y^2\,dA$$

The total moment of inertia of the finite area about X-X will be

$$I_{X-X} = \int dI_{X-X} = \int y^2\,dA \tag{125}$$

The moment of inertia is a product of four linear distances, and its units are in.^{4} or ft.^{4}.

Illustrative Example. The moment of inertia of the triangle shown in Fig. 270 about its base (X-X) is to be determined.

$$dA = b_1\,dy = \frac{h-y}{h}\,b\,dy$$

Applying equation (125),

$$I_{X-X} = \int y^2\,dA = \int b_1 y^2\,dy = \int_{y=o}^{y=h} \left(\frac{h-y}{h}\right) b\,y^2\,dy$$
$$= \frac{bh^3}{3} - \frac{bh^4}{4h} = \frac{bh^3}{12}$$

86. Formulas for Moments of Inertia of Plane Areas about Centroidal Axes. (Fig. 275)

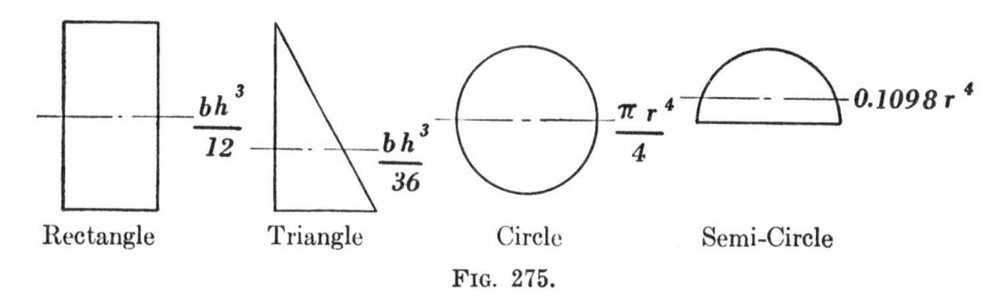

FIG. 275.

87. Polar Moment of Inertia. The polar moment of inertia of an area is the second moment of the area about an axis perpendicular to the plane of the area. For example, the polar moment of inertia of the elementary

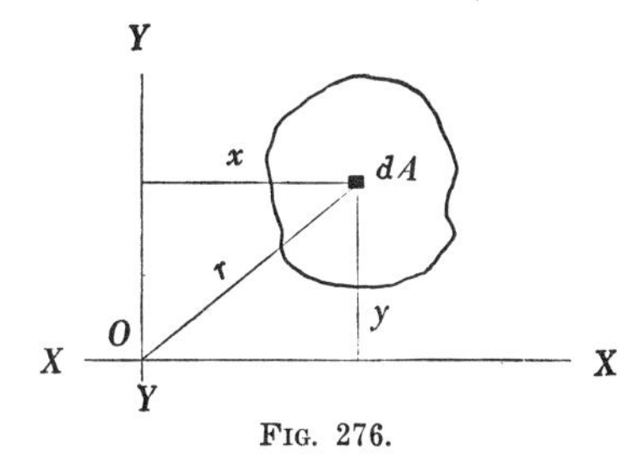

FIG. 276.

area, dA, shown in Fig. 276 about an axis at O, perpendicular to the plane of the area is

$$dI_P = r^2\,dA$$

and the polar moment of inertia of the entire finite area about the axis at O will be

$$I_P = \int r^2\,dA$$

But

$$r^2 = x^2 + y^2$$

and

$$I_P = \int (x^2 + y^2)\,dA = \int x^2\,dA + \int y^2\,dA = I_Y + I_X \qquad \textbf{(126)}$$

Then the *polar moment of inertia of an area about an axis at any point is equal to the sum of the second moments about a pair of mutually perpendicular axes through the given point.*

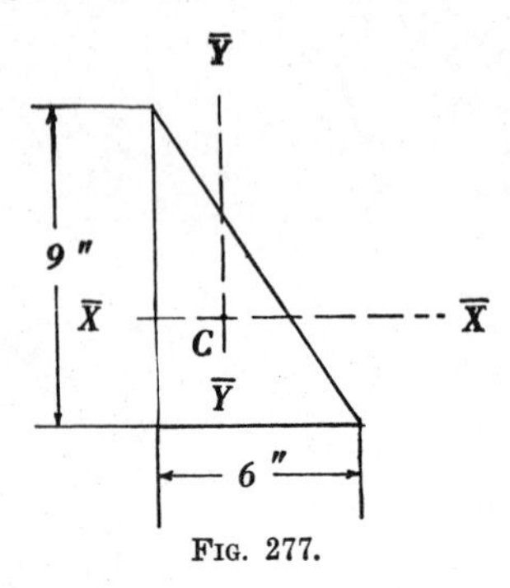

FIG. 277.

Illustrative Example. Determine the polar moment of inertia of the triangular area shown in Fig. 277 about an axis perpendicular to the plane of the area at point C, which is the centroid of the triangle.

$$I_X = \frac{6 \times (9)^3}{36} = 121.5 \text{ in.}^4$$

$$I_Y = \frac{9 \times (6)^3}{36} = 54.0 \text{ in.}^4$$

By equation (126), $I_P = I_X + I_Y = 121.5 + 54.0 = 175.5 \text{ in.}^4$

88. Parallel Axis Theorem. The moment of inertia of any area must frequently be determined when the axis of reference is not one of the centroidal axes covered by the formulas given in Art. 86.

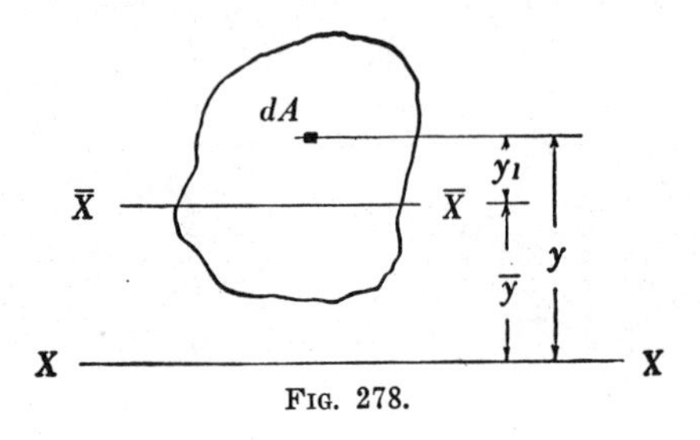

FIG. 278.

The moment of inertia of the elementary area, dA, of Fig. 278 about axis X-X is, by definition,

$$dI_X = y^2\, dA$$

But $$y = y_1 + \bar{y}$$

Then $$dI_X = (y_1 + \bar{y})^2\, dA$$

and the moment of inertia of the total area about X-X is

$$\begin{aligned} I_X &= \int (y_1 + \bar{y})^2 \, dA \\ &= \int y_1^2 \, dA + \int 2\bar{y}\, y_1 \, dA + \int \bar{y}^2 \, dA \\ &= I_{\bar{X}} + 2\bar{y} \int y_1 \, dA + \bar{y}^2 A \end{aligned}$$

where $I_{\bar{X}}$ is the moment of inertia of the area about the centroidal axis $\bar{X}$-$\bar{X}$, and A is the total area. $\int y_1 \, dA$, which appears in the second term, is the first moment of the area about a centroidal axis, which is zero, and

$$I_X = I_{\bar{X}} + \bar{y}^2 A \tag{127}$$

This expression is the transfer formula which enables us to determine the moment of inertia of an area about any axis when the moment of inertia about a parallel axis through the centroid of the area is known.

Illustrative Example. Determine the moment of inertia of the shaded area shown in Fig. 279 about the axis X-X.

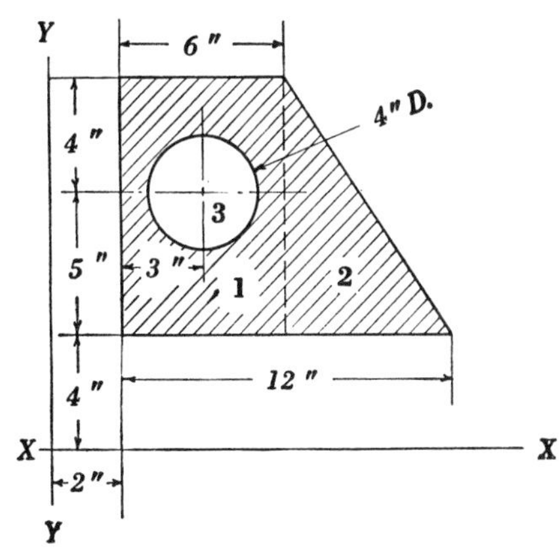

Fig. 279.

We shall divide the area into the component figures **1**, which is the 6- by 9-in. rectangle; **2**, the 6- by 9-in. triangle, and **3**, which is the circular hole.

Area **1**: $$I_{\bar{X}} = \frac{bh^3}{12} = \frac{6 \times (9)^3}{12} = 364.5 \text{ in.}^4$$

By equation (127),

$$I_{\bar{X}} = I_{\bar{X}} + \bar{y}^2 A = 364.5 + (8.5)^2 \times (6 \times 9) = 4266 \text{ in.}^4$$

Area **2**: $$I_{\bar{X}} = \frac{bh^3}{36} = \frac{6 \times (9)^3}{36} = 121.5 \text{ in.}^4$$

By equation (127),

$$I_X = I_{\bar{X}} + \bar{y}^2 A = 121.5 + (7)^2 \times \frac{6 \times 9}{2} = 1445 \text{ in.}^4$$

Area **3**: $I_{\bar{X}} = \frac{\pi r^4}{4} = \frac{\pi(2)^4}{4} = 12.56 \text{ in.}^4$

By equation (127),

$$I_X = I_{\bar{X}} + \bar{y}^2 A = 12.56 + (9)^2 \pi (2)^2 = 1030 \text{ in.}^4$$

Area **3** is negative, for it is a hole, and its moment of inertia must be subtracted from the sum of the moments of inertia of the two positive areas. The moment of inertia of the total area about axis X-X will be

$$I_X = 4266 + 1445 - 1030 = 4681 \text{ in.}^4$$

PROBLEMS

516. Determine the moment of inertia about the X-axis for the area of Prob. 510.
Ans. 566 in.^{4}

517. Determine the moment of inertia about the X-axis for the indicated area.
Ans. 632 in.^{4}

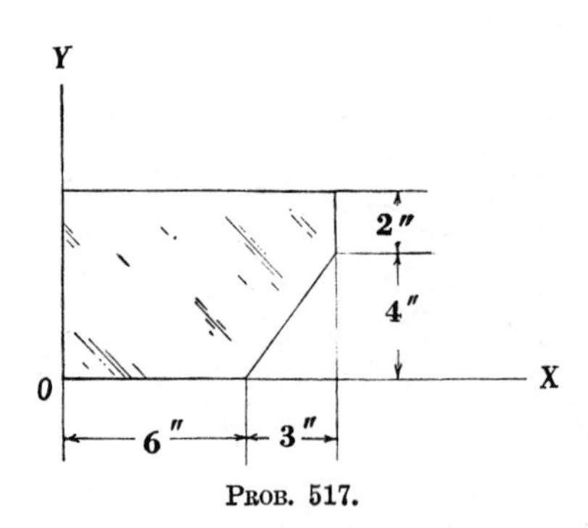

Prob. 517.

518. Determine the moment of inertia about the Y-axis for the area of Prob. 517.

519. Determine the moment of inertia about the X-axis of the indicated area.
Ans. 0.81 in.^{4}

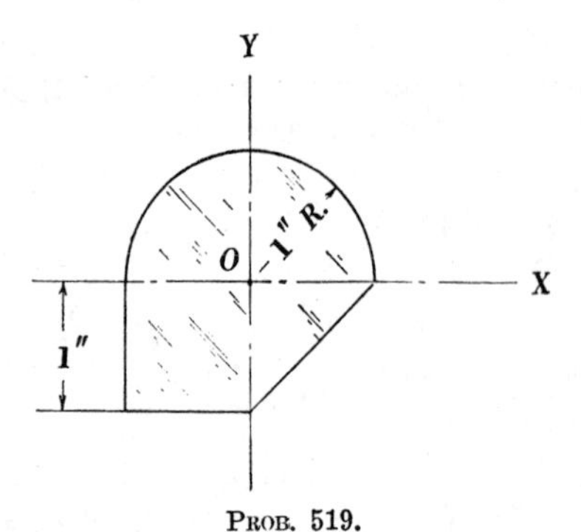

Prob. 519.

520. Determine the radius of gyration, relative to the Y-axis, of the area of Prob. 519.

521. Determine the polar moment of inertia at point a, for the indicated area.

Ans. 4015 in.^{4}

522. For the area of Prob. 521, determine the polar moment of inertia at point b.

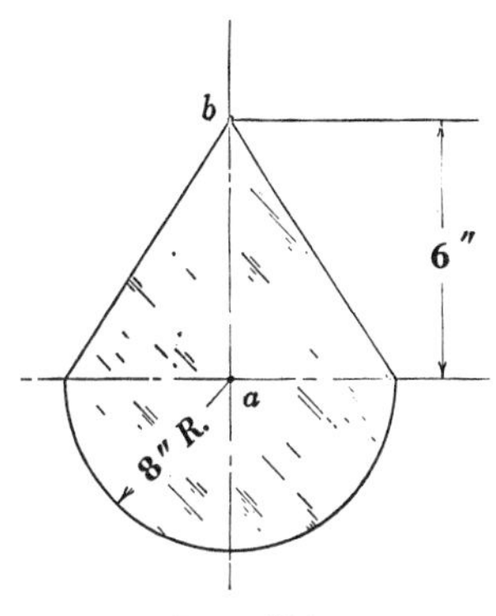

PROB. 521.

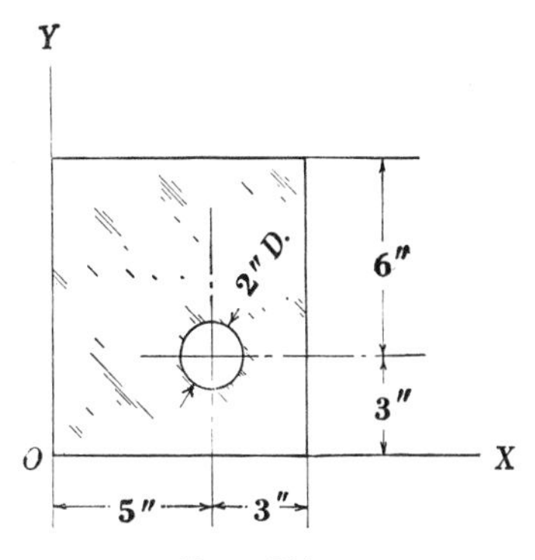

PROB. 524.

523. For the area given in Prob. 510, determine the polar moment of inertia at the centroid.

524. Determine the polar moment of inertia, at point O, for the indicated area.

Ans. 3370 in.^{4}

89. Product of Inertia. Another mathematical property of plane areas is of concern to the engineering designer. This is the *product of inertia*, which is defined as the product of an elementary area, dA (Fig. 274), times the product of the coordinate distances to any pair of mutually perpendicular axes, like X-X and Y-Y, or

$$dI_{XY} = x\,y\,dA$$

It will be noted that the product of inertia, like the moment of inertia, is a second moment, and its units, too, are inches^4 or feet^4.

The product of inertia of the total area of Fig. 274 relative to axes X-X and Y-Y is the sum of the elementary products of inertia, and

$$I_{X-Y} = \int dI_{X-Y} = \int x\,y\,dA \tag{128}$$

The values of the products of inertia of plane areas, like those of the first moments or moments of inertia, are determined by integration of the defining expression. For example, the product of inertia of the triangle shown in Fig. 270 about the axes X-X and Y-Y is, by equation (128),

$$I_{X-Y} = \int x\,y\,dA = \int\int x\,y\,dx\,dy$$

Since

$$x = b\,\frac{(h - y)}{h}$$

$$I_{XY} = \int_{x=o}^{x=\frac{b}{h}(h-y)} \int_{y=o}^{y=h} xy\,dx\,dy$$

$$= \frac{b^2h^2}{24}$$

It should be noted that, unlike moments of inertia, which must always be positive, products of inertia may be positive, negative, or zero. By definition, the product of inertia is a product of x times y times dA. Since values of x may be positive or negative, as may values of y, their product may be positive or negative. The nature of the sign of the product will depend upon the quadrant in which the area lies relative to the framework of reference axes.

The product of inertia of any area which has an axis of symmetry will be zero relative to a pair of mutually perpendicular axes, one of which is the axis of symmetry. In Fig. 280, for example, it will be noted that the

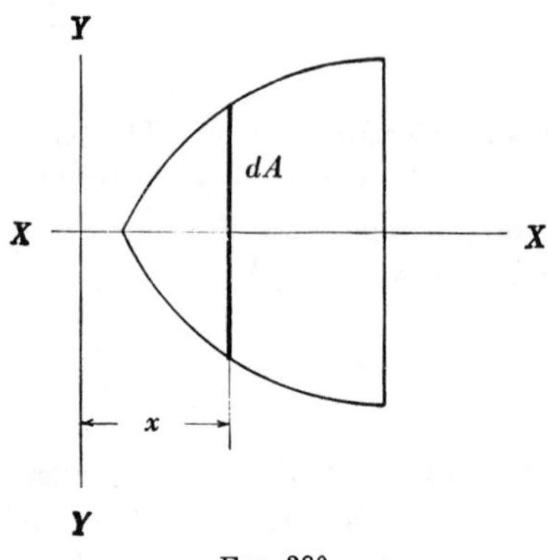

FIG. 280.

product of inertia of dA relative to axes X-X and Y-Y is $x\,y\,dA$. X-X is an axis of symmetry, and, therefore, passes through the centroid of the area. Then $y\,dA$ is the first moment of dA about a centroidal axis, and $x\,y\,dA$ is zero. It follows that $\int xy\,dA$ is zero, and the entire area will have a product of inertia equal to zero relative to axes XX and YY.

90. Parallel Axes. Transfer of Products of Inertia. The product of inertia of dA (Fig. 281) relative to X-X and Y-Y is

$$dI_{XY} = x\,y\,dA$$

But $\quad x = x_1 + \bar{x} \quad$ and $\quad y = y_1 + \bar{y}$

Then
$$dI_{X-Y} = (x_1 + \bar{x})(y_1 + \bar{y})dA$$
$$= (x_1y_1 + x_1\bar{y} + \bar{x}y_1 + \bar{x}\bar{y})\,dA$$

For the total area

$$I_{X-Y} = \int dI_{X-Y} = \int x_1y_1\,dA + \bar{y}\int x_1\,dA + \bar{x}\int y_1\,dA + \bar{x}\bar{y}\int dA$$

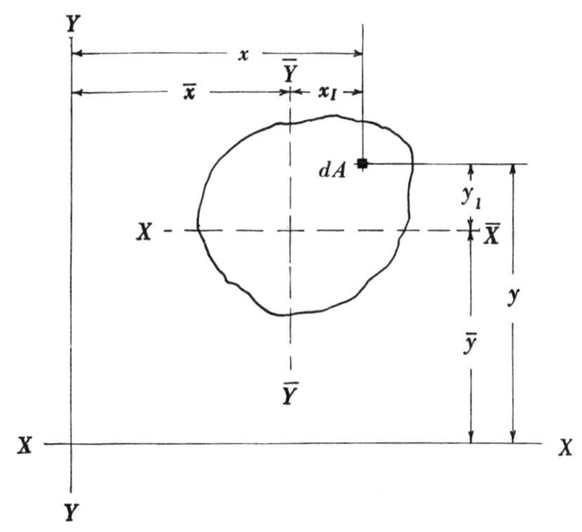

FIG. 281.

The second and third terms of this expression contain first moments of the area about centroidal areas $\bar{Y}$-$\bar{Y}$ and $\bar{X}$-$\bar{X}$, which are zero.

Then
$$I_{X-Y} = \int x_1y_1\,dA + \bar{x}\bar{y}\int dA$$
or
$$I_{X-Y} = I_{\bar{X}-\bar{Y}} + \bar{x}\bar{y}\,A \qquad \textbf{(129)}$$

This is the transfer expression which enables us to determine products of inertia of given areas about pairs of mutually perpendicular axes when the products of inertia of these areas about parallel pairs of axes through the centroids of the areas are known.

Illustrative Example I. Determine the product of inertia of the triangle shown in Fig. 270 about the centroidal axes X-X and Y-Y.

From the preceding article, the product of inertia about axes X-X and Y-Y is

$$I_{X-Y} = \frac{b^2h^2}{24}$$

Substituting in the transfer equation, transposing the terms of equation (129),

$$I_{\bar{X}-\bar{Y}} = I_{X-Y} - \bar{x}\bar{y}A$$

$$= \frac{b^2h^2}{24} - \left(+\frac{b}{3}\right)\left(+\frac{h}{3}\right)\left(\frac{bh}{2}\right)$$

$$= -\frac{b^2h^2}{72}$$

Illustrative Example II. Determine the product of inertia of the area shown in Fig. 279, relative to the axes X-X and Y-Y.

The area will again be divided into the rectangle **1**, the triangle **2**, and the circular hole **3**. By equation (129),

Area **1**: $I_{X-Y} = I_{\bar{X}-\bar{Y}} + \bar{x}\,\bar{y}A$
$= 0 + (+5)(+8.5)(6 \times 9) = +2295 \text{ in.}^4$

Area **2**: $I_{X-Y} = I_{\bar{X}-\bar{Y}} + \bar{x}\,\bar{y}A$

$$= -\frac{(6)^2(9)^2}{72} + (+10)(+7)\left(\frac{6 \times 9}{2}\right) = +1850 \text{ in.}^4$$

Area **3** (negative):

$$I_{X-Y} = I_{\bar{X}-\bar{Y}} + \bar{x}\bar{y}A$$
$$= 0 + (+5)(+9)[\pi(2)^2] = 565 \text{ in.}^4$$

Total: $I_{X-Y} = +2295 + 1850 - 565 = +3580 \text{ in.}^4$

PROBLEMS

525–528, inclusive. In each case, the product of inertia relative to the indicated X- and Y-axes is to be determined.

526. *Ans.* 70.9 in.^{4}

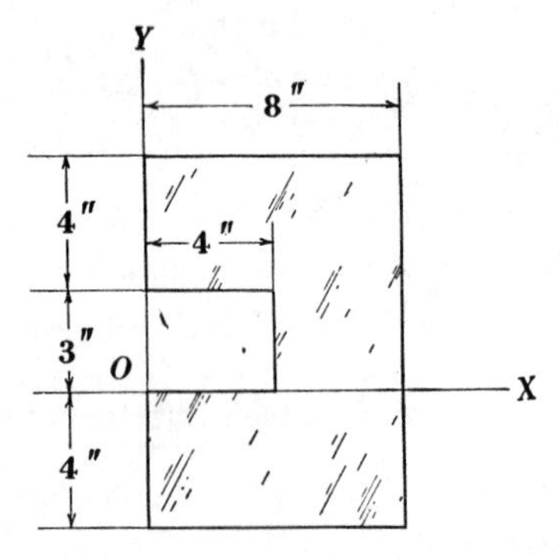

PROB. 525.

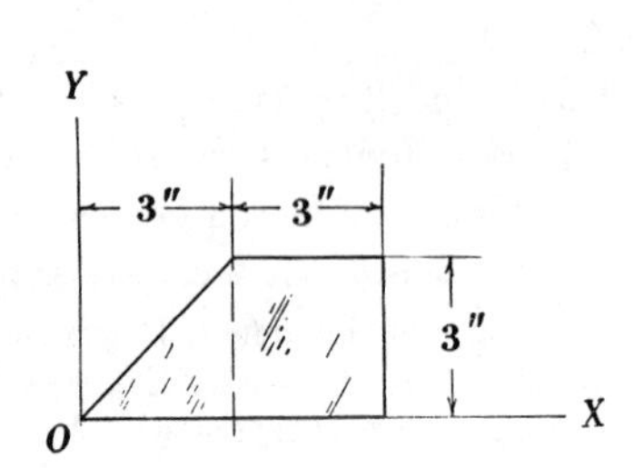

PROB. 526.

528. *Ans.* 632 in.^{4}

529. Determine I_{X-Y} for the area of Prob. 510. *Ans.* 306 in.^{4}

530. Determine I_{X-Y} for the area of Prob. 519. *Ans.* 0.208 in.^{4}

531. Determine I_{X-Y} for the area of Prob. 513.

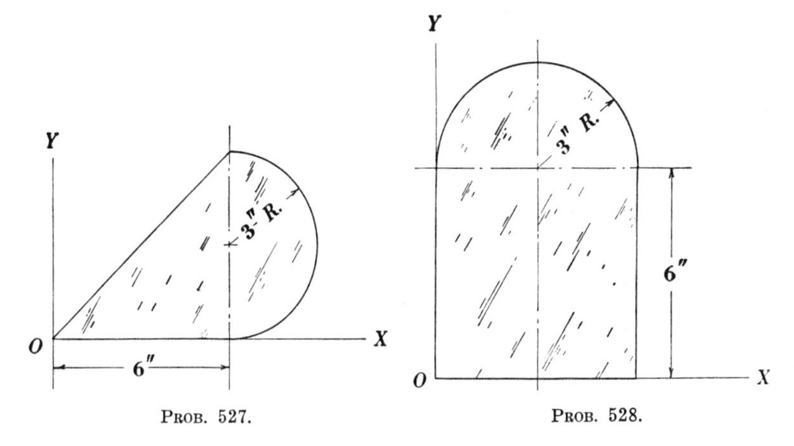

PROB. 527. PROB. 528.

91. Moments of Inertia about Inclined Axes. Principal Moments of Inertia. The moment of inertia of a plane area about an axis which, like X_1-X_1 (Fig. 282), is inclined at any angle θ with axis X-X may be evaluated as follows:

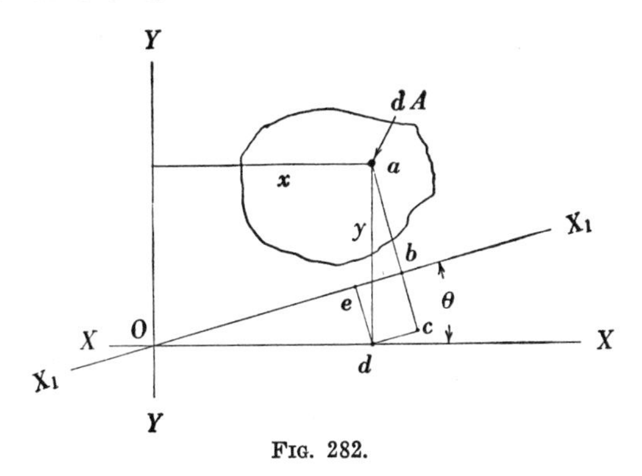

FIG. 282.

Line abc is drawn from point a at area dA perpendicular to axis X_1-X_1. Line ad is perpendicular to axis X-X and de is drawn, parallel to line abc, from point d. Line cd is parallel to X_1-X_1.

$$ab = ac - (bc = de)$$
$$= ad \cos\theta - Od \sin\theta$$

The normal from area dA to axis X_1-X_1 is ab, and we shall call this normal distance y_1, while ad is the coordinate y and Od the coordinate x of dA.

Then
$$y_1 = y \cos \theta - x \sin \theta$$

By definition, the moment of inertia of the elementary area dA about axis X_1-X_1 is

$$dI_{X_1} = y_1^2 \, dA$$

and the moment of inertia of the total finite area shown, about axis X_1-X_1 is

$$\begin{aligned} I_{X_1} &= \int (y_1)^2 \, dA \\ &= \int (y \cos \theta - x \sin \theta)^2 \, dA \\ &= \int y^2 \, dA \cos^2 \theta + \int x^2 \, dA \sin^2 \theta - \int 2xy \, dA \sin \theta \cos \theta \\ &= I_X \cos^2 \theta + I_Y \sin^2 \theta - 2I_{XY} \sin \theta \cos \theta \end{aligned} \quad \textbf{(130)}$$

It will be observed that I_{X_1} is varying sinusoidally with the angle θ and that there must, therefore, be some axis X_1-X_1 about which the moment of inertia of the area is maximum for the point A, and another axis X_1-X_1 about which the moment of inertia of the area is minimum. These moments are of great importance in mechanics and they are called the *principal moments of inertia* of the area at the given point. The axes about which the moments of inertia of the area are maximum and minimum are called the *principal axes of inertia.*

As in all cases where we seek maxima and minima, we differentiate the general expression and set the first derivative equal to zero. Differentiating equation (130) in this manner,

$$\frac{dI_{X1}}{d\theta} = -2I_X \sin \theta \cos \theta + 2I_Y \sin \theta \cos \theta - 2I_{XY} (\cos^2 \theta - \sin^2 \theta) = 0$$

Then
$$\frac{\sin 2\theta}{\cos 2\theta} = \tan 2\theta = -\frac{2I_{XY}}{I_X - I_Y} \quad \textbf{(131)}$$

This evaluation of the angle 2θ, which may be halved to determine θ, yields the location of the principal axes. There are two angles which have the same tangent, differing by 180°. Then equation (131) yields the location of two axes which are 180° apart. When 2θ is halved, two axes are determined which are 90° apart. These are the principal axes of inertia at the given point. When θ has been determined, equation (130) may be used to evaluate the principal moments of inertia.

Illustrative Example. The area shown in Fig. 283 has the following properties:

At point A,
$$I_X = 200 \text{ in.}^4$$
$$I_Y = 100 \text{ in.}^4$$
$$I_{X-Y} = +50 \text{ in.}^4$$

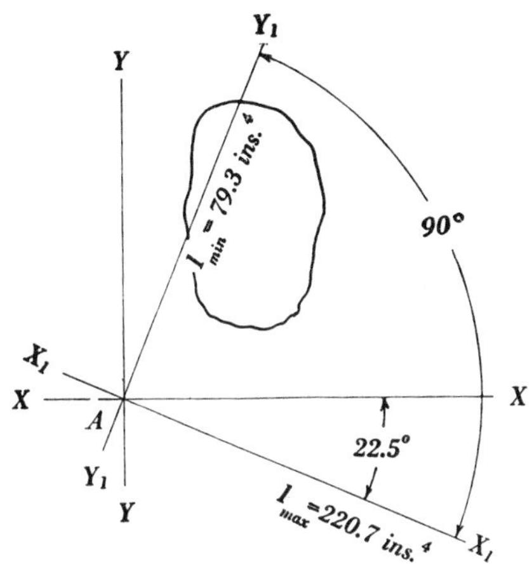

FIG. 283.

The principal axes are located by using the equation (131),

$$\tan 2\theta = -\frac{2I_{X-Y}}{I_X - I_Y}$$
$$= -\frac{2 \times 50}{200 - 100} = -1$$
$$2\theta = -45^\circ$$
$$\theta = -22.5^\circ$$

These principal axes are shown as X_1-X_1 and Y_1-Y_1 in Fig. 283.

The principal moments of inertia are determined by substitution in equation (130).

$$\theta = -22.5^\circ \quad I_{X_1} = I_X \cos^2 \theta + I_Y \sin^2 \theta - 2I_{XY} \sin \theta \cos \theta$$
$$= 200(0.9239)^2 + 100(0.3827)^2 + 2 \times 50 \times 0.9239 \times 0.3827$$
$$= 170.7 + 14.6 + 35.4 = 220.7 \text{ in.}^4$$
$$\theta = +67.5^\circ\text{:} \quad I_{X_1} = 200(0.3827)^2 + 100(0.9329)^2 - 2 \times 50 \times 0.3827 \times 0.9239$$
$$= 29.3 + 85.4 - 35.4 = 79.3 \text{ in.}^4$$

These principal moments of inertia, which have been plotted in Fig. 283, are the maximum and minimum moments of inertia of the given area relative to the axes which pass through point A.

The product of inertia of an area about inclined axes may also be expressed as a function of I_X, I_Y, I_{X-Y}, and the locating angle θ by means of the following equation:

$$I_{X_1Y_1} = I_{X-Y} (\cos^2 \theta - \sin^2 \theta) + (I_X - I_Y) \sin \theta \cos \theta \qquad \textbf{(133)}$$

The product of inertia of an area relative to a pair of principal axes is zero. This statement may be confirmed if we refer to the equation for the first derivative given on page 434.

$$-2I_X \sin\theta \cos\theta + 2I_Y \sin\theta \cos\theta - 2I_{X-Y} (\cos^2\theta - \sin^2\theta) = 0$$

If both sides of this equation are divided by minus 2, we have

$$(I_X - I_Y) \sin\theta \cos\theta + I_{X-Y} (\cos^2\theta - \sin^2\theta) = 0$$

Then $I_{X_1Y_1} = 0$, when X_1-X_1 and Y_1-Y_1 are principal axes.

92. Mohr's Circle for Moments of Inertia. The analytical solution of the problem of moments and products of inertia of plane areas relative to inclined axes is based upon equations (130) and (131). The form of these equations is identical with that of the equations which express the state of stress on inclined planes through a point of a loaded body (see Art. 5). Mohr's circle, which was discussed in Art. 6, presents a graphical solution of all equations of such form, and is available for our present application to moments and products of inertia. Its ease of application makes it as desirable a tool for this use as we found it to be in the problems of stress at a point.

The circle, for this application, is constructed with moments of inertia as abscissae and products of inertia as ordinates.

We shall illustrate its construction by applying it to the same problem which we solved, analytically, as an illustrative example in the preceding article. The circle may be drawn to exact scale, and the solution made upon purely graphical bases, or it may be drawn in sketch form to act as a guide to simple arithmetical calculations. We shall employ the latter method.

In Fig. 284-a we first lay out abscissa $Oa = I_X = 200$ in.^{4}, and then erect ordinate $ab = I_{X-Y} = +50$ in.^{4} (Positive products of inertia are laid out above the axis, negative products of inertia below.)

Now $Od = I_Y = 100$ in.^{4} is laid out, and $de = -I_{X-Y} = -50$ in.^{4} erected as ordinate.

It should be noted that I_{X-Y} is plotted with its proper sign as the ordinate associated with I_X, and with *reversed* sign as the ordinate associated with I_Y.

Points b and e are the ends of the diameter of the Mohr's circle.

The principal moments of inertia are represented by points f and g, for these points have ordinates equal to zero, which signifies that there is zero product of inertia about the axes represented by these two points

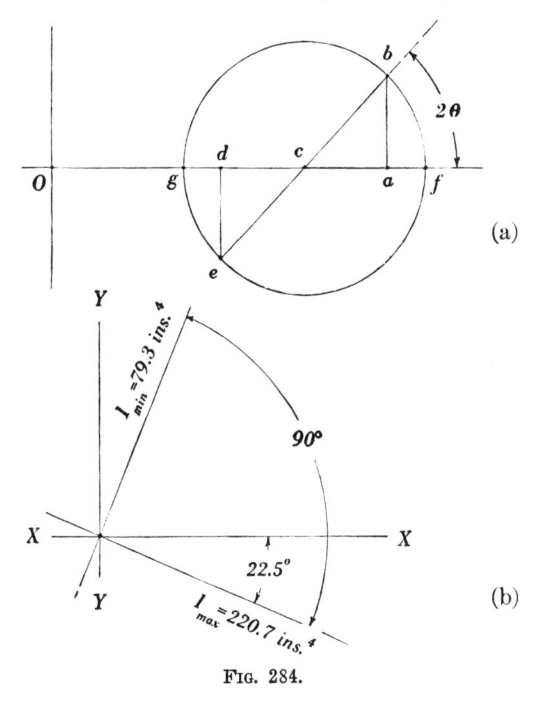

FIG. 284.

and they must therefore be principal axes of inertia. The maximum principal moment of inertia is

$$Of = Oc + \text{radius } (cb = cf)$$

$$Oc = 100 + \frac{1}{2}(200 - 100) = 150$$

$$\text{radius } cb = \sqrt{(50)^2 + (50)^2} = 70.7$$

Then $$Of = 150 + 70.7 = 220.7 \text{ in.}^4$$

The minimum principal moment of inertia is Og.

$$\begin{aligned} Og &= Oc - \text{radius } (cb = cg) \\ &= 150 - 70.7 = 79.3 \text{ in.}^4 \end{aligned}$$

To locate the principal axes, we note that the angular displacement from point b to point f is

$$2\theta = \tan^{-1}\left[\frac{ab}{ac} = \frac{50}{50} = 1\right]$$

$$2\theta = 45^\circ; \qquad \theta = 22.5^\circ$$

The direction of angular displacement from b to f is clockwise. Then the principal axis represented by point f is inclined at an angle of 22.5°, clockwise, from the X-X axis represented by point b.

The results of this solution agree with those previously obtained in the analytical solution, and are shown in Fig. 284-b.

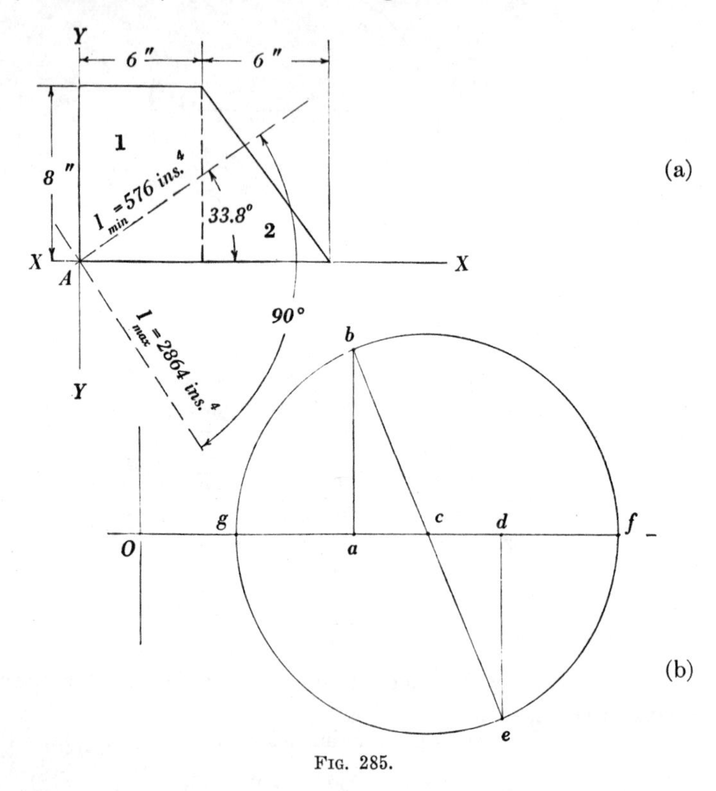

FIG. 285.

Illustrative Example I. Determine the principal moments of inertia at point A for the area shown in Fig. 285-a.

I_X: Area 1: $\dfrac{bh^3}{3} = \dfrac{6 \times (8)^3}{3} = 1024 \text{ in.}^4$

Area 2: $\dfrac{bh^3}{12} = \dfrac{6 \times (8)^3}{12} = 256 \text{ in.}^4$

Total $I_X = 1280 \text{ in.}^4$

I_Y: Area 1: $\dfrac{bh^3}{3} = \dfrac{8 \times (6)^3}{3} = 576 \text{ in.}^4$

Area 2: $\dfrac{bh^3}{36} + \bar{x}^2 A = \dfrac{8 \times (6)^3}{36} + (8)^2\left(\dfrac{6 \times 8}{2}\right) = 1584 \text{ in.}^4$

Total $I_Y = 2160 \text{ in.}^4$

I_{X-Y}: Area 1: $\dfrac{b^2h^2}{4} = \dfrac{(8)^2 \times (6)^2}{4} = +576 \text{ in}^4$

Area 2: $-\dfrac{b^2h^2}{72} + \bar{x}\bar{y}A$

$$= -\frac{(6)^2 \times (8)^2}{72} + (+8)\left(+\frac{8}{3}\right)\left(\frac{6 \times 8}{2}\right) = +480 \text{ in.}^4$$

$$\text{Total } I_{X-Y} = +1056 \text{ in.}^4$$

The Mohr's circle has been plotted as Fig. 285-b.

$$\begin{aligned} Oa &= I_X = 1280 \\ ab &= I_{X-Y} = +1056 \\ Od &= I_Y = 2160 \\ de &= I_{X-Y} = -1056 \end{aligned}$$

The radius of the Mohr's circle is

$$cb = \sqrt{(ca)^2 + (ab)^2} = \sqrt{(440)^2 + (1056)^2} = 1144$$

The maximum principal moment of inertia is

$$\begin{aligned} Of &= Oc + \text{radius } (cb = cf) \\ &= 1720 + 1144 = 2864 \text{ in.}^4 \end{aligned}$$

The minimum principal moment of inertia is

$$\begin{aligned} Og &= Oc - \text{radius } (cb = cg) \\ &= 1720 - 1144 = 576 \text{ in.}^4 \end{aligned}$$

The location of the principal axes is determined as follows:

$$\angle bca = 2\theta = \tan^{-1} \frac{1056}{440} = 67.6°$$

$$\theta = 33.8°$$

The angular displacement from b to g is counter-clockwise. Then the inclinations of the principal axes, with their accompanying principal moments of inertia, are as shown in Fig. 285-a.

Illustrative Example II. Determine the least radius of gyration of the right triangle shown in Fig. 286. (We have already noted, in the articles devoted to Column theory, the necessity for determining this property of cross-sectional areas.)

The radius of gyration of an area relative to any axis is

$$r = \sqrt{\frac{I}{A}}$$

where I is the moment of inertia of the area relative to the given axis and A is the amount of area.

The least radius of gyration will, therefore, become available when we determine the axis about which the moment of inertia of the area is a minimum. This axis must be a principal axis at the centroid of the area—for moments of inertia, by the parallel-axis theorem (Art. 88), are increasing as we move away from the centroid.

At the centroid, C, of the triangle (Fig. 286-a),

$$I_{\overline{X}} = \frac{bh^3}{36} = \frac{6 \times (12)^3}{36} = 288 \text{ in.}^4$$

$$I_{\overline{Y}} = \frac{bh^3}{36} = \frac{12 \times (6)^3}{36} = 72 \text{ in.}^4$$

$$I_{\overline{X}-\overline{Y}} = -\frac{b^2h^2}{72} = -\frac{(6)^2(12)^2}{72} = -72 \text{ in.}^4$$

These values are used to plot the Mohr's circle of Fig. 286-b:

$$Oa = I_{\overline{X}} = 288$$
$$ab = I_{\overline{X}-\overline{Y}} = -72$$
$$Od = I_Y = 72$$
$$de = -I_{X-Y} = +72$$

The radius of the circle is

$$cb = \sqrt{(ab)^2 + (ca)^2} = 129.8$$

The minimum principal moment of inertia will be

$$I_{\text{min.}} = Og = Oc - \text{radius}(cb = cg)$$
$$= 180 - 129.8 = 50.2 \text{ in.}^4$$

The least radius of gyration will be

$$r_{\text{min.}} = \sqrt{\frac{I_{\text{min.}}}{A}} = \sqrt{\frac{50.2}{36}} = 1.18 \text{ in.}$$

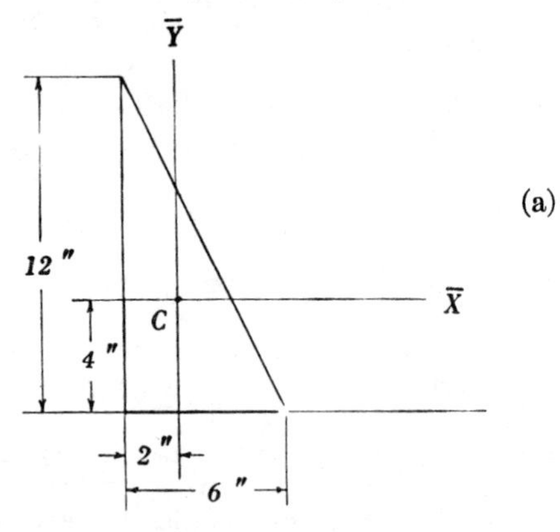

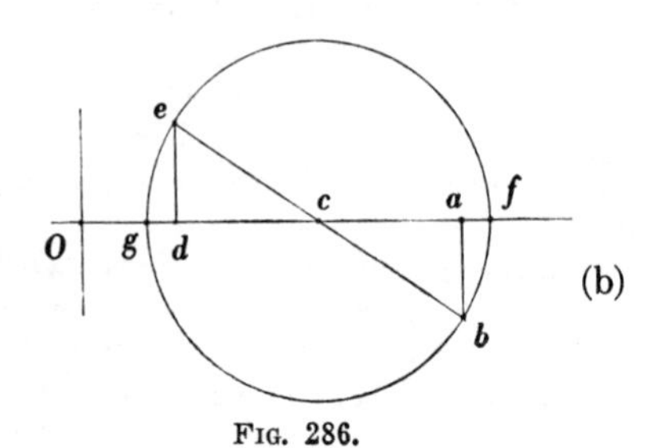

FIG. 286.

PROBLEMS

532. Locate the principal axes of inertia and determine the principal moments of inertia at point O of the area shown. *Ans.* 30 in.^{4} at $-18.5°$; 10 in.^{4} at $71.5°$

533. Locate the principal axes of inertia and determine the principal moments of inertia at the centroid of the indicated triangle. *Ans.* 141 in.^{4} at $-25.1°$; 35 in.^{4} at $64.9°$.

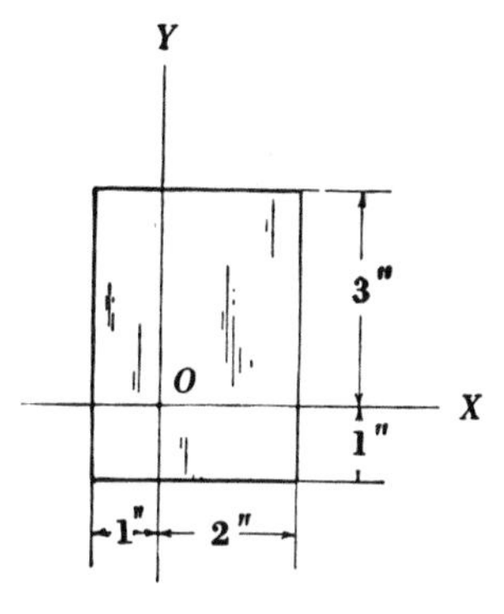

Prob. 532.

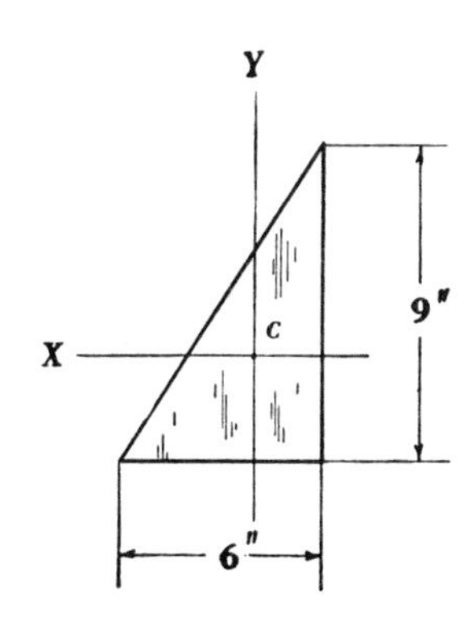

Prob. 533.

534. Locate the principal axes of inertia and determine the principal moments of inertia at point O of the indicated area.

535. Determine the least radius of gyration at point O of the area given in Prob. 534. *Ans.* 0.747 in.

536. Locate the principal axes of inertia and determine the principal moments of inertia at point O of the area shown.

537. Determine the least radius of gyration at point O of the area given in Prob. 536.

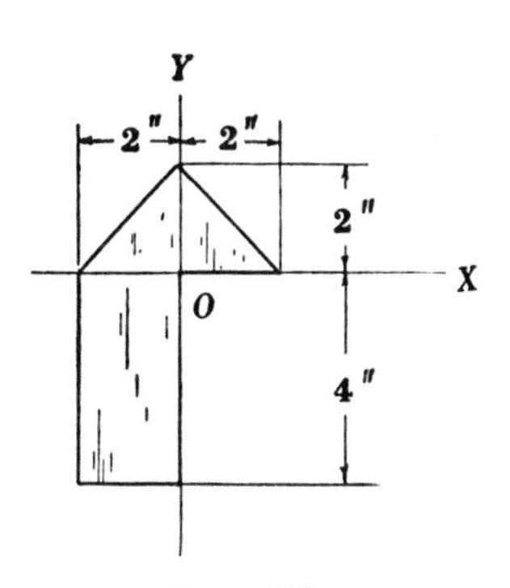

Prob. 534.

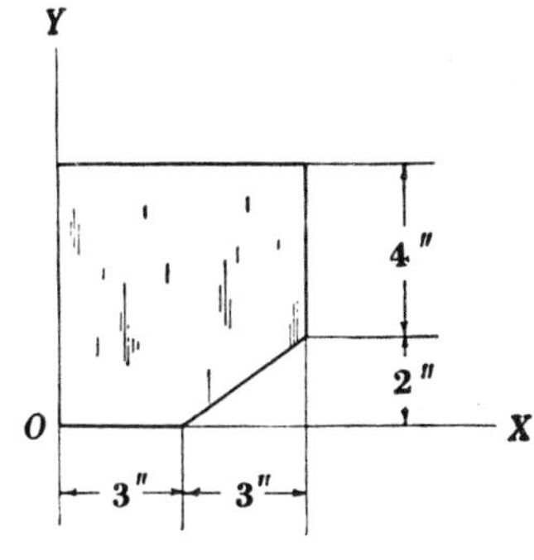

Prob. 536.

538. Locate the principal axes of inertia and determine the principal moments of inertia at point O of the area given in Prob. 519.

539. Determine the maximum moment of inertia of the indicated area at point O.
Ans. 385 in.^{4}

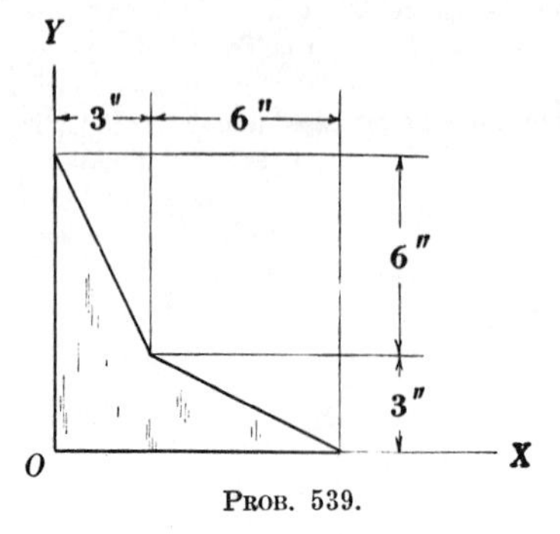

PROB. 539.

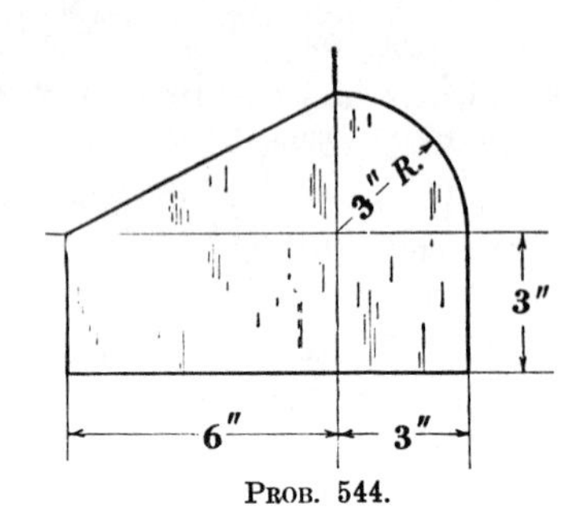

PROB. 544.

540. Determine the least radius of gyration of a 3- by 4- by 5-in. right triangle.
Ans. 0.56 in.

541. Determine the least moment of inertia at point O of the area given in Prob. 527

542. Locate the principal axes of inertia and determine the principal moments of inertia at point O of the area given in Prob. 517. *Ans.* 1550 in.^{4} at $-54.1°$; 153 in.^{4} at 35.9°.

543. Determine the least radius of gyration of the area given in Prob. 515.

544. Determine the least radius of gyration of the indicated area. *Ans.* 1.46 in.

PLANE STRAIN

93. Plane Strain. The plane strain relationships at any point of a loaded body (two-dimensional loading) may be announced by describing two linear strains, e_X and e_Y, along two axes, X and Y, at right angles, and an angular or shearing strain γ_{X-Y} which is the angular deformation of axes X and Y relative to each other. When these data are available, the linear strain along any axis A which is oblique to X and Y is given by the equation

$$e_A = e_X \cos^2 \theta + e_Y \sin^2 \theta - \gamma_{X-Y} \sin \theta \cos \theta \tag{134}$$

Equation (3) (page 19) expresses the normal *stress* on any oblique plane in terms of the normal and shear stresses on X- and Y- planes as

$$s_A = s_X \cos^2 \theta + s_Y \sin^2 \theta - 2s_{X-Y} \sin \theta \cos \theta$$

It will be noted that the form of equation (134) is identical with that of equation (3). It follows that any technique of solution of equation (3) is a proper method to employ in solving equation (134).

The solution of equation (3), including the location of the principal planes of stress and the determination of the principal stresses, was enhanced by the application of the convenient Mohr's circle, which expressed graphically the stress relationships.

To apply Mohr's circle to strain, we replace the terms s_A of equation (3) by e_A; s_X by e_X; s_Y by e_Y; and s_{X-Y} by $\gamma_{X-Y}/2$. The conventions used in plotting follow (linear strains are plotted as abscissae, and shearing strains as ordinates): Positive, or tensile, linear strains are plotted to the right of the origin; negative, or compressive linear strains are plotted to the left. The shearing strain is taken as positive and plotted above the origin if it tends to increase the unstrained right angle between the X and Y axes when loading occurs.

The determination of the principal strains now follows the same routine which we have previously employed in the determination of principal stresses or principal moments of inertia by Mohr's circle.

To illustrate this method of procedure, we shall employ the Mohr's circle in the following illustrative example.

Illustrative Example. Determine the principal strains at a point of a loaded body if

$$e_X = +700 \times 10^{-6} \text{ in./in.}$$
$$e_Y = +100$$
$$\gamma_{X-Y} = +800$$

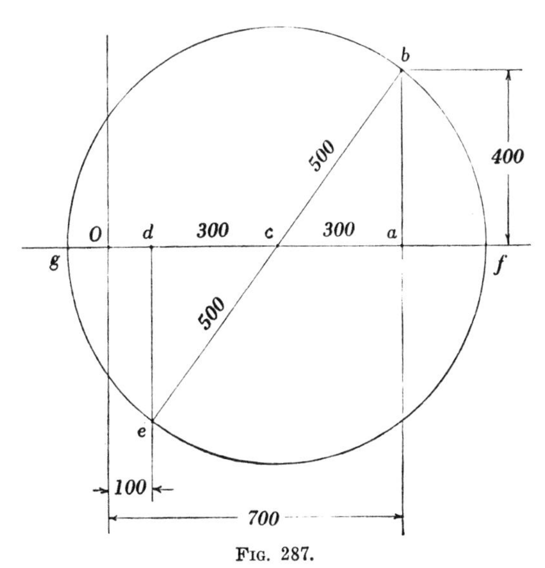

FIG. 287.

The Mohr's circle appears in Fig. 287. The numbers shown on the drawing represent strain $\times$ 10^6. (It is suggested that the reader review the plotting of

Mohr's circle for stress, as described in Art. 6.)

In the figure

$$Oa = e_X = +700$$

$$ab = \frac{\gamma_{X-Y}}{2} = +400$$

$$Od = e_Y = +100$$

$$de = -\frac{\gamma_{X-Y}}{2} = -400$$

The radius of the circle is

$$cb \text{ or } ce = \sqrt{(300)^2 + (400)^2} = 500$$

Then the maximum principal strain is

$$Of = +100 + 300 + 500 = +900 \times 10^{-6} \text{ in./in.}$$

and the minimum principal strain is

$$Og = +100 + 300 - 500 = -100 \times 10^{-6} \text{ in./in.}$$

94. Determination of Principal Stresses from Principal Strains. The determination of the principal stresses at a point in a loaded body follows when the principal strains have been determined, as in the preceding article, and when the modulus of elasticity, E, and Poisson's ratio, μ, of the material are known.

In Art. 14, the principal strains were expressed in the following equations:

Equation (25), $$e_1 = \frac{s_1}{E} - \mu\frac{s_2}{E}$$

Equation (26), $$e_2 = \frac{s_2}{E} - \mu\frac{s_1}{E}$$

where axes 1 and 2 are principal axes, and s_1 and s_2 are the principal stresses.

Equations (25) and (26) may be solved, simultaneously, to yield expressions for the principal stresses.

From equation (25), $$s_1 = e_1E + \mu s_2 \quad (1)$$

and, from equation (26), $$s_2 = e_2E + \mu s_1 \quad (2)$$

Substituting the value of s_2 given in equation (2) in equation (1),

$$s_1 = e_1E + \mu(e_2E + \mu s_1) = E(e_1 + \mu e_2) + \mu^2 s_1$$

$$s_1(1 - \mu^2) = E(e_1 + \mu e_2)$$

and $$s_1 = \frac{E(e_1 + \mu e_2)}{1 - \mu^2} \quad \textbf{(135)}$$

Similarly, $$s_2 = \frac{E(e_2 + \mu e_1)}{1 - \mu^2} \quad \textbf{(136)}$$

Illustrative Example. In the illustrative example of Art. 93, the principal strains were found to be

$$e_{max.} = +900 \times 10^{-6} \text{ in./in.}$$
$$e_{min.} = -100 \times 10^{-6} \text{ in./in.}$$

If the material is steel, with $E = 30 \times 10^6$ psi, and $\mu = 0.3$, the principal stresses are to be determined.

Applying equation (135),

$$s_1 = \frac{30 \times 10^6[+900 + 0.3(-100)] \times 10^{-6}}{1 - (0.3)^2}$$

$$= 28{,}700 \text{ psi}$$

and, applying equation (136),

$$s_2 = \frac{30 \times 10^6[-100 + 0.3(+900)] \times 10^{-6}}{1 - (0.3)^2}$$

$$= 5600 \text{ psi}$$

95. Strain Rosettes. The development of extremely accurate strain gages which are simple and convenient to use has presented stress analysts with a means of establishing the data that are needed to evaluate the principal stresses at critical points of loaded bodies.

The *resistance* gage takes advantage of the fact that when a wire is stretched, its diameter decreases, and its electrical resistance increases. This change in electrical resistance can be very sensitively measured and recorded by such apparatus as the Wheatstone bridge and the oscilloscope. To measure strain, a small grid of wire elements, protected by a paper covering, is cemented to the machine or structural part where the strain is to be observed. Current is passed through the grid, and a reading taken when the load is acting.

The resistance-gage method records linear strains. The Mohr's circle, which we discussed in the preceding article, was constructed upon data which furnished two linear strains and one angular strain. We must, therefore, consider the manner in which the linear strains furnished by the resistance gage can serve equally well in strain measurement.

Any circle is determined when the locations of three points on its circumference are known. If, for example, three strain gages are arranged in the pattern, or *rosette* (shown in Fig. 288) they will record the linear strain in three directions, **1**, **2**, and **3**. If the strains in these three directions are called e_1, e_2, and e_3, respectively, they may be used to start the construction of the circle of Fig. 289. As before, horizontal distances are abscissae representing linear strain, and vertical distances are ordinates representing shearing strain.

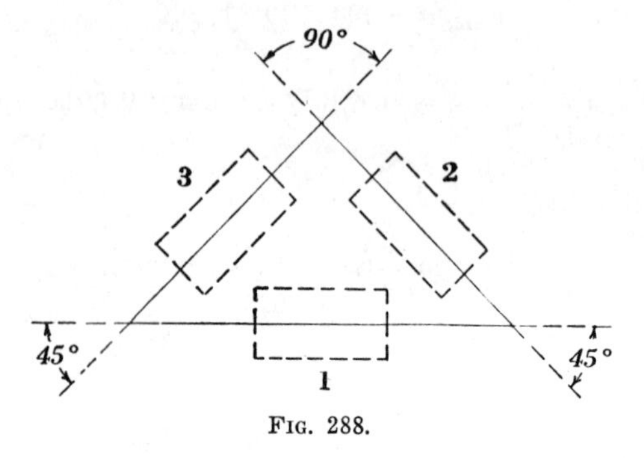

FIG. 288.

We first lay off three distances along the horizontal reference line through origin O, with magnitudes to scale,

$$Om = e_1$$
$$On = e_2$$
$$Ol = e_3$$

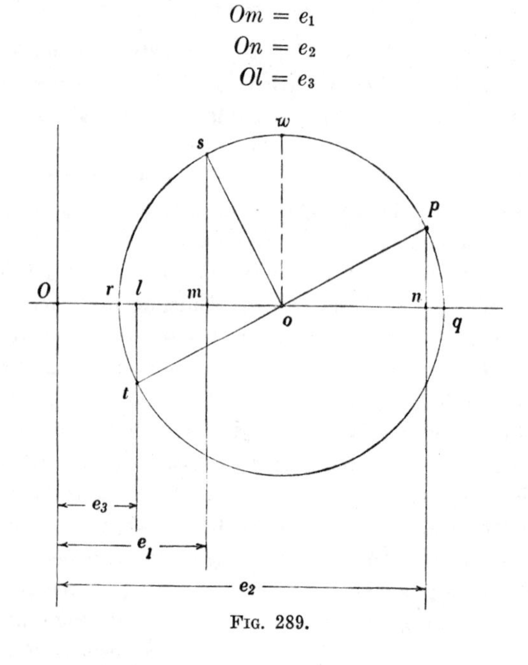

FIG. 289.

Vertical lines are now drawn through points l, m, and n. The distance ln is bisected to yield point o, which is the center of the Mohr's circle.

We must now establish the radius of the circle. If distance $np = om$ is laid off on the vertical line through point n, op is the radius.

The principal strains will be Oq and Or, and, as in the preceding article, these principal strains may be used in the determination of the principal stresses.

The proof that this geometrical construction has yielded the correct Mohr's circle for the given point of the loaded body follows.

Points p, s, and t have abscissae representing the linear strains in the directions of the strain gages, **1**, **2**, and **3**, respectively. Points p and t lie on a diameter of the circle, and are, therefore, 180° apart. On any Mohr's circle, angular distance is always twice that of angular displacement on the loaded body, and points p and t represent strain directions **2** and **3** which are 90° apart in the strain-gage pattern of Fig. 288.

Triangles osm and opn are by construction congruent right triangles. If vertical ow is erected through point o, we note that

$$\angle pow = \angle opn$$

and

$$\angle wos = \angle osm = \angle pon$$

But

$$\angle pon + \angle opn = 90^\circ$$

Then

$$\angle wos + \angle pow = \angle pos = 90^\circ$$

and points p and s are 90° apart on the Mohr's circle, which is consistent with the fact that the abscissae of p and s, representing strain directions **1** and **2**, are 45° apart in the pattern of Fig. 288.

While this general discussion of strain measurement has been illustrated by a pattern in which two 45° angles, and the remaining 90° angle have been used in forming the pattern of gages, other arrangements or rosettes may be employed. A growing literature is available in which detailed information concerning strain rosettes and their interpretation may be found.

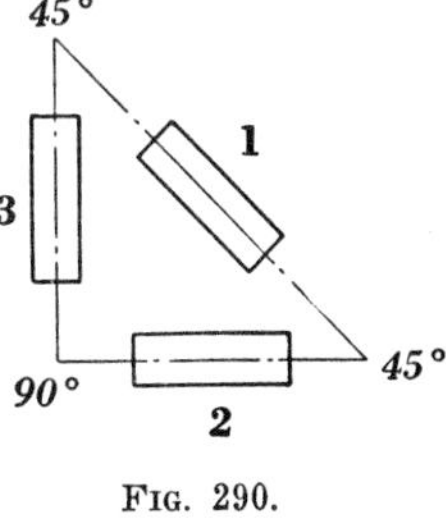

FIG. 290.

Illustrative Example. The strain gages at a point in a loaded body are placed in a 45° rosette (Fig. 290) and yield the following readings:

Gage **1**. $e_1 = +150 \times 10^{-6}$ in./in.
Gage **2**. $e_2 = +400 \times 10^{-6}$ in./in.
Gage **3**. $e_3 = +100 \times 10^{-6}$ in./in.

The principal strains are to be determined.

The Mohr's circle is shown in Fig. 291.

$$On = +400(\times 10^{-6});\ Om = +150\ (\times 10^{-6});\ Ol = +100\ (\times 10^{-6})$$

Bisecting ln, point o is located at 150 units from n, and 100 units from m. Distance np is made equal to 100 units ($= om$), and the radius of the circle is

$$op = \sqrt{(150)^2 + (100)^2} = 180$$

The maximum principal strain will be

$$Oq = +150 + 100 + 180 = +430(\times 10^{-6}\ \text{in./in.})$$

and the minimum principal strain will be

$$Or = +150 + 100 - 180 = +70(\times 10^{-6}\ \text{in./in.})$$

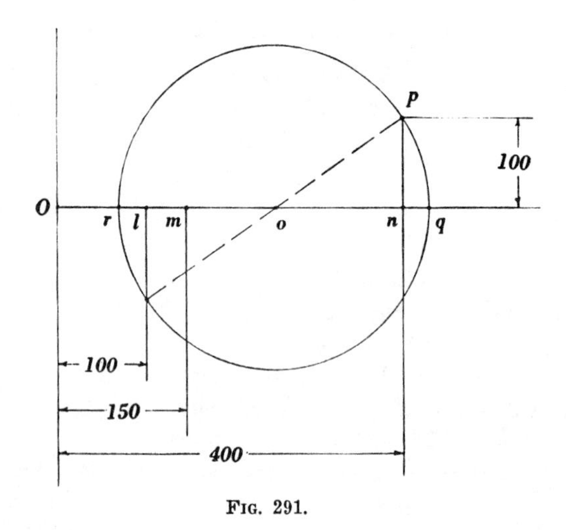

FIG. 291.

PROBLEMS

545. Determine the principal strains at a point of a loaded body if:
$e_X = 900 \times 10^{-6}$ in./in.
$e_Y = 100 \times 10^{-6}$ in./in.
$\gamma_{X-Y} = 400 \times 10^{-6}$ in./in.
Ans. $e_{\text{max.}} = 947 \times 10^{-6}$ in./in.; $e_{\text{min.}} = 53 \times 10^{-6}$ in./in.

546. Determine the principal strains at a point of a loaded body if
$e_X = 1000 \times 10^{-6}$ in./in.
$e_Y = -200 \times 10^{-6}$ in./in.
$\gamma_{X-Y} = 600 \times 10^{-6}$ in./in.

547. The suspended rod has a cross-sectional area of 0.8 sq. in. $E = 12 \times 10^6$ psi. $\mu = 0.3$. Determine the strain at an angle of 45° with right section A-A when a load of 4800 lb. is applied. *Ans.* 325×10^{-6} in./in.

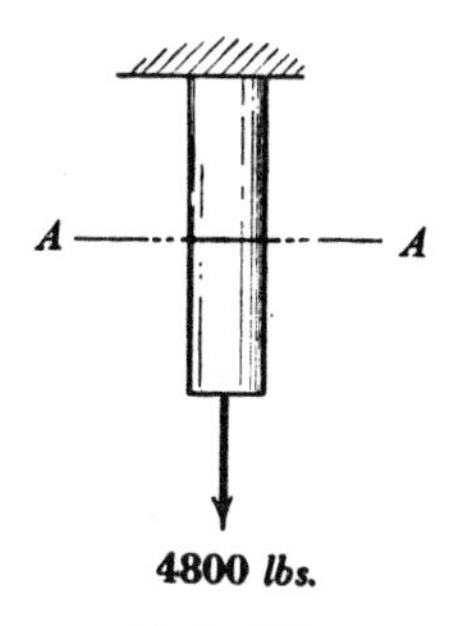

PROB. 547.

548–553, inclusive. In each case the strain gages form the 45° rosette shown in the figure. Determine the principal stresses.

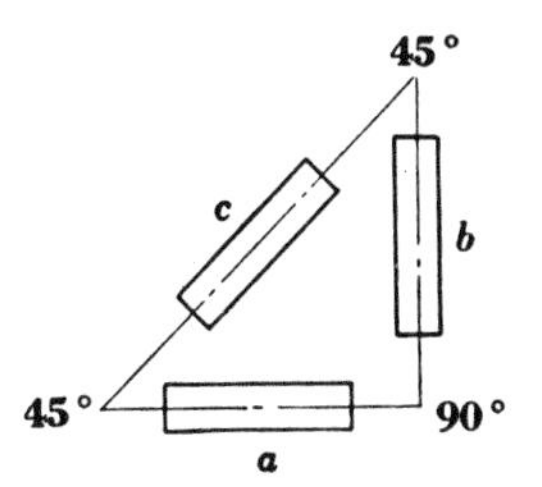

PROBS. 548-553.

548. $e_a = 900 \times 10^{-6}$ in./in.; $e_b = 300 \times 10^{-6}$ in./in.; $e_c = 500 \times 10^{-6}$ in./in. $E = 30 \times 10^6$ psi. $\mu = 0.3$. *Ans.* $s_{\text{max.}} = 33{,}000$ psi; $s_{\text{min.}} = 18{,}400$ psi.

549. $e_a = -600 \times 10^{-6}$ in./in.; $e_b = 200 \times 10^{-6}$ in./in.; $e_c = -300 \times 10^{-6}$ in./in. $E = 30 \times 10^6$ psi. $\mu = 0.3$.

550. $e_a = 180 \times 10^{-6}$ in./in.; $e_b = 640 \times 10^{-6}$ in./in.; $e_c = 200 \times 10^{-6}$ in./in. $E = 16 \times 10^6$ psi. $\mu = 0.36$.

551. $e_a = 600 \times 10^{-6}$ in./in; $e_b = -100 \times 10^{-6}$ in./in.; $e_c = 150 \times 10^{-6}$. in./in.; $E = 10.3 \times 10^6$ psi. $\mu = 1/3$. *Ans.* $s_{\text{max.}} = 6675$ psi; $s_{\text{min.}} = 1050$ psi.

552. $e_a = 1000 \times 10^{-6}$ in./in.; $e_b = 400$ in./in.; $e_c = 100 \times 10^{-6}$ in./in. $E = 30 \times 10^6$ psi. $\mu = 0.3$.

553. $e_a = 453 \times 10^{-6}$ in./in.; $e_b = -110 \times 10^{-6}$ in./in.; $e_c = 136 \times 10^{-6}$ in./in. $E = 30 \times 10^6$ psi. $\mu = 0.3$. *Ans.* $s_{\text{max.}} = 13{,}900$ psi; $s_{\text{min.}} = 820$ psi.

APPENDIX

TABLE I

Material	*Poisson's ratio*
Cast iron	0.27
Steel	0.30
Aluminum	0.33
Copper	0.36
Lead	0.43
Rubber	0.40
Concrete	0.14

TABLE II. MODULUS OF ELASTICITY

Material	*E*
Steel	30×10^6 psi
Cast iron, gray	15×10^6
Cast iron, malleable	25×10^6
Wrought iron	28×10^6
Brass	15×10^6
Bronze	12×10^6
Copper	16×10^6
Aluminum	10.3×10^6
Magnesium	6.5×10^6

TABLE III. COEFFICIENT OF LINEAR EXPANSION

Material	*Coefficient*
Steel	6.5×10^{-6} in./in./°F
Cast iron, gray	6.0×10^{-6}
Cast iron, malleable	6.6×10^{-6}
Wrought iron	6.7×10^{-6}
Brass	10.4×10^{-6}
Bronze	10.0×10^{-6}
Copper	9.3×10^{-6}
Aluminum	12.5×10^{-6}
Magnesium	14.5×10^{-6}

TABLE IV. MODULUS OF RIGIDITY

Material	*G*
Steel	12×10^6 psi
Cast iron, gray	6×10^6
Aluminum	4×10^6
Brass	5×10^6
Copper	6×10^6

NOTE: TABLE V. ALUMINUM COLUMNS. See page 343.
TABLE VI. PARABOLIC COLUMN FORMULAS. See page 345.
TABLE VII. STRUCTURAL TIMBER. See page 345.
TABLE VIII. MODULUS OF RESILIENCE. See page 391.

TABLE IX. WIDE-FLANGE SECTIONS

Design Properties

(Abridged List)*

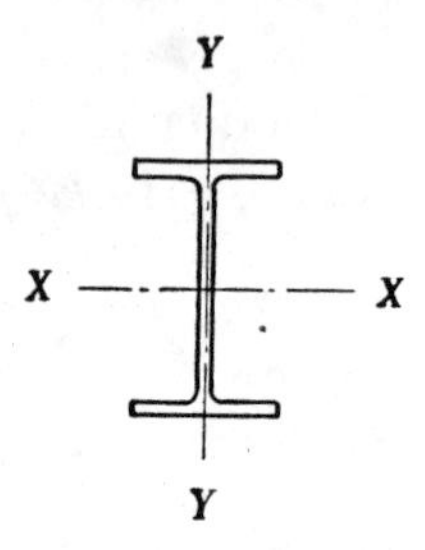

Nominal Depth	Weight per Foot- lb.	Area of Section in.²	Depth of Section in.	Axis X-X I in.⁴	Axis X-X S in.³	Axis X-X r in.	Axis Y-Y I in.⁴	Axis Y-Y S in.³	Axis Y-Y r in.
36	300	88.17	36.72	20290.2	1105.1	15.17	1225.2	147.1	3.73
	260	76.56	36.24	17233.8	951.1	15.00	1020.6	123.3	3.65
	240	70.60	36.00	15724.0	873.6	14.92	920.1	111.5	3.61
	170	49.98	36.16	10470.0	579.1	14.47	300.6	50.0	2.45
	150	44.16	35.84	9012.1	502.9	14.29	250.4	41.8	2.38
33	240	70.52	33.50	13585.1	811.1	13.88	874.3	110.2	3.52
	200	58.79	33.00	11048.2	669.6	13.71	691.7	87.8	3.43
	152	44.71	33.50	8147.6	486.4	13.50	256.1	44.3	2.39
	132	38.84	33.15	6856.8	413.7	13.29	207.8	36.1	2.31
30	210	61.78	30.38	9872.4	649.9	12.64	707.9	93.7	3.38
	190	55.90	30.12	8825.9	586.1	12.57	624.6	83.1	3.34
	172	50.65	29.88	7891.5	528.2	12.48	550.1	73.4	3.30
	132	38.83	30.30	5753.1	379.7	12.17	185.0	35.1	2.18
	116	34.13	30.00	4919.1	327.9	12.00	153.2	29.2	2.12
27	177	52.10	27.31	6728.6	492.8	11.36	518.9	73.7	3.16
	145	42.68	26.88	5414.3	402.9	11.26	406.9	58.3	3.09
	114	33.53	27.28	4080.5	299.2	11.03	149.6	29.7	2.11
	91	26.77	26.84	3129.2	233.2	10.81	109.0	21.8	2.02
24	160	47.04	24.72	5110.3	413.5	10.42	492.6	69.9	3.23
	130	38.21	24.25	4009.5	330.7	10.27	375.2	53.6	3.13
	100	29.43	24.00	2987.3	248.9	10.08	203.5	33.9	2.63
	74	21.77	23.87	2033.8	170.4	9.67	73.8	16.5	1.84
21	142	41.76	21.46	3403.1	317.2	9.03	385.9	58.8	3.04
	103	30.27	21.29	2268.0	213.1	8.66	119.9	26.4	1.99
	82	24.10	20.86	1752.4	168.0	8.53	89.6	20.0	1.93
	68	20.02	21.13	1478.3	139.9	8.59	60.4	14.6	1.74
	59	17.36	20.91	1246.8	119.3	8.47	49.2	12.0	1.68
18	124	36.45	18.64	2227.1	239.0	7.82	281.9	47.4	2.78
	114	33.51	18.48	2033.8	220.1	7.79	255.6	43.2	2.76
	96	28.22	18.16	1674.7	184.1	7.70	206.8	35.2	2.71
	85	24.97	18.32	1429.9	156.1	7.57	99.4	22.5	2.00
	70	20.56	18.00	1153.9	128.2	7.49	78.5	17.9	1.95

TABLE IX. WIDE-FLANGE SECTIONS—Continued

Nominal Depth	Weight per Foot-lbs.	Area of Section in.²	Depth of Section in.	Axis X-X			Axis Y-Y		
				I in.⁴	S in.³	r in.	I in.⁴	S in.³	r in.
	64	18.80	17.87	1045.8	117.0	7.46	70.3	16.1	1.93
	55	16.19	18.12	889.9	98.2	7.41	42.0	11.1	1.61
	50	14.71	18.00	800.6	89.0	7.38	37.2	9.9	1.59
16	114	33.51	16.64	1642.6	197.4	7.00	254.6	43.8	2.76
	96	28.22	16.32	1355.1	166.1	6.93	207.2	35.9	2.71
	78	22.92	16.32	1042.6	127.8	6.74	87.5	20.4	1.95
	64	18.80	16.00	833.8	104.2	6.66	68.4	16.1	1.91
	50	14.70	16.25	655.4	80.7	6.68	34.8	9.8	1.54
	40	11.77	16.00	515.5	64.4	6.62	26.5	7.6	1.50
14	426	125.25	18.69	6610.3	707.4	7.26	2359.5	282.7	4.34
	370	108.78	17.94	5454.2	608.1	7.08	1986.0	241.1	4.27
	300	88.20	17.00	4149.5	488.2	6.86	1546.0	191.2	4.19
	246	72.33	16.25	3228.9	397.4	6.68	1226.6	153.9	4.12
	202	59.39	15.63	2538.8	324.9	6.54	979.7	124.4	4.06
	158	46.47	15.00	1900.6	253.4	6.40	745.0	95.8	4.00
	127	37.33	14.62	1476.7	202.0	6.29	527.6	71.8	3.76
	103	30.26	14.25	1165.8	163.6	6.21	419.7	57.6	3.72
	84	24.71	14.18	928.4	130.9	6.13	225.5	37.5	3.02
	74	21.76	14.19	796.8	112.3	6.05	133.5	26.5	2.48
	58	17.06	14.06	597.9	85.0	5.92	63.7	15.7	1.93
	48	14.11	13.81	484.9	70.2	5.86	51.3	12.8	1.91
	43	12.65	13.68	429.0	62.7	5.82	45.1	11.3	1.89
	38	11.17	14.12	385.3	54.6	5.87	24.6	7.3	1.49
	30	8.81	13.86	289.6	41.8	5.73	17.5	5.2	1.41
12	190	55.86	14.38	1892.5	263.2	5.82	589.7	93.1	3.25
	133	39.11	13.28	1221.2	182.5	5.59	389.9	63.1	3.16
	92	27.06	12.62	788.9	125.0	5.40	256.4	42.2	3.08
	65	19.11	12.12	533.4	88.0	5.28	174.6	29.1	3.02
	64	18.83	12.31	528.3	85.8	5.29	119.0	23.7	2.51
	50	14.71	12.19	394.5	64.7	5.18	56.4	14.0	1.96
	36	10.59	12.24	280.8	45.9	5.15	23.7	7.2	1.50
	28	8.23	12.00	213.5	35.6	5.09	17.5	5.4	1.46
10	136	40.03	11.88	917.2	154.4	4.79	295.9	56.0	2.72
	100	29.43	11.12	625.0	112.4	4.61	206.6	39.9	2.65
	77	22.67	10.62	457.2	86.1	4.49	153.4	30.1	2.60
	60	17.66	10.25	343.7	67.1	4.41	116.5	23.1	2.57
	54	15.88	10.12	305.7	60.4	4.39	103.9	20.7	2.56
	45	13.24	10.12	248.6	49.1	4.33	53.2	13.3	2.00
	37	10.88	9.88	196.9	39.9	4.25	42.2	10.6	1.97
	29	8.53	10.22	157.3	30.8	4.29	15.2	5.2	1.34
	23	6.77	10.00	120.6	24.1	4.22	11.3	3.9	1.29
	21	6.19	9.90	106.3	21.5	4.14	9.7	3.4	1.25
8	67	19.70	9.00	271.8	60.4	3.71	88.6	21.5	2.12
	48	14.11	8.50	183.7	42.3	3.61	60.9	15.0	2.08
	35	10.30	8.12	126.5	31.1	3.50	42.5	10.6	2.03
	31	9.12	8.00	109.7	27.4	3.47	37.0	9.2	2.01
	27	7.93	8.03	94.1	23.4	3.44	20.8	6.4	1.62
	21	6.18	8.19	73.8	18.0	3.45	9.13	3.5	1.22
	17	5.00	8.00	56.4	14.1	3.36	6.72	2.6	1.16

TABLE IX. WIDE-FLANGE SECTIONS—Continued

Nominal Depth	Weight per Foot- lb.	Area of Section in.²	Depth of Section in.	Axis X-X I in.⁴	Axis X-X S in.³	Axis X-X r in.	Axis Y-Y I in.⁴	Axis Y-Y S in.³	Axis Y-Y r in.
6 (B)	27.5	8.11	6.46	59.7	18.5	2.71	19.1	6.2	1.53
	22.5	6.63	6.28	47.4	15.1	2.67	15.2	5.0	1.51
	18.0	5.31	6.11	36.4	11.9	2.62	11.7	3.9	1.48
	15.5	4.62	6.00	30.3	10.1	2.56	9.69	3.2	1.45
5 (B)	18.5	5.45	5.12	25.4	9.94	2.16	8.89	3.54	1.28
	13.5	3.98	4.86	17.1	7.02	2.07	6.05	2.43	1.23
4 (B)	13.0	3.82	4.16	11.3	5.45	1.72	3.76	1.85	0.99
	10.0	2.93	4.00	8.31	4.16	1.68	2.74	1.37	0.97
	7.5	2.22	3.87	6.06	3.13	1.65	1.96	0.99	0.94

TABLE X. AMERICAN STANDARD I-BEAM SECTIONS

Design Properties

(Abridged List)

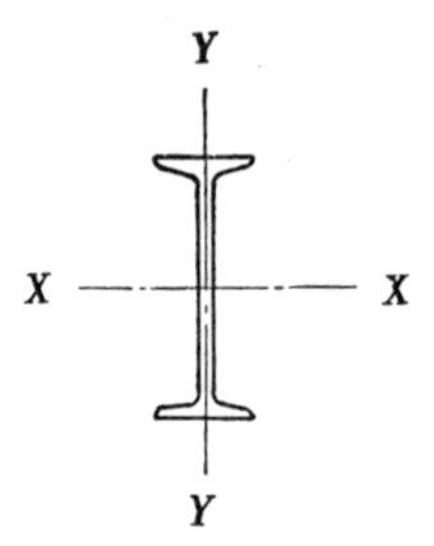

Depth in.	Weight per Foot-lb.	Area of Section in.²	Axis X-X			Axis Y-Y		
			I in.⁴	*S* in.³	*r* in.	*I* in.⁴	*S* in.³	*r* in.
24	120.0	35.13	3010.8	250.9	9.26	84.9	21.1	1.56
	110.0	32.18	2869.1	239.1	9.44	80.6	20.3	1.58
	100.0	29.25	2371.8	197.6	9.05	48.4	13.4	1.29
	90.0	26.30	2230.1	185.8	9.21	45.5	12.8	1.32
	79.9	23.33	2087.2	173.9	9.46	42.9	12.2	1.36
20	100.0	29.20	1648.3	164.8	7.51	52.4	14.4	1.34
	90.0	26.26	1550.3	155.0	7.68	48.7	13.7	1.36
	81.4	23.74	1466.3	146.6	7.86	45.8	13.1	1.39
	75.0	21.90	1263.5	126.3	7.60	30.1	9.4	1.17
	70.0	20.42	1214.2	121.4	7.71	28.9	9.2	1.19
	65.4	19.08	1169.5	116.9	7.83	27.9	8.9	1.21
18	70.0	20.46	917.5	101.9	6.70	24.5	7.8	1.09
	65.0	18.98	877.7	97.5	6.80	23.4	7.6	1.11
	60.0	17.50	837.8	93.1	6.92	22.3	7.3	1.13
	54.7	15.94	795.5	88.4	7.07	21.2	7.1	1.15
15	75.0	21.85	687.2	91.6	5.61	30.6	9.8	1.18
	70.0	20.38	659.6	87.9	5.69	28.8	9.3	1.19
	65.0	18.91	632.1	84.3	5.78	27.2	8.9	1.20
	60.8	17.68	609.0	81.2	5.87	26.0	8.7	1.21
	50.0	14.59	481.1	64.2	5.74	16.0	5.7	1.05
	42.9	12.49	441.8	58.9	5.95	14.6	5.3	1.08
12	55.0	16.04	319.3	53.2	4.46	17.3	6.2	1.04
	50.0	14.57	301.6	50.3	4.55	16.0	5.8	1.05
	45.0	13.10	284.1	47.3	4.66	14.8	5.5	1.06
	40.8	11.84	268.9	44.8	4.77	13.8	5.3	1.08
	35.0	10.20	227.0	37.8	4.72	10.0	3.9	0.99
	31.8	9.26	215.8	36.0	4.83	9.5	3.8	1.01
10	40.0	11.69	158.0	31.6	3.68	9.4	3.7	0.90
	35.0	10.22	145.8	29.2	3.78	8.5	3.4	0.91
	30.0	8.75	133.5	26.7	3.91	7.6	3.2	0.93
	25.4	7.38	122.1	24.4	4.07	6.9	3.0	0.97
8	25.5	7.43	68.1	17.0	3.03	4.7	2.2	0.80
	23.0	6.71	64.2	16.0	3.09	4.4	2.1	0.81
	18.4	5.34	56.9	14.2	3.26	3.8	1.9	0.84

TABLE X. AMERICAN STANDARD I-BEAM SECTIONS—Continued

Depth in.	Weight per Foot-lb.	Area of Section in.^{2}	Axis X-X			Axis Y-Y		
			I in.^{4}	S in.^{3}	r in.	I in.^{4}	S in.^{3}	r in.
7	20.0	5.83	41.9	12.0	2.68	3.1	1.6	0.74
	17.5	5.09	38.9	11.1	2.77	2.9	1.6	0.76
	15.3	4.43	36.2	10.4	2.86	2.7	1.5	0.78
6	17.25	5.02	26.0	8.7	2.28	2.3	1.3	0.68
	14.75	4.29	23.8	7.9	2.36	2.1	1.2	0.69
	12.5	3.61	21.8	7.3	2.46	1.8	1.1	0.72
5	14.75	4.29	15.0	6.0	1.87	1.7	1.0	0.63
	12.25	3.56	13.5	5.4	1.95	1.4	0.91	0.63
	10.0	2.87	12.1	4.8	2.05	1.2	0.82	0.65
4	10.5	3.05	7.1	3.5	1.52	1.0	0.70	0.57
	7.7	2.21	6.0	3.0	1.64	0.77	0.58	0.59
3	7.5	2.17	2.9	1.9	1.15	0.59	0.47	0.52
	5.7	1.64	2.5	1.7	1.23	0.46	0.40	0.53

TABLE XI. AMERICAN STANDARD CHANNEL SECTIONS

Design Properties

(Abridged List)

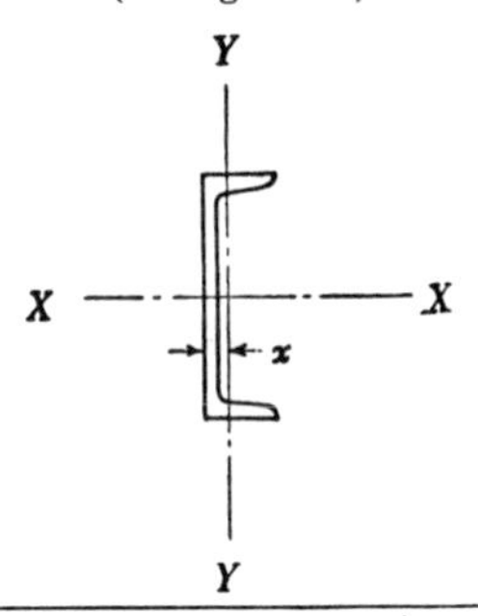

Depth in.	Weight per Foot-lb.	Area of Section in.²	Axis X-X			Axis Y-Y			
			I in.⁴	S in.³	r in.	I in.⁴	S in.³	r in.	x in.
18	51.9	15.18	622.1	69.1	6.40	17.1	5.3	1.06	0.87
	42.7	12.48	594.2	61.0	6.64	15.0	4.9	1.10	0.90
15	55.0	16.11	429.0	57.2	5.16	12.1	4.1	0.87	0.82
	50.0	14.64	401.4	53.6	5.24	11.2	3.8	0.87	0.80
	33.9	9.90	312.6	41.7	5.62	8.2	3.2	0.91	0.79
12	40.0	11.73	196.5	32.8	4.09	6.6	2.5	0.75	0.72
	30.0	8.79	161.2	26.9	4.28	5.2	2.1	0.77	0.63
	25.0	7.32	143.5	23.9	4.43	4.5	1.9	0.79	0.68
	20.7	6.03	128.1	21.4	4.61	3.9	1.7	0.81	0.70
10	35.0	10.27	115.2	23.0	3.34	4.6	1.9	0.67	0.69
	15.3	4.47	66.9	13.4	3.87	2.3	1.2	0.72	0.64
9	25.0	7.33	70.5	15.7	3.10	3.0	1.4	0.64	0.61
	13.4	3.89	47.3	10.5	3.49	1.8	0.97	0.67	0.61
8	21.25	6.23	47.6	11.9	2.77	2.2	1.1	0.60	0.59
	11.5	3.36	32.3	8.1	3.10	1.3	0.79	0.63	0.58
7	19.75	5.79	33.1	9.4	2.39	1.8	0.96	0.56	0.58
	9.8	2.85	21.1	6.0	2.72	0.98	0.63	0.59	0.55
6	15.5	4.54	19.5	6.5	2.07	1.3	0.73	0.53	0.55
	8.2	2.39	13.0	4.3	1.34	0.70	0.50	0.54	0.52
5	11.5	3.36	10.4	4.1	1.76	0.82	0.54	0.49	0.51
4	7.25	2.12	4.5	2.3	1.47	0.44	0.35	0.46	0.46
3	6.0	1.75	2.1	1.4	1.08	0.31	0.27	0.42	0.46

TABLE XII. EQUAL LEG ANGLES
(Abridged List)

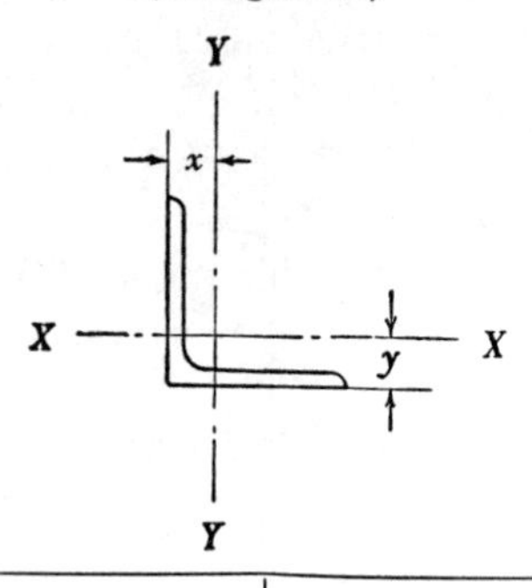

Size in.	Thickness in.	Weight per Foot-lb.	Area of Section in.^{2}	I in.^{4}	S in.^{3}	r in.	x or y in.	$r_{min.}$ in.
8 × 8	1	51.0	15.00	89.0	15.8	2.44	2.37	1.56
	¾	38.9	11.44	69.7	12.2	2.47	2.28	1.57
	½	26.4	7.75	48.6	8.4	2.50	2.19	1.59
6 × 6	1	37.4	11.00	35.5	8.6	1.80	1.86	1.17
	¾	28.7	8.44	28.2	6.7	1.83	1.78	1.18
	½	19.6	5.75	19.9	4.6	1.86	1.68	1.18
5 × 5	1	30.6	9.00	19.6	5.8	1.48	1.61	0.97
	¾	23.6	6.94	15.7	4.5	1.51	1.52	0.97
	½	16.2	4.75	11.3	3.2	1.54	1.43	0.98
	⅜	12.3	3.61	8.7	2.4	1.56	1.39	0.99
4 × 4	¾	18.5	5.44	7.7	2.8	1.19	1.27	0.78
	½	12.8	3.75	5.6	2.0	1.22	1.18	0.78
	⅜	9.8	2.86	4.4	1.5	1.23	1.14	0.79
	¼	6.6	1.94	3.0	1.1	1.25	1.09	0.80

TABLE XIII. UNEQUAL LEG ANGLES
(Abridged List)

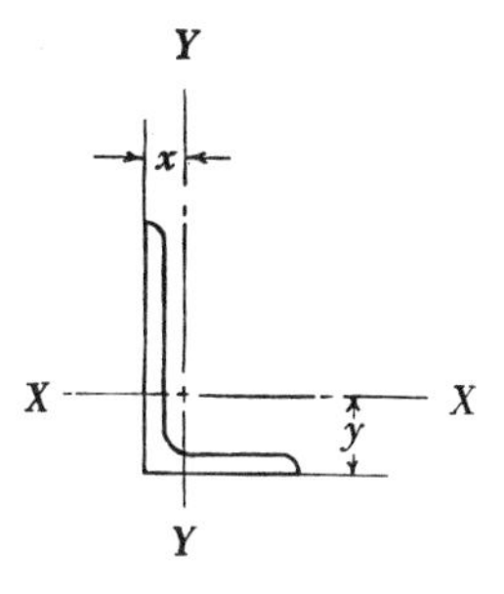

Size in.	Thickness in.	Weight per Foot- lb.	Area of Section in.^{2}	Axis X-X I in.^{4}	Axis X-X S in.^{3}	Axis X-X r in.	Axis X-X y in.	Axis Y-Y I in.^{4}	Axis Y-Y S in.^{3}	Axis Y-Y r in.	Axis Y-Y x in.	$r_{min.}$ in.
8 × 6	1	44.2	13.00	80.8	15.1	2.49	2.65	38.8	8.9	1.73	1.65	1.28
	¾	33.8	9.94	63.4	11.7	2.53	2.56	30.7	6.9	1.76	1.56	1.29
	½	23.0	6.75	44.3	8.0	2.56	2.47	21.7	4.8	1.79	1.47	1.30
8 × 4	1	37.4	11.00	69.6	14.1	2.52	3.05	11.6	3.9	1.03	1.05	0.85
	¾	28.7	8.44	54.9	10.9	2.55	2.95	9.4	3.1	1.05	0.95	0.85
	½	19.6	5.75	38.5	7.5	2.59	2.86	6.7	2.2	1.08	0.86	0.86
7 × 4	1	34.0	10.00	47.7	10.9	2.18	2.60	11.2	3.9	1.06	1.10	0.85
	¾	26.2	7.69	37.8	8.4	2.22	2.51	9.1	3.0	1.09	1.01	0.86
	½	17.9	5.25	26.7	5.8	2.25	2.42	6.5	2.1	1.11	0.92	0.87
	⅜	13.6	3.98	20.6	4.4	2.27	2.37	5.1	1.6	1.13	0.87	0.88
6 × 4	1	30.6	9.00	30.8	8.0	1.85	2.17	10.8	3.8	1.09	1.17	0.86
	¾	23.6	6.94	24.5	6.3	1.88	2.08	8.7	3.0	1.12	1.08	0.86
	½	16.2	4.75	17.4	4.3	1.91	1.99	6.3	2.1	1.15	0.99	0.87
	⅜	12.3	3.61	13.5	3.3	1.93	1.94	4.9	1.6	1.17	0.94	0.88
6 × 3½	¾	22.4	6.56	23.3	6.1	1.89	2.18	5.8	2.3	0.94	0.93	0.75
	½	15.3	4.50	16.6	4.2	1.92	2.08	4.3	1.6	0.97	0.83	0.76
	⅜	11.7	3.42	12.9	3.3	1.94	2.04	3.3	1.2	0.99	0.79	0.77
5 × 3½	¾	19.8	5.81	13.9	4.3	1.55	1.75	5.6	2.2	0.98	1.00	0.75
	½	13.6	4.00	10.0	3.0	1.58	1.66	4.1	1.6	1.01	0.91	0.75
	5/16	8.7	2.56	6.6	1.9	1.61	1.59	2.7	1.0	1.03	0.84	0.77
5 × 3	¾	18.5	5.44	13.2	4.2	1.55	1.84	3.5	1.6	0.80	0.84	0.64
	½	12.8	3.75	9.5	2.9	1.59	1.75	2.6	1.1	0.83	0.75	0.65
	5/16	8.2	2.40	6.3	1.9	1.61	1.68	1.8	0.75	0.85	0.68	0.66
4 × 3½	¾	17.3	5.06	7.3	2.8	1.20	1.34	5.2	2.2	1.01	1.09	0.72
	½	11.9	3.50	5.3	1.9	1.23	1.25	3.8	1.5	1.04	1.00	0.72
	5/16	7.7	2.25	3.6	1.3	1.26	1.18	2.6	1.0	1.07	0.93	0.73

TABLE XIII. UNEQUAL LEG ANGLES—Continued

Size in.	Thickness in.	Weight per Foot lb.	Area of Section in.^{2}	Axis X-X				Axis Y-Y				$r_{min.}$
				I in.^{4}	S in.^{3}	r in.	y in.	I in.^{4}	S in.^{3}	r in.	x in.	in.
4 × 3	3/4	16.0	4.69	6.9	2.7	1.22	1.42	3.3	1.6	0.84	0.92	0.64
	1/2	11.1	3.25	5.1	1.9	1.25	1.33	2.4	1.1	0.86	0.83	0.64
	1/4	5.8	1.69	2.8	1.0	1.28	1.24	1.4	0.60	0.90	0.74	0.65
3½ × 3	3/4	14.7	4.31	4.7	2.1	1.04	1.21	3.2	1.5	0.85	0.96	0.62
	1/2	10.2	3.00	3.5	1.5	1.07	1.13	2.3	1.1	0.88	0.88	0.62
	1/4	5.4	1.56	1.9	0.78	1.11	1.04	1.3	0.59	0.91	0.79	0.63
3½ × 2½	1/2	9.4	2.75	3.2	1.4	1.09	1.20	1.4	0.76	0.70	0.70	0.53
	1/4	4.9	1.44	1.8	0.75	1.12	1.11	0.78	0.41	0.74	0.61	0.54
3 × 2½	1/2	8.5	2.50	2.1	1.0	0.91	1.00	1.3	0.74	0.72	0.75	0.52
	1/4	4.5	1.31	1.2	0.56	0.95	0.91	0.74	0.40	0.75	0.66	0.53
3 × 2	1/2	7.7	2.25	1.9	1.0	0.92	1.08	0.67	0.47	0.55	0.58	0.43
	1/4	4.1	1.19	1.1	0.54	0.95	0.99	0.39	0.26	0.57	0.49	0.43
2½ x 2	1/2	6.8	2.00	1.1	0.70	0.75	0.88	0.64	0.46	0.56	0.63	0.42
	3/16	2.75	0.81	0.51	0.29	0.79	0.76	0.29	0.20	0.60	0.51	0.43
2½ × 1½	5/16	3.92	1.15	0.71	0.44	0.79	0.90	0.19	0.17	0.41	0.40	0.32
	3/16	2.44	0.72	0.46	0.28	0.80	0.85	0.13	0.11	0.42	0.35	0.33
2 × 1½	3/8	3.99	1.17	0.43	0.34	0.61	0.71	0.21	0.20	0.42	0.46	0.32
	1/8	1.44	0.42	0.17	0.13	0.64	0.62	0.09	0.08	0.45	0.37	0.33
1¾ × 1¼	1/4	2.34	0.69	0.20	0.18	0.54	0.60	0.09	0.10	0.35	0.35	0.27
	1/8	1.23	0.36	0.11	0.09	0.56	0.56	0.05	0.05	0.37	0.31	0.27

TABLE XIV. ALUMINUM STANDARD I-BEAMS
(Abridged List)*

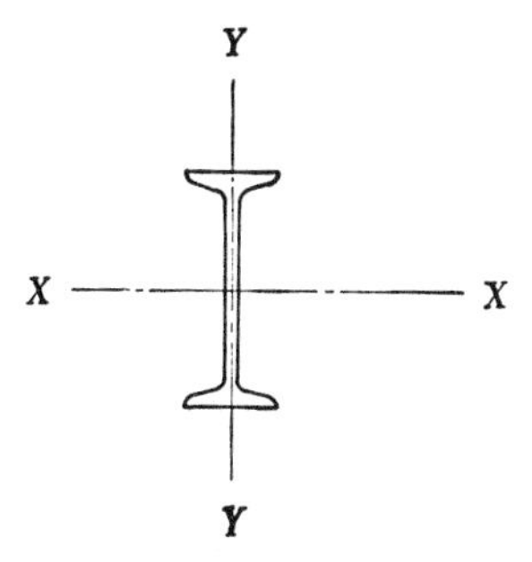

Depth in.	Weight per Foot- lb.	Area of Section in.^{2}	Axis X-X			Axis Y-Y		
			I in.^{4}	S in.^{3}	r in.	I in.^{4}	S in.^{3}	r in
12	17.78	14.70	304.84	50.81	4.56	15.71	5.74	1.03
	16.01	13.23	287.27	47.88	4.66	14.50	5.42	1.05
	12.44	10.28	229.36	38.23	4.72	9.87	3.89	0.98
	11.31	9.35	218.13	36.35	4.83	9.35	3.74	1.00
10	9.01	7.45	123.39	24.68	4.07	6.78	2.91	0.95
8	9.07	7.49	68.73	17.18	3.03	4.66	2.19	0.79
	7.30	6.03	60.92	15.23	3.18	3.99	1.95	0.81
	6.53	5.40	57.55	14.39	3.27	3.73	1.86	0.83
7	6.23	5.15	39.40	11.26	2.77	2.88	1.53	0.75
6	5.25	4.34	24.11	8.04	2.36	2.04	1.19	0.69
	4.43	3.66	22.08	7.36	2.46	1.82	1.09	0.71
5	5.25	4.34	15.22	6.09	1.87	1.66	1.01	0.62
	3.53	2.92	12.26	4.90	2.05	1.21	0.81	0.64
4	3.38	2.79	6.79	3.39	1.56	0.90	0.65	0.57
	2.72	2.25	6.06	3.03	1.64	0.76	0.57	0.58
3	2.67	2.21	2.93	1.95	1.15	0.59	0.47	0.52
	2.02	1.67	2.52	1.68	1.23	0.46	0.39	0.52

*Printed with the permission of the copyright owner, the Aluminum Company of America.

TABLE XV. ALUMINUM WIDE-FLANGE BEAMS

(Abridged List)*

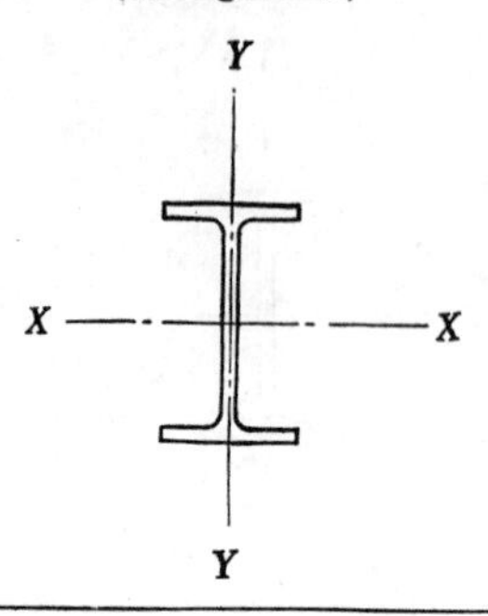

Nominal Size	Actual Depth in.	Weight per Foot-lb.	Area of Section in.^{2}	Axis X-X			Axis Y-Y		
				I in.^{4}	S in.^{3}	r in.	I in.^{4}	S in.^{3}	r in.
10 × 5¾	9.90	7.51	6.21	106.74	21.56	4.15	10.77	3.75	1.32
8 × 8	8.00	11.04	9.12	109.66	27.41	3.47	36.97	9.24	2.01
8 × 7	8.00	8.56	7.08	84.15	21.04	3.45	18.23	5.61	1.61
8 × 5	8.00	6.07	5.02	56.73	14.18	3.36	7.44	2.83	1.22
6 × 6	6.00	5.56	4.59	30.17	10.06	2.56	9.69	3.23	1.45
6 × 4	6.00	4.28	3.54	21.75	7.25	2.48	2.98	1.49	0.92

*See Note, Table XIV.

TABLE XVI. AREAS OF CIRCLES

Diameter in.	*Area* in.^{2}
⅛	0.0123
¼	0.0491
⅜	0.1104
½	0.1963
⅝	0.3068
¾	0.4418
13/16	0.5185
⅞	0.6013
15/16	0.6903
1	0.7854
1¼	1.227
1½	1.767
1¾	2.405
2	3.142
2½	4.909
3	7.069
4	12.566
5	19.635

TABLE XVII. AVERAGE PROPERTIES OF COMMON ENGINEERING METALS*

Material	*Tensile Strength* 1000 psi	*Yield Point* 1000 psi
Steel		
AISI 1020 (Plain Carbon)		
as rolled	70	45
cold drawn	70	48
AISI 1045 (Plain Carbon)		
as rolled	100	60
cold drawn	110	70
normalized	95	65
AISI 1112 (Free Cutting)		
as rolled	65	40
cold drawn	80	65
AISI 2315 (Nickel)		
as rolled	85	55
cold drawn	95	75
AISI 3140 (Nickel-Chromium)		
as rolled	110	75
annealed	95	65
AISI 4140 (Chromium-Molybdenum)		
hot-rolled, annealed	90	65
cold drawn, annealed	115	90
AISI 6150 (Chrome-Vanadium)	100–200	70–190
Steel, stainless, 502, annealed	60	25
309, annealed	90–100	34–45
Cast Iron, gray	20–60	
Iron, malleable	50–53	32–35
Aluminum,		
14S	60–68	37–60
61S	35–45	21–40
Magnesium,		
extruded shapes	40–50	26–33
forgings	36–46	23–31
sheet and plate	30–45	15–35
Monel metal, annealed	70–85	30–40
Copper, cold drawn	40–50	—
Copper-base alloys,		
wrought, hard		
aluminum bronze	90–100	35–60
manganese bronze	75	45
red brass	70–90	50–60
Copper-base alloys,		
cast		
aluminum bronze	70–95	25–50
structural bronze G	30–45	15–25
manganese bronze	60–90	20–40
red brass	30–38	12–17
Die-casting alloys		
aluminum	30–43	16–26
brass	45–58	25–30
magnesium	29–34	22
zinc	40–50	—

*These properties are markedly affected by alloying, heat-treatment, processing, etc. The values given in the table are intended only to present typical data for use in problems.

Index

ENGINEERING AND TECHNOLOGY

General and mathematical

ENGINEERING MATHEMATICS, Kenneth S. Miller. A text for graduate students of engineering to strengthen their mathematical background in differential equations, etc. Mathematical steps very explicitly indicated. Contents: Determinants and Matrices, Integrals, Linear Differential Equations, Fourier Series and Integrals, Laplace Transform, Network Theory, Random Function . . . all vital requisites for advanced modern engineering studies. Unabridged republication. Appendices: Borel Sets; Riemann-Stieltjes Integral; Fourier Series and Integrals. Index. References at Chapter Ends. xii + 417pp. 6 x 8½. S1121 Paperbound **$2.00**

MATHEMATICAL ENGINEERING ANALYSIS, Rufus Oldenburger. A book designed to assist the research engineer and scientist in making the transition from physical engineering situations to the corresponding mathematics. Scores of common practical situations found in all major fields of physics are supplied with their correct mathematical formulations—applications to automobile springs and shock absorbers, clocks, throttle torque of diesel engines, resistance networks, capacitors, transmission lines, microphones, neon tubes, gasoline engines, refrigeration cycles, etc. Each section reviews basic principles of underlying various fields: mechanics of rigid bodies, electricity and magnetism, heat, elasticity, fluid mechanics, and aerodynamics. Comprehensive and eminently useful. Index. 169 problems, answers. 200 photos and diagrams. xiv + 426pp. 5⅜ x 8½. S919 Paperbound **$2.50**

MATHEMATICS OF MODERN ENGINEERING, E. G. Keller and R. E. Doherty. Written for the Advanced Course in Engineering of the General Electric Corporation, deals with the engineering use of determinants, tensors, the Heaviside operational calculus, dyadics, the calculus of variations, etc. Presents underlying principles fully, but purpose is to teach engineers to deal with modern engineering problems, and emphasis is on the perennial engineering attack of set-up and solve. Indexes. Over 185 figures and tables. Hundreds of exercises, problems, and worked-out examples. References. Two volume set. Total of xxxiii + 623pp. 5⅜ x 8.
S734 Vol I Paperbound **$1.85**
S735 Vol II Paperbound **$1.85**
The set **$3.70**

MATHEMATICAL METHODS FOR SCIENTISTS AND ENGINEERS, L. P. Smith. For scientists and engineers, as well as advanced math students. Full investigation of methods and practical description of conditions under which each should be used. Elements of real functions, differential and integral calculus, space geometry, theory of residues, vector and tensor analysis, series of Bessel functions, etc. Each method illustrated by completely-worked-out examples, mostly from scientific literature. 368 graded unsolved problems. 100 diagrams. x + 453pp. 5⅝ x 8⅜. S220 Paperbound **$2.00**

THEORY OF FUNCTIONS AS APPLIED TO ENGINEERING PROBLEMS, edited by R. Rothe, F. Ollendorff, and K. Pohlhausen. A series of lectures given at the Berlin Institute of Technology that shows the specific applications of function theory in electrical and allied fields of engineering. Six lectures provide the elements of function theory in a simple and practical form, covering complex quantities and variables, integration in the complex plane, residue theorems, etc. Then 5 lectures show the exact uses of this powerful mathematical tool, with full discussions of problem methods. Index. Bibliography. 108 figures. x + 189pp. 5⅜ x 8.
S733 Paperbound **$1.35**

Aerodynamics and hydrodynamics

AIRPLANE STRUCTURAL ANALYSIS AND DESIGN, E. E. Sechler and L. G. Dunn. Systematic authoritative book which summarizes a large amount of theoretical and experimental work on structural analysis and design. Strong on classical subsonic material still basic to much aeronautic design . . . remains a highly useful source of information. Covers such areas as layout of the airplane, applied and design loads, stress-strain relationships for stable structures, truss and frame analysis, the problem of instability, the ultimate strength of stiffened flat sheet, analysis of cylindrical structures, wings and control surfaces, fuselage analysis, engine mounts, landing gears, etc. Originally published as part of the CALCIT Aeronautical Series. 256 Illustrations. 47 study problems. Indexes. xi + 420pp. 5⅜ x 8½.
S1043 Paperbound **$2.25**

FUNDAMENTALS OF HYDRO- AND AEROMECHANICS, L. Prandtl and O. G. Tietjens. The well-known standard work based upon Prandtl's lectures at Goettingen. Wherever possible hydrodynamics theory is referred to practical considerations in hydraulics, with the view of unifying theory and experience. Presentation is extremely clear and though primarily physical, mathematical proofs are rigorous and use vector analysis to a considerable extent. An Engineering Society Monograph, 1934. 186 figures. Index. xvi + 270pp. 5⅜ x 8.
S374 Paperbound **$1.85**

FLUID MECHANICS FOR HYDRAULIC ENGINEERS, H. Rouse. Standard work that gives a coherent picture of fluid mechanics from the point of view of the hydraulic engineer. Based on courses given to civil and mechanical engineering students at Columbia and the California Institute of Technology, this work covers every basic principle, method, equation, or theory of interest to the hydraulic engineer. Much of the material, diagrams, charts, etc., in this self-contained text are not duplicated elsewhere. Covers irrotational motion, conformal mapping, problems in laminar motion, fluid turbulence, flow around immersed bodies, transportation of sediment, general charcteristics of wave phenomena, gravity waves in open channels, etc. Index. Appendix of physical properties of common fluids. Frontispiece + 245 figures and photographs. xvi + 422pp. 5⅜ x 8. S729 Paperbound **$2.25**

WATERHAMMER ANALYSIS, John Parmakian. Valuable exposition of the graphical method of solving waterhammer problems by Assistant Chief Designing Engineer, U.S. Bureau of Reclamation. Discussions of rigid and elastic water column theory, velocity of waterhammer waves, theory of graphical waterhammer analysis for gate operation, closings, openings, rapid and slow movements, etc., waterhammer in pump discharge caused by power failure, waterhammer analysis for compound pipes, and numerous related problems. "With a concise and lucid style, clear printing, adequate bibliography and graphs for approximate solutions at the project stage, it fills a vacant place in waterhammer literature," WATER POWER. 43 problems. Bibliography. Index. 113 illustrations. xiv + 161pp. 5⅜ x 8½.
S1061 Paperbound **$1.65**

AERODYNAMIC THEORY: A GENERAL REVIEW OF PROGRESS, William F. Durand, editor-in-chief. A monumental joint effort by the world's leading authorities prepared under a grant of the Guggenheim Fund for the Promotion of Aeronautics. Intended to provide the student and aeronautic designer with the theoretical and experimental background of aeronautics. Never equalled for breadth, depth, reliability. Contains discussions of special mathematical topics not usually taught in the engineering or technical courses. Also: an extended two-part treatise on Fluid Mechanics, discussions of aerodynamics of perfect fluids, analyses of experiments with wind tunnels, applied airfoil theory, the non-lifting system of the airplane, the air propeller, hydrodynamics of boats and floats, the aerodynamics of cooling, etc. Contributing experts include Munk, Giacomelli, Prandtl, Toussaint, Von Karman, Klemperer, among others. Unabridged republication. 6 volumes bound as 3. Total of 1,012 figures, 12 plates. Total of 2,186pp. Bibliographies. Notes. Indices. 5⅜ x 8.
S328-S330 Clothbound, The Set **$17.50**

APPLIED HYDRO- AND AEROMECHANICS, L. Prandtl and O. G. Tietjens. Presents, for the most part, methods which will be valuable to engineers. Covers flow in pipes, boundary layers, airfoil theory, entry conditions, turbulent flow in pipes, and the boundary layer, determining drag from measurements of pressure and velocity, etc. "Will be welcomed by all students of aerodynamics," NATURE. Unabridged, unaltered. An Engineering Society Monograph, 1934. Index. 226 figures, 28 photographic plates illustrating flow patterns. xvi + 311pp. 5⅜ x 8.
S375 Paperbound **$1.85**

SUPERSONIC AERODYNAMICS, E. R. C. Miles. Valuable theoretical introduction to the supersonic domain, with emphasis on mathematical tools and principles, for practicing aerodynamicists and advanced students in aeronautical engineering. Covers fundamental theory, divergence theorem and principles of circulation, compressible flow and Helmholtz laws, the Prandtl-Busemann graphic method for 2-dimensional flow, oblique shock waves, the Taylor-Maccoll method for cones in supersonic flow, the Chaplygin method for 2-dimensional flow, etc. Problems range from practical engineering problems to development of theoretical results. "Rendered outstanding by the unprecedented scope of its contents . . . has undoubtedly filled a vital gap," AERONAUTICAL ENGINEERING REVIEW. Index. 173 problems, answers. 106 diagrams. 7 tables. xii + 255pp. 5⅜ x 8. S214 Paperbound **$1.45**

HYDRAULIC TRANSIENTS, G. R. Rich. The best text in hydraulics ever printed in English . . . by one of America's foremost engineers (former Chief Design Engineer for T.V.A.). Provides a transition from the basic differential equations of hydraulic transient theory to the arithmetic intergration computation required by practicing engineers. Sections cover Water Hammer, Turbine Speed Regulation, Stability of Governing, Water-Hammer Pressures in Pump Discharge Lines, The Differential and Restricted Orifice Surge Tanks, The Normalized Surge Tank Charts of Calame and Gaden, Navigation Locks, Surges in Power Canals—Tidal Harmonics, etc. Revised and enlarged. Author's prefaces. Index. xiv + 409pp. 5⅜ x 8½.
S116 Paperbound **$2.50**

HYDRAULICS AND ITS APPLICATIONS, A. H. Gibson. Excellent comprehensive textbook for the student and thorough practical manual for the professional worker, a work of great stature in its area. Half the book is devoted to theory and half to applications and practical problems met in the field. Covers modes of motion of a fluid, critical velocity, viscous flow, eddy formation, Bernoulli's theorem, flow in converging passages, vortex motion, form of effluent streams, notches and weirs, skin friction, losses at valves and elbows, siphons, erosion of channels, jet propulsion, waves of oscillation, and over 100 similar topics. Final chapters (nearly 400 pages) cover more than 100 kinds of hydraulic machinery: Pelton wheel, speed regulators, the hydraulic ram, surge tanks, the scoop wheel, the Venturi meter, etc. A special chapter treats methods of testing theoretical hypotheses: scale models of rivers, tidal estuaries, siphon spillways, etc. 5th revised and enlarged (1952) edition. Index. Appendix. 427 photographs and diagrams. 95 examples, answers. xv + 813pp. 6 x 9.
S791 Clothbound **$8.00**

FLUID MECHANICS THROUGH WORKED EXAMPLES, D. R. L. Smith and J. Houghton. Advanced text covering principles and applications to practical situations. Each chapter begins with concise summaries of fundamental ideas. 163 fully worked out examples applying principles outlined in the text. 275 other problems, with answers. Contents; The Pressure of Liquids on Surfaces; Floating Bodies; Flow Under Constant Head in Pipes; Circulation; Vorticity; The Potential Function; Laminar Flow and Lubrication; Impact of Jets; Hydraulic Turbines; Centrifugal and Reciprocating Pumps; Compressible Fluids; and many other items. Total of 438 examples. 250 line illustrations. 340pp. Index. 6 x 8⅞. S981 Clothbound **$6.00**

THEORY OF SHIP MOTIONS, S. N. Blagoveshchensky. The only detailed text in English in a rapidly developing branch of engineering and physics, it is the work of one of the world's foremost authorities—Blagoveshchensky of Leningrad Shipbuilding Institute. A senior-level treatment written primarily for engineering students, but also of great importance to naval architects, designers, contractors, researchers in hydrodynamics, and other students. No mathematics beyond ordinary differential equations is required for understanding the text. Translated by T. & L. Strelkoff, under editorship of Louis Landweber, Iowa Institute of Hydraulic Research, under auspices of Office of Naval Research. Bibliography. Index. 231 diagrams and illustrations. Total of 649pp. 5⅜ x 8½. Vol. I: S234 Paperbound **$2.00**
Vol. II: S235 Paperbound **$2.00**

THEORY OF FLIGHT, Richard von Mises. Remains almost unsurpassed as balanced, well-written account of fundamental fluid dynamics, and situations in which air compressibility effects are unimportant. Stressing equally theory and practice, avoiding formidable mathematical structure, it conveys a full understanding of physical phenomena and mathematical concepts. Contains perhaps the best introduction to general theory of stability. "Outstanding," Scientific, Medical, and Technical Books. New introduction by K. H. Hohenemser. Bibliographical, historical notes. Index. 408 illustrations. xvi + 620pp. 5⅜ x 8⅜. S541 Paperbound **$3.50**

THEORY OF WING SECTIONS, I. H. Abbott, A. E. von Doenhoff. Concise compilation of subsonic aerodynamic characteristics of modern NASA wing sections, with description of their geometry, associated theory. Primarily reference work for engineers, students, it gives methods, data for using wing-section data to predict characteristics. Particularly valuable: chapters on thin wings, airfoils; complete summary of NACA's experimental observations, system of construction families of airfoils. 350pp. of tables on Basic Thickness Forms, Mean Lines, Airfoil Ordinates, Aerodynamic Characteristics of Wing Sections. Index. Bibliography. 191 illustrations. Appendix. 705pp. 5⅜ x 8. S558 Paperbound **$3.25**

WEIGHT-STRENGTH ANALYSIS OF AIRCRAFT STRUCTURES, F. R. Shanley. Scientifically sound methods of analyzing and predicting the structural weight of aircraft and missiles. Deals directly with forces and the distances over which they must be transmitted, making it possible to develop methods by which the minimum structural weight can be determined for any material and conditions of loading. Weight equations for wing and fuselage structures. Includes author's original papers on inelastic buckling and creep buckling. "Particularly successful in presenting his analytical methods for investigating various optimum design principles," AERONAUTICAL ENGINEERING REVIEW. Enlarged bibliography. Index. 199 figures. xiv + 404pp. 5⅜ x 8⅜.
S660 Paperbound **$2.50**

Electricity

TWO-DIMENSIONAL FIELDS IN ELECTRICAL ENGINEERING, L. V. Bewley. A useful selection of typical engineering problems of interest to practicing electrical engineers. Introduces senior students to the methods and procedures of mathematical physics. Discusses theory of functions of a complex variable, two-dimensional fields of flow, general theorems of mathematical physics and their applications, conformal mapping or transformation, method of images, freehand flux plotting, etc. New preface by the author. Appendix by W. F. Kiltner. Index. Bibliography at chapter ends. xiv + 204pp. 5⅜ x 8½. S1118 Paperbound **$1.50**

FLUX LINKAGES AND ELECTROMAGNETIC INDUCTION, L. V. Bewley. A brief, clear book which shows proper uses and corrects misconceptions of Faraday's law of electromagnetic induction in specific problems. Contents: Circuits, Turns, and Flux Linkages; Substitution of Circuits; Electromagnetic Induction; General Criteria for Electromagnetic Induction; Applications and Paradoxes; Theorem of Constant Flux Linkages. New Section: Rectangular Coil in a Varying Uniform Medium. Valuable supplement to class texts for engineering students. Corrected, enlarged edition. New preface. Bibliography in notes. 49 figures. xi + 106pp. 5⅜ x 8.
S1103 Paperbound **$1.25**

INDUCTANCE CALCULATIONS: WORKING FORMULAS AND TABLES, Frederick W. Grover. An invaluable book to everyone in electrical engineering. Provides simple single formulas to cover all the more important cases of inductance. The approach involves only those parameters that naturally enter into each situation, while extensive tables are given to permit easy interpolations. Will save the engineer and student countless hours and enable them to obtain accurate answers with minimal effort. Corrected republication of 1946 edition. 58 tables. 97 completely worked out examples. 66 figures. xiv + 286pp. 5⅜ x 8½.
S974 Paperbound **$1.85**

GASEOUS CONDUCTORS: THEORY AND ENGINEERING APPLICATIONS, J. D. Cobine. An indispensable text and reference to gaseous conduction phenomena, with the engineering viewpoint prevailing throughout. Studies the kinetic theory of gases, ionization, emission phenomena; gas breakdown, spark characteristics, glow, and discharges; engineering applications in circuit interrupters, rectifiers, light sources, etc. Separate detailed treatment of high pressure arcs (Suits); low pressure arcs (Langmuir and Tonks). Much more. "Well organized, clear, straightforward," Tonks, Review of Scientific Instruments. Index. Bibliography. 83 practice problems. 7 appendices. Over 600 figures. 58 tables. xx + 606pp. 5⅜ x 8. S442 Paperbound **$3.25**

INTRODUCTION TO THE STATISTICAL DYNAMICS OF AUTOMATIC CONTROL SYSTEMS, V. V. Solodovnikov. First English publication of text-reference covering important branch of automatic control systems—random signals; in its original edition, this was the first comprehensive treatment. Examines frequency characteristics, transfer functions, stationary random processes, determination of minimum mean-squared error, of transfer function for a finite period of observation, much more. Translation edited by J. B. Thomas, L. A. Zadeh. Index. Bibliography. Appendix. xxii + 308pp. 5⅜ x 8. S420 Paperbound **$2.25**

TENSORS FOR CIRCUITS, Gabriel Kron. A boldly original method of analyzing engineering problems, at center of sharp discussion since first introduced, now definitely proved useful in such areas as electrical and structural networks on automatic computers. Encompasses a great variety of specific problems by means of a relatively few symbolic equations. "Power and flexibility . . . becoming more widely recognized," Nature. Formerly "A Short Course in Tensor Analysis." New introduction by B. Hoffmann. Index. Over 800 diagrams. xix + 250pp. 5⅜ x 8. S534 Paperbound **$2.00**

SELECTED PAPERS ON SEMICONDUCTOR MICROWAVE ELECTRONICS, edited by Sumner N. Levine and Richard R. Kurzrok. An invaluable collection of important papers dealing with one of the most remarkable devolopments in solid-state electronics—the use of the **p-n** junction to achieve amplification and frequency conversion of microwave frequencies. Contents: General Survey (3 introductory papers by W. E. Danielson, R. N. Hall, and M. Tenzer); General Theory of Nonlinear Elements (3 articles by A. van der Ziel, H. E. Rowe, and Manley and Rowe); Device Fabrication and Characterization (3 pieces by Bakanowski, Cranna, and Uhlir, by McCotter, Walker and Fortini, and by S. T. Eng); Parametric Amplifiers and Frequency Multipliers (13 articles by Uhlir, Heffner and Wade, Matthaei, P. K. Tien, van der Ziel, Engelbrecht, Currie and Gould, Uenohara, Leeson and Weinreb, and others); and Tunnel Diodes (4 papers by L. Esaki, H. S. Sommers, Jr., M. E. Hines, and Yariv and Cook). Introduction. 295 Figures. xiii + 286pp. 6½ x 9¼. S1126 Paperbound **$2.25**

THE PRINCIPLES OF ELECTROMAGNETISM APPLIED TO ELECTRICAL MACHINES, B. Hague. A concise, but complete, summary of the basic principles of the magnetic field and its applications, with particular reference to the kind of phenomena which occur in electrical machines. Part I: General Theory—magnetic field of a current, electromagnetic field passing from air to iron, mechanical forces on linear conductors, etc. Part II: Application of theory to the solution of electromechanical problems—the magnetic field and mechanical forces in non-salient pole machinery, the field within slots and between salient poles, and the work of Rogowski, Roth, and Strutt. Formery titled "Electromagnetic Problems in Electrical Engineering." 2 appendices. Index. Bibliography in notes. 115 figures. xiv + 359pp. 5⅜ x 8½. S246 Paperbound **$2.25**

Mechanical engineering

DESIGN AND USE OF INSTRUMENTS AND ACCURATE MECHANISM, T. N. Whitehead. For the instrument designer, engineer; how to combine necessary mathematical abstractions with independent observation of actual facts. Partial contents: instruments & their parts, theory of errors, systematic errors, probability, short period errors, erratic errors, design precision, kinematic, semikinematic design, stiffness, planning of an instrument, human factor, etc. Index. 85 photos, diagrams. xii + 288pp. 5⅜ x 8. S270 Paperbound **$2.00**

A TREATISE ON GYROSTATICS AND ROTATIONAL MOTION: THEORY AND APPLICATIONS, Andrew Gray. Most detailed, thorough book in English, generally considered definitive study. Many problems of all sorts in full detail, or step-by-step summary. Classical problems of Bour, Lottner, etc.; later ones of great physical interest. Vibrating systems of gyrostats, earth as a top, calculation of path of axis of a top by elliptic integrals, motion of unsymmetrical top, much more. Index. 160 illus. 550pp. 5⅜ x 8. S589 Paperbound **$2.75**

MECHANICS OF THE GYROSCOPE, THE DYNAMICS OF ROTATION, R. F. Deimel, Professor of Mechanical Engineering at Stevens Institute of Technology. Elementary general treatment of dynamics of rotation, with special application of gyroscopic phenomena. No knowledge of vectors needed. Velocity of a moving curve, acceleration to a point, general equations of motion, gyroscopic horizon, free gyro, motion of discs, the damped gyro, 103 similar topics. Exercises. 75 figures. 208pp. 5⅜ x 8. S66 Paperbound **$1.75**

STRENGTH OF MATERIALS, J. P. Den Hartog. Distinguished text prepared for M.I.T. course, ideal as introduction, refresher, reference, or self-study text. Full clear treatment of elementary material (tension, torsion, bending, compound stresses, deflection of beams, etc.), plus much advanced material on engineering methods of great practical value: full treatment of the Mohr circle, lucid elementary discussions of the theory of the center of shear and the "Myosotis" method of calculating beam deflections, reinforced concrete, plastic deformations, photoelasticity, etc. In all sections, both general principles and concrete applications are given. Index. 186 figures (160 others in problem section). 350 problems, all with answers. List of formulas. viii + 323pp. 5⅜ x 8. S755 Paperbound **$2.00**

PHOTOELASTICITY: PRINCIPLES AND METHODS, H. T. Jessop, F. C. Harris. For the engineer, for specific problems of stress analysis. Latest time-saving methods of checking calculations in 2-dimensional design problems, new techniques for stresses in 3 dimensions, and lucid description of optical systems used in practical photoelasticity. Useful suggestions and hints based on on-the-job experience included. Partial contents: strained and stress-strain relations, circular disc under thrust along diameter, rectangular block with square hole under vertical thrust, simply supported rectangular beam under central concentrated load, etc. Theory held to minimum, no advanced mathematical training needed. Index. 164 illustrations. viii + 184pp. 6⅛ x 9¼. S720 Paperbound **$2.00**

APPLIED ELASTICITY, J. Prescott. Provides the engineer with the theory of elasticity usually lacking in books on strength of materials, yet concentrates on those portions useful for immediate application. Develops every important type of elasticity problem from theoretical principles. Covers analysis of stress, relations between stress and strain, the empirical basis of elasticity, thin rods under tension or thrust, Saint Venant's theory, transverse oscillations of thin rods, stability of thin plates, cylinders with thin walls, vibrations of rotating disks, elastic bodies in contact, etc. "Excellent and important contribution to the subject, not merely in the old matter which he has presented in new and refreshing form, but also in the many original investigations here published for the first time," NATURE. Index. 3 Appendixes. vi + 672pp. 5⅜ x 8. S726 Paperbound **$3.25**

APPLIED MECHANICS FOR ENGINEERS, Sir Charles Inglis, F.R.S. A representative survey of the many and varied engineering questions which can be answered by statics and dynamics. The author, one of first and foremost adherents of "structural dynamics," presents distinctive illustrative examples and clear, concise statement of principles—directing the discussion at methodology and specific problems. Covers fundamental principles of rigid-body statics, graphic solutions of static problems, theory of taut wires, stresses in frameworks, particle dynamics, kinematics, simple harmonic motion and harmonic analysis, two-dimensional rigid dynamics, etc. 437 illustrations. xii + 404pp. 5⅜ x 8½. S1119 Paperbound **$2.00**

THEORY OF MACHINES THROUGH WORKED EXAMPLES, G. H. Ryder. Practical mechanical engineering textbook for graduates and advanced undergraduates, as well as a good reference work for practicing engineers. Partial contents: Mechanisms, Velocity and Acceleration (including discussion of Klein's Construction for Piston Acceleration), Cams, Geometry of Gears, Clutches and Bearings, Belt and Rope Drives, Brakes, Inertia Forces and Couples, General Dynamical Problems, Gyroscopes, Linear and Angular Vibrations, Torsional Vibrations, Transverse Vibrations and Whirling Speeds (Chapters on vibrations considerably enlarged from previous editions). Over 300 problems, many fully worked out. Index. 195 line illustrations. Revised and enlarged edition. viii + 280pp. 5⅝ x 8¾. S980 Clothbound **$5.00**

THE KINEMATICS OF MACHINERY: OUTLINES OF A THEORY OF MACHINES, Franz Reuleaux. The classic work in the kinematics of machinery. The present thinking about the subject has all been shaped in great measure by the fundamental principles stated here by Reuleaux almost 90 years ago. While some details have naturally been superseded, his basic viewpoint has endured; hence, the book is still an excellent text for basic courses in kinematics and a standard reference work for active workers in the field. Covers such topics as: the nature of the machine problem, phoronomic propositions, pairs of elements, incomplete kinematic chains, kinematic notation and analysis, analyses of chamber-crank trains, chamber-wheel trains, constructive elements of machinery, complete machines, etc., with main focus on controlled movement in mechanisms. Unabridged republication of original edition, translated by Alexander B. Kennedy. New introduction for this edition by E. S. Ferguson. Index. 451 illustrations. xxiv + 622pp. 5⅜ x 8½. S1124 Paperbound **$3.00**

ANALYTICAL MECHANICS OF GEARS, Earle Buckingham. Provides a solid foundation upon which logical design practices and design data can be constructed. Originally arising out of investigations of the ASME Special Research Committee on Worm Gears and the Strength of Gears, the book covers conjugate gear-tooth action, the nature of the contact, and resulting gear-tooth profiles of: spur, internal, helical, spiral, worm, bevel, and hypoid or skew bevel gears. Also: frictional heat of operation and its dissipation, friction losses, etc., dynamic loads in operation, and related matters. Familiarity with this book is still regarded as a necessary prerequisite to work in modern gear manufacturing. 263 figures. 103 tables. Index. x + 546pp. 5⅜ x 8½. S1073 Paperbound **$2.75**

Optical design, lighting

THE SCIENTIFIC BASIS OF ILLUMINATING ENGINEERING, Parry Moon, Professor of Electrical Engineering, M.I.T. Basic, comprehensive study. Complete coverage of the fundamental theoretical principles together with the elements of design, vision, and color with which the lighting engineer must be familiar. Valuable as a text as well as a reference source to the practicing engineer. Partial contents: Spectroradiometric Curve, Luminous Flux, Radiation from Gaseous-Conduction Sources, Radiation from Incandescent Sources, Incandescent Lamps, Measurement of Light, Illumination from Point Sources and Surface Sources, Elements of Lighting Design. 7 Appendices. Unabridged and corrected republication, with additions. New preface containing conversion tables of radiometric and photometric concepts. Index. 707-item bibliography. 92-item bibliography of author's articles. 183 problems. xxiii + 608pp. 5⅜ x 8½. S242 Paperbound **$2.85**

OPTICS AND OPTICAL INSTRUMENTS: AN INTRODUCTION WITH SPECIAL REFERENCE TO PRACTICAL APPLICATIONS, B. K. Johnson. An invaluable guide to basic practical applications of optical principles, which shows how to set up inexpensive working models of each of the four main types of optical instruments—telescopes, microscopes, photographic lenses, optical projecting systems. Explains in detail the most important experiments for determining their accuracy, resolving power, angular field of view, amounts of aberration, all other necessary facts about the instruments. Formerly "Practical Optics." Index. 234 diagrams. Appendix. 224pp. 5⅜ x 8. S642 Paperbound **$1.75**

APPLIED OPTICS AND OPTICAL DESIGN, A. E. Conrady. With publication of vol. 2, standard work for designers in optics is now complete for first time. Only work of its kind in English; only detailed work for practical designer and self-taught. Requires, for bulk of work, no math above trig. Step-by-step exposition, from fundamental concepts of geometrical, physical optics, to systematic study, design, of almost all types of optical systems. Vol. 1: all ordinary ray-tracing methods; primary aberrations; necessary higher aberration for design of telescopes, low-power microscopes, photographic equipment. Vol. 2: (Completed from author's notes by R. Kingslake, Dir. Optical Design, Eastman Kodak.) Special attention to high-power microscope, anastigmatic photographic objectives. "An indispensable work," J., Optical Soc. of Amer. "As a practical guide this book has no rival," Transactions, Optical Soc. Index. Bibliography. 193 diagrams. 852pp. 6⅛ x 9¼. Vol. 1 S366 Paperbound **$3.50**
Vol. 2 S612 Paperbound **$2.95**

Miscellaneous

THE MEASUREMENT OF POWER SPECTRA FROM THE POINT OF VIEW OF COMMUNICATIONS ENGINEERING, R. B. Blackman, J. W. Tukey. This pathfinding work, reprinted from the "Bell System Technical Journal," explains various ways of getting practically useful answers in the measurement of power spectra, using results from both transmission theory and the theory of statistical estimation. Treats: Autocovariance Functions and Power Spectra; Direct Analog Computation; Distortion, Noise, Heterodyne Filtering and Pre-whitening; Aliasing; Rejection Filtering and Separation; Smoothing and Decimation Procedures; Very Low Frequencies; Transversal Filtering; much more. An appendix reviews fundamental Fourier techniques. Index of notation. Glossary of terms. 24 figures. XII tables. Bibliography. General index. 192pp. 5⅜ x 8. S507 Paperbound **$1.85**

CALCULUS REFRESHER FOR TECHNICAL MEN, A. Albert Klaf. This book is unique in English as a refresher for engineers, technicians, students who either wish to brush up their calculus or to clear up uncertainties. It is not an ordinary text, but an examination of most important aspects of integral and differential calculus in terms of the 756 questions most likely to occur to the technical reader. The first part of this book covers simple differential calculus, with constants, variables, functions, increments, derivatives, differentiation, logarithms, curvature of curves, and similar topics. The second part covers fundamental ideas of integration, inspection, substitution, transformation, reduction, areas and volumes, mean value, successive and partial integration, double and triple integration. Practical aspects are stressed rather than theoretical. A 50-page section illustrates the application of calculus to specific problems of civil and nautical engineering, electricity, stress and strain, elasticity, industrial engineering, and similar fields.—756 questions answered. 566 problems, mostly answered. 36 pages of useful constants, formulae for ready reference. Index. v + 431pp. 5⅜ x 8. T370 Paperbound **$2.00**

METHODS IN EXTERIOR BALLISTICS, Forest Ray Moulton. Probably the best introduction to the mathematics of projectile motion. The ballistics theories propounded were coordinated with extensive proving ground and wind tunnel experiments conducted by the author and others for the U.S. Army. Broad in scope and clear in exposition, it gives the beginnings of the theory used for modern-day projectile, long-range missile, and satellite motion. Six main divisions: Differential Equations of Translatory Motion of a projectile; Gravity and the Resistance Function; Numerical Solution of Differential Equations; Theory of Differential Variations; Validity of Method of Numerical Integration; and Motion of a Rotating Projectile. Formerly titled: "New Methods in Exterior Ballistics." Index. 38 diagrams. viii + 259pp. 5⅜ x 8½. S232 Paperbound **$1.75**

LOUD SPEAKERS: THEORY, PERFORMANCE, TESTING AND DESIGN, N. W. McLachlan. Most comprehensive coverage of theory, practice of loud speaker design, testing; classic reference, study manual in field. First 12 chapters deal with theory, for readers mainly concerned with math. aspects; last 7 chapters will interest reader concerned with testing, design. Partial contents: principles of sound propagation, fluid pressure on vibrators, theory of moving-coil principle, transients, driving mechanisms, response curves, design of horn type moving coil speakers, electrostatic speakers, much more. Appendix. Bibliography. Index. 165 illustrations, charts. 411pp. 5⅜ x 8. S588 Paperbound **$2.25**

MICROWAVE TRANSMISSION, J. C. Slater. First text dealing exclusively with microwaves, brings together points of view of field, circuit theory, for graduate student in physics, electrical engineering, microwave technician. Offers valuable point of view not in most later studies. Uses Maxwell's equations to study electromagnetic field, important in this area. Partial contents: infinite line with distributed parameters, impedance of terminated line, plane waves, reflections, wave guides, coaxial line, composite transmission lines, impedance matching, etc. Introduction. Index. 76 illus. 319pp. 5⅜ x 8.
S564 Paperbound **$1.50**

MICROWAVE TRANSMISSION DESIGN DATA, T. Moreno. Originally classified, now rewritten and enlarged (14 new chapters) for public release under auspices of Sperry Corp. Material of immediate value or reference use to radio engineers, systems designers, applied physicists, etc. Ordinary transmission line theory; attenuation; capacity; parameters of coaxial lines; higher modes; flexible cables; obstacles, discontinuities, and injunctions; tunable wave guide impedance transformers; effects of temperature and humidity; much more. "Enough theoretical discussion is included to allow use of data without previous background," Electronics. 324 circuit diagrams, figures, etc. Tables of dielectrics, flexible cable, etc., data. Index. ix + 248pp. 5⅜ x 8. S459 Paperbound **$1.65**

RAYLEIGH'S PRINCIPLE AND ITS APPLICATIONS TO ENGINEERING, G. Temple & W. Bickley. Rayleigh's principle developed to provide upper and lower estimates of true value of fundamental period of a vibrating system, or condition of stability of elastic systems. Illustrative examples; rigorous proofs in special chapters. Partial contents: Energy method of discussing vibrations, stability. Perturbation theory, whirling of uniform shafts. Criteria of elastic stability. Application of energy method. Vibrating systems. Proof, accuracy, successive approximations, application of Rayleigh's principle. Synthetic theorems. Numerical, graphical methods. Equilibrium configurations, Ritz's method. Bibliography. Index. 22 figures. ix + 156pp. 5⅜ x 8.
S307 Paperbound **$1.85**

ELASTICITY, PLASTICITY AND STRUCTURE OF MATTER, R. Houwink. Standard treatise on rheological aspects of different technically important solids such as crystals, resins, textiles, rubber, clay, many others. Investigates general laws for deformations; determines divergences from these laws for certain substances. Covers general physical and mathematical aspects of plasticity, elasticity, viscosity. Detailed examination of deformations, internal structure of matter in relation to elastic and plastic behavior, formation of solid matter from a fluid, conditions for elastic and plastic behavior of matter. Treats glass, asphalt, gutta percha, balata, proteins, baker's dough, lacquers, sulphur, others. 2nd revised, enlarged edition. Extensive revised bibliography in over 500 footnotes. Index. Table of symbols. 214 figures. xviii + 368pp. 6 x 9¼. S385 Paperbound **$2.45**

THE SCHWARZ-CHRISTOFFEL TRANSFORMATION AND ITS APPLICATIONS: A SIMPLE EXPOSITION, Miles Walker. An important book for engineers showing how this valuable tool can be employed in practical situations. Very careful, clear presentation covering numerous concrete engineering problems. Includes a thorough account of conjugate functions for engineers—useful for the beginner and for review. Applications to such problems as: Stream-lines round a corner, electric conductor in air-gap, dynamo slots, magnetized poles, much more. Formerly "Conjugate Functions for Engineers." Preface. 92 figures, several tables. Index. ix + 116pp. 5⅜ x 8½. S1149 Paperbound **$1.25**

THE LAWS OF THOUGHT, George Boole. This book founded symbolic logic some hundred years ago. It is the 1st significant attempt to apply logic to all aspects of human endeavour. Partial contents: derivation of laws, signs & laws, interpretations, eliminations, conditions of a perfect method, analysis, Aristotelian logic, probability, and similar topics. xviii + 424pp. 5⅜ x 8. S28 Paperbound **$2.00**

SCIENCE AND METHOD, Henri Poincaré. Procedure of scientific discovery, methodology, experiment, idea-germination—the intellectual processes by which discoveries come into being. Most significant and most interesting aspects of development, application of ideas. Chapters cover selection of facts, chance, mathematical reasoning, mathematics, and logic; Whitehead, Russell, Cantor; the new mechanics, etc. 288pp. 5⅜ x 8. S222 Paperbound **$1.35**

FAMOUS BRIDGES OF THE WORLD, D. B. Steinman. An up-to-the-minute revised edition of a book that explains the fascinating drama of how the world's great bridges came to be built. The author, designer of the famed Mackinac bridge, discusses bridges from all periods and all parts of the world, explaining their various types of construction, and describing the problems their builders faced. Although primarily for youngsters, this cannot fail to interest readers of all ages. 48 illustrations in the text. 23 photographs. 99pp. 6⅛ x 9¼.
T161 Paperbound **$1.00**

PHYSICS

General physics

FOUNDATIONS OF PHYSICS, R. B. Lindsay & H. Margenau. Excellent bridge between semi-popular works & technical treatises. A discussion of methods of physical description, construction of theory; valuable for physicist with elementary calculus who is interested in ideas that give meaning to data, tools of modern physics. Contents include symbolism, mathematical equations; space & time foundations of mechanics; probability; physics & continua; electron theory; special & general relativity; quantum mechanics; causality. "Thorough and yet not overdetailed. Unreservedly recommended," NATURE (London). Unabridged, corrected edition. List of recommended readings. 35 illustrations. xi + 537pp. 5⅜ x 8.
S377 Paperbound **$2.75**

FUNDAMENTAL FORMULAS OF PHYSICS, ed. by D. H. Menzel. Highly useful, fully inexpensive reference and study text, ranging from simple to highly sophisticated operations. Mathematics integrated into text—each chapter stands as short textbook of field represented. Vol. 1: Statistics, Physical Constants, Special Theory of Relativity, Hydrodynamics, Aerodynamics, Boundary Value Problems in Math. Physics; Viscosity, Electromagnetic Theory, etc. Vol. 2: Sound, Acoustics, Geometrical Optics, Electron Optics, High-Energy Phenomena, Magnetism, Biophysics, much more. Index. Total of 800pp. 5⅜ x 8. Vol. 1 S595 Paperbound **$2.00**
Vol. 2 S596 Paperbound **$2.00**

MATHEMATICAL PHYSICS, D. H. Menzel. Thorough one-volume treatment of the mathematical techniques vital for classic mechanics, electromagnetic theory, quantum theory, and relativity. Written by the Harvard Professor of Astrophysics for junior, senior, and graduate courses, it gives clear explanations of all those aspects of function theory, vectors, matrices, dyadics, tensors, partial differential equations, etc., necessary for the understanding of the various physical theories. Electron theory, relativity, and other topics seldom presented appear here in considerable detail. Scores of definitions, conversion factors, dimensional constants, etc. "More detailed than normal for an advanced text . . . excellent set of sections on Dyadics, Matrices, and Tensors," JOURNAL OF THE FRANKLIN INSTITUTE. Index. 193 problems, with answers. x + 412pp. 5⅜ x 8. S56 Paperbound **$2.00**

THE SCIENTIFIC PAPERS OF J. WILLARD GIBBS. All the published papers of America's outstanding theoretical scientist (except for "Statistical Mechanics" and "Vector Analysis"). Vol I (thermodynamics) contains one of the most brilliant of all 19th-century scientific papers—the 300-page "On the Equilibrium of Heterogeneous Substances," which founded the science of physical chemistry, and clearly stated a number of highly important natural laws for the first time; 8 other papers complete the first volume. Vol II includes 2 papers on dynamics, 8 on vector analysis and multiple algebra, 5 on the electromagnetic theory of light, and 6 miscellaneous papers. Biographical sketch by H. A. Bumstead. Total of xxxvi + 718pp. 5⅝ x 8⅜.
S721 Vol I Paperbound **$2.50**
S722 Vol II Paperbound **$2.00**
The set **$4.50**

BASIC THEORIES OF PHYSICS, Peter Gabriel Bergmann. Two-volume set which presents a critical examination of important topics in the major subdivisions of classical and modern physics. The first volume is concerned with classical mechanics and electrodynamics: mechanics of mass points, analytical mechanics, matter in bulk, electrostatics and magnetostatics, electromagnetic interaction, the field waves, special relativity, and waves. The second volume (Heat and Quanta) contains discussions of the kinetic hypothesis, physics and statistics, stationary ensembles, laws of thermodynamics, early quantum theories, atomic spectra, probability waves, quantization in wave mechanics, approximation methods, and abstract quantum theory. A valuable supplement to any thorough course or text.
Heat and Quanta: Index. 8 figures. x + 300pp. 5⅜ x 8½. S968 Paperbound **$2.00**
Mechanics and Electrodynamics: Index. 14 figures. vii + 280pp. 5⅜ x 8½.
S969 Paperbound **$1.75**

THEORETICAL PHYSICS, A. S. Kompaneyets. One of the very few thorough studies of the subject in this price range. Provides advanced students with a comprehensive theoretical background. Especially strong on recent experimentation and developments in quantum theory. Contents: Mechanics (Generalized Coordinates, Lagrange's Equation, Collision of Particles, etc.), Electrodynamics (Vector Analysis, Maxwell's equations, Transmission of Signals, Theory of Relativity, etc.), Quantum Mechanics (the Inadequacy of Classical Mechanics, the Wave Equation, Motion in a Central Field, Quantum Theory of Radiation, Quantum Theories of Dispersion and Scattering, etc.), and Statistical Physics (Equilibrium Distribution of Molecules in an Ideal Gas, Boltzmann statistics, Bose and Fermi Distribution, Thermodynamic Quantities, etc.). Revised to 1961. Translated by George Yankovsky, authorized by Kompaneyets. 137 exercises. 56 figures. 529pp. 5⅜ x 8½. S972 Paperbound **$2.50**

ANALYTICAL AND CANONICAL FORMALISM IN PHYSICS, André Mercier. A survey, in one volume, of the variational principles (the key principles—in mathematical form—from which the basic laws of any one branch of physics can be derived) of the several branches of physical theory, together with an examination of the relationships among them. Contents: the Lagrangian Formalism, Lagrangian Densities, Canonical Formalism, Canonical Form of Electrodynamics, Hamiltonian Densities, Transformations, and Canonical Form with Vanishing Jacobian Determinant. Numerous examples and exercises. For advanced students, teachers, etc. 6 figures. Index. viii + 222pp. 5⅜ x 8½. S1077 Paperbound **$1.75**

Acoustics, optics, electricity and magnetism, electromagnetics, magneto-hydrodynamics

THE THEORY OF SOUND, Lord Rayleigh. Most vibrating systems likely to be encountered in practice can be tackled successfully by the methods set forth by the great Nobel laureate, Lord Rayleigh. Complete coverage of experimental, mathematical aspects of sound theory. Partial contents: Harmonic motions, vibrating systems in general, lateral vibrations of bars, curved plates or shells, applications of Laplace's functions to acoustical problems, fluid friction, plane vortex-sheet, vibrations of solid bodies, etc. This is the first inexpensive edition of this great reference and study work. Bibliography. Historical introduction by R. B. Lindsay. Total of 1040pp. 97 figures. 5⅜ x 8.
S292, S293, Two volume set, paperbound, **$4.70**

THE DYNAMICAL THEORY OF SOUND, H. Lamb. Comprehensive mathematical treatment of the physical aspects of sound, covering the theory of vibrations, the general theory of sound, and the equations of motion of strings, bars, membranes, pipes, and resonators. Includes chapters on plane, spherical, and simple harmonic waves, and the Helmholtz Theory of Audition. Complete and self-contained development for student and specialist; all fundamental differential equations solved completely. Specific mathematical details for such important phenomena as harmonics, normal modes, forced vibrations of strings, theory of reed pipes, etc. Index. Bibliography. 86 diagrams. viii + 307pp. 5⅜ x 8. S655 Paperbound **$2.00**

WAVE PROPAGATION IN PERIODIC STRUCTURES, L. Brillouin. A general method and application to different problems: pure physics, such as scattering of X-rays of crystals, thermal vibration in crystal lattices, electronic motion in metals; and also problems of electrical engineering. Partial contents: elastic waves in 1-dimensional lattices of point masses. Propagation of waves along 1-dimensional lattices. Energy flow. 2 dimensional, 3 dimensional lattices. Mathieu's equation. Matrices and propagation of waves along an electric line. Continuous electric lines. 131 illustrations. Bibliography. Index. xii + 253pp. 5⅜ x 8.
S34 Paperbound **$2.00**

THEORY OF VIBRATIONS, N. W. McLachlan. Based on an exceptionally successful graduate course given at Brown University, this discusses linear systems having 1 degree of freedom, forced vibrations of simple linear systems, vibration of flexible strings, transverse vibrations of bars and tubes, transverse vibration of circular plate, sound waves of finite amplitude, etc. Index. 99 diagrams. 160pp. 5⅜ x 8. S190 Paperbound **$1.50**

LIGHT: PRINCIPLES AND EXPERIMENTS, George S. Monk. Covers theory, experimentation, and research. Intended for students with some background in general physics and elementary calculus. Three main divisions: 1) Eight chapters on geometrical optics—fundamental concepts (the ray and its optical length, Fermat's principle, etc.), laws of image formation, apertures in optical systems, photometry, optical instruments etc.; 2) 9 chapters on physical optics—interference, diffraction, polarization, spectra, the Rayleigh refractometer, the wave theory of light, etc.; 3) 23 instructive experiments based directly on the theoretical text. "Probably the best intermediate textbook on light in the English language. Certainly, it is the best book which includes both geometrical and physical optics," J. Rud Nielson, PHYSICS FORUM. Revised edition. 102 problems and answers. 12 appendices. 6 tables. Index. 270 illustrations. xi +489pp. 5⅜ x 8½. S341 Paperbound **$2.50**

PHOTOMETRY, John W. T. Walsh. The best treatment of both "bench" and "illumination" photometry in English by one of Britain's foremost experts in the field (President of the International Commission on Illumination). Limited to those matters, theoretical and practical, which affect the measurement of light flux, candlepower, illumination, etc., and excludes treatment of the use to which such measurements may be put after they have been made. Chapters on Radiation, The Eye and Vision, Photo-Electric Cells, The Principles of Photometry, The Measurement of Luminous Intensity, Colorimetry, Spectrophotometry, Stellar Photometry, The Photometric Laboratory, etc. Third revised (1958) edition. 281 illustrations. 10 appendices. xxiv + 544pp. 5½ x 9¼. S319 Paperbound **$3.00**

EXPERIMENTAL SPECTROSCOPY, R. A. Sawyer. Clear discussion of prism and grating spectrographs and the techniques of their use in research, with emphasis on those principles and techniques that are fundamental to practically all uses of spectroscopic equipment. Beginning with a brief history of spectroscopy, the author covers such topics as light sources, spectroscopic apparatus, prism spectroscopes and graphs, diffraction grating, the photographic process, determination of wave length, spectral intensity, infrared spectroscopy, spectrochemical analysis, etc. This revised edition contains new material on the production of replica gratings, solar spectroscopy from rockets, new standard of wave length, etc. Index. Bibliography. 111 illustrations. x + 358pp. 5⅜ x 8½. S1045 Paperbound **$2.25**

FUNDAMENTALS OF ELECTRICITY AND MAGNETISM, L. B. Loeb. For students of physics, chemistry, or engineering who want an introduction to electricity and magnetism on a higher level and in more detail than general elementary physics texts provide. Only elementary differential and integral calculus is assumed. Physical laws developed logically, from magnetism to electric currents, Ohm's law, electrolysis, and on to static electricity, induction, etc. Covers an unusual amount of material; one third of book on modern material: solution of wave equation, photoelectric and thermionic effects, etc. Complete statement of the various electrical systems of units and interrelations. 2 Indexes. 75 pages of problems with answers stated. Over 300 figures and diagrams. xix +669pp. 5⅜ x 8. S745 Paperbound **$3.50**

MATHEMATICAL ANALYSIS OF ELECTRICAL AND OPTICAL WAVE-MOTION, Harry Bateman. Written by one of this century's most distinguished mathematical physicists, this is a practical introduction to those developments of Maxwell's electromagnetic theory which are directly connected with the solution of the partial differential equation of wave motion. Methods of solving wave-equation, polar-cylindrical coordinates, diffraction, transformation of coordinates, homogeneous solutions, electromagnetic fields with moving singularities, etc. Index. 168pp. 5⅜ x 8. S14 Paperbound **$1.75**

PRINCIPLES OF PHYSICAL OPTICS, Ernst Mach. This classical examination of the propagation of light, color, polarization, etc. offers an historical and philosophical treatment that has never been surpassed for breadth and easy readability. Contents: Rectilinear propagation of light. Reflection, refraction. Early knowledge of vision. Dioptrics. Composition of light. Theory of color and dispersion. Periodicity. Theory of interference. Polarization. Mathematical representation of properties of light. Propagation of waves, etc. 279 illustrations, 10 portraits. Appendix. Indexes. 324pp. 5⅜ x 8. S178 Paperbound **$2.00**

THE THEORY OF OPTICS, Paul Drude. One of finest fundamental texts in physical optics, classic offers thorough coverage, complete mathematical treatment of basic ideas. Includes fullest treatment of application of thermodynamics to optics; sine law in formation of images, transparent crystals, magnetically active substances, velocity of light, apertures, effects depending upon them, polarization, optical instruments, etc. Introduction by A. A. Michelson. Index. 110 illus. 567pp. 5⅜ x 8. S532 Paperbound **$2.45**

ELECTRICAL THEORY ON THE GIORGI SYSTEM, P. Cornelius. A new clarification of the fundamental concepts of electricity and magnetism, advocating the convenient m.k.s. system of units that is steadily gaining followers in the sciences. Illustrating the use and effectiveness of his terminology with numerous applications to concrete technical problems, the author here expounds the famous Giorgi system of electrical physics. His lucid presentation and well-reasoned, cogent argument for the universal adoption of this system form one of the finest pieces of scientific exposition in recent years. 28 figures. Index. Conversion tables for translating earlier data into modern units. Translated from 3rd Dutch edition by L. J. Jolley. x + 187pp. 5½ x 8¾. S909 Clothbound **$6.00**

ELECTRIC WAVES: BEING RESEARCHES ON THE PROPAGATION OF ELECTRIC ACTION WITH FINITE VELOCITY THROUGH SPACE, Heinrich Hertz. This classic work brings together the original papers in which Hertz—Helmholtz's protegé and one of the most brilliant figures in 19th-century research—probed the existence of electromagnetic waves and showed experimentally that their velocity equalled that of light, research that helped lay the groundwork for the development of radio, television, telephone, telegraph, and other modern technological marvels. Unabridged republication of original edition. Authorized translation by D. E. Jones. Preface by Lord Kelvin. Index of names. 40 illustrations. xvii + 278pp. 5⅜ x 8½. S57 Paperbound **$1.75**

PIEZOELECTRICITY: AN INTRODUCTION TO THE THEORY AND APPLICATIONS OF ELECTROMECHANICAL PHENOMENA IN CRYSTALS, Walter G. Cady. This is the most complete and systematic coverage of this important field in print—now regarded as something of scientific classic. This republication, revised and corrected by Prof. Cady—one of the foremost contributors in this area—contains a sketch of recent progress and new material on Ferroelectrics. Time Standards, etc. The first 7 chapters deal with fundamental theory of crystal electricity. 5 important chapters cover basic concepts of piezoelectricity, including comparisons of various competing theories in the field. Also discussed: piezoelectric resonators (theory, methods of manufacture, influences of air-gaps, etc.); the piezo oscillator; the properties, history, and observations relating to Rochelle salt; ferroelectric crystals; miscellaneous applications of piezoelectricity; pyroelectricity; etc. "A great work," W. A. Wooster, NATURE. Revised (1963) and corrected edition. New preface by Prof. Cady. 2 Appendices. Indices. Illustrations. 62 tables. Bibliography. Problems. Total of 1 + 822pp. 5⅜ x 8½.
S1094 Vol. I Paperbound **$2.50**
S1095 Vol. II Paperbound **$2.50**
Two volume set Paperbound **$5.00**

MAGNETISM AND VERY LOW TEMPERATURES, H. B. G. Casimir. A basic work in the literature of low temperature physics. Presents a concise survey of fundamental theoretical principles, and also points out promising lines of investigation. Contents: Classical Theory and Experimental Methods, Quantum Theory of Paramagnetism, Experiments on Adiabatic Demagnetization. Theoretical Discussion of Paramagnetism at Very Low Temperatures, Some Experimental Results, Relaxation Phenomena. Index. 89-item bibliography. ix + 95pp. 5⅜ x 8. S943 Paperbound **$1.25**

SELECTED PAPERS ON NEW TECHNIQUES FOR ENERGY CONVERSION: THERMOELECTRIC METHODS; THERMIONIC; PHOTOVOLTAIC AND ELECTRICAL EFFECTS; FUSION, Edited by Sumner N. Levine. Brings together in one volume the most important papers (1954-1961) in modern energy technology. Included among the 37 papers are general and qualitative descriptions of the field as a whole, indicating promising lines of research. Also: 15 papers on thermoelectric methods, 7 on thermionic, 5 on photovoltaic, 4 on electrochemical effect, and 2 on controlled fusion research. Among the contributors are: Joffe, Maria Telkes, Herold, Herring, Douglas, Jaumot, Post, Austin, Wilson, Pfann, Rappaport, Morehouse, Domenicali, Moss, Bowers, Harman, Von Doenhoef. Preface and introduction by the editor. Bibliographies. xxviii + 451pp. 6⅛ x 9¼. S37 Paperbound **$3.00**

SUPERFLUIDS: MACROSCOPIC THEORY OF SUPERCONDUCTIVITY, Vol. I, Fritz London. The major work by one of the founders and great theoreticians of modern quantum physics. Consolidates the researches that led to the present understanding of the nature of superconductivity. Prof. London here reveals that quantum mechanics is operative on the macroscopic plane as well as the submolecular level. Contents: Properties of Superconductors and Their Thermodynamical Correlation; Electrodynamics of the Pure Superconducting State; Relation between Current and Field; Measurements of the Penetration Depth; Non-Viscous Flow vs. Superconductivity; Micro-waves in Superconductors; Reality of the Domain Structure; and many other related topics. A new epilogue by M. J. Buckingham discusses developments in the field up to 1960. Corrected and expanded edition. An appreciation of the author's life and work by L. W. Nordheim. Biography by Edith London. Bibliography of his publications. 45 figures. 2 Indices. xviii + 173pp. 5⅝ x 8⅜. S44 Paperbound **$1.45**

SELECTED PAPERS ON PHYSICAL PROCESSES IN IONIZED PLASMAS, Edited by Donald H. Menzel, Director, Harvard College Observatory. 30 important papers relating to the study of highly ionized gases or plasmas selected by a foremost contributor in the field, with the assistance of Dr. L. H. Aller. The essays include 18 on the physical processes in gaseous nebulae, covering problems of radiation and radiative transfer, the Balmer decrement, electron temperatives, spectrophotometry, etc. 10 papers deal with the interpretation of nebular spectra, by Bohm, Van Vleck, Aller, Minkowski, etc. There is also a discussion of the intensities of "forbidden" spectral lines by George Shortley and a paper concerning the theory of hydrogenic spectra by Menzel and Pekeris. Other contributors: Goldberg, Hebb, Baker, Bowen, Ufford, Liller, etc. viii + 374pp. 6⅛ x 9¼. S60 Paperbound **$2.95**

THE ELECTROMAGNETIC FIELD, Max Mason & Warren Weaver. Used constantly by graduate engineers. Vector methods exclusively: detailed treatment of electrostatics, expansion methods, with tables converting any quantity into absolute electromagnetic, absolute electrostatic, practical units. Discrete charges, ponderable bodies, Maxwell field equations, etc. Introduction. Indexes. 416pp. 5⅜ x 8. S185 Paperbound **$2.00**

THEORY OF ELECTRONS AND ITS APPLICATION TO THE PHENOMENA OF LIGHT AND RADIANT HEAT, H. Lorentz. Lectures delivered at Columbia University by Nobel laureate Lorentz. Unabridged, they form a historical coverage of the theory of free electrons, motion, absorption of heat, Zeeman effect, propagation of light in molecular bodies, inverse Zeeman effect, optical phenomena in moving bodies, etc. 109 pages of notes explain the more advanced sections. Index. 9 figures. 352pp. 5⅜ x 8. S173 Paperbound **$1.85**

FUNDAMENTAL ELECTROMAGNETIC THEORY, Ronold P. King, Professor Applied Physics, Harvard University. Original and valuable introduction to electromagnetic theory and to circuit theory from the standpoint of electromagnetic theory. Contents: Mathematical Description of Matter—stationary and nonstationary states; Mathematical Description of Space and of Simple Media—Field Equations, Integral Forms of Field Equations, Electromagnetic Force, etc.; Transformation of Field and Force Equations; Electromagnetic Waves in Unbounded Regions; Skin Effect and Internal Impedance—in a solid cylindrical conductor, etc.; and Electrical Circuits—Analytical Foundations, Near-zone and quasi-near zone circuits, Balanced two-wire and four-wire transmission lines. Revised and enlarged version. New preface by the author. 5 appendices (Differential operators: Vector Formulas and Identities, etc.). Problems. Indexes. Bibliography. xvi + 580pp. 5⅜ x 8½. S1023 Paperbound **$2.75**

Hydrodynamics

A TREATISE ON HYDRODYNAMICS, A. B. Basset. Favorite text on hydrodynamics for 2 generations of physicists, hydrodynamical engineers, oceanographers, ship designers, etc. Clear enough for the beginning student, and thorough source for graduate students and engineers on the work of d'Alembert, Euler, Laplace, Lagrange, Poisson, Green, Clebsch, Stokes, Cauchy, Helmholtz, J. J. Thomson, Love, Hicks, Greenhill, Besant, Lamb, etc. Great amount of documentation on entire theory of classical hydrodynamics. Vol I: theory of motion of frictionless liquids, vortex, and cyclic irrotational motion, etc. 132 exercises. Bibliography. 3 Appendixes. xii + 264pp. Vol II: motion in viscous liquids, harmonic analysis, theory of tides, etc. 112 exercises, Bibliography. 4 Appendixes. xv + 328pp. Two volume set. 5⅜ x 8.
S724 Vol I Paperbound **$1.75**
S725 Vol II Paperbound **$1.75**
The set **$3.50**

HYDRODYNAMICS, Horace Lamb. Internationally famous complete coverage of standard reference work on dynamics of liquids & gases. Fundamental theorems, equations, methods, solutions, background, for classical hydrodynamics. Chapters include Equations of Motion, Integration of Equations in Special Gases, Irrotational Motion, Motion of Liquid in 2 Dimensions, Motion of Solids through Liquid-Dynamical Theory, Vortex Motion, Tidal Waves, Surface Waves, Waves of Expansion, Viscosity, Rotating Masses of liquids. Excellently planned, arranged; clear, lucid presentation. 6th enlarged, revised edition. Index. Over 900 footnotes, mostly bibliographical. 119 figures. xv + 738pp. 6⅛ x 9¼. S256 Paperbound **$3.75**

HYDRODYNAMICS, H. Dryden, F. Murnaghan, Harry Bateman. Published by the National Research Council in 1932 this enormous volume offers a complete coverage of classical hydrodynamics. Encyclopedic in quality. Partial contents: physics of fluids, motion, turbulent flow, compressible fluids, motion in 1, 2, 3 dimensions; viscous fluids rotating, laminar motion, resistance of motion through viscous fluid, eddy viscosity, hydraulic flow in channels of various shapes, discharge of gases, flow past obstacles, etc. Bibliography of over 2,900 items. Indexes. 23 figures. 634pp. 5⅜ x 8. S303 Paperbound **$2.75**

Mechanics, dynamics, thermodynamics, elasticity

MECHANICS, J. P. Den Hartog. Already a classic among introductory texts, the M.I.T. professor's lively and discursive presentation is equally valuable as a beginner's text, an engineering student's refresher, or a practicing engineer's reference. Emphasis in this highly readable text is on illuminating fundamental principles and showing how they are embodied in a great number of real engineering and design problems: trusses, loaded cables, beams, jacks, hoists, etc. Provides advanced material on relative motion and gyroscopes not usual in introductory texts. "Very thoroughly recommended to all those anxious to improve their real understanding of the principles of mechanics." MECHANICAL WORLD. Index. List of equations. 334 problems, all with answers. Over 550 diagrams and drawings. ix + 462pp. 5⅜ x 8.
S754 Paperbound **$2.00**

THEORETICAL MECHANICS: AN INTRODUCTION TO MATHEMATICAL PHYSICS, J. S. Ames, F. D. Murnaghan. A mathematically rigorous development of theoretical mechanics for the advanced student, with constant practical applications. Used in hundreds of advanced courses. An unusually thorough coverage of gyroscopic and baryscopic material, detailed analyses of the Coriolis acceleration, applications of Lagrange's equations, motion of the double pendulum, Hamilton-Jacobi partial differential equations, group velocity and dispersion, etc. Special relativity is also included. 159 problems. 44 figures. ix + 462pp. 5⅜ x 8.
S461 Paperbound **$2.25**

THEORETICAL MECHANICS: STATICS AND THE DYNAMICS OF A PARTICLE, W. D. MacMillan. Used for over 3 decades as a self-contained and extremely comprehensive advanced undergraduate text in mathematical physics, physics, astronomy, and deeper foundations of engineering. Early sections require only a knowledge of geometry; later, a working knowledge of calculus. Hundreds of basic problems, including projectiles to the moon, escape velocity, harmonic motion, ballistics, falling bodies, transmission of power, stress and strain, elasticity, astronomical problems. 340 practice problems plus many fully worked out examples make it possible to test and extend principles developed in the text. 200 figures. xvii + 430pp. 5⅜ x 8. S467 Paperbound **$2.00**

THEORETICAL MECHANICS: THE THEORY OF THE POTENTIAL, W. D. MacMillan. A comprehensive, well balanced presentation of potential theory, serving both as an introduction and a reference work with regard to specific problems, for physicists and mathematicians. No prior knowledge of integral relations is assumed, and all mathematical material is developed as it becomes necessary. Includes: Attraction of Finite Bodies; Newtonian Potential Function; Vector Fields, Green and Gauss Theorems; Attractions of Surfaces and Lines; Surface Distribution of Matter; Two-Layer Surfaces; Spherical Harmonics; Ellipsoidal Harmonics; etc. "The great number of particular cases . . . should make the book valuable to geophysicists and others actively engaged in practical applications of the potential theory," Review of Scientific Instruments. Index. Bibliography. xiii + 469pp. 5⅜ x 8. S486 Paperbound **$2.50**

THEORETICAL MECHANICS: DYNAMICS OF RIGID BODIES, W. D. MacMillan. Theory of dynamics of a rigid body is developed, using both the geometrical and analytical methods of instruction. Begins with exposition of algebra of vectors, it goes through momentum principles, motion in space, use of differential equations and infinite series to solve more sophisticated dynamics problems. Partial contents: moments of inertia, systems of free particles, motion parallel to a fixed plane, rolling motion, method of periodic solutions, much more. 82 figs. 199 problems. Bibliography. Indexes. xii + 476pp. 5⅜ x 8. S641 Paperbound **$2.50**

MATHEMATICAL FOUNDATIONS OF STATISTICAL MECHANICS, A. I. Khinchin. Offering a precise and rigorous formulation of problems, this book supplies a thorough and up-to-date exposition. It provides analytical tools needed to replace cumbersome concepts, and furnishes for the first time a logical step-by-step introduction to the subject. Partial contents: geometry & kinematics of the phase space, ergodic problem, reduction to theory of probability, application of central limit problem, ideal monatomic gas, foundation of thermo-dynamics, dispersion and distribution of sum functions. Key to notations. Index. viii + 179pp. 5⅜ x 8.
S147 Paperbound **$1.50**

ELEMENTARY PRINCIPLES IN STATISTICAL MECHANICS, J. W. Gibbs. Last work of the great Yale mathematical physicist, still one of the most fundamental treatments available for advanced students and workers in the field. Covers the basic principle of conservation of probability of phase, theory of errors in the calculated phases of a system, the contributions of Clausius, Maxwell, Boltzmann, and Gibbs himself, and much more. Includes valuable comparison of statistical mechanics with thermodynamics: Carnot's cycle, mechanical definitions of entropy, etc. xvi + 208pp. 5⅜ x 8. S707 Paperbound **$1.45**

PRINCIPLES OF MECHANICS AND DYNAMICS, Sir William Thomson (Lord Kelvin) and Peter Guthrie Tait. The principles and theories of fundamental branches of classical physics explained by two of the greatest physicists of all time. A broad survey of mechanics, with material on hydrodynamics, elasticity, potential theory, and what is now standard mechanics Thorough and detailed coverage, with many examples, derivations, and topics not included in more recent studies. Only a knowledge of calculus is needed to work through this book. Vol. I (Preliminary): Kinematics; Dynamical Laws and Principles; Experience (observation, experimentation, formation of hypotheses, scientific method); Measures and Instruments; Continuous Calculating Machines. Vol. II (Abstract Dynamics): Statics of a Particle—Attraction; Statics of Solids and Fluids. Formerly Titled "Treatise on Natural Philosophy." Unabridged reprint of revised edition. Index. 168 diagrams. Total of xlii + 1035pp. 5⅜ x 8½.
Vol. I: S966 Paperbound **$2.35**
Vol. II: S967 Paperbound **$2.35**
Two volume Set Paperbound **$4.70**

INVESTIGATIONS ON THE THEORY OF THE BROWNIAN MOVEMENT, Albert Einstein. Reprints from rare European journals. 5 basic papers, including the Elementary Theory of the Brownian Movement, written at the request of Lorentz to provide a simple explanation. Translated by A. D. Cowper. Annotated, edited by R. Fürth. 33pp. of notes elucidate, give history of previous investigations. Author, subject indexes. 62 footnotes. 124pp. 5⅜ x 8.
S304 Paperbound **$1.25**

MECHANICS VIA THE CALCULUS, P. W. Norris, W. S. Legge. Covers almost everything, from linear motion to vector analysis: equations determining motion, linear methods, compounding of simple harmonic motions, Newton's laws of motion, Hooke's law, the simple pendulum, motion of a particle in 1 plane, centers of gravity, virtual work, friction, kinetic energy of rotating bodies, equilibrium of strings, hydrostatics, sheering stresses, elasticity, etc. 550 problems. 3rd revised edition. xii + 367pp. 6 x 9. S207 Clothbound **$4.95**

THE DYNAMICS OF PARTICLES AND OF RIGID, ELASTIC, AND FLUID BODIES; BEING LECTURES ON MATHEMATICAL PHYSICS, A. G. Webster. The reissuing of this classic fills the need for a comprehensive work on dynamics. A wide range of topics is covered in unusually great depth, applying ordinary and partial differential equations. Part I considers laws of motion and methods applicable to systems of all sorts; oscillation, resonance, cyclic systems, etc. Part 2 is a detailed study of the dynamics of rigid bodies. Part 3 introduces the theory of potential; stress and strain, Newtonian potential functions, gyrostatics, wave and vortex motion, etc. Further contents: Kinematics of a point; Lagrange's equations; Hamilton's principle; Systems of vectors; Statics and dynamics of deformable bodies; much more, not easily found together in one volume. Unabridged reprinting of 2nd edition. 20 pages of notes on differential equations and the higher analysis. 203 illustrations. Selected bibliography. Index. xi + 588pp. 5⅜ x 8. S522 Paperbound **$2.45**

A TREATISE ON DYNAMICS OF A PARTICLE, E. J. Routh. Elementary text on dynamics for beginning mathematics or physics student. Unusually detailed treatment from elementary definitions to motion in 3 dimensions, emphasizing concrete aspects. Much unique material important in recent applications. Covers impulsive forces, rectilinear and constrained motion in 2 dimensions, harmonic and parabolic motion, degrees of freedom, closed orbits, the conical pendulum, the principle of least action, Jacobi's method, and much more. Index. 559 problems, many fully worked out, incorporated into text. xiii + 418pp. 5⅜ x 8.
S696 Paperbound **$2.25**

DYNAMICS OF A SYSTEM OF RIGID BODIES (Elementary Section), E. J. Routh. Revised 7th edition of this standard reference. This volume covers the dynamical principles of the subject, and its more elementary applications: finding moments of inertia by integration, foci of inertia, d'Alembert's principle, impulsive forces, motion in 2 and 3 dimensions, Lagrange's equations, relative indicatrix, Euler's theorem, large tautochronous motions, etc. Index. 55 figures. Scores of problems. xv + 443pp. 5⅜ x 8. S664 Paperbound **$2.50**

DYNAMICS OF A SYSTEM OF RIGID BODIES (Advanced Section), E. J. Routh. Revised 6th edition of a classic reference aid. Much of its material remains unique. Partial contents: moving axes, relative motion, oscillations about equilibrium, motion. Motion of a body under no forces, any forces. Nature of motion given by linear equations and conditions of stability. Free, forced vibrations, constants of integration, calculus of finite differences, variations, precession and nutation, motion of the moon, motion of string, chain, membranes. 64 figures. 498pp. 5⅜ x 8. S229 Paperbound **$2.45**

DYNAMICAL THEORY OF GASES, James Jeans. Divided into mathematical and physical chapters for the convenience of those not expert in mathematics, this volume discusses the mathematical theory of gas in a steady state, thermodynamics, Boltzmann and Maxwell, kinetic theory, quantum theory, exponentials, etc. 4th enlarged edition, with new material on quantum theory, quantum dynamics, etc. Indexes. 28 figures. 444pp. 6⅛ x 9¼.
S136 Paperbound **$2.65**

THE THEORY OF HEAT RADIATION, Max Planck. A pioneering work in thermodynamics, providing basis for most later work, Nobel laureate Planck writes on Deductions from Electrodynamics and Thermodynamics, Entropy and Probability, Irreversible Radiation Processes, etc. Starts with simple experimental laws of optics, advances to problems of spectral distribution of energy and irreversibility. Bibliography. 7 illustrations, xiv + 224pp. 5⅜ x 8.
S546 Paperbound **$1.75**

FOUNDATIONS OF POTENTIAL THEORY, O. D. Kellogg. Based on courses given at Harvard this is suitable for both advanced and beginning mathematicians. Proofs are rigorous, and much material not generally avaliable elsewhere is included. Partial contents: forces of gravity, fields of force, divergence theorem, properties of Newtonian potentials at points of free space, potentials as solutions of Laplace's equations, harmonic functions, electrostatics, electric images, logarithmic potential, etc. One of Grundlehren Series. ix + 384pp. 5⅜ x 8.
S144 Paperbound **$1.98**

THERMODYNAMICS, Enrico Fermi. Unabridged reproduction of 1937 edition. Elementary in treatment; remarkable for clarity, organization. Requires no knowledge of advanced math beyond calculus, only familiarity with fundamentals of thermometry, calorimetry. Partial Contents: Thermodynamic systems; First & Second laws of thermodynamics; Entropy; Thermodynamic potentials: phase rule, reversible electric cell; Gaseous reactions: van't Hoff reaction box, principle of LeChatelier; Thermodynamics of dilute solutions: osmotic & vapor pressures, boiling & freezing points; Entropy constant. Index. 25 problems. 24 illustrations. x + 160pp. 5⅜ x 8.
S361 Paperbound **$1.75**

THE THERMODYNAMICS OF ELECTRICAL PHENOMENA IN METALS and A CONDENSED COLLECTION OF THERMODYNAMIC FORMULAS, P. W. Bridgman. Major work by the Nobel Prizewinner: stimulating conceptual introduction to aspects of the electron theory of metals, giving an intuitive understanding of fundamental relationships concealed by the formal systems of Onsager and others. Elementary mathematical formulations show clearly the fundamental thermodynamical relationships of the electric field, and a complete phenomenological theory of metals is created. This is the work in which Bridgman announced his famous "thermomotive force" and his distinction between "driving" and "working" electromotive force. We have added in this Dover edition the author's long unavailable tables of thermodynamic formulas, extremely valuable for the speed of reference they allow. Two works bound as one. Index. 33 figures. Bibliography. xviii + 256pp. 5⅜ x 8. S723 Paperbound **$1.65**

TREATISE ON THERMODYNAMICS, Max Planck. Based on Planck's original papers this offers a uniform point of view for the entire field and has been used as an introduction for students who have studied elementary chemistry, physics, and calculus. Rejecting the earlier approaches of Helmholtz and Maxwell, the author makes no assumptions regarding the nature of heat, but begins with a few empirical facts, and from these deduces new physical and chemical laws. 3rd English edition of this standard text by a Nobel laureate. xvi + 297pp. 5⅜ x 8.
S219 Paperbound **$1.75**

THE MATHEMATICAL THEORY OF ELASTICITY, A. E. H. Love. A wealth of practical illustration combined with thorough discussion of fundamentals—theory, application, special problems and solutions. Partial Contents: Analysis of Strain & Stress, Elasticity of Solid Bodies, Elasticity of Crystals, Vibration of Spheres, Cylinders, Propagation of Waves in Elastic Solid Media, Torsion, Theory of Continuous Beams, Plates. Rigorous treatment of Volterra's theory of dislocations, 2-dimensional elastic systems, other topics of modern interest. "For years the standard treatise on elasticity," AMERICAN MATHEMATICAL MONTHLY. 4th revised edition. Index. 76 figures. xviii + 643pp. 6⅛ x 9¼.
S174 Paperbound **$3.25**

STRESS WAVES IN SOLIDS, H. Kolsky, Professor of Applied Physics, Brown University. The most readable survey of the theoretical core of current knowledge about the propagation of waves in solids, fully correlated with experimental research. Contents: Part I—Elastic Waves: propagation in an extended plastic medium, propagation in bounded elastic media, experimental investigations with elastic materials. Part II—Stress Waves in Imperfectly Elastic Media: internal friction, experimental investigations of dynamic elastic properties, plastic waves and shock waves, fractures produced by stress waves. List of symbols. Appendix. Supplemented bibliography. 3 full-page plates. 46 figures. x + 213pp. 5⅜ x 8½.
S1098 Paperbound **$1.75**

Relativity, quantum theory, atomic and nuclear physics

SPACE TIME MATTER, Hermann Weyl. "The standard treatise on the general theory of relativity" (Nature), written by a world-renowned scientist, provides a deep clear discussion of the logical coherence of the general theory, with introduction to all the mathematical tools needed: Maxwell, analytical geometry, non-Euclidean geometry, tensor calculus, etc. Basis is classical space-time, before absorption of relativity. Partial contents: Euclidean space, mathematical form, metrical continuum, relativity of time and space, general theory. 15 diagrams. Bibliography. New preface for this edition. xviii + 330pp. 5⅜ x 8.
S267 Paperbound **$2.00**

ATOMIC SPECTRA AND ATOMIC STRUCTURE, G. Herzberg. Excellent general survey for chemists, physicists specializing in other fields. Partial contents: simplest line spectra and elements of atomic theory, building-up principle and periodic system of elements, hyperfine structure of spectral lines, some experiments and applications. Bibilography. 80 figures. Index. xii + 257pp. 5⅜ x 8.
S115 Paperbound **$2.00**

THE PRINCIPLE OF RELATIVITY, A. Einstein, H. Lorentz, H. Minkowski, H. Weyl. These are the 11 basic papers that founded the general and special theories of relativity, all translated into English. Two papers by Lorentz on the Michelson experiment, electromagnetic phenomena. Minkowski's SPACE & TIME, and Weyl's GRAVITATION & ELECTRICITY. 7 epoch-making papers by Einstein: ELECTROMAGNETICS OF MOVING BODIES, INFLUENCE OF GRAVITATION IN PROPAGATION OF LIGHT, COSMOLOGICAL CONSIDERATIONS, GENERAL THEORY, and 3 others. 7 diagrams. Special notes by A. Sommerfeld. 224pp. 5⅜ x 8.
S81 Paperbound **$1.75**

EINSTEIN'S THEORY OF RELATIVITY, Max Born. Revised edition prepared with the collaboration of Gunther Leibfried and Walter Biem. Steering a middle course between superficial popularizations and complex analyses, a Nobel laureate explains Einstein's theories clearly and with special insight. Easily followed by the layman with a knowledge of high school mathematics, the book has been thoroughly revised and extended to modernize those sections of the well-known original edition which are now out of date. After a comprehensive review of classical physics, Born's discussion of special and general theories of relativity covers such topics as simultaneity, kinematics, Einstein's mechanics and dynamics, relativity of arbitrary motions, the geometry of curved surfaces, the space-time continuum, and many others. Index. Illustrations, vii + 376pp. 5⅜ x 8. S769 Paperbound **$2.00**

ATOMS, MOLECULES AND QUANTA, Arthur E. Ruark and Harold C. Urey. Revised (1963) and corrected edition of a work that has been a favorite with physics students and teachers for more than 30 years. No other work offers the same combination of atomic structure and molecular physics and of experiment and theory. The first 14 chapters deal with the origins and major experimental data of quantum theory and with the development of conceptions of atomic and molecular structure prior to the new mechanics. These sections provide a thorough introduction to atomic and molecular theory, and are presented lucidly and as simply as possible. The six subsequent chapters are devoted to the laws and basic ideas of quantum mechanics: Wave Mechanics, Hydrogenic Atoms in Wave Mechanics, Matrix Mechanics, General Theory of Quantum Dynamics, etc. For advanced college and graduate students in physics. Revised, corrected republication of original edition, with supplementary notes by the authors. New preface by the authors. 9 appendices. General reference list. Indices. 228 figures. 71 tables. Bibliographical material in notes, etc. Total of xxiii + 810pp. 5⅜ x 8⅜.
S1106 Vol. I Paperbound **$2.50**
S1107 Vol. II Paperbound **$2.50**
Two volume set Paperbound **$5.00**

WAVE MECHANICS AND ITS APPLICATIONS, N. F. Mott and I. N. Sneddon. A comprehensive introduction to the theory of quantum mechanics; not a rigorous mathematical exposition it progresses, instead, in accordance with the physical problems considered. Many topics difficult to find at the elementary level are discussed in this book. Includes such matters as: the wave nature of matter, the wave equation of Schrödinger, the concept of stationary states, properties of the wave functions, effect of a magnetic field on the energy levels of atoms, electronic spin, two-body problem, theory of solids, cohesive forces in ionic crystals, collision problems, interaction of radiation with matter, relativistic quantum mechanics, etc. All are treated both physically and mathematically. 68 illustrations. 11 tables. Indexes. xii + 393pp. 5⅜ x 8½. S1070 Paperbound **$2.25**

BASIC METHODS IN TRANSFER PROBLEMS, V. Kourganoff, Professor of Astrophysics, U. of Paris. A coherent digest of all the known methods which can be used for approximate or exact solutions of transfer problems. All methods demonstrated on one particular problem —Milne's problem for a plane parallel medium. Three main sections: fundamental concepts (the radiation field and its interaction with matter, the absorption and emission coefficients, etc.); different methods by which transfer problems can be attacked; and a more general problem—the non-grey case of Milne's problem. Much new material, drawing upon declassified atomic energy reports and data from the USSR. Entirely understandable to the student with a reasonable knowledge of analysis. Unabridged, revised reprinting. New preface by the author. Index. Bibliography. 2 appendices. xv + 281pp. 5⅜ x 8½.
S1074 Paperbound **$2.00**

PRINCIPLES OF QUANTUM MECHANICS, W. V. Houston. Enables student with working knowledge of elementary mathematical physics to develop facility in use of quantum mechanics, understand published work in field. Formulates quantum mechanics in terms of Schroedinger's wave mechanics. Studies evidence for quantum theory, for inadequacy of classical mechanics, 2 postulates of quantum mechanics; numerous important, fruitful applications of quantum mechanics in spectroscopy, collision problems, electrons in solids; other topics. "One of the most rewarding features . . . is the interlacing of problems with text," Amer. J. of Physics. Corrected edition. 21 illus. Index. 296pp. 5⅜ x 8. S524 Paperbound **$2.00**

PHYSICAL PRINCIPLES OF THE QUANTUM THEORY, Werner Heisenberg. A Nobel laureate discusses quantum theory; Heisenberg's own work, Compton, Schroedinger, Wilson, Einstein, many others. Written for physicists, chemists who are not specialists in quantum theory, only elementary formulae are considered in the text; there is a mathematical appendix for specialists. Profound without sacrifice of clarity. Translated by C. Eckart, F. Hoyt. 18 figures. 192pp. 5⅜ x 8. S113 Paperbound **$1.25**

BOOKS EXPLAINING SCIENCE AND MATHEMATICS

General

WHAT IS SCIENCE?, Norman Campbell. This excellent introduction explains scientific method, role of mathematics, types of scientific laws. Contents: 2 aspects of science, science & nature, laws of science, discovery of laws, explanation of laws, measurement & numerical laws, applications of science. 192pp. 5⅜ x 8. S43 Paperbound **$1.25**

THE COMMON SENSE OF THE EXACT SCIENCES, W. K. Clifford. Introduction by James Newman, edited by Karl Pearson. For 70 years this has been a guide to classical scientific and mathematical thought. Explains with unusual clarity basic concepts, such as extension of meaning of symbols, characteristics of surface boundaries, properties of plane figures, vectors, Cartesian method of determining position, etc. Long preface by Bertrand Russell. Bibliography of Clifford. Corrected, 130 diagrams redrawn. 249pp. 5⅜ x 8. T61 Paperbound **$1.60**

SCIENCE THEORY AND MAN, Erwin Schrödinger. This is a complete and unabridged reissue of SCIENCE AND THE HUMAN TEMPERAMENT plus an additional essay: "What is an Elementary Particle?" Nobel laureate Schrödinger discusses such topics as nature of scientific method, the nature of science, chance and determinism, science and society, conceptual models for physical entities, elementary particles and wave mechanics. Presentation is popular and may be followed by most people with little or no scientific training. "Fine practical preparation for a time when laws of nature, human institutions . . . are undergoing a critical examination without parallel," Waldemar Kaempffert, N. Y. TIMES. 192pp. 5⅜ x 8. T428 Paperbound **$1.35**

FADS AND FALLACIES IN THE NAME OF SCIENCE, Martin Gardner. Examines various cults, quack systems, frauds, delusions which at various times have masqueraded as science. Accounts of hollow-earth fanatics like Symmes; Velikovsky and wandering planets; Hoerbiger; Bellamy and the theory of multiple moons; Charles Fort; dowsing, pseudoscientific methods for finding water, ores, oil. Sections on naturopathy, iridiagnosis, zone therapy, food fads, etc. Analytical accounts of Wilhelm Reich and orgone sex energy; L. Ron Hubbard and Dianetics; A. Korzybski and General Semantics; many others. Brought up to date to include Bridey Murphy, others. Not just a collection of anecdotes, but a fair, reasoned appraisal of eccentric theory. Formerly titled IN THE NAME OF SCIENCE. Preface. Index. x + 384pp. 5⅜ x 8. T394 Paperbound **$1.50**

A DOVER SCIENCE SAMPLER, edited by George Barkin. 64-page book, sturdily bound, containing excerpts from over 20 Dover books, explaining science. Edwin Hubble, George Sarton, Ernst Mach, A. d'Abro, Galileo, Newton, others, discussing island universes, scientific truth, biological phenomena, stability in bridges, etc. Copies limited; no more than 1 to a customer, FREE

POPULAR SCIENTIFIC LECTURES, Hermann von Helmholtz. Helmholtz was a superb expositor as well as a scientist of genius in many areas. The seven essays in this volume are models of clarity, and even today they rank among the best general descriptions of their subjects ever written. "The Physiological Causes of Harmony in Music" was the first significant physiological explanation of musical consonance and dissonance. Two essays, "On the Interaction of Natural Forces" and "On the Conservation of Force," were of great importance in the history of science, for they firmly established the principle of the conservation of energy. Other lectures include "On the Relation of Optics to Painting," "On Recent Progress in the Theory of Vision," "On Goethe's Scientific Researches," and "On the Origin and Significance of Geometrical Axioms." Selected and edited with an introduction by Professor Morris Kline. xii + 286pp. 5⅜ x 8½. T799 Paperbound **$1.45**

BOOKS EXPLAINING SCIENCE AND MATHEMATICS

Physics

CONCERNING THE NATURE OF THINGS, Sir William Bragg. Christmas lectures delivered at the Royal Society by Nobel laureate. Why a spinning ball travels in a curved track; how uranium is transmuted to lead, etc. Partial contents: atoms, gases, liquids, crystals, metals, etc. No scientific background needed; wonderful for intelligent child. 32pp. of photos, 57 figures. xii + 232pp. 5⅜ x 8. T31 Paperbound **$1.50**

THE RESTLESS UNIVERSE, Max Born. New enlarged version of this remarkably readable account by a Nobel laureate. Moving from sub-atomic particles to universe, the author explains in very simple terms the latest theories of wave mechanics. Partial contents: air and its relatives, electrons & ions, waves & particles, electronic structure of the atom, nuclear physics. Nearly 1000 illustrations, including 7 animated sequences. 325pp. 6 x 9. T412 Paperbound **$2.00**

BOOKS EXPLAINING SCIENCE AND MATHEMATICS

Engineering, technology, applied science etc.

TEACH YOURSELF ELECTRICITY, C. W. Wilman. Electrical resistance, inductance, capacitance, magnets, chemical effects of current, alternating currents, generators and motors, transformers, rectifiers, much more. 230 questions, answers, worked examples. List of units. 115 illus. 194pp. 6⅞ x 4¼. Clothbound **$2.00**

ELEMENTARY METALLURGY AND METALLOGRAPHY, A. M. Shrager. Basic theory and descriptions of most of the fundamental manufacturing processes involved in metallurgy. Partial contents: the structure of metals; slip, plastic deformation, and recrystalization; iron ore and production of pig iron; chemistry involved in the metallurgy of iron and steel; basic processes such as the Bessemer treatment, open-hearth process, the electric arc furnace —with advantages and disadvantages of each; annealing, hardening, and tempering steel; copper, aluminum, magnesium, and their alloys. For freshman engineers, advanced students in technical high schools, etc. Index. Bibliography. 177 diagrams. 17 tables. 284 questions and problems. 27-page glossary. ix + 389pp. 5⅜ x 8. S138 Paperbound **$2.25**

BASIC ELECTRICITY, Prepared by the Bureau of Naval Personnel. Originally a training course text for U.S. Navy personnel, this book provides thorough coverage of the basic theory of electricity and its applications. Best book of its kind for either broad or more limited studies of electrical fundamentals . . . for classroom use or home study. Part 1 provides a more limited coverage of theory: fundamental concepts, batteries, the simple circuit, D.C. series and parallel circuits, conductors and wiring techniques, A.C. electricity, inductance and capacitance, etc. Part 2 applies theory to the structure of electrical machines—generators, motors, transformers, magnetic amplifiers. Also deals with more complicated instruments, synchros, servo-mechanisms. The concluding chapters cover electrical drawings and blueprints, wiring diagrams, technical manuals, and safety education. The book contains numerous questions for the student, with answers. Index and six appendices. 345 illustrations. x + 448pp. 6½ x 9¼. S973 Paperbound **$3.00**

BASIC ELECTRONICS, prepared by the U.S. Navy Training Publications Center. A thorough and comprehensive manual on the fundamentals of electronics. Written clearly, it is equally useful for self-study or course work for those with a knowledge of the principles of basic electricity. Partial contents: Operating Principles of the Electron Tube; Introduction to Transistors; Power Supplies for Electronic Equipment; Tuned Circuits; Electron-Tube Amplifiers; Audio Power Amplifiers; Oscillators; Transmitters; Transmission Lines; Antennas and Propagation; Introduction to Computers; and related topics. Appendix. Index. Hundreds of illustrations and diagrams. vi + 471pp. 6½ x 9¼. S1076 Paperbound **$2.75**

BASIC THEORY AND APPLICATION OF TRANSISTORS, Prepared by the U.S. Department of the Army. An introductory manual prepared for an army training program. One of the finest available surveys of theory and application of transistor design and operation. Minimal knowledge of physics and theory of electron tubes required. Suitable for textbook use, course supplement, or home study. Chapters: Introduction; fundamental theory of transistors; transistor amplifier fundamentals; parameters, equivalent circuits, and characteristic curves; bias stabilization; transistor analysis and comparison using characteristic curves and charts; audio amplifiers; tuned amplifiers; wide-band amplifiers; oscillators; pulse and switching circuits; modulation, mixing, and demodulation; and additional semiconductor devices. Unabridged, corrected edition. 240 schematic drawings, photographs, wiring diagrams, etc. 2 Appendices. Glossary. Index. 263pp. 6½ x 9¼. S380 Paperbound **$1.25**

TEACH YOURSELF HEAT ENGINES, E. De Ville. Measurement of heat, development of steam and internal combustion engines, efficiency of an engine, compression-ignition engines, production of steam, the ideal engine, much more. 318 exercises, answers, worked examples. Tables. 76 illus. 220pp. 6⅞ x 4¼. Clothbound **$2.00**

BOOKS EXPLAINING SCIENCE AND MATHEMATICS

Miscellaneous

ON THE SENSATIONS OF TONE, Hermann Helmholtz. This is an unmatched coordination of such fields as acoustical physics, physiology, experiment, history of music. It covers the entire gamut of musical tone. Partial contents: relation of musical science to acoustics, physical vs. physiological acoustics, composition of vibration, resonance, analysis of tones by sympathetic resonance, beats, chords, tonality, consonant chords, discords, progression of parts, etc. 33 appendixes discuss various aspects of sound, physics, acoustics, music, etc. Translated by A. J. Ellis. New introduction by Prof. Henry Margenau of Yale. 68 figures. 43 musical passages analyzed. Over 100 tables. Index. xix + 576pp. 6⅛ x 9¼. S114 Paperbound **$3.00**

TYCHO BRAHE: A PICTURE OF SCIENTIFIC LIFE AND WORK IN THE SIXTEENTH CENTURY, J. L. E. Dreyer. The definitive biography of a stormy Renaissance genius. Full discussion of Brahe's fascinating life and scientific achievements in readable, non-technical language by this century's foremost historian of astronomy. Unabridged reprinting. 15 illustrations. 5 full-page plates. Index. xiv + 405pp. 5⅜ x 8½. T1057 Paperbound **$2.00**

LOUIS PASTEUR, S. J. Holmes, former Professor of Zoology at the U. of California. A brief, highly readable biography of France's greatest man of science. Remarkably clear accounts of Pasteur's scientific investigations and discoveries (from the first youthful experiments in chemistry and crystallization to the triumphant researches into the diseases affecting wine, vinegar, silkworms, fowl, cattle, and men); also a warm and revealing picture of his private life. "A special appeal and unique value for the general reader," N. Y. Times. "All the essential facts," Nature (London). Unabridged republication of 1st edition. New preface by the author. Index. 17 illustrations. x + 149pp. 5⅜ x 8. T197 Paperbound **$1.00**

THE LIFE OF PASTEUR, R. Vallery-Radot. 13th edition of this definitive biography, cited in Encyclopaedia Britannica. Authoritative, scholarly, well-documented with contemporary quotes, observations; gives complete picture of Pasteur's personal life; especially thorough presentation of scientific activities with silkworms, fermentation, hydrophobia, inoculation, etc. Introduction by Sir William Osler. Index. 505pp. 5⅜ x 8. S51/ Paperbound **$2.00**

BIBLIOGRAPHIES

THE STUDY OF THE HISTORY OF MATHEMATICS & THE STUDY OF THE HISTORY OF SCIENCE, George Sarton. Scientific method & philosophy in 2 scholarly fields. Defines duty of historian of math., provides especially useful bibliography with best available biographies of modern mathematicians, editions of their collected works, correspondence. Observes combination of history & science, will aid scholar in understanding science today. Bibliography includes best known treatises on historical methods. 200-item critically evaluated bibliography. Index. 10 illustrations. 2 volumes bound as one. 113pp. + 75pp. 5⅜ x 8. T240 Paperbound **$1.25**

GUIDE TO THE LITERATURE OF MATHEMATICS AND PHYSICS, N. G. Parke III. Over 5000 entries included under approximately 120 major subject headings, of selected most important books, monographs, periodicals, articles in English, plus important works in German, French, Italian, Spanish, Russian (many recently available works). Covers every branch of physics, math, related engineering. Includes author, title, edition, publisher, place, date, number of volumes, number of pages. A 40-page introduction on the basic problems of research and study provides useful information on the organization and use of libraries, the psychology of learning, etc. This reference work will save you hours of time. 2nd revised edition. Indices of authors, subjects. 464pp. 5⅜ x 8. S447 Paperbound **$2.49**

Prices subject to change without notice.

Dover publishes books on art, music, philosophy, literature, languages, history, social sciences, psychology, handcrafts, orientalia, puzzles and entertainments, chess, pets and gardens, books explaining science, intermediate and higher mathematics, mathematical physics, engineering, biological sciences, earth sciences, classics of science, etc. Write to:

Dept. catrr.
Dover Publications, Inc.
180 Varick Street, N.Y. 14, N.Y.